D1617164

# COLLECTED WORKS OF JOHN STUART MILL

## VOLUME XXXI

The Collected Edition of the Works of John Stuart Mill has been planned and is being directed by an editorial committee appointed from the Faculty of Arts and Science of the University of Toronto, and from the University of Toronto Press. The primary aim of the edition is to present fully collated texts of those works which exist in a number of versions, both printed and manuscript, and to provide accurate texts of works previously unpublished or which have become relatively inaccessible.

# Miscellaneous Writings

## by JOHN STUART MILL

*Edited by*

JOHN M. ROBSON

University Professor and Professor of English,
Victoria College, University of Toronto

UNIVERSITY OF TORONTO PRESS

ROUTLEDGE

© *University of Toronto Press 1989*
*Toronto and Buffalo*
*Printed in Canada*
ISBN 0-8020-2728-8


*London: Routledge*
ISBN 0-415-04879-6

Printed on acid-free paper

---

**Canadian Cataloguing in Publication Data**
Mill, John Stuart, 1806–1873.
Collected works of John Stuart Mill
Edited by John M. Robson and others.
Includes bibliographical references.
Partial contents: v. 31. Miscellaneous writings /
edited by John M. Robson.
ISBN 0-8020-2728-8 (v. 31)
1. Philosophy. 2. Political science. 3. Economics.
I. Robson, John M., 1927–   . II. Title.
B1602.A2 1963      192      C64-000188-2 rev

---

**British Library Cataloguing in Publication Data**
Mill, John Stuart, 1806–1873
Miscellaneous writings. –
(Collected works of John Stuart Mill; V. 31).
I. Title. II. Robson, J.M. (John Mercel), 1927–   828'.708
ISBN 0-415-04879-6

This volume has been published with the assistance of a grant
from the Social Sciences and Humanities Research Council of Canada

# Contents

**Medical Reviews, 1834 and 1842**

APPENDICES

# Introduction

JOHN M. ROBSON

THE RANGE of volume titles in the *Collected Works* might suggest that "miscellaneous" is redundant in Mill's case; however, given that the current laws of the political economy of publishing rule out very slender volumes, his breadth of interest has defeated our taxonomical abilities. The label must nevertheless not be seen as denigrating: collectively these materials contribute substantially to a full understanding of Mill's life and thought, and many have independent value. The following comments are designed to make that statement plausible to any sceptics who may have strayed into these underpopulated Millian territories, although full mapping of them remains a task for cartographers as yet unsighted.

## JEREMY BENTHAM AND JAMES MILL

*Rationale of Judicial Evidence*

MILL'S FIRST MAJOR WORK was as an editor, and it is a credit to his capacity and temper that he was able to describe it in his *Autobiography* with such equanimity:

About the end of 1824, or beginning of 1825, Mr. Bentham, having lately got back his papers on Evidence from M. Dumont (whose *Traité des Preuves Judiciaires*, grounded on them, was then first completed and published), resolved to have them printed in the original, and bethought himself of me as capable of preparing them for the press; in the same manner as his *Book of Fallacies* had been recently edited by Bingham. I gladly[1] undertook this task, and it occupied nearly all my leisure for about a year, exclusive of the time afterwards spent in seeing the five large volumes through the press. Mr. Bentham had begun this treatise three times, at considerable intervals, each time in a different manner, and each time without reference to the preceding: two of the three times he had gone over nearly the whole subject.[2]

[1]In the Early Draft of the *Autobiography*, "gladly" does not appear.
[2]*Autobiography*, *Collected Works* [CW] (Toronto: University of Toronto Press, 1981), I, 117.

Bentham's project in fact dated back to the early 1800s, as Mill indicates in his Preface of 1827: "The papers, from which the work now submitted to the public has been extracted, were written by Mr. Bentham at various times, from the year 1802 to 1812."[3] There had been several attempts to shape manuscript into book before Etienne Dumont, who had already laboured mightily in the vineyard to squeeze out the 1802 vintage Bentham (*Traités de législation civile et pénale*), succeeded in 1823 with his French redaction, *Traité des preuves judiciaires*. In 1809, when Dumont had just commenced the work that took some fifteen years to complete, Bentham described the early states of the manuscripts to him, partly explaining in the process why Dumont was to take so long:

> In reading the old stuff of Years 1803 and 1804 (1804 was part of the way a 2d edition [i.e., version] of 1803) it would be an act of charity or of justice (place it to which account you please) if you would hold a *pencil* in your hand and mark by *cancelling lines* such passages as are clearly superseded by the edition of 1808, as on the opposite page: —[Bentham illustrated on a page of this letter.]
> still more if with pencil or better still if with pen you would, in such parts as may appear not superseded, make a memorandum indicative of the places in which they may with most propriety be respectively inserted: for example *in* such a Chapter: or *between* such and such a Chapter: viz in the edition of 1808 which contains 14 or 15 Chapters.
> If in this way you amend the French, it will be ingratitude in you to grudge doing the same service to the English.[4]

Not only Dumont was acting as a legal aide to Bentham. In the same letter Bentham says that "the whole of Book Circumstantial" in the version of 1808 had been "marginal-contented" by Herbert Koe, then his amanuensis.[5] The pattern is similar to that he adopted in most of his publications, which appeared as edited by disciples, so that, in Sydney Smith's words, Bentham was Bentham to the civilized world "after that eminent philosopher has been washed, trimmed, shaved and forced into clean linen."[6]

Never one to underestimate, Bentham looked for someone to take on "the coal-heavers work of revising, expunging various Sections and polishing," or, as he alternatively phrased it, "revision, with confrontation of the parts, that there may be no repetitions or inconsistencies, or gaps."[7] And even these editorial

[3]Below, p. 5. Subsequent references are given in parentheses in the text.
[4]*Correspondence*, VIII, ed. Stephen Conway (Oxford: Clarendon Press, 1988), 36 (11 July, 1809).
[5]*Ibid*. Mill himself learned from Bentham to "marginal-content" his essays; see, e.g., his early "Traité de Logique," in *Journals and Debating Speeches*, *CW*, XXVI–XXVII (Toronto: University of Toronto Press, 1988), 145–90.
[6]"Bentham's *Book of Fallacies*," *Edinburgh Review*, XLII (Aug. 1825), 367. Smith is actually referring to a second valetting by a reviewer, and indeed the *Rationale* after Mill's ministrations still is not fully groomed.
[7]In a letter to his brother Samuel on 20 August, 1806, Bentham says he is within a few days of completion, and goes on to the first comment quoted above; in another of 18–20 September, he says, "Evidence—viz: the large volume that I mean to publish in the first

labours take one only up to the press, not through it, as Dumont had earlier pointed out to Bentham: "Yet what a life—what a galley-slave life is an editor's! Correct as he may, faults will remain to tear his soul in pieces—an & is wanting—a word is omitted—a letter misplaced—stops in confusion. Truly a corrector of the press is a galley-slave!"[8]

In addition to Koe, James Mill, newly acquainted with Bentham and dependent on free-lance writing and editing, was enlisted as coal-heaver and galley-slave on the masses of "evidence" manuscript. Ever hopeful, Bentham wrote to his brother on 29 September, 1809: "Evidence—the editing it forms [James] Mill's sole business, and the business of striking out various sections so to fit it for the press goes on prosperously. I hope to see it ready for the press before Christmas—yes considerably before."[9] Mill exerted himself in his usual thorough fashion, giving "a lesson in reading Benthamic copy" to the printer, who became "far less frightened than he formerly was, or pretended to be"; Mill also was putting in hard days at sections such as "Circumstantial," which left him "not a little non plused, on more occasions than one, whether to take or reject—unwilling to lose, and yet unwilling to overload," and "Pre-appointed, . . . a remarkably interesting part, [which] is not for that reason a part the sooner to be got through."[10] Letters between Dumont and Bentham are full of badinage as well as hints about how the revisions were made,[11] but one letter from James Mill to Bentham best summarizes the labour:

I have this day got to the end of *Exclusion. Impossibility* then is all that remains; and I am at the end of the principal stage of my labours, viz. my operations upon your text,—*i.e.* among your various lections, the making choice of one—the completing of an expression, when, in the hurry of penmanship, it had been left incomplete, etc. Editorial notes, of which we have so often talked, are only thus far advanced, that a variety of rudiments are set down, with references to the places of the work where they should be introduced. But it has often happened to me to find, what I had thought might be added as a note in one place, was given admirably by yourself in another place, and a better place. And in truth, having surveyed the whole, the ground appears to me so completely trod, that I can hardly conceive anything wanting. It is not easy, coming after you, to find anything to pick up behind you. My

---

instance, is finished: arrears of marginal-contenting of d° finished within the value of 3 or 4 days work," and then makes the second remark quoted in the text. (*Correspondence*, VII, ed. John Dinwiddy [Oxford: Clarendon Press, 1988], 365, 381.)

[8]*Ibid.*, 12 (7 Mar., 1802).

[9]*Ibid.*, VIII, 46.

[10]James Mill to Bentham (25 July, 26 and 31 Oct., and 6 Nov., 1809), *ibid.*, 37, 47–8, 49, and 50.

[11]For example, Bentham to Dumont: "For Your [*sic*] miserable predilection in favour of *Evidence* I know of no other cause than the non-existence of it. Had it existence, it would contain, of course, like everything else from the same hand, '*formes trop abregées*' or *trop etendues*, or both together: besides containing words,—the Lord above knows how many,—any one of which, like '*forthcomingness*' would be sufficient to make the whole unreadable." (*Correspondence*, VII, 518 [7 Aug., 1808].)

memory, too, is so overmatched by the vast multiplicity of objects which the work involves, that I am afraid to trust myself in any kind of notes, save suggestions of cases, illustration by instances,—lest what I say should be an idea brought forward in some other part of the work. All this, however, is not intended to operate as an apology or pretext for indolence. Notes there shall be written, and very full ones,—whether these notes shall be printed, is another question.[12]

In October 1811, writing to James Madison, President of the United States, to demonstrate his competence to supply a comprehensive code, Bentham says:

The subject of evidence has been examined in its whole extent and sifted to the bottom. A work of mine on this subject under the title of *The Rationale of Evidence* enough to occupy two moderate sized quarto volumes, has been for some time in the hands of another friend of mine [i.e., James Mill], and will be in the Printers' hands in the course of about two months.[13]

But such was not to be, and James Mill's mighty efforts appear to have been wasted. In late November Bentham's attention turned to what became *An Introductory View of the Rationale of Evidence for the Use of Non-Lawyers as well as Lawyers*, of which 148 pages (about one-third of the whole) were printed by 1812, and the rest was written at that time, but the work was not published until Bowring's edition in 1843.[14]

And only in 1823 did a much abbreviated version of the *Rationale* itself appear in Dumont's redaction, *Traité des preuves judiciaires*, which was followed by an anonymous English translation of it, *A Treatise on Judicial Evidence*, in 1825. The younger Mill, saying nothing of his father's or anyone else's shaping hand, indicates that all was still to do when his call came.

[The] three masses of manuscript it was my business to condense into a single treatise; adopting the one last written as the groundwork, and incorporating with it as much of the two others as it had not completely superseded. I had also to unroll such of Bentham's involved and parenthetical sentences, as seemed to overpass by their complexity the measure of[15] what readers were likely to take the pains to understand. It was further Mr. Bentham's particular desire that I should, from myself, endeavour to supply any *lacunae*

[12]*Ibid.*, VIII, 57–8 (6 Dec., 1809).

[13]*Ibid.*, 208.

[14]J.S. Mill took a rather dismissive attitude to this work: "My notions of Mr. Bentham's intentions with respect to the 'Introduction to the Rationale' (though I confess it is but an indistinct notion) has always been that he intended to put it forth as a kind of feeler, at a time when he did not contemplate finishing the work itself for publication at an early period. My opinion is entirely adverse to publishing the Introduction at all; & if that is decided upon, the later in the collection it comes the better. I would much rather it followed, than preceded, the Rationale." (To John Hill Burton, *Earlier Letters*, ed. Francis E. Mineka, Vols. XII and XIII of *CW* [Toronto: University of Toronto Press, 1963], XIII, 368; 23 Jan., 1837 [*sic* for 1838].) However, the *Introductory View* was published at the beginning of Vol. VI of the collected edition, before the *Rationale*; see note 26 below.

[15]The Early Draft reads "to overpass in obscurity".

which he had left; and at his instance I read, for this purpose, the most authoritative treatises on the English Law of Evidence, and commented on a few of the objectionable points of the English rules,[16] which had escaped Bentham's notice. I also replied to the objections which had been made to some of his doctrines, by reviewers of Dumont's book, and added a few supplementary remarks on some of the more abstract parts of the subject, such as the theory of improbability and impossibility. The controversial part of these editorial additions was written in a more assuming tone, than became[17] one so young and inexperienced as I was: but indeed I had never contemplated coming forward in my own person; and, as an anonymous editor of Bentham, I fell into the tone of my author, not thinking it unsuitable to him or to the subject, however it might be so to me. My name as editor was put to the book after it was printed, at Mr. Bentham's positive desire, which I in vain attempted to persuade him to forego.[18]

The concluding sentences are borne out by correspondence both at the time of publication and when the work was reprinted for the Bowring edition of Bentham's *Works*. While the work was in press (it was published in mid-May 1827),[19] Bentham wrote on 18 April:

Dear John

It is matter of no small surprise to me to see the title page without your name to it. Nothing could be more clearly understood between us than that it should be there. I do not say that the word title page was used on that occasion—but such was the meaning. If what you have done has been written under a different impression, so much the worse for me—and if the book be good for any thing, for the [world?] at large.

To this Mill replied:

I certainly did not understand you to have expressed any desire that my name should be in the title page. Nevertheless, if you positively require it, I am willing that it should be so, rather than that you should imagine I had taken less pains with the work under the idea of its being (so far as I am concerned) anonymous. But I confess I should greatly prefer that my name should be omitted. That the work should be benefited by it is out of the question. I myself might be benefited inasmuch as it would prove that you thought me worthy to be the editor of a work of yours. But on the other hand very little of the labour which I have bestowed upon the book appears on the face of it, or can be known to any one who was not acquainted with the MS. If my name were annexed to it people would think that I wished to

[16]The Early Draft is more specific: "I read at his instance Phillipps on the Law of Evidence and part of Starkie and wrote comments [the cancelled version reads: "such comments as I could"] on those few among the defective points in the English rules of evidence."

[17]Mill's embarrassment over this tone, commented on below, is evident in his revision of the version in the Early Draft: "The tone of these additions, or at least of the controversial part of them, was more assuming than became" [an earlier version reads: "assuming, even to arrogance, and unbecoming"].

[18]*Autobiography*, *CW*, I, 117–19. Cf. the account in the Preface below, which contains the anodyne remark that the editor's task "has chiefly consisted in collating the manuscripts" (6).

[19]The *Examiner* on 13 May, 1827, said that it would appear "in a few days, in five thick volumes" (304).

make a parade either of your good opinion [of] me, or of the few notes which I have added.[20] The notes are not of sufficient value to make it of any consequence to the public to know who wrote them — I should be very sorry to be suspected of wishing to obtain a reputation at a cheap rate by appearing before the public under the shelter of your name.

Bentham's brief response on 24 April was decisive: "My dear John / Your name is of far too great importance to the work to be omitted in the title page to it." Mill's immediate acceptance is lost, but Bentham's confirmation (still on the 24th) is again typical: "Dear John / Amen. If you know not what that word means send to the Booksellers for a Hebrew Dictionary." "P.S. Name at the end of the Preface."[21]

So much for modesty and deference. After the *Rationale* was published, the editor's close friend, John Arthur Roebuck, reviewing the work in the house journal, the *Westminster Review*, gave little away:

On the labour of the editor we are hardly entitled to give an opinion; not knowing the state of the papers from which he has compiled the work, we are unable to judge in how much we are indebted to him for the order and regularity which the work at present evinces. The notes and additions he has supplied are few, but those few are judicious: they are short and to the purpose.[22]

And the *Law Magazine*, which says Mill edited the work "with great ability," and in a later article judges that he "contributed by far the most valuable part of the chapter on conclusive evidence,"[23] can have given only pleasure. But through William Empson's pen, the old enemy, the *Edinburgh Review*, gave the reviewer's sting that brought on Mill's allergic regret about his tone. In the course of a thorough thrashing of the author, Empson takes but a little breath before turning on the editor.

Mr Mill, junior, is not likely to have underrated the importance of the trust confided to him by Mr Bentham . . .; yet, unless they were persuaded, upon Hindoo principles, that he was born of a legal caste, and that therefore talents of this description must be hereditary; or unless they took the fiction, by which every Englishman is supposed to be acquainted with the law, for a reality, we think that both parties would have exercised a sounder discretion — the one in not reposing, the other in not accepting, such a charge. Considering that Mr Bentham's own experience of the law of England must have been long suspended, and can have been at best only an acquaintance with principles rather than details, an accurate knowledge of this despised part of jurisprudence became an indispensable qualification on the part of his assistant — the groom, to whom a colt, so naturally wild, and so peculiarly circumstanced, was made over to be physicked, broken in, and got ready for the fair. If it were likely that a pamphlet might be compiled of the minor inaccuracies of the original, there could be no object in leaving more than a given portion of them uncorrected; and it was surely quite unnecessary to add supplemental errors in the notes.

[20]The word "added" is crossed out but the word substituted for it ("appended[?]") is mostly torn away.
[21]Mill's letter is in *EL, CW*, XII, 18–19, where Bentham's letters are given in notes.
[22]*Westminster Review*, IX (Jan. 1828), 216.
[23]*Law Magazine*, I (1828–29), 185–219, and VI (1831), 356.

And perhaps equally unnecessary for the reviewer to add:

The cannon's roar in the text is, throughout, ludicrously accompanied by a discharge of the editor's pocket-pistol in the note. The deep growl that mutters from above, is followed by a snap and a snarl from below; so that, in the place of any instructive commentary, or even reproof, there is a long reproachful howl, which reminds one of nothing philosophical and scholastic — except possibly it may be the accompaniment with which a litter of young Cynics used to attend the lectures at Diogenes's Tub.[24]

The riposte in the *Westminster* to the *Edinburgh*'s attack on the *Rationale* included only a brief allusion to the youthful editor, in which the usual irony against the *Edinburgh* is blunt. Offering the reviewer's constant plea of limited space, the anonymous friend says:

We must leave Mr. Mill, junior, under rebuke for having found fault with the English law, lacking the knowledge of a craftsman; while it is confessed that the law should be level and accessible to all understandings — when the very accusation of ignorance becomes a condemnation of the thing indicated. . . .[25]

There can be no doubt that Mr. Mill, junior, agreed that he had taken the prudence out of jurisprudence, and when in 1837, a decade older and proportionately wiser, he was approached by John Hill Burton about the reprinting of the *Rationale* in the collected edition, his response indicates a lingering smart: "If it is proposed to reprint, along with the Rationale of Evidence, my preface & notes, I should like much to see the proofs, as there are various things in the notes which I regret having published. Otherwise I have nothing to suggest."[26] On Burton's

---

[24]*Edinburgh Review*, XLVIII (Dec. 1828), 464n–5n.

[25]"Bentham — *Edinburgh Review*," *Westminster Review*, X (Apr. 1829), 392. It may be that the defence was less sturdy because the Mills had by this time withdrawn from the *Westminster* stable.

[26]Without pausing, he in fact went on with a proposal: "I should rather have suggested putting the 'Introduction' after the Rationale itself — as being a sort of summary or résumé of it, a kind of Table Analytique, as I imagine it to be — & more dry & more abstruse than the work itself, consequently rather calculated to repel readers from it. But without having read the Introduction (except a small portion which was printed in Mr. B.'s lifetime) I cannot presume to judge." (*EL, CW*, XII, 361–2 [29 Nov., 1837].) Apart from the general sloppiness of the Bowring edition, the lack of any manuscripts meant that Mill's edition had to be used. Several notes were added, but except for the matters mentioned in letters to Burton on 15 December, 1837 (*Later Letters [LL]*, ed. Francis E. Mineka and Dwight N. Lindley, Vols. XIV–XVII of *CW* [Toronto: University of Toronto Press, 1972], XVII, 1982) and 25 October, 1838 (see the next note), nothing of Mill's was altered or removed. (Mill himself suggested in the first of these that the last paragraph of his note on the Belgic Code [92 below] be omitted, but it was not.) He had just a fortnight before his first letter to Burton indicated unambiguously to William Tait, the publisher of the Bowring edition, that he would not write a life, memoir, or critique of Bentham for the *Works* because he did not wish to be "in any way mixed up with their proceedings as [he liked] to avoid getting into a hornet's nest," and because he was planning "a very elaborate article, speaking [his] whole mind" about Bentham in "the proper place," the *Westminster*, as a review of the edition

urging, he took second thought, and suggested the suppression of the note at I, 126 (15–16 below), then adding:

But I should wish my signature, at the end of the preface, & all mention of my name, to be omitted. I never intended to put my name to the book in any shape, & only did so because Mr Bentham insisted on it, & I feared that if I persisted in my refusal he would think I had done my work so ill as to be ashamed to avow it.

I should also wish a paragraph to the effect of that on the opposite page, to be added in brackets, at the end of the preface.[27]

That paragraph was the basis of the addition to the preface in the Bowring edition, in which Mill anonymously apologizes for "the air of confident dogmatism perceptible in some of [the] notes and additions," excused partly by "their having been written in very early youth," and partly by his belief that they would be anonymous, and so should be "accordant with the spirit of the work itself, and in Mr. Bentham admissible. . . ." "His name," he concludes truthfully if in the exculpatory third person, "was subsequently affixed, contrary to his own strongly expressed wish, at the positive desire of the venerable author, who certainly had a right to require it."[28] After sending the paragraph to Burton, Mill wrote again to suggest further adding the words (quoted above from the final version) "and in Mr. Bentham admissible":

Otherwise I shall have the appearance of censuring the tone of the work, which I am very far indeed from intending. I still wish to suppress any direct mention of my name, not to prevent it from being known to the reader if he chuses to enquire about it which I know cannot be done, but because its suppression is as it were, an act of disavowal as to any appropriateness in the notes and additions to my present frame of mind, and because I do not like to perk in the face of the world in general that the person known by my name has written things which he is ashamed of, when my name has never in any instance been put to writings I am not [*sic*] ashamed of.[29]

One must not assume, however, that the experience was a disaster for Mill. His account, written, it should be recalled, some thirty years after the editing, concludes with a passage that emphasizes individual without entirely forgetting general utility:

The time occupied in this editorial work was extremely well employed in respect to my own improvement. The *Rationale of Judicial Evidence* is one of the richest in matter of all Bentham's productions. The theory of evidence being in itself one of the most important of

---

(*EL, CW*, XII, 357–8 [18 and 20 Nov., 1837]). His "Bentham" appeared in December 1838 (in *Essays on Ethics, Religion, and Society, CW*, X [Toronto: University of Toronto Press, 1969], 75–115).

[27]*LL, CW*, XVII, 1981 (9 Dec., 1837). Nearly a year later, evidently on Richard Doane's instigation, Burton suggested the omission of the note at II, 236 (22–3 below), and Mill agreed on the grounds that it was "of very trifling importance," though he did not "feel the force of the objection to it" (*LL, CW*, XVII, 1988–9 [25 Oct., 1838]).

[28]The addition of 1837 is printed below (10) following the original Preface.

[29]*EL, CW*, XIII, 368.

his subjects, and ramifying into most of the others, the book contains, very fully developed, a great proportion of all his best thoughts: while, among more special things, it comprises the most elaborate exposure of the vices and defects of English law, as it then was, which is to be found in his works; not confined to the law of evidence, but including, by way of illustrative episode, the entire procedure or practice of Westminster Hall. The direct knowledge, therefore, which I obtained from the book, and which was imprinted upon me much more thoroughly than it could have been by mere reading, was itself no small acquisition. But this occupation[30] did for me what might seem less to be expected; it gave a great start to my powers of composition. Everything which I wrote subsequently to this editorial employment, was markedly superior to anything that I had written before it.[31] Bentham's later style, as the world knows, was heavy and cumbersome, from the excess of a good quality, the love of precision. . . . But his earlier style . . . is a model of liveliness and ease combined with fulness of matter, scarcely ever surpassed: and of this earlier style there were many striking specimens in the manuscripts on Evidence, all of which I endeavoured to preserve. So long a course of this admirable writing had a considerable effect upon my own. . . .[32]

Given the striking stylistic differences between Mill's journalism and speeches in his apprentice years and in the early 1830s, there is no reason to question this assessment. Nor can one doubt that his practised diligence and beaverish industry were helped into habit by the work. Also, the sheer bulk of the *Rationale* calls for the kind of commendation too often denied to editors.[33] In this respect, the skill of the youngster would command the highest of meagre wages paid such diligent servants (present coal-heavers and galley-slaves excepted). The heaviest demands were made by Bentham's manuscripts themselves—the hand-writing execrable, the fragmentary state of the references and the allusiveness exhausting, the repetitions with variation mind-destroying.

As to the benefit to Mill of the content, some debate is possible, but the coincidence of Bentham's major themes[34] with Mill's own cast of thought is hardly accidental or trivial. In general, one can point to the epistemological,

---

[30]In the Early Draft Mill first wrote "day's work" which he altered to "year's work".

[31]In the Early Draft he wrote and then cancelled: "This was the effect of the familiarity I gained wtih Bentham's style as a writer."

[32]*Autobiography*, *CW*, I, 119.

[33]It has been estimated that the still extant manuscripts by Bentham on evidence, procedure, and judicial organization exceed 13,000 folios (William Twining, "Bentham's Writings on Evidence," *Bentham Newsletter*, No. 10 [June 1986], 3). And the manuscripts that Dumont and Mill used are not among them, having presumably been discarded in the printing.

[34]The bulk of the *Rationale* being so daunting, William Twining's amazingly clear and succinct summary should be recommended; indeed there is no substitute. He introduces his analysis by a one-paragraph "catechism" that indicates the central themes: the end being rectitude of decision; the system of procedure being the "Natural" rather than the prevailing "Technical" one; the greatest instrument the admission of all evidence unless irrelevant or superfluous, or leading to vexation, expense, or delay; and the means being legislative sanctions to make evidence "forthcoming" and non-mendacious, and to provide instructions to judges concerning the value and weight of various kinds of evidence. (William

psychological, and logical speculations in the *Rationale* as reflected throughout Mill's writings. The last is most obvious, though no pushing of slender inference would justify asserting that Mill's *System of Logic* grew directly and solely out of his editing of Bentham's *Rationale*, for he had begun the study of logic in early youth, had written his "Traité de Logique" (derivative as it was) in 1820–21, and had worked hard on the subject with his fellow "Students of Mental Philosophy" during the mid-1820s.[35] But he began seriously considering writing on "the science of science itself, the science of investigation—of method,"[36] not long after the appearance of the *Rationale*. And the interconnections are significant. In the first place, the examination of evidence is at the centre of induction.[37] Furthermore, Bentham's discussion of probability and improbability prompted some of Mill's more interesting notes (e.g., 17–18, 28–32) that adumbrate his speculations in the *Logic*.[38] Bentham's attention to psychological factors is less obviously manifest in Mill's work, but is consonant with his discussions not only in the *Logic* but in his social thought.

More pervasive, especially in Mill's newspaper writings at the time, and his strenuous propagandism for the Philosophic Radical programme, is what L.J. Hume identifies as Bentham's "single intellectual enterprise" between 1802 and 1822, "the development of a campaign against misrule in all its forms."[39] The centrality of the *Rationale* in this enterprise is obvious in such statements as "Evidence is the basis of Justice,"[40] and the young Mill, though not subtle about the meaning of "justice," certainly worked for his mentors' version of it. Probably the most telling example, linking cause with effect, is the note attacking the dicta of the moral-sense schools, beginning "An appropriate name for this class of phrases would be *covers for dogmatism*; an appellation indicating the property common to them all, of serving as cloaks for ipse-dixitism . . ." (15). This passage

---

Twining, *Theories of Evidence: Bentham and Wigmore* [Stanford: Stanford University Press, 1985], 27–8.)

[35]For the background and composition of Mill's *Logic*, see the Textual Introduction to *System of Logic*, Vols. VII–VIII of *CW* (Toronto: University of Toronto Press, 1973), VII.

[36]To John Sterling (20–22 Oct., 1831), *EL*, *CW*, XII, 79.

[37]John Henry Wigmore, the leading U.S. writer on evidence, used as an epigraph for his *Principles of Judicial Proof* a passage from Israel Zangwill's *The Big Bow Mystery*, which includes the comment that evidence is "the science of the sciences. What is the whole of inductive logic, as laid down (say) by Bacon and Mill, but an attempt to apprise the value of evidence. . . ." William Twining agrees so fully as to use the same passage as one of the epigraphs to his *Theories of Evidence*.

[38]See esp. Bk. III, Chap. xxv (*CW*, VII, 622–38), where the same passage in Hume's "Of Miracles" is cited, and the anecdote about the King of Siam's disbelief in ice is repeated.

[39]*Bentham and Bureaucracy* (Cambridge: Cambridge University Press, 1981), 166.

[40]*Rationale*, V, 1. Cf. "Evidence is the basis of justice: exclude evidence, you exclude justice" (*ibid.*, Pt. III, Chap. i).

echoes tone for tone the chapter in Bentham's *Introduction to the Principles of Morals and Legislation* that Mill repeatedly cited in his own polemical essays on ethics[41] — his reason for suppressing it in Bowring's edition is not at all obvious, as repetition is the norm rather than the exception in that edition, and Mill used the same material in his well-known essay on Bentham in the *London and Westminster* in 1838, and developed part of the argument further in his essay on Nature, written in the 1850s. Furthermore, the argument appears in other guise at 90, where the statement that the "love of justice" is not innate interestingly anticipates the final chapter of *Utilitarianism*.

Apart from absorbing general tenets, Mill must also have stocked his capacious mind with considerable information, for Bentham's quirky text is as full of matter as of mannerism, and abounds in suggestive and telling opinion. However, much of this matter (as well as the general tenets) was also found elsewhere in Bentham's and James Mill's writings (including the latter's Commonplace Books), as well as in the intense Radical discussions and ephemeral journalism, and tracing any specific notion in the younger Mill's work to the editing of the *Rationale* is uncertain. In his many general allusions to Bentham's thought he of course touches on ideas found in the *Rationale* as well as in other writings of a genius not liable to single utterance of insights, and, curiously enough, the central issue of the *Rationale* stayed with Mill, though it occupies almost no place in his own concerns. In a letter to Cliffe Leslie, the comment, late and solicited, is definite:

I agree with you in going the complete length with Bentham as to the admissibility of evidence. There are I believe frequent cases like that you mention, of practical mischief both to the accused & to others from his not being examined as a witness. The one point on which alone B seems to me to be wrong is in allowing the judge to interrogate.[42]

Apart from the fundamental issues raised in the *Rationale*, specific points and applications can be seen in Mill's writings, especially those of the 1820s, many of which, as he said, dwelt on "some defect of the law, or misdoings of the magistracy or the courts of justice,"[43] and, as he might have added, the inutility of oaths, the culpability of "Judge and Co.," and the absurdities of technical obstructions. However, on the whole Mill took comparatively little interest in

[41]See John M. Robson, "John Stuart Mill and Jeremy Bentham, with Some Observations on James Mill," in *Essays Presented to A.S.P. Woodhouse*, ed. M. MacLure and F.W. Watt (Toronto: University of Toronto Press, 1964), 245–68.

[42]*LL, CW*, XVII, 1558 (8 Feb., 1869). In a letter of 22 Sept., 1865, to Arthur John Williams, a law student, Mill says: "I am very desirous of promoting the abolition of the remaining exclusions of evidence, and will certainly support in Parliament any movement for that purpose" (Ms, College of Law, Nihon University, Tokyo; to appear in *Additional Letters*, ed. Marion Filipiuk, Michael Laine, and John M. Robson, *CW*, XXXII).

[43]*Autobiography, CW*, I, 91. For a discussion of these debts, see Ann P. Robson's introduction to the *Newspaper Writings*, Vols. XXII–XXV of *CW* (Toronto: University of Toronto Press, 1986), XXII, esp. xxxv–xxxviii.

most legal questions, the early decision not to enter the Inns of Court being as decisive as that not to go to Cambridge. His mind did not take a legal bent, and so, even allowing for his youth and inexperience, it is not surprising to find little obvious originality in his notes and additions, which had not even the energy derived from self-prompting. Still, Roebuck's remark quoted above hardly seems adequate (though it would be welcomed by the present editor): "The notes and additions [the editor] has supplied are few, but those few are judicious: they are short and to the purpose." First, Mill's contributions are not really few or short: they number about seventy, plus forty-two referential footnotes, and while some are perfunctory and several, appropriately brief, concern the text (e.g., 13, 24, 24–5), bring information up to date (e.g., 38, 45), or give internal references (e.g., 33), the majority are substantive, including definitions (e.g., 11, 12, 18), illustrations (e.g., 18–19), and corrections (e.g., 22–3, 28–30, 30–2, 49, 50—this last is specially interesting, as it uses information from James Mill's *History of India*).[44]

Were Mill's contributions "to the purpose"? To judge that they are seems apposite. In substance Mill did not overreach himself or his brief, although it must be admitted that Bentham's extravagant play of mind makes pontification about proper exclusion or inclusion difficult. The critic who has looked most closely at Bentham's writings on adjective law, William Twining, is enthusiastic about Mill's general contribution, saying that it

must rank as one of the most remarkable editorial feats in history. Anyone who has had occasion to work with Bentham manuscripts will recognise the magnitude of the task: the crabbed script, the convoluted prose, the tendency to repetition and, above all, the sheer volume of the material, are enough to daunt committed and experienced editors.

But, he adds,

The quality of the achievement is less easy to assess. Mill succeeded in organising the material into a reasonably coherent structure; he judiciously preserved many eloquent passages in Bentham's early, more direct, style; no doubt he made it more readable than the original manuscripts, although much of it falls far short of the clarity and simplicity of Dumont. Mill competently filled in a number of gaps; he was generally scrupulous in identifying passages of which he was the author and in indicating points where he disagreed with Bentham. His youth and his lack of training may have been an advantage in allowing him to approach the task boldly with few inhibitions, yet there is little to suggest that he misrepresented, distorted or suppressed any of Bentham's views.[45]

The longest of Mill's substantive additions, especially 70–83 and 84–90, quite justify Twining's judgment about the extraordinary nature of the editing.[46] In them

[44]From the terms of Mill's mandate, one would anticipate (and the *Edinburgh*'s reviewer would presumably have enjoyed) more quotation from authorities, as at 22 and 47.

[45]"Bentham's Writings on Evidence," 36, 37.

[46]Those who are in frequent contact with bright eighteen-year-olds might wish to consider the likely difficulties if one of them were asked to think carefully about the

particularly he seems to be saying what would be "in Mr. Bentham admissible," though he is less spectacular than his mentor; the imitation is so close, indeed, that at times two readings are needed to get at the syntax, though in Mill's passages no more are generally required to get at the sense.

Were Mill's contributions, in spite of his own later doubts, "judicious"? In rebuking the *Edinburgh* for its earlier sins (see esp. 57–64, 64–6), Mill did not go near the limits of the journal warfare of the time,[47] but should have expected the spirited rebuff he received after making such comments on the *Edinburgh*'s reviewer as: "But I waste time, and fill up valuable space, in arguing seriously against such solemn trifling" (66). The "pocket-pistol" comment presumably was prompted by the heavy irony against lawyers found throughout (see, e.g., 46, 46–8), as well as the attacks on religion (e.g., 54–5). And Mill's adoption of an ethical stance learned from his father is not endearing: "After an attentive consideration . . ., the reader will probably join with me . . ." (30). Apart from these local and political short-term reverberations, the evidence suggests, as he might have said, that a less bellicose and dismissive tone would have been appropriate, even though it would have left Bentham alone on the provocative salient he himself typically advanced.

### Analysis of the Phenomena of the Human Mind

THE CIRCUMSTANCES of Mill's other major editorial work were quite different; though his intimate study of his father's *Analysis* began even before he started work on the *Rationale* in 1824–25, his edition of the *Analysis* was one of his last literary projects, appearing in 1869. It must be seen, therefore, as a much more carefully considered endeavour, and one that reflects lifelong intellectual and indeed personal concerns.

The *Autobiography* gives the initial context. James Mill, says his son, "could only command the concentration of thought necessary for this work, during the complete leisure of his holiday of a month or six weeks annually"; and he commenced the *Analysis*

in the summer of 1822, in the first holiday he passed at Dorking; in which neighbourhood, from that time to the end of his life, with the exception of two years, he lived, as far as his

---

exclusion of various kinds of legal evidence, read the prevailing authorities, and then write a chapter like "Of the Rule, That Evidence Is to Be Confined to the Points in Issue" (84–90 below) that would not only deal with the questions, but do so in accordance with the conclusions of someone else's argument and in that person's manner and tone. In Mill's case, a grade of A+ would seem insulting.

[47]Compare the relevant instances of James Mill's and J.S. Mill's lengthy attacks on the *Edinburgh* in the *Westminster Review* in 1824 (the latter, with references to the former, is in *CW*, I, 291–325), or Macaulay's well-known vigorous demolitions of the Utilitarians in the *Edinburgh* (XLIX [Mar. 1829], 159–89; *ibid.* [June 1829], 273–99; and L [Oct. 1829], 99–125).

official duties permitted, for six months of every year. He worked at the *Analysis* during several successive vacations, up to the year 1829, when it was published, and allowed me to read the manuscript, portion by portion, as it advanced.[48]

After its publication J.S. Mill enlisted others in the regime of careful reading and study to which he attributed so much. Describing the activities of the "Students of Mental Philosophy," which met twice a week in George Grote's house, beginning in 1825 (that is, while the youthful employee of the East India Company was, very much *inter alia*, editing Bentham), Mill says that one of them read aloud a section of the work under study (they started with James Mill's *Elements of Political Economy*), after which discussion began, "any one who had an objection or other remark to make" being heard.

Our rule was to discuss thoroughly every point raised, whether great or small, prolonging the discussion until all who took part were satisfied with the conclusion they had individually arrived at; and to follow up every topic of collateral speculation which the chapter or the conversation suggested, never leaving it until we had untied every knot which we found. We repeatedly kept up the discussion of some one point for several weeks, thinking intently on it during the intervals of our meetings. . . .

After political economy, they turned to logic, and then "launched into analytic psychology," beginning with David Hartley.

When we had finished Hartley, we suspended our meetings; but, my father's *Analysis of the Mind* being published soon after, we reassembled for the purpose of reading it. With this our exercises ended. I have always dated from these conversations my own real inauguration as an original and independent thinker. It was also through them that I acquired, or very much strengthened, a mental habit to which I attribute all that I have ever done, or ever shall do, in speculation; that of never accepting half-solutions of difficulties as complete; never abandoning a puzzle, but again and again returning to it until it was cleared up; never allowing obscure corners of a subject to remain unexplored, because they did not appear important; never thinking that I perfectly understood any part of a subject until I understood the whole.[49]

It is surely not fanciful to hear an echo of this discussion in the Preface that Mill supplied for the edition of the *Analysis* in 1869. At its conclusion he suggests that the best way to approach the edition is to read James Mill's text first (perhaps a chapter at a time); when the "student has done all he can with the author's own exposition—has possessed himself of the ideas, and felt, perhaps, some of the difficulties, he will be in a better position for profiting by any aid that the notes may afford, and will be in less danger of accepting, without due examination, the opinion of the last comer as the best" (104).

[48]*Autobiography*, *CW*, I, 71.
[49]*Ibid.*, 123–7. The Early Draft contains a further sentence: "It became a mental necessity with me, to require for my own complete conviction what Moliere calls 'des clartés de tout,' and this qualified me to make things clear to others, which is probably what I have best succeeded in as an expository writer" (126). For other references to the "Students of Mental Philosophy," see the Introduction to *CW*, I, xii and n.

It cannot now be determined how much the detailed scrutiny by the Students of Mental Philosophy in 1829 contributed to the notes Mill wrote for the edition of 1869,[50] but it is certain that he himself had "become possessed . . . of the ideas, and felt . . . some of the difficulties," and one may assume, given his devotion to the *Analysis*, that many of the points tackled forty years later were originally puzzles that had been again and again returned to until cleared up. He was loyal almost to a fault to his father's writings, even paying for a reissue—without notes—of the little read and polemically narrow *Fragment on Mackintosh* after he had contracted with Longmans for the second edition of the *Analysis*.[51] Throughout his life he referred to the virtues of the *Analysis*, which it would appear he valued above the work that established James Mill's reputation and career, the generally more appreciated *History of British India*.

His first tribute appeared in 1833, in an appendix to Lytton Bulwer's *England and the English* that, if not directly written, was certainly prompted by Mill.

> As a searcher into original truths, the principal contribution which Mr. Mill has rendered to philosophy, is to be found in his most recent work, *The Analysis of the Phenomena of the Human Mind*. Nothing more clearly proves what I have before asserted, viz.—our indifference to the higher kind of philosophical investigation, than the fact, that no full account—no *criticism* of this work has appeared in either of our principal Reviews.[52]

[50]The only known account with any indication of the actual discussions of the Students of Mental Philosophy is in the Diary of Henry Cole (Victoria and Albert Museum). Cole had met Mill in November 1826, and was attending the meetings of the group in Grote's house in Threadneedle Street (he identifies the meetings by their location) by November 1827. He reports that Mill told him on 30 January, 1828, that the meetings were postponed "sine die." On his evidence they resumed to discuss James Mill's *Analysis* on 14 November, 1829, and he records meetings, most of which he attended, on 21 November, 6 January, 1830 ("Discussion on the Vividness of sensation—Mr. Mill seeming to imply that it could only be applied to such sensations as were either pleasurable or painful"), 9 January ("Why Custom should tend [to] render some ideas and sensations almost imperceptible and to add to others?"), 13 January ("discussion upon *custom* and several questions collateral"), 16 January, 10 February, 17 February ("the subject of whence arises our belief in the existence of *Matter* was postponed in consequence of the absence of Roebuck and Graham"), 20 February ("Our subject was resemblance—but nothing peculiar occured" [*sic*]), 6 March, 10 March ("Discussion on Matter"), 20 March ("Discussion on Matter resumed"), 24 March ("whence arises the belief in one's existence"), 27 March ("Dissociability of ideas"), and 31 March. This record concludes with Cole's rather unsettling comment on 20 September, 1830: "Reading Mr. Mill's Analysis of the Human Mind"—but one hopes he meant re-reading.

[51]In this respect his fealty is shown in the long quotations from the *Fragment on Mackintosh* inserted in his notes to the *Analysis*: see 227 on motives, a passage cited approvingly, and 233–9, a passage on moral sentiments, mainly cited as valuable, but also to justify attempts at correction, as at 239–41.

[52]That is, in the *Edinburgh* and *Quarterly*. One had appeared slightly belatedly in the *Westminster*, XIII (Oct. 1830), 265–92, probably by Southwood Smith. Though the Mills had distanced themselves from the *Westminster*, the author, in the few pages where the work ostensibly reviewed is mentioned (282–4), heartily lauds James Mill and the

After quickly summarizing the doctrine, and suggesting that some points should be contended, the notice continues:

> The moment in which this remarkable work appeared is unfortunate for its temporary success. Had it been published sixty years ago—or perhaps sixty years hence, it would perhaps have placed the reputation of its author beyond any of his previous writings.[53]

In the next year Mill recommended his "father's metaphysical work" warmly to J.P. Nichol, offering him a copy,[54] and there was no diminution of his admiration after James Mill's death, as is evident in the paragraph he contributed to Andrew Bisset's article on James Mill in the 7th ed. (1842) of the *Encyclopaedia Britannica*:

> Mr. Mill's ingenuity as a very acute and original metaphysician was abundantly displayed in his *Analysis of the Phenomena of the Human Mind*, published in 1829. In this work he evinced analytical powers rarely, if ever, surpassed; and which have placed him high in the list of those subtle inquirers who have attempted to resolve all the powers of the mind into a very small number of simple elements. Mr. Mill took up this analysis where Hartley had left it, and applied the same method to the more complex phenomena, which the latter did not attempt to explain. From the general neglect of metaphysical studies in the present age, this work, which, at some periods of our history, would have placed its author on a level, in point of reputation, with the highest names in the republic of letters, has been less read and appreciated than his other writings.[55]

Though in 1853, being busy with other work and probably disaffected from John Chapman, he resisted Chapman's suggestion that he publish "notes to the Analysis,"[56] he continued actively to promote and recommend it.[57] He became immersed again in the experientialists' battle with the intuitionists during the writing and revision of his *Examination of Sir William Hamilton's Philosophy* and was reminded of his early activities and friends during his campaign for the parliamentary borough of Westminster in 1865, so it is not surprising that his father's work should be in his mind during the parliamentary recess of 1867. He decided to settle down in Avignon to a "winter's work which will not be political or economical but psychological." "I am," he told his associate and friend W.T. Thornton, "going to prepare in concert with Bain a new edition of my father's Analysis of the Mind with notes and supplementary matter. This will be not only

---

*Analysis*; however, the great bulk of the article is devoted to matters ancillary—and not for the most part closely connected with the actual text.

[53]"A Few Observations on Mr. Mill," App. C of Edward Lytton Bulwer, *England and the English* (London: Bentley, 1833); in *CW*, I, 590.

[54]*EL*, *CW*, XII, 237 (14 Oct., 1834).

[55]Reprinted in *CW*, I, 595.

[56]*LL*, *CW*, XIV, 104 (25 Apr., 1853).

[57]See, e.g., letters to a bookseller, to Harriet Taylor Mill, to W.G. Ward, and to Florence May: *LL*, *CW*, XVII, 2008 (25 Apr., 1853); XIV, 193 (3 Apr., 1854); XV, 649 (28 Nov., 1859); and XVI, 1472–4 (before Nov. 1868).

very useful but a very great relief by its extreme unlikeness to parliamentary work & to parliamentary semi-work or idleness."[58]

Alexander Bain, mentioning that the work began in that recess, says it was finished in 1868, and comments: "I had necessarily a long correspondence with him on the allocation of topics; but each of us took our own line in regard to the doctrines."[59] An undated but obviously preliminary list in Mill's hand of "Notes required" seriously underestimates the work to be done:

1. On latent feelings; & the question whether sensations of which we have no memory, have ever been in consciousness.
2. On the ignoring in the Analysis, of all direct action on ideas by external stimuli operating on the brain: no production of ideas being recognised save by sensations & association.
3. (Bain) The nervous character of ideation.
4. (Bain) The parts of speech.
5. To correct the philology of conjunctions & prepositions.[60]

At that point Bain clearly had been recruited, but the lack of a name against the final point suggests that the philologist Alexander Findlater had not yet been asked, and there is no indication that the assistance of George Grote (probably James Mill's most consistent admirer) had been solicited on questions of Greek philosophy.

Mill's account in his *Autobiography* (written soon after the publication of the edition early in 1869) deals with these matters, and emphasizes his continued hopes for the *Analysis*'s much-delayed success as well as his explanation for its failure:

... I commenced (and completed soon after I had left Parliament) the performance of a duty to philosophy and to the memory of my father, by preparing and publishing an edition of the *Analysis of the Phenomena of the Human Mind* with notes bringing up the doctrines of that admirable book to the latest improvements in science and in speculation.[61] This was a joint undertaking: the psychological notes being furnished in about equal proportions by Mr. Bain and myself, while Mr. Grote supplied some valuable contributions on points in the history of philosophy incidentally raised, and Dr. Andrew Findlater supplied the deficiencies in the book which had been occasioned by the imperfect philological knowledge of the time when it was written.[62] Having been originally published at a time when the current of metaphysical speculation ran in a quite opposite direction to the psychology of Experience and Association, the *Analysis* had not obtained the amount of immediate success which it deserved, though it had made a deep impression on many

[58]*LL, CW*, XVI, 1320 (19 Oct., 1867).
[59]*J.S. Mill. A Criticism: with Personal Recollections* (London: Longmans, Green, 1882), 129. Bain discusses the work in detail in his *Autobiography* (London: Longmans, Green, 1904), 289–91.
[60]Ms. in the John Stuart Mill Papers, Yale University.
[61]The text itself was not altered, except to correct a few typographical errors.
[62]In fact Mill supplied the Preface and 111 notes (not all "psychological"), Bain contributed 50 (including many of the most significant and lengthy); Findlater 17 (all in the first volume); and Grote only 3, but very long.

individual minds, and had largely contributed, through those minds, to create that more favourable atmosphere for the Association Psychology of which we now have the benefit. Admirably adapted for a class-book of the Experience Metaphysics, it only required to be enriched, and in some cases corrected, by the results of more recent labours in the same school of thought, to stand, as it now does, in company with Mr. Bain's treatises, at the head of the systematic works on Analytic psychology.[63]

There can be no doubt that, as in the *Autobiography* itself, in the new edition of the *Analysis* the two motives, loyal devotion to his father and active service in the war against intuitionism, were genuine, united, and indeed inseparable. Though in early near-apostate moments, especially when manoeuvring to stay close to John Sterling, he could admit doubts, the saving words are present—for example in the following passage, "your need," "bad moods," "if I could":

I am very far from agreeing, in all things, with the "Analysis," even on its own ground —though perhaps, from your greater distance, the interval between me & it may appear but trifling. But I can understand your need of something beyond it & deeper than it, & I have often bad moods in which I would most gladly postulate like Kant a different ultimate foundation "subjectiver bedürfnisses willen" if I could.[64]

Normally the allegiance is clear. In a passage not found in the Early Draft of his *Autobiography*, he says of his father:

leaving out of the reckoning all that portion of his labours in which he benefitted by what Bentham had done, and counting only what he achieved in a province in which Bentham had done nothing, that of analytic psychology, he will be known to posterity as one of the greatest names in that most important branch of speculation, on which all the moral and political sciences ultimately rest, and will mark one of the essential stages in its progress.[65]

And he emphasizes the link between his own major work and the *Analysis* when explaining the polemical purpose of his *System of Logic*:

the chief strength of this false philosophy [the intuitive] in morals, politics, and religion, lies in the appeal which it is accustomed to make to the evidence of mathematics and of the cognate branches of physical science. To expel it from these, is to drive it from its stronghold: and because this had never been effectually done, the intuitive school, even after what my father had written in his *Analysis of the Mind*, had in appearance, and as far as published writings were concerned, on the whole the best of the argument.[66]

Again, explaining his purpose in assailing Hamilton, Mill says:

That philosophy [the intuitional metaphysics], not always in its moderate forms, had ruled the thought of Europe for the greater part of a century. My father's *Analysis of the Mind*, my own *Logic*, and Professor Bain's great treatise, had attempted to reintroduce a better mode of philosophizing, latterly with quite as much success as could be expected. . . .[67]

[63]*Autobiography*, *CW*, I, 288–9.
[64]*EL*, *CW*, XIII, 406–7 (28 Sept., 1839).
[65]*Autobiography*, *CW*, I, 213.
[66]*Ibid.*, 233; the Early Draft contains this passage.
[67]*Ibid.*, 270; this passage is in the final section, written after the appearance of the new edition of the *Analysis*.

About the intentions, then, nothing more need be said. About the effect, there is little to be claimed specifically for the *Analysis*. Of course, though the details are moot and the history tangled, twentieth-century Anglo-American philosophy drew much impetus from the experientialist school and much of its energy from opposing the heirs of the intuitionists, and experimental psychologists, who have shown little interest in their antecedents, owe a considerable debt to the associationists. But it cannot be argued that the second edition of James Mill's *Analysis* in itself contributed much more to the tradition than its first edition. And that little more—a very little—is traceable to interest in John Stuart Mill's notes, which have attracted some modest attention in relation not to his father or to the experiential school but to his own thought.

Mill's notes to the *Analysis*, like those to the *Rationale*, may be categorized according to purpose and content. A few are merely locative (e.g., 107, 108), while many are critical of James Mill's terminology (e.g., 104–5, 123, 153, 198–9). Not surprisingly, there are frequent eulogies of author and work: "This exposition of Naming . . . is one of those specimens of clear and vigorous statement, going straight to the heart of the matter, and dwelling on it just long enough and no longer than necessary, in which the *Analysis* abounds" (122–3); "The doctrine of this chapter ["Conception"] is as just as it is admirably stated" (141).[68]

Many of the most interesting notes involve an expansion and elucidation of James Mill's ideas.[69] But the dominant kind are those in which such expansion and elucidation are marked by overt or strongly implied criticism. He is hardest on James Mill in the discussions of general names, classification, connotation and denotation, memory and expectation, the import of propositions, attention, will, and belief.[70] But the tone is appropriately gentle, as befits the relation between this editor and author: "The theory of Predication here set forth, stands in need of further elucidation, and perhaps of some correction and addition" (128). Mill can, however, be forthright: "I am unable to feel the force of this remark" (132). Probably the best illustrations of his tone come in passages where he strives for balance:

The reason assigned by the author for considering association by resemblance as a case of association by contiguity, is perhaps the least successful attempt at a generalisation and simplification of the laws of mental phenomena, to be found in the work. It ought to be remembered that the author, as the text shews, attached little importance to it. And perhaps, not thinking it important, he passed it over with a less amount of patient thought than he usually bestowed on his analyses. (120.)

[68]Cf. 131, 133–4. Such remarks occur also in the midst of notes that contain criticisms: "As is well shewn in the text . . ." (126).

[69]See, for instance, 117–19, 157, 202–3; the last instances cases where the point is slight.

[70]Belief, a matter not extensively treated in this way by Mill elsewhere, and one on which he differed from Bain, is the subject of the longest note (159–74).

That the pleasures or pains of another person can only be pleasurable or painful to us through the association of our own pleasures or pains with them, is true in one sense, which is probably that intended by the author, but not true in another, against which he has not sufficiently guarded his mode of expression (219).[71]

For students of J.S. Mill's thought, there is much to engage the attention. Generally, his associationism is laid out in much more detail here then elsewhere, especially if one takes into account his explicit and implied approval of James Mill's account and his explicit acceptance or modification of the views of Bain[72] and Spencer.[73] In Bain's words: "The work contains perhaps the best summary of his psychological opinions, although the *Hamilton* shows them in the more stirring shape of polemics."[74] That "stirring shape" can, of course, be discerned, as Hamilton, Mackintosh, and other intuitionists are not spared. The battle is joined most obviously at 117–19, and in the final chapters, but there are skirmishes throughout (e.g., 181–3), and no one could escape the conclusion that the rallying cry on all fronts is "Experience!"

As a result, useful parallel accounts and modifications of questions that occupy Mill elsewhere are found in these notes. Matters dealt with in his *System of Logic* recur, for instance in reference to syllogism (175). His brisk encounters with Samuel Bailey over Berkeley's theory of vision are revived (156),[75] and the account of personal identity (211–13) recalls parts of his *Examination of Sir William Hamilton's Philosophy*. The most compelling modifications relate to moral theory, the notes to Chaps. xix ff., especially in their bearing on the development of moral feeling through sympathy, being essential to a full appreciation of Mill's utilitarianism (particularly the long note at 231–42).[76] Another interesting discussion, not duplicated elsewhere in his limited accounts of aesthetic issues, is that of beauty (223–6), where he reveals an acquaintance with aspects of Coleridge's and Ruskin's views.[77]

---

[71]For typical examples of such critical passages early in the text, see 112–14, 115–16, 120–1, and 127.

[72]Frequently Mill praises Bain's notes which, when there is overlap, precede his. In their annotation, Bain says: "Coincidence of view was the rule, the discrepancy seldom went beyond the mode of statement, the chief exception being the topic of Belief" (*J.S. Mill*, 129). The coincidence may also be seen in Mill's "Bain's Psychology," in *Essays on Philosophy and the Classics*, Vol. XI of *CW* (Toronto: University of Toronto Press, 1978), 339–73.

[73]Note especially the very long quotation from Spencer's *Principles*, 205–10.

[74]*J.S. Mill*, 129.

[75]See "Bailey on Berkeley's Theory of Vision," *CW*, XI, 245–69.

[76]It seems uncharitable in Mill to omit references to Bentham in these contexts. And it is mildly annoying that when discussing evidence, though treating it in terms of belief, he does not allude to Bentham, and refers the subject to logic (175–6; cf. *CW*, VII, 554–603).

[77]Bain's comment should, however, be noted. Mentioning that James Mill's account of the aesthetic is gravely deficient, he says: "John Mill himself confessed that he was unable

Here, indeed, interpretation moves close to biography. The notes contain a few pleasing personal touches, as when in using a typical philosopher's illustration, he says he has seen Lafayette (174); for the fact, see his *Autobiography, CW*, I, 179. Also, he refers to ascending Skiddaw (212–13), an experience that occupies an important place in his walking tour of the Lake District.[78] His mention of the effect of music (222) has individual experience at its core, and when he then refers to the colour of flowers the feeling is powerfully manifest:

My own memory recals to me the intense and mysterious delight which in early childhood I had in the colours of certain flowers; a delight far exceeding any I am now capable of receiving from colour of any description, with all its acquired associations. And this was the case at far too early an age, and with habits of observation far too little developed, to make any of the subtler combinations of form and proportion a source of much pleasure to me. This last pleasure was acquired very gradually, and did not, until after the commencement of manhood, attain any considerable height. (223.)

Once more, the evidence of the gradual growth of pleasure in form and proportion is found in his walking-tour journals, where the Romantic picturesque is applied in personal ways. In the same passage dealing with colour and music, Mill's apparently general comment has at its heart his interpretation of his own sensibility in comparison with that of his wife:

The susceptibility to the physical pleasures produced by colours and musical sounds, (and by forms if any part of the pleasure they afford is physical), is probably extremely different in different organisations. In natures in which any one of these susceptibilities is originally faint, more will depend on association. The extreme sensibility of this part of our constitution to small and unobvious influences, makes it certain that the sources of the feelings of beauty and deformity must be, to a material extent, different in different individuals. (223.)[79]

The main biographical interest, however, must centre on Mill's comments about his father. When his discussion in the *Autobiography* of James Mill's denigration of the feelings is recalled, the note to the *Analysis* in which he says that the author undervalued the role of the "animal" as compared with the "mental, or intellectual" part of human nature stands out boldly (220–1). In another passage in the *Autobiography* Mill shortly but memorably mentions one of James Mill's shortcomings: "A defect running through his otherwise admirable modes of instruction, as it did through all his modes of thought, was that of trusting too much

---

to grapple with the Sublime and the Beautiful without an amount of study which he could not devote to the topic" (Bain, *Autobiography*, 290–1). But see *CW*, XI, 363–4.

[78]See *CW*, XXVII, 537–9.

[79]For discussion of this issue, see John M. Robson, "Artist and Scientist: Harriet Taylor and John Stuart Mill," *Queen's Quarterly*, 73 (Summer 1966), 167–86, and "Mill on Women and Other Poets," *Victorian Studies Association Newsletter*, No. XII (Nov. 1973), 75–80.

to the intelligibleness of the abstract, when not embodied in the concrete."[80] In the Preface to the *Analysis*, he expands on the failure, though with his usual sense of needed justification:

an opening was made for some mistakes, and occasional insufficiency of analysis, by a mental quality which the author exhibits not unfrequently in his speculations, though as a practical thinker both on public and on private matters it was quite otherwise; a certain impatience of detail. The bent of his mind was towards that, in which also his greatest strength lay; in seizing the larger features of a subject—the commanding laws which govern and connect many phenomena. Having reached these, he sometimes gives himself up to the current of thoughts which those comprehensive laws suggest, not stopping to guard himself carefully in the minutiae of their application, nor devoting much of his thoughts to anticipating all the objections that could be made, though the necessity of replying to some of them might have led him to detect imperfections in his analyses. (102–3.)

The most telling parallel, however, is found between the accounts of James Mill's character and moral effect on the young in the *Autobiography* and in the Preface to the *Analysis*. It is tempting to quote the former at length, but one extract will perhaps be sufficient to suggest the whole.

My father's moral inculcations were at all times mainly those of the "Socratici viri": justice, temperance (to which he gave a very extended application), veracity, persever-ance, readiness to encounter pain and especially labour; regard for the public good; estima-tion of persons according to their merits, and of things according to their intrinsic useful-ness; a life of exertion, in contradiction to one of self-indulgent sloth. These and other moralities he conveyed in brief sentences, uttered as occasion arose, of grave exhortation, or stern reprobation and contempt.[81]

With that account one must compare the passage in the Preface:

The moral qualities which shone in his conversation were, if possible, more valuable to those who had the privilege of sharing it, than even the intellectual. They were precisely such as young men of cultivated intellect, with good aspirations but a character not yet thoroughly formed, are likely to derive most benefit from. A deeply rooted trust in the general progress of the human race, joined with a good sense which made him never build unreasonable or exaggerated hopes on any one event or contingency; an habitual estimate of men according to their real worth as sources of good to their fellow-creatures, and an unaffected contempt for the weaknesses or temptations that divert them from that object, —making those with whom he conversed feel how painful it would be to them to be counted by him among such backsliders; a sustained earnestness, in which neither vanity nor personal ambition had any part, and which spread from him by a sympathetic contagion to those who had sufficient moral preparation to value and seek the opportunity; this was the mixture of qualities which made his conversation almost unrivalled in its salutary moral effect. He has been accused of asperity, and there was asperity in some few of his writings; but no party spirit, personal rivalry, or wounded *amour-propre* ever stirred it up. (101.)[82]

---

[80]*CW*, I, 27.

[81]*Ibid.*, 49. The passage continues with an account of James Mill's moral character that gives clear indications of its effect on John Mill and other young associates.

[82]The reference to "asperity" undoubtedly derives from the remarks attributed to

Few sons have done so much to praise while explaining—but then few fathers have needed both so much.

## BOTANICAL WRITINGS

MOST STUDENTS of Mill's thought, as well as those casually acquainted with his writings and reputation, would find it odd that the *Examiner*'s collective obituary of Mill included a section entitled "His Botanical Studies," by Henry Trimen.[83] But in fact Mill's passion for field botany began early and continued—indeed may be said to have contributed—to his death.

One can date the initiation quite accurately. Sir Samuel Bentham and family took their young guest with them on a tour of the Pyrenees and vicinity in August and September of 1820, during which George Bentham, who was to become one of the leading botanists of the century, was making the observations that led to his first book, *Catalogue des plantes indigènes des Pyrénées et du Bas-Languedoc* (1826). He introduced the fourteen-year-old Mill, six years his junior, to the pleasures of gathering and, emphatically, of *cataloguing*. When the party settled down in Montpellier for the winter celebrated in Mill studies as the hothouse forcing-ground of his precocity, Mill immediately reported in his notebook, *inter* important *alia*, the activity that became as incessant as he could manage: "Je m'occupai pendant toute la journée à écrire mon journal, à arranger mes plantes, et à lire l'oraison *Milonienne* de Ciceron."[84] Such entries occur frequently.[85]

Not entirely coincidentally, Mill's only reference in the *Autobiography* to his botanical passion comes in the midst of his vivid account of his true inception into the utilitarian faith, when it "burst" upon him, the "feeling rushed" upon him, that "a new era in thought" was commencing; the "vista of improvement" that Jeremy

---

Bentham in the "Memoir" by Bowring that closes his edition of Bentham's works. For the background, and Mill's reply, which is here echoed, see "Letter to the Editor of the Edinburgh Review, on James Mill," *CW*, I, 533–8.

[83]The tributes, published in the *Examiner* on 17 May, 1873, 502–18, were gathered and published as *John Stuart Mill: His Life and Works*, ed. H.R. Fox Bourne (London: Dalton; New York: Holt, 1873; the quotations below are from the latter). Trimen, who knew Mill slightly, was on the staff of the British Museum, and coedited the *Journal of Botany*. The only discursive article dealing with the subject is Simon Curtis's "The Philosopher's Flowers," *Encounter*, LXXX (Feb. 1988), 26–33, which gives interesting details about the collection in Avignon described below.

[84]"French Journal and Notebook," *CW*, XXVI, 125 (entry for 16 Oct., 1820). The succeeding entries provide more evidence.

[85]Mill regrettably seems to have had little to do with George Bentham after the latter's return to England in the late 1820s. A friendly letter, in response to one prompted by Mill's gift to him of his *System of Logic*, dwells on botanical matters, including specimens and books, and implies some further contact (*EL, CW*, XIII, 577 [14 Mar., 1843]).

Bentham opened up was "sufficiently large and brilliant to light up" his life. Typically for Mill, this personal dedication depended on a method that offered clarity and evidence; one of the central persuasive elements in Bentham's *Traités* was its classification of offences. Typically for Bentham, the model was scientific: "The Linnaeus of Natural History the world has had for some time past. The Linnaeus of Ethics is yet to come."[86]

Mill's comment in the *Autobiography* emphasizes the links:

Logic, and the dialectics of Plato, which had formed so large a part of my previous training, had given me a strong relish for accurate classification. This taste had been strengthened and enlightened by the study of botany, on the principles of what is called the Natural Method, which I had taken up with great zeal, though only as an amusement,[87] during my stay in France; and when I found scientific classification applied to the great and complex subject of Punishable Acts, under the guidance of the ethical principle of Pleasurable and Painful Consequences, followed out in the method of detail introduced into these subjects by Bentham, I felt taken up to an eminence from which I could survey a vast mental domain, and see stretching out into the distance intellectual results beyond all computation.[88]

The lesson is applied in Mill's *System of Logic*, especially in Bk. IV, Chap. viii, Sect. 5. After describing the "natural arrangement" based on "natural groups," Mill deals with the general value of classification:

Although the scientific arrangements of organic nature afford as yet the only complete example of the true principles of rational classification, whether as to the formation of groups or of series, those principles are applicable to all cases in which mankind are called upon to bring the various parts of any extensive subject into mental co-ordination. They are as much to the point when objects are to be classed for purposes of art or business, as for those of science. The proper arrangement, for example, of a code of laws, depends on the same scientific conditions as the classifications in natural history; nor could there be a better preparatory discipline for that important function, than the study of the principles of a natural arrangement, not only in the abstract, but in their actual application to the class of phenomena for which they were first elaborated, and which are still the best school for learning their use. Of this the great authority on codification, Bentham, was perfectly aware: and his early *Fragment on Government*, the admirable introduction to a series of writings unequalled in their department, contains clear and just views (as far as they go) on the meaning of a natural arrangement, such as could scarcely have occurred to any one who lived anterior to the age of Linnaeus and Bernard de Jussieu.[89]

[86]*Deontology*, in *Deontology, together with A Table of the Springs of Action and Article on Utilitarianism*, ed. Amnon Goldworth (Oxford: Clarendon Press, 1983), 219.
[87]In the Early Draft, following his wife's suggestion, he rejected "a mere amusement" (*CW*, I, 68).
[88]*Autobiography*, *CW*, I, 69. The full account of the experience is on 67–71.
[89]*CW*, VIII, 731–2. Trimen quotes part of this passage in arguing that Mill's interest in classification was stimulated by botany: "The views expressed so clearly in these chapters are chiefly founded on the actual needs experienced by the systematic botanist; and the argument is largely sustained by references to botanical systems and arrangements. Most botanists agree with Mr. Mill in his objections to Dr. Whewell's views of a natural classification by resemblance to 'types,' instead of in accordance with well-selected characters. . . ." (47.)

It would have been inappropriate in that context for Mill to have said that he had been taken by Bentham's writings "up to an eminence" whence he "could survey a vast mental domain," and indeed, while admitting the great importance of classification to his thought, it would be silly pretence to assert that his botanical excursions always took him up to these heights: it was the ethical vision that inspired him. Nonetheless, his moral philosophy came, through a complicated personal development, to incorporate aesthetic feelings; his intense appreciation of landscape, first stimulated on the same journey that introduced him to botany, helped shape the poetic values that he found essential to moral practice.[90] And, holding as closely as he could to the dictum *mens sana in corpore sano*, he certainly worked for mental as for physical health in his constant and admirable walking regime, which allowed for continuous stooping to the vegetable level without evident damage to his sacroiliac.

The central purposes of his *Autobiography* not being biographical, he gives merely a passing reference to what was actually a fully realized avocation, alluding to his early habit of "taking long rural walks" on Sundays, and to his holiday "tours, chiefly pedestrian," with chosen companions, followed later in life by "longer journeys or excursions, alone or with other friends."[91] It is in the records of these walks, tours, and journeys—sufficiently pedestrian in style—that one can see the importance to Mill of his passion.

The evidence comes in several forms, physical as well as literary. As early as September 1828 Mill was able to engage Henry Cole for several evenings "pleasantly enough in the examination of his Hortus Siccus"—an arranged collection of dried plants—from which Mill gave him several specimens.[92] By 1840 the collection in the family's Kensington Square house, according to Caroline Fox, amounted to an "immense herbarium";[93] it continued to expand, and his Avignon collection was housed in a herbarium specially built for him in 1868 by his stepdaughter, Helen Taylor.[94]

[90]For the initial experience, see *CW*, I, 59. The importance is revealed in his essays on poetry, also in *CW*, I, and in *Journals and Speeches*, *CW*, XXVI–XXVII (see the Introduction to those volumes, xli–liv). For critical comment, see John M. Robson, "J.S. Mill's Theory of Poetry," *University of Toronto Quarterly*, XXIX (July 1960), 420–38.

[91]*CW*, I, 85–7.

[92]Entries for 4, 11, 18, and 25 Sept., 1828, in Cole's Diary, Victoria and Albert Museum.

[93]Caroline Fox, *Memories of Old Friends*, ed. Horace N. Pym, 2nd ed., 2 vols. (London: Smith, Elder, 1882), I, 189.

[94]Insisting on his pleasure at being out of the House of Commons, Mill described (in Bentham's terms) his Avignon retreat to W.T. Thornton on 16 January, 1869: "The terrace, you must know, as it goes round two sides of the house, has got itself dubbed the 'semi-circumgyratory.' In addition to this, Helen has built me a *herbarium*—a little room fitted up with closets for my plants, shelves for my botanical books, & a great table whereon to manipulate them all. Thus you see with my herbarium, my vibratory, & my semi-circumgyratory I am in clover & you may imagine with what scorn I think of the H. of

xxxii *Introduction*

These collections, which included Indian plants given to Mill by his colleague, Dr. Royle, a surgeon and naturalist who was in charge of the East India Company's correspondence relating to vegetable productions,[95] are now preserved in herbaria in at least four countries: in England in the collection of the Royal Botanic Gardens at Kew and the Holmesdale Natural Historical Club Museum in Reigate, Surrey;[96] in France at the Musée Requien, Avignon; in the United States at the Academy of Natural Sciences in Philadelphia, the National Arboretum in Washington, and Harvard University; and in Australia in the Royal Botanic Gardens and National Herbarium, South Yarra, Victoria.

The Avignon collection, consisting mainly of plants from the department of Vaucluse (with some English and a few other specimens), was at Mill's request put at the disposal of his friend and botanical collaborator, Jean Henri Fabre. It includes ten loose-leaf volumes containing about 1000 specimens with labels giving the plant's name and the date of its accession, the collection beginning in 1859, when Mill took up residence in Avignon following his wife's death, and continuing virtually up to his own death.[97]

The other collections (with the exception of that in the Holmesdale Natural Historical Club Museum, the provenance of which is unknown) were all originally part of the gift by Helen Taylor to Joseph Dalton Hooker, the Director of the Royal Botanic Gardens at Kew. She made the offer on 27 September, 1873, saying Hooker could have a choice of specimens for his own "private or any public collection."[98] He responded favourably, saying that in his view the plants should go to the National Collection at Kew, and on 9 February, 1874, she reported that the "packages" of his selection were now ready for shipment, and said he was free to choose from the many duplicates for his own collection.[99] A year later, four

---

C., which, comfortable club as it is said to be, could offer me none of these comforts, or more properly speaking these necessaries of life." (*LL*, *CW*, XVII, 1549.)

[95]These, as of more exotic interest than Mill's European collections, have made tracing the steps in the dispersal somewhat easier.

[96]Some records mistakenly indicate that some of his plants are at Cambridge University because of the common confusion arising from the location of Harvard University in Cambridge, Massachusetts.

[97]For an account of this collection, with a very condensed summary of Mill's career as a botanist, see Curtis, "The Philosopher's Flowers," in which places from which the plants were gathered are listed on 29–31.

[98]A.l.s., Royal Botanic Gardens, "Kew Herbarium—Presentations to," 1900, Vol. 2, ff. 527–9.

[99]A.l.s., Royal Botanic Gardens, English letters 1843/1900, Vol. 103, ff. 23–4. Typical of her punctiliousness (or waspishness), is her explanation of the terms: "I have seen a statement in some of the newspapers to the effect that Mr Mill bequeathed his herbarium to the National Collection at Kew. This statement is entirely erroneous, as I believe you are aware. Had it been true, I should of course have had nothing to do but to despatch the whole collection at once to Kew, and if to you, to you, only in your official capacity. But the fact is

cases were shipped (at her expense), and she said on 20 March, 1875 (assuming that they had arrived) that she was "very glad" to accept his suggestion that he donate the duplicates to "Cambridge University, U.S."[100]

On 7 April, 1875, Hooker addressed a formal letter to the Secretary of the Royal Gardens saying that the gift, "of considerable extent and in excellent condition" had been received, and that an official letter of thanks should be sent to Helen Taylor. He commented:

> These collections are of both scientific value and historical interest, on account of the eminence of their former possessor as a philosopher and writer, and because his botanical tastes and acquirements were well and widely known. In early life Mr Mill was a diligent observer and collector of British plants, and made some important discoveries relating to the Flora of these Islands, and he continued collecting and observing wherever he resided or travelled up to a very short period before his death.[101]

Subsequently Hooker's annual report included an account of the gift:

> The complete herbarium of the late J. Stuart Mill was presented after his death by Miss Helen Taylor. Although better known for his philosophical and other writings Mr. Mill collected diligently in the neighbourhood of London and in his later years travelled extensively in south Europe. The range of his specimens extends from the Pyrenees to the Bithynian Olympus, and Greece is particularly well represented partly by plants gathered by his own hands and partly by a collection procured from Professor Van Heldreich of Athens. Amongst plants from Asia Minor is a new and very distinct species of flat-leaved *Sedum* which has been described by Mr. Baker in the Journal of Botany under the name of *Sedum Millii*. A selection of about 2,530 species has been made for the Kew Herbarium, and it is Miss Taylor's wish that the remainder be presented to Harvard University, U.S.A. and to the Botanical Museum of the Melbourne Gardens.[102]

What happened to the specimens not chosen by Hooker originally, which consequently remained in France, is not known; probably they are the non-Vaucluse items in the Musée Requien. Also a record of the donation to Melbourne has not been located. The rest of Helen Taylor's gift took a complicated route: Hooker consulted, as he had indicated he would, Asa Gray, Director of the herbarium at Harvard (now named after him). Gray agreed to accept the material Hooker did not wish to retain at Kew, and when it arrived, made a selection from

---

that Mr Mill left his Herbarium to me, leaving the disposal entirely to my discretion, and with no expression of any wish on the subject. [In her letter of 27 September, 1873, she had expressly said that it was Mill's "wish" that Fabre have the Vaucluse plants.] Aware of his high respect for yourself I asked your advice as to the best disposition to be made of the major part of it: and you were kind enough to favour me with your advice, recommending me to prcsent it to the National Collection at Kew."

[100]A.l.s., *ibid*.

[101]Autograph draft, Royal Botanic Gardens, "Kew Herbarium—Presentations to," 1900, Vol. 2, f. 528.

[102]*Report on the Progress and Condition of the Royal Gardens at Kew, During the Year 1875*, 14. For the reference to Baker, see n136 below.

it, which is now at Harvard.[103] He then, in consultation with John H. Redfield, a scientific friend in Philadelphia, donated the bulk of the collection to the Academy of Natural Sciences of Philadelphia, which was in the process of revitalizing its collections. On its receipt in April 1878, this portion of Mill's herbarium contained some 3000 species,[104] most of which are still in the Academy's collection. Some, however, were traded by Redfield, then Conservator of the Botanical Section in the Academy, to Isaac Martindale, another active supporter; his collection eventually was purchased by the U.S. National Arboretum in 1964, and in it were some 200 sheets attributable to Mill.

The written records of Mill's botanical passion run from single labels,[105] through lists and notebooks, references in journals and letters, and anecdotes by others, to the articles included in this volume, and the books in his library. Like all dedicated observers in that heyday of natural history, Mill knew the value of lists; like many, he was obsessive in keeping them; like few, he was famous enough to have them preserved. Short lists are in the Mill papers at Yale and Johns Hopkins and in the Mill-Taylor Collection of the London School of Economics,[106] but the main itemized records fill five notebooks in the Mill-Taylor Collection.[107]

[103]There are no pre-1898 accession records for the Gray herbarium, and the Mill items are evidently not identified as his. There are many sheets marked "ex herb. hook" or "ex herb. kew," several of which are of Royle's Indian collections, and so almost certainly originated in the Taylor gift.

[104]Dr. David G. Frodin of the Department of Botany, Academy of Natural Sciences of Philadelphia, to whom I am indebted for some of the detail above, supplied this figure; in its official letter of thanks to Asa Gray, the Academy says: "2000 specimens of plants from the collection of the late John Stuart Mill, principally from Europe and Asia" (Royal Botanic Gardens, "Kew Herbarium—Presentations to," 1900, Vol. 2, f. 529).

[105]The University of Bristol Library has a single signed label (presumably collected for its signature) for Cirsium oleraccum, gathered "near Brussels."

[106]At Yale there are two folios giving findings near Orange in France. Item 35 in the Johns Hopkins' collection also gives French items, from Gard, Hénault, Bouches-du-Rhône, and Drôme. Item 12 in Vol. LIX of the Mill-Taylor Collection, a single sheet which probably originally enclosed a specimen, dates from his first enthusiasm; it reads: "Buxus sempervirens L. / Restinclière, garrigues / 1821 Février." In Vol. LXVIII, item 14, a letter of 6 August, 1842, to Henry Cole, has on its verso a list headed: "Plants found in the neighbourhood of London but not in Surrey."

[107]Vol. XXXI contains (in this order) undated entries from Marseille, Italy, the Brenner Pass, Austria, Germany, and Coblentz; then France, Italy and Sicily, and Greece; then Italy again, and St. Gothard-Switzerland; and finally the Lake District and the Wye Valley (f. 22v).

Vol. XXXII contains a running record of what Mill collected, month by month, from October 1858 to October 1868, recording excursions mainly in the south of France, but also in the Pyrenees, Greece and Switzerland, the United Kingdom, and Austria.

Vol. XXXIII evidently follows Vol. XXXII, having monthly lists from April 1869 to May 1873 (when Mill died). Up to July 1870, all the entries are from France; then they are from various English and Scottish stations (August 1870 to July 1871); then again from France until June 1872, when there are some entries from Italy and the Alps. English finds

Mill's walking-tour journals from 1827 to 1832 are mainly topographical in detail, but they sufficiently indicate that, in spite of the respectable distances covered, he took time to stoop and study. On the second day of the first trip, for example, he reports that an otherwise dull walk near Bognor "however afforded the Atriplex laciniata and littoralis, Hordeum maritimum, Phleum arenarium and Beta maritima."[108] This is typical, being simply a list that is revelatory only to the inditer and the initiate. Mill's role as instructor[109] occasionally appears: "I will enumerate the plants which a young botanist may expect to find" in the Vale of Aylesbury.[110] But only a few passages evoke feelings attractive to more general readers: in Upper Yewdale, "a complete Alpine valley,"

for the first time we saw some alpine plants, particularly the bright yellow Saxifrage, one of the most beautiful of our mountain plants whose golden flowers grow in tufts up the moist sides of this dell. . . . The pass [beyond Tilberthwaite] contains much boggy ground, which is completely covered with that delightful shrub, the sweet gale, also called the Dutch myrtle, from its myrtle like appearance and smell: here and in Langdale, whole acres are covered with it, and the air is perfumed by it to a great distance. Mixed with its little bushes, a more delicate plant the Lancashire bog asphodel raises its bright yellow spikes.[111]

Generally more interesting and happy evidence is found in the diary of Mill's friend Henry Cole and in Mill's correspondence to and concerning his family and friends. Indeed Cole's diary again supplies unique information. The first botanical reference is dated 4 September, 1828: "Drank tea with John Mill and employed the evening in the examination of a portion of his Botanical Specimens of which he liberally made me several presents." On the next day he "Botanized in Battersea fields and Breakfasted with J. Mill," and from 11 to 25 September he employed three evenings, "pleasantly enough in the examination of [Mill's] Hortus

---

appear again in August, September, and November 1872, and April 1873, before the final list from Orange in May.

Vol. XXXIV is undated, except that near the beginning Mill writes "also in 1863." Its sections are headed: "Species and habitats unverified in Surrey" (ff. 1v–23v), and "Additional Habitats not verified" (ff. 25v–60r).

Vol. XXXV contains several separate items: a pencilled list without dates or locations, lists of Greek finds (mostly on Olympus), with a list of corrections, and lists headed: "*Entre Broussa et la mer*," "*Partie basse et boisée du Mont Olympe au dessous du plateau*" and "*Plateau du Mont Olympe*," "*Partie alpine du Mont Olympe*," and "*Thérapia et Buyukdéré*." Finally there is a letter from Alexander Irvine to Mill, and a scrap in Irvine's hand giving directions, with a hand-drawn map on the verso, to a botanical station.

[108]More finds are recorded in the next few sentences: see "Walking Tour of Sussex," *CW*, XXVII, 457 (21 July, 1827).

[109]Having inducted Henry Cole, he continued to cultivate him: see below, and *EL*, *CW*, XII, 534–5 (6 Aug., 1842), with the matter cited in n106 above.

[110]"Walking Tour of Berkshire, Buckinghamshire, Oxfordshire, and Surrey," *CW*, XXVII, 490 (10 July, 1828).

[111]"Walking Tour of Yorkshire and the Lake District," *ibid.*, 518 (14 July, 1831).

Siccus."[112] Cole also records that on 12 June, 1829, he went to Battersea Fields "in company with John Mill and his brother [presumably James, then aged about 13] to seek for the Orchis latifolia which (as is usual in most cases where there is a specific proposal) we could not find." And a year later, on 29 June, 1830, he reports that when he called on Mill he found him "exulting in his discovery of the Martigon Lily at Dorking."[113]

Mill's correspondence also has some delightful moments. In 1837, writing in Greek to his brother Henry, aged seventeen, Mill says (translated and with place names interpreted): "In the wet parts of the source of River [Riverhead] I have seen a large plant and want to have it. But perhaps you have found it either in [Riverhead] or in [the Weald?]."[114] And two years later he writes to his mother from Venice: "Among other fruits of my journey [in Italy] I have botanized much, & come back loaded with plants. By the bye among those I want Henry to dry for me, I forgot to mention the common elder."[115] After Henry's death in 1840, there is evidence of even closer collaboration with the youngest boy in the family, George, who contributed three articles to the *Phytologist*; in the most impressive of these, "List of the Flowering Plants in the Neighbourhood of Great Marlow, Bucks, in the Early Part of the Summer 1843" (I [June 1844], 983–95), John undoubtedly collaborated.[116]

Nothing is known of Mill's sisters' botanical interests, and his wife was perceived as too delicate for field pursuits. She, however, took or was induced to adopt an interest in his hobby. For instance, he reports to her from St. Hélier during his continental search for health in 1854: "I have made a good many excellent captures of plants." And again from Morlaix, recalling an earlier trip with her and her daughter Helen, he comments: "I have got few plants yet in France—the botanizing at Vire & Dinan in 1844 seems to have exhausted this part of the country."[117] Indeed in almost every one of his daily letters in this series there is some reference to botany, usually conveying the pleasure and often the fun of the game.

When I got to the inn [in Palermo] I was not even tired, except indeed my arms with the weight of plants I carried, to the edification & amidst the apostrophes of the public—who were full of questions & remarks—the most complimentary of which was one I overheard, one woman having given a shout of astonishment (all speaking here by the common people is shouting) when another quietly remarked to her that it was for my bella & was a

[112]On the last of these evenings he first met James Mill, though he had already been in the house several times (Cole's Diary, Victoria and Albert Museum).

[113]*Ibid.*

[114]*EL, CW,* XIII, 743n (6 July, 1837).

[115]*Ibid.,* 399 (19 May, 1839).

[116]For a fuller account, see John M. Robson, "George Grote Mill: Another Field Botanist," *Mill News Letter,* XXII (Winter 1987), 9–16. The collaboration is noted by Trimen, 45.

[117]*LL, CW,* XIV, 210 (13 June, 1854), and 216–17 (19 June, 1854).

galanteria. I wish indeed it had been for my bella, & a day never passes when I do not wish to bring flowers home to her. You see by this how beautiful the flowers are: this time, besides some lovely blue flowers, there were some noble specimens of the tall yellow asphodel of our gardens, which grew quite comfortably out of the rocks of Pellegrino & were gathered for me by an enterprising goatherd. On entering the town I was actually stopped at the octroi—I was asked what those were: "plants" I said—"what do they serve for?" "per sciente". what did I bring them for? "for curiosity"—"there was nothing doganale"—they were quite satisfied & dismissed me with the pleased animated look & voice which everybody here has on every occasion.

Complaints such as the following are not to be taken seriously when the voice is an addict's:

I was not at all tired, except the hand which carried the plants, for the load . . . was quite painful to mind & body. I never felt so much the embarras des richesses. Determining them with imperfect books takes several hours in every 24: it is now past 12 & I have only determined about a third, the rest must remain in water & in the tin case till tomorrow—to be determined by daylight—nor have I been able to change a single paper. I am here in the season of flowers as well as of all other beauty.[118]

The reports continued at home as well as abroad: "On Monday morning there was a Scotch mist but I made out my walk over Wrynose & down the Duddon to Broughton & though I could not see much of the mountains in Little Langdale it was still very fine & I found a rare fern & a rare mint, peppermint to wit, which I have never found before."[119] And when, after her mother's death, Helen Taylor became his almost constant companion, she not only received the botanical news, but joined him on several trips that included, as was mandatory for him, collecting samples. Even she, much more physically active than her mother, sometimes found Mill too much for her. For instance, after climbing the Pic du Midi through ice and snow, she comments from a warm ground-level, to her brother Algernon on 16 July, 1859: "Mr. Mill is still well, although he suffers from the great heat. Nevertheless as he walks all the mornings, determines plants all the afternoons and often sits up till 2 o'clock drying papers, and does not suffer from fatigue he must be getting better."[120] The most significant series of letters from Mill to Helen Taylor concerns a major attempt to catalogue the collection in his Blackheath house, during January and February 1860, when he suggests to Helen, who was in Avignon, that she can "trace [his] progress" in Charles Cardale Babington's *Manual of British Botany*.[121]

Of course Mill's non-familial correspondence also reflects his botanical

[118]*Ibid.*, 341 (24 Feb., 1855), from Palermo, and 429 (21 and 23 Apr., 1855), from Athens.

[119]*Ibid.*, XV, 537 (16 Sept., 1857), from Settle. Cf. *ibid.*, 538, 564, and 566–7.

[120]Mill-Taylor Collection, Vol. XXIV, no. 712.

[121]*LL*, *CW*, XV, 667 (2 Feb., 1860), from Blackheath. For the other references to his mighty labour, see *ibid.*, 661, 664, 667, 671, 673, 675, 678, 680, 681–2, 684, 686, and 687.

activities. Throughout his life, his letters written during or after tours report interesting findings to sympathetic ears (and at least temporarily sedentary legs). An early example reveals Mill in May 1830 moving towards acquaintance with William Jackson Hooker, the leading English botanist of the day, and author of the just-published *British Flora*. Through the agency of Henry Cole, who knew Hooker, Mill sends his notes on the work, giving additional stations, especially for *Oenanthe aprifloria* and *Vicia sativa*. He adds:

As I am very favourably situated for observing the plants of Surrey, which have hardly been observed at all since Ray's time if we except those in the immediate vicinity of London, which are figured in Curtis's *Flora Londinensis* and many of which appear to have become extinct in the situations where Curtis found them, I may possibly be able hereafter to make other communications of a nature similar to this, if the present one should prove to be of any use. I have explored some parts of the County very fully, and almost every part of it more or less, but I expect to make many more discoveries before I have done.[122]

The immediate result was an exchange of specimens; the gradual one, Mill's acceptance by the botanical community.[123] He walked with some of the most avid collectors, and corresponded widely. The most extensive single letter is worth extracting at length, because it suggests much that may have been lost in non-extant correspondence. His friend Henry S. Chapman, in New Zealand, wrote concerning the possibility of importing useful plants (a proper enough concern for utilitarians, especially since the school's founder had been concerned with importing and exporting plants useful as well as decorative). Mill replied, "I lost no time in asking Dr. Royle for the Himalayan seeds," and "seeds of any useful plants that are likely to suit your climate." He had arranged for them to be sent directly by Dr. Jameson, a botanist who had pioneered tea planting in India, and was Superintendent of the East India Company's botanical garden at Saharunpore. He asked Chapman to send Jameson New Zealand seeds for trial in India, and he added, turning to the personal:

Many thanks for thinking of ferns for me. If you have anybody there who can name them it would be useful, as there are probably no books here on the botany of New Zealand; but if not, I will find someone to name and describe them here, as in any case there are likely to be new ones among them. Any other plants would be interesting as well as ferns, — all is fish that comes to my net, and there may be among plants picked up indiscriminately in a new country, as many and as interesting nondescripts as there were in Graham's Mexican collection.[124]

The concluding reference indicates the network involved: George John Graham, one of Mill's closest friends in the 1820s, travelling in Mexico from 1827 to 1829,

[122]*EL, CW*, XII, 50–1 (26 May, 1830).
[123]See *ibid.*, 67–8 and 69–70.
[124]*Ibid.*, XIII, 685 (12 Nov., 1845). Chapman delivered at least the ferns to Mill, who returned thanks for the "beautiful set of ferns which arrived safe, in perfect condition, and gave [him] great pleasure" (*ibid.*, 732 [29 Feb., 1848]).

had collected some 400 specimens of Mexican plants; his collection is mentioned by George Bentham in his *Plantae Hartwegianae* (1839). Mill botanized with Royle,[125] and with two of the main supporters of the *Phytologist*, its second publisher, William Pamplin, with whom Mill became friendly, and its final editor, Alexander Irvine, who became one of Mill's favourite walking companions.

All this activity did not mean that Mill confused collecting with extirpation. In company with other botanists, he objected strenuously to the Royal Horticultural Society's offering in 1864 "three prizes for the three best herbaria of every county in England, and three additional prizes for the best of these best," because the result would be "the extinction of nearly all the rare species in our already so scanty flora." In his view, expressed in a letter to the editor of the *Gardeners' Chronicle*, the invitation included the temptation to "all the dabblers in plant collection, a race whose selfish rapacity certainly needs no additional temptation, . . . to hunt out all the rare plants in every part of the country and to carry off all they find, or destroy what they do not carry off, in order that not only they may themselves possess the plant, but that their competitors may not."[126]

All of Mill's botanical writings intended for publication appeared in *The Phytologist: A Botanical Journal*, except for his loyal notice of the *Phytologist* in the *Westminster Review* in 1843. The journal, which began publication in June 1841, was initially conducted by George Luxford, was owned (and printed) by another botanical enthusiast, Edward Newman, and was published by yet another, John Van Voorst. From May 1855 to March 1863 the editor was Alexander Irvine.[127] Typical of its times, the *Phytologist* signalled the importance of natural theology by the inscription in a medallion, "Wisdom of God in Creation," in all volumes in the first series, and by religious epigraphs in Greek and Latin in both

---

[125]See *LL*, *CW*, XIV, 41–2 and 59.

[126]26 Jan., 1864, quoted in the obituary of Mill in the *Gardeners' Chronicle*, 17 May, 1873, 679; see Anna J. Mill, "J.S.M., Conservationist," *Mill News Letter*, X (Winter 1975), 2–3. The letter will be included in *Additional Letters*, *CW*, XXXII.

[127]As is often the case with such specialized, or "class," journals, the publishing history has difficult patches. The monthly numbers sold for sixpence until June 1842, when the price was raised to a shilling, and the issues were enlarged to 32 pages from 24 (having been increased from 16 in January 1842). Counting on faithful readers, the editors did not worry if some numbers ended in mid-article, and if the pagination guiding the binding into volumes was far from regular. The first series, edited by Luxford, was suspended when he died in June 1854, as the back wrapper, following p. 216, announces. (A cumulative index was issued with this number.) One concluding number, however, identified as No. clix, was issued two and a half years later, long after the publication in May 1855 of the first number of the new series, which was also called No. clix. (The printer of the New Series was John Edward Taylor.) The publisher of the first series, Van Voorst, advertised his last number on the front wrapper in the number for February 1857 of the new series, calling it the "Supplementary Number of the 'Phytologist,' completing Mr. Newman's Series." Perhaps it was automatically sent to subscribers to the new series. (Irvine hints at the problems in n.s. II [Jan. 1857], 1–2.)

series. Mill was evidently not troubled by this devotion, which in any case did not flavour the journal's articles.

Mill's contributions appeared from the first number in June 1841 until October 1862, not long before the journal ceased publication. They are not regularly distributed, however, seven of the ten in the first series being from 1841, and nothing appearing between 1845 and 1856, when the first of his eighteen in the second series appeared. They are similarly unequal in length and significance, some dealing with single species, and one, "Botany in Spain," four parts printed in five instalments, being a comparatively full record of a walking tour with Helen Taylor.[128] Not the least of the conclusions to be drawn from it is just how energetic they both were; the two intervening years had, evidently, brought her up to his competitive standards.

Like many of the articles in the *Phytologist*, some of Mill's contributions are mere extracts from letters intended for publication in full or in part. One can only guess whether he sent material to the first series that was not published, but under Irvine's editorship each number included a list of "Communications Received" that gives firmer evidence.[129] Commonly there are close to twenty names in the list; Mill's name or initials appear comparatively frequently—a few dedicated readers outdid him by writing virtually every month. It would appear that mention in this list did not preclude publication of an actual extract elsewhere in the same or succeeding issues, though there were no regular quotations from correspondence until 1862, except for 1858, when three extracts from Mill appeared. Undoubtedly some of the "communications" received from Mill were printed, but certainly not all of his articles were listed as communications.[130]

Further evidence of his passion, not in itself persuasive or exciting for the general reader, comes from his collection of reference works. It is not now possible to determine the extent of Mill's botanical library, especially that portion of it that was in his Avignon home. The following titles, however, were included in the gift of his library to Somerville College, Oxford, in 1907 (those marked with

---

[128]Mill had also botanized in northern Spain in July 1859, a year before the trip that resulted in "Botany of Spain." See his letters of 22 June to Pasquale Villari (*LL*, *CW*, XV, 628), and of 14 Aug., 1859 to Henri Bordère, a botanist of the Hautes Pyrénées (to be found in *Additional Letters*, *CW*, XXXII).

[129]Such lists are, of course, a common feature of class journals. There was no regular section replying to correspondents until 1862.

[130]There are no originals of any of his letters to the *Phytologist*, so only references to their reception can be given. In n.s. I: Apr. 1856, 304; Oct. 1856, 440; Nov. 1856, 484. In n.s. II: May 1857, 72; Aug. 1857, 192; Sept. 1857, 224; Oct. 1857, 256; Jan. 1858, 328; July 1858, 512; Sept. 1858, 568; Nov. 1858, 632. In n.s. IV: Jan. 1860, 32; Oct. 1860, 320. In n.s. V: Feb. 1861, 64; Apr. 1861, 128; May 1861, 160; July 1861, 224; Aug. 1861, 256; Sept. 1861, 288; Oct. 1861, 320; Nov. 1861, 352. In n.s. VI: Feb. 1862, 64; Apr. 1862, 128; Sept. 1862, 256; Oct. 1862, 314 (the extract in the editor's mention of the correspondence is given as the last item in the text below); Jan. 1863, 416; Feb. 1863, 448; and Mar. 1863, 480 (the last number of the *Phytologist*).

an asterisk are no longer in the collection): C.C. Babington, *Manual of British Botany*, 5th ed. (London, 1862); A. de Brébisson, *Flore de la Normandie*, Pt. 1: *Phanérogamie* (Caen, 1836); J.A. Brewer, *Flora of Surrey* (London, 1863), and *A New Flora of the Neighbourhood of Reigate, Surrey* (London, 1856); W.A. Bromfield, *Flora Vectensis: Being a Systematic Description of the . . . Flowering Plants . . . Indigenous to the Isle of Wight*, ed. W.J. Hooker and T.B. Salter (London, 1856); George Louis le Clerc Buffon, *Histoire naturelle* (first 15 vols. of 1st ed. of 44 vols.) (Paris, 1749–67); M.H. Cowell, *A Floral Guide for East Kent* (Faversham, 1839); T.B. Flower, *Flora of the Isle of Thanet* (Ramsgate, 1842); E.F. Forster, *Flora of Tunbridge Wells* (London, 1816); G. Francis, *An Analysis of the British Ferns and Their Allies* (London, 1837); *\*Observations on Modern Gardening* (London, 1770); G.S. Gibson, *Flora of Essex* (London, 1852); Joseph Dalton Hooker, *The Student's Flora of the British Islands* (London, 1870); William Jackson Hooker, *The British Flora*, 3rd ed., 2 vols. (London, 1835); \*Alexander Irvine, *Illustrated Handbook of British Plants* (London, 1858); John Lindley, *A Natural System of Botany; or, A Systematic View of the Organisation, Natural Affinities, and Geographic Distribution, of the Whole Vegetable Kingdom*, 2nd ed. (London, 1836); Edward Newman, *A History of British Ferns, and Allied Plants* (London, 1844); \*Daniel Oliver, *Lessons in Elementary Botany* (Leipzig and Cambridge, 1864); *\*Phytologist*, 15 vols.; G.E. Smith, *Flora of South Kent* (1829); H.C. Watson, *Compendium of the Cybele Britannica*, 4 vols. [one missing] (London, 1868–70), and *Part 1 of Supplement to the Cybele Britannica* (London, 1860). Many of these are well worn, though some must have been difficult to carry in the field.

What they demonstrate in the company of all the other evidence is the remarkable devotion that Mill gave to his avocation. In an age of amateurs, he made a mark, though not a top one. Henry Trimen's assessment is convincng; Mill's notes in the *Phytologist*, he says, though "always clear and accurate," give no "inkling of the great intellectual powers of the writer." They are, he continues,

merely such notes as any working botanical collector is able to supply in abundance. Mainly content with the pursuit as an outdoor occupation, with such an amount of home-work as was necessary to determine the names and affinities of the species, Mr. Mill never penetrated deeply into the philosophy of botany, so as to take rank among those who have, like Herbert Spencer, advanced that science by original work either of experiment or generalization, or have entered into the battle-field where the great biological questions of the day are being fought over.[131]

His slight contributions—slight compared to his work in other areas as well as to the major labours of others in this—are not quite trivial. Best known is the aid he gave in the preparation of Brewer's *Flora of Surrey*.[132] In fact, in the *Flora* stations observed by him are given for virtually every genus and on virtually every

[131]"His Botanical Studies," 46–7.

[132]See, e.g., Ray Desmond, *Dictionary of British and Irish Botanists and Horticulturists* (London: Taylor and Francis, 1977), 437, and Trimen, 44–5.

page. Surrey was his special territory, but certainly not his only one. Mountstuart Grant Duff reports: "I remember once, in the division lobby, asking him whether it was true that he was preparing a Flora of the department of Vaucluse. 'Yes,' he said, 'I make a Flora of every district in which I settle. I made a Flora of Surrey.'"[133] That remark is open to a narrow interpretation, and in fact the only other comparable endeavour seems to have been his collaboration with Fabre, whom he met in 1859, on the flora of Vaucluse.[134] Some of Mill's identifications have been mentioned in the specialist literature,[135] and the taxonomy records his name in the mushroom *Stuartella* and in *Sedum Millii*.[136]

On balance, it would seem, however, that the private outweighed the public utility of Mill's botanizing. The glimpses into his daily life and pleasures certainly help correct the view of him as a joyless moral machine. A letter from Mill to Herbert Spencer, not himself known for playful exuberance,[137] is welcome evidence:

My murderous propensities are confined to the vegetable world. I take as great a delight in the pursuit of plants as you do in that of salmon, and find it an excellent incentive to exercise. Indeed I attribute the good health I am fortunate enough to have, very much to my great love for exercise, and for what I think the most healthy form of it, walking.

My late attack at Paris [at the end of June] was choleraic, dangerous for a few hours, and leaving me a little weak, but I am now quite recovered, thanks partly to having wandered about the Dunes at Calais and the Downs at Dover in pursuit of specimens for my herbarium.[138]

And Henry Trimen's snapshot is evocative:

The writer of this notice well remembers meeting, a few years since, the (at that time) parliamentary logician, with his trousers turned up out of the mud, and armed with the tin insignia of his craft, busily occupied in the search after a marsh-loving rarity in a typical spongy wood on the clay to the north of London.[139]

All in all, it is fitting that Mill's death was related to his loved avocation. On Saturday, 3 May, 1873, he made a fifteen-mile botanizing walk in Orange with

---

[133]*Notes from a Diary, 1886–88*, I, 187, quoted in *Journal of Botany*, XLII (1904), 297.

[134]The idea originated, according to Fabre, with himself, as a means of honouring and utilizing the collections of Requien: "Un homme de bien, dont nous déplorons tous le perte récente, Stuart Mill, concertait ses efforts avec les miens dans cette entreprise" (J. Véran, "Le Souvenir de Stuart Mill à Avignon," *Revue des Deux Mondes* [1937], 215). This passage is quoted by Curtis, "The Philosopher's Flowers," 28–31, who gives a usefully succinct account of their relations, based in part on Lucien Gérin, "L'amité entre Henri Fabre et Stuart Mill et la destruction de la maison de ce dernier, stigmatisée par l'écrivain Henri Bosco," *Bulletin des Amis d'Orange*, No. 84 (1981), 3–5, which in turn quotes extensively from an article by Bosco in *Les Nouvelles Littéraires*, 7 Dec., 1961.

[135]See Desmond, *Dictionary*, 437, and the references there given.

[136]See J.G. Baker, "On a New Species of *Sedum* Discovered by the Late John Stuart Mill in Asia Minor," *Journal of Botany*, XIII (1875), 236–7.

[137]For curious details about his private life, see the peculiarly moving account in "Two," *The Home Life of Herbert Spencer* (London, 1906).

[138]*LL, CW*, XVII, 1620 (6 July, 1869), from Blackheath.

[139]"His Botanical Studies," 47.

Fabre, and had lunch with him before returning to Avignon, where he developed a chill on the Monday, and died on Wednesday, 7 May, of the erysipelas endemic to the area. His last extant letter was to Fabre, concerning their trip,[140] and what seems to have been his last written word is a notation of a plant located on that final—and happy—+excursion.

# MEDICAL REVIEWS AND APPENDICES

## MEDICAL REVIEWS

MILL'S INTEREST in medicine, which was much more personal than theoretical, is very little evident in his published works, though not infrequently obvious in his correspondence. The only published items directly bearing on the subject are the two slight reviews here included, "King's Lecture on the Study of Anatomy," from the *Monthly Repository* in 1834, and "Carpenter's Physiology," from the *Westminster Review* in 1842. It will be noted that in both Mill emphasizes the importance of systematic method, praising the Continental physiologists for their powers of generalization, which the English were only beginning to emulate. His botanical bent is also shown in his praise of Carpenter for including the physiology of plants in his discussion. Anyone interested in Mill and medicine, however, should turn to his letters, especially those to his wife, and to a manuscript of twelve pages suggesting the proper preventive care and medication appropriate for visitors to Egypt.[141]

## APPENDIX A: WILLS AND DEED OF GIFT

IN 1853, following his marriage, Mill made a short and conventional will, confirming not surprisingly his devotion to his wife by leaving everything to her,

---

[140]"S'il ne s'agissait que d'herboriser une seule fois à Orange il vaudrait mieux certainement ne le faire qu'à quelque temps d'ici; mais il me reste, grace à vos découvertes, tant d'espèces précieuses à receuillir dans cette région qui toutes ne mûrissent pas en même temps, que j'ai envie d'y faire, ce printemps, plus d'une course dont le plaisir comme le fruit sera beaucoup plus grand pour moi s'il m'est permis de les faire avec vous. Je me propose donc de me rendre à Orange Samedi prochain par le train qui y arrive à 11.46 . . . et de revenir ici par le train qui passe par Orange à 5.40." (*LL, CW*, XVII, 1952–3 [30 Apr., 1873], from Avignon.)

[141]Though the manuscript (in the John Stuart Mill Papers at Yale) is in Mill's hand, it seems simply to be copied from some manuscript source; at one place, for instance, Mill indicates an uncertain reading by putting a word in square brackets with a mark of interrogation. Mill and Helen Taylor had planned a trip to Egypt in 1859, but abandoned it when difficulties arose over the completion of the memorial tombstone to Harriet Taylor Mill (Helen Taylor to Algernon Taylor, from St. Veran, 23 Oct., 1859, Mill-Taylor Collection, XXIV, 713).

and in the event of her death, to her daughter, Helen Taylor; they were, with his friends William Ellis and William Thomas Thornton, appointed executors. After Harriet Taylor Mill's death, he bought a plot in the Avignon cemetery, and a house and its land nearby; subsequently he drew up a French will in February 1859, securing these properties to Helen Taylor. In January 1864 he confirmed that will and added a codicil willing her additional properties he had acquired in the neighbourhood, as well as any he might acquire in the future. Another codicil in January 1867 added to her legacy all real and personal property that he possessed in Avignon and environs. To evade provisions of the French law of inheritance, he made all these provisions unnecessary by a deed of gift ("donation") to Helen Taylor in February 1869 that conveyed to her all his real property in the district, and the contents of the house (including 982 volumes).

Finally, in 1872 Mill added a long codicil to his English will, cancelling earlier codicils to it not now known, reconfirming Helen Taylor as executor (and, failing her, Ellis and Thornton). He also appointed Helen Taylor as literary executor, and left to her the manuscript of the *Autobiography* to be published as she saw fit, with the aim of protecting his reputation against any "pretended" biography; she also was entrusted with the decision to add to the autobiographical memoir a selection of his letters, all others to be destroyed. His French will was mentioned, and his wish that his mortal remains be buried in the tomb of his wife in Avignon. He further specified legacies not only to Helen Taylor and her brother Algernon and his children, but also to his sister Mary Elizabeth Colman and her children, and to his alternate executors, was well as to the Royal Society for the Prevention of Cruelty to Animals (£500), the Land Tenure Reform Association (£500), and to the first university in the United Kingdom "to throw open all its degrees to female students" (£6000). His copyrights he left to John Morley for support of a periodical "which shall be open to the expression of all opinions and shall have all its articles signed with the name of the writer." These bequests, however, were subject to Helen Taylor's predeceasing him, which of course she did not, and it is not known which provisions she carried out, except that she expressly denied responsibility to carry out the gift to the university first to admit women.[142]

APPENDICES B AND C: "THE VIXEN, AND CIRCASSIA" AND "THE SPANISH QUESTION"

WHILE MILL was not as interventionist an editor as Francis Jeffrey of the *Edinburgh* or Charles Dickens of *Household Words* and *All the Year Round*, his temper and

---

[142]Professor William Knight of St. Andrews wrote to Helen Taylor on 8 March, 1881, saying that he anticipated that women would soon be admitted to the University, and asking about Mill's bequest. She replied on 11 March: "Your letter of the 8th reached me only late last night and I hasten to say that Mr Mill did not make a bequest as you seem to have been informed. I rejoice much to hear that you are engaged on so good a work and heartily wish you all success." (Mill-Taylor Collection, British Library of Political and Economic Science.)

talents were tested by some articles commissioned for or submitted to the *London and Westminster* during his stewardship from 1835 to 1840. In the manuscript list of his published works he included four articles to which he felt his contribution sufficiently justified the claim of co-authorship. Two of these are related to his specific interests, and are consequently included in earlier thematic volumes of the *Collected Works*.[143] The others, "The Vixen, and Circassia" and "The Spanish Question," both appeared in 1837,[144] reflecting particular international issues of the day and so calling for comment in the periodical, but neither involving a special concern of Mill's. They contribute, however, to an appreciation of his role and activity as editor, especially when read with his correspondence of the period, and his editorial notes to the *London and Westminster*, which are reprinted in Volume I of the *Collected Works*. "The Spanish Question" is known to have posed problems that were undoubtedly recurrent: Mill first wrote to William Napier, experienced on the ground and in print about Spanish military matters, gently proposing that he contribute on the subject or name someone who could; Mill himself offered to supply comments on British foreign policy and the general question of intervention. Napier declined, but gave important details in his letter, and suggested Charles Shaw as a substitute; in his reply Mill indicated that Shaw was not appropriate, as his work would be reviewed in the article, and said that an (unnamed) author had been found.[145]

### APPENDIX D: QUESTIONS BEFORE THE SELECT COMMITTEE ON METROPOLITAN LOCAL GOVERNMENT IN 1867

DURING HIS PARLIAMENTARY CAREER, probably the closest Mill came to dealing effectively with constituency matters was through his part in the campaign for municipal government for the metropolis. He spoke often on the issue, and served

---

[143]"Taylor's *Statesman*," co-authored with George Grote, in *Essays on Politics and Society*, Vols. XVIII-XIX of *CW* (Toronto: University of Toronto Press, 1977), XIX, 617–47, and "Guizot's Lectures on European Civilization," co-authored with Joseph Blanco White, in *Essays on French History and Historians*, Vol. XX of *CW* (Toronto: University of Toronto Press, 1985), 367–93.

[144]Co-author of the first was Charles Buller; the *Wellesley Index to Victorian Periodicals* suggests on internal evidence that the co-author of the second was William Cooke Taylor, the favourable referee who in 1842 recommended publication of Mill's *Logic* to the publisher William Parker, and whose hand Mill then recognized (Bain, *John Stuart Mill*, 66n).

[145]*LL*, *CW*, XVII, 1964 (26 Apr., 1836), and 1972 (5 June, 1837). A comment about the article to William Molesworth, proprietor of the review, reveals more woes: "The editorial errors you speak of must be those (very bad to be sure) in a portion of the article on Spain, which I wrote myself. These errors remained uncorrected, or rather were miscorrected because the proof came to my house when I was out of town & so was printed off before I saw it. This was not Robertson's [the sub-editor's] fault, & I will take care it shall not happen again. Some such errors are inevitable when articles come in late, but I shall take care they do not happen frequently." (*Ibid.*, 1976 [29 Aug., 1837].)

actively on the Select Committee considering the proposal. The Committee issued three reports, two in 1866, and a third in 1867.[146] Mill's interest in efficiency, fairness, and responsible leadership emerges in his questions, which thus help fill in the detail of his political beliefs and activities, especially in his interaction with sympathetic witnesses whose appearance was called for by his allied reformers.

### APPENDIX E: MILL AT THE POLITICAL ECONOMY CLUB

AN INTERESTING GLIMPSE into Mill's combined intellectual and social life, similar to those deriving from the records of his debating activities, is provided by the records of the Political Economy Club, founded in 1821. He was elected to it in 1836, and became a member of its ruling Committee in 1840, as did his friend Edwin Chadwick. His father was one of its founding members (a portion of the draft rules is in his hand),[147] though he seldom attended and resigned in 1835, presumably because of ill-heath; and George Grote was the first treasurer. The membership, originally limited to thirty, and raised to thirty-five in 1847, was not thoroughly orthodox but economically eclectic, including businessmen, politicians (cabinet ministers were honorary members after 1834), civil servants, and men of letters, as well as writers on economics. The meetings, on the first Monday of each month from December through June, were held successively during Mill's membership in the Freemason's Tavern (until 1850), the Thatched House Tavern (1850–61), the St. James's Restaurant (1861–67), and Willis's Rooms (1867–77); the original subscription was five guineas. The sessions began with a dinner at 6:30 p.m., and the discussion often lasted until 11, with the speakers remaining seated.

The proposed questions (often more than one for each meeting) were printed and circulated before each meeting, and the proposer, if present, opened the discussion, originally and through Mill's period speaking without a text. Mill was an active member, as the list of topics in Appendix E shows, and his prominence is indicated by the passing of a resolution regretting his death, a rare practice, and by the subscription of £50 from the Club's funds towards his proposed memorial.[148]

His questions cover, not surprisingly, a wide range of topics, from technical definitions, through queries about the practical effects of measures, to broad social and moral issues. They not infrequently reflect Mill's pondering over matters that

---

[146]For Mill's questions and the witnesses' responses given in the First and Second Reports, see *Public and Parliamentary Speeches*, Vols. XXVIII–XXIX of *CW* (Toronto: University of Toronto Press, 1988), XXIX, App. B, 437–542. The material from the Third Report was inadvertently omitted from that volume.

[147]See *Political Economy Club*, IV (1882). James Mill's draft, which included a "grotesque proposal for a nightly catechism of Members," was much revised before acceptance (*Political Economy Club*, VI [1921], xi).

[148]*Ibid.*, xvi–xvii.

appear prominently in his writings, not only in his *Principles of Political Economy* (first published in 1848, and much revised in later editions), but also in his newspaper articles on Ireland, his parliamentary evidence on the Bank Act and on income tax, and his comments in various essays on co-operation. There are also inferences to be drawn about his life from his absences in the record in 1854 when he was travelling for his health, and in 1859–60, after his wife's death, when he stayed for much of the year in semi-retirement in Avignon. His final appearance is interesting in that he gave attendance at the Club as the reason for his return to London early in July 1865;[149] he in fact became caught up reluctantly in the successful campaign for his election on 11 July as Member of Parliament for Westminster.

Initially I made the claim that the miscellaneous writings in this volume contribute substantially to a full understanding of Mill's life and thought, and that many have independent value: that claim can be substantiated only by a careful analysis of them, each in context, and the comments above are intended merely to make it plausible. In any case, taken with the great bulk of his better-known writings in earlier volumes, these materials certainly demonstrate that Mill's character and behaviour were much richer and more varied than narrow stereotypes have suggested. And if he is taken as representative of *homo victorianus*, that species too must be seen as vital, compelling, and emphatically not to be confined in a museum's *hortus siccus*.

## THE TEXTS

IN THIS VOLUME, as the edition draws to a close after some thirty years, it seems appropriate to admit that our filing system includes a drawer labelled miscellaneous, in which there is a folder labelled miscellaneous, in which. . . . Considering what those dots conceal, I should further confess that the temptation to include in this volume all the various bits and pieces connected with Mill has been very great. An inoculation of common sense, however, not unrelated to a cost-benefit regime, has controlled the impulse. Omitted, therefore, are some slight manuscripts not connected to other writings,[150] including those that are merely copies of passages by others (most notably the Egyptian medical notes mentioned above), and Mill's comments on Grote's manuscripts. As indicated above, we have had to exclude his manuscript botanical lists. Also omitted are marginalia: Mill was not a great

---

[149]*LL, CW,* XVI, 1058 and 1061.

[150]Those that have textual bearing have been included in earlier volumes either in appendices or textual notes. Several fragments in Harriet Taylor Mill's hand have survived, as well as the record of a couple of word games played presumably in the Taylors' drawing room; to exclude these was perhaps my most painful decision.

annotator of books, most of his pencilled marks being merely crosses or lines against passages or page references on fly leaves; few suggest more than that a passage interested him.

This volume is divided into three sections, reflecting subject matter and genre, and appendices. The first part consists of Mill's editorial contributions to Jeremy Bentham's *Rationale of Judicial Evidence* (1827) and to the second edition of James Mill's *Analysis of the Phenomena of the Human Mind* (1869). Both of these sets of materials exist only in printed form, except for a manuscript fragment of the latter. These exhibit a curious inversion of original intention, in that Mill's annotations become the text, and the text becomes annotation: to give the context, passages explaining, summarizing, and quoting Bentham's and James Mill's texts, in italic type (and also within square brackets when not direct quotations), introduce Mill's comments. Economy is here necessary, and only when the actual wording of the original is essential are these introductory passages lengthy; when Mill's comment is virtually self-explanatory, the editorial note is merely locative. Page references to the original are given at the end of each discrete passage; though many of Mill's additions are in footnotes, these references do not include "n." To avoid confusion, references incorporated in the original text are moved to footnotes. For consistency, "Vol." and "p(p)." are added to original references as necessary.

The second section contains Mill's published writings on botany, which appeared in the *Phytologist* between 1841 and 1862, plus a review of the *Phytologist* in the *Westminster Review* (1843), and a "Calendar of Odours" he prepared for Caroline Fox. All of these are extant in only one version, and present no special textual problems.

The text proper concludes with two brief notices of the printed version of a medical lecture and of a textbook, the first printed in the *Monthly Repository* (1834), the second in the *Westminster Review* (1842). Again there is only one version of each, and no special problems.

The appendices include five textual items. Appendix A, containing Mill's English and French wills, has the manuscript documents as copy-texts; despite the urge to punctuate lawyer's forms, these are reproduced diplomatically, except that "and" is substituted for "&" and "etc." for "&c." Appendices B and C, co-authored reviews from the *London and Westminster Review*, exist only in the one printed form, as do Appendix D, taken from *Parliamentary Papers*, and Appendix E, taken from the printed record of the Political Economy Club: in each case there are no competing versions. The two remaining appendices are lists of textual emendations and of persons and works cited in the texts and Appendices A through E. The distinct challenges in preparing the index to such a volume have been met and overcome by the skills and diligence of Dr. Jean O'Grady.

Editorial notes to each item identify the copy-text, indicate whence such titles as are not original have been derived (as in the case of several of the botanical articles), and supply other specific explanatory material, such as the description of the item in Mill's own list of his published writings and any corrections found in his own copy. Editorial footnotes (signalled by numeric series within each item) give personal identifications, bibliographic detail, and such limited historical comment as seems necessary for comprehension. Notes in the originals are signalled by the series *, †, ‡, etc.; occasionally references within the text have been moved to footnotes for consistency, and some have been corrected.

There being no competing versions of any of the items, except for the manuscript fragment of a note to James Mill's *Analysis*, there are few textual notes, each of which is explained in its place.

## EDITORIAL EMENDATIONS

THE ONLY EDITORIAL INTERVENTIONS in printed texts, except for Mill's editions of Bentham and James Mill, are made for consistency; special instances are given in Appendix F with, as necessary, explanations for the changes. Headings have been restyled. Other general practices include: "2dly" and similar forms are given as "2ndly"; ordinals attached to rulers' names are given in the form "Charles I"; "&c." is given as "etc."; terms mentioned rather than used are given in italic (sometimes this involves removing quotation marks)—this alteration is especially needed in the notes to James Mill's *Analysis*, where the practice is normal in James Mill's text, but, surprisingly, not in the notes. The titles of works published separately are given in italic and parts of works in quotation marks. Foreign words and phrases are normalized in italic type. Long quotations have been set in smaller type, and the quotation marks deleted. An apparent exception to this practice appears in the editorial notes to Bentham's *Rationale* in places where Mill says quotation marks signal passages written by Bentham that he has incorporated within sections of his own. Square brackets appear when page references are added to the text to conform to Mill's own practice in particular items. Volume and page references in the original have been standardized and corrected as necessary.[151] In the notes to the *Analysis*, "i.e." is normalized in italic.

[151]In the following list the page and line reference is followed by the original reading; the altered reference is given in square brackets.
26n.2    ch. i [Chap. viii] [*as in fact; corrected in Bowring's ed.*]
29.34    sect. 9 [Sect. 10] [*as in fact*]
32.13    (p. 285) [(pp. 285–6)]
45n.1    p. 340 [(pp. 340–1)]
*350n.18*    90 [99, 101]
*351n.10*    418 [417–22]
*352n.2*    180 [180–1]
*352n.4*    9 [9–10]
*353n.2*    47 [46–7]

## ACKNOWLEDGMENTS

FOR PERMISSION to publish manuscript materials, we are indebted to the National Provincial Bank, residual legatees of Mary Taylor, Mill's step-granddaughter. We are most grateful to the librarians and staff of the British Library, the British Library of Political and Economic Science, the Farlow Reference Library of Harvard University, the Institute for Historical Research (University of London), Somerville College Oxford, the University of London Library, the Library of University College London, the University of Toronto Library, the Victoria University Library, and the Yale University Library. We have been graciously assisted by David G. Frodin of the Academy of Natural Sciences of Philadelphia, G. Lucas, S. FitzGerald, and L.E. Thompson of the Royal Botanic Gardens, Kew, Hollis G. Bedell of the Botany Libraries, Harvard University, and J.H. Ross of the Royal Botanic Gardens and National Herbarium, Yarra, Victoria, Australia. Among those scholars who gave generously of their time and attention are John Beattie, Stephen Conway, Lawrence Dewan, Robert Fenn, and Anthony Lewis. Joan Bulger, our copy-editor, has continued with the aid and co-operation of her production and design colleagues to prolong my joy at working with the University of Toronto Press. As always, my thanks to the Editorial Committee of the *Collected Works*, most signally to Ann P. Robson, who on many a joint ante-jentacular circumgyration proved conclusively, with rationale and analysis abounding, that weeds editorial are but flowers stylistic in the wrong place. Attentive readers will appreciate how much of the work of the edition is the result of the unstinted dedication and labour (not all mental) of my co-workers, especially Marion Filipiuk, who found our way through the thickets of Bentham and James Mill, Jean O'Grady, whose green thumb and environmental care made the botanical lists yield what fruit they have, and Rea Wilmshurst, whose gimlet eye and clutterless mind saved us from many an error. They were assisted in all but command by Michele Green, Jonathan Cutmore, Jannifer Smith-Rubenzahl, and Elizabeth King.

| | |
|---|---|
| *353n.5* | 410 [410–11] |
| *354n.4* | 49 [48–9] |
| *355n.3* | 24 [23–4] |
| *356n.1* | 25 [24–5] |
| *356n.3* | 29 [28] |

# EDITIONS OF JEREMY BENTHAM AND JAMES MILL

## 1827, 1869

# JEREMY BENTHAM'S RATIONALE OF JUDICIAL EVIDENCE

1827

## EDITOR'S NOTE

Extracts from *Rationale of Judicial Evidence, Specially Applied to English Practice. From the Manuscripts of Jeremy Bentham, Esq. Bencher of Lincoln's Inn*. 5 vols. London: Hunt and Clarke, 1827. Preface signed "John S. Mill." Identified in Mill's bibliography as "The Preface, Additions and Editorial Notes to the Rationale of Judicial Evidence by Jeremy Bentham" (MacMinn, p. 8). In the text below, Mill's contributions are printed in normal roman type, with volume and page references to the edition of 1827 in parentheses at the end. In the original, Mill's contributions are usually attributed at the end by "*Editor*" or "Ed."; these are here omitted. In a few cases, specially noted, the attribution was not attached to passages obviously Mill's. Where necessary, passages of Bentham's own text are quoted or summarized in italic type; the summaries are enclosed in square brackets. Unless otherwise indicated, Mill's footnotes are appended to the conclusion of the quoted or summarized text.

# Jeremy Bentham's Rationale
# of Judicial Evidence

## PREFACE

THE PAPERS, from which the work now submitted to the public has been extracted, were written by Mr. Bentham at various times, from the year 1802 to 1812. They comprise a very minute exposition of his views on all the branches of the great subject of Judicial Evidence, intermixed with criticisms on the law of Evidence as it is established in this country, and with incidental remarks on the state of that branch of law in most of the continental systems of jurisprudence.

Mr. Bentham's speculations on Judicial Evidence have already been given to the world, in a more condensed form, by M. Dumont, of Geneva, in the *Traité des Preuves Judiciaires*, published in 1823: one of the most interesting among the important works founded on Mr. Bentham's manuscripts, with which that "first of translators and *redacteurs*," as he has justly been termed, has enriched the library of the continental jurist.[1] The strictures, however, on English law, which compose more than one-half of the present work, were judiciously omitted by M. Dumont, as not sufficiently interesting to a continental reader to compensate for the very considerable space which they would have occupied. To an English reader—to him at least who loves his country sufficiently well to desire that what is defective in her institutions should be amended, and, in order to its being amended, should be known—these criticisms will not be the least interesting portion of the work. As is usual in the critical and controversial part of Mr. Bentham's writings, the manner is forcible and perspicuous. The occasional obscurity, of which his style is accused, but which in reality is almost confined to the more intricate of the theoretical discussions, is the less to be regretted, as the nature of the subject is of itself sufficient to render the work a sealed letter to those who read merely for amusement. They who really desire to possess useful knowledge do not grudge the trouble necessary to acquire it.

---

[1]Pierre Etienne Louis Dumont (1759–1829), Swiss jurisprudentialist and publicist, was mainly responsible, through his French redactions, for Bentham's international reputation. *Traité des preuves judiciaires. Ouvrage extrait des manuscrits de M. Jérémie Bentham, jurisconsulte anglais*, 2 vols. (Paris: Bossange, 1823) was translated into English as *A Treatise on Judicial Evidence, Extracted from the Manuscripts of Jeremy Bentham Esq. by M. Dumont* (London: Baldwin, *et al.*, 1825).

The task of the Editor has chiefly consisted in collating the manuscripts. Mr. Bentham had gone over the whole of the field several times, at intervals of some length from one another, with little reference on each occasion to what he had written on the subject at the former times. Hence, it was often found that the same topic had been treated two and even three times; and it became necessary for the Editor to determine, not only which of the manuscripts should supply the basis of the chapter, but likewise how great a portion of each of those which were laid aside might usefully be incorporated with that which was retained. The more recent of the manuscripts has in most cases been adopted as the ground-work, being generally that in which the subjects were treated most comprehensively and systematically; while the earlier ones often contained thoughts and illustrations of considerable value, with passages, and sometimes whole pages, written with great spirit and pungency. Where these could conveniently be substituted for the corresponding passages in the manuscript chosen as the basis of the work, the substitution has been made. Where this was thought inexpedient, either on account of the merit of the passages which would thus have been superseded, or because their omission would have broken the thread of the discussion, the Editor (not thinking himself justified in suppressing anything which appeared to him to be valuable in the original) has *added* the passage which was first written, instead of *substituting* it for that which was composed more recently. From this cause it may occasionally be found in perusing the work, that the same ideas have been introduced more than once, in different dresses. But the Editor hopes that this will never prove to be the case, except where either the merit of both passages, or the manner in which one of them was interwoven with the matter preceding and following it, constituted a sufficient motive for retaining both.

The plan of the work having been altered and enlarged at different times, and having ultimately extended to a much wider range of subjects than were included in the original design, it has not unfrequently happened that the same subject has been discussed incidentally in one book, which was afterwards treated directly in another. In some of these cases the incidental discussion has been omitted, as being no longer necessary; but in others it contained important matter, which was not to be found in the direct and more methodical one, and which, from the plan on which the latter was composed, it was not found possible to introduce in it. In such cases both discussions have usually been retained.

The work, as has been already observed, not having been written consecutively, but part at one time, and part at another, and having always been regarded by the author as an unfinished work, it has sometimes, (though but rarely) occurred, that while one topic was treated several times over, another, of perhaps equal importance, was not treated at all. Such deficiencies it was the wish of Mr. Bentham that the Editor should endeavour to supply. In compliance with this wish, some cases of the exclusion of evidence in English law, which were not noticed by Mr. Bentham, have been stated and commented upon in the last chapter of the book on Makeshift Evidence, and in two chapters of the sixth part of the Book on Exclusion.* He has likewise subjoined to some of the chapters in the latter book, a vindication of the doctrines which they contain, against the strictures of an able writer in the *Edinburgh Review*.[2] A few miscellaneous notes are scattered here and there, but sparingly: nor could anything, except the distinctly expressed wish of the Author, have induced the Editor to think that any additions of his could enhance the value of a work on such a subject, and from such a hand.

For the distribution of the work in Chapters and Sections, the Editor alone is responsible. The division into Books is all that belongs to the Author.

The original manuscripts contained, under the title of Causes of the Exclusion of Evidence, a treatise on the principal defects of the English system of Technical Procedure. This extensive subject may appear not to be so intimately connected with the more limited design of a work which professes to treat of Judicial Evidence only, as to entitle a dissertation upon it to a place in these pages. On examination, however, the parenthetical treatise was thought to be not only so instructive, but so full of point and vivacity, that its publication could not but be acceptable to the readers of the present work: and the additional bulk, in a work which already extended beyond four volumes, was not deemed a preponderant objection, especially as the dissertation, from the liveliness and poignancy with which it exposes established absurdities, gives in some degree a relief to the comparative abstruseness of some other parts of the work. It stands as the eighth in order of the ten books into which the work is divided.[3]

A few of the vices in the detail of English law, which are complained of both in

---

*[On "Makeshift Evidence," see Vol. III, pp. 573–86 (Bk. VI, Chap. xii) (pp. 38–45 below); on "Exclusion," Vol. V, pp. 570–610 (Bk. IX, Pt. VI, the conclusion of Chap. iv and Chap. v) (pp. 70–90 below).] The Editor has not thought it necessary to consult, on the state of the existing law, any other authorities than the compilations of Phillipps, Starkie, and others. These works were sufficiently authoritative for his purpose; and if the state of the law be such, that even those experienced lawyers can have misunderstood it, this simple fact proves more against the law than any remarks which the Editor can have grounded on the misconception. [Samuel March Phillipps (1780–1862), *A Treatise on the Law of Evidence* (1814), 6th ed., 2 vols. (London: Butterworth; Dublin, Cooke, 1824); Thomas Starkie (1782–1849), *A Practical Treatise of the Law of Evidence, and Digest of Proofs in Civil and Criminal Proceedings*, 3 vols. (London: Clarke, 1824); "others" consulted by Mill include two cited below, Geoffrey Gilbert (1674–1726), *The Law of Evidence*, 2nd ed. (London: Owen, 1760); and Samuel Bealey Harrison (1802–67), *Evidence: Forming a Title of the Code of Legal Proceedings, According to the Plan Proposed by Crofton Uniacke, Esq.* (London: Butterworth, 1825).]

[2]Mill added to parts of Bk. IX, in Vol. V, pp. 57–9 (Pt. III, Chap. iii) (pp. 51–2 below), pp. 313–25 (Pt. III, Chap. v) (pp. 57–64 below), pp. 345–9 (Pt. IV, Chap. v) (pp. 64–6 below), and pp. 352–4 (Pt. V, Chap. i) (pp. 66–8 below), in reply to Thomas Denman (1779–1854), "Law of Evidence: Criminal Procedure: Publicity," *Edinburgh Review*, XL (Mar. 1824), 169–207 (a review of Dumont's *Traité*).

[3]"On the Causes of the Exclusion of Evidence—The Technical System of Procedure," Vol. IV, pp. 1–475.

this book and in other parts of the work, have been either wholly or partially remedied by Mr. Peel's recent law reforms;[4] and some others may be expected to be removed, if the recommendations of the late Chancery Commission be carried into execution.[5] The changes, however, which will thus be effected in a system of procedure founded altogether upon wrong principles, will not be sufficient to render that system materially better; in some cases, perhaps, they will even tend to render it worse: since the *malâ fide* suitor has always several modes of distressing his adversary by needless delay or expense, and these petty reforms take away at most one or two, but leave it open to him to have recourse to others, which, though perhaps more troublesome to himself, may be even more burdensome to his *bonâ fide* adversary than the former. Thus, for instance: in one of the earlier chapters of Book VIII, the reader will find an exposure of one of those contrivances for making delay which were formerly within the power of the dishonest suitor; I mean that of groundless writs of error.[6] Mr. Peel has partially (and *but* partially) taken away this resource,[7] and the consequence, as we are informed, has been, not that improper delay has not been obtained, but that it has been obtained by way of demurrer,[8] or by joining issue and proceeding to trial; either of which expedients (though perhaps somewhat less efficacious to the party seeking delay) are equally, if not more, oppressive in the shape of expense to the party against whom they are employed, than the proceedings in error.

The truth is, that, bad as the English system of jurisprudence is, its parts harmonize tolerably well together; and if one part, however bad, be taken away, while another part is left standing, the arrangement which is substituted for it may, for the time, do more harm by its imperfect adaptation to the remainder of the old system, than the removal of the abuse can do good. The objection so often urged by lawyers as an argument against reforms, "That in so complicated and intricate a system of jurisprudence as ours, no one can foretell what the consequences of the slightest innovation may be," is perfectly correct;[9] although the inference to be drawn from it is not, as they would have it to be understood, that the system ought

[4]Robert Peel (1788–1850), as Home Secretary, was responsible for the legal reforms enacted in 5 George IV, c. 41 (1824), and 6 George IV, cc. 25, 84, and 96 (1825).

[5]"Report Made to His Majesty by the Commissioners Appointed to Enquire into the Practice of Chancery," *Parliamentary Papers* [*PP*], 1826, XV, 1–120.

[6]Vol. IV, pp. 63–71 (Bk. VIII, Chap. iv, Sect. 1).

[7]By 6 George IV, c. 96.

[8]A pleading that admits the facts but denies that they entitle the opponent to legal relief; the action stops until that issue is resolved.

[9]The exact words of the quotation have not been located, but cf. John Freeman Mitford (1748–1830), Baron Redesdale, *Considerations Suggested by the Report Made to His Majesty under a Commission, Authorizing the Commissioners to Make Certain Improvements Respecting the Court of Chancery* (London: Hatchard, 1826), pp. 4–5, 24–5. The British Library's copies of the 1st and 2nd eds. of this pamphlet were Bentham's; the former is annotated in his hand: "Paragon of dulness, blindness, and senility" (title-page), and "Blame nobody" (p. 10).

not to be reformed, but that it ought to be reformed thoroughly, and on a comprehensive plan; not piecemeal, but at once. There are numerous cases in which a gradual change is preferable to a sudden one; because its immediate consequences can be more distinctly foreseen. But in this case, the consequences even of a sudden change can be much more easily foreseen than those of a gradual one. Whatever difficulties men might at first experience (though the difficulties which they would experience have been infinitely exaggerated) in adapting their conduct to a system of procedure entirely founded on rational, and therefore on new, principles; none are more ready than lawyers themselves to admit that still greater difficulty would be felt in adapting it to a system partly rational and partly technical.

For such a thorough reform, or rather re-construction of our laws, the public mind is not yet entirely prepared. But it is rapidly advancing to such a state of preparation. It is now no longer considered as a mark of disaffection towards the state, and hostility to social order and to law in general, to express an opinion that the existing law is defective, and requires a radical reform. Thus much Mr. Peel's attempts have already done for the best interests of his country; and they will in time do much more. A new spirit is rising in the profession itself. Of this the recent work of Mr. Humphreys, obtaining, as it has done, so great circulation and celebrity, is one of the most gratifying indications.[10] The reform which he contemplates in one of the most difficult, as well as important branches of the law, is no timid and trifling attempt to compromise with the evil, but goes to the root at once.* And the rapidity with which this spirit is spreading among the young and rising lawyers, notwithstanding the degree in which their pecuniary interest must be affected by the removal of the abuses, is one of the most cheering signs of the times,[11] and goes far to shew, that the tenacity with which the profession has usually clung to the worst parts of existing systems, was owing not wholly to those sinister interests[12] which Mr. Bentham has so instructively expounded, but, in part at least, to the extreme difficulty which a mind conversant only with one set of securities feels in conceiving that society can possibly be held together by any other.

It has appeared to the Editor superfluous to add one word in recommendation of

[10]James Humphreys (d. 1830), *Observations on the Actual State of the English Laws of Real Property, with the Outlines of a Code* (London: Murray, 1826).

*It may not be impertinent here to remark, that the suggestions of Mr. Humphreys, admirable as they are, have received most valuable improvements from Mr. Bentham's pen.—See an article in the *Westminster Review*, No. XII. [Bentham, "Bentham on Humphrey's *Property Code*," *Westminster Review*, VI (Oct. 1826), 446–507.]

[11]Cf. Matthew, 16:3.

[12]A key term for Bentham; see, e.g., its definition and application in *Rationale of Judicial Evidence*, Bk. I, Chap. ix, and Bk. IX, Pt. III, Chap. i; cf. *Plan of Parliamentary Reform*, in *Works*, ed. John Bowring, 11 vols. (Edinburgh: Tait, 1843), Vol. III, pp. 440, 446.

the work. The vast importance of the subject, which is obvious to all men, and the consideration that it has now for the first time been treated philosophically, and by such a master, contain in themselves so many incitements of curiosity to every liberal mind, to every mind which regards knowledge on important subjects as an object of desire, that volumes might be written without adding to their force.

\*    \*    \*    \*    \*

## ADDITION TO PREFACE, DECEMBER 1837[13]

AT AN INTERVAL of more than ten years from the first publication of this work, the original Editor feels that an apology is due from him for the air of confident dogmatism perceptible in some of his notes and additions, and for which he can only urge the palliation of their having been written in very early youth—a time of life at which such faults are more venial than at any other, because they generally arise, not so much from the writer's own self-conceit, as from confidence in the authority of his teachers. It is due, however, to himself to state, that the tone of some of the passages in question would have been felt by him, even then, to be unbecoming, as proceeding from himself individually: he wrote them in the character of an anonymous Editor of Mr. Bentham's work, who, in the trifling contributions which the author desired at his hands, considered (so far as mere manner was concerned) rather what would be accordant with the spirit of the work itself, and in Mr. Bentham admissible, than what would be decorous from a person of his years and his limited knowledge and experience.[14] His name was subsequently affixed, contrary to his own strongly expressed wish, at the positive desire of the venerable author, who certainly had a right to require it.[15]

\*    \*    \*    \*    \*

*The exclusive rules relative to evidence belong to the adjective branch of the law: the effect of them is to frustrate and disappoint the expectations raised by the substantive branch. The maintenance of them has this effect perpetually: the*

---

[13]This paragraph was added to the Preface when the *Rationale* was reprinted in Bentham's *Works*, ed. Bowring, which appeared in separate fascicles that were gathered into the volumes of the collected edition in 1843. This fascicle first appeared in 1839. In the *Works* the paragraph is in Vol. VI, p. 203.

[14]Cf. Mill's comment in his *Autobiography*, *CW*, Vol. I, pp. 117–19.

[15]See Mill's letter to Bentham, ca. 24 Apr., 1827, *EL*, *CW*, Vol. XII, pp. 18–19.

*abolition of them, even though by the judicial power, would have no such effect, but the contrary.*

The terms, *adjective* and *substantive*, applied to law, are intended to mark an important distinction, first pointed out to notice by this author;[16] viz. the distinction between the commands which refer directly to the ultimate ends of the legislator, and the commands which refer to objects which are only the means to those ends. The former are as it were the laws themselves; the latter are the prescriptions for carrying the former into execution. They are, in short, the rules of procedure. The former Mr. Bentham calls the substantive law, the latter the adjective. (Vol. I, p. 5.)

\*     \*     \*     \*     \*

[*Bentham argues (Vol. I, pp. 18–20) that in searching for matters of fact, human beings are faced "every day, and almost every waking hour," with "questions of evidence." He mentions specifically domestic management, natural philosophy, technology, medicine, and then mathematics, noting that in the last "the evidentiary facts" are "feigned," but nonetheless persuasion depends on evidence.*]

The difference, in respect of evidence, between questions of mathematics and questions of purely experimental science, of chemistry, for example, is merely this; that the evidence applicable to the former, is that description of evidence which is founded upon general reasoning; while the evidence applicable to the latter, is evidence of that description which is derived immediately from matters of fact, presenting themselves to our senses. To point out the peculiar properties of these two kinds of evidence, and to distinguish them from one another, belongs rather to a treatise on logic than to a work like the present; which, considering evidence almost exclusively in regard to its connection with judicature, excludes all general speculations which have no immediate bearing upon that subject. (Vol. I, p. 20.)

\*     \*     \*     \*     \*

[*Bentham refers again to the substantive and adjective branches of law.*]

See ante, p. 5—note. (Vol. I, p. 25.)

\*     \*     \*     \*     \*

[16]See Bentham, *Principles of International Law* (written 1786–89), *Works*, Vol. II, p. 539.

*The state of the facts, as well as the state of the law, being such as to confer on the
plaintiff a title to such or such a right, or to satisfaction on the score of such or such
a wrong; if evidence, and that of a sufficient degree of* probative force *to satisfy the
judge, of the existence of the necessary matter of fact, be wanting; the law, in that
instance, fails of receiving its due execution and effect; and, according to the
nature of the case, injustice in the shape of non-collation of rights where due,
non-administration of compensation where due, or non-administration of punishment where due, is the consequence. [Mill's note is appended to "non-collation."]*

By collation of rights, Mr. Bentham means that species of service which the judge
renders to any person by putting him in possession of a certain right. Non-collation
of rights has place when that service is not rendered,—when the person in question
is not put in possession of the right.

So, collative facts are those facts which have been appointed by the legislator to
give commencement to a right: thus, under English law, in the case of the right to a
landed estate, collative facts are, a conveyance executed in a particular form, a
devise, and the like: in the case of the rights of a husband over a wife, and *vice
versâ*, the collative fact is the ceremony of marriage, and so on. Collative facts are
also sometimes called by Mr. Bentham *investitive* facts.

In like manner, *ablative*, or *divestitive* facts, are those which take away rights:
as in the case of property, gift or sale to another party: in the case of several of the
rights of a father over his child, the child's coming of age, etc. etc.[17] (Vol. I,
p. 26.)

\*    \*    \*    \*    \*

*[It is one] natural and proper object of the legislator's care, viz. to see that the
necessary evidence be* forthcoming.

There are many other judicial purposes for which it is necessary that things and
persons should be forthcoming, besides that of being presented to the judge in the
character of sources of evidence. The subject of Forthcomingness, therefore,
belongs to the general subject of Procedure. And as the arrangements necessary to
secure the forthcomingness of persons and things to serve as sources of evidence,
do not differ from those which are necessary to secure their forthcomingness for
any other judicial purpose, they do not properly form part of the subject of the
present work. (Vol. I, p. 27.)

\*    \*    \*    \*    \*

[17]For Bentham's discussion of these terms, see Vol. IV, p. 256 (Bk. VIII, Chap. xvi).

*Of evidence* sine lite. *An example of this is, where, to enable a man to receive money from an officer employed in the payment of public money, evidence shewing his title must be produced. Here, as elsewhere, the object is to guard against deception in the most effectual way possible, without preponderant or unnecessary vexation, expense, and delay.*

On this subject a few pages had been written by Mr. Bentham, but he had never completed the enquiry, and the manuscript in the hands of the Editor was so incomplete that he has thought it best to suppress it.[18] (Vol. I, p. 37.)


\*   \*   \*   \*   \*


[*Bentham proposes (Vol. I, pp. 103–6) a scale to measure the value of witnesses' evidence.*]

M. Dumont, in a note to the *Traité des Preuves Judiciaires*, has brought forward several objections against the scale which Mr. Bentham has suggested for the measurement of degrees of persuasion and probative force. It is fair that the reader should have the means of judging for himself, what degree of validity these objections possess. I quote from a recently published and very well executed translation of Mr. Dumont's work.

I do not dispute the correctness of the author's principles; and I cannot deny that, where different witnesses have different degrees of belief, it would be extremely desirable to obtain a precise knowledge of these degrees, and to make it the basis of the judicial decision; but I cannot believe that this sort of perfection is attainable in practice. I even think, that it belongs only to intelligences superior to ourselves, or at least to the great mass of mankind. Looking into myself, and supposing that I am examined in a court of justice on various facts, if I cannot answer "Yes" or "No" with all the certainty which my mind can allow, if there be degrees and shades, I feel myself incapable of distinguishing between two and three, between four and five, and even between more distant degrees. I make the experiment at this very moment; I try to recollect who told me a certain fact; I hesitate, I collect all the circumstances, I think it was A rather than B: but should I place my belief at No. 4, or No. 7? I cannot tell.
A witness who says, "I am doubtful," says nothing at all, in so far as the judge is concerned. It serves no purpose, I think, to enquire after the degrees of doubt. But these different states of belief, which, in my opinion, it is difficult to express in numbers, display themselves to the eyes of the judge by other signs. The readiness of the witness, the distinctness and certainty of his answers, the agreement of all the circumstances of his story with each other,—it is this which shows the confidence of the witness in himself. Hesitation, a painful searching for the details, successive connexions of his own testimony,—it is this which announces a witness who is not at the *maximum* of certainty. It belongs to the judge to appreciate these differences, rather than to the witness himself, who would be greatly embarrassed if he had to fix the numerical amount of his own belief.

---

[18]This note is not signed "Editor," but obviously is Mill's.

Were this scale adopted, I should be apprehensive that the authority of the testimony would often be inversely as the wisdom of the witnesses. Reserved men—men who knew what doubt is—would, in many cases, place themselves at inferior degrees, rather than at the highest; while those of a positive and presumptuous disposition, above all, passionate men, would almost believe they were doing themselves an injury, if they did not take their station immediately at the highest point. The wisest thus leaning to a diminution, and the least wise to an augmentation, of their respective influence on the judge, the scale might produce an effect contrary to what the author expects from it.

The comparison with wagers and insurances does not seem to me to be applicable. Testimony turns on past events; wagers turn on future events: as a witness, I know, I believe, or I doubt; as a wagerer, I know nothing, but I conjecture, I calculate probabilities: my rashness can injure nobody but myself; and if a wagerer feels that he has gone too far, he often diminishes the chances of loss by betting on the other side.

It appears to me, that, in judicial matters, the true security depends on the degree in which the judges are acquainted with the nature of evidence, the appreciation of testimony, and the different degrees of proving power. These principles put a balance into their hands, in which witnesses can be weighed much more accurately than if they were allowed to assign their own value; and even if the scale of the degrees of belief were adopted, it would still be necessary to leave judges the power of appreciating the intelligence and morality of the witnesses, in order to estimate the confidence due to the numerical point of belief at which they have placed their testimony.

These are the difficulties which have presented themselves to me, in meditating on this new method.[19]

On these observations of M. Dumont it may, in the first place, be remarked that, if applicable at all, they are applicable only to the use of the scale by the witness, not to the use of it by the judge, which latter use, however, is perhaps the more important of the two. In the next place, even as regards the witness, I doubt whether any great weight should be attached to the objections. For, first, what almost all of them seem to imply is, that, because we cannot in all cases attain the degree of exactness which is desirable, therefore we ought to neglect the means of attaining that degree of exactness which is in our power. The witness who does not know the degree of his persuasion,—the witness to whom the scale would be useless, will not call for it: the judge will at all events have the same means of appreciating *his* testimony, as he has now, and will not be the more likely to be deceived by a witness who does not use the scale, because it has happened to him to have received the testimony of one who does.

Secondly, the most formidable in appearance of all M. Dumont's objections—I mean that which is contained in his third paragraph—seems to me, if it prove anything, to prove much more than M. Dumont intended. The wise, says he, will place their degree of persuasion lower than they ought, the foolish, higher than they ought: the effect therefore of the scale is to give greater power to the foolish than they otherwise would have, and less power to the wise. But if this be true, what does it prove? that different degrees of persuasion should not be suffered to be indicated at all; that no one should be suffered to say he doubts. It is not the scale

[19]Dumont, note in Bentham, *Treatise on Judicial Evidence*, p. 45n.

which does the mischief, if mischief there be. There are but two sorts of witnesses, the wise and the foolish: grant to them the privilege of expressing doubt, or any degree of persuasion short of the highest, and the foolish, says M. Dumont, will make no use of the privilege, the wise will make a bad use. But if so, would it not be better to withhold the privilege altogether? Is it the scale which makes all the difference?

The truth seems to me to be, that the scale will neither add to the power of the foolish witness, nor unduly diminish that of the wise one. It will not add to the power of the foolish witness, because he cannot place his persuasion higher than the highest point in the scale; and this is no more than he could do without it. It will not unduly diminish the power of the wise witness; because the wise witness will know tolerably well what degree of persuasion he has grounds for, and will therefore know tolerably well whereabouts to place himself in the scale. That he would be likely to place himself too low, seems to me a mere assumption. The wiser a man becomes, the more certainly will he doubt, where evidence is insufficient, and scepticism justifiable; but as his wisdom increases, so also will his confidence increase, in all those cases in which there is sufficient evidence to warrant a positive conclusion. (Vol. I, pp. 106–9.)

\* \* \* \* \*

*When, by a consideration of any kind, a man is determined to maintain a proposition of any kind, and finds it not tenable on the ground of reason and experience; to conceal his distress, he has recourse to some phrase, in and by which the truth of the proposition is, somehow or other, assumed.*

*Thus, in the moral department of science; having a set of obligations which they were determined to impose upon mankind, or such part of it at any rate as they should succeed in engaging by any means to submit to the yoke; phrases, in no small variety and abundance, have been invented by various persons, for the purpose of giving force to their respective wills, and thus performing for their accommodation the functions of a law. Law of nations, moral sense, common sense, understanding, rule of right, fitness of things, law of reason, right reason, natural justice, natural equity, good order, truth, will of God, repugnancy to nature.*

An appropriate name for this class of phrases would be *covers for dogmatism*; an appellation indicating the property common to them all, of serving as cloaks for ipse-dixitism, for that fallacy which has been termed by the logicians *petitio principii*.

To say that an act is right or wrong, because it is conformable or disconformable to the law of nature, is merely to say that it is right or wrong because it is

conformable or disconformable to right or wrong. What law has nature? What is
nature itself? Is it a poetical and imaginary personage, which I suppose nobody
ever seriously believed to have any real existence? Is it the physical and
psychological world, considered as a whole? Take the word in either sense, "law
of nature" is a phrase which can have no meaning; and he who uses it means
nothing by it, except his own opinions, or his own feelings; which he thus
endeavours to erect into a standard, to which the opinions and feelings of others are
to conform.

   To say, in like manner, that an act is right or wrong because it is conformable or
disconformable to conscience, or moral sense, is to say that it is right or wrong,
because I, the speaker, approve or disapprove of it. For what is conscience, or
moral sense, except my own feeling of approbation or disapprobation? By what
other test am I to determine what is conformable to conscience, what is
conformable to the moral sense?

   The moralists, or pretended moralists, who make use of these words, may be
said to belong to the *dogmatical school* of ethics: since they give their own
approbation or disapprobation, as a reason for itself, and a standard for the
approbation or disapprobation of every one else. This appellation will distinguish
them from those who think that morality is not the province of dogmatism, but of
reason, and that propositions in ethics need proof, as much as propositions in
mathematics. (Vol. I, p. 126.)

*   *   *   *   *

*[In a "Note by the Author," Bentham mentions an article by Richard Price
(1723–91), "On the Importance of Christianity, the Nature of Historical
Evidence, and Miracles," in* Four Dissertations *(London: Millar and Cadell,
1767), pp. 359–439. Bentham summarizes part of Price's argument thus:]
Imagine a lottery, says he, with a million of blanks to a prize: take No. 1, No.
1,000,001, or any intermediate number; and suppose yourself to hear of its
gaining the prize: would you find any difficulty in believing it? No, surely: yet here
is an improbability of a million to one: and yet you believe it without difficulty. If
this ratio does not import sufficient improbability, instead of millions take billions:
or, instead of billions, trillions, and so on.*

   *Well then, since we must stop somewhere, we will stop at a trillion. This being
the nominal ratio, what is the consequence? Answer—That the real ratio is that of
1 to 1. One little circumstance of the case had escaped the observation of the
mathematical divine. Of the trillion and one, that some one ticket should gain the
prize, is matter of necessity: and of them all, every one has exactly as good a
chance as every other. Mathematicians, it has been observed, (so fond are they of*

*making display of the hard-earned skill acquired by them, in the management of their instrument) are apt not to be so scrupulous as might be wished in the examination of the correctness and completeness of the data which they assume, and on which they operate. [Mill appended the following "Farther Note by the Editor."]*

When Dr. Price affirms that we continually believe, on the slightest possible evidence, things in the highest degree improbable,[20] he confounds two ideas, which are totally distinct from one another, and would be seen to be such, did they not unfortunately happen to be called by the same name: these are, improbability in the ordinary sense, and mathematical improbability. In the latter of these senses there is scarcely any event which is not improbable: in the former, the only improbable events are extraordinary ones.

In the language of common life, an improbable event means an event which is disconformable to the ordinary course of nature.* This kind of improbability constitutes a valid reason for disbelief; because, universal experience having established that the course of nature is uniform, the more widely an alleged event differs from the ordinary course of nature, the smaller is the probability of its being true.

In the language of mathematics, the word improbability has a totally different meaning. In the mathematical sense of the word, every event is improbable, of the happening of which it might have been said *à priori* that the odds were against it. In this sense, almost all events which ever happened are improbable: not only those events which are disconformable, but even those events which are in the highest degree conformable, to the course, and even to the most ordinary course, of nature.

A corn merchant goes into a granary, and takes up a handful of grain as a sample; there are millions of grains in the granary, which had an equal chance of being taken up. According to Dr. Price, events which happen daily, and in every corner, are extraordinary, and highly improbable. The chances were infinitely great against my placing my foot, when I rise from my chair, on the precise spot where I have placed it; going on, in this manner, from one example to another, nothing can happen that is not infinitely improbable.[†]

True it is, in all these cases (as well as in that of the lottery, supposed by Dr. Price[21] there is what would be called, in the language of the doctrine of chances, an improbability, in the ratio of as many as you please to one: yet it would obviously be absurd to make this a reason for refusing our belief to the alleged event; and why? Because, though it is in one sense an improbable event, it is not an

[20]Price, "On the Importance of Christianity," pp. 407–12.

*See Book V, "Circumstantial," Chap. xvi, "Improbability and Impossibility." [Vol. III, pp. 283–307, esp. Sect. 5, pp. 304–7. Cf. Mill's note to that passage, pp. 30–2 below.]

†[Bentham,] *Traité des Preuves Judiciaires*—translation [i.e., *Treatise on Judicial Evidence*], p. 282.

[21]Price, "On the Importance of Christianity," pp. 410–11.

extraordinary event; there is not in the case so much as a shadow of disconformity even to the most ordinary course of nature. Mathematically improbable events happen every moment: experience affords us no reason for refusing our belief to *them*. Extraordinary events happen rarely: and as respects them, consequently, experience *does* afford a valid reason for doubt, or for disbelief. The only question in any such case is, which of two things would be most disconformable to the ordinary course of nature; that the event in question should have happened; or that the witnesses by whom its occurrence is affirmed, should have been deceivers or deceived. (Vol. I, pp. 137–8.)

\*    \*    \*    \*    \*

[*Bentham refers to revenge and malice as dyslogistic terms.*]

The word *dyslogistic* is employed by Mr. Bentham in the sense of *vituperative*; as opposed to *eulogistic*. (Vol. I, p. 146.)[22]

\*    \*    \*    \*    \*

[*Bentham argues that in general the "moral or popular sanction" operates to promote truth, but that there are exceptions when there is a conflict between the interest of the whole and those of "smaller communities or aggregations of individuals" within it. For instance (Vol. I, pp. 214–15),*] *The whole community has its popular or moral sanction upon an all-comprehensive scale; the several communities of thieves, smugglers, and all other communities having particular interests acting in opposition to the general interest—all those recognized, or not recognized, as being included in the more comprehensive class or denomination of malefactors,—have each of them a sort of section of the popular or moral sanction to itself.*

Instances in which particular classes have joined in making one moral rule for their conduct among themselves, another and a totally different rule for their conduct towards all other persons, are not unfrequent. Such is uniformly found to be the case, where particular classes are possessed of so much power, as to be in a great degree independent of the good or ill opinion of the community at large. In the moral code of the West India slaveholders, many acts which would be among the worst of crimes if committed against a white man, are perfectly innocent when the subject of them is a negro. For white and black, substitute Mahomedan and Christian, and the same observation holds good with respect to Turkey. Substitute

[22]Again the note is not signed "Editor" but obviously is Mill's.

orthodox and heretic, it at one time held good in all Catholic, not to say in all Christian countries; as well with regard to the other virtues in general as to that of veracity in particular. (Vol. I, p. 215.)

\*     \*     \*     \*     \*

[*In discussing the effect of the religious sanction in procuring complete and correct testimony, Bentham comments:*] *The age in which the text of the sacred writings was first committed to writing, was not, in the instance of any of the book-religions, an age in which any such qualities as those of precision, accuracy, and particularity of explanation, belonged in any considerable degree to the public mind. To reduce the precept to a state adapted to practice, it has become more and more the custom to fill up from the precepts of the moral sanction, the reputed deficiencies manifested in these particulars by the religious sanction. In a delineation, which at this time of day should come to be given, of what the religious sanction prescribes in relation to truth and falsehood; the exceptions above mentioned as applied by the moral sanction to the general requisition of veracity and verity—the particular allowances as well as counter-prescriptions made by the moral sanction, in favour of the several classes of falsehoods, designated as above by the several appellations of falsehoods of duty, falsehoods of humanity, and falsehoods of urbanity,—would probably not be omitted.*

Mr. Bentham might have quoted, in illustration of this remark, the following passage from Paley—a writer of undisputed piety, who, in a system of morals professing to be founded upon the will of God as its principle, makes no difficulty in giving a licence to falsehood, in several of its necessary or allowable shapes.

There are falsehoods which are not lies, that is, which are not criminal; as, where the person to whom you speak has no right to know the truth, or, more properly, where little or no inconveniency results from the want of confidence in such cases; as where you tell a falsehood to a madman, for his own advantage; to a robber, to conceal your property; to an assassin, to defeat or divert him from his purpose. The particular consequence is, by the supposition, beneficial; and as to the general consequence, the worst that can happen is, that the madman, the robber, the assassin, will not trust you again; which (beside that the first is incapable of deducing regular conclusions from having been once deceived, and the two last not likely to come a second time in your way), is sufficiently compensated by the immediate benefit which you propose by the falsehood.\*

(Vol. I, pp. 233–4.)

\*     \*     \*     \*     \*

\*[William Paley (1743–1805), *Principles of*] *Moral and Political Philosophy* [(1785), 15th ed., 2 vols. (London: Faulder, 1804)], Bk. III, Chap. xv [Vol. I, pp. 207–9].

*[To illustrate the inefficiency of the religious sanction in preventing "wilful and deliberate falsehood," Bentham cites] Cases in which, under the influence of a manifestly-operating sinister interest in the shape of wealth, power, dignity, or reputation, such declarations of opinion are made, as, from the nature of the facts asserted, cannot, consistently with the nature of the human mind, be in all points true; but without any particular proof of falsity operating in the case of one such false declarer more than another. To this head may be referred all solemn declarations of opinion on the subject of controverted points respecting facts out of the reach of human knowledge, delivered in the shape of pre-appointed formularies; adopted and authenticated by the signature of the witness in question, or otherwise; the declaration enforced or not by the ceremony of an oath.*

Every person taking orders in the English church, signs a declaration of his full belief in the whole of the thirty-nine articles of that church. Some of the most pious members of it have not, however, scrupled to declare, that it is not necessary that this declaration should be true: that it is allowable for a person who does not believe in the whole, but only in a part, of the thirty-nine articles, to sign a declaration professing himself to believe in the whole.[23] (Vol. I, p. 239.)

*       *       *       *       *

*[Continuing his assault on the religious sanction, Bentham says:] To depend, on every the most important occasion of life, upon the force of a principle which, on the occasions here in question, not to speak of other occasions, has been demonstrated by experience to be nearly, if not altogether, without force, would continue to lead, as it has led, to mischievous error and deception, to an indefinite extent. The topic of oaths, and the topic of exclusionary rules, grounded on the supposition of a deficiency of sensibility to the force of the religious sanction, will furnish proofs and illustrations.*

See Book II, Securities, Chapter vi, and Book IX, Exclusion, Part III, Chap. v. [Vol. V, pp. 125–45.]

Cases no doubt there are, and those very numerous, in which the religious

---

[23]The first "pious" clergyman to put forward this view was Francis Blackburne (1705–87), in his *The Confessional; or, A Full and Free Inquiry into the Right, Utility, Edification and Success of Establishing Systematic Confessions of Faith and Doctrine in Protestant Churches* (London: Bladon, 1766). Also significant in the controversy was Richard Watson (1737–1816), Bishop of Llandaff; see his *A Letter to the Members of the Honourable House of Commons, Respecting the Petition for Relief in the Matter of Subscription* (London: Boyer and Nichols, 1772).

sanction appears to exercise a much stronger influence than is here ascribed to it. That which is really the effect of the moral sanction, or of the legal sanction, or of both, is continually ascribed to the influence of the religious sanction. From causes which it would be easy, but foreign to the present purpose, to explain, religious persons are apt to suppose, that an act, if virtuous, is more virtuous, if vicious, more excusable, when the motive which prompted it belonged to the religious class, than when it belonged to any other: and even in some cases, that an act which, if produced by any other motive, would be vicious, becomes virtuous by having a motive of this class for its cause. Thus it becomes the interest of every one, to whom the reputation of virtue is an object of desire, to persuade others, and even himself, that as many as possible of his actions, be they good or bad, emanate from that class of motives. (Vol. I, pp. 246–7.)

\*   \*   \*   \*   \*

[*Bentham's list of securities for trustworthiness of testimony concludes with "Investigation," which he describes as*] *arrangements designed or tending to promote the discovery of one article of evidence through the medium of another: the discovery of a lot of testimonial evidence, for example, of a sort fit to be lodged in the budget of ultimately employable evidence; whether the article, by means of which it is discovered, be, or be not, itself fit to be so disposed of, fit to be attended to in that character: the finding out, for example, a person who was an eye-witness of the transaction, by the examination of a person who was not himself an eye-witness of it, but heard the other speak of himself as having been so.*

*Arrangements competent to the process of investigation, as here described, are in every case necessary, to preserve the aggregate mass of evidence from being untrustworthy and deceptitious on the score of incompleteness.*

This last article in the list of securities, which, as the reader will have seen, is a security, not for the correctness of any one article of evidence, but for the completeness of the whole mass, belongs to the head of Forthcomingness, which was reserved by the Author to form part of a work on Procedure.[24] (Vol. I, p. 281.)

\*   \*   \*   \*   \*

[24]See *Principles of Judicial Procedure* (1837), in *Works*, Vol. II, pp. 52–7 and 116–17 (Chap. x, "Judicial Communication," and Chap. xx, "Prehension"). This reference is supplied by Bowring in *Works*, Vol. VI, p. 285.

[*Mill appended the following note to a discursive footnote by Bentham on the absurdities of rules concerning cross-examination of witnesses.*]

Mr. Phillipps's *Law of Evidence*, Vol. I, p. 256, says, "If a witness should appear to be in the interest of the opposite party, or unwilling to give evidence, the court will in its discretion allow the examination-in-chief to assume something of the form of a cross-examination." It appears therefore that this rule of judge-made law has to a great degree been set aside by other judge-made law, subsequently enacted. (Vol. II, pp. 48–9.)

*       *       *       *       *

[*Bentham considers the benefit and "vexation" of confining a witness, when*] *What is manifest is, that the price thus considered as capable of being paid for an additional security against the liberation of a guilty defendant by mendacious testimony, is not a small one. . . .*

*Whatsoever be the species of delinquency, of the vexation in question the magnitude will be the same. The proportion between the two mischiefs, between the two benefits, or between the benefit on one hand and the price paid for it in the shape of mischief ( viz. vexation) on the other hand, will depend in every case upon the magnitude, that is, upon the mischievousness, of the offence.*

It seems, however, that there can be scarcely any cases in which an extraneous witness, not suspected of being in any way implicated in the offence of which the defendant stands accused, can with propriety be subjected to confinement: particularly to such close confinement as is here in question. Not that, if there were no better means of warding off the danger of deception from his testimony, there might not be cases of so much importance that even this remedy, expensive as it is, would be fit to be employed. But I see no reason why the same arrangement which is proposed by Mr. Bentham to be adopted in the case of a defendant, (viz. *vivâ voce* interrogation as soon as possible after his person can be secured),[25] should not, *when necessary*, be adopted likewise in the case of an extraneous witness; or why, if sufficient in the one case, it should not be sufficient in the other. I admit that it would be absurd, in the view of obviating the danger of mendacity-serving suggestion, to receive in every cause the evidence of every witness in the first instance, and thus try the cause from beginning to end, in order to facilitate the trying of it again at a subsequent period: but if (as Mr. Bentham maintains) a strong suspicion that the witness means to give false evidence, renders even confinement

[25]*Rationale*, Vol. II, p. 232.

of his person, if necessary to the prevention of deception from that cause, a justifiable measure, that same degree, or even a less degree, of suspicion, would surely justify the subjecting him to a preliminary examination; which, though it would not prevent him from subsequently receiving mendacity-serving information, would at any rate render such information of little use to him for his mischievous purpose. Observe also, that this arrangement would obviate, not only the danger of suggestion *ab extrà*, but that of premeditation: confinement of his person, were it ever so close, could be a security only against the former. (Vol. II, p. 236.)

*     *     *     *     *

[*Bentham's list of the advantages of "preappointed evidence" in cases involving contracts includes prevention of (1) "non-notoriety and oblivion," (2) "uncertainty" as to "import," (3) "spurious contracts," (4) "unfairly obtained" contracts, and (5) "injury to third persons"; it concludes with (6) "Production of revenue to government," concerning which he says:*] In this, the last upon the list of purposes, we see an advantage altogether void of all natural connection with the five preceding ones, and with the general object and use of evidence. But, when the connection is once formed, it contributes a material assistance to those other original and direct purposes: inasmuch as the advantage derived from the institution in this point of view is carried to account, and serves to set in the scale against whatever articles are chargeable upon it on the side of disadvantage.

This last might perhaps without impropriety be struck out of the list of uses: since a tax on contracts, in whatever manner laid on, is either a law-tax, that is, a tax upon justice, which is perhaps the worst of all taxes, or a tax upon the transfer of property, which is one of the worst, or both together. (Vol. II, p. 456.)

*     *     *     *     *

[*Bentham proposes to deal with types of "evidentiary facts" as bearing on the probability of "principal facts," that is, "facts on the belief of which judicial decision depends." The fourth of these principal facts "considered as probabilized" is "Unauthenticity" of*] any instrument being, or purporting to be, of ancient date. For the circumstances capable of serving in the character of evidentiary facts to probabilize *this principal fact*, unauthenticity,—*or (which is the same thing in other words), to* disprobabilize *the* authenticity *of the instrument,—see a table of evidentiary facts of this description, taken principally from* Le Clerc's Ars Critica.

No such table is to be found in the MS.[26] (Vol. III, p. 24.)

\* \* \* \* \*

[*The fifth of these principal facts is*] Posteriora priorum: *any supposed* antecedent *acts in a number of supposed successive acts (whether forbidden by law or not), considered as following one another in a supposed naturally connected series: for example, as being, or being supposed to be, conducive to one and the same end; such as, in a law-suit,* success, viz. *on either side of the suit.*

*Correspondent evidentiary facts,—any acts proved to have been performed, and considered as having been performed in consequence of such supposed antecedent acts; for example, in pursuit of the same end.*

*See a table of evidentiary facts of this description taken from Comyns's* Digest of English Law.

This table, as well as that which is subsequently mentioned, is also wanting.[27] (Vol. III, p. 24.)

\* \* \* \* \*

[*The following note is appended to the title, "Of Improbability and Impossibility," of Chap. xvi of Book V.*]

In putting together the scattered papers from which this work was compiled, considerable difficulty was felt in assigning its proper place to what Mr. Bentham had written on the subject of improbability and impossibility.

[26]In Bowring's edition an appended note reads: "The portion of Le Clerc's work which was made use of, is evidently the 2nd section of Part III, ('De locis et scriptis spuriis à genuinis dignoscendis.') *Vide Ars Critica*, London [Clavel, *et al.*], 1698, Vol. II, p. 367." The cited section of the work by Jean Leclerc (1657–1736) runs from p. 367 to p. 410.

[27]In the Bowring edition, a note is appended to Mill's footnote: "[But see the Addenda to Evidence, Tit. Testmoigne, Com. Dig. Hammond's Edit.—*Ed. of this Collection.*]" The reference is to the list of cases, from which Bentham presumably constructed his lost tables, in the "Addenda" to the article "Testmoigne—Evidence," in John Comyns (d. 1740), *A Digest of the Laws of England* (1762–67), 5th ed., 8 vols. ed. Anthony Hammond (London: Butterworth, *et al.*, 1822), Vol. VII, pp. 432–46.

Had it been in the power of the editor to select that arrangement which appeared to him best suited to the nature of the subject, he would have placed so much of the present chapter as is merely explanatory of the *nature* of improbability and impossibility, in the first book, entitled THEORETIC GROUNDS; and so much of it as relates to the *probative force* of improbability and impossibility, considered as articles of *circumstantial evidence*, in the present book. It appeared to him, however, on perusing the manucript, that the mode in which Mr. Bentham had treated the subject did not admit of any such separation of it into two parts, as he had at first contemplated. The only question, therefore, which remained, was, whether to place the chapter under the head of Theoretic Grounds, or under that of Circumstantial Evidence? and, on consideration, he has thought it better to postpone the more general and explanatory matter to the present book, than to separate this one species of circumstantial evidence from the rest. (Vol. III, p. 258.)

\*     \*     \*     \*     \*

[*To begin his discussion of "Impossible facts distinguished from verbal contradictions," Bentham says:*] *It having been shewn that improbability and impossibility, applied to a matter of fact, are merely terms expressing a certain strength of persuasion of the non-existence of that fact; what remains is to shew, what are the grounds, on which such a persuasion is liable to be entertained: to shew, in other words, in what consists the improbability or impossibility of any alleged fact.*

*Previously, however, to entering upon this inquiry, it will be necessary to discard out of the list of impossible facts, articles that might be in danger of being considered as included in it. These are:*

*1. Contradictions in terms: or, as they might be termed, verbal impossibilities. Examples: Two and two are not so many as four:—Two and two are more than four:—The same thing is, and is not, at the same time.*

*The truth is, that in these cases no matter of fact at all is asserted; consequently none of which it can be said that it is impossible.*

This may be illustrated by the following passage from Locke:

All propositions, wherein two abstract terms are affirmed one of another, are barely about the signification of sounds. For since no abstract idea can be the same with any other but itself, when its abstract name is affirmed of any other term, it can signify no more but this, that it may or ought to be called by that name; or that these two names signify the same idea. Thus, should any one say, *that parsimony is frugality*, that *gratitude is justice*; that this or that action is, or is not, *temperate*; however specious these and the like propositions may at first sight seem, yet when we come to press them, and examine nicely what they contain, we shall find that it all amounts to nothing, but the signification of those terms.*

(Vol. III, p. 268.)

\* \* \* \* \*

*[The second category, after contradictions in terms, discussed in the preceding note, is "Inconceivable facts," concerning which Bentham says:] Sometimes to this class, sometimes to the former, belong the opposites of a variety of propositions of a mathematical nature: e.g. that two and two should be either more or less than equal to four: that two right lines should of themselves enclose a space.*

These propositions, even such an one as the last, viz. that two right lines cannot enclose a space, are but verbal contradictions. The terms *straight line*, and *space*, and *enclose*, are all general terms, and to affirm them one of another, is merely to say that they are of this or that meaning. It is merely to say that the meaning we ascribe to the term space, or rather to the term enclosure of space, is inconsistent with the meaning we ascribe to the term two straight lines. When we pass from names to things, and take two straight rods in our hands, we have the evidence of our senses, that they cannot enclose a space. If they touch at any one part, they diverge from one another at every other part. If they touch at more than one part, they coincide, and then are equivalent to one straight line. What we mean by an enclosure, is such a line, or continuance of lines, that a body departing from any one point can pass on without turning back till it come to that point again, without having met in its progress any place where the line was interrupted, any place where there was not a portion of line. An enclosure is a line or conjunction of lines, which beginning at one point is continued till it comes to that point again. Two straight lines are lines which departing from one point never meet, but continually diverge. What is affirmed, then, is, that lines which do meet, in the manner thus described, and lines which in that manner do not meet, are not the same lines. The question, then, either is about the physical fact, the rods, to which the evidence of sense and experience is applicable; or it is about the meaning of general terms. (Vol. III, pp. 268–9.)

\* \* \* \* \*

*[John Locke (1632–1704),] Essay Concerning Human Understanding [((1690), in Works*, new ed., 10 vols. (London: Tegg, *et al.*, 1823)], Bk. IV, Chap. viii, Sect. 12 [Vol. III, p. 52].

[*Bentham asserts that supposed "disconformity" between matters of fact and what someone believes to be "the established course of nature" may be of three kinds: facts "disconformable in toto," such as a body being at the same time in two places; facts "disconformable in degree," such as a man being sixty feet tall; and facts "disconformable in specie," such as a unicorn. He continues:*] *It is manifest, that, in the two last of these classes, the incredibility of the fact rises only to a greater or less degree of improbability, not to that of impossibility. The supposed facts are not* repugnant *to the established course of nature; they are only not conformable to it: they are facts which are not yet known to exist, but which, for aught we know, may exist; though, if true, they would belong to the class of extraordinary facts, and therefore require a greater degree of evidence to establish their truth than is necessary in the case of a fact exactly resembling the events which occur every day.*

It will be attempted to be shewn in a subsequent note,[28] that even what Mr. Bentham calls impossibilities *in toto*, are in reality nothing more than facts in a high degree improbable. (Vol. III, p. 284.)

\* \* \* \* \*

[*Bentham gives (Vol. III, pp. 285–6) the "primum mobiles, or causes of motion and rest," that modify the law of gravitation, as:*]
*1. The centrifugal force.*
*2. The force of cohesion,—the attraction observed to take place amongst the homogeneous parts of the same whole.*
*3. The force of chemical attraction: to which, perhaps, may be to be added repulsion. . . .*
*4. The force of repulsion or elasticity, given to the particles of other matter by caloric, when, being united with them, it forms a gas.*
*5. The force of expansion and contraction (repulsion and re-attraction) produced by the addition and subtraction of caloric to and from other bodies in the states of solidity and liquidity.*
*6. The force of electrical and galvanic attraction and repulsion.*
*7. The force of magnetic attraction and repulsion.*
*8. The force of muscular motion put in action by the will.*
*9. The force of muscular motion put in action by the vital power, in the case of the involuntary motions that take place in living animals.*
*10. The force of muscular motion put in action in the way of animal galvanism.*
*11. The force of vegetation.*

[28]See the next entry.

*[He concludes the discussion by considering whether new primum mobiles may not be found:]* as to the discovery of new causes of motion, causes apparently distinct from, and not referable to, any of those above enumerated, I am not disposed to regard it as in any degree improbable. Yet, as to any causes adequate to the production of any such effect as the effect in question; in the discoveries just spoken of there is not any thing that would prevent me from regarding it as being, in the sense above determined, practically impossible. Why? Because it appears to me practically impossible, that, after so long a course of physical experience and experiment, any primum mobile, of a force adequate to the production of an effect of such magnitude, can have remained undetected. As to the power of steam, the application of it to any useful purpose is not so old as a century and a half; but the existence of it as a source of motion, could never have been altogether a secret to any one who ever boiled a pot with a cover to it.

It may, perhaps, be doubted, whether, until our knowledge shall have attained a perfection far beyond what it has attained, or is ever likely to attain, such an attribute as impossibility *in toto*, can, in the sense in which Mr. Bentham uses the words, be predicated of any conceivable phenomenon whatever.

Mr. Bentham has given a list (whether complete or incomplete is of no consequence for the present purpose) of the various forces by which gravitation is known to be, under certain circumstances, counteracted: and assuming this list to be complete, he proceeds to infer [p. 287], that "any motion which, being in a direction opposite to that of the attraction of gravitation, should not be referable to any one of those particular causes of motion, may be pronounced impossible:" and for practical purposes, no doubt it may; but if metaphysical accuracy be sought for, I doubt whether even in this case the impossibility in question be any thing more than a very high degree of improbability. For,

1st. Suppose the catalogue of all the known forces which may operate to the production of motion, (or, as Mr. Bentham calls them, the primum mobiles,) to be at present complete: does it follow that it will always remain so? Is it possible to set limits to the discoveries which mankind are capable of making in the physical sciences? Are we justified in affirming that we are acquainted with all the moving forces which exist in nature? Before the discovery (for instance) of galvanism, it will be allowed, we should not have been justified in making any such assertion.[29] In what respect are circumstances changed since that time? except that we are now acquainted with one force more than we were before. By what infallible mark are

---

[29]The phenomenon, named after its discoverer, Luigi Galvani (1737–98), was made known in his "De viribis electricitatis in motu musculari commentarius," *De Bononiensi Scientiarum et Artium Instituto atque Academia Commentarii* (1791), VII, 363–418. The theory was corrected, however, by Alessandro Volta (1745–1827), in a letter to Sir Joseph Banks (20 Mar., 1800), *Philosophical Transactions of the Royal Society of London*, XC, Pt. II (1800), 403–31.

we to determine, when we have come to the knowledge of all the properties of matter?

Mr. Bentham himself acknowledges [p. 289] that the discovery of new moving forces is not impossible; but the discovery of new forces, adequate to the production of such an effect as that of raising a heavy body from the floor to the ceiling of a room without any perceptible cause, he does consider impossible; because (says he) had any force, adequate to the production of such an effect, been in existence, it must have been observed long ago.* No doubt, the improbability of the existence of any such force, increases in proportion to the magnitude of the effect; but it may be permitted to doubt, whether it ever becomes an impossibility. Had our grandfathers been told, that there existed a force in nature, which was capable of setting gold, silver, and almost all the other metals on fire, and causing them to burn with a bright blue, green, or purple flame,—of converting the earths into bright metallic substances by the extrication of a particular kind of air; etc. etc.,—they surely might have said, with fully as much justice as we can at present, that if any cause had existed in nature, adequate to the production of such remarkable effects, they could not have failed to have been aware of it before.

2ndly. Suppose it certain that all the great moving forces, to one or more of which all the phenomena of the universe must be referable, were known to us; we should not, to any practical purpose, be farther advanced than before. We might indeed, in a general way, be assured of the impossibility of every phenomenon not referable to some one or more of these forces as its cause: but that any *given* alleged phenomenon is in this predicament, is more than we could possibly be assured of; until we knew not only all the moving forces which exist, but all the possible varieties of the operation of all those forces, and all the forms and shapes under which it is possible for them to manifest themselves; until, in short, we knew all which it is possible to know of the universe. How can I be sure that a given phenomenon which has no perceptible cause, is not the effect of electricity, unless I knew what all the effects of electricity are? And so of all the other laws of nature. As, however, it is very improbable that we ever shall know all the laws of nature in all their different combinations and manifestations, and as, moreover, it is difficult to see how, even if we did know them all, we could ever be certain that we did so; it seems that we never can pronounce, with perfect certainty, of any conceivable event, that it is impossible. See even Mr. Bentham himself, *infra*, Sect. 10, *ad finem* [Vol. III, pp. 371–2].

Although, however, it could not be pronounced, of the story told by Mr. Bentham, that the event which it relates is impossible, thus much may with safety

*In this instance, Mr. Bentham really breaks down the distinction between his impossibility *in toto*, and impossibility *in degree*. Causes may exist (says he) which are not yet known to us, adequate to the production of *some* effect; but not adequate to the production of *so great* an effect. If so, however, this impossible fact is impossible in degree only, and not *in toto*.

be pronounced, that, if it did happen, it was not produced by witchcraft.[30] I can conceive the existence of sufficient evidence to convince me of the occurrence of the event, improbable though it be. I cannot conceive the existence of any evidence, which could convince me that witchcraft was the cause of it. The reason is this: suppose the fact proved, the question remains,—Is it referable to witchcraft, or to some natural cause?—Of extraordinary events, produced by natural causes, many have come within my experience: of events produced by witchcraft, none whatever. That extraordinary events from natural causes have frequently occurred, there is abundant evidence: while there cannot, in the nature of things, be any evidence, that any event has ever been occasioned by witchcraft. There may be evidence that a particular event has uniformly followed the will of a particular person supposed to be a witch; but that the supposed witch brought about the given effect, not by availing herself of the laws of nature, but through the agency of an evil spirit, counteracting those laws,—this can never be more than an inference: it is not in the nature of things that any person should have personal knowledge to that effect; unless he has that perfect acquaintance with all the laws of nature, which alone can enable him to affirm with certainty that the given effect did not arise from any of those laws. What alleged witch, or magician, was ever suspected of producing more extraordinary effects than are daily produced by natural means, in our own times, by jugglers? Omniscience alone, if witchcraft were possible, could enable any one not in the secret, to distinguish it from jugglery. It is no wonder, then, that no evidence can *prove* witchcraft; since there *never can be* any evidence of it, good or bad, trustworthy or the reverse. All the evidence that has ever been adduced of witchcraft is,—testimony, in the first place, to an extraordinary event, and, in the next place, to somebody's *opinion* that this event was supernatural; but to nothing else whatever. (Vol. III, pp. 289–92.)

\*    \*    \*    \*    \*

[*The following note, headed* "'Further Remarks by the Editor,'" *completes Bk. V, Chap. xvi, Sect. 5, "On the Three Modes of Disconformity to the Course of Nature."*]

After an attentive consideration of the characters by which Mr. Bentham endeavours to distinguish his three classes from one another,[31] the reader will probably join with me in reducing these three classes to two; viz. 1. facts *repugnant* to the course of nature so far as known to us, and 2. facts merely

[30] An account of a man's levitating, taken, Bentham says, from a book on "witchcraft and apparitions."
[31] See p. 27 above.

*deviating* from it: or (to express the same meaning in more precise language) 1. facts *contrary* to experience; 2. facts *not conformable* to experience.

The discovery of a new species of animal, presents a specimen of a fact *not conformable* to experience. The discovery (were such a thing possible) of an animal belonging to any of the already known species, but unsusceptible of death, or decay, would be a fact *contrary* to experience.

This distinction was pointed out by Hume;* but, having pointed it out, he knew not how to apply it: and the misapplication which it seemed to me that he had made of it, led me for a long time to imagine that there was no foundation for the distinction itself. Having, however, by further reflection, satisfied myself of its reality, I will attempt, if possible, to make my conception of it intelligible to the reader.

All that our senses tell us of the universe, consists of certain *phenomena*, with their *sequences*. These sequences, that is to say, the different orders in which different phenomena succeed one another, have been discovered to be invariable. If they were not so; if, for example, that food, the reception of which into the stomach was yesterday followed by health, cheerfulness, and strength, were, if taken to-day, succeeded by weakness, disease, and death; the human race, it is evident, would have long ago become extinct. Those sequences, then, which are observed to recur constantly, compose what is termed the *order of nature*: and any one such sequence is, by rather an inappropriate metaphor, stiled a *law* of nature.

When a new discovery is made in the natural world, it may be either by the disruption of an old sequence, or by the discovery of a new one. It may be discovered, that the phenomenon A, which was imagined to be in all cases followed by the phenomenon B, is, in certain cases, not followed by it; or it may be discovered that the phenomenon C is followed by a phenomenon D, which, till now, was not known to follow it.

In the former case, the newly discovered fact is *contrary* to experience; in the latter case, it is merely *not conformable* to it. In the first case it is *repugnant* to what had been imagined to be the order of nature; in the second case, it merely *deviates* from it.

The first time that the sensitive plant was discovered, its characteristic property was a fact *not conformable* to experience. A new sequence was discovered; but no sequence was broken asunder; the plant had not been known to possess this property, but neither had it been known not to possess it, not having been known at all.

But if a stone projected into the air were, without any perceptible cause, to remain suspended, instead of falling to the ground; here would be not merely a new

*See his Essay on Miracles. [David Hume (1711–76), "Of Miracles," Sect. x of *An Inquiry Concerning Human Understanding*, in *Essays and Treatises on Several Subjects* (1758), new ed., 2 vols. (London: Cadell; Edinburgh: Bell and Bradfute, and Duncan, 1793), Vol. II, pp. 124–47, esp. p. 129.]

sequence, but the disruption of an old one: a phenomenon (projection of a stone into the air) which, from past experience, had been supposed to be universally followed by another phenomenon (the fall of the stone), is found, in the case in question, not to be so followed. Here then is a fact *contrary* to experience.

The error, then, (as it appears to me) of Hume, did not consist in making the distinction between facts contrary, and facts not conformable, to experience; it consisted in imagining, that, although events not conformable to experience may properly be believed, events contrary to experience cannot. That an event is not fit to be credited which supposes the non-universality of a sequence previously considered to be universal, is so far, in my conception, from being true, that the most important of all discoveries in physics have been those whereby what were before imagined to be universal laws of nature, have been proved to be subject to exception. Take Mr. Bentham's own list (pp. 285–6)[32] of the exceptions to the law of gravitation: suppose all these unknown, the law might have been supposed universal, and the exceptions, when discovered, would have been so many violations of it: but do not these exceptions, with the exceptions again to them, and so on, compose by far the most valuable part of physical science? (Vol. III, pp. 304–7.)

*     *     *     *     *

[*Bentham discusses cases in which facts that could properly have been objected to on rational grounds as improbable have been proved true. The first of these is water turning to ice, a fact that was incredible to the King of Siam, according to an anecdote reported by Locke.*][33]

This being one of the chapters which was written twice over by Mr. Bentham, the last time without reference to the first; the story of the King of Siam is told twice over at full length. As, however, it is brought to view for two very different purposes, viz. the first time, to illustrate the principle that the credibility of a fact relative to a particular individual depends upon his acquaintance with the course of nature, and the second time, to exemplify the effect of improbability as an article of circumstantial evidence; and as, moreover, the illustrations which accompany the story, in the two places in which it is introduced, are different; it has not been thought advisable to strike it out in either place. (Vol. III, p. 333.)

*     *     *     *     *

[32]Listed at p. 27 above.
[33]*Essay Concerning Human Understanding*, *Works*, Vol. III, p. 99. Bentham tells the story in Vol. III, pp. 319–22 and 333–6 (Bk. V, Chap. xvi). Mill repeats the instance in his *System of Logic*, *CW*, Vol. VII, p. 627.

[*Concerning such nonsense as that an old woman can move "through the air at pleasure on a broomstick," or a man can introduce "his body into a quart bottle," we have as full proof of their falsity*] *as, for the governance of human conduct, a man needs to have; it is only by a mixture of ignorance and rash confidence, that either of them could be pronounced, in the strict sense of the word impossibility,* impossible: *since, to the production of either of these effects, there needs but the existence of some power in nature with which we are not as yet acquainted.*

Compare this with page 289, and the note at the bottom of that page.[34] (Vol. III, p. 372.)

\*    \*    \*    \*    \*

[*Attempting in Sect. xi of Chap. xvi to assert, in connection with "alibi evidence," a distinction between "facts impossible* per se, *and facts impossible* si alia," *Bentham says:*] *There are two occasions on which the evidence, or argument, indicated by the words* impossibility *and* incredibility, *are capable of presenting themselves.*

*1. On the one side ( say that of the demandant ), a fact is deposed to by a witness: on the other side ( viz. that of the defendant ), no testimony is adduced, but it is averred that the supposed fact, as thus deposed to, is in its own nature incredible; or, what comes to the same thing, improbable to such a degree as to be incredible. Say, for example, a fact pretended to have taken place in the way of witchcraft: a man lifted up slowly, without any exertion of will on his part, or connexion with any other, from the ground into the air; or an old woman, by an exertion of volition on her part, riding in the air at pleasure on a broomstick.*

*2. On the one side ( say again that of the demandant ), a fact is deposed to by a witness, as before: on the other hand, it is averred to be impossible, —impossible not in its own nature, as before, but for this reason, viz. that the existence of it is incompatible with the existence of another fact, which in this view is deposed to by other evidence: say the testimony of a superior number of witnesses. The defendant cannot, at the time alleged, have been committing the offence in London; for at that same time he was at York, a place above two hundred miles distant. The instance here given is that which is commonly known by the name of* alibi. *It supposes the incompatibility of a man's existing in one place at any given point of time, with the existence of the same man in any other place at the same point of time: or, in other words, of a man's existing in two places at once.*

"For the purpose of the present inquiry, these two kinds of impossibility are exactly alike. The nature of the impossibility is in both cases the same; in both

[34]See pp. 28–30 above.

cases it consists in disconformity to the established course of nature. The difference is, that, in the first of the two cases, there is but one event mentioned, and that event is one which, taken by itself, cannot be true;—in the second case there are two events mentioned, either of which, taken by itself, may be true, but both together cannot.

"In the first case, therefore, the impossibility being supposed, we immediately set it down that the testimony of the affirming witnesses is false:—in the second place, we have to choose which of the two testimonies we shall disbelieve; that of the witnesses who affirm the one fact, or that of the witnesses who affirm the other fact.

"If I am told that, on such a day, at such an hour, John Brown leaped over the moon, I at once reject the assertion as being incredible: this is impossibility of the first kind. If A tells me, that, on such a day, at such an hour, John Brown was in London; and B tells me, that, on the same day, and at the same hour, the same individual was at York; I pronounce with equal readiness that both stories cannot be true, but it remains a question for subsequent consideration, which of them it is that is false: and this is impossibility of the second kind."* (Vol. III, pp. 372–4.)

\* \* \* \* \*

[*The following note is appended to the title, "Of* ex parte *preappointed written evidence," of Sect. 2 of Bk. VI, Chap. ii ( "Of Extrajudicially Written Evidence" ). The next section is entitled "Of adscititious evidence; i.e. evidence borrowed from another cause." Mill completed the chapter; see the next entry.*]

This and the following section were left by the author in the state of mere fragments. Several *memoranda*, far too incoherent to be inserted, prove it to have been his intention to enter more fully both into the subject of *ex parte* preappointed evidence, and into that of adscititious evidence. It does not appear, however, that he carried this intention into effect. (Vol. III, p. 422.)

\* \* \* \* \*

[*The following note appears at the end of Bentham's discussion, in Bk. VI, Chap. ii, Sect. 2, of "evidence* alio in foro." *Mill's contribution follows immediately in the text.*]

\*N.B. The paragraphs in inverted commas are inserted by the Editor. They appeared necessary to complete the section, which is composed of mere fragments, written at different times by the author, and which the Editor was obliged to connect together as he best could.

Here ends all that Mr. Bentham had written on the subject of adscititious evidence, with the exception of some loose memoranda. What follows was chiefly made up from these memoranda by the editor.

The course proper to be taken, in respect to adscititious evidence, will be found to vary, according as the document in question is a previous *decision*, or the whole or some part of the *minutes of the evidence* delivered in a previous cause.

In respect of the propriety of admission, both these species of adscititious evidence stand nearly on the same ground. Neither of them ought to be admitted, when better evidence from the same source is, without preponderant inconvenience, to be had; neither of them ought to be rejected, when it is not.

There is not, probably, that system of judicial procedure in existence, (how bad soever the mode of taking evidence that it employs), which does not afford a greater probability of right decision than of wrong; and in general the presumption of right decision is a very strong one. True it is that no decision of a court of justice, certifying the existence of a fact, affords ground for believing it, any farther than as such decision renders probable the existence, at the time when it was pronounced, of *evidence* sufficient to support it: and if the original evidence, on which the decision in the former cause was grounded, were forthcoming in the present, that evidence would be preferable, as a foundation for decision, to the mere opinion formerly pronounced on the ground of that same evidence by a judge. But it scarcely ever happens that evidence which has once been presented, admits of being again presented in as perfect a form as before. All that important species of evidence which is constituted by the deportment of the witness in the presence of the judge, is, in most cases, irrecoverably lost: such evidence as can be obtained now, might not be sufficient to warrant the former decision, and yet the decision, when pronounced, may have been perfectly borne out by the evidence on that occasion adduced. On the other hand, it is true that, in very many cases, by recurring to the original sources, sufficient evidence of the fact might even now be obtained, not, however, without more or less of delay, vexation, and expense: for the avoidance of which, it is often proper that the previous decision, though an inferior kind of evidence, should be received as a substitute, in the place of a superior kind.

As to the minutes of the evidence delivered in the former cause; it is sufficiently manifest that they ought not to be admitted, if recurrence to the original sources of evidence be practicable, without preponderant inconvenience; if the witnesses in the former cause be capable of being examined, or such written or real evidence as it may have afforded be capable of being exhibited, in the present: unless when there may be a use in comparing two testimonies delivered by the same witness on two different occasions. But if (no matter from what cause) recurrence to the original sources be either physically or prudentially impracticable, the minutes of the former evidence should be admitted, and taken for what they are worth. If the evidence in question be oral testimony, being generally upon oath, subject to punishment in case of intentional falsehood, and to counter-interrogation, it is at any rate better than hearsay evidence, which, at its origin, had none of these securities: if it be real evidence, the official minutes of it are the very best kind of reported real evidence, of which hereafter.

A question of greater nicety is, whether in any, and, if in any, in what cases, adscititious evidence shall be taken for conclusive?

In the case of minutes of evidence, the short answer is, never. The testimony of a witness, or of any number of witnesses, even if delivered in the cause in hand, and under all the securities which can be taken in the cause in hand for its correctness and completeness, ought not to be, nor, under any existing system of law that I know of, would be, taken for conclusive: much less a mere note of the testimony which they delivered on a former occasion, subject perhaps, indeed, to the same set of securities, but perhaps to a set in any degree inferior to those which there may, in the cause in hand, be the means of subjecting them to.

The case of a *decision* is more complicated. For the purpose of a prior cause, a decision has been given which supposes proof made of a certain fact; and the question is, whether, on the ground of such decision, such fact shall be taken for true,—shall be considered as being sufficiently and conclusively proved,—for the purpose of the decision to be given in a posterior cause?

It must of course be assumed, that the prior decision *necessarily* supposes evidence of the fact in question to have been presented to the judge, sufficient to create in his mind a persuasion of its existence: for there would be manifest impropriety in making the decision conclusive evidence of any fact not absolutely necessary to its legality; with whatever degree of *probability* the existence of such fact might be inferred from it.

1. Let the parties be the same; and the tribunal either the same tribunal, or one in which the same or equally efficient securities are taken for rectitude of decision. In this case, unless where a new trial of the former cause would be proper, the decision in the former cause ought to be taken as conclusive evidence (for the purpose of the posterior cause) of every fact, proof of which it *necessarily* implies. A lawyer would say, *Quia interest reipublicae ut sit finis litium*.[35] Not choosing to content myself with vague and oracular generalities, which are as susceptible of being employed in defence of bad arrangements of procedure as of good ones, I place the propriety of the rule upon the following more definite ground: that, as every person who would have an opportunity of applying the security of counter-interrogation in the second cause, has had such an opportunity in the first; and as the rules of evidence which were observed in the former trial, were, by supposition, as well calculated for the extraction of the truth, as those which would be to be acted upon in the present; the judge on the second occasion would have no

---

[35]"It concerns the state that there be an end to litigation."

advantage, in seeking after the truth, over the judge on the first, to counterbalance the disadvantage necessarily consequent upon lapse of time: and the decision of the first judge (though strictly speaking it be only evidence of evidence) is more likely to be correct, than that which the second judge might pronounce on the occasion of the posterior cause.

The case is different if fresh evidence happen to have been brought to light subsequently to the first trial, or if there be any reason for suspecting error or *mala fides* on the part of the first judge. But, in either of these cases, a new trial of the former cause would be proper. If the fact be sufficiently established for the purpose of the first cause, it is sufficiently established for the purpose of any subsequent cause between the same parties. It is only when there appears reason to think that it was improperly considered as established in the first cause, that there can be any use in going through the trouble of establishing it again in the second.

The above remarks apply also to the case in which the parties to the second cause are not the actual parties to the first, but persons who claim in their right, their executors, for example, or heirs-at-law; or even persons claiming under the same deed, or, in any other way, upon the same title; all those, in short, who in English law language are quaintly called *privies* in blood, in estate, and in law: for though these have not had an opportunity of cross-examining the witnesses in the former cause, other persons representing the same interest have.

2. Suppose the parties different, that is, with different interests, and the same reasons do not apply. The deficiency in respect of securities for trustworthiness, which constitutes the inferiority of adscititious evidence, may now have place to an indefinite extent, and is always likely to have place to some extent. It will very often happen that there was some part of the facts, known to the witnesses in the former cause, which would have made in favour of one or other party to the present cause; but which did not come to light, because, there being no one among the parties to the former cause in whose favour it would have made, it found no one to draw it out by interrogation. The former decision, therefore, although conclusive against the parties to the former cause, and all who claim under them, ought not to be conclusive against a third party. If it were, an opportunity would be given for a particular modification of the characteristic fraud: a feigned suit instituted by one conspirator against another, and judgment suffered by the latter to go against him, with the view of establishing a false fact, to be afterwards made use of in a suit against some other person.

The above observations constitute what foundation there is for the rule of English law, that *res inter alios acta* is not evidence:[36] of which hereafter. Note, *en passant*, the character of jurisprudential logic: a decision *inter alios* is not *conclusive* evidence, therefore not *admissible*.

---

[36]In full, *res inter alios acta alteri nocere non debet*: "Things transacted between strangers do not injure those who are not parties to them."

3. Lastly, suppose the tribunals different, and governed by different rules: and let the rules of the tribunal which tried the first cause be less calculated to insure rectitude of decision than those of the tribunal which tries the second. In this case, with or without the deficiency in point of security, arising from the difference of the parties, there is at any rate the deficiency which arises from the imperfection of the rules: the impropriety, therefore, of making the decision conclusive, is manifest. Its probative force will evidently vary, in proportion to the imperfection of the rules which govern the practice of the court by which it was pronounced; always considered with reference to the main end, rectitude of decision.

The probative force will be greater, *caeteris paribus*, when the court from which the evidence is borrowed is in the same, than when it is in a different, country; on account of the greater difficulty, in the latter case, of obtaining proof of the existence of the characteristic fraud. But this presumption is much less strong than that which arises from a difference in the mode of extraction.

We shall see hereafter to how great an extent nearly all the above rules are violated in English law. (Vol. III, pp. 426–33.)

\*    \*    \*    \*    \*

[*The following note is appended to Bentham's list of the means (of varying reliability) of making transcripts: writing with pen and ink, printing with moveable types and stereotypes, engraving, sculpture, and painting.*]

Add to these *lithography*, which, when this work was written, had scarcely been applied to the multiplication of copies of a written document.[37] (Vol. III, p. 472.)

\*    \*    \*    \*    \*

[*The first paragraph of the following passage appears in the text in square brackets and italics at the end of Bentham's discussion in Bk. VI, Chap. xii ("Aberrations of English Law in Regard to Makeshift Evidence"). Mill's contribution follows immediately in normal roman type.*]

The papers from which the above remarks on the aberrations of English law have been compiled, were written by Mr. Bentham at different times, and left by him in a very incomplete and fragmentitious state. It appears that he had intended to give some account of what is done by English law in regard to all the different kinds of makeshift evidence, but never completed his design. The remainder of this

---

[37]Lithography was invented in 1796 by a German, Alois Senefelder (1771–1834).

chapter, (with the exception of a fragment, which for distinction's sake has been printed in inverted commas,) is the result of a partial attempt to fill up the void which had thus been left in the body of the work.

5. Few questions have been more agitated in English law than those which relate to the admissibility of, and the effect, to be given to, different articles of *adscititious* evidence.* The subject occupies sixty closely printed nominal octavo, real quarto pages, in Phillipps's exposition of the law of evidence.[38] Of a subject thus extensive, more than a very general view cannot be expected to be given in the present work: nor is it necessary for our purpose to go beyond the more prominent features.

One remarkable circumstance is, that the whole body of the rules of law relating to this subject, are, with a very small number of exceptions, exclusionary. Either the decision given in a former cause is said not to be evidence; and then it is that decision which is excluded; or it is said to be conclusive evidence: and then an exclusion is put upon the whole mass of evidence, howsoever constituted, which might have been capable of being presented on the other side.

In saying this, enough has already been said to satisfy any one, who has assented to what was said in a former chapter concerning adscititious evidence,[39] that nearly the whole of the established rules on this subject, except to the extent of the single and very limited case in which it was there seen that exclusion is proper, are bad. Accordingly, the rule that a judgment directly upon the point is conclusive in any future cause between the same parties, is a good rule: it is almost the only one that is.

Even this rule is cut into by one exception: that verdicts in criminal proceedings are not only not conclusive, but are not even *admissible* evidence, in civil cases.[†] For this exception, two reasons are given: the one, founded on a mere technicality; the other on a view, though a narrow and partial one, of the justice of the case. The first is, that it is *res inter alios acta*: the parties in the civil cause cannot, it is said, have been also the parties in the previous criminal one, the plaintiff in a criminal proceeding being the king. It is obvious, however, that the king's being plaintiff is in this case a mere *fiction*. Although the party in whose favour the previous verdict is offered in evidence, was not called the *plaintiff* in the former proceeding, there is nothing whatever to hinder him from having been the *prosecutor*, who is substantially the plaintiff. Now if he was the prosecutor, and his adversary the defendant, it is evident that the cause *is* between the same parties; that it is *not*, in reality, *res inter alios acta*; and that if it be treated as such, justice is sacrificed, as it so often is, to a fiction of law.

*See Chap. ii of this book. [See also pp. 35–8 above.]
[38]Phillipps, *Treatise*, Vol. I, pp. 299–363.
[39]I.e., in Chap. ii of Bk. VI.
[†]Phillipps, Vol. I, p. 317, *et seqq*.

The other reason is, "that the party in the civil suit, in whose behalf the evidence is supposed to be offered, might have been a witness on the prosecution."* This is true. He *might* have been a witness; and the previous verdict might have been obtained by his evidence. But it *might* be, that the contrary was the case. Whether he was a witness, or not, is capable of being ascertained. If he was not a witness, why adhere to a rule, which cannot have the shadow of a ground but upon the supposition that he was? But suppose even that he was a witness, and that the verdict which he now seeks to make use of, was obtained from the jury by means of his own testimony. This will often be a very good reason for distrust; but it never can be sufficient reason for exclusion. Under a system of law, indeed, which does not suffer a party to give evidence directly in his own behalf, it is consistent enough to prevent him from doing the same thing in a roundabout way. A proposition, however, which will be maintained in the sequel of this work, is, that in no case ought the plaintiff to be excluded from testifying in what lawyers indeed would call his own behalf, but which, by the aid of counter-interrogation, is really, if his cause is bad, much more his adversary's behalf than his own.[40] Should this opinion be found to rest on sufficient grounds, the reason just referred to for not admitting the former verdict as evidence, will appear to be, on the contrary, a strong reason for admitting it.

Thus much may suffice, as to the first rule relating to this subject in English law: a rule which has been seen to be as reasonable, as the above-mentioned exception to it is unreasonable. We shall find few instances, in the succeeding rules, of an approach even thus near to the confines of common sense.

For, first, a judgment is not evidence, even between the same parties, "of any matter which came collaterally in question, nor of any matter incidentally cognizable, nor of any matter to be inferred by argument from the judgment."[†] By the words *not evidence*, lawyers sometimes mean one thing, sometimes another: here, however, *not admissible* in evidence, is what is meant. That it ought not to be *conclusive* as to any fact but such as the judgment, if conformable to law, necessarily supposes to have been proved, is no more than we have seen in a former chapter: that, however, because it ought not to be made conclusive, it ought not to be admissible, is an inference which none but a lawyer would ever think of drawing. A common man's actions are received every day as circumstantial evidence of the motive by which he was actuated; why not those of a judge?

*Ibid.*, p. 319.
[40]See Vol. V, pp. 359–80 (Bk. IX, Pt. V, Chap. ii).
†C.J. De Grey, in the Duchess of Kingston's case, *apud* Phillipps, Vol. I, p. 304. [Phillipps is quoting the judgment of Chief Justice William de Grey (1719–81), 1st Baron Walsingham, in the case of Elizabeth Chudleigh (1720–88), Countess of Bristol, who contracted a second marriage with the Duke of Kingston, on a charge of bigamy. See Thomas Bayley Howell and Thomas Jones Howell, *A Complete Collection of State Trials*, 34 vols. (London: Longman, *et al.*, 1809–28), Vol. XX, cols. 355–652.]

The next rule is, that a verdict or judgment on a former occasion, is not evidence against any one who was a stranger to the former proceeding: that is, who was not a party, nor stood in any such relation to a party, as will induce lawyers to say that he was *privy* to the verdict. The reason why a judgment under these circumstances is not evidence, is, that it is *res inter alios acta*. But we have seen already* that its being *res inter alios acta*, though a sufficient reason for receiving it with suspicion, is no reason for excluding it.

The more special reason, by which, in the case now under consideration, this general one is corroborated, is, that the party "had no opportunity to examine witnesses, or to defend himself, or to appeal against the judgment."† This being undeniable, it would be very improper, no doubt, to take the judgment for *conclusive*. On this ground, what is the dictate of unsophisticated common sense? A very obvious one. As the party has not had an opportunity to examine witnesses, to defend himself, or to appeal against the judgment, at a former period, let him have an opportunity of doing all these things now: let him have leave to impeach the validity of the grounds on which the former judgment was given, and to shew, by comments on the evidence, or by adducing fresh evidence, that it was an improper one: but do not shut out perhaps the only evidence which is now to be had against him, merely because it would be unjust, on the ground of that evidence, to condemn him without a hearing. In the nature of a judgment is there any thing which renders a jury less capable of appreciating that kind of evidence, than any other kind, at its just value? But it is useless to argue against one particular case of the barbarous policy which excludes all evidence that seems in any degree exposed to be untrustworthy. The proofs which will be hereafter‡ adduced of the absurdity of the principle, are proofs of its absurdity in this case, as in every other.

Another curious rule is, that, as a judgment is not evidence *against* a stranger, the contrary judgment shall not be evidence *for* him. If the rule itself is a curious one, the reason given for it is still more so: "nobody can take benefit by a verdict, who had not been prejudiced by it, had it gone contrary:"[41] a maxim which one would suppose to have found its way from the gaming-table to the bench. If a party be benefited by one throw of the dice, he will, if the rules of fair play are observed, be prejudiced by another: but that the consequence should hold when applied to justice, is not equally clear. This rule of *mutuality* is destitute of even that semblance of reason, which there is for the rule concering *res inter alios acta*. There is reason for saying that a man shall not lose his cause in consequence of the verdict given in a former proceeding to which he was not a party; but there is no reason whatever for saying that he shall not lose his cause in consequence of the verdict in a proceeding to which he *was* a party, merely because his adversary was

*Vide* Chap. ii.
†Phillipps, Vol. I, p. 309.
‡See Bk. IX, "Exclusion," Pt. III [Chap. ii], "Deception." [Vol. V, pp. 9–33.]
[41]Phillipps, Vol. I, p. 309, quoting Gilbert, *The Law of Evidence*, pp. 34–5.

not. It is right enough that a verdict obtained by A against B should not bar the claim of a third party C; but that it should not be evidence in favour of C against B, seems the very height of absurdity. The only fragment of a reason which we can find in the books, having the least pretension to rationality, is this, that C, the party who gives the verdict in evidence, may have been one of the witnesses by means of whose testimony it was obtained. The inconclusiveness of this reason we have already seen.

The rule, that a judgment *inter alios* is not evidence, which, like all other rules of law, is the perfection of reason,[42] is in a variety of instances set aside by as many nominal exceptions, but real violations, all of which are also the perfection of reason. To the praise of common sense, at least, they might justly lay claim, if they did no more, in each instance, than abrogate the exclusionary rule. But if the rule be bad in one way, the exceptions, as usual, are bad in the contrary way.

One of the exceptions relates to an order of removal, executed, and either not appealed against, or, if appealed against, confirmed by the quarter sessions. This, as between third parishes, who were not parties to the order, is admissible evidence, and therefore (such is jurisprudential logic) conclusive: the officers, therefore, of a third parish, in which the pauper may have obtained a settlement, have it in their power, by merely keeping the only witnesses who could prove the settlement out of the way till after the next quarter sessions, or at farthest for three months, to rid their parish for ever of the incumbrance. The reason of this is, "that there may be some end to litigation:"* a reason which is a great favourite with lawyers, and very justly. Litigation, understand in those who cannot pay for it, is a bad thing: let no such person presume to apply for justice. One is tempted, however, to ask, whether justice be a thing worth having, or no? and if it be, at what time it is desirable that litigation should be at an end? after justice is done, or before? It would be ridiculous to ask, for what reason it is of so much greater importance that litigation between parishes should have an end, than litigation between individuals; since a question of this sort would imply (what can by no means be assumed) that *reason* had something to do with the matter.

What is called a judgment *in rem* in the exchequer, is, as to all the world, admissible, and conclusive. The sentence of a court of admiralty, is, in like manner, as against all persons, admissible, and conclusive. So is even that of a foreign court of admiralty. The sentence of ecclesiastical courts, in some particular instances; this, like the others, is admissible, and, like the others, conclusive. It is useless to swell the list. Equally useless would it be to enter into a detailed exposition of the badness of these several rules. The reader by whom the spirit of

[42]For this maxim, ironically dwelt on by the Benthamites, see Edward Coke (1552–1634), *The First Part of the Institutes of the Lawes of England; or, A Commentarie upon Littleton* (London: Society of Stationers, 1628), p. 97 (Lib. II, Cap. vi, Sect. 138).

*Phillipps, Vol. I, p. 312.

the foregoing remarks has been imbibed, will make the application to all these cases for himself.

The law recognizes no difference in effect, between the decision of a court abroad, and that of a court at home. The sentence of any foreign court, of competent jurisdiction, directly deciding a question, is conclusive, if the same question arise incidentally between the same parties in this country; in all other cases, it is inadmissible. The case of debt, in which it is admissible, but not conclusive, is partially, and but partially, an exception: for even in this case the foreign judgment is, as to some points, conclusive.*

To make no allowance for the different chance which different courts afford for rectitude of decision, would be consistent enough as between one court and another in the same country; in England at least, the rules of the several courts, howsoever different among themselves, being each of them within its own sphere the perfection of reason, any such allowance as is here spoken of would be obviously absurd: that must be equally good every where, which is every where the best possible. Of foreign judicatories, however, taken in the lump, similar excellence has not, we may venture to affirm, been ever predicated by any English lawyer; nor is likely to be by any Englishman; for Englishmen, how blind soever to the defects of their own institutions, have usually a keen enough perception of the demerits, whether of institutions or of any thing else, if presented to them without the bounds of their own country. Were a consistent regard paid to the dictates of justice, what could appear more absurd than to give the effect of conclusive evidence to the decisions of courts in which nearly all the vices of English procedure prevail, unaccompanied by those cardinal securities, publicity and cross-examination, which go so far to make amends for all those vices, and which alone render English judicature endurable? Yet the rule which, in so many cases, excludes those decisions altogether, errs nearly as much on the contrary side; for, the difficulty of bringing witnesses and other evidence from another country being generally greater than that of bringing them from another and perhaps not a distant part of the same country, there is the greater probability that the decision in question may be the only evidence obtainable.[43]

After what has been observed concerning the admissibility of prior decisions in English law, little need be said on that of prior depositions. Wherever the decision itself is said to be *res inter alios acta*, the depositions on which it was grounded are so too; and are consequently excluded. In other cases they are generally admissible: though to this there are some exceptions. Happily nobody ever thought of making them conclusive.[†]

"Among the causes which have contributed to heap vexation upon suitors on the

---

*Ibid.*, pp. 330–4.
[43]Cf. *ibid.*, pp. 327–34.
[†]Here commences the fragment [by Bentham] alluded to in p. 574 [p. 39 above].

ground of evidence, one has been the scramble for jurisdiction, *i.e.* for fees, between the common law courts, and the courts called courts of equity. Such was the hostility, the common law courts refused to give credit to whatever was done under authority of their rivals. Depositions in equity were not admissible evidence at common law. When the work of iniquity is wrought by judicial hands, there must always be a pretence; but no pretence has been too thin to serve the purpose. It consists always in some word or phrase: and any one word that comes uppermost is sufficient.

"The pretence on this occasion was,—a court of equity is not a court of record. A better one would have been, to have said, it is not a tennis court. The consequence would have been equally legitimate; and the defects of the common law courts, and the effrontery of the conductors of the business, would not have been placed in so striking a point of view.

"With much better reason (if reason had any thing to do in the business) might the equity courts have refused the application of courts of record to the common law courts. In every cause, the evidence, and that alone, is the essence of the cause; in it is contained whatever constitutes the individual character of the cause, and distinguishes it from all other causes of the same species: to a cause, the evidence is what the kernel is to the nut. In a court of equity, this principal part of the cause, though not made up in the best manner, is at any rate put upon record, or, in plain English, committed to writing, and preserved. In a court of law this is never done. The evidence, like the leaves of the Sibyl, is committed to the winds.[44] What goes by the name of the record is a compound of sense and nonsense, with excess of nonsense: the sense composed of a minute quantity of useful truth, drowned and rendered scarce distinguishable by a flood of lies, which would be more mischievous if they were less notorious.

"In the court of exchequer, the same judges constitute one day a court of equity, another day a court of law. What if the occasion for the rejection of the evidence had presented itself in this court? In the hands of an English judge, the *jus mentiendi* is the sword of Alexander.[45] On the declared ground of iniquity, stopping every day their own proceedings, why scruple to refuse credit to their own acts?"

It is now, however, fully settled, that the answer of the defendant, as well as the depositions of witnesses, in chancery, are evidence in a court of law; and that "a

---

[44]See Dionysius of Halicarnassus (fl. 30–8 B.C.), *The Roman Antiquities* (Greek and English), trans. Earnest Cary, 7 vols. (London: Heinemann; Cambridge, Mass.: Harvard University Press, 1937–63), Vol. II, p. 464 (Bk. IV, Sect. lxii).

[45]I.e., the judge's power of creating fictions enables him to cut through difficult cases; for the sword of Alexander and the Gordian knot, see Plutarch (fl. A.D. 50–120), *Life of Alexander*, in *Lives* (Greek and English), trans. Bernadotte Perrin, 11 vols. (London: Heinemann; Cambridge, Mass.: Harvard University Press, 1914–26), Vol. VII, p. 272 (xviii).

decree of the court of chancery may be given in evidence, on the same footing, and under the same limitations, as the verdict or judgment of a court of common law."*

The exemplifications which we undertook to give of the defects of English law in relation to makeshift evidence, may here end. To what purpose weary the reader with the dull detail of the cases in which casually-written or *ex-parte* preappointed evidence are excluded, with the equally long, and equally dull, list of the cases in which, though exclusion would be just as reasonable (if it were reasonable at all), admission, and not exclusion, is the rule? To know that the established systems are every where radically wrong, wrong in the fundamental principles upon which they rest, and wrong just so far as those principles are consistently applied; this, to the person who regards the happiness of mankind as worth pursuing, and good laws as essential to happiness, is in a pre-eminent degree important and interesting. But, for one who, by a comprehensive survey of the grand features, has satisfied himself that the system is rotten to the core; for such a person to know that it is somewhat more tolerable in one part than in another part; that principles which are mischievous in all their applications, are a little more or a little less mischievous in one application than in another; that, in this or that portion of the field of law, vicious theories are consistently carried out, and yield their appropriate fruit in equally vicious practice, while in this or that odd corner they are departed from; would in general be a sort of knowledge as destitute of instruction, as it always and necessarily must be of amusement. (Vol. III, pp. 573–86.)

* * * * *

[*Examining the "delay, vexation, and expense" of the "corruptive" "fee-gathering principle," Bentham begins with "Sham writs of error—King's Bench an open delay-shop."*]

The reader will remember that this was written previously to Mr. Peel's recent law reforms. By one of these, a partial, and but a partial, remedy, was applied to the abuse here in question;[46] which, however, will equally serve the purpose of history, and of illustration. (Vol. IV, p. 64.)

* * * * *

*Phillipps, Vol. I, pp. 340–1.
[46] 6 George IV, c. 96 (1825), "An Act for Preventing Frivolous Writs of Error."

*[Under "natural procedure," Bentham argues, the genuine claim would be obvious, and there would be no surprises. As it is,] where information is by either party really wanted, generally speaking, he has this alternative: either he applies for it by motion, (a cause within a cause), getting it, or not getting it; or he does without it as well as he can.*

So utterly unfit is the initial document called the *declaration*, in the opinion of judges themselves, for any such purpose as that of informing the defendant what claim it is that is made upon him,—that a practice has grown up of compelling the plaintiff to give in, together with the declaration, another document, called a bill of particulars, which shall *really* specify, what the declaration *pretends* to specify, the nature of the demand. According to the judges, then, who have introduced this practice, the declaration is waste paper: utterly useless with reference to the purpose for what it is pretended to be meant; productive only of a mass of expense to the defendant. The bill of particulars really giving the information, all the information that is wanted; the question, why the declaration is not abolished, is a question for those who are capable of penetrating the mysteries of the judicial conscience. (Vol. IV, p. 285.)

\*  \*  \*  \*  \*

*[The following comment, headed "Note by the Editor," appears in the midst of Bentham's account in Bk. VIII, Chap. xxviii, of remedies for the flaws in technical procedure. Bentham comments:] As far as concerns the organization of the existing courts of natural procedure, they are susceptible of great improvements: but in respect of the mode of procedure, two single features, (viz. appearance of the parties before the judge, and* vivâ voce *examination of the parties, but especially the former) are enough to render them as much superior to the best of the regular courts, as the military tactics of European are to those of Asiatic powers. They afford no work for lawyers: the wonder is not great that they should not be to the taste of lawyers.*

It is proper to observe here, that the praise bestowed by Mr. Bentham upon the existing courts of natural procedure, is confined, in the strictest sense, to the *procedure* of these courts, and by no means extends to the constitution of the courts themselves. In many of these courts, it is well known that justice is very badly administered. What, however, we may be very certain of, is, that the cause of this bad administration of justice is not the absence of the technical rules; and that if, over and above all other sources of badness, the practice of these courts were afflicted, in addition, with the rules of technical procedure, they would be not only no better, but beyond comparison worse, than they are.

The real and only cause of the badness of the courts of natural procedure, (in so far as they are bad), is that which is the cause of the mal-administration of so many other departments of the great field of government; *defect of responsibility* on the part of those persons, to whom the administration of them is entrusted.

Causes of such defect of responsibility:

1. Defect of publicity. In the case of a justice of peace, administering judicature, alone, or in conjunction with a brother justice, at his own house, or on his bowling green, or wherever he happens to be, publicity does not exist in any degree. In the case of courts of conscience,[47] there is (I believe) nominal, but there can scarcely be said to be effectual, publicity; since the apparent unimportance of the cause prevents the proceedings in it from being reported in the newspapers, and would prevent it, even if reported, from attracting in general any portion, sufficient to operate as a security, of public attention.

2. Number of judges. In many of the courts of conscience, the tribunal is composed of a considerable number of officers; though any greater number than one, or at most two, (one to officiate when the other is sick, or, from any other cause, unavoidably absent), can serve no purpose but that of dividing, and in that manner virtually destroying, responsibility.

3. Defect of appeal. In a great variety of cases, no appeal lies from the decision of individual justices of peace, except to the Quarter Sessions, that is to say, from the justices individually to the justices collectively. How fruitless an appeal of this sort must in general be (not to speak of its expense) is evident enough. What little value it has, is mainly owing to the greater effectual publicity attendant on the proceedings of a court of general sessions, which are generally reported in the local papers, and always excite more or less of interest in the neighbourhood.

4. The judges exempt from punishment, or even loss of office, in the event of misconduct.

If the party injured by the decision of a justice of peace is able and willing to go to the expense of a motion for a criminal information in the King's Bench, or an indictment at Nisi Prius, or an action against the justice for damages; and if, having done so, he can prove, to the satisfaction of the judges, the existence of what is called *malice** on the part of the magistrate, by whose unjust decision he has been injured; all these things being supposed, he may then have some chance of seeing some punishment inflicted upon his oppressor; though even then probably a very

---

[47]Dating from Tudor times, and abolished finally in 1846 by 9 & 10 Victoria, c. 95, courts of conscience (or courts of request) dealt with cases not sufficiently important to be brought before Chancery.

*In an action against a justice, according to Mr. Starkie, the plaintiff cannot recover more than twopence damages, nor any costs, unless it be alleged in the declaration that the acts with which the justice is charged were done maliciously, and without any reasonable or probable cause. [Starkie, *Practical Treatise*, Vol. II, p. 799, referring to 43 George III, c. 141 (1803).]

inadequate one; the prevailing doctrine being, that the proceedings of an unpaid magistrate ought to be construed *liberally* and *indulgently*, as otherwise no *gentleman* will consent to take upon himself the office.[48]

But, without the above preliminaries, who ever heard of an English justice of peace who was so much as suspended from the commission, on the ground of any misconduct, however gross? And a country justice must either have very bad luck, or play his cards extremely ill, if, out of every thousand cases of misdecision, there be so much as one or two in which all these conditions meet. (Vol. IV, pp. 443–6.)

\*    \*    \*    \*    \*

[*The following note is appended to the heading of a section dealing with another "remedy," "Abolition of fees."*]

This, as the reader will observe, was written before the recent act, which, in the instance of the twelve judges, commuted fees for salaries.[49] The evil, however, still subsists, in regard to a vast variety of judicial offices. (Vol. IV, p. 450.)

\*    \*    \*    \*    \*

[*Bentham says:*] *On the score of vexation to the public at large, by the disclosure of facts comprizable under the denomination of secrets of state, no decision appears to have been ever pronounced. Why? Because no known case ever presented itself, in which a decision to that effect was called for on that ground. In this instance, as in every other, it depends upon chance to open the mouth of jurisprudence.* [*To that comment he appends a note on the habit courts of judicature have of declaring—that is, making—law, which concludes:*] *More law, law covering a greater extent in the field of legislation, is thus made by a single judge, in a quarter of a minute, and at the expense of a couple of words, than the legislature would make in a century, by statutes upon statutes, after committees upon committees.* [*Mill's note, in square brackets, continues Bentham's note, though it refers rather to Bentham's text.*]

[48]See George Holme-Sumner (1760–1838), then M.P. for Surrey, Speech on Commitments by Magistrates (2 Mar., 1824), and Speech on Commitments and Convictions (27 May, 1824), *PD*, n.s., Vol. X, cols 646–7, and Vol. XI, col. 908; the reference occurs in Mill's speech on reform of August 1824 (*CW*, Vol. XXVI, p. 274).

[49]6 George IV, c. 84 (1825). The twelve judges were the Chief Baron of the Exchequer, the Chief Justices of King's Bench and Common Pleas, the three puisne barons, and the six puisne judges. In Bowring's edition a further note is appended, saying the commutation was not fully settled until the passing of 2 & 3 William IV, c. 116 (1832).

Mr. Bentham seems to have overlooked one remarkable case, in which a witness was forbidden to disclose something which the judge thought proper to consider, or to pretend to consider, as a state secret. I allude to the case of Plunkett *v.* Cobbett, in which Lord Ellenborough refused to suffer a witness, who was a member of parliament, to be examined concerning words spoken in parliament: and this by reason of his duty, and in particular of his oath, by which he was bound not to reveal the counsels of the nation.*

To support this inference, the two following falsehoods must have been taken for true: 1. That words spoken in parliament were state secrets; 2. That in no case ought state secrets to be revealed. (Vol. IV, pp. 541–2.)

*    *    *    *    *

[*Continuing his onslaught on the needless expense of the law, Bentham remarks:*] *Be the delinquency of the defendant ever so enormous, the expense of prosecution ever so great, reimbursement is not to be thought of. Why not? Because, to receive money under the name of costs is "beneath the royal dignity."*

The iniquity of this rule has forced the judges to take upon themselves the responsibility of allowing to the prosecutor a sum of money under the name of expenses: this however they do or leave undone as they please: consequently the most frivolous reasons frequently suffice for leaving it undone. It is asserted in the eighty-fourth number of the *Edinburgh Review*, p. 403, that, in a recent case, a judge refused to allow the prosecutor his expenses, because one of the witnesses for the prosecution offended him by his demeanour.[50] (Vol. IV, p. 547.)

*    *    *    *    *

[*On "Abolition of taxes upon justice," Bentham says:*] *In speaking of this or any other expedient for obtaining pecuniary supplies for the relief of this species of distress, it is impossible to avoid thinking of the factitious loads by which it has*

---

*Phillipps, Vol. I, p. 274. [In 1804 William Conyngham Plunket (1764–1854), the Solicitor General, successfully sued William Cobbett (1762–1835) for derogatory comments in the latter's *Weekly Register*. Edward Law (1750–1818), Lord Ellenborough, refused to hear the evidence of John Foster (1740–1828), M.P. for Louth, as to what was said in the House of Commons. See Howell, *State Trials*, Vol. XXIX, cols. 53–80, esp. 71–2.]

[50]Henry Thomas Cockburn (1779–1854), "Office of the Public Prosecutor," *Edinburgh Review*, XLII (Aug. 1825), 403.

*everywhere been aggravated. I speak not here of what has been done by the judge for his own profit; but of what has been done by the finance minister for his own use. The subject has elsewhere been treated pretty much at large. See* Protest against Law Taxes.[51]

The reader will observe, that this work was written before the late repeal of the stamp duties on law proceedings,[52] which has been justly deemed one of the most meritorious acts of the present enlightened administration. The arguments in the text, however, are general, and apply equally to all nations. (Vol. IV, p. 624.)

*    *    *    *    *

*[In Bk. IX, Pt. III, Chap. ii, Sect. 2, Bentham attacks judges, concerned with precedent and their own interest, for exclusionary principles.]*

It seems much more probable, that the exclusion of evidence originated in the ignorance of an uncivilized age, than in the sinister interest of the judge. In a rude state of society, where the art of extracting truth from the lips of a witness is not understood, and where testimonies are counted, not weighed,[53] it seems to have been the universal practice to strike out of the account the testimony of all witnesses who were considered to be under the influence of any mendacity-promoting cause. Exclusionary rules of evidence have nowhere been carried so far as under the systems of procedure which have been the least fettered with technicalities. Take, for instance, the Hindoo law of evidence. See Mill's *History of British India*, Bk. II, Chap. iv.[54] (Vol. V, p. 27.)

*    *    *    *    *

*[Continuing his onslaught on foolish exclusions of evidence, Bentham says:] One decision I meet with, that would be amusing enough, if to a lover of mankind there could be any thing amusing in injustice. A man is turned out of court for a*

---

[51]Bentham, *A Protest against Law-Taxes, Showing the Peculiar Mischievousness of All Such Impositions As Add to the Expense of Appeal to Justice* (printed 1793, published 1795), in *Works*, Vol. II, pp. 573–83.

[52]5 George IV, c. 41 (1824).

[53]This old legal maxim was adapted by Samuel Taylor Coleridge (1772–1834) in a passage Mill in later writings refers to; see *Second Lay Sermon* (1817), 2nd ed., in *On the Constitution of Church and State, and Lay Sermons* (London: Pickering, 1839), p. 409.

[54]James Mill (1773–1836), father of J.S. Mill, *The History of British India*, 3 vols. (London: Baldwin, *et al.*, 1817 [1818]), Vol. I, pp. 162–7.

*liar,—not for any interest that he has, but for one which he supposed himself to have, the case being otherwise. Instead of turning the man out of court, might not the judge have contented himself with setting him right? . . . The pleasant part of the story is, that the fact on which the exclusion was grounded could not have been true. For, before the witness could be turned out of court for supposing himself to have an interest, he must have been informed of his having none: consequently, at the time when he was turned out, he must have ceased to suppose that he had any.*

*Another offence for which I find a man pronounced a liar, seems to make no bad match with the foregoing: it was for being a man of honour. "Oh ho! you are a man of honour, are you? Out with you, then; you have no business here." Being asked whether he did not look upon himself as bound in honour to pay costs for the party who called him, supposing him to lose the cause, and whether such was not his intention; his answer was in the affirmative, and he was rejected. It was taken for granted that he would be a liar. Why? Because he had shewn he would not be one. If instead of saying yes he had said no, who could have refused to believe him? and what would have become of the pretence?*

*By the supposition, the witness is a man of super-ordinary probity: moral obligation, naked moral obligation, has on him the force of law. What is the conclusion of the exclusionist? That this man of uncommonly nice honour will be sure to perjure himself, to save himself from incurring a loss which he cannot be compelled to take upon himself.*

Both these extravagancies have been set aside by later decisions. A witness cannot now, according to Phillipps, be excluded on account of his believing himself to be interested, nor on account of his considering himself bound in honour to pay the costs.* The former point, however, seems to be still doubtful.[†]

Another of the absurdities of English law, in respect to the exclusion grounded on pecuniary interest, is very well exposed in the following passage, extracted from a review of the *Traités des Preuves Judiciaires*, in the 79th Number of the *Edinburgh Review*:

Take as an example the case of forgery. Unless the crime has been committed in the presence of witnesses, it can only be *proved* (in the proper sense of the word) by the individual whose name is said to have been forged. Yet that person is the only one whom the law of England prohibits from proving the fact; a strange prohibition, for which some very strong reason will naturally be sought. The reason to be found in *the books* is this, that the party has an interest in pronouncing that paper forged, for the enforcement of which he may be sued if it is genuine:[55] and this would be true, if the event of the criminal inquiry were admitted to affect his interest, when the holder proceeds in a civil suit to enforce the supposed obligation. But it is also an indisputable rule, that the issue of the trial for forgery, whether condemnation or discharge, is not permitted to have the least effect upon this

---

*See Phillipps, Vol. I, pp. 50–1.
[†]See *ibid.*, note (1) to p. 52.
[55]See, e.g., *ibid.*, Vol. I, pp. 113–14.

liability: the criminal may be convicted, and yet the party whose name appears to the instrument, may be fixed with the debt in a civil proceeding; or he may be acquitted, and yet the genuineness of the handwriting may hereafter be questioned, and its falsehood established. How, then, can the anomaly of this exclusion be explained? It seems that legal antiquarians have preserved the tradition of a practice which is said to have prevailed in former times,—when a person was convicted of forgery, the forged instrument was *damned*; *i.e.* delivered up to be destroyed in open court. The practice, if it ever existed, now lives but in the memory of the learned; the disabling consequences, however, survive it to this hour. The trial proceeds in the presence of the person whose name is said to have been forged, who alone knows the fact, and has no motive for misrepresenting it. His statement would at once convict the pursuer [*qu.* prisoner?] if guilty, or, if innocent, relieve him from the charge. But the law declares him incompetent; and he is condemned to sit by, a silent spectator, hearing the case imperfectly pieced out by the opinions and surmises of other persons, on the speculative question, whether or not the handwriting is his. And this speculation, incapable under any circumstances of satisfying a reasonable mind, decides upon the life of a fellow-citizen, in a system which habitually boasts of requiring always the very best evidence that the nature of the case can admit![56]

(Vol. V, pp. 57–9.)


\*     \*     \*     \*     \*


[*Bentham considers exceptions to the general rule that evidence of witnesses is excluded when they have pecuniary interest in the outcome. The first exception is discussed under the heading, "Interest against interest."* ] *Unless the rule, out of which the exception is taken, be supposed to be bad* in toto, *the reason of the exception (if it has any) supposes all other circumstances equal, and the quantity of money creative of the interest the same on both sides. Against the truth of this supposition, there is exactly infinity to one. The number of possible ratios is infinite: of these the ratio of equality is one. Of the proportion between interest and interest, the exception takes no cognizance: no mention of it is made.*

It must be acknowledged, that, in many of the cases in which this exception has been allowed, it has been, from the nature of the case, unquestionably certain that the interest, at least the pecuniary interest, was equal on both sides; thus, the accepter of a bill of exchange is an admissible witness in an action by indorser against drawer, to prove that he had no effects of the drawer's in his hands; because, whichever way the suit may be decided, he is equally liable. On the other hand, there are many cases in which the interest is not really, but only nominally the same on both sides. Thus, a pauper is a good witness for either parish, in a settlement case: why? because (we are told) it is the same thing to him whether he has a settlement in one parish or in another;[57] true, it may be the same thing; but it

---

[56]Denman, "Law of Evidence," pp. 176–7. The square-bracketed query is Mill's.
[57]Starkie, *Practical Treatise*, Vol. II, p. 751.

may also be a very different thing, since different parishes give very different allowances to their poor. (Vol. V, p. 63.)

\*     \*     \*     \*     \*

[*In discussing (Bk. IX, Pt. III, Chap. iv, Sect. 1) perjury as one of the improper grounds for exclusion because of improbity, Bentham says, in a footnote which Mill's comment (in square brackets) concludes:*] *Where a witness, who at the time of the transaction was an uninterested one, has since given himself an interest in the cause, as, for instance, by a wager, English lawyers have decided—and with indisputable justice—that, by this act of the witness, the party shall not be deprived of the benefit of his testimony. The damage which a man is not allowed to do by an act otherwise so innocent as that of a wager, shall he be allowed to do it by so criminal an act as perjury?*

It is rather curious, that, while the attesting witness, if he has happened to perjure himself since he signed his name, would not, I suppose, be admitted to prove his own signature, he is admitted to disprove it: "a person who has set his name as a subscribing witness to a deed or will, is admissible to impeach the execution of the instrument;"* although by so doing he confesses himself to have been guilty of a crime which differs from the worst kind of perjury only in the absence of oath, from forgery only in name. (Vol. V, pp. 86–7.)

\*     \*     \*     \*     \*

[*Looking to experience for support of his views on exclusion based on improbity, Bentham says:*] *Inquiring among professional friends the degree of observance given to the rules excluding witnesses on the ground of improbity, I learn that judges may, in this point of view, be divided into three classes. Some, treating the objection as an objection to credit, not to competency, admit the witness, suffer his evidence to go to the jury, presenting the objection at the same time, warning the jury of the force of it, and when thus warned, leaving them to themselves. If, after this warning, the jury convict a man of whose guilt the judge from whom they have thus received the warning, is not satisfied; from thence follows, as a matter of course, a recommendation to mercy, from whence follows, as a matter also of course, a pardon. Another class suffer the testimony to be given, but if they do not*

*Phillipps on Evidence, Vol. I, p. 39, and the cases there referred to. [The cases referred to in the sentence quoted are Lowe *v.* Joliffe, 1 Black. Rep. 365. 7 T.R. 604.611. 6 East, 195, and 1 Ves. & Beam, 208.]

*find it corroborated by other testimony, direct the jury to acquit, paying no regard to it. A third class, again, if they understand that no other evidence is to follow, refuse, in spite of all authorities, so much as to suffer the jury to hear the evidence.*

The reader should be informed that these pages were written somewhere about the year 1803. Whether any greater degree of unanimity exists on the bench, in regard to these matters, at the present day, perhaps nobody knows: it is hardly worth knowing. (Vol. V, p. 95.)

\*    \*    \*    \*    \*

[*In condemning exclusions based on religious opinions, Bentham says:*] *Speculation, quoth somebody. No; cases of evidence excluded on account of atheism have every now and then presented themselves in practice.* [*To this he appends the following note, which Mill's comment (in square brackets) concludes:*] *The books exhibit several cases of this sort; and from private information it has happened to me to hear of several not mentioned in any book.*

Such a case occurred only a few months ago. One of Carlile's shopmen had been robbed.[58] His evidence was refused, and justice denied to him, on the ground of what lawyers affectedly call *defect of religious principle*.[59] (Vol. V, pp. 132–3.)

\*    \*    \*    \*    \*

[*Bentham asserts that the question "Are you an atheist?" not only offends "against the dictates of reason and justice," but is*] *repugnant to the known rules of actually existing law. In virtue of a statute still in force,* [*Mill's note is here appended*] *a declaration to any such effect subjects the individual to penalties of high severity: and the rule, that no man shall, in return to any question, give an answer that can have the effect of subjecting him to any sort of penalty, is the firmly-established fruit of that mischievous superstition, the war upon which will form the business of the ensuing Part.*

Since this was written (July 1806) the statute against blasphemy has been

[58]Richard Carlile (1790–1843), a much prosecuted free-thinking author and printer; his shopman was John Christopher. For the case, see "Gross Perversion of Law and Justice," *Examiner*, 17 July, 1825, pp. 447–8.

[59]The title of Pt. I, Chap. iii, of Phillipps's *Treatise* is "Of Incompetency from Defect of Religious Principle" (Vol. I, p. 20).

repealed:[60] but the Lord Chancellor, (by virtue of that power of superseding the will of the legislature, which judges never hesitate to assume to themselves whenever they need it), has taken upon himself to declare, that to deny the Trinity is still an offence at common law.[61] (Vol. V, p. 133.)

\* \* \* \* \*

[*Concerning the exclusion of evidence from "persons excommunicated," Bentham says:*] *You omit paying your attorney's bill: if the bill is a just one, and you able to pay it, this is wrong of you; but if unable, your lot (of which immediately) will be just the same. If the business done, was done in a court called a common law court, your attorney is called an attorney, and the case belongs not to this purpose. If in a court called an ecclesiastical court, the attorney is called a proctor: you are imprisoned, and so forth; but first you must be excommunicated. For this crime, or for any other, no sooner are you excommunicated, than a discovery is made, that, being "excluded out of the church," you are "not under the influence of any religion:" you are a sort of atheist. To your own weak reason it appears to you that you believe; but the law, which is the perfection of reason, knows that you do not. Being omniscient, and infallible, and so forth, she knows that, were you to be heard, it would be impossible you should speak true: therefore, you too are posted off upon the excluded list, along with atheists, catholics, and quakers.*

*Forbidden by his religion, a quaker will not pay tithes: sued in the spiritual court, he is excommunicated. As a witness, he is now incompetent twice over: once by being a quaker, and again by being excommunicate. Why by being excommunicate? Answer, per Mr. Justice Buller, — "because he is not under the influence of any religion."*[62]

Since these two paragraphs were written (July 1806), the incompetency of excommunicated persons to give evidence has been removed by the statute 53 George III, c. 127 (Phillipps, Vol. I, p. 26). (Vol. V, p. 140.)

\* \* \* \* \*

[60]9 & 10 William III, c. 32 (1698), An Act for the More Effectual Suppressing of Blasphemy and Prophaneness, was repealed by 53 George III, c. 160 (1813).

[61]John Scott (1751–1838), Lord Eldon, Speech on the Unitarian Marriage-Bill (4 May, 1824), *PD*, n.s., Vol. 11, cols. 438–40.

[62]Francis Buller (1746–1800), *An Introduction to the Law Relative to Trials at Nisi Prius* (London: Bathurst, 1772), p. 292.

[*With heavy irony, echoed by Mill in his note, Bentham discusses the legal means by which "competency" is restored to a witness. The first of these is the "Burning Iron" applied to the hands of those guilty of "clergyable felonies." He comments, in part:*] Other punishments may run their course; other punishments, whatever may be their duration, may have run their course, and the incredibility remain unextinguished. It is not time, but heat, that works the cure. Neither does whipping possess any such virtue as that of a restorative to veracity: for whipping is not fire. A conviction of an offence, for which whipping is the sentence, expels the veracity; but the execution of the sentence does not in this case bring it back again. To a plain understanding, the incredibility might as well be whipped out as burnt out, or the new credibility whipped in as burnt in: but this, it seems, is not law. There is no purifier like fire.

There are cases indeed, in which whipping, or fine, or transportation, or any other kinds of punishment, have all the virtue of burning: but this is only when they have been substituted for it by act of parliament:[63] in all other cases, nothing but burning will serve. The benefit of clergy has of itself no virtue; burning, or a statutory substitute is indispensable. "In Lord Warwick's case," says Phillipps (Vol. I, p. 32) "one who had been convicted of manslaughter, and allowed his clergy, but not burnt in the hand, was called as a witness for the prisoner; and on an objection to his competency, the lords referred it to the judges present, who thought he was not a competent witness, as the statute had made the burning in the hand a condition precedent to the discharge."[64] (Vol. V, p. 172.)

\* \* \* \* \*

[*The second means of restoring competency (see the previous entry) is "A Great Seal," on which Bentham says:*] The sort of great seal to be employed on this occasion, is that which is employed for granting pardons. Supposing (what has sometimes happened) the ground of the pardon to have been the persuasion of the convict's innocence, the restoration of the admissibility would, under the rule of consistency, be a necessary consequence: in every other case, whatever propriety there might be, consistency is out of the question. An experiment was once made by

[63]Branding was first instituted by 4 Henry VII, c. 13 (1487); transportation was substituted by 4 George I, c. 11 (1717), and fine or whipping by 19 George III, c. 74 (1779).

[64]In the trial for murder (1699) of Edward Rich (1673–1701), Earl of Warwick, the judges, Edward Nevil (d. 1705), George Treby (ca. 1644–1700), and Edward Ward (1638–1714), ruled that the proposed witness, French, was not competent, referring to 18 Elizabeth, c. 7 (1576). For an account, see Howell, *State Trials*, Vol. XIII, cols. 939–1032, esp. 1015–19.

*another sort of seal, called a privy seal: the experiment failed: the seal was not found to be big enough. [To this passage Bentham appends the following note, which Mill's comment (in square brackets) concludes:] The English of this is, that it belongs to the Chancellor, not to the Lord Privy Seal (or at least not to the Lord Privy Seal alone) to grant pardons. Understand, in a direct way: for in an indirect way, as above shewn [See Bk. VIII, "Technical Procedure," Chap. xiv, "Nullification."], it belongs to any body.*

A statute of the last session but one, (6 Geo. IV, c. 25) enacts, that a pardon under the sign manual, and countersigned by a Secretary of State, shall have the same effect as a pardon under the great seal. (Vol. V, p. 173.)

\* \* \* \* \*

*[Bentham asserts sadly that to expect relief from law taxes is hopeless,] unless the moment (perhaps an ideal one) should ever arrive, that should produce a financier to whom the most important interests of the people should be dearer than his own momentary ease.*

That time is happily come.[65] (Vol. V, p. 222.)

\* \* \* \* \*

*[The following lengthy passage, headed "Farther Remarks by the Editor," concludes Sect. 2, "Lawyer and Client," of Bk. IX, Chap. v, "Examination of the Cases in Which English Law Exempts One Person from Giving Evidence against Another."]*

In the notice of the *Traité des Preuves Judiciaires*, in the *Edinburgh Review*,\* the rule which excludes the testimony of the professional assistant, is with much earnestness defended.[66] The grounds of the defence, in so far as they are intelligible to me, reduce themselves to those which follow:

1. The first argument consists of two steps, whereof the former is expressed, the latter understood; and either of them, if admitted, destroys the other. The proposition which is asserted is, that the aid which is afforded to an accused person by his advocate, is of exceedingly great importance to justice. The proposition

[65]I.e., with Peel's reforms, cited in n4 above.
\*No. 79, March 1824 [Vol. XL, pp. 169–207, by Thomas Denman].
[66]Denman, pp. 183–7; *Traité*, Vol. II, pp. 137–40 (cf. *Treatise*, pp. 246–7).

which is insinuated is, that of this aid he would be deprived, if his advocate were rendered subject to examination.—If the only purpose, for which an advocate can be of use, be to assist a criminal in the concealment of his guilt, the last proposition is true: but what becomes of the former? If, on the other hand (as is sufficiently evident) an advocate be needful on other accounts than this,—if he be of use to the innocent, as well as to the guilty, to the man who has nothing to conceal, as well as to the man who has; what is to hinder an innocent, or even a guilty defendant, from availing himself of his advocate's assistance for all purposes, except that of frustrating the law?

2. The second argument consists but of one proposition: it is, that Lord Russell's attorney would have been a welcome visitor, with his notes in his pocket, to the office of the solicitor of the Treasury. To the exalted personages, whose desire it was to destroy Lord Russell, any person would, it is probable, have been a welcome visitor, who came with information in his pocket tending to criminate the prisoner.[67] From this, what does the reviewer infer? That no information tending to criminate the prisoner should be received? That the truth should not, on a judicial occasion, be ascertained? Not exactly: only that one means, a most efficient means, of ascertaining it, should be rejected. Are we to suppose, then, that on every judicial occasion the thing which is desirable is, that the laws should not be executed? then, indeed, the reviewer's conclusion would be liable to no other objection than that of not going nearly far enough; since all other kinds of evidence might, and indeed ought, on such a supposition, to be excluded likewise.

So long as the law treats any act as a crime which is not a crime, so long it will, without doubt, be desirable that some acts which are legally crimes should escape detection: and by conducing to that end, this or any other exclusionary rule may palliate, in a slight degree, the mischiefs of a bad law. To make the conclusion hold universally, what would it be necessary to suppose? Only that the whole body of the law is a nuisance, and its frustration, not its execution, the end to be desired.

Laws are made to be executed, not to be set aside. For the sake of weakening this or that bad law, would you weaken all the laws? How monstrous must that law be, which is not better than such a remedy! Instead of making bad laws, and then, by exclusionary rules, undoing with one hand a part of the mischief which you have been doing with the other, would it not be wiser to make no laws but such as are fit to be executed, and then to take care that they be executed on all occasions?

3. The third argument is of that ingenious and sometimes very puzzling sort, called a dilemma. If the rule were abolished, two courses only, according to the reviewer, the lawyer would have: he must enter into communication with the

---

[67]Lord William Russell (1639–83), convicted in 1683 of plotting to assassinate Charles II in the Rye-House Plot, was represented by Edward Ward (see n61 above), John Holt (1642–1710), and Henry Pollexfen (1632–91), against the Crown's case argued by Heneage Finch (ca. 1647–1719), George Jeffreys (1648–89), and Robert Sawyer (1633–92). See Howell, *State Trials*, Vol. IX, cols. 577–886.

opposite party from the beginning, to which course there would be objections; or he must wait till he had satisfied himself that his client was in the wrong, and must enter into communication with the opposite party *then*; to which course there would be other objections. What the force of these objections may be, it is not necessary, nor would it be pertinent, to inquire: since neither justice nor Mr. Bentham demand that he should enter into communication with the opposite party at all. What is required is only, that if, upon the day of trial, the opposite party should choose to call for his evidence, it may not be in his power, any more than in that of any other witness, to withhold it.

One would not have been surprised at these arguments, or even worse, from an indiscriminate eulogizer of "things as they are;"[68] this, however, is by no means the character of the writer of this article: it is the more surprising, therefore, that he should have been able to satisfy himself with reasons such as the three which we have examined. Not that these are all the reasons he has to give: the following paragraph seems to be considered by him as containing additional reasons to the same effect:

Even in the very few instances where the accused has intrusted his defender with a full confession of his crime, we hold it to be clear that he may still be lawfully defended. The guilt of which he may be conscious, and which he may have so disclosed, he has still a right to see distinctly proved upon him by legal evidence. To suborn wretches to the commission of perjury, or procure the absence of witnesses by bribes, is to commit a separate and execrable crime; to tamper with the purity of the judges is still more odious: but there is no reason why any party should not, by fair and animated arguments, demonstrate the insufficiency of that testimony, on which alone a righteous judgment can be pronounced to his destruction. Human beings are never to be run down like beasts of prey, without respect to the laws of the chase. If society must make a sacrifice of any one of its members, let it proceed according to general rules, upon known principles, and with clear proof of necessity: "let us carve him as a feast fit for the gods, not hew him as a carcass for the hounds."[69] Reversing the paradox above cited from Paley,[70] we should not despair of finding strong arguments in support of another, and maintain that it is desirable that guilty men should sometimes escape, by the operation of those general rules which form the only security for innocence.[71]

In reading the above declamation, one is at a loss to discover what it is which the writer is aiming at. Does he really think that, all other things being the same, a system of procedure is the better, for affording to criminals a chance of escape? If this be his serious opinion, there is no more to be said; since it must be freely admitted that, reasoning upon this principle, there is no fault to be found with the rule. If it be your object not to find the prisoner guilty, there cannot be a better way

[68]A Benthamite ironic catch-phrase, presumably deriving from the title of *Things As They Are; or, The Adventures of Caleb Williams* (1794), by William Godwin (1756–1836).
[69]William Shakespeare (1564–1616), *Julius Caesar*, II, i, 173–4; in *The Riverside Shakespeare*, ed. G. Blakemore Evans (Boston: Houghton Mifflin, 1974), p. 1113.
[70]See *Principles of Moral and Political Philosophy*, Vol. II, pp. 332–3.
[71]Denman, p. 186.

than refusing to hear the person who is most likely to know of his guilt, if it exist. The rule is perfectly well adapted to its end: but is that end the true end of procedure? This question surely requires no answer.

But if the safety of the innocent, and not that of the guilty, be the object of the reviewer's solicitude; had he shewn how an innocent man could be endangered by his lawyer's telling all he has to tell, he would have delivered something more to the purpose than any illustration which the subject of carcasses and hounds could yield. If he can be content for one moment to view the question with other than fox-hunting eyes, even he must perceive that, to the man who, having no guilt to disclose, has disclosed none to his lawyer, nothing could be of greater advantage than that this should appear; as it naturally would if the lawyer were subjected to examination.

"There is no reason why any party should not, by fair and animated arguments, demonstrate the insufficiency of that testimony, on which alone a righteous judgment can be pronounced to his destruction." This, if I rightly understand it, means, that incomplete evidence ought not, for want of comments, to be taken for complete: we were in no great danger of supposing that it ought. But the real question is,—should you, because your evidence is incomplete, shut out other evidence which would complete it? After the lawyer has been examined, is the evidence incomplete notwithstanding? then is the time for your "fair and animated arguments." Is it complete? then what more could you desire?

The denunciation which follows, against *hunting down* human beings without respect for the laws of the chase, is one of those proofs which meet us every day, how little, as yet, even instructed Englishmen are accustomed to look upon judicature as a means to an end, and that end the execution of the law. They speak and act, every now and then, as if they regarded a criminal trial as a sort of game, partly of chance, partly of skill, in which the proper end to be aimed at is, not that the truth may be discovered, but that both parties may have fair play: in a word, that whether a guilty person shall be acquitted or punished, may be, as nearly as possible, an even chance.

I had almost omitted the most formidable argument of all, which was brought forward by M. Dumont, not as decisive, but as deserving of consideration, and which the reviewer, who adopts it, terms "a conclusive *reductio ad absurdum*."[72] This consists in a skilful application of the words *spy* and *informer* (espion, délateur), two words forming part of a pretty extensive assortment of vaguely vituperative expressions, which possess the privilege of serving as conclusive objections against any person or thing which it is resolved to condemn, and against which, it is supposed, no other objections can be found.

Spies and informers are bad people; a lawyer who discloses his client's guilt is a spy and an informer; he is therefore a bad man, and such disclosure is a bad

---

[72]*Ibid.*, p. 184; Bentham, *Treatise*, p. 247n.

practice, and the rule by which it is prohibited is a good rule. Such, when analysed into its steps, is the argument which we are now called upon to consider.

But to form a ground for condemning any practice, it is not enough to apply to the person who practises it an opprobrious name: it is necessary, moreover, to point out some pernicious tendency in the practice; to shew that it produces more evil than good. It cannot be pretended that the act of him, who, when a crime comes to his knowledge, (be it from the malefactor's own lips, or from any other source), being called upon judicially to declare the truth, declares it accordingly, is a pernicious act. On the contrary, it is evident that it is a highly useful act: the evil occasioned by it being, at the very worst, no more than the punishment of the guilty person; an evil which, in the opinion of the legislature, is outweighed by the consequent security to the public. Call this man, therefore, an informer or not, as you please; but if you call him an informer, remember to add, that the act which constitutes him one, is a meritorious act.

M. Dumont expresses an apprehension that no honourable man would take upon him the functions of an advocate, if compelled to put on what he is pleased to call the character of an informer. Further reflection would, I think, have convinced him that this apprehension is chimerical. There is scarcely any thing in common between the two characters of an informer and of a witness. The antipathy which exists against the former extends not to the latter. A witness, as such, does not take money for giving evidence, as an informer frequently does for giving information. The act of an informer is spontaneous: he is a man who goes about of his own accord doing mischief to others: so at least it appears to the eyes of unreflecting prejudice. The evidence of the witness may be more fatal to the accused than the indications given by the informer; but it has the appearance of not being equally spontaneous: he tells what he knows, because the law compels him to say something, and because being obliged to speak, he will speak nothing but the truth: but for any thing that appears, if he had not been forced, he would have held his tongue and staid away. An honourable man, acting in the capacity of an advocate, would, by giving true evidence, incur the approbation of all lovers of justice, and would not incur the disapprobation of any one: what, therefore, is there to deter him? unless it be a hatred of justice.

The reviewer adds, that M. Dumont's argument "might be assisted with a multiplicity of reasonings:" these, as he has not stated them, Mr. Bentham, probably, may be pardoned for being ignorant of. The reviewer is modest enough to content himself with the "single and very obvious remark, that the author evidently presumes the guilt from the accusation:"[73] a remark which could have had its source in nothing but the thickest confusion of ideas. Had Mr. Bentham recommended condemnation without evidence, or any other practice which would be indiscriminately injurious to all accused persons, innocent or guilty; it might

[73]Denman, pp. 184–5.

then have been said of him, with some colour of justice, that he presumed the guilt from the accusation. But when, of the practice which he recommends, it is a characteristic property to be a security to the innocent, a source of danger to the guilty alone,—under what possible pretence can he be charged with presuming the existence of guilt?—though he may be charged, sure enough, with desiring that where there is guilt, it may be followed by punishment; a wish probably blameable in the eyes of the reviewer, who thinks it "desirable that guilty men should sometimes escape."

Thus weak are all the arguments which could be produced against this practice, by men who would have been capable of finding better arguments, had any better been to be found. It may appear, and perhaps ought to appear, surprising, that men generally unprejudiced, and accustomed to think, should be misled by sophistry of so flimsy a texture as this has appeared to be. Unhappily, however, there is not any argument so palpably untenable and absurd, which is not daily received, even by instructed men, as conclusive, if it makes in favour of a doctrine which they are predetermined to uphold. In the logic of the schools, the premises prove the conclusion. In the logic of the affections, some cause, hidden or apparent, having produced a prepossession, this prepossession proves the conclusion, and the conclusion proves the premises. You may then scatter the premises to the winds of heaven, and the conclusion will not stand the less firm:—the affections being still enlisted in its favour, and the shew, not the substance, of a reason being that which is sought for,—if the former premises are no longer defensible, others of similar quality are easily found. The only mode of attack which has any chance of being successful, is to look out for the cause of the prepossession, and do what may be possible to be done towards its removal: when once the feeling, the real support of the opinion, is gone, the weakness of the ostensible supports, the so called reasons, becomes manifest, and the opinion falls to the ground.

What is plainly at the bottom of the prepossession in the present case, is a vague apprehension of danger to innocence. There is nothing which, if listened to, is so sure to mislead as vague fears.[74] Point out any specific cause of alarm, any thing upon which it is possible to lay your hand, and say, from this source evil of this or that particular kind is liable to flow; and there may be some chance of our being able to judge whether the apprehension is or is not a reasonable one. Confine yourself to vague anticipations of undefined evils, and your fears merit not the slightest regard: if you cannot tell what it is you are afraid of, how can you expect any one to participate in your alarm? One thing is certain: that, if there be any reason for fear, that reason must be capable of being pointed out: and that a danger which does not admit of being distinctly stated, is no danger at all. Let any one,

---

[74]"Vague fears" is a repeated heading in James Mill's Commonplace Books, Vol. I, ff. 37r and 161r, and Vol. III, ff. 101r, 141v, 145r, 146r, and 148r; J.S. Mill obviously consulted these Commonplace Books in his apprentice years.

therefore, ask himself,—supposing the law good, and the accused innocent,—what possible harm can be done him by making his professional assistant tell all that he knows?

He may have told to his lawyer, and his lawyer, if examined, may disclose, circumstances which, though they afford no inference against him, it would have been more agreeable to him to conceal. True; but to guard him against any such unnecessary vexation, he will have the considerate attention of the judge: and this inconvenience, after all, is no more than what he may be subjected to by the deposition of any other witness, and particularly by that of his son, or his servant, or any other person who lives in his house, much more probably than by that of his lawyer.

Whence all this dread of the truth? Whence comes it that any one loves darkness better than light, except it be that his deeds are evil?[75] Whence but from a confirmed habit of viewing the law as the enemy of innocence,—as scattering its punishments with so ill-directed and so unsparing a hand, that the most virtuous of mankind, were all his actions known, could no more hope to escape from them than the most abandoned of malefactors? Whether the law be really in this state, I will not take upon myself to say: sure I am, that if it be, it is high time it should be amended. But if it be not, where is the cause of alarm? In men's consciousness of their own improbity. Children and servants hate tell-tales; thieves hate informers, and peaching accomplices; and, in general, he who feels a desire to do wrong, hates all things, and rules of evidence among the rest, which may, and he fears will, lead to his detection.

Thus much in vindication of the proposed rule. As for its advantages, they are to be sought for not so much in its direct, as in its indirect, operation. The party himself having been, as he ought to be, previously subjected to interrogation; his lawyer's evidence, which, though good of its kind, is no better than hearsay evidence, would not often add any new facts to those which had already been extracted from the lips of the client. The benefit which would arise from the abolition of the exclusionary rule, would consist rather in the higher tone of morality which would be introduced into the profession itself. A rule of law which, in the case of the lawyer, gives an express license to that wilful concealment of the criminal's guilt, which would have constituted any other person an accessary in the crime, plainly declares that the practice of knowingly engaging one's self as the hired advocate of an unjust cause, is, in the eye of the law, or (to speak intelligibly) in that of the law-makers, an innocent, if not a virtuous practice. But for this implied declaration, the man who in this way hires himself out to do injustice or frustrate justice with his tongue, would be viewed in exactly the same light as he who frustrates justice or does injustice with any other instrument. We should not then hear an advocate boasting of the artifices by which he had trepanned a deluded

---

[75]John, 3:19.

jury into a verdict in direct opposition to the strongest evidence; or of the effrontery with which he had, by repeated insults, thrown the faculties of a *bonâ fide* witness into a state of confusion, which had caused him to be taken for a perjurer, and as such disbelieved. Nor would an Old Bailey counsel any longer plume himself upon the number of pickpockets whom, in the course of a long career, he had succeeded in rescuing from the arm of the law. The professional lawyer would be a minister of justice, not an abettor of crime; a guardian of truth, not a suborner of mendacity: and not at *his* hands only, in another sphere, whether as a private man or as a legislator, somewhat more regard for truth and justice might be expected than now, when resistance to both is his daily business, and, if successful, his greatest glory; but, through his medium, the same salutary influence would speedily extend itself to the people at large. Can the paramount obligation of these cardinal virtues ever be felt by them as it ought, while they imagine that, on such easy terms as those of putting on a wig and gown, a man obtains, and on the most important of all occasions, an exemption from both? (Vol. V, pp. 313–25.)

*   *   *   *   *

[*Having commented that a wife's evidence is admissible against her husband when he is accused of inflicting personal injury on her, Bentham adds a note on the exclusion of a first wife's evidence in cases of bigamy, on the grounds that she is the only lawful wife. Mill's comment (in square brackets) completes the footnote.*]

Technical law is never consistent, even in its badness. On a prosecution for bigamy, the first husband or wife is not admissible to prove the fact of the former marriage. But, after a long period of uncertainty, it has been settled as late as the year 1817, that in any collateral suit or proceeding between third persons, the rule is quite different:[76] a person may therefore be incidentally charged with bigamy by the testimony of the first wife or husband, and with the effect of punishment, viz. in the shape of loss of character; a punishment not the less real, for being inflicted by other hands than those of the executioners of the law. (Vol. V, pp. 336–7.)

*   *   *   *   *

[*Bk. IX, Pt. IV, Chap. v, on exclusion of evidence by husbands and wives, is concluded by Mill's comments, headed* "Further remarks by the Editor."]

The exclusion of the testimony of husband and wife, for or against each other, is in

---

[76]The King against the Inhabitants of All Saints, Worcester (3 May, 1817), 105 *English Reports* 1215–18.

the number of the exclusions which, in an article already alluded to, are defended by the *Edinburgh Review*:

> yet not entirely, [says the reviewer,] on account of that dread entertained by the English law, of conjugal feuds, though these are frequently of the most deadly character. But the reason just given, in the case of the priest, applies; [this refers to the opinion of Mr. Bentham, that the disclosure, by a catholic priest, of the secrets confided to him by a confessing penitent, should not be required or permitted][77] for the confidence between married persons makes their whole conversation an unreserved confession; and they also could never be contradicted but by the accused: while external circumstances might be fabricated with the utmost facility, to give apparent confirmation to false charges. But our stronger reason is, that the passions must be too much alive, where the husband and wife contend in a court of justice, to give any chance of fair play to the truth. It must be expected, as an unavoidable consequence of the connexion by which they are bound, that their feelings, either of affection or hatred, must be strong enough to bear down the abstract regard for veracity, even in judicial depositions.[78]

Want of space might form some excuse to this writer for not having said more; but it is no apology for the vagueness and inconclusiveness of what he *has* said.

The confidence, say you, between married persons makes their whole conversation an unreserved confession? So much the better: their testimony will be the more valuable. It is a strange reason for rejecting an article of evidence, that it is distinguished from other articles by its fulness and explicitness.

The reviewer must have read Mr. Bentham very carelessly, to suppose that his reason for excluding the testimony of the priest is, because the discourse of the penitent is an "unreserved confession:" this would be a reason for admitting, not for rejecting, the evidence. The true reason for the exclusion in the case of the confessor, is, that punishment attaching itself upon the discharge of a religious duty would in effect be punishment for religious opinions. Add to which, that the confidence reposed by the criminal in his confessor has not for its object the furtherance, nor the impunity, of offences; but for its effect, as far as it goes, the prevention of them. To seal the lips of the wife gives a facility to crime: to seal those of the confessor gives none; but, on the contrary, induces a criminal to confide the secret of his guilt to one whose only aim will in general be to awaken him to a sense of it. Lastly, it is to be remembered that, by compelling the disclosure in the case of the confessor, no information would ultimately be gained: the only effect being, that, on the part of the criminal, no such revelations would be made. Not so in the case of the wife, who may have come to a knowledge of the crime independently of any voluntary confession by her criminal husband.

That the testimony of the wife could not be contradicted but by the accused person, her husband, and *vice versâ*,—which, if true, would be a good reason for distrusting, but no reason for rejecting, their evidence,—is, in the majority of

[77]Mill's interpolated comment, in parenthesis in the original, refers to Vol. IV, pp. 586–92 (Bk. IX, Pt. II, Chap. vi).
[78]Denman, p. 179.

cases, not true. What the husband and wife have told one another in secret, no one but they two can know; and, consequently, what either of them says on the subject of it, nobody but the other has it in his power to contradict. But is not this likewise the case between the criminal and his accomplice, or between the criminal and any other person, with respect to any fact which occurred when they two were the only persons present? while, with respect to all other facts, the testimony of husband or wife would, if false, be just as capable of being refuted by counter-evidence as the testimony of any other witness.

The aphorism on which the reviewer founds what he calls his "stronger reason," one would not have wondered at meeting with in a German tragedy; but it is certainly what one would never have looked for in a discourse upon the law of evidence. Strange as it may sound in sentimental ears, I am firmly persuaded that many, nay most, married persons pass through life without either loving or hating one another to any such uncontrollable excess. Suppose them however to do so, and their "feelings," whether of affection or of hatred, to be "strong enough to bear down the abstract regard for veracity:" will they, in addition to this "abstract regard,"—a curious sort of a regard,—be strong enough to bear down the fear of punishment and of shame? Will they render the witness proof against the vigilance and acuteness of a sagacious and experienced cross-examiner? Or rather, are not the witnesses who are under the influence of a strong passion, precisely those who, when skilfully dealt with, are least capable of maintaining the appearance of credibility, even when speaking the truth; and, *à fortiori*, least likely to obtain credit for a lie?

But I waste time, and fill up valuable space, in arguing seriously against such solemn trifling. (Vol. V, pp. 345–9.)

\*    \*    \*    \*    \*

[*The following note occurs in the midst of Bentham's argument that justice is deprived of valuable evidence by the exclusion of evidence by "a party to the cause, for or against himself" (Bk. IX, Pt. V, Chap. i).*]

The *Edinburgh Review*, in an article which has been several times referred to, makes a long attack upon "the French method of interrogating persons under a charge" with a view to the extraction of their self-criminative testimony.[79] It is not necessary to enter particularly into the objections advanced by the reviewer against this practice. They may all be summed up in two propositions, neither of which seems very likely to be disputed: 1. that an innocent man may very possibly be unable to furnish, all at once, those explanations which are necessary to make his

[79]*Ibid.*, p. 187.

innocence appear; and 2. that, such inability on the part of a prisoner not being conclusive evidence of his guilt, it would be very wrong to treat it as if it were so.

The reviewer does not state whether his objection extends to the examination of the prisoner on the occasion of the *definitive* trial: but we may presume that it does not, since his arguments do not apply to that case. By that time, the prisoner may reasonably be supposed to be prepared with all such explanations as the circumstances will admit of; and if he is not, I fear it will go hard with him, whether the insufficient explanations which he does give, are given through his advocate only, or partly from the lips of his advocate and partly from his own.

But, even against the preliminary interrogation of the prisoner as soon as possible after his apprehension, the objections, it is evident, are altogether inconclusive. That non-response and evasive responsion are strong articles of circumstantial evidence against a prisoner, is what will hardly be denied:—that, by an inconsiderate judge, more than the due weight may be attached to them, is a casualty to which they are liable, in common with all other sorts of circumstantial evidence, but not more liable than other sorts. Were the possibility of deception a sufficient ground for putting an exclusion upon evidence, can it be necessary to say, that no evidence would be admitted at all? But the exclusionists never seem to consider, that if deception may arise from evidence, it is still more likely to arise from the want of evidence.

After all, the reviewer, when he comes to his practical conclusion, explains away the whole effect of his previous arguments, and ends by prescribing

a middle course, which leaves the party to judge and act for himself. If he is blessed with self-command, and is in possession of the means of at once refuting his pursuers, why should his vindication be delayed? but as he may be incompetent to do so, or unprovided with the necessary proofs, let him be calmly told by the magistrate, that no unfair inference will be drawn from his reserving his defence for a more convenient season.[80]

That *something* of this sort should be told him, is obviously proper; to which I will add, that no promise could be more safely given than a promise not to draw any *unfair* inferences; though it may be doubted how far such an assurance would quiet the alarms of an innocent prisoner, until he should be informed *what* inferences the magistrate would consider unfair. The proper thing to tell him would be, that if, from the unexpectedness of the accusation, he felt his faculties to be in too bewildered a state to qualify him for making a clear statement of the truth (and of this the magistrate would be in some measure able to judge), or if any sufficient reason rendered him unable or averse to give the necessary explanations without delay, he would be at liberty to say as little or as much as he pleased; but that if, when the trial should come on, and he should come to be finally examined, the explanations afforded by him should appear to be such as might with equal facility and propriety have been given on the spot; his having refrained from giving

[80]*Ibid.*, p. 191.

them at that time, would be considered as strong evidence (though even then, not conclusive evidence) of his guilt. (Vol. V, pp. 352–4.)

\*    \*    \*    \*    \*

[*Bentham examines, in Bk. IX, Pt. V, Chap. iii, the inconsistencies of English law concerning the admissibility of defendant's evidence. He treats first criminal cases, and then turns to civil ones, on which he says, in part:*] *Speak indeed he* [*the defendant*] *may; if mere speaking will content him, without speaking to any purpose. For, in cases of this class, defendant and plaintiff standing on even ground, and without any nook for compassion (real or hypocritical) to plant itself upon, and cry, Hear him! hear him! whatever he may (if he have courage) insist upon saying, will be watched by men with sieves in their hands; and whatever testimony he may take upon him to throw in along with his matter of argument and observations, will be carefully separated, and forbidden to be lodged in the budget of evidence.*

There is one case, according to Phillipps, in which the evidence of the defendant is allowed to be given in his own behalf, on the occasion of an action in the common law courts. The case I allude to, is that of an action for a malicious prosecution, "where it seems," says Phillipps, "to have been understood; that the evidence which the defendant himself gave on the trial of the indictment, may, under certain circumstances, be received in his favour on the trial of the action." (Phillipps, Vol. I, p. 66.)

Observe that in this, as in so many other cases, evidence which might without any trouble be obtained in a good shape, is carefully put into a bad one. What the defendant said on the first occasion, may be received in his favour on the second; though by what evidence, except hearsay evidence, he can be proved to have said it (unless the judge's notes happen to have been preserved) is not clear: while the defendant himself, who is there in court, ready to be examined, and without the slightest inconvenience in the shape of delay, vexation, or expense, stands peremptorily debarred from opening his mouth.

Whether he is allowed in this case to give evidence for himself, or no,—certain however it is, that in this one case his wife is allowed to give evidence for him, which, in the opinion of Phillipps, seems to be the same thing. The reason given by Lord Holt for admitting in evidence the oath of the defendant's wife, to prove the felony committed, is as follows: "For otherwise, one that should be robbed would be under an intolerable mischief: if he prosecuted for such robbery, and the party should be acquitted, the prosecutor would be liable to an action for a malicious prosecution, without the possibility of making a good defence, though the cause of prosecution were ever so pregnant."[81] The reason is a good one; but admit its goodness, and what becomes of the exclusionary rule? (Vol. V, pp. 388–9.)

\* \* \* \* \*

[*Arguing against the requirement of a second witness in cases of perjury, Bentham points to the error in*] *supposing that any rational conclusion can be drawn from the mere circumstance of number, as between accusers and defendants, without taking into the account the particular circumstances of each case.*

It is on the same ridiculous plea, that the testimony of a single witness has been determined in English law to be insufficient to ground a conviction for perjury: "because," we are told, "there would only be one oath against another."[82] Irrefragable logic this, if all oaths be exactly of equal value, no matter what may be the character of the swearer, and to the action of what interests he may be exposed. It is on the same ground, that no decree can be made, in equity, on the oath of one witness, against the defendant's answer on oath. (See the following section.) (Vol. V, p. 469.)

\* \* \* \* \*

[*After pointing out that in English law, two witnesses are required to support a conviction of treason, Bentham has high sport with the notion that the king is less protected from assassination than any subject. Mill's note is appended to this comment:*] *Picking a pocket of a handkerchief, value one shilling, is capital felony; its being the king's pocket does not make it treason: for picking the king's pocket of his handkerchief, a man might be hanged on the testimony of a single witness: shooting the king being treason, a man may shoot the king in the presence of any body he pleases, and not a hair of the murderer's head can be touched for it. Blessed laws! under which it is as safe again, to shoot the king as to pick his pocket!*

This singular rule of evidence is now no longer in force as regards any direct

[81]Phillipps, Vol. I, p. 66, citing Holt, 87 *English Reports* 969 (Johnson *v.* Browning).
[82]The judgment of Chief Justice Thomas Parker (ca. 1666–1732), Earl of Macclesfield, in 101 *English Reports* 690.

attempt against the person of the king, but it still subsists as regards any other kind of treason.[83] (Vol. V, p. 487.)

*       *       *       *       *

*[Mill's self-explanatory note, the first paragraph below (in italics and square brackets), appears at the end of Bentham's part of Bk. IX, Pt. VI, Chap. iv, "Exclusion by Rendering a Particular Species of Evidence Conclusive." Mill's part of the chapter follows immediately in normal type.]*

This chapter having been left unfinished by the Author, what follows has been added to it by the Editor. A few paragraphs, which for distinction have been put in inverted commas, consist of fragments, written at different times by Mr. Bentham: for the remainder the Editor is alone responsible.

This is not the only sort of case in which the sworn, but uncrossexamined and self-serving testimony of a party to the suit, is received as conclusive, that is, to the exclusion of counter-evidence. "The practice in chancery," we are informed by Phillipps,* "invariably is, that a party is entitled only to extracts of letters, if the other party will swear that the passages extracted are the only parts relating to the subject matter."

There is another rule, by which a man's own testimony is rendered conclusive evidence in his favour, and that too on such a subject as that of his own character. The witness indeed in this case is not a party in the suit; but for any thing that appears, he may be the vilest of malefactors; and he is, at any rate, under the influence of an interest, which is one of the strongest of all interests in the bulk of mankind, while even in the vilest it cannot be a weak one. A witness, as we have seen,[†] is not compellable to answer any question, the answer to which, if true, might tend to degrade his character: if, however, he chooses to answer, the party

[83]Bentham's comment is, for unknown reasons, out of date. The statute that required two witnesses for a conviction on a charge of treason was 7 & 8 William III, c. 3 (1695), sect. 2. The requirement was altered, however, by 39 & 40 George III, c. 93 (1800); one witness was sufficient for conviction on a charge in which any direct attempt was made upon the life of the sovereign.

Mill ignores the fact that Bentham's assertion that picking a pocket of a handkerchief is a capital felony was no longer true either. It had been a capital felony by virtue of 8 Elizabeth, c. 4 (1565), but the penalty for felonious theft from the person had been altered by 48 George III, c. 129 (1808) to transportation.

*Vol. I, p. 421.

†Book III, "Extraction," Chap. iv, "Discreditive Interrogation" [Vol. II, pp. 59–79].

who asks the question is bound by his answer, and is not allowed to falsify it by counter-evidence.*

The above seem to be the only instances worth mentioning, in which an article of orally delivered testimonial evidence has in English law been made conclusive. The instances in which similar effect has been given to an article of circumstantial evidence are innumerable; and many of them have been already brought to view.

1. As often as a decision has been given against either of the parties in a suit, on no other ground than that of his having failed, at a particular stage of the suit, to perform any operation which has been rendered necessary at that stage by technical rules, to the obtainment of justice; so often has the non-performance of that operation been taken as evidence, and conclusive evidence, of what is called in the language of lawyers *want of merits*, that is, of the badness of his cause.

"Of the justice of the demand, whatsoever it be, that happens to be made upon the defendant, provided the suit does not happen to be called a criminal one, non-resistance on his part is regarded and acted upon as sufficient evidence; and to the plaintiff possession is given of the object of his demand, just as if the justness of it had been proved. Even a lawyer will not pretend that on any ground of reason the inference is a conclusive one. Pecuniary inability, especially under the load of factitious expense imposed every where by the technical system, is another cause equally adequate to the production of the effect. In every part of the empire of the technical system, and more particularly in England, this inability will have place in the case of a vast majority of the body of the people.

"If a presumption thus slight were not received in proof of the justice of the plaintiff's claim, and in the character of conclusive evidence,—if such direct proof of it as were to be had, were in every instance to be required,—a number of *malâ fide* suits, with the produce of which, the coffers of the man of law are at present swelled, would have no existence.

"Thus it is, that under the technical system, every court calling itself a court of justice is in effect an open shop, in which, for the benefit of the shopkeeper and his associates, licenses are sold at a fixed, or at least at a limited, price,—empowering the purchaser to oppress and ruin at his choice any and every individual, obnoxious to him or not, on whom indigence or terror impose the inability of opposing effectual resistance.

*In the disapprobation bestowed upon this rule, it is of course implied, that the case is one of those in which the production of evidence to discredit the character of the witness, is in itself proper; for which cases, see Book V, "Circumstantial," Chap. xiii, "Of motives, means," etc., Sect. 3 and 4, "Character Evidence." [Vol. III, pp. 193–207.] If not, it is proper to exclude any such evidence, after he has answered, only because it is proper to exclude it, whether he answers or no. But if the case be one in which it would have been proper to adduce evidence against his character without putting any questions to himself, it is difficult to see what impropriety there can be in doing exactly the same thing after you have interrogated him and got his answer, if you do not believe his answer to be true.

"The real condition in which the great majority of the people, in the capacity of suitors, have been placed by the factitious expenses manufactured by the man of law, is an object too reproachful to him to be suffered to remain undisguised. In this, as in every other part of the system, extortion and oppression find in mendacity an ever-ready instrument. The real condition in which the suitor has been involved, the misfortune of defencelessness through indigence, is put out of sight: a crime is imputed to him in its stead: and for that crime, not only without proof, but under the universally notorious consciousness of his innocence, he is punished. *Contempt* is the word constantly employed to designate this imaginary crime. The real, the universally notorious, causes of his inaction, are fear and impotence. But a man cannot be punished avowedly for fear: he cannot be punished for impotence: mankind would not submit themselves to tyranny so completely without a mask. Adding calumny to mendacity, they pretend to regard his inaction as originating in *contempt*; and it is on this mendacious accusation of their own forging, that they ground the ruin they inflict on him under the name of punishment."

In equity, the defendant, who, from his own poverty or ignorance, or the carelessness of his lawyer, is so unfortunate as not to put in an answer to the plaintiff's bill, stands a great chance (if a poor man) of being a prisoner for life. He is committed to gaol for the *contempt*: and as he is not released without payment of fees,—unless he has money to pay these fees, or can find some one else who will pay them for him, he must remain there all his life. Instances of this sort have not unfrequently, through the medium of the newspapers, been presented to the public eye.

2. As often as a contract, or any other legally operative instrument, is pronounced *null and void*, on account of the non-observance of any *formality*; so often, the sort of exclusion of which we are here treating, has place. A man claims a landed estate, under the will of the last proprietor. The will is produced in court: it is found to have the signatures of two witnesses only, instead of three;[84] or one of the three is proved to have put his name to the will in the absence of the testator: the will is rejected, and the party loses his estate. The rejection of the will may, perhaps, be considered as a *penalty*, for non-compliance with that injunction of the law which requires that certain formalities should be observed. Considered in this point of view, it has been shewn in a previous Book* to be unnecessary and objectionable. But it may also be regarded as grounded on the presumption that the will was spurious, or unfairly obtained. Here then is this one circumstance, viz. non-observance of legally prescribed formalities, received as conclusive evidence of spuriousness or unfairness. The fallacy of this supposition has also been made

[84]As required by 29 Charles II, c. 3 (1676).
*See Book IV, "Preappointed" [Vol. II, pp. 435–700 (Chap. v, esp. Sect. 2, pp. 518–28)].

sufficiently manifest in the Book already referred to. This article of circumstantial evidence, which is conclusive in law, is so far from being conclusive in reason, that it scarcely amounts even to the slightest presumption, until two things be ascertained: first, that the party *knew* that these formalities were prescribed; and secondly, that compliance with them was in his *power*. That spurious or unfair instruments have not frequently been *prevented* by the peremptory requisition of these formalities, is more than I would undertake to say: but an assertion which one may venture upon without much danger of mistake, is, that there is scarcely an instance of any instrument's having been actually *set aside* for the want of them, in which there was not a considerable, if not a preponderant, probability of its being genuine.

3. Almost all *estoppels* are exclusions of the sort now under consideration. You are estopped, say the lawyers, from proving so and so: the meaning of which is, that they will not permit you to prove it. For this they have sometimes one pretext, sometimes another: something which you yourself have said or done; or something which has been said or done by somebody else.

There is a great variety of instances in which they tell you that you are estopped by a previous decision, either of the same court, or of some other court of justice: these have been already noticed under the head of adscititious evidence.* At other times you are estopped by what they term an *admission*. You are said to make an admission, if you say or do any thing, or if any other person says or does any thing for you, which a judge construes as an acknowledgment on your part, that a certain event has happened; that is, any thing from which he chooses to infer its happening: after which, though every body, who knows any thing about the matter, knows that it has not happened, and would say so if asked, the judge, to save the trouble of asking, chooses to act exactly as if it had.

Admissions are of two kinds, express or presumed; and the former are either admissions upon record, or admissions not upon record. It is a rule with lawyers, that no evidence can be received to dispute admissions upon record,[†] that is, admissions in the pleadings. If this rule went no farther than to confine the evidence to such points as are actually in dispute between the parties, it would be a good rule. In a law book, a man may reckon himself fortunate if he hits upon a rule which has a reason: if he expect, that where the reason stops, the rule will stop too, it is very rarely that he will not be disappointed. One example will serve as well as a thousand. When a man, against whom an action is brought for a sum of money, denies that the plaintiff is entitled to the whole sum which he claims, but admits that he has a just claim upon him for a smaller sum,—the practice is, for the defendant to pay into court the amount of the sum which he acknowledges to be

---

*See Book VI, "Makeshift" [esp. Chap. ii, Sect. 3, "Of Adscititious Evidence; i.e. Evidence Borrowed from Another Cause" (Vol. III, pp. 424–33); see also pp. 35–8 above].

[†]Phillipps, Vol. I, p. 159.

due, that it may remain in deposit until the cause is decided. This payment, lawyers choose to call an "acknowledgment upon record;" and now mark the consequence: "the party cannot recover it back, although he has paid it wrongfully, or by mistake."*

As for extrajudicial admissions, it is not always that they are even receivable; when they are, they are generally taken for conclusive: for it may be observed, in regard to this part of the law of evidence, as in regard to so many other parts of it, that neither the lawyers by whom it was made, nor the lawyers by whom it has been expounded, ever seem to know that there is any middle course between taking an article of evidence for conclusive, and rejecting it altogether. Accordingly, in reading the *dicta* of judges, or the compilations of institutional writers from those *dicta*, one is continually at a loss to know what they mean. In speaking of this or that evidentiary circumstance, what they tell you concerning it, is, that it is *evidence*: now and then superadding, as it were for the sake of variety, the epithet *good* to the general appellative, evidence. Would you know whether they mean that it is *conclusive*, or only that it is *admissible*? Observe their *actions*: see whether they send it to a jury: for any thing that you can collect from their *words*, they are as likely to mean the one as the other.

The following will serve as an example, as well of the ambiguity of which I have been speaking, as of the sort of logic which passes for irrefragable, under the dominion of technical rules. When a party, interested in the cause, makes an admission against his interest, if he has not made it by mistake, it is nearly the best evidence against him that you can have: *ergo*, it ought to be taken for conclusive against him, when he *has* made it by mistake; *ergo*, the admission of a person who is merely a nominal plaintiff, and who is *not interested in the cause*, ought to be conclusive against the person who is. So, at least, it was decided in the case of Bauerman *v.* Radenius,[†] in which the admission of the plaintiffs on the record, though not the parties really interested, was received as conclusive, and the plaintiffs were nonsuited. I say, received as conclusive; because, when a plaintiff is nonsuited, that is to say, when his claim is dismissed by the judge without going to a jury, it is because, if he had gone to a jury, the jury *must have found a verdict against him*; which would have been a bar to any future prosecution of the same claim: whereas a nonsuit leaves it still in his power to bring a fresh action, after remedying the defect which would have compelled the jury to find against him. The court of King's Bench afterwards *affirmed*, that is, confirmed, the nonsuit: on which occasion Mr. Justice Lawrence said, "The present plaintiffs either have or have not an interest: but it must be considered that they have an interest, in order to support the action; and if they have, an admission made by them that they have no cause of action, is admissible evidence."[85] This judge, here, with much *naïveté*,

---

*Ibid., p. 175.
[†]*Ibid.*, p. 84 [citing 101 *English Reports* 1186–90].
[85]Phillipps, Vol. I, p. 175, citing Soulden Lawrence (1751–1814).

displays the manner in which, under the influence of technical rules, what is known to be false is taken for true, in order that what is evidently unjust may be done. He knew as well as the nominal plaintiffs knew, that they had *not* an interest in the cause: but what of that? The law knew that they had.

There is an overflow of legal learning, on the question, what effect to your prejudice shall be given to the admission of your *agent*: and here again recurs the usual alternative: it is either not received, or it is received as conclusive: it either excludes all other evidence, or it is itself excluded. Thus, in one case,* "a letter from the defendant's clerk, informing the plaintiff that a policy had been effected, was held to be *good evidence* [meaning here *conclusive* evidence] of the existence of the policy; and the defendant *was not allowed to prove* that the letter had been written by mistake, and that the policy had not been made:" while, in another case,† "where the fact sought to be established, was, that a bond had been executed by the defendant to the plaintiff, which the defendant had got possession of, the Master of the Rolls *refused to admit*, as evidence of this fact, the declaration of the defendant's agent, who had been employed to keep the bond for the plaintiff's benefit, and who, on its being demanded by the plaintiff, informed him that it had been delivered to the defendant." It might seem to a cursory reader, on comparing these two decisions, either that the predilection of judges for bad evidence was such, that, rejecting an admission in other cases, they were willing to receive it upon the single condition of its being made by *mistake*; or that, in laying down rules of evidence, blind caprice was the only guide. In this apparent inconsistency, however, there is a principle, though no one would have thought it: it is this: that the admissions of an agent are not to be received, unless "made by him, either at the time of his making an agreement about which he is employed, or in acting within the scope of his authority."[86] It is not, that what he says on these occasions is more likely to be true than what he says on other occasions: it is, that "it is impossible to say a man is precluded from questioning or contradicting any thing that any person may have asserted, as to his conduct or agreement, merely because that person has been an agent:"[87] and as it would be unjust to preclude him from contradicting it, it is not permitted so much as to be heard.

Besides these express admissions, there is an extensive assortment of presumed ones; when a man "precludes himself from disputing a fact, by the tenour of his conduct and demeanour:"‡ the meaning of which is, that the court will *presume an*

*Harding *v.* Carter, *apud* Phillipps, Vol. I, p. 97n.
†Fairlie *v.* Hastings [32 *English Reports* 791–3], *ibid.*, p. 95.
[86]*Ibid.*
[87]*Ibid.*, p. 96.
‡See an abstract or digest of the Law of Evidence, recently published by Mr. Harrison, on the plan of Crofton Uniacke, Esq., p. 8. [I.e., Samuel Harrison, *Evidence*; the "plan" of Crofton Uniacke (1783–1852) is embodied in his *The New Jury Law* (London: Clarke, 1825).]

*admission* from any thing that a man does, which they think he would not have done if the fact had not been true. This is the principle: but as to the extent of its application, there is no criterion of it except the Index to the Reports. It has usually been applied only to cases in which the presumption afforded by the act is really strong, and might reasonably be held conclusive in the *absence* of counter-evidence, though certainly not to the *exclusion* of counter-evidence, since there is not so much as one of the cases in which the presumption is not liable to fail. Without touching upon the grounds of failure which are peculiar to this or that case, there is one obvious ground which is common to them all. A man's actions can never prove the truth of a fact, except in so far as his *belief* of it is evidence of its truth: and to hinder a man from proving that a thing did not happen, because at some former period he believed that it did, even if you were sure that he believed it (which in general you are not, it being only inferred from his actions), would be unjust in any case, but is more especially absurd, when the fact in question is one of those complicated, and frequently recondite, facts, which are constitutive of *title*.

Take a few instances.

"By accounting with a person as farmer of the tolls of a turnpike, a party is estopped from disputing the validity of his title, when sued by account stated for those tolls.

"By paying tithes to the plaintiff on former occasions, a defendant admits the right of the plaintiff to an action for not setting out tithes.

"Where a party rented glebe lands of a rector, and had paid him rent, he was not permitted, in an action for use and occupation, to dispute his lessor's title, by proving that his presentation was simoniacal.

"In actions of use and occupation, when the tenant has occupied by the permission of the plaintiff, he cannot dispute the plaintiff's title, although he may shew that it is at an end.

"In an action of ejectment, by a landlord against his tenant, the tenant cannot question the title of his landlord, although he is at liberty to shew that it has expired."*

In all these instances, the presumption upon which, if upon any thing, the decision must have been grounded, is, that if the plaintiff had not really had a good title, the defendant would not have paid rent, tithe, etc. to him, as the case may be. To justify the rendering this presumption conclusive, it would be necessary, among a crowd of other suppositions, to suppose that a tenant never paid rent to the *de facto* landlord, without first demanding his title deeds, and going over them with a lawyer, for the purpose of assuring himself that they did not contain any flaw.

4. A whole host of exclusions lurk in the admired rule, that the best evidence which the nature of the case admits of, is to be required: a rule which seems to

*Harrison, *ut suprà*, pp. 9–10.

please every body, and with the more reason, as, having no distinct meaning of its own, it is capable of receiving any which any one thinks proper to attach to it. There is a charm, too, in the sound of the words *best evidence*, which no lawyer, and scarcely any non-lawyer, is able to resist. The following seems to be nearly the train of thought (in so far as any thing like thought can be said to have place) which passes through the mind of the submissive and admiring student, when he hears this maxim delivered *ex cathedrâ*, as something which, like Holy Writ, is to be believed and adored. Good evidence, it naturally occurs to him, is a good thing: *à fortiori* therefore (it is unnecessary to say), the best evidence cannot but be a good thing: what, however, can be more proper, than always to require, and insist upon having, the best of every thing? How admirable, therefore, the rule which requires the best evidence (whether it is to be had or no); and how admirable the system of law, which is in a great measure made up of such rules!

As a preliminary to praising this rule, a desirable thing would be, to understand it: for this, however, you have no chance but by looking at the practice: the attempt to find a meaning for the words would be lost labour. The meaning attached to it by lawyers has been different, according to the different purposes which they have had to serve by it. One use which they have made of it, is, to serve as a reason for excluding an inferior and less trustworthy sort of evidence, when a more trustworthy sort, from the same source, is to be had: as, for example, a transcript, when the original is in existence and forthcoming. Applied to this purpose, the rule, if it were not so vague, would be justly entitled to the appellation of a good rule: the purpose, at any rate, (with the limitations which have been seen in the Book on Makeshift Evidence), must be allowed to be a good purpose. Another use which has been made by lawyers, at times, of this rule, is, to enable a judge, at no greater expense than that of calling a particular sort of evidence the best evidence, to treat it as conclusive in favour of the party who produces it; or the non-production of it as conclusive against the party who, it is supposed, ought to have produced it; in both cases putting an exclusion upon all other evidence: and it is in this application of the rule, that it presents a demand for consideration in this place.

"Take a sample of their best evidence,—of that best evidence which, by such its *bestness*, puts an exclusion upon all other evidence.

"Speculative Position or Antecedent;—Written evidence is better than parol evidence. Practical Inference or Conclusion;—Therefore, in case of a contract, when there exists written evidence of it, with certain formalities for its accompaniments, oral evidence is, or is not, to be admitted, in relation to the purport of such contract. Is, or is not; whichever is most agreeable and convenient to the judge. Such is the plain and true account of the matter: for distinctions are spun out of distinctions; and, the light of reason, by which they would be all consumed, being effectually shut out, on and on the thread might continue to be spun without end.

"Observe the inconsistency.

"In English law, circumstantial evidence of the weakest kind, comparison of hands, by persons acquainted, or not acquainted, with the hand of the person in question,—or even the bare tenour of the instrument, *i.e.* the circumstance of its purporting upon the face of it to have been executed (*i.e.* recognized) by the person or persons therein mentioned,—this circumstance, if coupled with the evidentiary circumstance *ex custodiâ*, is (if the assumed date of the instrument be as much as thirty years anterior to the day of production) held sufficient, and, in default of counter-evidence, conclusive.

"A dozen or a score of alleged percipient witnesses, all ready to concur in deposing that, to the provisions in the instrument mentioned, this or that other had been agreed to be added or substituted,—shall they be received, and heard to say as much? Oh, no; that must not be; it is against our rule about *best evidence*."

The general rule on this subject, is, that oral evidence is not admissible "to contradict, or vary, or add to, the terms of a written agreement."* Cut down as this rule is, by almost innumerable exceptions, there is still enough of it left to do much mischief. The exceptions, if their practical effect be looked to, are reasonable, as narrowing *pro tanto* the extent of a bad rule: in principle, however, there is scarce one of them which is tenable, unless it be first granted that the rule is absurd. It would be difficult, for example, to discover how, in respect of the propriety of admitting oral evidence to shew the abandonment of a written agreement, it should make any difference whether the agreement was or was not under seal; or why, in equity, on a bill for the specific performance of a written agreement, evidence to prove that, by reason of accident or mistake, the written instrument does not correctly express the agreement, should, if tendered by the defendant, be in certain cases admitted; if tendered by the plaintiff, refused. The origin of the exceptions to this rule, as well as to so many other technical rules, is visible enough. They were established by the same sort of authority which established the rules, viz. that of judges, deciding *pro hâc vice*,[88] under the guidance of no principle, but in accordance with the interest or whim of the moment, or frequently with the laudable view of doing justice, notwithstanding technical rules. A judge sees plainly, that, in this or that particular case, if he adhere to the rule, he will do injustice; and without daring to set it aside, or even allowing himself to suppose that a rule which had descended from wise ancestors could be other than a good one, he has honesty enough to wish to do justice in the cause in hand, and accordingly cuts into the rule with a new exception for every new instance which presents itself to him of its mischievous operation, taking care never to carry the exception one jot farther than is strictly necessary for his immediate purpose: another judge follows, and takes another nibble at the rule,

*Phillipps, Vol. I, p. 530.
[88]I.e., for this one occasion.

always upon the same diminutive scale; and so on. Hence it comes, that, at length, after the lapse of a few centuries, the body of the law, considered as a whole, has become a little more just, and a great deal more unintelligible:—while the law books have degenerated from the primitive simplicity of the old textbooks, where every thing was comprehended under a few simple principles, (in which, whatever trespasses you might find against justice or common sense, you will find none against consistency,—and which would be perfect, if conduciveness to human happiness were a quality that could, without inconvenience, be dispensed with in law); and have swelled into an incoherent mass of mutually conflicting decisions, none of them covering more than a minute spot in the field of law, and which the most practised memory would vainly strive to retain, or the most consummate logic to reduce to a common principle.

Oral evidence, it seems, is receivable to *explain*, in many cases in which it would not be receivable to *vary*, the terms of an agreement. The general rule is, that, in case of a *latent* ambiguity,—that is to say, an ambiguity which does not appear on the face of the instrument, but is raised by extrinsic evidence,—extrinsic evidence will be received to explain it: thus, if a testator bequeaths to John Stiles his estate of Blackacre, and it appears that he has two estates known by that name, oral evidence will be received to shew which of the two he meant. Provided always, that there be no possibility of giving effect to the instrument *in terminis*,[89] without the aid of other evidence:* for if it have a definite meaning, though a different one from that of the testator, it does not signify. When they cannot by any means contrive to give execution to the *ipsissima verba* of the will, then, it seems, they will condescend to inquire what the testator intended.

Not so when the ambiguity is *patent*, that is, apparent on the face of the instrument. In this case, the door is inexorably shut upon all extrinsic evidence; and if the intention of the party cannot be inferred from the context, "the clause will be void, on account of its uncertainty."[90] You are unskilled in composition: after making mention in your will of two persons, your brother and your younger son, you bequeath to *him* an estate: in this case it may possibly admit of dispute, to which of the two you meant to bequeath it; what, however, can admit of no dispute, is, that you meant to bequeath it to one or other of them: as, therefore, it is doubtful whether you intended that A should have it, or B, the judge will not give it to either of them, but gives it to C, the heir-at-law, whom it is certain you intended not to have it. Or, if he gives it to either of the two persons who, and who alone, can

[89]I.e., solely in its own terms.
*"The question on the admissibility of parol evidence, in such cases, will depend principally upon this,—namely, whether the evidence is necessary to give an effective operation to the devise, or whether, without that evidence, there appears to be sufficient to satisfy the terms of the devise and the intention of the testator, as expressed on the face of the will." (Phillipps, Vol. I, p. 515.)
[90]*Ibid.*, p. 519.

possibly have been meant, he gives it upon the slightest imaginable presumption from the context. There were twenty persons standing by when you executed the will, all of whom knew perfectly well, from your declarations at the time, which of the two parties in question you meant, but none of whom he will suffer to be heard. And this is what lawyers call requiring the best evidence.

For this rule two reasons have been given: one a technical, that is, avowedly an irrational one; the other, one which pretends to be rational. The technical reason is the production of Lord Bacon: it is this: "the law will not couple and mingle *matter of specialty*, which is *of the higher account*, with *matter of averment*, which is *of inferior account* in law."[91] For those to whose conceptions the incongruity of so irregular a mixture might fail to present itself in colours sufficiently glaring, a subsequent lord chancellor brought forth the following less recondite reason; that the admission of oral evidence in explanation of patent ambiguities, "would tend to put it in the power of witnesses to make wills for testators:"[92] an objection which would be very strong against any one mode of proof, if it did not unhappily apply to every other.

All hearing of evidence lets in *some* danger of falsehood. What, however, was probably meant, is, that the admissibility of oral evidence to explain a will, would frustrate the intention of the law in requiring preappointed evidence, a better sort of evidence than oral, and less likely to be false. If this be the meaning, it is enunciated far too generally. It is true that preappointed evidence, considered as a *genus*, is better than oral. But it is not true that every particular article of the former is better than the best conceivable article of the latter. It is not true that the signature of three witnesses is better, *caeteris paribus*, than the oral depositions of twenty. Yet this rule excludes the latter evidence, on the plea of its inferiority to the former.*

[91]*Ibid.*, pp. 519–20, quoting from Francis Bacon (1561–1626), *Maxims of the Law* (1630), in *Works*, ed. James Spedding, *et al.*, 14 vols. (London: Longmans, *et al.*, 1857–74), Vol. VII, pp. 385–7 (Rule 25).
[92]Phillipps, Vol. I, p. 520, citing the judgment of Lord Chancellor Philip Yorke (1690–1764), Earl of Hardwicke, in Castleton *v.* Turner, in 28 *English Reports* 140–2.
*[Mill here appends a passage from Bentham in a note:] The refusal to put upon the words used by a man in penning a deed or a will, the meaning which it is all the while acknowledged he put upon it himself, is an enormity, an act of barefaced injustice, unknown every where but in English jurisprudence. It is, in fact, making for a man a will that he never made; a practice exactly upon a par (impunity excepted) with forgery.

Lawyers putting upon it their own sense: yes, their own sense. But which of all possible senses is their own sense? They are as far from agreeing with one another, or each with himself, as with the body of the people. In evident reason and common justice, no one will ought to be taken as a rule for any other; no more than the evidence in one cause is a rule for the evidence to different facts in another cause. It is not from this or that word, or string of words, in a will, but from all the words taken together,—nor yet only from all the words taken together, but from all the words, compared wtih every relevant fact that is

Another consequence of the technical maxim, that written evidence is better than parol, (a maxim which, like almost all other general maxims of technical law, is not true in more than half the cases which it extends to), is the exclusion, in a great number of cases, of oral evidence to prove that there *exists* a written document evidentiary of a particular fact. The judges, on the occasion of a reference made to them in the course of the late queen's trial, declared that "the contents of every written paper are, according to the ordinary and well-established rules of evidence, to be proved by the paper itself, and by that alone, if the paper be in existence."* Good: provided always it be a necessary consequence, that a paper is forthcoming, because it is in existence. Upon the strength of this rule, the judges decided, that the supposed writer of a letter could not be questioned concerning the contents of the letter, unless the letter itself were first produced, and the witness asked whether he wrote it. Thus, the only evidence, perhaps, which you have got, and that too of so good a kind as the testimony of a writer concerning what he himself has written, is excluded, because another sort of evidence is not produced, which would be better if you could get it, but which, in all probability, you cannot get. The superior evidence, though not forthcoming to any practical purpose, cannot be shewn not to exist; and it is therefore said to be *forthcoming*, to the purpose of excluding all inferior evidence.

A volume might be filled with specimens of the injustice and absurdity which are the fruit of the rule requiring the best evidence. Take this example among others. A written instrument, with certain formalities, being the best evidence; if, in the written instrument, any one of these formalities be omitted, neither the agreement, nor any other evidence of the transaction, will be received. Thus,

a written instrument which requires a stamp, cannot be admitted in evidence, unless it be duly stamped; and no parol evidence will be received of its contents. If, therefore, the instrument produced is the only legal proof of the transaction, and that cannot be admitted

---

ascertainable respecting the situation of his property, of his family, of his connexions, that the intention of the testator is to be gathered.

To these diseases of jurisprudence, attempts have been made to apply a remedy by jurisprudence. But the attempt, if not treacherous, has been shallow. The result never has been, never can be, any thing better than a further extent given to the application of the *double fountain* principle. (See the chapter so intituled. [Vol. IV, pp. 384–7 (Bk. VIII, Chap. xxiii), "Eighteenth Device—Double Fountain Principle."]) No; it is not a case for Telephus with his spear; it is a case for Hercules with his searing-iron. Jurisprudence pruned by jurisprudence, is the hydra decollated, and left to pullulate: the only searing-iron is the legislative sceptre.

*Phillipps, Vol. I, p. 281. [The question arose during the trial in 1820 of Queen Caroline (1768–1821), who was accused of adultery. The judges were William Draper Best (1767–1845), Baron Wynford; Robert Dallas (1756–1824); and George Sowley Holroyd (1758–1831). For their ruling, see Charles Abbott (1762–1832), Baron Tenterden, Speech in the Debate on the Bill of Pains and Penalties (1 Sept., 1820), *PD*, n.s., Vol. 2, col. 1184.]

for want of a proper stamp, the transaction cannot be proved at all; as, in an action for use and occupation, if it appear that the defendant held under a written agreement, which for want of a stamp cannot be received, the plaintiff will not be allowed to go into general evidence; for the agreement is the *best evidence* of the nature of the occupation.*

An agreement on *unstamped* paper not being itself receivable, it follows naturally enough, that if it be lost, parol evidence will not be received of its contents; nor even if it be wrongfully destroyed by the other party: notwithstanding another technical rule, that no one is allowed to take advantage of his own wrong.[93] But you can never guess from the terms of a rule, to what cases it will be applied.

Take the following still more barefaced piece of absurdity, as a final specimen of the operation of this vaunted rule.

The acts of state of a foreign government can only be proved by copies of such acts, properly authenticated. Thus, in the case of Richardson *v.* Anderson, where the counsel on the part of the defendant proposed to give in evidence a book purporting to be a collection of treaties concluded by America, and to be published by the authority of the American government; and it was proposed, further, to prove, by the American minister resident at this court, that the book produced was the rule of his conduct; this evidence was offered as equivalent to a regular copy of the archives in Washington: but Lord Ellenborough rejected the evidence, and held, that it was necessary to have a copy examined with the archives.[†]

We may expect in time to see a judge arise, who, more tenacious of consistency than his predecessors, will refuse to take notice of the existence of the city of London, unless an examined copy of the charter of the corporation be given in evidence to prove it.

Can any exposure make this piece of technicality more ridiculous than it is made by merely stating it?

5. I shall notice only one more instance of the species of disguised exclusion which forms the subject of the present chapter. The sort of evidence which, in this instance, is taken for conclusive, is the species of official document called a record.

Records, [says Phillipps,] are the memorials of the proceedings of the legislature, and of the king's courts of justice, preserved in rolls of parchment; and they are considered of such authority, that no evidence is allowed to contradict them. Thus, if a verdict, finding several issues, were to be produced in evidence, the opposite party would not be allowed to shew, that no evidence was offered on one of the issues, and that the finding of the jury was indorsed on the postea by mistake.[‡]

On this piece of absurdity, after what has already been said, it can scarcely be necessary to enlarge. Somehow or other, however, lawyers seem to have found

---

*Phillipps, Vol. I, p. 486.
[93]See Coke, *Institutes*, p. 148 (II, xii, 222).
†Phillipps, Vol. I, pp. 382–3.
‡*Ibid.*, p. 299.

out, that, like every thing else which is human, so even a record,—however high its "authority," and however indisputable its title to the appellation bestowed upon it by Lord Chief Baron Gilbert, "a diagram" (whatever be meant by a diagram) "for the demonstration of right" (whatever be meant by the demonstration of right),—is still, notwithstanding it be written upon parchment, liable to error:[94] for they have found it necessary to determine that a record shall be conclusive proof only "that the decision or judgment of the court was as is there stated," and not "as to the truth of allegations which were not material nor traversable."[95] This is fortunate: the fact of the judgment being one of the very few matters, contained in what is called a record, which, unless by mistake, are generally true. But, however fallible in respect of other facts, in respect of this one fact they hold it to be infallible; and its infallibility, itself needing no proof, supersedes all proof of the contrary; which, therefore, as it cannot prove any thing, it would be loss of time to hear: accordingly it is not heard, but inexorably excluded.* (Vol. V, pp. 570–96.)

\* \* \* \* \*

[94]Gilbert, *Law of Evidence*, p. 7.
[95]Phillipps, Vol. I, p. 300.
*[Mill concludes the chapter with an appended note giving a comment of Bentham's:] We have seen in how many cases the words *conclusive evidence* cover a real exclusion: it remains to bring to notice one case in which they do not. This is when an act, designated by a distinct expression, is termed *evidence* of the same act designated by an indistinct one.

The clouds in which, partly by imbecility, partly by improbity, the field of legislation has been involved, are, in some places, of so thick a texture, that no small labour is requisite to pierce through them. Even in statute law, the phraseology employed by the professional penman in whom the legislator has reposed his confidence, has, in but too many instances, been so unhappily or so dexterously chosen, as to present no fixed sense, no sense distinct enough for use. In this case, what has been the resource? To describe an act in more distinct terms, to consider it as an act different from the act described in the less distinct terms, and to speak of the unauthoritatively, but more distinctly described act, as evidence of the authoritatively, but less distinctly expressed one.

Thus, in the case of an offence bearing relation to the police, certain acts have been spoken of as being *evidence* of vagrancy. Stript of its disguise, what, in this case, was the plain fact? That vagrancy was one sort of act, the acts in question another sort? and that, these acts being regarded as proved, vagrancy was regarded as a distinct act, the existence of which had been rendered preponderantly probable by the other? No such thing: but the acts in question were determinate, the signification of the word vagrancy, not. What was the consequence? That on the ground of the statute interdicting vagrancy, a rule of jurisprudential law was enacted, interpretative of the statute law: a rule of jurisprudential law, applying to the acts in question the final consequences attached by the statute to the indistinct appellation.

## OF THE RULE, THAT EVIDENCE IS TO BE CONFINED
## TO THE POINTS IN ISSUE.*

THIS RULE, though good in principle, is frequently, as it is administered, an instrument of mischief; partly from being combined with a bad system of pleading, partly from the perverse application which has been made of it to purposes for which it was never intended. Being an exclusionary rule, it demands consideration in this place: and the occasion seems a suitable one for taking notice, not of the bad effects in the way of exclusion only, but of the bad effects of other descriptions, which are the fruit of it.

Nothing can be more proper than to exclude all evidence irrelevant to the points in dispute: and if the points in issue on the pleadings were always the points, and all the points, in dispute, nothing could be more proper than to exclude all evidence irrelevant to the points in issue. Unhappily, however, to determine what are the points in dispute, though the professed object of all systems of pleading, is very imperfectly attained even under the best; and the points really at issue are often very different from the points *in issue*, as they appear on the pleadings.

In so far as the representation given in the pleadings of the state of the question between the parties, fails to accord with the real state; in so far, at least, as any point (that is, of course, any material point) which is really in dispute, is omitted or mis-stated in the pleadings; in so far, the rule, which requires that the evidence be confined to the points in issue, those points not being the points in dispute, operates to the exclusion of all evidence which bears only upon the real points in dispute. This includes all cases of quashing, grounded on what is called a *flaw* in the pleadings: as, for instance, the case of a misnomer. If you indict a man under the name of John Josiah Smith, and it turns out that his real name is John Joseph Smith, though nobody has the least doubt of his being the person meant, and though he himself would not have the effrontery to declare upon oath a belief that he was not, it is no matter, the indictment is quashed: because, the only question at issue, as indicated by the indictment, relating to the supposed guilt of Josiah, proof, however convincing, of the criminality of Joseph, is *foreign to the issue*. On the same ground, in an action for non-residence, the designation of the parish by the name of St. Ethelburgh, instead of Saint Ethelburgha, was held to be (as lawyers term it) a fatal variance. On another occasion, the ground of the quashing was, that a party to a bill of exchange had been called Couch, instead of Crouch: on another, that the prisoner was charged with having personated M'Cann, while the evidence went to shew, that the man whom he had personated was M'Carn. It was not that, in any of these instances, any real doubt existed as to the purport of the charge; nor was it that, in the guilt of defrauding two persons with names so different as *M'Cann* and *M'Carn* are, there was deemed to be any such difference

*This chapter [Bk. IX, Pt. VI, Chap. v] has been added by the Editor.

in point of enormity as could justify so great a diversity of treatment: it was, that the unbending spirit of technical rules requires that you should prove, *verbatim et literatim*, the very thing which you have asserted, and, whatever may be the real issue, ties you down to the nominal one. That the substitution of an *r* for an *n* could in any other way be effected than by dropping the proceeding and beginning *de novo*, is what you will never get any Common Lawyer to understand.

It is the same when any other circumstance, legally material, is misdescribed in the pleadings; as when the declaration stated an absolute promise, and a conditional one was proved; and when a declaration for assaulting a constable in the execution of his office, alleged that he was constable of a particular parish, and the proof was that he was sworn in for a liberty, of which the parish was part: a notable reason for depriving the plaintiff of justice, or putting him to the expense of another suit to obtain it!*

The root of the evil here lies in the system of pleading. To eradicate it entirely, that whole system must be abolished: the mode in which what is called pleading is now conducted, namely, by a sort of written correspondence between two attorneys, must give place to oral pleading, by the parties themselves, in the presence of the judge; when either no such mistakes as the above would be made, or, if made, they would be instantly rectified. Even under the present vicious system, however, the quashing of the suit might be avoided much oftener than it is. There are mistakes that are of consequence, there are others which are of none: there are mistakes by which the opposite party may have been misled, there are others by which he cannot. It is just, certainly, that after a party has intimated to his adversary his intention of proving a certain case, he should be allowed to prove that case, and no other: since, if there were no such rule, the other party might be taken by surprise: he might come prepared with evidence to rebut what he imagined was the claim against him, and might find, on going to trial, that the one really brought was quite different. This being the reason, what then is the practical rule? Let the remedy be confined to the single case, in which alone there is any evil to be remedied. If the opposite party has really been misled, or put to any inconvenience by the error, he cannot, one would think, have any reasonable objection to saying so: nor to delivering the assertion under all those securities which are taken for the truth of testimony in any other case. Unless, therefore, he is willing, under these securities, to declare that, in consequence of the error, he has been either prevented from bringing the necessary evidence, or induced to bring evidence which was not necessary, let the error be rectified, and the cause go on as it would have done if there had been no error. If he *be* willing to make such a declaration, and if his adversary admit, or fail to disprove its truth, let the necessary delay (when any delay is necessary) be granted: and let the party by whose fault the error was

*See the title *Variance*, in Starkie's *Law of Evidence* [Vol. III, pp. 1561–2].

occasioned, be subjected to the obligation of indemnifying the other for all *bonâ fide* expenses which he can prove to have been occasioned him by it.

If the rule, in the cases above examined, is attended with bad effects, it is not that it is a bad rule, but (as has been already intimated) that it is accompanied by a bad system of pleading. There is, however, another set of cases, in which the rule is applied in a sense in which it is altogether absurd: facts being shut out, under pretence of their not being the facts at issue, which, though unquestionably not the facts at issue, are of the highest importance as evidentiary of those which are.

Thus, the custom of one manor is not to be given in evidence to explain the custom of another manor; unless it be first proved, that both manors were formerly one, or were held under one lord; or unless the custom is laid as a general custom of the country, or of that particular district. Why? Because customs are "different in different manors, and in their nature distinct."[96] But although the customs of different manors are *different*, they may nevertheless be *analogous*; and though the custom of one manor cannot of itself *prove* that of another, it may assist in clearing up apparent inconsistencies in it, or in obviating an argument grounded on its supposed improbability. There is also another reason, of still greater weight, which we owe to the ingenuity of Lord Chief Justice Raymond: "for," says he, "if this kind of evidence were to be allowed, the consequence seems to be, that it would let in the custom of one manor into another, and in time bring the customs of all manors to be the same."* In the contemplation of so overwhelming a calamity, it is no wonder that Lord Raymond should have lost sight of whatever inconvenience might happen to be sustained by the party in the right, from losing his cause for want of such explanations as a reference to the custom of a neighbouring manor might have afforded; especially if advertence be had to the appalling fact, that the customs of all manors would come to be the same, if suffered to be shewn for what they are. The reader will not, of course, indulge in any such vain fancy, as that the custom which is good for one manor, can be good, or even endurable, for the manor adjoining; or that the inhabitants of one village could even exist, under rules and regulations which bind the inhabitants of another village as well as themselves.

Again; "in a question between landlord and tenant, whether rent was payable quarterly or half-yearly, evidence of the mode in which other tenants of the same landlord paid their rent, is not admissible."† Yet what can be more strictly relevant? the determining motive in such cases usually being the landlord's convenience, which may reasonably be presumed to be the same in the case of one farmer as of another.

Mr. Harrison gives an abstract of eight cases decided under the rule that

---

[96]Phillipps, Vol. I, p. 162.
*Ibid*. [quoting Chief Justice Robert Raymond (1673–1733)].
†Harrison, *ut suprà*, p. 132.

evidence is to be confined to the points in issue; seven of which include this same sort of absurdity.

It cannot be pretended, that the evidence thus shut out is irrelevant: and to maintain, as a general maxim, that evidence of relevant facts is to be excluded, because those facts are not expressly averred in the pleadings, would be too great a stretch of technicality, even for a lawyer. For the above decisions, however, no better reason can be given; unless that of Lord Chief Justice Raymond, which Mr. Phillipps styles an "argument of inconvenience,"[97] be so considered.

With as good reason might any other article of circumstantial evidence be excluded. A murder, suppose, has been committed: the prisoner was near the spot; he was known to be a personal enemy of the deceased, and at a former interview he had threatened to kill him: stains of blood were found upon his linen when he was apprehended, and he had a bloody knife in his pocket. What then? None of these facts are in issue: it is not said in the indictment, that he was an enemy of the deceased, nor yet that he had used threatening language towards him; he is not charged with soiling his linen; and though, indeed, it is alleged in the indictment, that he killed and slew the deceased with a knife, value sixpence, it is nowhere imputed to him that he stained the knife. At this rate, the plaintiff would need to include in the declaration every fact which, in the character of an evidentiary fact, he might have occasion to bring to the notice of the judge.

We have now considered the rule in both its applications: its abusive application, which can never be other than mischievous; and its legitimate application, which, to be purely beneficial, wants only to be combined with a rational mode of pleading. Suppose the system of pleading reformed; this rule, to be a good one, would only need to be always employed in its legitimate, and never in its abusive, sense. When thus restricted, however, what does it really mean? Only, that evidence is not to be admitted of any facts, except either those on which the decision immediately turns, or other facts which are evidentiary of them.

General as this rule is, greater particularity will not, in this instance, be found to be attainable; since the question, on what facts the decision turns, is a question, not of evidence, but of the substantive branch of the law: it respects the *probandum*, not the *probans*: it does not belong to the inquiry, by what sort of evidence the facts of the case may be proved; it belongs to the inquiry, what are the facts of which the law has determined that proof shall be required, in order to establish the plaintiff's claim.

This circumstance, obvious as it is, might easily be overlooked by one who had studied the subject only in the compilations of the English institutional writers; who, not content with directing that the evidence be confined to the points in issue, have farther proceeded, under the guise of laying down rules of evidence, to declare, on each occasion, what the points in issue are.

[97]Phillipps, Vol. I, p. 162.

One whole volume[98] out of two which compose Mr. Phillipps's treatise on the Law of Evidence,—with a corresponding portion of the other treatises extant concerning that branch of the law,—is occupied in laying down rules concerning the *sort of evidence* which should be required in different sorts of actions or suits at law. But why should different forms of action require different sorts of evidence? The *securities* by which the trustworthiness of evidence is provided for, and the *rules* by which its probative force is estimated, if for every sort of cause they are what they ought to be, must be the same for one sort of cause as for another. The difference is not in the nature of the proof; it is in the nature of the facts required to be proved. There is no difference as between different forms of action, in reason, or even in English law, in respect of the rules relating to the competency of witnesses; nor, in general, to the admissibility or the proof of written documents; nor in respect of any other of the general rules of evidence. What Mr. Phillipps (I mention him only as a representative of the rest) professes, under each of the different forms of action, to tell you, is, what facts, in order to support an action in that form, it is necessary that you should prove.

Now what are these facts? In every cause, either some *right* is claimed, or redress demanded for some *wrong*. By a wrong, is of course meant a violation of a right. Some one or more of those facts, therefore, by which rights are conferred, or taken away, or violated, must at any rate be proved: and if proof of any other fact be necessary, it can only be as evidentiary of these. If, therefore, a man professes to tell you all the facts, some one or more or all of which you must prove, in order to get a decision in your favour; he must furnish you, among other things, with a complete list of all the facts which confer or take away, and all the acts which violate, all the rights, which have been constituted and sanctioned by law. This, accordingly, is what Mr. Phillipps and others of his brethren attempt to do. But, to enumerate the facts which confer or take away rights, is the main business of what is called the civil branch of the law: to enumerate the acts by which rights are violated, in other words to define *offences*, is the main business of the penal branch. What, therefore, the lawyers give us, under the appellation *law of evidence*, is really, in a great part of it, civil and penal law.

Another part of it consists of rules, which are called rules of evidence, but which are really rules of pleading. These are laid down under the guise of instructions for adapting the evidence to the pleadings. It is not often, however, that a man has it in his power to mould the evidence as he pleases: but he always has the power,—that is to say, his lawyers have it for him,—of moulding the pleadings (those on his own side at least) as he pleases. These rules, therefore, for adapting the evidence to the pleadings, are, in fact, rules for adapting the pleadings to the evidence.

Two examples will illustrate the intermixture of the substantive law with the law of evidence; and one of them will also afford a specimen of the intermixture of rules of evidence with rules of pleading.

[98]I.e., Vol. II.

Under the title Burglary, Mr. Starkie begins by saying, that on an indictment for burglary, it is essential to prove, 1st, a felonious breaking and entering; 2ndly, of the dwelling-house; 3rdly, in the night-time; 4thly, with intent to commit a felony.[99] He then proceeds to inform us, that there must be evidence of an actual or constructive breaking: for if the entry was obtained through an open door or window, it is no burglary. That the lifting up a latch, taking out a pane of glass, lifting up folding-doors, breaking a wall or gates which protect the house, the descent down a chimney, the turning a key where the door is locked on the inside,—constitute a sufficient breaking. That where the glass of the window was broken, but the shutter within was not broken, it was doubted whether the breaking was sufficient, and no judgment was given; and so on in the same strain. Who does not see that all this is an attempt,—a lame one, it must be confessed, (which is not the fault of the compiler), but still an attempt,—to supply that *definition* of the offence of burglary, which the substantive law has failed to afford?

The title "burglary" consists of twelve octavo pages, not one line of which is law of evidence.[100] It is all, like the part above extracted, penal law; except three pages, which are occupied in stating how the ownership of the dwelling-house, in which the offence was committed, must be laid in the indictment; and which therefore belong to pleading.

To take our next example from the non-penal branch of the law: when Mr. Phillipps, in treating of the sort of evidence required to support an action of *trover*, informs us, that the plaintiff in this action must prove that he had either the absolute property in the goods, or at least a special property, such as a carrier has, or a consignee or factor, who are responsible over to their principal; and further, that he must shew either his actual possession of the goods, or his right to immediate possession; and that he must prove a wrongful conversion of the goods by the defendant, and that the denial of goods to him who has a right to demand them, is a wrongful conversion; and that the defendant may shew that the property belonged to him, or to another person under whom he claims, or that the plaintiff had before recovered damages against a third person for a conversion of the same goods, or that he was joint tenant of the property with the plaintiff, or tenant in common, or parcener, or had a *lien* on the goods, or a hundred other things which it would be of no use to enumerate;[101] what can be more plain, than that he is here telling us, not by what evidence an action of trover is to be sustained, but in what cases such an action will lie: that he is telling us, in fact, what we are to prove, not by what evidence we are to prove it; that he is enumerating the *investitive* facts, which will give to the plaintiff a right to the service which he claims to be rendered to him at the charge of the defendant; and the *divestitive* facts, by which that right will be taken away from him.

[99]Starkie, *Practical Treatise*, Vol. II, pp. 318–19.
[100]*Ibid.*, pp. 318–30; the "three pages" mentioned below are 325–9 (only a few words on pp. 325 and 329).
[101]Phillipps, Vol. II, pp. 168–73.

Yet, of this sort of matter the whole of the chapter, a few sentences excepted, is composed; and this it is that composes the greatest part of almost all the other chapters in the volume; which yet does not include any sorts of causes except those which, in form at least, are non-penal.

I do not mention this as matter of blame to the institutional writers from whose compilations the above examples are drawn. There are some things really belonging to the subject of evidence, which it is necessary to state in treating separately of each particular kind of action; viz. the nature of the corresponding *preappointed* evidence, (if the law has rendered any such evidence necessary to support the claim that is the subject of the action); and also the nature and amount of the evidence which the law renders sufficient to establish a *primâ facie* case, and throw the *onus probandi* upon the other side. With this matter really belonging to Evidence, it may be convenient to mix up such matters belonging to civil and penal law, as ought to be adverted to by the professional agent of the party who brings the action. The arrangement which is best for the practitioner, or the student of the law, differs as much from that which is best for the philosopher, as the alphabetical arrangement of words in a dictionary differs from the methodical classification of them in a philosophical grammar. (Vol. V, pp. 597–610.)

\*     \*     \*     \*     \*

[*Bentham argues that "the greater the affliction" of the sufferer in a suit appears to a witness, the less likely is "mendacious testimony," one reason being that, "at least in a civilized state of society," the "love of justice . . . may be considered as having more or less hold on every human heart."*]

This love of justice, commonplace moralists, and even a certain class of philosophers, would be likely to call an original principle of human nature. Experience proves the contrary: by any attentive observer of the progress of the human mind in early youth, the gradual growth of it may be traced.

Among the almost innumerable associations by which this love of justice is nourished and fostered, that one to which it probably owes the greatest part of its strength, arises from a conviction which cannot fail to impress itself upon the mind of every human being possessed of an ordinary share of intellect,—the conviction, that if other persons in general were habitually and universally to disregard the rules of justice in their conduct towards him, his destruction would be the speedy consequence: and that by every single instance of disregard to those rules on the part of any one, (himself included), the probability of future violations of the same nature is more or less increased. (Vol. V, p. 638.)

\*     \*     \*     \*     \*

[*In discussing the effect on testimony of "interest derived from sexual connections," Bentham considers the possibility that a wife's adultery will affect her probity in a case involving her husband. He appends the following note, which Mill's comment (in square brackets) concludes:*] Among the Lacedaemonians and Romans, though adultery was no more dispunishable than horse-stealing, a man would lend his wife to a friend as he would his horse. To whatsoever degree illaudable, the custom does not the less prove the rashness of any opinion that should regard adultery on the part of the wife as a proof of the extinction of that partiality, by which, in a cause in which the husband is party, her testimony will naturally be drawn towards the husband's side.

In France, before the revolution, the effect even of notorious adultery in diminishing that partiality was as nothing. (Vol. V, p. 671.)


\*     \*     \*     \*     \*


[*The following note concludes the* Rationale.]

## NOTE ON THE BELGIC CODE[102]

THE CODE recently promulgated for the kingdom of the Netherlands, forms in many respects, so far as regards the law of evidence, an advantageous contrast with most European systems of jurisprudence.

Its superiority is most decided in the department of *preappointed* evidence, particularly under the head of contracts: formalities being, as it is fit they should be, *prescribed*, but not *peremptorily* so. A contract, although informally drawn up, may yet, if signed by the parties, be received in evidence. There is also a system of registration for written contracts. It is an article of this code, that oral evidence is not admissible to prove the existence, or to disprove or add to or alter the contents, of a written contract in form; but to this exclusionary rule there are two curious exceptions, one in favour of the poor, the other in favour of the mercantile classes: if the property dependant on the contract do not exceed the value of one hundred florins, or if the transaction which gave rise to the contract be a commercial transaction, oral evidence may be heard. These exceptions render the code more wise and just, but much less consistent.

In the department of testimonial evidence, the only absolute exclusions are those of the husband or wife of a party to the cause, and all relatives of a party in the direct line: but the relatives and connexions of a party in any collateral line (as well

[102]Code Civil, in *Journal Officiel du Royaume des Pays-Bas*, Vols. 17–21 (1822–26). The Code was laid out in separate acts, not in sequential order, between 14 June, 1822, and 23 March, 1826.

as those of the husband or wife of a party) to the fourth degree, are said to be *reproché* (in the Dutch version of the code, *gewraakt*); as are also the presumptive heir, or servant of a party, all persons directly or indirectly interested (pecuniarily) in the cause, and all persons who have been convicted of robbery, theft, or swindling, or who have suffered any *afflictive* or *infamizing* punishment.

It is probable, though not clearly apparent on the face of the code, that the words *reproché* and *gewraakt* refer to the old rule of the Roman law, by which the evidence of two witnesses is conclusive evidence (*plena probatio*) in certain cases:[103] and the meaning of these phrases probably is, that a witness belonging to any of the classes above enumerated, shall not be considered a witness to *that* purpose, viz. the purpose of forming a *plena probatio*, in conjunction with one other witness. If this be the meaning of the apparently exclusionary rule, it tends, *pro tanto*, to diminish the mischievousness of the monstrous principle of law to which it constitutes an exception.

It seems that the parties themselves cannot be heard in evidence under this code; with this exception, however, that a party may be required to admit or deny his own signature; and several other exceptions closely resembling the *juramentum expurgatorium* and the *juramentum suppletorium* of the Roman law, which have already been explained.[104]

Among the bad rules of Roman law which are adopted in this code, is that which constitutes the evidence of a single witness insufficient to form the ground of a decision. The place of a second witness may, however, in many instances, be supplied by a written document, which is in such cases termed a *commencement de preuve par écrit*.

A rule deserving of imitation in this code, is that which permits children under fifteen years of age to give their testimony without oath. Their title to credence evidently does not depend upon their capacity to understand the nature of a religious ceremony, but upon their power of giving a clear, consistent, and probable narrative of what they have seen or heard.

On the whole, this new code, so far at least as regards the department of evidence, may be pronounced, though still far from perfect, considerably better than either the English system, or the other continental modifications of the Roman law. (Vol. V, pp. 745–7.)

---

[103]See Johann Gottlieb Heineccius (1681–1741), *Elementa juris civilis, secundum ordinem institutionum et pandectarum* (1727), in *Operum ad universam juris prudentiam*, 8 vols. (Geneva: Cramer Heirs and Philibert Bros., 1744–49), Vol. V, p. 374 (IV, XII, iii, 118).

[104]*Ibid.*, p. 245 (III, XII, ii, 28). Bentham's explanation is in Vol. I, pp. 409–10 (Bk. II, Chap. vi).

JAMES MILL'S ANALYSIS
OF THE PHENOMENA OF THE HUMAN MIND

1869

## EDITOR'S NOTE

Extracts from James Mill, *Analysis of the Phenomena of the Human Mind, New Ed. with Notes Illustrative and Critical by Alexander Bain, Andrew Findlater, and George Grote, Edited with Additional Notes by John Stuart Mill*, 2 vols. (London: Longmans, *et al.*, 1869). Identified in Mill's bibliography as "The Preface and many of the notes to the edition of 'Mill's Analysis of the Human Mind' published in 1869" (MacMinn, p. 98). The first edition of the *Analysis*, 2 vols. (London: Baldwin and Cradock), appeared in 1829. In the text below, J.S. Mill's contributions are printed in normal roman type, with the original page references in parentheses at the end. In the original, J.S. Mill's contributions are usually signalled at the end by "Editor" or "Ed."; these are here omitted. Where necessary, passages of James Mill's own text are quoted or summarized in italic type; the summaries are enclosed in square brackets. The one manuscript fragment, in the Yale University John Stuart Mill Papers, is signalled as a variant.

# James Mill's Analysis
# of the Phenomena of the Human Mind

## PREFACE TO THE PRESENT EDITION

IN THE STUDY of Nature, either mental or physical, the aim of the scientific enquirer is to diminish as much as possible the catalogue of ultimate truths. When, without doing violence to facts, he is able to bring one phenomenon within the laws of another; when he can shew that a fact or agency, which seemed to be original and distinct, could have been produced by other known facts and agencies, acting according to their own laws; the enquirer who has arrived at this result, considers himself to have made an important advance in the knowledge of nature, and to have brought science, in that department, a step nearer to perfection. Other accessions to science, however important practically, are, in a scientific point of view, mere additions to the materials: this is something done towards perfecting the structure itself.

The manner in which this scientific improvement takes place is by the resolution of phenomena which are special and complex into others more general and simple. Two cases of this sort may be roughly distinguished, though the distinction between them will not be found on accurate examination to be fundamental. In one case it is the order of the phenomena that is analysed and simplified; in the other it is the phenomena themselves. When the observed facts relating to the weight of terrestrial objects, and those relating to the motion of the heavenly bodies, were found to conform to one and the same law, that of the gravitation of every particle of matter to every other particle with a force varying as the inverse square of the distance, this was an example of the first kind.[1] The order of the phenomena was resolved into a more general law. A great number of the successions which take place in the material world were shewn to be particular cases of a law of causation pervading all Nature. The other class of investigations are those which deal, not with the successions of phenomena, but with the complex phenomena themselves, and disclose to us that the very fact which we are studying is made up of simpler

---

[1]By Isaac Newton (1642–1727), in *Philosophia naturalis principia mathematica* (1687), in *Opera*, ed. Samuel Horsley, 5 vols. (London: Nichols, 1779–85), Vol. III, p. 11 (Prop. II, Theorem ii).

facts: as when the substance Water was found to be an actual compound of two other bodies, hydrogen and oxygen; substances very unlike itself, but both actually present in every one of its particles.[2] By processes like those employed in this case, all the variety of substances which meet our senses and compose the planet on which we live, have been shewn to be constituted by the intimate union, in a certain number of fixed proportions, of some two or more of sixty or seventy bodies, called Elements or Simple Substances, by which is only meant that they have not hitherto been found capable of further decomposition.[3] This last process is known by the name of chemical analysis: but the first mentioned, of which the Newtonian generalization is the most perfect type, is no less analytical. The difference is, that the one analyses substances into simpler substances; the other, laws into simpler laws. The one is partly a physical operation; the other is wholly intellectual.

Both these processes are as largely applicable, and as much required, in the investigation of mental phenomena as of material. And in the one case as in the other, the advance of scientific knowledge may be measured by the progress made in resolving complex facts into simpler ones.

The phenomena of the Mind include multitudes of facts, of an extraordinary degree of complexity. By observing them one at a time with sufficient care, it is possible in the mental, as it is in the material world, to obtain empirical generalizations of limited compass, but of great value for practice. When, however, we find it possible to connect many of these detached generalizations together, by discovering the more general laws of which they are cases, and to the operation of which in some particular sets of circumstances they are due, we gain not only a scientific, but a practical advantage; for we then first learn how far we can rely on the more limited generalizations; within what conditions their truth is confined; by what changes of circumstances they would be defeated or modified.

Not only is the order in which the more complex mental phenomena follow or accompany one another, reducible, by an analysis similar in kind to the Newtonian, to a comparatively small number of laws of succession among simpler facts, connected as cause and effect; but the phenomena themselves can mostly be shown, by an analysis resembling those of chemistry, to be made up of simpler phenomena. "In the mind of man," says Dr. Thomas Brown, in one of his Introductory Lectures,

all is in a state of constant and ever-varying complexity, and a single sentiment may be the slow result of innumerable feelings. There is not a single pleasure, or pain, or thought, or emotion, that may not, by the influence of that associating principle which is afterwards to

[2]By Henry Cavendish (1731–1810) in 1781; three years later he published "Experiments on Air," *Philosophical Transactions of the Royal Society of London*, LXXIV (1784), Pt. I, pp. 119–53.
[3]The periodic table was the work of the Russian chemist Dimitri Ivanovich Mendeléeff (1834–1907), who first announced his discovery in 1869.

come under our consideration, be so connected with other pleasures, or pains, or thoughts, or emotions, as to form with them, for ever after, an union the most intimate. The complex, or seemingly complex, phenomena of thought, which result from the constant operation of this principle of the mind, it is the labour of the intellectual inquirer to analyse, as it is the labour of the chemist to reduce the compound bodies on which he operates, however close and intimate their combination may be, to their constituent elements. . . . From the very instant of its first existence, the mind is constantly exhibiting phenomena more and more complex: sensations, thoughts, emotions, all mingling together, and almost every feeling modifying, in some greater or less degree, the feelings that succeed it; and as, in chemistry, it often happens that the qualities of the separate ingredients of a compound body are not recognizable by us in the apparently different qualities of the compound itself,—so in this spontaneous chemistry of the mind, the compound sentiment that results from the association of former feelings has, in many cases, on first consideration, so little resemblance to these constituents of it, as formerly existing in their elementary state, that it requires the most attentive reflection to separate, and evolve distinctly to others, the assemblages which even a few years may have produced.[4]

It is, therefore, "scarcely possible to advance even a single step, in intellectual physics, without the necessity of performing some sort of analysis, by which we reduce to simpler elements some complex feeling that seems to us virtually to involve them."[5]

These explanations define and characterize the task which was proposed to himself by the author of the present treatise, and which he concisely expressed by naming his work an *Analysis of the Phenomena of the Human Mind*. It is an attempt to reach the simplest elements which by their combination generate the manifold complexity of our mental states, and to assign the laws of those elements, and the elementary laws of their combination, from which laws, the subordinate ones which govern the compound states are consequences and corollaries.

The conception of the problem did not, of course, originate with the author; he merely applied to mental science the idea of scientific inquiry which had been matured by the successful pursuit, for many generations, of the knowledge of external nature. Even in the particular path by which he endeavoured to reach the end, he had eminent precursors. The analytic study of the facts of the human mind began with Aristotle; it was first carried to a considerable height by Hobbes and Locke, who are the real founders of that view of the Mind which regards the greater part of its intellectual structure as having been built up by Experience. These three philosophers have all left their names identified with the great fundamental law of Association of Ideas;[6] yet none of them saw far enough to perceive that it is through this law that Experience operates in moulding our thoughts and forming

[4]Thomas Brown (1778–1820), *Lectures on the Philosophy of the Human Mind* (1820), 19th ed. (1 vol. issue) (Edinburgh: Black; London: Longman, 1851), pp. 60, 62.

[5]*Ibid.*, p. 60.

[6]The references are general to the works of the great Greek exponent of analytic thought, Aristotle (384–322 B.C.), and the two major founders of British philosophy of mind, Thomas Hobbes (1588–1679), and John Locke.

our thinking powers. Dr. Hartley was the man of genius who first clearly discerned
that this is the key to the explanation of the more complex mental phenomena,
though he, too, was indebted for the original conjecture to an otherwise forgotten
thinker, Mr. Gay.[7] Dr. Hartley's treatise (*Observations on Man*) goes over the
whole field of the mental phenomena, both intellectual and emotional, and points
out the way in which, as he thinks, sensations, ideas of sensation, and association,
generate and account for the principal complications of our mental nature. If this
doctrine is destined to be accepted as, in the main, the true theory of the Mind, to
Hartley will always belong the glory of having originated it. But his book made
scarcely any impression upon the thought of his age. He incumbered his theory of
Association with a premature hypothesis respecting the physical mechanism of
sensation and thought;[8] and even had he not done so, his mode of exposition was
little calculated to make any converts but such as were capable of working out the
system for themselves from a few hints. His book is made up of hints rather than of
proofs. It is like the production of a thinker who has carried his doctrines so long in
his mind without communicating them, that he has become accustomed to leap
over many of the intermediate links necessary for enabling other persons to reach
his conclusions, and who, when at last he sits down to write, is unable to recover
them. It was another great disadvantage to Hartley's theory, that its publication so
nearly coincided with the commencement of the reaction against the Experience
psychology, provoked by the hardy scepticism of Hume. From these various
causes, though the philosophy of Hartley never died out, having been kept alive by
Priestley, the elder Darwin,[9] and their pupils, it was generally neglected, until at
length the author of the present work gave it an importance that it can never again
lose. One distinguished thinker, Dr. Thomas Brown, regarded some of the mental
phenomena from a point of view similar to Hartley's, and all that he did for
psychology was in this direction; but he had read Hartley's work either very
superficially, or not at all: he seems to have derived nothing from it, and though he

[7]The basic text for the Associationist philosophers was David Hartley (1705–57),
*Observations on Man, His Frame, His Duty, and His Expectations*, 2 pts. (Bath: Leake and
Frederick; London: Hitch and Austen, 1749). The treatise by John Gay (1699–1745),
*Dissertation Concerning the Fundamental Principle and Immediate Criterion of Virtue*,
was published as a preface to William King (1650–1729), *Essay on the Origin of Evil*
(Cambridge: Thurlbourn, 1731).
[8]Hartley, *Observations*, Pt. I, pp. 7–9 and 16–34. This perceived defect in the work led
Joseph Priestley (1773–1804), mentioned below, to excise the physiological account in his
edition, *Hartley's Theory of the Human Mind* (London: Johnson, 1775), which J.S. Mill
and his friends used during their intense study of the subject (see *Autobiography*, *CW*, Vol.
I, pp. 125–7).
[9]Erasmus Darwin (1731–1802), Charles Darwin's grandfather, in his *Zoonomia; or, The
Laws of Organic Life* (1794–96), 3rd ed., 4 vols. (London: Johnson, 1801), esp. Vol. I,
pp. 61–6 and 127–34.

made some successful analyses of mental phenomena by means of the laws of association, he rejected, or ignored, the more searching applications of those laws; resting content, when he arrived at the more difficult problems, with mere verbal generalizations, such as his futile explanations by what he termed "relative suggestion."[10] Brown's psychology was no outcome of Hartley's; it must be classed as an original but feebler effort in a somewhat similar direction.

It is to the author of the present volumes that the honour belongs of being the reviver and second founder of the Association psychology. Great as is this merit, it was but one among many services which he rendered to his generation and to mankind. When the literary and philosophical history of this century comes to be written as it deserves to be, very few are the names figuring in it to whom as high a place will be awarded as to James Mill. In the vigour and penetration of his intellect he has had few superiors in the history of thought: in the wide compass of the human interests which he cared for and served, he was almost equally remarkable: and the energy and determination of his character, giving effect to as single-minded an ardour for the improvement of mankind and of human life as I believe has ever existed, make his life a memorable example. All his work as a thinker was devoted to the service of mankind, either by the direct improvement of their beliefs and sentiments, or by warring against the various influences which he regarded as obstacles to their progress: and while he put as much conscientious thought and labour into everything he did, as if he had never done anything else, the subjects on which he wrote took as wide a range as if he had written without any labour at all. That the same man should have been the author of the *History of India* and of the present treatise, is of itself sufficiently significant. The former of those works, which by most men would have been thought a sufficient achievement for a whole literary life, may be said without exaggeration to have been the commencement of rational thinking on the subject of India: and by that, and his subsequent labours as an administrator of Indian interests under the East India Company, he effected a great amount of good, and laid the foundation of much more, to the many millions of Asiatics for whose bad or good government his country is responsible. The same great work is full of far-reaching ideas on the practical interests of the world; and while forming an important chapter in the history and philosophy of civilization (a subject which had not then been so scientifically studied as it has been since) it is one of the most valuable contributions yet made even to the English history of the period it embraces. If, in addition to the *History* and to the present treatise, all the author's minor writings were collected; the outline treatises on nearly all the great branches of moral and political science which he drew up for the *Supplement to the Encyclopaedia*

[10]"On the Phenomena of Relative Suggestion" is the main title of Lecture XLV in Brown's *Lectures*.

*Britannica*, and his countless contributions to many periodical works;[11] although advanced thinkers have outgrown some of his opinions, and include, on many subjects, in their speculations, a wider range of considerations than his, every one would be astonished at the variety of his topics, and the abundance of the knowledge he exhibited respecting them all. One of his minor services was, that he was the first to put together in a compact and systematic form, and in a manner adapted to learners, the principles of Political Economy[12] as renovated by the genius of Ricardo: whose great work,[13] it may be mentioned by the way, would probably never have seen the light, if his intimate and attached friend Mr. Mill had not encouraged and urged him, first to commit to paper his profound thoughts, and afterwards to send them forth to the world. Many other cases might be mentioned in which Mr. Mill's private and personal influence was a means of doing good, hardly inferior to his public exertions. Though, like all who value their time for higher purposes, he went little into what is called society, he helped, encouraged, and not seldom prompted, many of the men who were most useful in their generation: from his obscure privacy he was during many years of his life the soul of what is now called the advanced Liberal party; and such was the effect of his conversation, and of the tone of his character, on those who were within reach of its influence, that many, then young, who have since made themselves honoured in the world by a valuable career, look back to their intercourse with him as having had a considerable share in deciding their course through life. The most distinguished of them all, Mr. Grote, has put on record, in a recent publication, his sense of these obligations, in terms equally honourable to both.[14] As a converser, Mr. Mill has had few equals; as an argumentative converser, in modern times probably none. All his mental resources seemed to be at his command at any moment, and were then freely employed in removing difficulties which in his writings for the public he often did not think it worth while to notice. To a logical acumen which has always been acknowledged, he united a clear appreciation of the practical side of things, for which he did not always receive credit from those

[11]For a comprehensive listing of these writings, most of which have never been collected, see Robert A. Fenn, *James Mill's Political Thought* (New York and London: Garland, 1987), pp. 161–85. The best known of his contributions from 1816 to 1823 to the *Supplement* to the 4th, 5th, and 6th editions of the *Encyclopaedia Britannica*, including "Government," "Jurisprudence," "Liberty of the Press," "Prisons and Prison Discipline," "Colonies," "Law of Nature," and "Education," were gathered in much discussed volumes (esp. *Essays* [1825]) in the 1820s.

[12]Mill, *Elements of Political Economy* (London: Baldwin, *et al.*, 1821), with 2nd ed., revised, 1824, and 3rd ed., revised, 1826.

[13]David Ricardo (1772–1823), economist and M.P., *On the Principles of Political Economy and Taxation* (London: Murray, 1817).

[14]George Grote (1794–1871), historian of Greece and M.P., close friend of J.S. Mill, "John Stuart Mill on the Philosophy of Sir William Hamilton," *Westminster Review*, LXXXV (Jan. 1866), 4–5.

who had no personal knowledge of him, but which made a deep impression on those who were acquainted with the official correspondence of the East India Company conducted by him. The moral qualities which shone in his conversation were, if possible, more valuable to those who had the privilege of sharing it, than even the intellectual. They were precisely such as young men of cultivated intellect, with good aspirations but a character not yet thoroughly formed, are likely to derive most benefit from. A deeply rooted trust in the general progress of the human race, joined with a good sense which made him never build unreasonable or exaggerated hopes on any one event or contingency; an habitual estimate of men according to their real worth as sources of good to their fellow-creatures, and an unaffected contempt for the weaknesses or temptations that divert them from that object,—making those with whom he conversed feel how painful it would be to them to be counted by him among such backsliders; a sustained earnestness, in which neither vanity nor personal ambition had any part, and which spread from him by a sympathetic contagion to those who had sufficient moral preparation to value and seek the opportunity; this was the mixture of qualities which made his conversation almost unrivalled in its salutary moral effect. He has been accused of asperity, and there was asperity in some few of his writings; but no party spirit, personal rivalry, or wounded *amour-propre* ever stirred it up.[15] Even when he had received direct personal offence, he was the most placable of men. The bitterest and ablest attack ever publicly made on him was that which was the immediate cause of the introduction of Mr. Macaulay into public life.[16] He felt it keenly at the time, but with a quite impersonal feeling, as he would have felt anything that he thought unjustly said against any opinion or cause which was dear to him; and within a very few years afterwards he was on terms of personal friendship with its author, as Lord Macaulay himself, in a very creditable passage of the preface to his collected *Essays*, has, in feeling terms, commemorated.[17]

At an early period of Mr. Mill's philosophical life, Hartley's work had taken a strong hold of his mind; and in the maturity of his powers he formed and executed the purpose of following up Hartley's leading thought, and completing what that thinker had begun. The result was the present work, which is not only an immense advance on Hartley's in the qualities which facilitate the access of recondite

[15]The reference is undoubtedly to the remarks in Bowring's edition of Bentham, given greater currency by repetition in the *Edinburgh Review*, to which J.S. Mill replied in his "Letter to the Editor of the Edinburgh Review" (Jan. 1844), *CW*, Vol. I, pp. 533–8.

[16]Thomas Babington Macaulay (1800–59) attacked James Mill in his series, "Mill's Essay on Government: Utilitarian Logic and Politics," "Bentham's Defence of Mill: Utilitarian System of Philosophy," and "Utilitarian Theory of Government, and the 'Greatest Happiness Principle,'" *Edinburgh Review*, XLIX (Mar. and June 1829), 159–89 and 273–99, and L (Oct. 1829), 99–125.

[17]Macaulay, "Preface," *Critical and Historical Essays*, 3 vols. (London: Longman, *et al.*, 1843), Vol. I, p. viii.

thoughts to minds to which they are new, but attains an elevation far beyond Hartley's in the thoughts themselves. Compared with it, Hartley's is little more than a sketch, though an eminently suggestive one: often rather showing where to seek for the explanation of the more complex mental phenomena, than actually explaining them. The present treatise makes clear, much that Hartley left obscure: it possesses the great secret for clearness, though a secret commonly neglected—it bestows an extra amount of explanation and exemplification on the most elementary parts. It analyses many important mental phenomena which Hartley passed over, and analyses more completely and satisfactorily most of those of which he commenced the analysis. In particular, the author was the first who fully understood and expounded (though the germs of this as of all the rest of the theory are in Hartley) the remarkable case of Inseparable Association: and inasmuch as many of the more difficult analyses of the mental phenomena can only be performed by the aid of that doctrine, much had been left for him to analyse.

I am far from thinking that the more recondite specimens of analysis in this work are always successful, or that the author has not left something to be corrected as well as much to be completed by his successors. The completion has been especially the work of two distinguished thinkers in the present generation, Professor Bain and Mr. Herbert Spencer; in the writings of both of whom, the Association Psychology has reached a still higher development.[18] The former of these has favoured me with his invaluable collaboration in annotating the present work. In the annotations it has been our object not only to illustrate and enforce, but to criticise, where criticism seemed called for. What there is in the work that seems to need correction, arises chiefly from two causes. First, the imperfection of physiological science at the time at which it was written, and the much greater knowledge since acquired of the functions of our nervous organism and their relations with the mental operations. Secondly, an opening was made for some mistakes, and occasional insufficiency of analysis, by a mental quality which the author exhibits not unfrequently in his speculations, though as a practical thinker both on public and on private matters it was quite otherwise; a certain impatience of detail. The bent of his mind was towards that, in which also his greatest strength lay; in seizing the larger features of a subject—the commanding laws which govern and connect many phenomena. Having reached these, he sometimes gives himself up to the current of thoughts which those comprehensive laws suggest, not stopping to guard himself carefully in the minutiae of their application, nor devoting much of his thoughts to anticipating all the objections that could be made,

[18]Alexander Bain (1818–1903), the main philosophic disciple and biographer of both James and J.S. Mill, developed associationist theory in his *The Senses and the Intellect* (1855), 2nd ed. (London: Longmans, Green, 1864), and *The Emotions and the Will* (1859), 2nd ed. (London: Longmans, Green, 1865). Herbert Spencer (1820–1903), the synthetic psychologist and sociologist, contributed to associationism especially in his *Principles of Psychology* (London: Longman, *et al.*, 1855).

though the necessity of replying to some of them might have led him to detect imperfections in his analyses. From this cause (as it appears to me), he has occasionally gone further in the pursuit of simplification, and in the reduction of the more recondite mental phenomena to the more elementary, than I am able to follow him; and has left some of his opinions open to objections, which he has not afforded the means of answering. When this appeared to Mr. Bain or myself to be the case, we have made such attempts as we were able to place the matter in a clearer light; and one or other, or both, have supplied what our own investigations or those of others have provided, towards correcting any shortcomings in the theory.

Mr. Findlater, of Edinburgh, Editor of *Chambers' Cyclopaedia*, has kindly communicated, from the rich stores of his philological knowledge, the corrections required by the somewhat obsolete philology which the author had borrowed from Horne Tooke.[19] For the rectification of an erroneous statement respecting the relation of the Aristotelian doctrine of General Ideas to the Platonic, and for some other contributions in which historical is combined with philosophical interest, I am indebted to the illustrious historian of Greece and of the Greek philosophy.[20] Mr. Grote's, Mr. Bain's and Mr. Findlater's notes are distinguished by their initials; my own, as those of the Editor.

The question presented itself, whether the annotations would be most useful, collected at the end of the work, or appended to the chapters or passages to which they more particularly relate. Either plan has its recommendations, but those of the course which I have adopted seemed to me on the whole to preponderate. The reader can, if he thinks fit, (and, if he is a real student, I venture to recommend that he should do so) combine the advantages of both modes, by giving a first careful

[19]Andrew Findlater (1810–85), Scots teacher and editor, contributed several notes dealing with semantic and philological corrections of ideas and terminology taken by James Mill from John Horne Tooke (1736–1812), Radical politician and nominalist philosopher, Επεα πτεροεντα; or, *The Diversions of Purley* (1786), 2nd ed., 2 vols. (London: Johnson, 1798, 1805). See esp. *Analysis*, Vol. I, pp. 216–22.

[20]In a lengthy note (Vol. I, pp. 271–87, esp. pp. 273–4), Grote deals with "General Ideas" in Aristotle and Plato. He makes special reference to Aristotle's *Metaphysics*, Bk. I, Sect. ix, 990[b] and 991[a] (trans. Hugh Tredennick, 2 vols. [London: Heinemann; New York: Putnam's Sons, 1933], Vol. I, pp. 62, 66–8), and *Posterior Analytics*, Bk. I, Sect. xi, 77[a], and Sect. xxiv, 85[a-b] (trans. Hugh Tredennick and E.S. Forster [London: Heinemann; Cambridge, Mass.: Harvard University Press, 1960], pp. 74, 136–40); and to Plato's *Parmenides*, 126[a]–137[b] (in *Cratylus, Parmenides, Greater Hippias, Lesser Hippias*, trans. H.N. Fowler [London: Heinemann; New York: Macmillan, 1914], pp. 198–236), *Phaedo*, 74[a]–75[b] (in *Euthyphro, Apology, Crito, Phaedo, Phaedrus*, trans. H.N. Fowler [London: Heinemann; Cambridge, Mass.: Harvard University Press, 1947], pp. 256–60), *Republic*, Bk. VII, Sect. ii, 514[a]–517[a] (trans. Paul Shorey, 2 vols. [London: Heinemann; Cambridge, Mass.: Harvard University Press, 1946], Vol. II, pp. 118–28), and *Symposium*, 210[e]–211[d] (in *Lysis, Symposium, Gorgias*, trans. W.R.M. Lamb [London: Heinemann: New York: Putnam's Sons, 1925], pp. 204–6).

reading to the book itself, or at all events to every successive chapter of the book, without paying any attention to the annotations. No other mode of proceeding will give perfectly fair play to the author, whose thoughts will in this manner have as full an opportunity of impressing themselves on the mind, without having their consecutiveness broken in upon by any other person's thoughts, as they would have had if simply republished without comment. When the student has done all he can with the author's own exposition—has possessed himself of the ideas, and felt, perhaps, some of the difficulties, he will be in a better position for profiting by any aid that the notes may afford, and will be in less danger of accepting, without due examination, the opinion of the last comer as the best.

*   *   *   *   *

[*James Mill, dealing with smell as a sensation, remarks:*] *The word smell, beside denoting the* sensation *and the* object, *denotes also the* organ, *in such phrases as the following; "Sight and Hearing are two of the inlets of my knowledge, and Smell is a third;" "The faculty by which I become sensible of odour is my Smell."*

It may be questioned whether, in the phrases here cited, the word *Smell* stands for the olfactory organ. It would perhaps be most correct to say, that in these cases it denotes the abstract capacity of smelling, rather than the concrete physical instrument. Even when smell is said to be one of the five senses, it may fairly be doubted whether a part of the meaning intended is, that it is one of the five *organs* of sensation. Nothing more seems to be meant, than that it is one of five distinguishable *modes* of having sensations, whatever the intrinsic difference between those modes may be.

In the author's footnote he recognises that the abstract power of smelling enters into this particular application of the word *Smell*; and refers to a subsequent part of the treatise for the meaning of Power.[21] But he thinks that along with the power, or as part of the conception of Power, the material organ is also signified. It seems to

---

[21] [James Mill's note (Vol. I, p. 15) reads:] It will naturally occur to some of my readers, that, in the term sense of smelling, the idea of power is also included. They will say, that when we speak of the sense of smelling, we mean not only the organ, but the function of the organ, or its power of producing a certain effect. This is undoubtedly true; but when the real meaning of the language is evolved, it only amounts to that which is delivered in the text. For what does any person mean when he says that, in the sense of smelling, he has the power of smelling? Only this, that he has an organ, and that when the object of that organ is presented to it, sensation is the consequence. In all this, there is nothing but the organ, the object, and the sensation, conceived in a certain order. This will more fully appear when the meaning of the relative terms, cause and effect, has been explained. [See Vol. II, pp. 42–3, for the discussion of relative terms; for "power," to which J.S. Mill refers, see Vol. II, pp. 84–5, and p. 198 below.]

me that the organ does not enter in either of these modes, into the signification of the word. We can imagine ourselves ignorant that we possess physical organs; or aware that we possess them, but not aware that our sensations of smell are connected with them. Yet on either of these suppositions the "power of smelling" would be perfectly intelligible, and would have the same meaning to us which it has now. (Vol. I, p. 14.)

\* \* \* \* \*

[*The final sentence of the section on hearing reads:*] *"Sense of hearing" is thus seen to be the name of a very complex idea, including five distinguishable ingredients, the idea of the organ of hearing, the idea of the sensation, the idea of the object of hearing, the idea of a synchronous order, and the idea of a successive order.*

In the case of hearing, as of smell, one of the ambiguities brought to notice by the author is of questionable reality. It is doubtful if *hearing* is ever used as a name of the organ. To the question supposed in the text, "by which of my organs do I have the knowledge of sound" the correct answer would surely be, not "my hearing"[22]—an expression which, so applied, could only be accepted as elliptical,—but "my organ of hearing," or (still better) "my ear." Again, the phrase "I have the sense of hearing" signifies that I have a capacity of hearing, and that this capacity is classed as one of sense, or in other words, that the feelings to which it has reference belong to the class Sensations: but the organ, though a necessary condition of my having the sensations, does not seem to be implied in the name. (Vol. I, pp. 19–20.)

\* \* \* \* \*

[*Having averred that* sight *is used as "a name of the object," James Mill goes on to say that it also "is sometimes employed as a name of the organ." He then says:*] *An old man informs us, that his sight is failing, meaning that his eyes are failing.*

The example given does not seem to me to prove that *sight* is ever employed as a name of the organ. When an old man says that his sight is failing, he means only that he is less capable of seeing. His eyes might be failing in some other respect, when he would not say that his sight was failing. The term "sense of sight," like

[22]Vol. I, p. 18.

sense of hearing or of smell, stands, as it seems to me, for the capability, without reference to the organ. (Vol. I, p. 23.)

\*    \*    \*    \*    \*

[*To illustrate his belief that* vision *denotes the object as well as the feeling, James Mill says:*] *What vision was that? would be a very intelligible question, on the sudden appearance and disappearance of something which attracted the eye.*

*Vision*, I believe, is used to denote the object of sight, only when it is supposed that this object is something unreal, *i.e.*, that it has not any extended and resisting substance behind it: or rhetorically, to signify that the object looks more like a phantom than a reality; as when Burke calls Marie Antoinette, as once seen by him, a delightful vision.[23] (Vol. I, p. 24.)

\*    \*    \*    \*    \*

[*James Mill observes that the "feelings" of taste are very often united with those of smell,*] *the two organs being often affected by the same thing, at the same time. In that case, though we have two sensations, they are so intimately blended as to seem but one; and the flavour of the apple, the flavour of the wine, appears to be a simple sensation, though compounded of taste and smell.*

Some physiologists have been of opinion that a large proportion of what are classed as tastes, including all flavours, as distinguished from the generic tastes of sweet, sour, bitter, etc., are really affections of the nerves of smell, and are mistaken for tastes only because they are experienced along with tastes, as a consequence of taking food into the mouth.[24] (Vol. I, p. 25.)

\*    \*    \*    \*    \*

[23]In his *Reflections on the Revolution in France* (1790), Edmund Burke (1729–97) says: "It is now sixteen or seventeen years since I saw the queen of France [Marie Antoinette (1755–93)], then the dauphiness, at Versailles; and surely never lighted on this orb, which she hardly seemed to touch, a more delightful vision" (*Works*, 8 vols. [London: Dodsley, and Rivington, 1792–1827], Vol. III, p. 110).

[24]See, e.g., William Benjamin Carpenter (1813–85), *Principles of Human Physiology* (1842), 6th ed., ed. Henry Power (London: Churchill, 1864), pp. 617 and 622; and Balthasar Anthelme Richerand (1779–1840), *Elements of Physiology*, trans. G.J.M. de Lys, ed. with notes by James Copland, 4th ed. (London: Longman, *et al.*, 1824), p. 302n (Copland's note).

[*Concerning* taste, *James Mill says there is the same complexity of meaning as in the other terms of sensation, including reference to the organ.*]

The statement that "taste" is sometimes employed as a name of the organ, seems to me, like the similar statements respecting the names of our other senses, disputable. (Vol. I, p. 27.)

\*     \*     \*     \*     \*

[*Once more James Mill says that a term,* touch, *refers to the object.*] *If I were to call a piece of fine and brilliant velvet a fine sight, another person might say, it is a fine touch as well as fine sight.*

It is more true of the word *touch*, than of the names of our other senses, that it is occasionally employed to denote the organ of touch; because that organ, being the whole surface of the body, has not, like the organs of the special senses, a compact distinctive name. But it may be doubted if the word *touch* ever stands for the object of touch. If a person made use of the phrase in the text, "it is a fine touch as well as a fine sight," he would probably be regarded as purchasing an epigrammatic turn of expression at the expense of some violence to language. (Vol. I, p. 32.)

\*     \*     \*     \*     \*

[*James Mill explains his use of the word* connotes *in the following footnote, to which J.S. Mill's note is appended.*] *The use, which I shall make, of the term* connotation, *needs to be explained. There is a large class of words, which denote two things, both together; but the one perfectly distinguishable from the other. Of these two things, also, it is observable, that such words express the one,* primarily, *as it were; the other, in a way which may be called* secondary. *Thus,* white, *in the phrase* white horse, *denotes two things, the colour, and the horse; but it denotes the colour* primarily, *the horse* secondarily. *We shall find it very convenient, to say, therefore, that it* notes *the primary,* connotes *the secondary, signification.*

Reasons will be assigned further on, why the words *to connote* and *connotation* had better be employed, not as here indicated, but in a different and more special sense.[25] (Vol. I, p. 34.)

\*     \*     \*     \*     \*

[25]See pp. 145 and 148–51 below.

[*With reference to sensations of "disorganization," caused by lacerations, cuts, bruises, burnings, poisonings, inflammation, etc., James Mill comments:*] *Most of those sensations are of the painful kind; though some are otherwise. Some slight, or locally minute inflammations, produce a sensation called itching, which is far from disagreeable, as appears from the desire to scratch, which excites it.*

The author, in this passage, uses the word *itching* out of its ordinary sense; making it denote the pleasant sensation accompanying the relief by scratching, instead of the slightly painful, and sometimes highly irritating, sensation which the scratching relieves. (Vol. I, pp. 37–8.)

*   *   *   *   *

[*James Mill points out that*] *there are some muscles of the body in constant and vehement action, as the heart, of the feelings attendant upon the action of which we seem to have no cognisance at all. That this is no argument against the existence of those feelings, will be made apparent, by the subsequent explanation of other phenomena, in which the existence of certain feelings, and an acquired incapacity of attending to them, are out of dispute.*

The paradox, of feelings which we have no cognisance of—feelings which are not felt—will be discussed at large in a future note.[26] (Vol. I, p. 42.)

*   *   *   *   *

[*James Mill, having asserted that just as each sense has "its separate class of sensations, so each has its separate class of ideas" (Vol. I, p. 54), argues that in the case of muscular action, the will is involved as antecedent.*] *Thus the idea of resistance is the thought, or idea, of the feelings we have, when we will to contract certain muscles, and feel the contraction impeded.*

Rather, when we will to contract certain muscles, and the contraction takes place, but is not followed by the accustomed movement of the limb; what follows, instead, being a sensation of pressure, proportioned to the degree of the contraction. It is not the muscular contraction itself which is impeded by the resisting object: that contraction takes place: but the outward effect which it was

[26]See pp. 138–41 below.

the tendency, and perhaps the purpose, of the muscular contraction to produce, fails to be produced. (Vol. I, p. 58.)

\*     \*     \*     \*     \*

*Hunger, and thirst, are also names of ideas, which chiefly refer to sensations in the same part of our system.*[27]

I venture to think that it is not a philosophically correct mode of expression, to speak of indigestion, or of hunger and thirst, as names of ideas. Hunger and thirst are names of definite sensations; and indigestion is a name of a large group of sensations, held together by very complicated laws of causation. If it be objected, that the word indigestion, and even the words hunger and thirst, comprehend in their meaning other elements than the immediate sensations; that the meaning, for instance, of hunger, includes a deficiency of food, the meaning of indigestion a derangement of the functions of the digestive organs; it still remains true that these additional portions of meaning are physical phenomena, and are not our thoughts or ideas of physical phenomena; and must, therefore, in the general partition of human consciousness between sensations and ideas, take their place with the former, and not with the latter. (Vol. I, p. 60.)

\*     \*     \*     \*     \*

*[J.S. Mill's footnote is appended to the end of Chap. ii, "Ideas" (following a long note by Bain).]*

A question which, as far as I know, has been passed over by psychologists, but which ought not to be left unanswered, is this: Can we have ideas of ideas? We have sensations, and we have copies of these sensations, called ideas of them: can we also have copies of these copies, constituting a second order of ideas, two removes instead of one from sensation?

Every one will admit that we can think of a thought. We remember ourselves remembering, or imagine ourselves remembering, an object or an event, just as we remember or imagine ourselves seeing one. But in the case of a simple idea of sensation, *i.e.* the idea or remembrance of a single undivided sensation, there seems nothing to distinguish the idea of the idea, from the idea of the sensation itself. When I imagine myself thinking of the colour of snow, I am not aware of any

---

[27]A corrective footnote by Alexander Bain intervenes between James Mill's sentence and J.S. Mill's footnote.

difference, even in degree of intensity, between the image then present to my mind of the white colour, and the image present when I imagine myself to be seeing the colour.

The case, however, is somewhat different with those combinations of simple ideas which have never been presented to my mind otherwise than as ideas. I have an idea of Pericles;[28] but it is derived only from the testimony of history: the real Pericles never was present to my senses. I have an idea of Hamlet, and of Falstaff;[29] combinations which, though made up of ideas of sensation, never existed at all in the world of sense; they never were anything more than ideas in any mind. Yet, having had these combinations of ideas presented to me through the words of Shakespeare, I have formed what is properly an idea not of an outward object, but of an idea in Shakespeare's mind; and I may communicate my idea to others, whose idea will then be an idea of an idea in my mind. My idea of Pericles, or my idea of any person now alive whom I have never seen, differs from these in the circumstance that I am persuaded that a real object corresponding to the idea does now, or did once, exist in the world of sensation: but as I did not derive my idea from the object, but from some other person's words, my idea is not a copy of the original, but a copy (more or less imperfect) of some other person's copy: it is an idea of an idea.

Although, however, the complex idea I have of an object which never was presented to my senses, is rightly described as an idea of an idea; my remembrance of a complex idea which I have had before, does not seem to me to differ from the remembered idea as an idea differs from a sensation. There is a distinction between my visual idea of Mont Blanc and the actual sight of the mountain, which I do not find between my remembrance of Falstaff and the original impression from which it was derived. My present thought of Falstaff seems to me not a copy but a repetition of the original idea; a repetition which may be dimmed by distance, or which may, on the contrary, be heightened by intermediate processes of thought; may have lost some of its features by lapse of time, and may have acquired others by reference to the original sources; but which resembles the first impression not as the thought of an object resembles the sight of it, but as a second or third sight of an object resembles the first. This question will meet us again in the psychological examination of Memory, the theory of which is in no small degree dependent upon it. (Vol. I, pp. 68–9.)

\*    \*    \*    \*    \*

[28]The Greek statesman and orator (d. 429 B.C.)
[29]Central characters in, respectively, *Hamlet* and *Henry IV Part I*, by Shakespeare. (Falstaff appears also in *Henry IV Part II* and *The Merry Wives of Windsor*, but Mill's later reference is specific to *Henry IV Part I*.)

*[James Mill avers that] we have three cases of vividness, of which we can speak with some precision: the case of sensations, as compared with ideas; the case of pleasurable and painful sensations, and their ideas, as compared with those which are not pleasurable or painful; and the case of the more recent, compared with the more remote.*

If it be admitted that in the three cases here specified the word *vividness*, as applied to our impressions, has a definite meaning, it seems to follow that this meaning may be extended in the way of analogy, to other cases than these. There are, for example, sensations which differ from some other sensations like fainter feelings of the same kind, in much the same manner as the idea of a sensation differs from the sensation itself: and we may, by extension, call these sensations less vivid. Again, one idea may differ from another idea in the same sort of way in which the idea of a sensation had long ago differs from that of a similar sensation received recently: that is, it is a more faded copy—its colours and its outlines are more effaced: this idea may fairly be said to be less vivid than the other.

The author himself, a few pages farther on, speaks of some complex ideas as being more "obscure" than others, merely on account of their greater complexity.[30] Obscurity, indeed, in this case, means a different quality from the absence of vividness, but a quality fully as indefinite.

Mr. Bain, whose view of the subject will be found further on,[31] draws a fundamental distinction (already indicated in a former note)[32] between the attributes which belong to a sensation regarded in an intellectual point of view, as a portion of our knowledge, and those which belong to the element of Feeling contained in it; Feeling being here taken in the narrower acceptation of the word, that in which Feeling is opposed to Intellect or Thought. To sensations in their intellectual aspect Mr. Bain considers the term *vividness* to be inapplicable: they can only be distinct or indistinct. He reserves the word *vividness* to express the degree of intensity of the sensation, considered in what may be called its emotional aspect, whether of pleasure, of pain, or of mere excitement.

Whether we accept this restriction or not, it is in any case certain, that the property of producing a strong and durable association without the aid of repetition, belongs principally to our pleasures and pains. The more intense the pain or pleasure, the more promptly and powerfully does it associate itself with its accompanying circumstances, even with those which are only accidentally present. In the cases mentioned in the text, a single occurrence of the painful sensation is sufficient to produce an association, which neither time can wear out nor counter-associations dissolve, between the idea of the pain and the ideas of the

---

[30]Vol. I, p. 94.
[31]*Ibid.*, pp. 116–17.
[32]*Ibid.*, pp. 62–8.

sensations which casually accompanied it in that one instance, however intrinsically indifferent these may be. (Vol. I, pp. 85–6.)

*    *    *    *    *

[*James Mill asserts that there are some ideas we cannot "combine," because*] *a strong association excludes whatever is opposite to it. I cannot associate the two ideas of assafoetida, and the taste of sugar. Why? Because the idea of assafoetida is so strongly associated with the idea of another taste, that the idea of that other taste rises in combination with the idea of assafoetida, and of course the idea of sugar does not rise. I have one idea associated with the word* pain. *Why can I not associate pleasure with the word* pain? *Because another indissoluble association springs up, and excludes it. This is, therefore, only a case of indissoluble association; but one of much importance, as we shall find when we come to the exposition of some of the more complicated of our mental phenomena.*

Some further elucidation seems needful of what is here said, in so summary a manner, respecting ideas which it is not in our power to combine: an inability which it is essential to the analysis of some of the more complex phenomena of mind that we should understand the meaning of. The explanation is indicated, but hardly more than indicated, in the text.

It seems to follow from the universal law of association, that any idea could be associated with any other idea, if the corresponding sensations, or even the ideas themselves, were presented in juxtaposition with sufficient frequency. If, therefore, there are ideas which cannot be associated with each other, it must be because there is something that prevents this juxtaposition. Two conditions hence appear to be required, to render ideas incapable of combination. First, the sensations must be incapable of being had together. If we cannot associate the taste of assafoetida with the taste of sugar, it is implied, that we cannot have the taste of assafoetida along with the taste of sugar. If we could, a sufficient experience would enable us to associate the ideas. Here, therefore, is one necessary condition of the impossibility of associating certain ideas with one another. But this condition, though necessary, is not sufficient. We are but too capable of associating ideas together though the corresponding external facts are really incompatible. In the case of many errors, prejudices, and superstitions, two ideas are so closely and obstinately associated, that the man cannot, at least for the time, help believing that the association represents a real coexistence or sequence between outward facts, though such coexistence or sequence may contradict a positive law of the physical world. There is therefore a further condition required to render two ideas unassociable, and this is, that one of them shall be already associated with some idea which excludes the other. Thus far the analysis is carried in the author's text. But the question remains, what ideas exclude one another? On careful consideration I can only find one case of such exclusion: when one of the ideas either contains, or raises up by association, the idea of the absence of the other. I am aware of no case of absolute incompatibility of thought or of imagination, except between the presence of something and its absence; between an affirmative and the corresponding negative. If an idea irresistibly raises up the idea of the absence of a certain sensation, it cannot become associated with the idea of that sensation; for it is impossible to combine together in the same mental representation, the presence of a sensation and its absence.

We are not yet, however, at the end of the difficulty; for it may be objected, that the idea of the absence of anything is the idea of a negation, of a nullity; and the idea of nothing must itself be nothing—no idea at all. This objection has imposed upon more than one metaphysician; but the solution of the paradox is very simple. The idea of the presence of a sensation is the idea of the sensation itself along with certain accompanying circumstances: the idea of the absence of the sensation is the idea of the same accompanying circumstances without the sensation. For example: my idea of a body is the idea of a feeling of resistance, accompanying a certain muscular action of my own, say of my hand; my idea of no body, in other words, of empty space, is the idea of the same or a similar muscular action of my own, not attended by any feeling of resistance. Neither of these is an idea of a mere negation; both are positive mental representations: but inasmuch as one of them includes the negation of something positive which is an actual part of the other, they are mutually incompatible: and any idea which is so associated with one of them as to recall it instantly and irresistibly, is incapable of being associated with the other.

The instance cited by the author from Dr. Brown, is a good illustration of the law.[33] We can associate the ideas of a plane and of a convex surface as two surfaces side by side; but we cannot fuse the two mental images into one, and represent to ourselves the very same series of points giving us the sensations we receive from a plane surface and those we receive from a convex surface both at once. That this cannot but be so, is a corollary from the elementary law of association. Not only has no instance ever occurred in our experience of a surface which gave us at the same moment both these sets of sensations; but whenever in our experience a surface originally plane, came to give us the sensations we receive from a convex surface (as for instance when we bend a flat sheet of paper), it, at the very same moment, ceased to be, or to appear, a plane. The commencement of the one set of sensations has always been simultaneous with the cessation of the other set, and this experience, not being affected by any change of circumstances, has the constancy and invariability of a law of nature. It forms a

---

[33]James Mill (Vol. I, p. 97) quotes from Brown, *Lectures*, pp. 187–8: "I cannot blend my notions of the two surfaces, a plane, and a convex, as one surface, both plane and convex, more than I can think of a whole which is less than a fraction of itself, or a square of which the sides are not equal."

correspondingly strong association; and we become unable to have an idea of either set of sensations, those of planeness or those of convexity, without having the idea of the disappearance of the other set, if they existed previously. I believe it will be found that all the mental incompatibilities, the impossibilities of thought, of which so much is made by a certain class of metaphysicians, can be accounted for in a similar manner. (Vol. I, pp. 97–100.)

*    *    *    *    *

*[The opening paragraphs of Sect. 10 of Chap. iii ("The Association of Ideas") read:] It not unfrequently happens in our associated feelings, that the antecedent is of no importance farther than as it introduces the consequent. In these cases, the consequent absorbs all the attention, and the antecedent is instantly forgotten. Of this a very intelligible illustration is afforded by what happens in ordinary discourse. A friend arrives from a distant country, and brings me the first intelligence of the last illness, the last words, the last acts, and death of my son. The sound of the voice, the articulation of every word, makes its sensation in my ear; but it is to the ideas that my attention flies. It is my son that is before me, suffering, acting, speaking, dying. The words which have introduced the ideas, and kindled the affections, have been as little heeded, as the respiration which has been accelerated, while the ideas were received.*

*It is important in respect to this case of association to remark, that there are large classes of our sensations, such as many of those in the alimentary duct, and many in the nervous and vascular systems, which serve, as antecedents, to introduce ideas, as consequents; but as the consequents are far more interesting than themselves, and immediately absorb the attention, the antecedents are habitually overlooked; and though they exercise, by the trains which they introduce, a great influence on our happiness or misery, they themselves are generally wholly unknown.*

*That there are connections between our ideas and certain states of the internal organs, is proved by many familiar instances. Thus, anxiety, in most people, disorders the digestion. It is no wonder, then, that the internal feelings which accompany indigestion, should excite the ideas which prevail in a state of anxiety. Fear, in most people, accelerates, in a remarkable manner, the vermicular motion of the intestines. There is an association, therefore, between certain states of the intestines, and terrible ideas; and this is sufficiently confirmed by the horrible dreams to which men are subject from indigestion; and the hypochondria, more or less afflicting, which almost always accompanies certain morbid states of the digestive organs. The grateful food which excites pleasurable sensations in the mouth, continues them in the stomach; and, as pleasures excite ideas of their causes, and these of similar causes, and causes excite ideas of their effects, and so on, trains of pleasurable ideas take their origin from pleasurable sensations in the stomach. Uneasy sensations in the stomach, produce analogous effects. Disagreeable sensations are associated with disagreeable circumstances; a train is introduced, in which, one painful idea following another, combinations, to the last degree afflictive, are sometimes introduced, and the sufferer is altogether overwhelmed by dismal associations.*

The law of association laid down in this section ranks among the principal of what may be termed the laws of Obliviscence. It is one of the widest in its action, and most important in its consequences of all the laws of the mind; and the merit of the author, in the large use he makes of it, is very great, as, though it is the key that unlocks many of the more mysterious phenomena of the mind, it is among the least familiar of the mental laws, and is not only overlooked by the great majority of psychologists, but some, otherwise of merit, seem unable to see and understand the law after any quantity of explanation.

The first, however, of the examples by which the author illustrates this law, is not marked by his usual felicity. Its shortcomings are pointed out by Mr. Bain in the preceding note.[34] The internal feelings (says the author) which accompany indigestion, introduce trains of ideas (as in the case of horrible dreams, and of hypochondria) which are acutely painful, and may embitter the whole existence, while the sensations themselves, being comparatively of little interest, are unheeded and forgotten. It is true that the sensations in the alimentary canal, directly produced by indigestion, though (as every one knows) in some cases intense, are in others so slight as not to fix the attention, and yet may be followed by melancholy trains of thought, the connection of which with the state of the digestion may be entirely unobserved: but by far the most probable supposition appears to be, that these painful trains are not excited by the sensations, but that they and the sensations are joint or successive effects of a common organic cause. It is difficult to comprehend how these obscure sensations can excite the distressing trains of ideas by the laws of association; for what opportunity have these sensations usually had of becoming associated, either synchronously or successively, with those ideas? The explanation, in the text, of this difficulty, seems surprisingly insufficient. Anxiety, in most people, disorders the digestion; and consequently, according to the author, the sensations of indigestion excite the ideas which prevail in a state of anxiety. If that were the true explanation, the only persons with whom indigestion would depress the spirits, would be those who had suffered previous depression of spirits, sufficient in duration and intensity to disorder the digestion, and to keep it disordered long enough to effect a close and inseparable cohesion between even very slight sensations of indigestion and painful ideas excited by other causes. Surely this is not the fact. The theory has a

---

[34]Bain's footnote (Vol. I, p. 102) immediately precedes this footnote by J.S. Mill.

true application in the case of the confirmed hypochondriac. When the sensations have been repeatedly experienced along with the melancholy trains of thought, a direct association is likely to grow up between the two; and when this has been effected, the first touch of the sensations may bring back in full measure the miserable mental state which had coexisted with them, thus increasing not only the frequency of its recurrence, but, by the conjunction of two exciting causes, the intensity of the misery. But the origin of the state must be looked for elsewhere, and is probably to be sought in physiology.

The other example in the text seems still less relevant. Fear tends to accelerate the peristaltic motion, therefore there is a connection between certain states of the intestines and terrible ideas. To make this available for the author's purpose, the consequence of the connection ought to be, that acceleration of the peristaltic motion excites ideas of terror. But does it? The state of indigestion characteristic of hypochondria is not looseness of the bowels, but is commonly attended with the exact opposite. The author's usual acuteness of discernment seems to have been, in these cases, blunted by an unwillingness to admit the possibility that ideas as well as sensations may be directly affected by material conditions. But if, as he admits, ideas have a direct action on our bodily organs, a *prima facie* case is made out for the localization of our ideas, equally with our sensations, in some part of our bodily system; and there is at least no antecedent presumption against the supposition that the action may be reciprocal—that as ideas sometimes derange the organic functions, so derangements of organic functions may sometimes modify the trains of our ideas by their own physical action on the brain and nerves, and not through the associations connected with the sensations they excite. (Vol. I, pp. 102–5.)

\* \* \* \* \*

[*The concluding paragraph of Chap. iii, Sect. 10 reads:*] *In illustration of the fact, that sensations and ideas, which are essential to some of the most important operations of our minds, serve only as antecedents to more important consequents, and are themselves so habitually overlooked, that their existence is unknown, we may recur to the remarkable case which we have just explained, of the ideas introduced by the sensations of sight. The minute gradations of colour, whch accompany varieties of extension, figure, and distance, are insignificant. The figure, the size, the distance, themselves, on the other hand, are matters of the greatest importance. The first having introduced the last, their work is done. The consequents remain the sole objects of attention, the antecedents are forgotten; in the present instance, not completely; in other instances, so completely, that they cannot be recognised.*[35]

[35]A footnote by Bain again intervenes between the text and J.S. Mill's footnote.

The reader, it may be hoped, is now familiar with the important psychological fact, so powerfully grasped and so discerningly employed by Hartley and the author of the *Analysis*,—that when, through the frequent repetition of a series of sensations, the corresponding train of ideas rushes through the mind with extreme rapidity, some of the links are apt to disappear from consciousness as completely as if they had never formed part of the series. It has been a subject of dispute among philosophers which of three things takes place in this case. Do the lost ideas pass through the mind without consciousness? Do they pass consciously through the mind and are they then instantly forgotten? Or do they never come into the mind at all, being, as it were, overleaped and pressed out by the rush of the subsequent ideas?

It would seem, at first sight, that the first and third suppositions involve impossibilities, and that the second, therefore, is the only one which we are at liberty to adopt. As regards the first, it may be said—How can we have a feeling without feeling it, in other words, without being conscious of it? With regard to the third, how, it may be asked, can any link of the chain have been altogether absent, through the pressure of the subsequent links? The subsequent ideas are only there because called up by it, and would not have arisen at all unless it had arisen first, however short a time it may have lasted. These arguments seem strong, but are not so strong as they seem.

In favour of the first supposition, that feelings may be unconsciously present, various facts and arguments are adduced by Sir William Hamilton in his *Lectures*; but I think I have shewn in another work, that the arguments are inconclusive, and the facts equally reconcilable with the second of the three hypotheses.[36] That a feeling should not be felt appears to me a contradiction both in words and in nature. But, though a feeling cannot exist without being felt, the organic state which is the antecedent of it may exist, and the feeling itself not follow. This happens, either if the organic state is not of sufficient duration, or if an organic state stronger than itself, and conflicting with it, is affecting us at the same moment. I hope to be excused for quoting what I have said elsewhere on this subject (*Examination of Sir William Hamilton's Philosophy*, Chap. xv).

In the case, for instance, of a soldier who receives a wound in battle, but in the excitement of the moment is not aware of the fact, it is difficult not to believe that if the wound had been accompanied by the usual sensation, so vivid a feeling would have forced itself to be attended to and remembered. The supposition which seems most probable is, that the nerves of the particular part were affected as they would have been by the same cause in any other circumstances, but that, the nervous centres being intensely occupied with other impressions, the affection of the local nerves did not reach them, and no sensation was

[36]William Hamilton (1788–1856), *Lectures on Metaphysics and Logic*, ed. Henry Longueville Mansel and John Veitch, 4 vols. (Edinburgh and London: Blackwood, 1859–60), Vol. I, pp. 338–63, and Vol. II, pp. 244–6. Mill's reply (quoted below) is in his *An Examination of Sir William Hamilton's Philosophy* (London: Longman, *et al.*, 1865), in *CW*, Vol. IX (Toronto: University of Toronto Press, 1979), pp. 282–4.

excited. In like manner, if we admit (what physiology is rendering more and more probable) that our mental feelings, as well as our sensations, have for their physical antecedents particular states of the nerves; it may well be believed that the apparently suppressed links in a chain of association, those which Sir William Hamilton considers as latent, really are so; that they are not, even momentarily, felt; the chain of causation being continued only physically, by one organic state of the nerves succeeding another so rapidly that the state of mental conciousness appropriate to each is not produced. We have only to suppose, either that a nervous modification of too short duration does not produce any sensation or mental feeling at all, or that the rapid succession of different nervous modifications makes the feelings produced by them interfere with each other, and become confounded in one mass. The former of these suppositions is extremely probable, while of the truth of the latter we have positive proof. An example of it is the experiment which Sir W. Hamilton quoted from Mr. Mill, and which had been noticed before either of them by Hartley.[37] It is known that the seven prismatic colours, combined in certain proportions, produce the white light of the solar ray. Now, if the seven colours are painted on spaces bearing the same proportion to one another as in the solar spectrum, and the coloured surface so produced is passed rapidly before the eyes, as by the turning of a wheel, the whole is seen as white. The physiological explanation of this phenomenon may be deduced from another common experiment. If a lighted torch, or a bar heated to luminousness, is waved rapidly before the eye, the appearance produced is that of a ribbon of light; which is universally understood to prove that the visual sensation persists for a certain short time after its cause has ceased. Now, if this happens with a single colour, it will happen with a series of colours: and if the wheel on which the prismatic colours have been painted, is turned with the same rapidity with which the torch was waved, each of the seven sensations of colour will last long enough to be contemporaneous with all the others, and they will naturally produce by their combination the same colour as if they had, from the beginning, been excited simultaneously. If anything similar to this obtains in our consciousness generally (and that it obtains in many cases of consciousness there can be no doubt) it will follow that whenever the organic modifications of our nervous fibres succeed one another at an interval shorter than the duration of the sensations or other feelings corresponding to them, those sensations or feelings will, so to speak, overlap one another, and becoming simultaneous instead of successive, will blend into a state of feeling, probably as unlike the elements out of which it is engendered, as the colour white is unlike the prismatic colours. And this may be the source of many of those states of internal or mental feeling which we cannot distinctly refer to a prototype in experience, our experience only supplying the elements from which, by this kind of mental chemistry, they are composed. The elementary feelings may then be said to be latently present, or to be present but not in consciousness. The truth, however, is that the feelings themselves are not present, consciously or latently, but that the nervous modifications which are their usual antecedents have been present, while the consequents have been frustrated, and another consequent has been produced instead.

In this modified form, therefore, the first of the three hypotheses may possibly be true. Let us now consider the third, that of the entire elision of some of the ideas which form the associated train. This supposition seemed to be inadmissible, because the loss of any link would, it was supposed, cause the chain itself to break off at that point. To make the hypothesis possible, it is only, however, necessary to

[37]Hamilton, *Lectures*, Vol. II, p. 147; Mill, *Analysis*, Vol. I, pp. 90–1; Hartley, *Observations*, Pt. I, p. 9.

suppose, that, while the association is acquiring the promptitude and rapidity which it ultimately attains, each of the successive ideas abides for a brief interval in our consciousness after it has already called up the idea which is to succeed it. Each idea in the series, though introduced, not by synchronous, but by successive association, is thus, during a part of its continuance, synchronous with the idea which introduced it: and as the rapidity of the suggestions increases by still further repetition, an idea may become synchronous with another which was originally not even contiguous to it, but separated from it by an intervening link; or may come into immediate instead of mediate sequence with such an idea. When either of these states of things has continued for some time, a direct association of the synchronous or of the successive kind will be generated between two ideas which are not proximate links in the chain; A will acquire a direct power of exciting C, independently of the intervening idea B. If, then, B is much less interesting than C, and especially if B is of no importance at all in itself, but only by exciting C, and has therefore nothing to make the mind dwell on it after C has been reached, the association of A with C is likely to become stronger than that of A with B: C will be habitually excited directly by A; as the mind runs off to the further ideas suggested by C, B will cease to be excited at all; and the train of association, like a stream which breaking through its bank cuts off a bend in its course, will thenceforth flow in the direct line AC, omitting B. This supposition accounts more plausibly than either of the others for the truly wonderful rapidity of thought, since it does not make so large a demand as the other theories on our ability to believe that a prodigious number of different ideas can successively rush through the mind in an instant too short for measurement.

The result is, that all the three theories of this mental process seem to be quite possible; and it is not unlikely that each of them may be the real process in some cases, either in different persons, or in the same persons under different circumstances. I can only remit the question to future psychologists, who may be able to contrive crucial experiments for deciding among these various possibilities. (Vol. I, pp. 106–10.)

\* \* \* \* \*

[*In considering whether resemblance, "an alleged principle of association," can be included under other laws, James Mill says:*] *I believe it will be found that we are accustomed to see like things together. When we see a tree, we generally see more trees than one; when we see an ox, we generally see more oxen than one; a sheep, more sheep than one; a man, more men than one. From this observation, I think, we may refer resemblance to the law of frequency, of which it seems to form only a particular case.*

The reason assigned by the author for considering association by resemblance as a case of association by contiguity, is perhaps the least successful attempt at a generalisation and simplification of the laws of mental phenomena, to be found in the work. It ought to be remembered that the author, as the text shews, attached little importance to it. And perhaps, not thinking it important, he passed it over with a less amount of patient thought than he usually bestowed on his analyses.

Objects, he thinks, remind us of other objects resembling them, because we are accustomed to see like things together. But we are also accustomed to see like things separate. When two combinations incompatible with one another are both realised in familiar experience, it requires a very great preponderance of experience on one side to determine the association specially to either. We are also much accustomed to see unlike things together; I do not mean things contrasted, but simply unlike. Unlikeness, therefore, not amounting to contrast, ought to be as much a cause of association as likeness. Besides, the fact that when we see (for instance) a sheep, we usually see more sheep than one, may cause us, when we think of a sheep, to think of an entire flock; but it does not explain why, when we see a sheep with a black mark on its forehead, we are reminded of a sheep with a similar mark, formerly seen, though we never saw two such sheep together. It does not explain why a portrait makes us think of the original, or why a stranger whom we see for the first time reminds us of a person of similar appearance whom we saw many years ago. The law by which an object reminds us of similar objects which we have been used to see along with it, must be a different law from that by which it reminds us of similar objects which we have not been used to see along with it. But it is the same law by which it reminds us of dissimilar objects which we have been used to see along with it. The sight of a sheep, if it reminds us of a flock of sheep, probably by the same law of contiguity, reminds us of a meadow; but it must be by some other law that it reminds us of a single sheep previously seen, and of the occasion on which we saw that single sheep.

The attempt to resolve association by resemblance into association by contiguity must perforce be unsuccessful, inasmuch as there never could have been association by contiguity without a previous association by resemblance. Why does a sensation received this instant remind me of sensations which I formerly had (as we commonly say), along with it? I never had them along with this very sensation. I never had this sensation until now, and can never have it again. I had the former sensations in conjunction not with it, but with a sensation exactly like it. And my present sensation could not remind me of those former sensations unlike itself, unless by first reminding me of the sensation like itself, which really did coexist with them. There is thus a law of association anterior to, and presupposed by, the law of contiguity: namely, that a sensation tends to recall what is called the idea of itself, that is, the remembrance of a sensation like itself, if such has previously been experienced. This is implied in what we call *recognising* a sensation, as one which has been felt before; more correctly, as undistinguishably resembling one which has been felt before. The law in question was scientifically enunciated, and included, I believe for the first time, in the list of Laws of Association, by Sir William Hamilton, in one of the Dissertations appended to his edition of Reid:[38] but the fact itself is recognised by the author of the *Analysis*, in various passages of his work; more especially in the second section of the fourteenth chapter.[39] There is, therefore, a suggestion by resemblance—a calling up of the idea of a past sensation by a present sensation like it—which not only does not depend on association by contiguity, but is itself the foundation which association by contiguity requires for its support.

When it is admitted that simple sensations remind us of one another by direct resemblance, many of the complex cases of suggestion by resemblance may be analysed into this elementary case of association by resemblance, combined with an association by contiguity. A flower, for instance, may remind us of a former flower resembling it, because the present flower exhibits to us certain qualities, that is, excites in us certain sensations, resembling and recalling to our re-membrance those we had from the former flower, and these recall the entire image of the flower by the law of association by contiguity. But this explanation, though it serves for many cases of complex phenomena suggesting one another by resemblance, does not suffice for all. For, the resemblance of complex facts often consists, not solely, or principally, in likeness between the simple sensations, but far more in likeness of the manner of their combination, and it is often by this, rather than by the single features, that they recall one another. After we had seen, and well observed, a single triangle, when we afterwards saw a second there can be little doubt that it would at once remind us of the first by mere resemblance. But the suggestion would not depend on the sides or on the angles, any or all of them; for we might have seen such sides and such angles uncombined, or combined into some other figure. The resemblance by which one triangle recalls the idea of another is not resemblance in the parts, but principally and emphatically in the manner in which the parts are put together. I am unable to see any mode in which this case of suggestion can be accounted for by contiguity; any mode, at least, which would fit all cases of the kind. (Vol. I, pp. 111–14.)

\* \* \* \* \*

[*The*] *union of two complex ideas into one, Dr. Hartley has called a duplex idea.*

I have been unable to trace in Hartley the expression here ascribed to him. In every

[38]Hamilton, "Note D.\*\*\* Outline of a Theory of Mental Reproduction, Suggestion, or Association," "Dissertations on Reid," in *The Works of Thomas Reid*, ed. Hamilton (Edinburgh: Maclachlan and Stewart; London: Longman, *et al.*, 1846), pp. 913–15.
[39]*Analysis*, Vol. II, pp. 6–88, esp. 10–12.

passage that I can discover, the name he gives to a combination of two or more complex ideas is that of a *decomplex* idea.[40] (Vol. I, p. 115.)

\* \* \* \* \*

[*A comprehensive note by Bain, appended to the end of Chap. iii, "The Association of Ideas," is followed by J.S. Mill's footnote.*]

The author and Mr. Bain agree in rejecting Contrast as an independent principle of association.[41] I think they might have gone further, and denied it even as a derivative one. All the cases considered as examples of it seem to me to depend on something else. I greatly doubt if the sight or thought of a dwarf has intrinsically any tendency to recall the idea of a giant. Things certainly do remind us of their own absence, because (as pointed out by Mr. Bain) we are only conscious of their presence by comparison with their absence; and for a further reason, arising out of the former, *viz.* that, in our practical judgments, we are led to think of the case of their presence and the case of their absence by one and the same act of thought, having commonly to choose between the two. But it does not seem to me that things have any special tendency to remind us of their positive opposites. Black does not remind us of white more than of red or green. If light reminds us of darkness, it is because darkness is the mere negation, or absence, of light. The case of heat and cold is more complex. The sensation of heat recalls to us the absence of that sensation: if the sensation amounts to pain, it calls up the idea of relief from it; that is, of its absence, associated by contiguity with the pleasant feeling which accompanies the change. But cold is not the mere absence of heat; it is itself a positive sensation. If heat suggests to us the idea of the sensation of cold, it is not because of the contrast, but because the close connection which exists between the outward conditions of both, and the consequent identity of the means we employ for regulating them, cause the thought of cold and that of heat to be frequently presented to us in contiguity. (Vol. I, pp. 125–6.)

\* \* \* \* \*

[*J.S. Mill's note comes at the end of Chap. iv, "Naming."*]

This exposition of Naming in its most general aspect, needs neither explanation nor comment. It is one of those specimens of clear and vigorous statement, going

---

[40]See, e.g., Pt. I, p. 77.

[41]James Mill deals with the matter perfunctorily in Vol. I, pp. 112–14; Bain at somewhat greater length in his *The Senses and the Intellect*, pp. 579–84.

straight to the heart of the matter, and dwelling on it just long enough and no longer than necessary, in which the *Analysis* abounds. (Vol. I, p. 133.)

\* \* \* \* \*

*Names, to be useful, cannot exceed a certain number. They could not otherwise be remembered. It is, therefore, of the greatest importance that each name should accomplish as much as possible. To this end, the greater number of names stand, not for individuals only, but classes. [For example, red, sweet, hot, loud, rose, stone, iron, ox.]*

Economy in the use of names is a very small part of the motive leading to the creation of names of classes. If we had a name for every individual object which exists in the universe, and could remember all those names, we should still require names for what those objects or some of them have in common; in other words, we should require classification, and class-names. This will be obvious if it is considered that had we no names but names of individuals, we should not have the means of making any affirmation respecting any object; we could not predicate of it any qualities. But of this more largely in a future note.[42] (Vol. I, p. 137.)

\* \* \* \* \*

[*James Mill comments that when wishing to name simple ideas, for instance those of sight, one has available only red, blue, violet, etc., all of which are the names of the sensations. Awkward expressions result, such as "my sensation of red, my idea of red." Similarly, "sound of a trumpet," "flight of a bird," "light," "pain," and "heat" are the names "of the sensation as well as the idea."*]

In strict propriety of language all these are names only of sensations, or clusters of sensations; not of ideas. A person studious of precision would not, I think, say heat, meaning the idea of heat, or a tree, when he meant the idea of a tree. He would use heat as the name only of the sensation of heat, and tree as the name of the outward object, or cluster of sensations; and if he had occasion to speak of the idea, he would say, my idea (or the idea) of heat; my idea (or the idea) of a tree. (Vol. I, p. 140.)

\* \* \* \* \*

[42]See pp. 142–3 below.

[*J.S. Mill's note comes at the end of "Nouns Substantive," Sect. 1 of Chap. iv, "Naming," in which James Mill refers to "complex ideas which, though derived ... from the senses, are put together in a great degree at our discretion, as the ideas of a centaur, a mountain of gold, of comfort, of meanness; all that class of ideas ... which Mr. Locke has called mixed modes"*[43] *(Vol. 1, pp. 137–8). He then mentions their arbitrary and individual formation, using other instances cited by J.S. Mill (*ibid., *pp. 140–1).*]

There is some need for additional elucidation of the class of complex ideas distinguished (under the name of Mixed Modes) by Locke, and recognised by the author of the *Analysis*, as "put together in a great degree at our discretion;" as "those which the mind forms arbitrarily," so that "the ideas of which they are composed are more or less numerous according to pleasure, and each man of necessity forms his own combination." From these and similar phrases, interpreted literally, it might be supposed that in the instances given, a centaur, a mountain of gold, comfort, meanness, fear, courage, temperance, ignorance, republic, aristocracy, monarchy, piety, good manners, prudence—the elements which constitute these several complex ideas are put together premeditatedly, by an act of will, which each individual performs for himself, and of which he is conscious. This, however, happens only in cases of invention, or of what is called creative imagination. A centaur and a mountain of gold are inventions: combinations intentionally made, at least on the part of the first inventor; and are not copies or likenesses of any combination of impressions received by the senses, nor are supposed to have any such outward phenomena corresponding to them. But the other ideas mentioned in the text, those of courage, temperance, aristocracy, monarchy, etc., are supposed to have real originals outside our thoughts. These ideas, just as much as those of a horse and a tree, are products of generalization and abstraction: they are believed to be ideas of certain points or features in which a number of the clusters of sensations which we call real objects agree: and instead of being formed by intentionally putting together simple ideas, they are formed by stripping off, or rather, by not attending to, such of the simple sensations or ideas entering into the clusters as are peculiar to any of them, and establishing an extremely close association among those which are common to them all. These complex ideas, therefore, are not, in reality, like the creations of mere imagination, put together at discretion, any more than the complex ideas, compounded of the obvious sensible qualities of objects, which we call our ideas of the objects. They are formed in the same manner as these, only not so rapidly or so easily, since the particulars of which they are composed do not obtrude themselves upon the senses, but suppose a perception of qualities and sequences not immediately obvious. From this circumstance results the consequence noticed by the author, that this class of complex ideas are often of different composition in

[43]Locke, *Essay*, Vol. I, pp. 293–301 (Bk. II, Chap. xxii, "Of Mixed Modes").

different persons. For, in the first place, different persons abstract their ideas of this sort from different individual instances; and secondly, some persons abstract much better than others; that is, take more accurate notice of the obscurer features of instances, and discern more correctly what are those in which all the instances agree. This important subject will be more fully entered into when we reach that part of the present work which treats of the ideas connected with General Terms.[44] (Vol. I, pp. 142–3.)

*     *     *     *     *

[*"Nouns Adjective," Sect. 2 of Chap. iv, concludes:*] *Beside the use of adjectives, in dividing great classes into smaller ones, without multiplication of names; they sometimes answer another purpose. It often happens that, in the cluster of sensations or ideas which have one name; we have occasion to call attention particularly to some one ingredient of the cluster. Adjectives render this service, as well as that of marking a class. This rose, I say, is red; that rose is yellow: this stone is hot, that stone is cold. The term, red rose, or yellow rose, is the name of a class. But when I say, this rose is red, where an individual is named, I mark emphatically the specific difference; namely, red, or yellow; which constitutes that subdivision of the genus rose, to which the individual belongs.*

In the concluding paragraph we find the first recognition by the author that class names serve any purpose, or are introduced for any reason, except to save multiplication of names. Adjectives, it is here said, answer also the purpose of calling attention to some one ingredient of the cluster of sensations combined under one name. That is to say, they enable us to *affirm* that the cluster contains that ingredient: for they do not merely call attention to the ingredient, or remind the hearer of it: the hearer, very often, did not know that the cluster contained the ingredient, until he was apprised by the proposition.

But surely it is not only adjectives which fulfil either office, whether of giving information of an ingredient, or merely fixing the attention upon it. All general names do so, when used as predicates. When I say that a distant object which I am pointing at is a tree, or a building, I just as much call attention to certain ingredients in the cluster of sensations constituting the object, as I do when I say, This rose is red. So far is it from being true that adjectives are distinguished from substantives by having this function in addition to that of economizing names, that it is, on the contrary, much more nearly true of adjectives than of the class-names which are nouns substantive, that the economizing of names is the principal motive for their institution. For though general names of some sort are indispensable to

[44]Chap. viii, "Classification," Vol. I, pp. 260–8, and J.S. Mill's appended note, pp. 142–3 below.

predication, adjectives are not. As is well shewn in the text, the peculiarity, which really distinguishes adjectives from other general names, is that they mark cross divisions. All nature having first been marked out into classes by means of nouns substantive, we might go on by the same means subdividing each class. We might call the large individuals of a class by one noun substantive and the small ones by another, and these substantives would serve all purposes of predication; but to do this we should need just twice as many additional nouns substantive as there are classes of objects. Since, however, the distinction of large and small applies to all classes alike, one pair of names will suffice to designate it. Instead therefore of dividing every class into sub-classes, each with its own name, we draw a line across all the classes, dividing all nature into large things and small, and by using these two words as adjectives, that is, by adding one or other of them as the occasion requires to every noun substantive which is the name of a class, we are able to mark universally the distinction of large and small by two names only, instead of many millions. (Vol. I, pp. 149–50.)

\*    \*    \*    \*    \*

[*In "Verbs," Sect. 3 of Chap. iv, James Mill says:*] *When the name of an act is applied to an agent, the agent is either the person speaking, the person spoken to, or some other person. The word denoting the action is, by what are called the Persons of the verb, made to connote these diversities. Thus* amo *notes the act, and connotes the person speaking as the actor;* amas *notes the act, and connotes the person spoken to, as the actor;* amat *notes the act, and connotes some person, as the actor, who is neither the person speaking, nor the person spoken to.*

There is here a fresh instance of the oversight already pointed out, that of not including in the function for which general names are required, their employment in Predication. *Amo, amas,* and *amamus,* cannot, I conceive, with any propriety be called names of actions, or names at all. They are entire predications. It is one of the properties of the kind of general names called verbs, that they cannot be used except in a Proposition or Predication, and indeed only as the predicate of it: (for the infinitive is not a verb, but the abstract of a verb). What else there is to distinguish verbs from other general names will be more particularly considered further on.[45] (Vol. I, p. 154.)

\*    \*    \*    \*    \*

[45]See J.S. Mill's next note, and that at pp. 133–4 below, which refers to Andrew Findlater's note at Vol. I, pp. 178–82.

[*James Mill discusses "the contrivances" used to make verbs,*] *the marks or names of action, by their connotative powers, a more and more effectual instrument of notation. Accurately speaking, they are adjectives, so fashioned as to connote, a threefold distinction of agents, with a twofold distinction of their number, a threefold distinction of the manner of the action, and a threefold distinction of its time; and, along with all this, another important particular, . . . the* COPULA *in* PREDICATION.

The imperfection of this theory of Verbs is sufficiently apparent. They are, says the author, a particular kind of Adjectives. Adjectives, according to the preceding Section, are words employed to enable us, without inconvenient multiplication of names, to subdivide great classes into smaller ones. Can it be said, or would it have been said by the author, that the only, or the principal reason for having Verbs, is to enable us to subdivide classes of objects with the greatest economy of names?

Neither is it strictly accurate to say that Verbs are always marks of motion, or of action, even including, as the author does, by an extension of the meaning of those terms, every process which is attended with a feeling of effort. Many verbs, of the kind which grammarians call neuter or intransitive verbs, express rest, or inaction: as *sit*, *lie*, and in some cases, *stand*. It is true however that the verbs first invented, as far as we know anything of them, expressed forms of motion, and the principal function of verbs still is to affirm or deny action. Or, to speak yet more generally, it is by means of verbs that we predicate events. Events, or changes, are the most important facts, to us, in the surrounding world. Verbs are the resource which language affords for predicating events. They are not the names of events; all names of events are substantives, as *sunrise*, *disaster*, or infinitives, as *to rise*, and infinitives are logically substantives. But it is by means of verbs that we assert, or give information of, events; as, The sun rises, or, Disaster has occurred. There is, however, a class of neuter verbs already referred to, which do not predicate events, but states of an unchanging object, as *lie*, *sit*, *remain*, *exist*. It would be incorrect, therefore, to give a definition of Verbs which should limit them to the expression of events. I am inclined to think that the distinction between nouns and verbs is not logical, but merely grammatical, and that every word, whatever be its meaning, must be reputed a verb, which is so constructed grammatically that it can only be used as the predicate of a proposition. Any meaning whatever is, in strictness, capable of being thrown into this form: but it is only certain meanings, chiefly actions or events, which there is, in general, any motive for putting into this particular shape. (Vol. I, pp. 155–6.)

\*     \*     \*     \*     \*

[*In "Predication," Sect. 4 of Chap. iv, James Mill refers to predication as*] *the*

*grand expedient, by which language is enabled to mark not only sensations and*
*ideas, but also the order of them.*

The theory of Predication here set forth, stands in need of further elucidation, and
perhaps of some correction and addition.

The account which the author gives of a Predication, or Proposition, is, first,
that it is a mode of so putting together the marks of sensations and ideas, as to mark
the order of them. Secondly, that it consists in substituting one name for another,
so as to signify that a certain name (called the predicate), is a mark of the same idea
which another name (called the subject) is a mark of.[46]

It must be allowed that a predication, or proposition, is intended to mark some
portion of the order either of our sensations or of our ideas, *i.e.*, some part of the
coexistences or sequences which take place either in our minds, or in what we term
the external world. But what sort of order is it that a predication marks? An order
supposed to be believed in. When *John*, or *man*, are said to be marks of an
individual object, all there is in the matter is that these words, being associated
with the idea of the object, are intended to raise that idea in the mind of the person
who hears or reads them. But when we say, John is a man, or, John is an old man,
we intend to do more than call up in the hearer's mind the images of John, of a man,
and of an old man. We intend to do more than inform him that we have thought of,
or even seen, John and a man, or John and an old man, together. We inform him of
a fact respecting John, namely, that he *is* an old man, or at all events, of our belief
that this is a fact. The characteristic difference between a predication and any other
form of speech, is, that it does not merely bring to mind a certain object (which is
the only function of a mark, merely as such); it *asserts* something respecting it.
Now it may be true, and I think it is true, that every assertion, every object of
Belief,—everything that can be true or false—that can be an object of assent or
dissent—is some order of sensations or of ideas: some coexistence or succession
of sensations or ideas actually experienced, or supposed capable of being
experienced. And thus it may appear in the end that in expressing a belief, we are
after all only declaring the order of a group or series of sensations or ideas. But the
order which we declare is not an imaginary order; it is an order believed to be real.
Whatever view we adopt of the psychological nature of Belief, it is necessary to
distinguish between the mere suggestion to the mind of a certain order among
sensations or ideas—such as takes place when we think of the alphabet, or the
numeration table—and the indication that this order is an actual fact, which is
occurring, or which has occurred once or oftener, or which, in certain definite
circumstances, always occurs; which are the things indicated as true by an
affirmative predication, and as false by a negative one.

That a predication differs from a name in doing more than merely calling up an
idea, is admitted in what I have noted as the second half of the author's theory of

[46]Vol. I, pp. 160–1.

Predication. That second half points out that every predication is a communication, intended to act, not on the mere ideas of the listener, but on his persuasion or belief: and what he is intended to believe, according to the author, is, that of the two names which are conjoined in the predication, one is a mark of the same idea (or let me add, of the same sensation or cluster of sensations) of which the other is a mark. This is a doctrine of Hobbes, the one which caused him to be termed by Leibnitz, in words which have been often quoted, "plus quam nominalis."[47] It is quite true that when we predicate B of A—when we assert of A that it is a B—B must, if the assertion is true, be a name of A, *i.e.*, a name applicable to A; one of the innumerable names which, in virtue of their signification, can be used as descriptive of A: but is this the information which we want to convey to the hearer? It is so when we are speaking only of names and their meaning, as when we enunciate a definition. In every other case, what we want to convey is a matter of fact, of which this relation between the names is but an incidental consequence. When we say, John walked out this morning, it is not a correct expression of the communication we desire to make, that "having walked out this morning" or "a person who has walked out this morning" are two of the innumerable names of John. They are only accidentally and momentarily names of John by reason of a certain event, and the information we mean to give is, that this event has happened. The event is not resolvable into an identity of meaning between names, but into an actual series of sensations that occurred to John, and a belief that any one who had been present and using his eyes would have had another series of sensations, which we call seeing John in the act of walking out. Again, when we say, Negroes are woolly-haired, we mean to make known to the hearer, not that woolly-haired is a name of every negro, but that wherever the cluster of sensations signified by the word *negro*, are experienced, the sensations signified by the word *woolly-haired* will be found either among them or conjoined with them. This is an order of sensations: and it is only in consequence of it that the name *woolly-haired* comes to be applicable to every individual of whom the term *negro* is a name.

There is nothing positively opposed to all this in the author's text: indeed he must be considered to have meant this, when he said, that by means of substituting one name for another, a predication marks the order of our sensations and ideas. The omission consists in not remarking that what is distinctively signified by a predication, as such, is Belief in a certain order of sensations or ideas. And when this has been said, the Hobbian addition, that it does so by declaring the predicate to be a name of everything of which the subject is a name, may be omitted as surplusage, and as diverting the mind from the essential features of the case.

---

[47]Hobbes, *Leviathan; or, the Matter, Form, and Power of a Commonwealth Ecclesiastical and Civil* (1651), in *The English Works*, ed. William Molesworth, 11 vols. (London: Bohn, 1839–45), Vol. III, p. 23 (Pt. I, Chap. iv); Gottfried Wilhelm von Leibniz (1646–1716), *Dissertatio de stilo philosophico Nizolii* (1670), in *Opera philosophica*, 2 pts., ed. Johann Eduard Erdmann (Berlin: Eichler, 1840), Pt. I, p. 69 (Sect. xxviii).

Predication may thus be defined, a form of speech which expresses a belief that a certain coexistence or sequence of sensations or ideas, did, does, or, under certain conditions, would take place: and the reverse of this when the predication is negative. (Vol. I, pp. 161–4.)

*     *     *     *     *

[*Continuing his discussion of predication, James Mill says:*] *We have already seen, perhaps at sufficient length, the manner in which, and the end for which, the Genus, and the Species are predicated of any subject. It is, that the more comprehensive name, may be substituted for the less comprehensive; so that each of our marks may answer the purpose of marking, to as great an extent as possible. In this manner we substitute the word* man, *for example, for the word* Thomas, *when we predicate the Species of the individual, in the proposition, "Thomas is a man;" the word* animal, *for the word* man, *when we predicate the Genus of the Species, in the proposition, "man, is an animal."*

If what has been said in the preceding note is correct, it is a very inadequate view of the purpose for which a generic or specific name is predicated of any subject, to say that it is in order that "the more comprehensive name may be substituted for the less comprehensive, so that each of our marks may answer the purpose of marking to as great an extent as possible." The more comprehensive and the less comprehensive name have each their uses, and the function of each not only could not be discharged with equal convenience by the other, but could not be discharged by it at all. The purpose, in predicating of anything the name of a class to which it belongs, is not to obtain a better or more commodious name for it, but to make known the fact of its possessing the attributes which constitute the class, and which are therefore signified by the class-name. It is evident that the name of one class cannot possibly perform this office vicariously for the name of another. (Vol. I, p. 165.)

*     *     *     *     *

[*Having dealt with* Genus *and* Species, *James Mill turns to the other three Classical predicables,* Differentia, Proprium, *and* Accidens.]

The author says, that no very distinct boundaries are marked by the three terms, *Differentia*, *Proprium*, and *Accidens*, nor do they effect a scientific division.[48] As

[48]Vol. I, p. 166.

used, however, by the more accurate of the school logicians, they do mark out distinct boundaries, and do effect a scientific division.

Of the attributes common to a class, some have been taken into consideration in forming the class, and are included in the signification of its name. Such, in the case of man, are rationality, and the outward form which we call the human. These attributes are its Differentiae; the fundamental differences which distinguish that class from the others most nearly allied to it. The school logicians were contented with one Differentia, whenever one was sufficient completely to circumscribe the class. But this was an error, because one attribute may be sufficient for distinction, and yet may not exhaust the signification of the class-name. All attributes, then, which are part of that signification, are set apart as Differentiae. Other attributes, though not included among those which constitute the class, and which are directly signified by its name, are consequences of some of those which constitute the class, and always found along with them. These attributes of the class are its Propria. Thus, to be bounded by three straight lines is the Differentia of a triangle: to have the sum of its three angles equal to two right angles, being a consequence of its Differentia, is a Proprium of it. Rationality is a Differentia of the class *Man*: to be able to build cities is a Proprium, being a consequence of rationality, but not, as that is, included in the meaning of the word *Man*. All other attributes of the class, which are neither included in the meaning of the name, nor are consequences of any which are included, are Accidents, however universally and constantly they may be true of the class; as blackness, of crows.

The author's remark, that these three classes of Attributives differ from one another only in the accident of their application,[49] is most just. There are not some attributes which are always Differentiae, and others which are always Propria, or always Accidents. The same attribute which is a Differentia of one genus or species, may be, and often is, a Proprium or an Accidens of others, and so on. (Vol. I, pp. 168–9.)

\*     \*     \*     \*     \*

[*James Mill argues that*] *all Predication, is Predication of Genus or Species, since the Attributives classed under the titles of* Differentia, Proprium, Accidens, *cannot be used but as part of the name of a Species. But we have seen, above, that Predication by Genus and Species is merely the substitution of one name for another, the more general for the less general; the fact of the substitution being marked by the* Copula. *It follows, if all Predication is by Genus and Species, that all Predication is the substitution of one name for another, the more for the less general.*

[49]*Ibid.*, p. 167.

*It will be easy for the learner to make this material fact familiar to himself, by attending to a few instances. Thus, when it is said that man is rational, the term* rational *is evidently elliptical, and the word* animal *is understood. The word* rational, *according to grammatical language, is an adjective, and is significant only in conjunction with a substantive. According to logical language, it is a connotative term, and is without a meaning when disjoined from the object, the property or properties of which it connotes.*

I am unable to feel the force of this remark. Every predication ascribes an attribute to a subject. Differentiae, Propria, and Accidents, agree with generic and specific names in expressing attributes, and the attributes they express are the whole of their meaning. I therefore cannot see why there should not be Predication of any of these, as well as of Genus and Species. These three Predicables, the author says, cannot be used but as part of the name of a genus or species: they are adjectives, and cannot be employed without a substantive understood. Allowing this to be logically, as it is grammatically, true, still the comprehensive and almost insignificant substantive, "thing" or "being," fully answers the purpose; and the entire meaning of the predication is contained in the adjective. These adjectives, as the author remarks, are connotative terms; but so, on his own shewing elsewhere, are all concrete substantives, except proper names. Why, when it is said that man is rational, must "the word *animal*" be "understood?" Nothing is understood but that the being, Man, has the attribute of reason. If we say, God is rational, is animal understood? It was only the Greeks who classed their gods as ζῶα ἀθάνατα.[50]

The exclusion of the three latter Predicables from predication probably recommended itself to the author as a support to his doctrine that all Predication is the substitution of one name for another, which he considered himself to have already demonstrated so far as regards Genus and Species. But proofs have just been given that in the predication of Genus and Species no more than in that of Differentia, Proprium, or Accidens, is anything which turns upon names the main consideration. Except in the case of definitions, and other merely verbal propositions, every proposition is intended to communicate a matter of fact: This subject has that attribute—This cluster of sensations is always accompanied by that sensation.

Let me remark by the way, that the word *connote* is here used by the author in what I consider its legitimate sense—that in which a name is said to connote a property or properties belonging to the object it is predicated of. He afterwards

---

[50]"Immortal beings": see esp. Homer (ca. 700 B.C.), *Iliad* (Greek and English), trans. Augustus Taber Murray, 2 vols. (London: Heinemann; Cambridge, Mass.: Harvard University Press, 1924), Vol. I, pp. 42, 204, 222, 224, 280, 308; and *Odyssey* (London: Heinemann; Cambridge, Mass.: Harvard University Press, 1919), Vol. I, pp. 4, 6, 206, 228; and cf. Pindar (ca. 518-ca. 446 B.C.), *The Odes* (Greek and English), trans. John Sandys (London: Heinemann; Cambridge, Mass.: Harvard University Press, 1946), p. 534.

casts off this use of the term, and introduces one the exact reverse: but of this hereafter.[51] (Vol. I, pp. 169–71.)

\*    \*    \*    \*    \*

[*Immediately following the text quoted in the previous entry, James Mill remarks:*] *With respect, however, to such examples as this last, namely, all those in which the predicate consists of the genus and differentia, the proposition is a mere definition; and the predicate, and the subject, are precisely equivalent. Thus, "rational animal" is precisely the same class as "man;" and they are only two names for the same thing; the one a simple, or single-worded name; the other a complex, or doubled-worded, name. Such propositions therefore are, properly speaking, not Predications at all. When they are used for any other purpose than to make known, or to fix, the meaning of a term, they are useless, and are denominated identical propositions.*

In this passage the author virtually gives up the part of his theory of Predication which is borrowed from Hobbes.[52] According to his doctrine in this place, whenever the predicate and the subject are exactly equivalent, and "are only two names for the same thing," the predication serves only "to make known, or to fix, the meaning of a term," and "such propositions are, properly speaking, not Predications at all." (Vol. I, p. 171.)

\*    \*    \*    \*    \*

[*James Mill argues in detail (Vol. I, pp. 174–8) the pernicious effects of the copula verb's being used also to denote existence, citing the verb* to be *in English. To this passage is appended a note by Findlater (pp. 178–82) in which he shows how this confusion is avoided in non-Indo-European languages. J.S. Mill's note follows immediately on Findlater's.*]

The interesting and important philological facts adduced by Mr. Findlater, confirm and illustrate in a very striking manner the doctrine in the text, of the radical distinction between the functions of the copula in predication, and those of the substantive verb; by shewing that many languages have no substantive verb, no verb expressive of mere existence, and yet signify their predications by other means; and that probably all languages began without a substantive verb, though they must always have had predications.

[51]See pp. 148–51 below.
[52]See pp. 128–9 above.

The confusion between these two different functions in the European languages, and the ambiguity of the verb *To Be*, which fulfils them both, are among the most important of the minor philosophical truths to which attention has been called by the author of the *Analysis*. As in the case of many other luminous thoughts, an approach is found to have been made to it by previous thinkers. Hobbes, though he did not reach it, came very close to it, and it was still more distinctly anticipated by Laromiguière, though without any sufficient perception of its value. It occurs in a criticism on a passage of Pascal, and in the following words.

Quand on dit, l'être est, etc. le mot *est*, ou le verbe, n'exprime pas la même chose que le mot *être*, sujet de la définition. Si j'énonce la proposition suivante: Dieu est existant, je ne voudrais pas dire assurément, Dieu existe existant: cela ne ferait pas un sens; de même, si je dis que Virgile est poëte, je ne veux pas donner à entendre que Virgile existe. Le verbe *est*, dans la proposition, n'exprime donc pas l'existence réelle; il n'exprime qu'un rapport spécial entre le sujet et l'attribut, le rapport du contenant au contenu. . . .*

Having thus hit upon an unobvious truth in the course of an argument directed to another purpose, he passes on and takes no further notice of it.

It may seem strange that the verb which signifies existence should have been employed in so many different languages as the sign of predication, if there is no real connection between the two meanings. But languages have been built up by the extension of an originally small number of words, with or without alterations of form, to express new meanings, the choice of the word being often determined by very distant analogies. In the present case, the analogy is not distant. All our predications are intended to declare the manner in which something affects, or would affect, ourselves or others. Our idea of existence is simply the idea of something which affects or would affect us somehow, without distinction of mode. Everything, therefore, which we can have occasion to assert of an existing thing, may be looked upon as a particular mode of its existence. Since snow is white, and since snow exists, it may be said to exist white; and if a sign was wanted by which to predicate white of snow, the word exists would be very likely to present itself. But most of our predications do relate to existing things: and this being so, it is in the ordinary course of the human mind that the same sign should be adhered to when we are predicating something of a merely imaginary thing (an abstraction, for instance) and that, being so used, it should create an association between the abstraction and the notion of real existence. (Vol. I, pp. 182–4.)

\* \* \* \* \*

*[Pierre Laromiguière (1756–1837),] *Leçons de philosophie* [1815–18], 7me ed. [2 vols. (Paris: Hachette, 1858)], Vol. I, p. 307. [The criticism is of Blaise Pascal (1623–62), *De l'esprit géométrique* (1658), printed in the Appendix to Vol. II of Laromiguière's *Leçons*, esp. pp. 471–4.]

[*To illustrate the sequences in trains of thought connected by cause and effect, James Mill says:*] *let me suppose that I have a flint and steel in my hand, which I am about to strike, one against the other, but at that instant perceive a barrel of gunpowder open, close before me. I withhold the stroke in consequence of the train of thought which suggests to me the ultimate effect. If I have occasion to mark the train, I can only do it by a series of Predications, each of which marks a sequence in the train of causes and effects. "I strike the flint on the steel," first sequence. "The stroke produces a spark," second sequence. "The spark falls on gunpowder," third sequence. "The spark ignites the gunpowder," fourth sequence. "The gunpowder ignited makes an explosion," fifth sequence. The ideas contained in these propositions must all have passed through my mind, and this is the only mode in which language enables me to mark them in their order.*

It is necessary again to notice the consistent omission, throughout the author's theory of Predication, of the element Belief. In the case supposed, the ideas contained in all the propositions might have passed through the mind, without our being led to assert the propositions. I might have thought of every step in the series of phenomena mentioned, might have pictured all of them in my imagination, and have come to the conclusion that they would not happen. I therefore should not have made, either in words or in thought, the predication, This gunpowder will explode if I strike the flint against the steel. Yet the same ideas would have passed through my mind in the same order, in which they stand in the text. The only deficient link would have been the final one, the Belief. (Vol. I, p. 187.)

\*     \*     \*     \*     \*

[*To illustrate sequences connected by being "included under the same name" (Vol. I, p. 186), James Mill refers (p. 188) to syllogism as the leading example.*] *Let us consider the following very familiar instance. "Every tree is a vegetable: every oak is a tree: therefore, every oak is a vegetable." This is evidently a process of naming. The primary idea is that of the object called an oak; from the name* oak, *I proceed to the name* tree, *finding that the name* oak, *is included in the name* tree; *and from the name* tree, *I proceed to the name* vegetable, *finding that the name* tree *is included in the name* vegetable, *and by consequence the name* oak. *This is the series of thoughts, which is marked in order, by the three propositions or predications of the syllogism.*

For the present I shall only remark on this theory of the syllogism, that it must stand or fall with the theory of Predication of which it is the sequel. If, as I have maintained, the propositions which are the premises of the syllogism are not correctly described as mere processes of naming, neither is the formula by which a third proposition is elicited from these two a process of mere naming. What it is, will be considered hereafter.[53] (Vol. I, p. 188.)

*	*	*	*	*

[*Discussing the predications in geometry, James Mill comments:*] *The amount of the three angles of a triangle, is twice a right angle. I arrive at this conclusion, as it is called, by a process of reasoning: that is to say, I find out a name "twice a right angle," which much more distinctly points out to me a certain quantity, than my first name, "amount of the three angles of a triangle;" and the process by which I arrive at this name is a successive change of names, and nothing more; as any one may prove to himself by merely observing the steps of the demonstration.*

I cannot see any propriety in the expression that when we infer the sum of the three angles of a triangle to be twice a right angle, the operation consists in finding a second name which more distinctly points out the quantity than the first name. When we assent to the proof of this theorem, we do much more than obtain a new and more expressive name for a known fact; we learn a fact previously unknown. It is true that one result of our knowledge of this theorem is to give us a name for the sum of the three angles, "the marking power of which is perfectly known to us:"[54] but it was not for want of knowing the marking power of the phrase "sum of the three angles of a triangle" that we did not know what that sum amounted to. We knew perfectly what the expression "sum of the three angles" was appointed to mark. What we have obtained, that we did not previously possess, is not a better mark for the same thing, but an additional fact to mark—the fact which is marked by predicating of that sum, the phrase "twice a right angle." (Vol. I, p. 191.)

*	*	*	*	*

[*Treating a matter to which he later returns, the class of words which are names of names, James Mill says:*] WORD *is a* generical *name for all Names. It is not the name of a Thing, as chair is the name of a thing, or watch, or picture. But word is a name for these several names; chair is a word, watch is a word, picture is a word, and so of all other names. Thus grammatical and logical terms are names of names. The word* noun, *is the name of one class of words,* verb *of another,* preposition *of another, and so on. The word* sentence, *is the name of a series of words put together for a certain purpose; the word* paragraph, *the same; and so*

[53]See p. 175 below.
[54]Vol. I, p. 190.

oration, discourse, essay, treatise, *etc. The words* genus *and* species, *are not names of things, but of names. Genus is not the name of any thing called animal or any thing called body; it is a name of the* names *animal, body, and so on; the* name *animal is a* genus, *the* name *body is a* genus; *and in like manner is the* name *man a* species, *the* name *horse, the* name *crow, and so on. The name* proposition, *the* name *syllogism, are names of a series of words put together for a particular purpose; and so is the term* definition; *and the term* argument. *It will be easily seen that these words enter into Predication precisely on the same principles as other words. Either the more distinct is predicated of the less distinct, its equivalent; or the more comprehensive of the less comprehensive. Thus we say, that nouns and verbs are declinables; preposition and adverb indeclinables; where the more comprehensive terms are predicated of the less. Thus we say, that adjectives and verbs are attributes; where the more distinct is predicated of the less.*

This exposition of the class of words which are properly names of names, belongs originally to Hobbes,[55] and is highly important. They are a kind of names, the signification of which is very often misunderstood, and has given occasion to much hazy speculation. It should however be remarked that the words *genus* and *species* are not solely names of names; they are ambiguous. A genus never indeed means (as many of the schoolmen supposed) an abstract entity, distinct from all the individuals composing the class; but it often means the sum of those individuals taken collectively; the class as a whole, distinguished on the one hand from the single objects comprising it, and on the other hand from the class name. (Vol. I, pp. 192–3.)

\* \* \* \* \*

[*In "Adverbs," Sect. vi of Chap. iv, to illustrate his assertion that adverbs are always employed to modify the subject or predicate of a proposition, James Mill comments (Vol. I, p. 199):*] *"Anciently," is an adverb of time. It is of the same import as the expression, "In distant past time." It is applied to modify the subject, or predicate, of a proposition, as in the following example: "A number of men anciently in England had wives in common." "Had wives in common," is the predicate of the above proposition, and it is modified, or limited, in respect to time, by the word "anciently." [He goes on to deal with adverbs of place, quality, and relation; J.S. Mill's note comes at the end of the section.*]

In many cases, and even in some of the examples given, the adverb does not modify either the subject or the predicate, but the application of the one to the

[55]Hobbes, "Computation or Logic" (in Latin, 1655), Pt. I of *Elements of Philosophy*, in *English Works*, Vol. I, p. 21 (Chap. ii, Sect. 10).

other. "Anciently," in the proposition cited, is intended to limit and qualify not men, nor community of wives, but the practice by men of community of wives: it is a circumstance affecting not the subject or the predicate, but the predication. The qualification of past and distant time attaches to the fact asserted, and to the copula, which is the mark of assertion. The reason of its seeming to attach to the predicate is because, as the author remarked in a previous section, the predicate, when a verb, includes the copula. (Vol. I, p. 200.)

*     *     *     *     *

[*At the end of Chap. v, "Consciousness," a long note by Bain, commenting generally on the term, is appended (Vol. I, pp. 226–9); J.S. Mill's note follows it.*]

Those psychologists who think that being conscious of a feeling is something different from merely having the feeling, generally give the name Consciousness to the mental act by which we refer the feeling to ourself; or, in other words, regard it in its relation to the series of many feelings, which constitutes our sentient life. Many philosophers have thought that this reference is necessarily involved in the fact of sensation: we cannot, they think, have a feeling, without having the knowledge awakened in us at the same moment, of a Self who feels it. But of this as a primordial fact of our nature, it is impossible to have direct evidence; and a supposition may be made which renders its truth at least questionable. Suppose a being, gifted with sensation but devoid of memory; whose sensations follow one after another, but leave no trace of their existence when they cease. Could this being have any knowledge or notion of a Self? Would he ever say to himself, *I* feel; this sensation is *mine*? I think not. The notion of a Self is, I apprehend, a consequence of Memory. There is no meaning in the word *Ego* or *I*, unless the I of to-day is also the I of yesterday; a permanent element which abides through a succession of feelings, and connects the feeling of each moment with the remembrance of previous feelings. We have, no doubt, a considerable difficulty in believing that a sentient being can exist without the consciousness of Itself. But this difficulty arises from the irresistible association which we, who possess Memory, form in our early infancy between every one of our feelings and our remembrance of the entire series of feelings of which it forms a part, and consequently between every one of our feelings and our Self. A slight correction, therefore, seems requisite to the doctrine of the author laid down in the present chapter.[56] There is a mental process, over and above the mere having a feeling, to which the word Consciousness is sometimes, and it can hardly be said improperly, applied, *viz.* the reference of the feeling to our Self. But this process, though

[56]See esp. Vol. I, p. 224.

separable in thought from the actual feeling, and in all probability not accompanying it in the beginning, is, from a very early period of our existence, inseparably attendant on it, though, like many other mental processes, it often takes place too rapidly to be remembered at the next instant.

Other thinkers, or perhaps the same thinkers on other occasions, employ the word *Consciousness* as almost a synonyme of *Attention*. We all know that we have a power, partly voluntary, though often acting independently of our will, of *attending* (as it is called) to a particular sensation or thought. The essence of Attention is that the sensation or thought is, as it were, magnified, or strengthened: it becomes more intense as a whole, and at the same time more distinct and definite in its various parts, like a visible object when a stronger light is thrown upon it: while all other sensations or thoughts which do or which might present themselves at the same moment are blunted and dimmed, or altogether excluded. This heightening of the feeling we may call, if we please, heightening the consciousness of the feeling; and it may be said that we are made more conscious of the feeling than we were before: but the expression is scarcely correct, for we are not more conscious of the feeling, but are conscious of more feeling.

In some cases we are even said to be, by an act of attention, made conscious of a feeling of which we should otherwise have been unconscious: and there is much difference of opinion as to what it is which really occurs in this case. The point has received some consideration in a former Note,[57] but there may be advantage in again recalling it to remembrance. It frequently happens (examples of it are abundant in the *Analysis*) that certain of our sensations, or certain parts of the series of our thoughts, not being sufficiently pleasurable or painful to compel attention, and there being no motive for attending to them voluntarily, pass off without having been attended to; and, not having received that artificial intensification, they are too slight and too fugitive to be remembered. We often have evidence that these sensations or ideas have been in the mind; because, during their short passage, they have called up other ideas by association. A good example is the case of reading from a book, when we must have perceived and recognized the visible letters and syllables, yet we retain a remembrance only of the sense which they conveyed. In such cases many psychologists think that the impressions have passed through the mind without our being conscious of them.[58] But to have feelings unconsciously, to have had them without being aware, is something like a contradiction. All we really know is that we do not remember having had them; whence we reasonably conclude that if we had them, we did not attend to them; and this inattention to our feelings is what seems to be here meant

---

[57]See pp. 117–19 above.
[58]See Hartley, *Observations*, Pt. I, p. 288; and Spencer, *Principles of Psychology*, p. 232; cf. Bain, *The Senses and the Intellect*, p. 329 and n, and *The Emotions and the Will*, pp. 557–8.

by being unconscious of them. Either we had the sensations or other feelings without attending to them, and therefore immediately forgot them, or we never, in reality, had them. This last has been the opinion of some of the profoundest psychologists. Even in cases in which it is certain that we once had these feelings, and had them with a lively consciousness (as of the letters and syllables when we were only learning to read) yet when through numberless repetitions the process has become so rapid that we no longer remember having those visual sensations, these philosophers think that they are elided,—that we cease to have them at all. The usual impressions are made on our organs by the written characters, and are transmitted to the brain, but these organic states, they think, pass away without having had time to excite the sensations corresponding to them, the chain of association being kept up by the organic states without need of the sensations. This was apparently the opinion of Hartley; and is distinctly that of Mr. Herbert Spencer. The conflicting suppositions are both consistent with the known facts of our mental nature. Which of them is the true, our present knowledge does not, I think, enable us to decide.

The author of the *Analysis* often insists on the important doctrine that we have many feelings, both of the physical and of the mental class, which, either because they are permanent and unchangeable, or for the contrary reason, that they are extremely fugitive and evanescent, and are at the same time uninteresting to us except for the mental processes they originate, we form the habit of not attending to; and this habit, after a time, grows into an incapacity; we become unable to attend to them, even if we wish. In such cases we are usually not aware that we have had the feelings; yet the author seems to be of opinion that we really have them. He says, for example, in the section on Muscular Sensations: "We know that the air is continually pressing upon our bodies. But the sensation being continual, without any call to attend to it, we lose from habit, the power of doing so. The sensation is as if it did not exist."[59] Is it not the most reasonable supposition that the sensation does not exist; that the necessary condition of sensation is change; that an unchanging sensation, instead of becoming latent, dwindles in intensity, until it dies away, and ceases to be a sensation? Mr. Bain expresses this mental law by saying, that a necessary condition of Consciousness is change; that we are conscious only of changes of state.[60] I apprehend that change is necessary to consciousness of feeling, only because it is necessary to feeling: when there is no change, there is, not a permanent feeling of which we are unconscious, but no feeling at all.

In the concluding chapter of Mr. Bain's great work, there is an enumeration of

---

[59]Vol. I, p. 41.
[60]See *The Senses and the Intellect*, p. 325, and *The Emotions and the Will*, pp. 566–8.

the various senses in which the word *Consciousness* is used.[61] He finds them no fewer than thirteen. (Vol. I, pp. 229–32.)

\*   \*   \*   \*   \*

[*J.S. Mill's note comes at the end of Chap. vi, "Conception."*]

The doctrine of this chapter is as just as it is admirably stated. A conception is nothing whatever but a complex idea, and to conceive is to have a complex idea. But as there must always have been some cause why a second name is used when there is already a first, there is generally some difference in the occasions of their employment: and a recognition of this difference is necessary to the completeness of the exposition. It seems to me that *conception* and *to conceive* are phrases appropriated to the case in which the thing conceived is supposed to be something external to my own mind. I am not said to conceive my own thoughts; unless it be in the case of an invention, or mental creation; and even then, to conceive it, means to imagine it realized, so that it may be presented to myself or others as an external object. To conceive something is to understand what it is; to adapt my complex idea to something presented to me objectively. I am asked to conceive an iceberg: it is not enough that I form to myself some complex idea; it must be a complex idea which shall really resemble an iceberg, *i.e.* what is called an iceberg by other people. My complex idea must be made up of the elements in my mind which correspond to the elements making up the idea of an iceberg in theirs.

This is connected with one of the most powerful and misleading of the illusions of general language. The purposes of general names would not be answered, unless the complex idea connected with a general name in one person's mind were composed of essentially the same elements as the idea connected with it in the mind of another. There hence arises a natural illusion, making us feel as if, instead of ideas as numerous as minds, and merely resembling one another, there were one idea, independent of individual minds, and to which it is the business of each to learn to make his private idea correspond. This is the Platonic doctrine of Ideas in all its purity:[62] and as half the speculative world are Platonists without knowing it, hence it also is that in the writings of so many psychologists we read of *the* conception or *the* concept of so and so; as if there was a concept of a thing or of a class of things, other than the ideas in individual minds—a concept belonging to everybody, the common inheritance of the human race, but independent of any of

[61]*The Emotions and the Will*, pp. 555–61.
[62]See, e.g., Plato, *Parmenides*, pp. 198–236 (126[a]–137[b]), and *Republic*, pp. 420–2 (596[a]–598[e]).

the particular minds which conceive it. In reality, however, this common concept is but the sum of the elements which it is requisite for the purposes of discourse that people should agree with one another in including in the complex idea which they associate with a class name. As we shall presently see, these are only a part, and often but a small part, of each person's complex idea, but they are the part which it is necessary should be the same in all. (Vol. I, pp. 236–7.)

\*     \*     \*     \*     \*

[*In Chap. viii, "Classification," developing further a position mentioned earlier, James Mill says:*] *Man first becomes acquainted with individuals. He first names individuals. But individuals are innumerable, and he cannot have innumerable names. He must make one name serve for many individuals. It is thus obvious, and certain, that men were led to class solely for the purpose of economizing in the use of names. Could the processes of naming and discourse have been as conveniently managed by a name for every individual, the names of classes, and the idea of classification, would never have existed. But as the limits of the human memory did not enable men to retain beyond a very limited number of names; and even if it had, as it would have required a most inconvenient portion of time, to run over in discourse, as many names of individuals, and of individual qualities, as there is occasion to refer to in discourse, it was necessary to have contrivances of abridgement; that is, to employ names which marked equally a number of individuals, with all their separate properties; and enabled us to speak of multitudes at once.*

The doctrine that "men were led to class solely for the purpose of economizing in the use of names," is here reasserted in the most unqualified terms. The author plainly says that if our memory had been sufficiently vast to contain a name for every individual, the names of classes and the idea of classification would never have existed. Yet how (I am obliged to ask) could we have done without them? We could not have dispensed with names to mark the points in which different individuals resemble one another: and these are class-names. The fact that we require names for the purpose of making affirmations—of predicating qualities—is in some measure recognised by the author, when he says "it would have required a most inconvenient portion of time to run over in discourse as many names of individuals *and of individual qualities* as there is occasion to refer to in discourse." But what is meant by an individual quality? It is not *individual* qualities that we ever have occasion to predicate. It is true that the qualities of an object are only the various ways in which we or other minds are affected by it, and these affections are not the same in different objects, except in the sense in which the word *same* stands for exact similarity. But we never have occasion to predicate of an object the individual and instantaneous impressions which it produces in us. The only meaning of predicating a quality at all, is to affirm a resemblance. When we ascribe a quality to an object, we intend to assert that the object affects us in a manner similar to that in which we are affected by a known class of objects. A quality, indeed, in the custom of language, does not admit of individuality: it is supposed to be one thing common to many; which, being explained, means that it is the name of a resemblance among our sensations, and not a name of the individual sensations which resemble. Qualities, therefore, cannot be predicated without general names; nor, consequently, without classification. Wherever there is a general name there is a class: classification, and general names, are things exactly coextensive. It thus appears that, without classification, language would not fulfil its most important function. Had we no names but those of individuals, the names might serve as marks to bring those individuals to mind, but would not enable us to make a single assertion respecting them, except that one individual is not another. Not a particle of the knowledge we have of them could be expressed in words. (Vol. I, pp. 260–2.)

\* \* \* \* \*

[*At the conclusion of Chap. viii, George Grote supplies a long note (Vol. I, pp. 271–87) on the Socratic philosophers' notions of classification and abstraction; J.S. Mill's note follows immediately.*]

Rejecting the notion that classes and classification would not have existed but for the necessity of economizing names, we may say that objects are formed into classes on account of their resemblance. It is natural to think of like objects together; which is, indeed, one of the two fundamental laws of association. But the resembling objects which are spontaneously thought of together, are those which resemble each other obviously, in their superficial aspect. These are the only classes which we should form unpremeditatedly, and without the use of expedients. But there are other resemblances which are not superficially obvious; and many are not brought to light except by long experience, or observation carefully directed to the purpose; being mostly resemblances in the manner in which the objects act on, or are acted on by, other things. These more recondite resemblances are often those which are of greatest importance to our interests. It is important to us that we should think of those things together, which agree in any particular that materially concerns us. For this purpose, besides the classes which form themselves in our minds spontaneously by the general law of association, we form other classes artificially, that is, we take pains to associate mentally together things which we wish to think of together, but which are not sufficiently associated by the spontaneous action of association by resemblance. The grand instrument we employ in forming these artificial associations, is general names. We give a common name to all the objects, we associate each of the objects with the name, and by their common association with the name they are knit together in close association with one another.

But in what manner does the name effect this purpose, of uniting into one complex class-idea all the objects which agree with one another in certain definite particulars? We effect this by associating the name in a peculiarly strong and close manner with those particulars. It is, of course, associated with the objects also; and the name seldom or never calls up the ideas of the class-characteristics unaccompanied by any other qualities of the objects. All our ideas are of individuals, or of numbers of individuals, and are clothed with more or fewer of the attributes which are peculiar to the individuals thought of. Still, a class-name stands in a very different relation to the definite resemblances which it is intended to mark, from that in which it stands to the various accessory circumstances which may form part of the image it calls up. There are certain attributes common to the entire class, which the class-name was either deliberately selected as a mark of, or, at all events, which guide us in the application of it. These attributes are the real meaning of the class-name—are what we intend to ascribe to an object when we call it by that name. With these the association of the name is close and strong: and the employment of the same name by different persons, provided they employ it with a precise adherence to the meaning, ensures that they shall all include these attributes in the complex idea which they associate with the name. This is not the case with any of the other qualities of the individual objects, even if they happen to be common to all the objects, still less if they belong only to some of them. The class-name calls up, in every mind that hears or uses it, the idea of one or more individual objects, clothed more or less copiously with other qualities than those marked by the name; but these other qualities may, consistently with the purposes for which the class is formed and the name given, be different with different persons, and with the same person at different times. What images of individual horses the word *horse* shall call up, depends on such accidents as the person's taste in horses, the particular horses he may happen to possess, the descriptions he last read, or the casual pecularities of the horses he recently saw. In general, therefore, no very strong or permanent association, and especially no association common to all who use the language, will be formed between the word *horse* and any of the qualities of horses but those expressly or tacitly recognised as the foundations of the class. The complex ideas thus formed consisting of an inner nucleus of definite elements always the same, imbedded in a generally much greater number of elements indefinitely variable, are our ideas of classes; the ideas connected with general names; what are called General Notions: which are neither real objective entities, as the Realists held, nor mere names, as supposed to be maintained by the Nominalists, nor abstract ideas excluding all properties not common to the class, such as Locke's famous Idea of a triangle that is neither equilateral nor isosceles nor scalene.[63] We cannot represent to ourselves a triangle with no properties but those common to all triangles: but we may represent it to ourselves sometimes in one of those three forms, sometimes in another, being aware all the while that all of them are equally consistent with its being a triangle.

One important consequence of these considerations is, that the meaning of a class-name is not the same thing with the complex idea associated with it. The complex idea associated with the name *man*, includes, in the mind of every one, innumerable simple ideas besides those which the name is intended to mark, and in the absence of which it would not be predicated. But this multitude of simple ideas which help to swell the complex idea are infinitely variable, and never exactly the same in any two persons, depending in each upon the amount of his knowledge, and the nature, variety, and recent date of his experience. They are therefore no part of the meaning of the name. They are not the association common to all, which it was intended to form, and which enables the name to be used by all in the same manner, to be understood in a common sense by all, and to serve, therefore, as a vehicle for the communication, between one and another, of the same thoughts. What does this, is the nucleus of more closely associated ideas, which is the constant element in the complex idea of the class, both in the same mind at different times, and in different minds.

It is proper to add, that the class-name is not solely a mark of the distinguishing class-attributes, it is a mark also of the objects. The name *man* does not merely signify the qualities of animal life, rationality, and the human form, it signifies all individual men. It even signifies these in a more direct way than it signifies the attributes, for it is predicated of the men, but not predicated of the attributes; just as the proper name of an individual man is predicated of him. We say, This is a man, just as we say, This is John Thompson: and if John Thompson is the name of one man, *Man* is, in the same manner, a name of all men. A class name, being thus a name of the various objects composing the class, signifies two distinct things, in two different modes of signification. It signifies the individual objects which *are* the class, and it signifies the common attributes which constitute the class. It is predicated only of the objects; but when predicated, it conveys the information that these objects possess those attributes. Every concrete class-name is thus a connotative name. It marks both the objects and their common attributes, or rather, that portion of their common attributes in virtue of which they have been made into a class. It *denotes* the objects, and, in a mode of speech lately revived from the old logicians, it *connotes* the attributes. The author of the *Analysis* employs the word *connote* in a different manner; we shall presently examine which of the two is best.[64]

We are now ready to consider whether the author's account of the ideas

[63]Locke, *Essay*, *Works*, Vol. III, pp. 27–8 (Bk. IV, Chap. vii, Sect. 9).
[64]See pp. 148–51 below.

connected with General Names is a true and sufficient one. It is best expressed in his own words.

The word *Man*, we shall say, is first applied to an individual; it is first associated with the idea of that individual, and acquires the power of calling up the idea of him; it is next applied to another individual, and acquires the power of calling up the idea of him; so of another, and another, till it has become associated with an indefinite number, and has acquired the power of calling up an indefinite number of those ideas indifferently. What happens? It does call up an indefinite number of the ideas of individuals, as often as it occurs, and calling them up in close connexion, it forms them into a species of complex idea. . . . When the word *man* calls up the ideas of an indefinite number of individuals, not only of all those to whom I have individually given the name, but of all those to whom I have in imagination given it, or imagine it will ever be given, and forms all those ideas into one,—it is evidently a very complex idea, and therefore indistinct; and this indistinctness has doubtless been the main cause of the mystery which has appeared to belong to it. That this however is the process, is an inevitable result of the laws of association.[65]

In brief, my idea of a Man is a complex idea compounded of the ideas of all the men I have ever known and of all those I have ever imagined, knit together into a kind of unit by a close association.

The author's description of the manner in which the class-association begins to be formed, is true and instructive; but does any one's idea of a man actually include all that the author finds in it? By an inevitable result of the laws of association, it is impossible to form an idea of a man in the abstract; the class-attributes are always represented in the mind as part of an image of an individual, either remembered or imagined; this individual may vary from time to time, and several images of individuals may present themselves either alternatively or in succession: but is it necessary that the name should recal images of all the men I ever knew or imagined, or even all of whom I retain a remembrance? In no person who has seen or known many men, can this be the case. Apart from the ideas of the common attributes, the other ideas whether of attributes or of individual men, which enter into the complex idea, are indefinitely variable not only in kind but in quantity. Some people's complex idea of the class is extremely meagre, that of others very ample. Sometimes we know a class only from its definition, *i.e.* from an enumeration of its class-attributes, as in the case of an object which we have only read of in scientific books: in such a case the idea raised by the class-name will not be limited to the class-attributes, for we are unable to conceive any object otherwise than clothed with miscellaneous attributes: but these, not being derived from experience of the objects, may be such as the objects never had, nor could have; while nevertheless the class, and the class-name, answer their proper purpose; they cause us to group together all the things possessing the class-attributes, and they inform us that we may expect those attributes in anything of which that name is predicated.

[65]Vol. I, pp. 264–5.

The defect, as it seems to me, of the view taken of General Names in the text, is that it ignores this distinction between the meaning of a general name, and the remainder of the idea which the general name calls up. That remainder is uncertain, variable, scanty in some cases, copious in others, and connected with the name by a very slight tie of association, continually overcome by counter-associations. The only part of the complex idea that is permanent in the same mind, or common to several minds, consists of the distinctive attributes marked by the class-name. Nothing else is universally present, though something else is always present: but whatever else be present, it is through these only that the class-name does its work, and effects the end of its existence. We need not therefore be surprised that these attributes, being all that is of importance in the complex idea, should for a long time have been supposed to be all that is contained in it. The truest doctrine which can be laid down on the subject seems to be this—that the idea corresponding to a class-name is the idea of a certain constant combination of class-attributes, accompanied by a miscellaneous and indefinitely variable collection of ideas of individual objects belonging to the class. (Vol. I, pp. 287–93.)

\*     \*     \*     \*     \*

[*In treating of "Abstraction" (Chap. ix), James Mill turns to the generalizing of adjectives that serve to differentiate.*] *Let us take the word "black" for an example; and let us suppose that we apply this adjective first to the word* man. *We say "black man." But we speedily see that for the same reason for which we say black man we may say black horse, black cow, black coat, and so on. The word* black *is thus associated with innumerable modifications of the sensation black. By frequent repetition, and the gradual strengthening of the association, these modifications are at last called up in such rapid succession that they appear commingled, and no longer many ideas, but one.* Black *is therefore no longer an individual but a general name. It marks not the particular black of a particular individual; but the black of every individual, and of all individuals.*

The example which the author has here selected of a general name, sets in a strong light the imperfection of the theory of general names, laid down by him in the preceding chapter. A name like "black," which marks a simple sensation, is an extreme case of the inapplicability of the theory. Can it be maintained that the idea called up in our minds by the word *black*, is an idea compounded of ideas of black men, black horses, black cows, black coats, and the like? If I can trust my own consciousness, the word need not, and generally does not, call up any idea but that of a single black surface. It is still not an abstract idea, but the idea of an individual object. It is not a mere idea of colour; it is that, combined with ideas of extension and figure, always present but extremely vague, because varying, even from one moment to the next. These vague ideas of an uncertain extension and figure, combined with the perfectly definite idea of a single sensation of colour, are, to my consciousness, the sole components of the complex idea associated with the word *black*. I am unable to find in that complex idea the ideas of black men, horses, or other definite things, though such ideas may of course be recalled by it.

In such a case as this, the idea of a black colour fills by itself the place of the inner nucleus of ideas knit together by a closer association, which I have described as forming the permanent part of our ideas of classes of objects, and the meaning of the class-names. (Vol. I, p. 297.)

\*     \*     \*     \*     \*

[*James Mill returns to the term* connotative, *saying:*] *I shall find much convenience in using the term* NOTATION *to point out the sensation or sensations which are peculiarly marked by such words, the term* CONNOTATION *to point out the clusters which they mark along with this their principal meaning.*

*Thus the word,* black, NOTES *that of which black is more peculiarly the name, a particular colour; it* CONNOTES *the clusters with the names of which it is joined: in the expression,* black man, *it connotes man;* black horse, *it connotes horse; and so of all other cases. The ancient Logicians used these terms, in the inverse order; very absurdly, in my opinion.*

The word *Connote*, with its substantive *Connotation*, was used by the old logicians in two senses; a wider, and a narrower sense. The wider is that in which, up to this place, the author of the *Analysis* has almost invariably used it; and is the sense in which he defined it, in a note to section 5 of his first chapter.

There is a large class of words which denote two things both together; but the one perfectly distinguishable from the other. Of these two things, also, it is observable, that such words express the one primarily as it were; the other in a way which may be called secondary. Thus *white*, in the phrase white horse, denotes two things, the colour and the horse; but it denotes the colour primarily, the horse secondarily. We shall find it very convenient to say, therefore, that it *notes* the primary, *connotes* the secondary signification.[66]

This use of terms is attended with the difficulty, that it may often be disputed which of the significations is primary and which secondary. In the example given, most people would agree with the author that the colour is the primary signification; the word being associated with the objects, only through its previous association with the colour. But take the other of the two words, *horse*. That too is connotative, and in the same manner. It signifies any and every individual horse,

[66]*Ibid.*, pp. 33–4. See p. 107 above.

and it also signifies those attributes common to horses, which led to their being classed together and receiving that common name. Which, in this case, is the primary, and which the second signification? The author would probably say, that in this case, unlike the other, horse is the primary signification, the attributes the secondary. Yet in this equally with the former case, the attributes are the foundation of the meaning: a thing is called a horse to express its resemblance to other horses; and the resemblance consists of the common attributes. The question might be discussed, pro and con, by many arguments, without any conclusive result. The difference between primary and secondary acceptations is too uncertain, and at best too superficial, to be adopted as the logical foundation of the distinction between the two modes of signification.

The author, however, has, throughout the preceding chapters, regarded words as *connoting* any number of things which though included in their signification, are not, in his judgment, what they primarily signify. He said, for example, that a verb notes an action, and connotes the agent (as either me, thee, or some third person), the number of agents (as one or more), the time (as past, present, or future), and three modes, "that in which there is no reference to anything preceding, that in which there is a reference to something preceding, and that in which reference is made to the will of one of the Persons."[67] I cite this complicated case, to shew by a striking example the great latitude with which the author uses the word *Connote*.

But in the present chapter he follows the example of some of the old logicians in adopting a second and more restricted meaning, expressive of the peculiar connotation which belongs to all concrete general names; *viz.* that twofold manner of signification, by which every name of a class signifies, on the one hand, all and each of the individual things composing the class, and on the other hand the common attributes, in consideration of which the class is formed and the name given, and which we intend to affirm of every object to which we apply the name. It is difficult to overrate the importance of keeping in view this distinction, or the danger of overlooking it when not made prominent by an appropriate phrase. The word *Connote*, which had been employed for this purpose, had fallen into disuse. But, though agreeing with the old logicians in using the word *Connote* to express this distinction, the author exactly reverses their employment of it. In their phraseology, the class-name connotes the attributes: in his, it notes the attributes, and connotes the objects. And he declares that in his opinion, their mode of employing the term is very absurd.[68]

We have now to consider which of these two modes of employing it is really the most appropriate.

A concrete general name may be correctly said to be a mark, in a certain way,

[67]*Ibid.*, pp. 154–5.
[68]*Ibid.*, p. 299.

both for the objects and for their common attributes. But which of the two is it conformable to usage to say that it is the name of? Assuredly, the objects. It is they that are called by the name. I am asked, what is this object called? and I answer, a horse. I should not make this answer if I were asked what are these attributes called. Again, I am asked, what is it that is called a horse? and I answer, the object which you see; not the qualities which you see. Let us now suppose that I am asked, what is it that is called black; I answer, all *things* that have this particular colour. Black is a name of all black things. The name of the colour is not black, but blackness. The name of a thing must be the name which is predicated of the thing, as a proper name is predicated of the person or place it belongs to. It is scarcely possible to speak with precision, and adhere consistently to the same mode of speech, if we call a word the name of anything but that which it is predicated of. Accordingly the old logicians, who had not yet departed widely from the custom of common speech, considered all concrete names as the names of objects, and called nothing the name of an attribute but abstract names.

Now there is considerable incongruity in saying that a word connotes, that is, signifies secondarily, the very thing which it is a name of. To connote, is to mark something along with, or in addition to, something else. A name can hardly be said to mark the thing which it is a name of in addition to some other thing. If it marks any other thing, it marks it in addition to the thing of which it is itself the name. In the present case, what is marked in addition, is that which is the cause of giving the name; the attributes, the possession of which by a thing entitles it to that name. It therefore seems more conformable to the original acceptation of the word *Connote*, that we should say of names like *man* or *black* that they connote humanity or blackness, and *de*note, or are names of, men and black objects; rather than, with the author of the *Analysis*, that they note the attributes, and connote the things which possess the attributes.

If this mode of using the terms is more consonant to propriety of language, so also is it more scientifically convenient. It is of extreme importance to have a technical expression exclusively consecrated to signify the peculiar mode in which the name of a class marks the attributes in virtue of which it is a class, and is called by the name. The verb "to note," employed by the author of the *Analysis* as the correlative of "to connote," is far too general to be confined to so specific a use, nor does the author intend so to confine it. "To connote," on the contrary, is a phrase which has been handed down to us in this restricted acceptation, and is perfectly fitted to be used as a technical term. There is no more important use of a term than that of fixing attention upon something which is in danger of not being sufficiently taken notice of. This is emphatically the case with the attribute-signification of the names of objects. That signification has not been seen clearly, and what has been seen of it confusedly has bewildered or misled some of the most distinguished philosophers. From Hobbes to Hamilton, those who have attempted to penetrate the secret of the higher logical operations of the intellect have continually missed the mark for want of the light which a clear conception of the connotation of general names spreads over the subject. There is no fact in psychology which more requires a technical name; and it seems eminently desirable that the words *Connote* and *Connotative* should be exclusively employed for this purpose; and it is for this purpose that I have myself invariably employed them.

In studying the *Analysis*, it is of course necessary to bear in mind that the author does not use the words in this sense, but sometimes in a sense much more vague and indefinite, and, when definite, in a sense the reverse of this. It may seem an almost desperate undertaking, in the case of an unfamiliar term, to attempt to rectify the usage introduced by the actual reviver of the word: and nothing could have induced me to attempt it, but a deliberate conviction that such a technical expression is indispensable to philosophy, and that the author's mode of employing these words unfits them for the purpose for which they are needed, and for which they are well adapted. I fear, however, that I have rarely succeeded in associating the words with their precise meaning, anywhere but in my own writings.[69] The word *Connote*, not unfrequently meets us of late in philosophical speculations, but almost always in a sense more lax than the laxest in which it is employed in the *Analysis*, meaning no more than *to imply*. To such an extent is this the case, that able thinkers and writers do not always even confine the expression to names, but actually speak of Things as connoting whatever, in their opinion, the existence of the Things implies or presupposes. (Vol. I, pp. 299–304.)

\*  \*  \*  \*  \*

[*James Mill asserts that he has shown*] *the real nature of* ABSTRACT *terms; a subject which has in general presented such an appearance of mystery. They are simply the* CONCRETE *terms, with the connotation dropped. And this has in it, surely, no mystery at all.*

After having said that a concrete general name notes an attribute, that is, one of the sensations in a cluster, and connotes the objects which have the attribute, *i.e.* the clusters of which that sensation forms a part;[70] the author proceeds to say that an abstract name is the concrete name with the connotation dropped.

This seems a very indirect and circuitous mode of making us understand what an abstract name signifies. Instead of aiming directly at the mark, it goes round it. It tells us that one name signifies a part of what another name signifies, leaving us to

[69]Most emphatically in his *System of Logic*, Bk. I, Chap. ii, Sect. 5 (*CW*, Vol. VII, pp. 30–40).

[70]Vol. I, p. 299; see pp. 148–51 above.

infer what part. A connotative name with the connotation dropped, is a phrase requiring to be completed by specifying what is the portion of signification left. The concrete name with its connotation signifies an attribute, and also the objects which have the attribute. We are now instructed to drop the latter half of the signification, the objects. What then remains? The attribute. Why not then say at once that the abstract name is the name of the attribute? Why tell us that *x* is *a* plus *b* with *b* dropped, when it was as easy to tell us that *x* is *a*?

The noticeable thing however is that if *a* stands merely for the sensation, *x* really is a little more than *a*: the connotation (in the author's sense of the term) of the concrete name is not *wholly* dropped in the abstract name. The term *blackness*, and every other abstract term, includes in its signification the existence of a black object, though without declaring what it is. That is indeed the distinction between the name of an attribute, and the name of a kind or type of sensation. Names of sensations by themselves are not abstract but concrete names. They mark the type of the sensation, but they do not mark it as emanating from any object. "The sensation of black" is a concrete name, which expresses the sensation apart from all reference to an object. "Blackness" expresses the same sensation with reference to an object, by which the sensation is supposed to be excited. Abstract names thus still retain a limited amount of connotation in both the author's senses of the term—the vaguer and the more specific sense. It is only in the sense to which I am anxious to restrict the term, that any abstract name is without connotation.

An abstract name, then, may be defined as the name of an attribute; and, in the ultimate analysis, as the name of one or more of the sensations of a cluster; not by themselves, but considered as part of any or all of the various clusters, into which that type of sensations enters as a component part. (Vol. I, pp. 304–5.)

*     *     *     *     *

[*James Mill says that the "infinitive mood" is an "abstract term,"*] *with this peculiarity, that, though it leaves out the connotation of the* actor, *it retains the connotation of* time.

The infinitive mood does not always express time. At least, it often expresses it aoristically, without distinction of tense. "To love" is as abstract a name as "love," "to fear," as "fear": they are applied equally to past, present, and future. The infinitives of the past and future, as *amavisse, amaturus esse*, do, however, include in their signification a particular time. (Vol. I, p. 306.)

*     *     *     *     *

[*James Mill suggests that in Latin the formation of abstract terms from verbs (by the addition of* tio*) is the cause of their having both active and passive signification, and laments that the defect has been handed on to English.*] *This ambiguity the Greek language happily avoided: thus it had* πρᾶχις *and* πρᾶγμα, *the first for the active signification of* actio, *the latter the passive.*

I apprehend that πραγμα is not an abstract but a concrete term, and does not express the attribute of being done, but the thing done—the effect which results from the completed action. (Vol. I, p. 308.)

\* \* \* \* \*

[*To James Mill's discussion in Chap. x, "Memory," of the act of trying to remember, Bain adds the following note, to which J.S. Mill's note, in square brackets, is appended:*] *This process seems best expressed by laying down a law of Compound or Composite Association; under which a plurality of feeble links of connexion may be a substitute for one powerful and self-sufficing link.*

The laws of compound association are the subject of one of the most original and profound chapters of Mr. Bain's treatise.\* (Vol. I, p. 323.)

\* \* \* \* \*

*That words alone, without ideas, suggest one another in a train, is proved by our power of repeating a number of words of an unknown language.*

There is here a lapse, of mere expression. The meaning is not that words suggest one another without ideas; words do not suggest words, but the ideas of words. The author intended to say that words, or the ideas of them, often suggest the ideas of other words (forming a series) without suggesting along with them any ideas of the things which those words signify. (Vol. I, p. 327.)

\* \* \* \* \*

[*James Mill asserts that, in memory,*] *there is not only the idea of the thing remembered; there is also the idea of my having seen it. Now these two, 1, the idea*

\*The Senses and the Intellect, Pt. II, Chap. iii [pp. 558–84].

*of the thing, 2, the idea of my having seen it, combined, make up, it will not be doubted, the whole of that state of consciousness which we call memory.*

The doctrine which the author thinks "will not be doubted" is more than doubted by most people, and in my judgment rightly. To complete the memory of seeing the thing, I must have not only the idea of the thing, and the idea of my having seen it, but the belief of my having seen it; and even this is not always enough; for I may believe on the authority of others that I have seen a thing which I have no remembrance of seeing. (Vol. I, p. 329.)

*        *        *        *        *

[*J.S. Mill's note is appended to the end of Chap. x, "Memory."*]

The only difficulty about Memory, when once the laws of Association are understood, is the difference between it and Imagination; but this is a difference which will probably long continue to perplex philosophers. The author finds in Memory, besides the idea of the fact remembered, two other ideas: "the idea of my present self, the remembering self, and the idea of my past self, the remembered or witnessing self:"[71] and a supposed rapid repetition in thought, of the whole of the impressions which I received between the time remembered and the time of remembering. But (apart from the question whether we really do repeat in thought, however summarily, all this series) explaining memory by Self seems very like explaining a thing by the thing. For what notion of Self can we have, apart from Memory? The fact of remembering, *i.e.* of having an idea combined with the belief that the corresponding sensation was actually felt *by me*, seems to be the very elementary fact of Self, the origin and foundation of the idea; presupposed in our having the very complex notion of a Self, which is here introduced to explain it. As, however, the author admits that the phenomenon of Belief, and the notions of Time and of Personal Identity, must be taken into account in order to give a complete explanation of Memory, any further remarks had better be deferred until these subjects have been regularly brought under our consideration.[72] (Vol. I, pp. 339–40.)

*        *        *        *        *

*I take* MEMORY *first, and* JUDGMENT *last, from no other principle of arrange-*

[71]Vol. I, p. 330.
[72]See the following note and those on Belief (pp. 159–74), on Time (p. 204), and on Identity (pp. 211–13) below.

*ment, than facility of exposition; and I have in this way found it convenient to treat of* JUDGMENT *as a case of* BELIEF.

How is it possible to treat of Belief without including in it Memory and Judgment? Memory is a case of belief. In what does Memory differ from Imagination, except in the belief that what it represents did really take place? Judgment, in its popular acceptation, is Belief resulting from deliberate examination, in other words, Belief grounded on evidence: while in its philosophical sense it is coextensive, if not synonymous, with Belief itself. I do not know how it is possible to distinguish a judgment from any other process of the mind, except by its being an act of belief. (Vol. I, p. 342.)

\*　\*　\*　\*　\*

[*James Mill argues that*] to have a sensation, and to believe that we have it, *are not distinguishable things. When I say "I have a sensation," and say, "I believe that I have it," I do not express two states of consciousness, but one and the same state. A sensation is a feeling; but a feeling, and the belief of it are the same thing. The observation applies equally to ideas. When I say I have the idea of the sun, I express the same thing, exactly, as when I say, that I believe I have it. The feeling is one, the names, only, are two. [A note to this passage by Bain, which is followed by J.S. Mill's note, reads:] In the case of a present reality, belief has no place; it can be introduced only by a fiction or a figure. The believing state comes into operation when something thought of is still remote, and attainable by an intermediate exertion. The fact "I see the sun" is full fruition: the fact that I can see the sun by going out of doors affords scope for belief or disbelief.*

The difference between Mr. Bain and the author is but in language and classification. It is necessary for the reader of the *Analysis* to remember, that the author uses the word *Belief* as the most general term for every species of conviction or assurance; the assurance of what is before our eyes, as well as of that which we only remember or expect; of what we know by direct perception, as well as of what we accept on the evidence of testimony or of reasoning: all this we are convinced or persuaded of; all this, in the author's language, we believe. Mr. Bain, on the other hand, like Sir William Hamilton and many others, restricts the term to those cases of conviction which are short of direct intuition.[73] (Vol. I, p. 343.)

\*　\*　\*　\*　\*

[73]Bain, *The Emotions and the Will*, pp. 524–5; Hamilton, "Dissertations on Reid," pp. 759–60 (Note A). The "many others" would include Henry Longueville Mansel (1820–71),

*Besides the sensation of colour, I have . . . the belief of a certain distance, at which I see the rose; and that of a certain figure, consisting of leaves disposed in a certain form. I believe that I see this distance and form; in other words, perceive it by the eye, as immediately as I perceive the colour. Now this last part of the process has been explained by various philosophers. There is no dispute, or uncertainty, about the matter. All men admit, that this, one of the most remarkable of all cases of belief, is wholly resolvable into association.*

"All men admit." Certainly not all men; though, at the time when the author wrote, it might be said, with some plausibility, all psychologists. Unfortunately this can no longer be said: Mr. Samuel Bailey has demanded a rehearing of the question, and has pronounced a strong and reasoned opinion on the contrary side; and his example has been followed by several other writers: but without, in my opinion, at all weakening the position which since the publication of Berkeley's *Essay on Vision*, had been almost unanimously maintained by philosophers.[74] (Vol. I, p. 345.)

\* \* \* \* \*

*That a cause means, and can mean nothing to the human mind, but constant antecedent, is no longer a point in dispute.*

Here again the author takes too sanguine a view of the amount of agreement hitherto attained among metaphysical philosophers. "That a cause means, and can mean, nothing to the human mind but constant antecedent" is so far from being "no longer a point in dispute" that it is denied with vehemence by a large numerical majority of philosophers; and its denial is perhaps the principal badge of one of the

---

*The Philosophy of the Conditioned* (London and New York: Strachan, 1866), pp. 18–19, 126n, and James McCosh (1811–94), *An Examination of Mr. J.S. Mill's Philosophy* (London: Macmillan, 1866), pp. 36–7; both of these have reference to J.S. Mill's discussion of the matter in his *Examination of Sir William Hamilton's Philosophy*, *CW*, Vol. IX, pp. 60–5.

[74]The view held by both Mills was first advanced by George Berkeley (1685–1753) in his *An Essay towards a New Theory of Vision* (1709), in *Works*, 3 vols. (London: Priestley, 1820), Vol. I, pp. 225–316. It was challenged by Samuel Bailey (1791–1870) in his *A Review of Berkeley's Theory of Vision* (London: Ridgway, 1842), and *A Letter to a Philosopher* (London: Ridgway, 1843). J.S. Mill controverted him in "Bailey on Berkeley's Theory of Vision" (1842 and 1843), *CW*, Vol. XI, pp. 245–69. Others who opposed Berkeley's opinion included David Brewster (1781–1868), "The Sight and How to See," *North British Review*, XXVI (Nov. 1856), 145–84, and Thomas Kingsmill Abbott (1829–1913), *Sight and Touch* (London: Longman, *et al.*, 1864).

two schools which at this, as at most other times, bisect the philosophical world—the intuitional school and the experiential. (Vol. I, p. 352.)

\*     \*     \*     \*     \*

[*James Mill asserts that the name given to the "supposed cause of supposed causes" is the "*Substratum,*" and comments that in a regressive search there is no reason to stop there.*] *The Barbarian, in accounting for the support of the earth, placed it on the back of a great elephant, and the great elephant on the back of a great tortoise; but neither himself, nor those whom he instructed, were carried by their habits of association any farther.*

It is a question worth considering, why that demand for a cause of everything, which has led to the invention of so many fabulous or fictitious causes, so generally stops short at the first step, without going on to imagine a cause of the cause. But this is quite in the ordinary course of human proceedings. It is no more than we should expect, that these frivolous speculations should be subject to the same limitations as reasonable ones. Even in the region of positive facts—in the explaining of phenomena by real, not imaginary, causes—the first semblance of an explanation generally suffices to satisfy the curiosity which prompts the inquiry. The things men first care to inquire about are those which meet their senses, and among which they live; of these they feel curious as to the origin, and look out for a cause, even if it be but an abstraction. But the cause once found, or imagined, and the familiar fact no longer perplexing them with the feeling of an unsolved enigma, they do not, unless unusually possessed by the speculative spirit, occupy their minds with the unfamiliar antecedent sufficiently to be troubled respecting it with any of the corresponding perplexity. (Vol. I, p. 354.)

\*     \*     \*     \*     \*

[*James Mill says:*] *There are certain things which I consider as marks or signs of sensations in other creatures. The Belief follows the signs, and with a force, not exceeded in any other instance. But the interpretation of signs is wholly a case of association, as the extraordinary phenomena of language abundantly testify.* [*Bain comments, in a note to which J.S. Mill's comment is appended (in square brackets):*] *This is true in by far the greater number of instances. Nevertheless, there are some of the signs of feeling that have an intrinsic efficacy, on very manifest grounds. While the meanings of the smile and the frown could have been reversed, if the association had been the other way, there is an obvious suitability*

*in the harsh stunning tones of the voice to signify anger and to inspire dread, and a
like suitability in the gentle tones to convey affection and kindly feeling. We might
have contracted the opposing associations, had the facts been so arranged, just as
in times of peace, we associate joy with deafening salvos of artillery; and as loud,
sharp-pealing laughter serves in the expression of agreeable feeling. But there is a
gain of effect when the signs employed are such as to chime in, by intrinsic
efficacy, with the associated meanings. On this coincidence depend the refine-
ments of elocution, oratory, and stage display.*

The fact here brought to notice by Mr. Bain is, that certain of the natural expressions of emotion have a kind of analogy to the emotions they express, which
makes an opening for an instinctive interpretation of them, independently of
experience. But if this be so (and there can be little doubt that it is so) the
suggestion takes place by resemblance, and therefore still by association. (Vol. I,
p. 356.)

*   *   *   *   *

*[James Mill says (Vol. I, p. 362):] The fundamental law of association is, that
when two things have been frequently found together, we never perceive or think of
the one without thinking of the other. [He goes on to elucidate, ending the passage
with the remark:] I can no more have the idea of a stone let go in the air, and not
have the idea of its dropping to the ground, than I can have the idea of the stone,
and not have it, at the same time.*

The theory maintained so powerfully and with such high intellectual resources by
the author, that Belief is but an inseparable association, will be examined at length
in a note at the end of the chapter.[75] Meanwhile let it be remarked, that the case of
supposed inseparable association given in this passage, requires to be qualified in
the statement. We cannot, indeed, think of a stone let go in the air, without having
the idea of its falling; but this association is not so strictly inseparable as to disable
us from having the contrary idea. There are analogies in our experience which
enable us without difficulty to form the imagination of a stone suspended in the air.
The case appears to be one in which we can conceive both opposites, falling and
not falling; the incompatible images not, of course, combining, but alternating in
the mind. Which of the two carries belief with it, depends on what is termed
Evidence. (Vol. I, p. 364.)

*   *   *   *   *

[75]See pp. 159–74 below.

[*In a footnote, James Mill comments:*] *Locke, at a period subsequent to the publication of his* Essay, *seems to have become more sensible of the importance of association. These are his words:*—*"I think I shall make some other additions to be put into your Latin translation, and particularly concerning the connexion of ideas, which has not, that I know, been hitherto considered, and has, I guess, a greater influence upon our minds, than is usually taken notice of."* * [*J.S. Mill's note is appended, in square brackets.*]

*a*When Locke wrote the letter here quoted, he had not yet written the chapter of his *Essay* which treats of the Association of Ideas. That chapter did not appear in the original edition, but was first inserted in the fourth, published in 1690.[76] The intention, therefore, which he expressed to Molineux, has received its fulfilment; and the passage quoted further on in the text, is part of the "addition" which he contemplated.*a* (Vol. I, p. 377.)

\* \* \* \* \*

[*To the end of Chap. xi, "Belief," a note by Bain is appended, followed by J.S. Mill's.*]

The analysis of Belief presented in this chapter, brings out the conclusion that all cases of Belief are simply cases of indissoluble association: that there is no generic distinction, but only a difference in the strength of the association, between a case of belief and a case of mere imagination: that to believe a succession or coexistence between two facts is only to have the ideas of the two facts so strongly and closely associated, that we cannot help having the one idea when we have the other.

If this can be proved, it is the greatest of all the triumphs of the Association Psychology. To first appearance, no two things can be more distinct than thinking of two things together, and believing that they are joined together in the outward world. Nevertheless, that the latter state of mind is only an extreme case of the former, is, as we see, the deliberate doctrine of the author of the *Analysis*; and it has also in its favour the high psychological authority of Mr. Herbert Spencer.[77]

*Locke, Letter to Molyneux, 26 Apr., 1695. [In *Works*, Vol. IX, p. 357. Thomas Molyneux (1661–1733), a doctor, was a close friend of Locke's.]

[76]Mill is obviously in error here; the 1st ed. appeared in 1690 (and the letter was written in 1695). Bk. II, Chap. xxxiii, "Of the Association of Ideas" (*Works*, Vol. II, pp. 148–57), was added to the 4th ed., but it appeared in 1700 (London: Churchill and Manslip).

[77]See his *Principles of Psychology*, esp. Pt. IV, pp. 517, 529, 580.

a–aWhen Locke wrote the letter here quoted, he had not yet written the chapter of his Essay treating of the Association of Ideas; which did not appear in the first edition, but was inserted in the fourth, published in 1690. The intention therefore, which he expressed to Molineux, was fulfilled; and the passage quoted in the text further on is part of the "addition" which he contemplated. [*headed:* vol. i, p. 290]

Mr. Bain, in the preceding note, as well as in his systematic work, looks at the phenomenon from another side, and pronounces that what constitutes Belief is the power which an idea has obtained over the Will.[78] It is well known and understood that a mere idea may take such possession of the mind as to exercise an irresistible control over the active faculties, even independently of Volition, and sometimes in opposition to it. This, which Mr. Bain calls the power of a Fixed Idea, is exemplified in the cases of what is called fascination: the impulse which a person looking from a precipice sometimes feels to throw himself down it; and the cases of crimes said to have been committed by persons who abhor them, because that very horror has filled their minds with an intense and irrepressible idea of the act. Since an idea is sometimes able to overpower volition, it is no wonder that an idea should determine volition; as it does whenever we, under the influence of the idea of a pleasure or of a pain, will that which obtains for us the pleasure or averts the pain. In this voluntary action, our conduct is grounded upon a relation between means and an end; (that is, upon a constant conjunction of facts in the way of causation, ultimately resolvable into a case of resemblance and contiguity): in common and unanalytical language, upon certain laws of nature on which we rely. Our reliance is the consequence of an association formed in our minds between the supposed cause and its effect, resulting either from personal experience of their conjunction, from the teachings of other people, or from accidental appearances. Now, according to Mr. Bain, when this association between the means and the end, the end calling up the idea of the means, arrives at the point of giving to the idea thus called up a command over the Will, it constitutes Belief. We believe a thing, when we are ready to act on the faith of it; to face the practical consequences of taking it for granted: and therein lies the distinction between believing two facts to be conjoined, and merely thinking of them together.[79] Thus far Mr. Bain: and with this I fully agree. But something is still wanting to the completeness of the analysis. The theory as stated, distinguishes two antecedents, by a difference not between themselves, but between their consequents. But when the consequents differ, the antecedents cannot be the same. An association of ideas is or is not a Belief, according as it has or has not the power of leading us to voluntary action: this is undeniable: but when there is a difference in the effects there must be a difference in the cause: the association which leads to action must be, in some respect or other, different from that which stops at thought. The question, therefore, raised, and, as they think, resolved, by the author of the *Analysis* and by Mr. Spencer, still demands an answer. Does the difference between the two cases consist in this, that in the one case the association is dissoluble, in the other it is so much more closely riveted, by repetition, or by the intensity of the associated feelings, as to be no longer dissoluble? This is the question we are compelled to face.

---

[78]Bain, *The Emotions and the Will*, pp. 524ff.
[79]*Ibid.*, pp. 525–6.

I

In the first place, then, it may be said—If Belief consisted in an indissoluble association, Belief itself would be indissoluble. An opinion once formed could never afterwards be destroyed or changed. This objection is good against the *word* indissoluble. But those who maintain the theory do not mean by an indissoluble association, one which nothing that can be conceived to happen could possibly dissolve. All our associations of ideas would probably be dissoluble, if experience presented to us the associated facts separate from one another. If we have any associations which are, in practice, indissoluble, it can only be because the conditions of our existence deny to us the experiences which would be capable of dissolving them. What the author of the *Analysis* means by indissoluble associations, are those which we cannot, by any mental effort, at present overcome. If two ideas are, at the present time, so closely associated in our minds, that neither any effort of our own, nor anything else which can happen, can enable us now to have the one without its instantly raising up the other, the association is, in the author's sense of the term, indissoluble. There would be less risk of misunderstanding if we were to discard the word indissoluble, and confine ourselves to the expression which the author employs as its equivalent, inseparable. This I will henceforth do, and we will now enquire whether Belief is nothing but an inseparable association.

In favour of this supposition there is the striking fact, that an inseparable association very often suffices to command belief. There are innumerable cases of Belief for which no cause can be assigned, except that something has created so strong an association between two ideas that the person cannot separate them in thought. The author has given a large assortment of such cases, and has made them tell with great force in support of his theory. Locke, as the author mentions, had already seen, that this is one of the commonest and most fertile sources of erroneous thought;[80] deserving to be placed high in any enumeration of Fallacies. When two things have long been habitually thought of together, and never apart, until the association between the ideas has become so strong that we have great difficulty, or cannot succeed at all, in separating them, there is a strong tendency to believe that the facts are conjoined in reality; and when the association is closer still, that their conjunction is what is called Necessary. Most of the schools of philosophy, both past and present, are so much under the influence of this tendency, as not only to justify it in principle, but to erect it into a Law of Things. The majority of metaphysicians have maintained, and even now maintain, that there are things which, by the laws of intelligence, cannot be separated in thought, and that these things are not only always united in fact, but united by necessity: and, again, other things, which cannot be united in thought—which cannot be thought of together, and that these not only never do, but it is impossible they ever

[80]In Vol. I, pp. 378–80, James Mill quotes from Bk. II, Chap. xxxiii, of Locke's *Essay*.

should, coexist in fact. These supposed necessities are the very foundation of the Transcendental schools of metaphysics, of the Common Sense school, and many others which have not received distinctive names. These are facts in human nature and human history very favourable to the supposition that Belief is but an inseparable association, or at all events that an inseparable association suffices to create Belief.

On the contrary side of the question it may be urged, that the inseparable associations which are so often found to generate Beliefs, do not generate them in everybody. Analytical and philosophical minds often escape from them, and resist the tendency to believe in an objective conjunction between facts merely because they are unable to separate the ideas. The author's typical example of an inseparable association, (and there can be none more suited to the purpose,) is the association between sensations of colour and the tangible magnitudes, figures, and distances, of which they are signs, and which are so completely merged with them into one single impression, that we believe we see distance, extension, and figure, though all we really see is the optical effects which accompany them, all the rest being a rapid interpretation of natural signs.[81] The generality of mankind, no doubt, and all men before they have studied the subject, believe what the author says they do; but a great majority of those who have studied the subject believe otherwise: they believe that a large portion of the facts which we seem to see, we do not really see, but instantaneously infer. Yet the association remains inseparable in these scientific thinkers as in others: the retinal picture suggests to them the real magnitude, in the same irresistible manner as it does to other people. To take another of the author's examples: when we look at a distant terrestrial object through a telescope, it appears nearer; if we reverse the telescope it appears further off.[82] The signs by which we judge of distance from us, here mislead, because those signs are found in conjunction with real distances widely different from those with which they coexist in our ordinary experience. The association, however, persists, and is irresistible, in one person as much as in another; for every one recognises that the object, thus looked at, *seems* nearer, or farther off, than we know it to be. But does this ever make any of us, except perhaps an inexperienced child, *believe* that the object is at the distance at which we seem to see it? The inseparable association, though so persistent and powerful as to create in everybody an optical illusion, creates no *de*lusion, but leaves our belief as conformable to the realities of fact as if no such illusive appearance had presented itself. Cases similar to this are so frequent, that cautious and thoughtful minds, enlightened by experience on the misleading character of inseparable associations, learn to distrust them, and do not, even by a first impulse, believe a connexion in fact because there is one in thought, but wait for evidence.

Following up the same objection, it may be said that if belief is only an

[81]The first example appears in Vol. I, pp. 94–6. Cf. pp. 345, 346, and 369.
[82]*Ibid.*, p. 347.

inseparable association, belief is a matter of habit and accident, and not of reason. Assuredly an association, however close, between two ideas, is not a sufficient *ground* of belief; is not *evidence* that the corresponding facts are united in external nature. The theory seems to annihilate all distinction between the belief of the wise, which is regulated by evidence, and conforms to the real successions and coexistences of the facts of the universe, and the belief of fools, which is mechanically produced by any accidental association that suggests the idea of a succession or coexistence to the mind: a belief aptly characterized by the popular expression, believing a thing because they have taken it into their heads.

Indeed, the author of the *Analysis* is compelled by his theory to affirm that we actually believe in accordance with the misleading associations which generate what are commonly called illusions of sense. He not only says that we believe we see figure and distance—which the great majority of psychologists since Berkeley do not believe;[83] but he says, that in the case of ventriloquy "we cannot help believing" that the sound proceeds from the place, of which the ventriloquist imitates the effect; that the sound of bells opposed by the wind, not only appears farther off, but is believed to come from farther off, although we may know the exact distance from which it comes; that "in passing on board ship, another ship at sea, we *believe* that she has all the motion, we none:" nay even, that when we have turned ourselves round with velocity several times, "we believe that the world is turning round."[84] Surely it is more true to say, as people generally do say, "the world *seems* to us to turn round." To me these cases appear so many experimental proofs, that the tendency of an inseparable association to generate belief, even when that tendency is fully effectual in creating the irresistible appearance of a state of things that does not really exist, may yet be impotent against reason, that is, against preponderant evidence.

In defence of these paradoxes, let us now consider what the author of the *Analysis* might say. One thing he would certainly say: that the belief he affirms to exist in these cases of illusion, is but a momentary one; with which the belief entertained at all other times may be at variance. In the case, for instance, of those who, from an early association formed between darkness and ghosts, feel terror in the dark though they have a confirmed disbelief in ghosts, the author's opinion is that there is a temporary belief, at the moment when the terror is felt.[85] This was also the opinion of Dugald Stewart:[86] and the agreement (by no means a solitary one) between two thinkers of such opposite tendencies, reminds one of the saying "Quand un Français et un Anglais sont d'accord, il faut bien qu'ils aient raison."[87]

[83]Berkeley, *Essay*, esp. pp. 237, 240–4, and 258–9.
[84]*Analysis*, Vol. I, pp. 370–1.
[85]*Ibid.*, pp. 372–3.
[86]Dugald Stewart (1753–1828), *Elements of the Philosophy of the Human Mind*, 3 vols. (London: Strahan and Cadell, *et al.*, 1792–1827), Vol. I, pp. 143–4 (Chap. iii).
[87]François Marie Arouet Voltaire (1694–1778), "Lettre XXII. Sur M. Pope et quelques autres poètes fameux," in *Lettres sur les Anglais, ou Lettres philosophiques* (1733), in *Oeuvres complètes*, 66 vols. (Paris: Renouard, 1817–25), Vol. XXIV, p. 136.

Yet the author seems to adopt this notion not from observation of the case, but from an antecedent opinion that "dread implies belief, and an uncontrollable belief," which, he says, "we need not stay to prove."[88] It is to be wished, in this case, that he had staid to prove it: for it is harder to prove than he thought. The emotion of fear, the physical effect on the nervous system known by that name, may be excited, and I believe often is excited, simply by terrific imaginations. That these imaginations are, even for a moment, mistaken for menacing realities, may be true, but ought not to be assumed without proof. The circumstance most in its favour (one not forgotten by the author) is that in dreams, to which may be added hallucinations, frightful ideas are really mistaken for terrible facts. But dreams are states in which all other sensible ideas are mistaken for outward facts. Yet sensations and ideas are intrinsically different, and it is not the normal state of the human mind to confound the one with the other.

Besides, this supposition of a momentary belief in ghosts breaking in upon and interrupting an habitual and permanent belief that there are no ghosts, jars considerably with the doctrine it is brought to support, that belief is an inseparable association. According to that doctrine, here are two inseparable associations, which yet are so far from exclusively possessing the mind, that they alternate with one another, each Inseparable implying the separation of the other Inseparable. The association of darkness with the absence of ghosts must be anything but inseparable, if there only needs the presence of darkness to revive the contrary association. Yet an association so very much short of inseparable, is accompanied, at least in the absence of darkness, by a full belief. Darkness is in this case associated with two incompatible ideas, the idea of ghosts and that of their absence, but with neither of them inseparably, and in consequence the two associations alternately prevail, as the surrounding circumstances favour the one or the other; agreeably to the laws of Compound Association, laid down with great perspicuity and reach of thought by Mr. Bain in his systematic treatise.[89]

To the argument, that the inseparable associations which create optical and other illusions, do not, when opposed by reason, generate the false belief, the author's answer would probably be some such as the following. When the rational thinker succeeds in resisting the belief, he does so by more or less completely overcoming the inseparableness of the association. Associations may be conquered by the formation of counter-associations. Mankind had formerly an inseparable association between sunset and the motion of the sun, and this inseparable association compelled them to believe that in the phenomenon of sunset the sun moves and the earth is at rest. But Copernicus, Galileo,[90] and after

[88]*Analysis*, Vol. I, p. 372.

[89]I.e., in *The Senses and the Intellect*; see p. 153 above.

[90]The revolution in views of the solar system was prompted by Nicolaus Copernicus (1473–1543), *De revolutionibus orbium coelestium libri VI* (Nuremberg: Petreium, 1543); and Galileo Galilei (1564–1642), *Sidereus nuncias* (Venice: Baglionum, 1610), and

them, all astronomers, found evidence, that the earth moves and the sun is at rest: in other words, certain experiences, and certain reasonings from those experiences, took place in their minds, the tendency of which was to associate sunset with the ideas of the earth in motion and the sun at rest. This was a counter-association, which could not coexist, at least at the same instant, with the previous association connecting sunset with the sun in motion and the earth at rest. But for a long time the new associating influences could not be powerful enough to get the better of the old association, and change the belief which it implied. A belief which has become habitual, is seldom overcome but by a slow process. However, the experiences and mental processes that tended to form the new association still went on; there was a conflict between the old association and the causes which tended to produce a new one; until, by the long continuance and frequent repetition of those causes, the old association, gradually undermined, ceased to be inseparable, and it became possible to associate the idea of sunset with that of the earth moving and the sun at rest; whereby the previous idea of the sun moving and the earth at rest was excluded for the time, and as the new association grew in strength, was at last thrown out altogether. The argument should go on to say that after a still further prolongation of the new experiences and reasonings, the old association became impossible and the new one inseparable; for, until it became inseparable, there could, according to the theory, be no belief. And this, in truth, does sometimes happen. There are instances in the history of science, even down to the present day, in which something which was once believed to be impossible, and its opposite to be necessary, was first seen to be possible, next to be true, and finally came to be considered as necessarily true, and its opposite (once deemed necessary) as impossible, and even inconceivable; insomuch that it is thought by some that what was reputed an impossibility, might have been known to be a necessity. In such cases, the quality of inseparableness has passed, in those minds at least, from the old association to the new one. But in much the greatest number of cases the change does not proceed so far, and both associations remain equally possible. The case which furnished our last instance is an example. Astronomers, and all educated persons, now associate sunset with motion confined to the earth, and firmly believe this to be what really takes place; but they have not formed this association with such exclusiveness and intensity as to have become unable to associate sunset with motion of the sun. On the contrary, the visible appearance still suggests motion of the sun, and many people, though aware of the truth, find that they cannot by any effort make themselves *see* sunset any otherwise than as the sinking of the sun below the earth. My own experience is different: I find that I can represent the phenomenon to myself in either light; I can, according to the manner in which I direct my thoughts, see sunset either as the

---

*Dialogo . . . sopra i due massimi sistemi del mondo tolemaico, e copernicano* (Florence: Landini, 1632), the work that led to the major religious controversy.

earth tilting above the sun, or as the sun dipping below the earth: in the same manner as when a railway train in motion passes another at rest, we are able, if we prevent our eyes from resting on any third object, to imagine the motion as being either in the one train or in the other. How, then, can it be said that there is an inseparable association of sunset with the one mode of representation, and a consequent inability to associate it with the other? It is associated with both, and the one of the two associations which is nearest to being inseparable is that which belief does not accompany. The difference between different people in the ability to represent to themselves the phenomenon under either aspect, depends rather on the degree of exercise which they have given to their imagination in trying to frame mental pictures conformable to the two hypotheses, than upon those considerations of reason and evidence which yet may determine their belief.

The question still remains, what is there which exists in the hypothesis believed, and does not exist in the hypothesis rejected, when we have associations which enable our imagination to represent the facts agreeably to either hypothesis? In other words, what is Belief?

I think it must be admitted, that when we can represent to ourselves in imagination either of two conflicting suppositions, one of which we believe, and disbelieve the other, neither of the associations can be inseparable; and there must therefore be in the fact of Belief, which exists in only one of the two cases, something for which inseparable association does not account. We seem to have again come up, on a different side, to the difficulty which we felt in the discussion of Memory, in accounting for the distinction between a fact remembered, and the same fact imagined. There is a close parallelism between the two problems. In both, we have the difference between a fact and a representation in imagination; between a sensation, or combination of sensations, and an idea, or combination of ideas. This difference we all accept as an ultimate fact. But the difficulty is this. Let me first state it as it presents itself in the case of Memory. Having in our mind a certain combination of ideas, in a group or a train, accompanying or succeeding one another; what is it which, in one case, makes us recognize this group or train as representing a group or train of the corresponding sensations, remembered as having been actually felt by us, while in another case we are aware that the sensations have never occurred to us in a group or train corresponding to that in which we are now having the ideas? This is the problem of Memory. Let me now state the problem of Belief, when the belief is not a case of memory. Here also we have ideas connected in a certain order in our own mind, which makes us think of a corresponding order among the sensations, and we believe that this similar combination of the sensations is a real fact: *i.e.* whether we ever felt it or not, we confidently expect that we should feel it under certain given conditions. In Memory, we believe that the realities in Nature, the sensations and combinations of sensations presented to us from without, *have* occurred to us in an order which agrees with that in which we are representing them to ourselves in thought: in those cases of Belief which are not cases of Memory, we believe, not that they have occurred, but that they would have occurred, or would occur, in that order.

What is it that takes place in us, when we recognize that there is this agreement between the order of our ideas and the order in which we either had or might have had the sensations which correspond to them—that the order of the ideas represents a similar order either in our actual sensations, or in those which, under some given circumstances, we should have reason to expect? What, in short, is the difference *to our minds* between thinking of a reality, and representing to ourselves an imaginary picture? I confess that I can perceive no escape from the opinion that the distinction is ultimate and primordial. There is no more difficulty in holding it to be so, than in holding the difference between a sensation and an idea to be primordial. It seems almost another aspect of the same difference. The author himself says, in the chapter on Memory, that, a sensation and an idea being different, it is to be expected that the remembrance of having had a sensation should be different from the remembrance of having had an idea, and that this is a sufficient explanation of our distinguishing them.[91] If this, then, is an original distinction, why should not the distinction be original between the remembrance of having had a sensation, and the actually having an idea (which is the difference between Memory and Imagination); and between the expectation of having a sensation, and the actually having an idea (which is the difference between Belief and Imagination)? Grant these differences, and there is nothing further to explain in the phenomenon of Belief. For every belief is either the memory of having had a sensation (or other feeling), or the expectation that we should have the sensation or feeling in some given state of circumstances, if that state of circumstances could come to be realized.

II

That all belief is either Memory or Expectation, will be clearly seen if we run over all the different objects of Belief. The author has already done so, in order to establish his theory; and it is now necessary that we should do the same.

The objects of Belief are enumerated by the author in the following terms:—
1. Events, real existences. 2. Testimony. 3. The truth of propositions.[92] He intended this merely as a rough grouping, sufficient for the purpose if it includes everything: for it is evident that the divisions overlap one another, and it will be seen presently that the last two are but cases of the first.

Belief in events he further divides into belief in present events, in past events, and in future events. Belief in present events he subdivides into belief in immediate existences present to my senses, and belief in immediate existences not present to

---

[91]Vol. I, pp. 328–36.
[92]*Ibid.*, p. 344.

my senses. We see by this that he recognises no difference, in a metaphysical sense, between existences and events, because he regards, with reason, objects as merely the supposed antecedents of events. The distinction, however, requires to be kept up, being no other than the fundamental difference between simultaneousness, and succession or change.

Belief in immediate existences present to my senses, is either belief in my sensations, or belief in external objects. Believing that I feel what I am at this moment feeling, is, as the author says, only another name for having the feeling;[93] with the idea, however, of Myself, associated with it; of which hereafter.

The author goes on to analyse Belief in external objects present to our senses; and he resolves it into a present sensation, united by an irresistible association with the numerous other sensations which we are accustomed to receive in conjunction with it. The Object is thus to be understood as a complex idea, compounded of the ideas of various sensations which we have, and of a far greater number of sensations which we should expect to have if certain contingencies were realized. In other words, our idea of an object is an idea of a group of possibilities of sensation, some of which we believe we can realize at pleasure, while the remainder would be realized if certain conditions took place, on which, by the laws of nature, they are dependent. As thus explained, belief in the existence of a physical object, is belief in the occurrence of certain sensations, contingently on certain previous conditions. This is a state of mind closely allied to Expectation of sensations. For—though we use the name Expectation only with reference to the future, and even to the probable future—our state of mind in respect to what *may* be future, and even to what *might have been* future, is of the same general nature, and depends on the same principles, as Expectation. I believe that a certain event will positively happen, because the known conditions which always accompany it in experience have already taken place. I believe that another event will certainly happen *if* the known conditions which always accompany it take place, and those conditions I can produce when I please. I believe that a third event will happen if its conditions take place, but I must wait for those conditions; I cannot realize them at pleasure, and may never realize them at all. The first of these three cases is positive expectation, the other two are conditional expectation. A fourth case is my belief that the event would have happened at any former time if the conditions had taken place at that time. It is not consonant to usage to call this Expectation, but, considered as a case of belief, there is no essential difference between it and the third case. My belief that I should have heard Cicero had I been present in the Forum, and my belief that I shall hear Mr. Gladstone if I am present in the House of Commons,[94] can nowise be regarded as essentially different phenomena. The one

[93]*Ibid*.

[94]William Ewart Gladstone (1809–98), the leading Liberal politician, at that time Prime Minister and M.P. for Greenwich.

we call Expectation, the other not, but the mental principle operative in both these cases of belief is the same.

The author goes on to say, that the belief that we should have the sensations if certain conditions were realized, that is, if we had certain other sensations, is merely an inseparable association of the two sets of sensations with one another, and their inseparable union with the idea of ourselves as having them.[95] But I confess it seems to me that all this may exist in a case of simple imagination. The author would himself admit that the complex idea of the object, in all its fulness, may be in the mind without belief. What remains is its association with the idea of ourselves as percipients. But this also, I cannot but think, we may have in the case of an imaginary scene, when we by no means believe that any corresponding reality exists. Does the idea of our own personality never enter into the pictures in our imagination? Are we not ourselves present in the scenes which we conjure up in our minds? I apprehend we are as constantly present in them, and as conscious of our presence, as we are in contemplating a real prospect. In either case the vivacity of the other impressions eclipses, for the most part, the thought of ourselves as spectators, but not more so in the imaginary, than in the real, spectacle.

It appears to me, then, that to account for belief in external objects, we must postulate Expectation; and since all our expectations, whether positive or contingent, are a consequence of our Memory of the past (as distinguished from a representation in fancy), we must also postulate Memory. The distinction between a mere combination of ideas in thought, and one which recals to us a combination of sensations as actually experienced, always returns on our hands as an ultimate postulate.

The author proceeds to shew how this idea of a mere group of sensations, actual or contingent, becomes knit up with an idea of a permanent Something, lying, as it were, under these sensations, and causing them; this further enlargement of the complex idea taking place through the intimate, or, as he calls it, inseparable association, generated by experience, which makes us unable to imagine any phenomenon as beginning to exist without something anterior to it which causes it.[96] This explanation seems to me quite correct as far as it goes; but, while it accounts for the difficulty we have in not ascribing our sensations to some cause or other, it does not explain why we accept, as in fact we do, the group itself as the cause. I have endeavoured to clear up this difficulty elsewhere (*Examination of Sir William Hamilton's Philosophy*), and in preference to going over the ground a second time, I subjoin, at the end of the volume, the chapter containing the explanation.[97] That chapter supplies all that appears to me to be further necessary

---

[95]Vol. I, p. 349.

[96]*Ibid.*, pp. 349–51.

[97]Chap. xi, "The Psychological Theory of the Belief in an External World," *CW*, Vol. IX, pp. 177–87, is reprinted as an Appendix to Vol. I of the *Analysis*, pp. 440–53.

on the subject of belief in outward objects; which is thus shewn to be a case of Conditional Expectation.

It is unnecessary to follow the author into the minute consideration of Belief in the existence of objects not present, since the explanation already given equally applies to them. My belief in the present existence of St. Paul's is correctly set forth by the author as consisting of the following elements: I believe that I have seen St. Paul's: I believe that I shall see St. Paul's, when I am again in St. Paul's Churchyard: I believe that I should see St. Paul's, if I were in St. Paul's Churchyard at this instant.[98] All this, as he justly remarks, is Memory or Expectation. And this, or some part of this, is the whole of what is in any case meant by belief in the real existence of an external object. The author adds, I also believe that if any creature whose senses are analogous to my own, is now in St. Paul's Churchyard, it has the present sensation of that edifice. But this belief is not necessary to my belief in the continued existence of St. Paul's. For that, it suffices that I believe I should myself see it. My belief that other creatures would do so, is part of my belief in the real existence of other creatures like myself; which is no more mysterious, than our belief in the real existence of any other objects some of whose properties rest not on direct sensation, but on inference.

Belief in past existences, when those existences have been perceived by ourselves, is Memory.[99] When the past existences are inferred from evidence, the belief of them is not Memory, but a fact of the same nature as Expectation; being a belief that we *should have had* the sensations if we had been cotemporary with the objects, and had been in the local position necessary for receiving sensible impressions from them.

We now come to the case of Belief in testimony.[100] But testimony is not itself an object of belief. The object of belief is what the testimony asserts. And so in the last of the author's three cases, that of assent to a proposition.[101] The object of belief, in both these cases, is an assertion. But an assertion is something asserted, and what is asserted must be a fact, similar to some of those of which we have already treated. According to the author, belief in an assertion is belief that two names are both of them names of the same thing: but this we have felt ourselves obliged to discard, as an inadequate explanation of the import of any assertions, except those which are classed as merely verbal. Every assertion concerning Things, whether in concrete or in abstract language, is an assertion that some fact, or group of facts, has been, is, or may be expected to be, found, wherever a certain other fact, or group of facts, is found. Belief in this, is therefore either remembrance that we did have, or expectation that we shall have, or a belief of the same nature with expectation that in some given circumstances we should have, or

---

[98]Vol. I, p. 355.
[99]Cf. *ibid.*, pp. 358–60.
[100]*Ibid.*, pp. 381–6.
[101]*Ibid.*, pp. 386–93.

should have had, direct perception of a particular fact. Belief, therefore, is always a case either of Memory or of Expectation; including under the latter name conditional as well as positive expectation, and the state of mind similar to expectation which affects us in regard to what *would* have been a subject of expectation, if the conditions of its realization had still been possible.

It may be objected, that we may believe in the real existence of things which are not objects of sense at all. We may. But we cannot believe in the real existence of anything which we do not conceive as capable of acting in some way upon our own or some other being's consciousness; though the state of consciousness it produces may not be called a sensation. The existence of a thing means, to us, merely its capacity of producing an impression of some sort upon some mind, that is, of producing some state of consciousness. The belief, therefore, in its existence, is still a conditional expectation of something which we should, under some supposed circumstances, be capable of feeling.

To resume: Belief, as I conceive, is more than an inseparable association, for inseparable associations do not always generate belief, nor does belief always require, as one of its conditions, an inseparable association: we can believe that to be true which we are capable of conceiving or representing to ourselves as false, and false what we are capable of representing to ourselves as true. The difference between belief and mere imagination, is the difference between recognising something as a reality in nature, and regarding it as a mere thought of our own. This is the difference which presents itself when Memory has to be distinguished from Imagination; and again when Expectation, whether positive or contingent (*i.e.* whether it be expectation that we shall, or only persuasion that in certain definable circumstances we should, have a certain experience) has to be distinguished from the mere mental conception of that experience.

### III

Let us examine, once more, whether the speculations in the text afford us any means of further analysing this difference.

The difference presents itself in its most elementary form in the distinction between a sensation and an idea. The author admits this distinction to be ultimate and primordial. "A sensation is different from an idea, only because it is felt to be different."[102] But, after having admitted that these two states of consciousness are distinguishable from each other in and by themselves, he adds, that they are also distinguishable by their accompaniments. "The accompaniments of a sensation are always generically different from those of an idea. . . . The accompaniments of a sensation, are all the simultaneous *objects of sensation*, together with all those which, to a certain extent, both preceded and followed it. The accompaniments of

[102]*Ibid.*, p. 334.

an idea are not the simultaneous objects of sensation, but *other ideas*; namely, the neighbouring parts, antecedent and consequent, of the mental train."[103] There can be no doubt that in those individual cases in which ideas and sensations might be confounded, namely, when an idea reaches or approaches the vivacity of a sensation, the indication here pointed out helps to assure us that what we are conscious of is, nevertheless, only an idea. When, for instance, we awake from a dream, and open our eyes to the outward world, what makes us so promptly recognise that this and not the other is the real world, is that we find its phenomena connected in the accustomed order of our objects of sensation. But though this circumstance enables us, in particular instances, to refer our impression more instantaneously to one or the other class, it cannot be by this that we distinguish ideas at first from sensations; for the criterion supposes the distinction to be already made. If we judge a sensation to be a sensation because its accompaniments are other sensations, and an idea to be an idea because its accompaniments are other ideas, we must already be able to distinguish those other sensations from those other ideas.

A similar remark is applicable to a criterion between sensations and ideas, incidentally laid down by Mr. Bain in the First Part of his systematic treatise. "A mere picture or *idea* remains the same whatever be our bodily position or bodily exertions; the sensation that we call the *actual* is entirely at the mercy of our movements, shifting in every possible way according to the varieties of action that we go through."* This test, like the author's, may serve in cases of momentary doubt; but sensations in general must have been already distinguished from ideas, before we could have hit upon this criterion between them. If we had not already known the difference between a sensation and an idea, we never could have discovered that one of them is "at the mercy of our movements," and that the other is not.

It being granted that a sensation and an idea are *ipso facto* distinguishable, the author thinks it no more than natural that "the copy of the sensation should be distinguishable from the revival of the idea, when they are both brought up by association."[104] But he adds, that there is another distinction between the memory of a sensation, and the memory of an idea, and it is this. In all Memory the idea of self forms part of the complex idea; but in the memory of sensation, the self which enters into the remembrance is "the sentient self, that is, seeing and hearing:" in the memory of an idea, it is "not the sentient self, but the conceptive self, self having an idea. But" (he adds) "myself percipient, and myself imagining, or conceiving, are two very different states of consciousness: of course the ideas of these states of consciousness, or these states revived by association, are very different ideas."[105]

---

[103]*Ibid.*, p. 335.
*The Senses and the Intellect*, 2nd ed., p. 381.
[104]Vol. I, p. 334.
[105]*Ibid.*, p. 336.

Concerning the fact there is no dispute. Myself percipient, and myself imagining or conceiving, are different states, because perceiving is a different thing from imagining; and being different states, the remembrance of them is, as might be expected, different. But the question is, in what does the difference between the remembrances consist? The author calls one of them the *idea* of myself perceiving, and the other the idea of myself imagining, and thinks there is no other difference. But how do the *idea* of myself having a sensation, and the idea of myself having an idea of that sensation, differ from one another? since in either case an idea of the sensation is all that I am having now. The thought of myself perceiving a thing at a former time, and the thought of myself imagining the thing at that former time, are both at the present moment facts of imagination—are now merely ideas. In each case I have an ideal representation of myself, as conscious in a manner very similar in the two cases; though not exactly the same, since in the one case I remember to have been conscious of a sensation, in the other, to have been conscious only of an idea of that sensation: but, in either case, that past consciousness enters only as an idea, into the consciousness I now have by recollection. In what, then, as far as mere ideas are concerned, do my present mental representations of the two cases differ? Will it be said, that the idea of the sensation is one thing, the idea of the idea of the sensation another thing? Or are they both the same idea, namely, the idea of the sensation; and is the element that is present in the one case, but absent in the other, not an idea but something else? A difference there is admitted to be between the remembrance of having had a sensation, and the remembrance of having merely thought of the sensation, *i.e.* had the idea of it: is this difference a difference in the ideas I have in the two cases, or is the idea the same, but accompanied in the one case by something not an idea, which does not exist in the other? for if so, this something is a Belief.

I have touched upon this question in a former note,[106] and expressed my inability to recognise, in the idea of an idea, anything but the idea itself; in the thought of a thought, anything but a repetition of the thought. My thought of Falstaff, as far as I can perceive, is not a copy but a repetition of the thought I had of him when I first read Shakespeare: not indeed an exact repetition, because all complex ideas undergo modification by time, some elements fading away, and new ones being added by reverting to the original sources or by subsequent associations; but my first mental image of Falstaff, and my present one, do not differ as the thought of a rose differs from the sight of one; as an idea of sensation differs from the sensation. On this point the author was perhaps of the same opinion, since we found him contrasting the "copy" of the sensation with the "revival" of the idea, as if the latter was a case of simple repetition, the former not. It would have been well if he had made this point a subject of express discussion; for if his opinion upon it was what, from this passage, we may suppose it to have been, it involves a serious difficulty. If (he says) a sensation and an idea "are

[106]See pp. 109–10 above.

distinguishable in the having, it is likely that the copy of the sensation should be distinguishable from the revival of the idea." But the copy of the sensation is the idea; so that, on this shewing, the idea is distinguishable from its own revival, that is, from the same idea when it occurs again. The author's theory would thus require him to maintain that an idea revived is a specifically different idea, and not the same idea repeated: since otherwise the two states of mind, so far as regards the ideas contained in them, are undistinguishable, and it is necessary to admit the presence in Memory of some other element.

Let us put another case. Instead of Falstaff, suppose a real person whom I have seen: for example General Lafayette.[107] My idea of Lafayette is almost wholly, what my idea of Falstaff is entirely, a creation of thought: only a very small portion of it is derived from my brief experience of seeing and conversing with him. But I have a remembrance of having seen Lafayette, and no remembrance of having seen Falstaff, but only of having thought of him. Is it a sufficient explanation of this difference to say, that I have an idea of myself seeing and hearing Lafayette, and only an idea of myself thinking of Falstaff? But I can form a vivid idea of myself seeing and hearing Falstaff. I can without difficulty imagine myself in the field of Shrewsbury, listening to his characteristic soliloquy over the body of Hotspur; or in the tavern in the midst of his associates, hearing his story of his encounter with the men in buckram.[108] When I recal the scene, I can as little detach it from the idea of myself as present, as I can in the case of most things of which I was really an eye-witness. The spontaneous presence of the idea of Myself in the conception, is always that of myself as percipient. The idea of myself as in a state of mere imagination, only substitutes itself for the other when something reminds me that the scene is merely imaginary.

I cannot help thinking, therefore, that there is in the remembrance of a real fact, as distinguished from that of a thought, an element which does not consist, as the author supposes, in a difference between the mere ideas which are present to the mind in the two cases. This element, howsoever we define it, constitutes Belief, and is the difference between Memory and Imagination. From whatever direction we approach, this difference seems to close our path. When we arrive at it, we seem to have reached, as it were, the central point of our intellectual nature, presupposed and built upon in every attempt we make to explain the more recondite phenomena of our mental being. (Vol. I, pp. 402–23.)

\* \* \* \* \*

[107]Marie Jean Paul Roch Yves Gilbert du Motier, marquis de Lafayette (1757–1834), French military hero and statesman, whom Mill met in 1830.

[108]*Henry IV Part I*, V, iv, 111–28, and II, iv, 114–283; in the *Riverside Shakespeare*, pp. 880 and 859–61.

[*J.S. Mill's note is appended to Chap. xii, "Ratiocination."* ]

This chapter, which is of a very summary character, is a prolongation of the portion of the chapter on Belief, which examines the case of belief in the truth of a proposition; and must stand or fall with it. The question considered is, how, from belief in the truth of the two premises of a syllogism, we pass into belief in the conclusion. The exposition proceeds on the untenable theory of the import of propositions, on which I have so often had occasion to comment. That theory, however, was not necessary to the author for shewing how two ideas may become inseparably associated through the inseparable association of each of them with a third idea: and inasmuch as an inseparable association between the subject and predicate, in the author's opinion, constitutes belief, an explanation of ratiocination conformable to that given of belief follows as a matter of course.

Although I am unable to admit that there is nothing in belief but an inseparable association, and although I maintain that there may be belief without an inseparable association, I can still accept this explanation of the formation of an association between the subject and predicate of the conclusion, which, when close and intense, has, as we have seen, a strong tendency to generate belief. But to shew what it is that gives the belief its validity, we must fall back on logical laws, the laws of evidence. And independently of the question of validity, we shall find in the reliance on those laws, so far as they are understood, the source and origin of all beliefs, whether well or ill founded, which are not the almost mechanical or automatic products of a strong association—of the lively suggestion of an idea. We may therefore pass at once to the nature of Evidence, which is the subject of the next chapter.

I venture to refer, in passing, to those chapters in my *System of Logic*, in which I have maintained, contrary to what is laid down in this chapter, that Ratiocination does not *consist* of Syllogisms; that the Syllogism is not the analysis of what the mind does in reasoning, but merely a useful formula into which it can translate its reasonings, gaining thereby a great increase in the security for their correctness.[109] (Vol. I, pp. 426–7.)

*    *    *    *    *

[*J.S. Mill's note is appended to Chap. xiii, "Evidence."* ]

This chapter on Evidence is supplementary to the chapter on Belief, and is intended to analyse the process of weighing and balancing opposing grounds for believing.

[109]*System of Logic*, Bk. II, esp. Chaps. i-iii (*CW*, Vol. VII, pp. 157–209).

Evidence is either of individual facts (not actually perceived by oneself), or of general truths. The former is the only case to which much attention is paid in the present chapter; which very happily illustrates it, by the case of navigators having to decide on the existence or non-existence of inhabitants in a newly discovered island. The process of balancing the evidence for and against, is depicted in a very lively manner. Let us see whether the mental facts set down in the exposition, are precisely those which take place.

When the sailors have seen prints of a foot, resembling those of a man, the idea is raised of a man making the print. When they afterwards see a monkey, whose feet leave traces almost similar, the idea is also raised of a monkey making the print, and the state of their minds, the author says, is doubt. Of this state he gives the following analysis.

There is here a double association with the print of the foot. There is the association of a man, and there is the association of a monkey. First, the print raises the idea of a man, but the instant it does so, it raises also the idea of a monkey. The idea of the monkey, displacing that of the man, hinders the first association from the fixity which makes it belief; and the idea of man, displacing that of monkey, hinders the second association from that fixity which constitutes belief.[110]

This passage deserves to be studied; for without having carefully weighed it, we cannot be certain that we are in complete possession of the author's theory of Belief.

There are two conflicting associations with the print of the foot. The picture of a man making it, cannot co-exist with that of a monkey making it. But the two may alternate with one another. Had the association with a man been the only association, it would, or might (for on this point the author is not explicit) have amounted to belief. But the idea of the monkey and that of the man alternately displacing one another, hinder either association from having the fixity which would make it belief.

This alternation, however, between the two ideas, of a monkey making the footprint and of a man making it, may very well take place without hindering one of the two from being accompanied by belief. Suppose the sailors to obtain conclusive evidence, testimonial or circumstantial, that the prints were made by a monkey. It may happen, nevertheless, that the remarkable resemblance of the foot prints to those of a man, does not cease to force itself upon their notice: in other words, they continue to associate the idea of a man with the footsteps; they are reminded of a man, and of a man making the footsteps, every time they see or think of them. The double association, therefore, may subsist, and the one which does not correspond with the fact may even be the most obtrusive of the two, while yet the other conception may be the one with which the men believe the real facts to have corresponded.

[110]Vol. I, p. 430.

All the rest of the exposition is open to the same criticism. The author accounts very accurately for the presence of all the ideas which the successive appearance of the various articles of evidence arouses in the mind. But he does not shew that the belief, which is ultimately arrived at, is constituted by the expulsion from the mind of one set of these ideas, and the exclusive possession of it by the other set. It is quite possible that neither of the associations may acquire the "fixity" which, according to the apparent meaning of the author, would defeat the other association altogether, and drive away the conception which it suggests; and yet, one of the suppositions may be believed and the other disbelieved, according to the balance of evidence, as estimated by the investigator. Belief, then, which has been already shewn not to require an inseparable association, appears not to require even "fixity"—such fixity as to exclude the idea of the conflicting supposition, as it does exclude the belief.

The problem of Evidence divides itself into two distinguishable enquiries: what effect evidence ought to produce, and what determines the effect that it does produce: how our belief ought to be regulated, and how, in point of fact, it is regulated. The first enquiry—that into the nature and probative force of evidence; the discussion of what proves what, and of the precautions needed in admitting one thing as proof of another—are the province of Logic, understood in its widest sense: and for its treatment we must refer to treatises on Logic, either inductive or ratiocinative.[111] All that would be in place here, reduces itself to a single principle: In all cases, except the case of what we are directly conscious of (in which case, as the author justly observes, the evidence and the belief are one and the same thing)—in all cases, therefore, in which belief is really grounded on evidence, it is grounded, in the ultimate result, on the constancy of the course of nature. Whether the belief be of facts or of laws, and whether of past facts or of those which are present or future, this is the basis on which it rests. Whatever it is that we believe, the justification of the belief must be, that unless it were true, the uniformity of the course of nature would not be maintained. A cause would have occurred, not followed by its invariable effect; an effect would have occurred, not preceded by any of its invariable causes; witnesses would have lied, who have always been known to speak the truth; signs would have proved deceptive, which in human experience have always given true indication. This is obvious, whatever case of belief on evidence we examine. Belief in testimony is grounded on previous experience that testimony is usually conformable to fact: testimony in general (for even this may with truth be affirmed); or the testimony of the particular witness, or the testimony of persons similar to him. Belief that the sun will rise and set to-morrow, or that a stone thrown up into the air will fall back, rests on experience that this has been invariably the case, and reliance that what has hitherto occurred

---

[111]For instance, in Mill's own *System of Logic*, Bk. III, Chaps. xx-xxiii (*CW*, Vol. VII, pp. 554–603).

will continue to occur hereafter. Belief in a fact vouched for by circumstantial evidence, rests on experience that such circumstances as are ascertained to exist in the case, never exist unaccompanied by the given fact. What we call evidence, whether complete or incomplete, always consists of facts or events tending to convince us that some ascertained general truths or laws of nature must have proved false, if the conclusion which the evidence points to is not true.

Belief on evidence is therefore always a case of the generalizing process; of the assumption that what we have not directly experienced resembles, or will resemble, our experience. And, properly understood, this assumption is true; for the whole course of nature consists of a concurrence of causes, producing their effects in a uniform manner; but the uniformity which exists is often not that which our first impressions lead us to expect. Mr. Bain has well pointed out, that the generalizing propensity, in a mind not disciplined by thought, nor as yet warned by its own failures, far outruns the evidence, or rather, precedes any conscious consideration of evidence; and that what the consideration of evidence has to do when it comes, is not so much to make us generalize, as to limit our spontaneous impulse of generalization, and restrain within just bounds our readiness to believe that the unknown will resemble the known.[112] When Mr. Bain occasionally speaks of this propensity as if it were instinctive, I understand him to mean, that by an original law of our nature, the mere suggestion of an idea, so long as the idea keeps possession of the mind, suffices to give it a command over our active energies. It is to this primitive mental state that the author's theory of Belief most nearly applies. In a mind which is as yet untutored, either by the teachings of others or by its own mistakes, an idea so strongly excited as for the time to keep out all ideas by which it would itself be excluded, possesses that power over the voluntary activities which is Mr. Bain's criterion of Belief;[113] and any association that compels the person to have the idea of a certain consequence as following his act, generates, or becomes, a real expectation of that consequence. But these expectations often turning out to have been ill grounded, the unduly prompt suggestion comes to be associated, by repetition, with the shock of disappointed expectation; and the idea of the desired consequent is now raised together with the idea not of its realization, but of its frustration: thus neutralizing the effect of the first association on the belief and on the active impulses. It is in this stage that the mind learns the habit of looking out for, and weighing, evidence. It presently discovers that the expectations which are least often disappointed are those which correspond to the greatest and most varied amount of antecedent experience. It gradually comes to associate the feeling of disappointed expectation with all those promptings to expect, which, being the result of accidental associations, have no, or but little, previous experience

[112]*The Emotions and the Will*, pp. 539–40.
[113]See p. 160 above.

conformable to them: and by degrees the expectation only arises when memory represents a considerable amount of such previous experience; and is strong in proportion to the quantity of the experience. At a still later period, as disappointment nevertheless not unfrequently happens notwithstanding a considerable amount of past experience on the side of the expectation, the mind is put upon making distinctions in the kind of past experiences, and finding out what qualities, besides mere frequency, experience must have, in order not to be followed by disappointment. In other words, it considers the conditions of right inference from experience; and by degrees arrives at principles or rules, more or less accurate, for inductive reasoning. This is substantially the doctrine of the author of the *Analysis*. It must be conceded to him, that an association, sufficiently strong to exclude all ideas that would exclude itself, produces a kind of mechanical belief; and that the processes by which this belief is corrected, or reduced to rational bounds, all consist in the growth of a counter-association, tending to raise the idea of a disappointment of the first expectation: and as the one or the other prevails in the particular case, the belief, or expectation, exists or does not exist, exactly as if the belief were the same thing with the association. It must also be admitted that the process by which the belief is overcome, takes effect by weakening the association; which can only be effected by raising up another association that conflicts with it. There are two ways in which this counter-association may be generated. One is, by counter-evidence; by contrary experience in the specific case, which, by associating the circumstances of the case with a contrary belief, destroys their association with the original belief. But there is also another mode of weakening, or altogether destroying, the belief, without adducing contrary experience: namely, by merely recognising the insufficiency of the existing experience; by reflecting on other instances in which the same amount and kind of experience have existed, but were not followed by the expected result. In the one mode as in the other, the process of dissolving a belief is identical with that of dissolving an association; and to this extent—and it is a very large extent—the author's theory of Belief must be received as true.

I cannot, however, go beyond this, and maintain with the author that Belief is identical with a strong association; on account of the reason already stated, *viz.* that in many cases—indeed in almost all cases in which the evidence has been such as required to be investigated and weighed—a final belief is arrived at without any such clinging together of ideas as the author supposes to constitute it; and we remain able to represent to ourselves in imagination, often with perfect facility, both the conflicting suppositions, of which we nevertheless believe one and reject the other. (Vol. I, pp. 433–9.)

\*   \*   \*   \*   \*

*[J.S. Mill's note is appended to the introductory paragraph of Chap. xiv, "Some Names Which Require a Particular Explanation":]* We have now seen that, in what we call the mental world, Consciousness, there are three grand classes of phenomena, the most familiar of all the facts with which we are acquainted,— SENSATIONS, IDEAS, and the TRAIN OF IDEAS. We have examined a number of the more complicated cases of Consciousness; and have found, that they all resolve themselves into the three simple elements, thus enumerated. We also found it necessary to shew, for what ends, and in what manner, marks were contrived of sensations and ideas, and by what combinations they were made to represent, expeditiously, trains of those states of consciousness. Some marks or names, however, could not be explained, till some of the more complicated states of consciousness were unfolded; these also are names so important, and so peculiar in their mode of signification, that a very complete understanding of them is required. It is to the consideration of these remarkable cases of Naming that we now proceed.

Under the modest title of an explanation of the meaning of several names, this chapter presents us with a series of discussions of some of the deepest and most intricate questions in all metaphysics. Like Plato, the author introduces his analysis of the most obscure among the complex general conceptions of the human mind, in the form of an enquiry into the meaning of their names.[114] The title of the chapter gives a very inadequate notion of the difficulty and importance of the speculations contained in it, and which make it, perhaps, the profoundest chapter of the book. It is almost as if a treatise on chemistry were described as an explanation of the names *air, water, potass, sulphuric acid*, etc. (Vol. II, p. 2.)

\*     \*     \*     \*     \*

*[J.S. Mill's note is appended to Sect. 1, "Names of Names," of Chap. xiv.]*

A right understanding of the words which are names of names, is of great importance in philosophy. The tendency was always strong to believe that whatever receives a name must be an entity or being, having an independent existence of its own; and if no real entity answering to the name could be found,

[114]See Plato, *Gorgias*, in *Lysis, Symposium, Gorgias* (Greek and English), trans. W.R.M. Lamb (London: Heinemann; Cambridge, Mass: Harvard University Press, 1925), pp. 260–78 (447c–453a); *Protagoras*, in *Laches, Protagoras, Meno, Euthydemus* (Greek and English), trans. W.R.M. Lamb (London: Heinemann; Cambridge, Mass.: Harvard University Press, 1952), pp. 98–106 (311$^b$–313$^c$); and *Theaetetus*, in *Theaetetus, Sophist* (Greek and English), trans. H.N. Fowler (London: Heinemann; New York: Putnam's Sons, 1921), pp. 20–8 (146$^b$–148$^d$).

men did not for that reason suppose that none existed, but imagined that it was something peculiarly abstruse and mysterious, too high to be an object of sense. The meaning of all general, and especially of all abstract terms, became in this way enveloped in a mystical haze; and none of these have been more generally misunderstood, or have been a more copious source of futile and bewildering speculation, than some of the words which are names of names. *Genus*, *Species*, *Universal*, were long supposed to be designations of sublime hyperphysical realities; *Number*, instead of a general name of all numerals, was supposed to be the name, if not of a concrete thing, at least of a single property or attribute.

This class of names was well understood and correctly characterized by Hobbes, of whose philosophy the distinction between names of names and of things was a cardinal point.[115] (Vol. II, p. 5.)

\*  \*  \*  \*  \*

[*In Chap. xiv, Sect. 2, "Relative Terms," James Mill says:*] *If it is asked, why we give names in pairs? The general answer immediately suggests itself; it is because the things named present themselves in pairs; that is, are joined by association. But as many things are joined in pairs by association, which do not receive relative names, the cause may still be inquired of the classification. What is the reason that some pairs do, while many more do not, receive relative names? The cause is the same by which we are guided in imposing other names. As the various combinations of ideas are far too numerous for naming, and we are obliged to make a selection, we name those which we find it of most importance to have named, omitting the rest. It is a question of convenience, solved by experience. It will be seen more distinctly hereafter, that relative names are one of the contrivances for epitomising; and that they enable us to express ourselves with fewer words than we should be able to do without them.*

No part of the *Analysis* is more valuable than the simple explanation here given of a subject which has seemed so mysterious to some of the most enlightened and penetrating philosophers, down even to the present time. The only difference between relative names and any others consists in their being given in pairs; and the reason of their being given in pairs is not the existence between two things, of a mystical bond called a Relation, and supposed to have a kind of shadowy and abstract reality, but a very simple peculiarity in the concrete fact which the two names are intended to mark.

In order to make quite clear the nature of this peculiarity, it will be desirable to advert once more to the double mode of signification of concrete general names,

[115]As before, the reference is to "Computation or Logic," *English Works*, Vol. I, p. 21.

*viz.* that while they denote (or are names of) objects, they connote some fact relating to those objects. The fact connoted by any name, relative or not, is always of the same nature; it is some bodily or mental feeling, or some set of bodily or mental feelings, accompanying or produced by the object. But in the case of the ordinary names of objects, this fact concerns one object only, or rather only that one object and the sentient mind. The peculiarity in the case of relative names is, that the fact connoted concerns two objects, and cannot be understood without thinking of them both. It is a phenomenon in which two objects play a part. There is no greater mystery in a phenomenon which concerns two objects, than in a phenomenon which concerns only one. For example; the fact connoted by the word *cause*, is a fact in which the thing which is the cause, is implicated along with another thing which is the effect. The facts connoted by the word *parent*, and also by the word *son* or *daughter*, are a long series of phenomena of which both the parent and the child are parts; and the series of phenomena would not be that which the name *parent* expresses, unless the child formed a part of it, nor would it be that which the name *son* or *daughter* expresses, unless the parent formed a part of it. Now, when in a series of phenomena of any interest to us two objects are implicated, we naturally give names expressive of it to both the objects, and these are relative names. The two correlative names denote two different objects, the cause and the effect, or the parent and son; but though what they denote is different, what they connote is in a certain sense the same: both names connote the same set of facts, considered as giving one name to the one object, another name to the other. This set of facts, which is connoted by both the correlative names, was called by the old logicians the ground of the relation, *fundamentum relationis*. The *fundamentum* of any relation is the facts, fully set out, which are the reason of giving to two objects two correlative names. In some cases both objects seem to receive the same name; in the relation of likeness, both objects are said to be like; in the relation of equality, both are said to be equal. But even here the duality holds, on a stricter examination: for the first object (A) is not said to be like, absolutely, but to be like the second object (B); the second is not said to be like absolutely, but to be like the first. Now though "like" is only one name, "like A" is not the same name as "like B," so that there is really, in this case also, a pair of names.

From these considerations we see that objects are said to be related, when there is any fact, simple or complex, either apprehended by the senses or otherwise, in which they both figure. Any objects, whether physical or mental, are related, or are in a relation, to one another, in virtue of any complex state of consciousness into which they both enter; even if it be a no more complex state of consciousness than that of merely thinking of them together. And they are related to each other in as many different ways, or in other words, they stand in as many distinct relations to one another, as there are specifically distinct states of consciousness of which they both form parts. As these may be innumerable, the possible relations not only of any one thing with others, but of any one thing with the same other, are infinitely numerous and various. But they may all be reduced to a certain number of general heads of classification, constituting the different kinds of Relation: each of which requires examination apart, to ascertain what, in each case, the state of consciousness, the cluster or train of sensations or thoughts, really is, in which the two objects figure, and which is connoted by the correlative names. This examination the author accordingly undertakes: and thus, under the guise of explaining names, he analyses all the principal cases which the world and the human mind present, of what are called Relations between things. (Vol. II, pp. 7–10.)

\* \* \* \* \*

[*James Mill analyzes Relative Terms into groups (Vol. II, pp. 8–10):*]
   *I. The only, or at least the principal, occasions, for naming simple sensations, or simple ideas, in pairs, seem to be these:*
   *1. When we take them into simultaneous view, as such and such;*
   *2. When we take them into simultaneous view, as antecedent and consequent.*
   *II. The principal occasions on which we name the complex ideas, called objects, in pairs, are these four:*
   *1. When we speak of them as having an order in space;*
   *2. When we speak of them as having an order in time;*
   *3. When we speak of them as agreeing or disagreeing in quantity;*
   *4. As agreeing or disagreeing in quality.*
   *III. The occasions on which we name the complex ideas of our own formation in pairs, are,*
   *1. When we speak of them as composed of the same or different simple ideas;*
   *2. When we speak of them as antecedent and consequent.*
[*He then (Vol. II, p. 10) turns to the first:*]
   *I. 1. We speak of two sensations, as* Same *or* Different, Like *or* Unlike.
[*J.S. Mill's note comes at the end of the discussion of I, 1.*]

The author commences his survey of Relations with the most universal of them all, Likeness and Unlikeness; and he examines these as subsisting between simple sensations or ideas; for whatever be the true theory of likeness or unlikeness as between the simple elements, the same, in essentials, will serve for the likenesses or unlikenesses of the wholes compounded of them.
   Examining, then, what constitutes likeness between two sensations (meaning two exactly similar sensations experienced at different times); he says, that to feel the two sensations to be alike, is one and the same thing with having the two sensations. Their being alike is nothing but their being felt to be alike; their being

unlike is nothing but their being felt to be unlike. The feeling of unlikeness is merely that feeling of change, in passing from the one to the other, which makes them two, and without which we should not be conscious of them at all. The feeling of likeness, is the being reminded of the former sensation by the present, that is, having the idea of the former sensation called up by the present, and distinguishing them as sensation and idea.

It does not seem to me that this mode of describing the matter explains anything, or leaves the likenesses and unlikenesses of our simple feelings less an ultimate fact than they were before. All it amounts to is, that likeness and unlikeness are themselves only a matter of feeling: and that when we have two feelings, the feeling of their likeness or unlikeness is inextricably interwoven with the fact of having the feelings. One of the conditions, under which we have feelings, is that they are like and unlike: and in the case of simple feelings, we cannot separate the likeness or unlikeness from the feelings themselves. It is by no means certain, however, that when we have two feelings in immediate succession, the feeling of their likeness is not a third feeling which follows instead of being involved in the two. This question is expressly left open by Mr. Herbert Spencer, in his *Principles of Psychology*;[116] and I am not aware that any philosopher has conclusively resolved it. We do not get rid of any difficulty by calling the feeling of likeness the same thing with the two feelings that are alike: we have equally to postulate likeness and unlikeness as primitive facts—as an inherent distinction among our sensations; and whichever form of phraseology we employ makes no difference in the ulterior developments of psychology. It is of no practical consequence whether we say that a phenomenon is resolved into sensations and ideas, or into sensations, ideas, and their resemblances, since under the one expression as under the other the resemblance must be recognised as an indispensable element in the compound.

When we pass from resemblance between simple sensations and ideas, to resemblance between complex wholes, the process, though not essentially different, is more complicated, for it involves a comparison of part with part, element with element, and therefore a previous discrimination of the elements. When we judge that an external object, compounded of a number of attributes, is like another external object; since they are not, usually, alike in all their attributes, we have to take the two objects into simultaneous consideration in respect to each of their various attributes one after another: their colour, to observe whether that is similar; their size, whether that is similar; their figure, their weight, and so on. It comes at last to a perception of likeness or unlikeness between simple sensations: but we reduce it to this by *attending* separately to one of the simple sensations forming the one cluster, and to one of those forming the other cluster, and if possible adjusting our organs of sense so as to have these two sensations in immediate juxtaposition: as when we put two objects, of which we wish to

[116]Spencer, *Principles*, pp. 312–16 and esp. 317.

compare the colour, side by side, so that our sense of sight may pass directly from one of the two sensations of colour to the other. This act of attention directed successively to single attributes, blunts our feeling of the other attributes of the objects, and enables us to feel the likeness of the single sensations almost as vividly as if we had nothing but these in our mind. Having felt this likeness, we say that the sensations are like, and that the two objects are like in respect of those sensations: and continuing the process we pronounce them to be either like or unlike in each of the other sensations which we receive from them. (Vol. II, pp. 17–20.)

\* \* \* \* \*

[*The next section, 1, 2, begins (Vol. II, p. 18):*] *2. The only other relative terms applicable to simple sensations and ideas, are those which denote them as* Antecedent *and* Consequent. [*Once more J.S. Mill's note appears at the end of the discussion.*]

The next relation which the author examines is that of succession, or Antecedent and Consequent. And here again we have one of the universal conditions to which all our feelings or states of consciousness are subject. Whenever we have more feelings than one, we must have them either simultaneously or in succession; and when we are conscious of having them in succession, we cannot in any way separate or isolate the succession from the feelings themselves. The author attempts to carry the analysis somewhat farther. He says that when we have two sensations in the order of antecedent and consequent, the consequent calls up the idea of the antecedent; and that this fact, that a sensation calls up the idea of another sensation directly, and not through an intermediate idea, *constitutes* that other sensation the antecedent of the sensation which reminds us of it—is not a *consequence* of the one sensation's having preceded the other, but is literally all we mean by the one sensation's having preceded the other. There seem to be grave objections to this doctrine. In the first place, there is no law of association by which a consequent calls up the idea of its antecedent. The law of successive association is that the antecedent calls up the idea of the consequent, but not conversely; as is seen in the difficulty of repeating backwards even a form of words with which we are very familiar. We get round from the consequent to the antecedent by an indirect process, through the medium of other ideas; or by going back, at each step, to the beginning of the train, and repeating it downwards until we reach that particular link. When a consequent directly recalls its antecedent, it is by synchronous association, when the antecedent happens to have been so prolonged as to coexist with, instead of merely preceding, the consequent.

The next difficulty is, that although the direct recalling of the idea of a past sensation by a present, without any intermediate link, does not take place from consequent to antecedent, it does take place from like to like: a sensation recalls the idea of a past sensation resembling itself, without the intervention of any other idea. The author, however, says, that "when two sensations in a train are such that if one exists, it has the idea of the other along with it by its immediate exciting power, and not through any intermediate idea; the sensation, the idea of which is thus excited, is called the antecedent, the sensation which thus excites that idea is called the consequent."[117] If this therefore were correct, we should give the names of antecedent and consequent not to the sensations which really are so, but to those which recall one another by resemblance.

Thirdly and lastly, to explain antecedence, *i.e.* the succession between two feelings, by saying that one of the two calls up the idea of the other, that is to say, is followed by it, is to explain succession by succession, and antecedence by antecedence. Every explanation of anything by states of our consciousness, includes as part of the explanation a succession between those states; and it is useless attempting to analyse that which comes out as an element in every analysis we are able to make. Antecedence and consequence, as well as likeness and unlikeness, must be postulated as universal conditions of Nature, inherent in all our feelings whether of external or of internal consciousness. (Vol. II, pp. 22–4.)

\* \* \* \* \*

[*Abstract terms, James Mill argues,*] *derive their meaning wholly from their concretes. . . . The same, in its abstract sense, is the case with line, though we have not words by which we can convey the conception with equal clearness. If we had an abstract term, separate from the concrete, the troublesome association in question would have been less indissoluble, and less deceptive. If we had such a word as* Lineness, *or* Linth, *for example, we should have much more easily seen, that our idea is the idea of the physical line; and that linth without a line, as breadth without something broad, length without something long, are just nothing at all.*

This conception of a geometrical line, as the abstract, of which a physical line is the corresponding concrete, is scarcely satisfactory. An abstract name is the name of an attribute, or property, of the things of which the concrete name is predicated. It is, no doubt, the name of some part, some one or more, of the sensations composing the concrete group, but not of those sensations simply and in themselves; it is the name of those sensations regarded as belonging to some group. *Whiteness*, the abstract name, is the name of the colour white, considered as the colour of some physical object. Now I do not see that a geometrical line is

[117]Vol. II, p. 21.

conceived as an attribute of a physical object. The attribute of objects which comes nearest to the signification of a geometrical line, is their length: but length does not need any name but its own; and the author does not seem to mean that a geometrical line is the same thing as length. He seems to have fallen into the mistake of confounding an abstract with an ideal. The line which is meant in all the theorems of geometry I take to be as truly concrete as a physical line; it denotes an object, but one purely imaginary; a supposititious object, agreeing in all else with a physical line, but differing from it in having no breadth. The properties of this imaginary line of course agree with those of a physical line, except so far as these depend on, or are affected by, breadth. The lines, surfaces, and figures contemplated by geometry are abstract, only in the improper sense of the term, in which it is applied to whatever results from the mental process called Abstraction. They ought to be called ideal. They are physical lines, surfaces, and figures, idealized, that is, supposed hypothetically to be perfectly what they are only imperfectly, and not to be at all what they are in a very slight, and for most purposes wholly unimportant, degree. (Vol. II, pp. 28–9.)

\*  \*  \*  \*  \*

[*In his discussion of relative terms that apply to the synchronous order, that is, in space, James Mill comments:*] *We never perceive, what we call an object, except in the synchronous order. Whatever other sensations we receive, the sensations of the synchronous order, are always received along with them. When we perceive a chair, a tree, a man, a house, they are always situated so and so, with respect to other objects. As the sensations of position are thus always received with the other sensations of an object, the idea of Position is so closely associated with the idea of the object, that it is wholly impossible for us to have the one idea without the other. It is one of the most remarkable cases of indissoluble association; and is that feeling which men describe, when they say that the idea of space forces itself upon their understandings, and is necessary.*

Under the head, as before, of Relative Terms, we find here an analysis of the important and intricate complex ideas of Extension and Position. It will be convenient to defer any remarks on this analysis, until it can be considered in conjunction with the author's exposition of the closely allied subjects of Motion and Space.[118] (Vol. II, p. 36.)

\*  \*  \*  \*  \*

[118]See pp. 205–11 below.

*[Turning to relative terms in the successive order, that is, in time, James Mill says:] Of successions, that is, the order of objects as antecedent and consequent, some are constant, some not constant. Thus, a stone dropped in the air always falls to the ground. This is a case of constancy of sequence. Heavy clouds drop rain, but not always. This is a case of casual sequence.*

This is surely an improper use of the word *Casual*. Sequences cannot be exhaustively divided into invariable and casual, or (as by the author a few pages further on) into constant and fortuitous. Heavy clouds, though they do not always drop rain, are not connected with it by mere accident, as the passing of a waggon might be. They are connected with it through causation: they are one of the conditions on which, when united, rain is invariably consequent, though it is not invariably consequent on that single condition. This distinction is essential to any system of Inductive Logic, in which it recurs at every step. (Vol. II, pp. 37–8.)

*       *       *       *       *

*[Continuing his account of relative terms in the successive order, James Mill says, after treating* Doctor *and* Patient *as properly "one name, though made up of two parts," that* Father *and* Son *are similarly] the two extremities of a train of great length and intricacy, very imperfectly understood. They also, both together, compose, as may easily be seen, but one name.* Father *is a word which connotes* Son, *and whether* Son *is expressed or not, the meaning of it is implied. In like manner* Son *connotes* Father; *and, stripped of that connotation, is without a meaning. Taken together, therefore, they are one name, the name of the complex idea of that train of which* father *is the one extremity,* son *the other.*

It seems hardly a proper expression to say that *Physician* and *Patient*, or that *Father* and *Son*, are one name made up of two parts. When one of the parts is a name of one person and the other part is the name of another, it is difficult to see how the two together can be but one name. *Father* and *Son* are two names, denoting different persons: but what the author had it in his mind to say, was that they connote the same series of facts, which series, as the two persons are both indispensable parts of it, gives names to them both, and is made the foundation or *fundamentum* of an attribute ascribed to each.

With the exception of this questionable use of language, which the author had recourse to because he had not left himself the precise word *Connote*, to express what there is of real identity in the signification of the two names; the analysis which follows of the various complicated cases of relation seems philosophically unexceptionable. The complexity of a relation consists in the complex composition of the series of facts or phenomena which the names connote, and which is the *fundamentum relationis*. The names signify that the person or thing, of which they are predicated, forms part of a group or succession of phenomena along with the other person or thing which is its correlate: and the special nature of that group or series, which may be of extreme complexity, constitutes the speciality of the relation predicated. (Vol. II, pp. 39–40.)

\* \* \* \* \*

[*J.S. Mill's note comes at the end of James Mill's third subsection on relative terms, dealing with quantity.*]

After analysing Position and Extension under the head of Relative Terms, the author now, under the same head, gives the analysis of Quantity and Quality. To what he says on the subject of Quantity it does not appear necessary to add anything. He seems to have correctly analysed the phenomenon down to a primitive element, beyond which we have no power to investigate. As Likeness and Unlikeness appeared to be properties of our simple feelings, which must be postulated as ultimate, and which are inseparable from the feelings themselves, so may this also be said of More and Less. As some of our feelings are like, some unlike, so there is a mode of likeness or unlikeness which we call Degree: some feelings otherwise like are unlike in degree, that is one is unlike another in intensity, or one is unlike another in duration; in either case one is distinguished as more, or greater, the other as less. And the fact of being more or less only means that we feel them as more or less. The author says in this case, as he had said in the other elementary cases of relation, that the more and the less being different sensations, to trace them and to distinguish their difference are not two things but one and the same thing. It matters not, since there the difference still is, unsusceptible of further analysis. The author's apparent simplification amounts only to this, that differences of quantity, like all other differences of which we take cognizance, are differences merely in our feelings; they exist only as they are felt. But (as we have already said of resemblance, and of antecedence and consequence) they must be postulated as elements. The distinction of more and less is one of the ultimate conditions under which we have all our states of consciousness. (Vol. II, pp. 53–4.)

\* \* \* \* \*

[*James Mill's fourth subsection on relative terms, on quality, is followed by J.S. Mill's note:*]

As in the case of Quantity, so in that of Quality, it is needless to add anything to the author's very sufficient elucidation. I merely make the usual reserves with respect to the use of the word *Connotation*. The concrete names which predicate qualities (for of abstract relative names the author is not yet speaking) are said by him to be the names of our sensations; *green*, for instance, and *red*. But it is the abstract names alone which are this: the names *greenness*, and *redness*. And even the abstract names signify something more than only the sensations: they are names of the sensations considered as derived from an object which produces them. The concrete name is a name not of the sensation, but of the object, of which alone it is predicable: we talk of green objects, but not of green sensations. It however connotes the quality *greenness*, that is, it connotes that particular sensation as produced by, or proceeding from, the object; as forming one of the group of sensations which constitutes the object. This, however, is but a difference, though a very important one, in terminology. It is strictly true, that the real meaning of the word is the sensations; as, in all cases, the meaning of a connotative word resides in the connotation (the attributes signified by it), though it is the name of, or is predicable of, only the objects which it denotes. (Vol. II, pp. 60–1.)

\* \* \* \* \*

[*J.S. Mill's note is appended to a clause, "In the case of objects, that which is named, is, clusters of ideas," in James Mill's discussion of "clusters, formed by arbitrary association," that "receive names in pairs," when "they consist of the same or different simple ideas" :*]

Say rather, in the case of objects, what is named is clusters of sensations, supplemented by possibilities of sensation. If an object is but a cluster of ideas, what is there to distinguish it from a mere thought? (Vol. II, p. 62.)

\* \* \* \* \*

[*Continuing the discussion of arbitrarily associated simple ideas giving rise to relative terms, James Mill deals (Vol. II, pp. 63–4) with equal and unequal, greater and less. J.S. Mill's note comes at the end of the discussion.*]

In this passage the author has got as near as it is perhaps possible to get, to an analysis of the ideas of More and Less. We say there is *more* of something, when, to what there already was, there has been superadded other matter of the same kind. And when there is no actual superadding, but merely two independent masses of the same substance, we call that one the greater which produces the same impression on our senses which the other would produce if an addition were made to it. So with differences of intensity. One sweet taste is called sweeter than another because it resembles the taste which would be produced by adding more sugar: and so forth. In all these cases there is presupposed an original difference in the sensations produced in us by the greater mass and by the smaller: but according to the explanation now offered, the idea which guides the application of the terms is that of physical juxtaposition. (Vol. II, pp. 64–5.)

\*   \*   \*   \*   \*

[*James Mill continues his discussion of relative terms by considering (Vol. II, pp. 65–9) successive ideas, which call forth terms such as* antecedent *and* consequent, prior *and* posterior, first *and* second. *In the course of the argument, he asks (p. 67):*] *if thoughts are reciprocally Cause and Effect, that is to say, if, in trains of thought, the same antecedent is regularly followed by the same consequent, how happens it that all trains of thought are not the same?* [*His answer is that the sensations giving rise to the ideas, and contributing to the "trains," vary greatly. J.S. Mill's note is appended to the end of this argument.*]

The author may seem to be anticipating a difficulty which few will feel, when he asks how it happens that all trains of thought are not the same. But what he is enquiring into is not why this happens, but how its happening is consistent with the doctrine he has just laid down. He is guarding against a possible objection to his proposition, that "the succession of two thoughts" has "that constancy to which we apply the terms Cause and Effect."[119] If (he says) it is by direct causation that an idea raises up another idea with which it is associated; and if it be the nature and the very meaning of a cause, to be invariably followed by its effect; how is it, he asks, that any two minds, which have once had the same idea, do not coincide in their whole subsequent history? And how is it that the same mind, when it gets back to an idea it has had before, does not go on revolving in an eternal round?

Of this difficulty he gives a solution, good as far as it goes—that it is because the train of ideas is interrupted by sensations, which are not the same in different minds, nor in the same mind at every repetition, and which even when they are the same, are connected in different minds with different associations. This is true, but is not the whole truth, and a still more complete explanation of the difficulty might have been given. The author has overlooked a part of the laws of association, of which he was perfectly aware, but to which he does not seem to have been always sufficiently alive. The first point overlooked is, that one idea seldom, perhaps never, entirely fills and engrosses the mind. We have almost always a considerable number of ideas in the mind at once; and it must be a very rare occurrence for any two persons, or for the same person twice over, to have exactly the same collection

[119]Vol. II, p. 67.

of ideas present, each in the same relative intensity. For this reason, were there no other, the ideas which the mental state excites by association are almost always more or less different.

A second point overlooked is, that every sensation or idea is far from recalling, whenever it occurs, all the ideas with which it is associated. It never recalls more than a portion of them, and a portion different at different times. The author has not, in any part of the *Analysis*, laid down any law that determines which among the many ideas associated with an idea or sensation, shall be actually called up by it in a given case. The selection which it makes among them depends on the truth already stated, that we seldom or never have only one idea at a time. When we have several together, they all exercise their suggesting power, and each of them aids, impedes, or modifies the suggesting power of the others. This important case of Association has been treated in a masterly manner by Mr. Bain, both in his larger treatise and in his *Compendium*, under the name of Compound Association, and he lays down the following as its most general law. "Past actions, sensations, thoughts, or emotions, are recalled more easily when associated either through contiguity or similarity, with more than one present object or impression."* It follows that when we have several ideas in our mind, none of which is able to call up all the ideas associated with it, those ideas will usually have the preference which are associated with more than one of the ideas already present. An idea A, coexisting in the mind with an idea B, will not select the same idea from among those associated with it, that it would if it occurred alone or with a different accompaniment. If there be any one of the ideas associated with A which is also associated with B, this will probably be one of those called up by their joint action. If there be any idea associated with A which not only is not associated with B, but whose negation is associated with B, this idea will probably be prevented from arising. If there are any sensations which have usually been presented in conjunction, not with A alone, or with B alone, but with the combination AB, still more likely is it that the ideas of these will be recalled when A and B are thought of together, even though A or B by themselves might in preference have recalled some other.

These considerations will be found of primary importance in explaining and accounting for the course of human thought. They enable us, for example, to understand what it is that keeps a train of thought coherent, *i.e.* that maintains it of a given quality, or directs it to a given purpose. The ideas which succeed one another in the mind of a person who is writing a treatise on some subject, or striving to persuade or conciliate a tribunal or a deliberative assembly, are suggested one by another according to the general laws of association. Yet the ideas recalled are not those which would be called up on any common occasion by the same antecedents, but are those only which connect themselves in the writer's

*[*Mental and Moral Science: A*] *Compendium of Psychology and Ethics*, [2 vols. (London: Longmans, Green, 1868), Vol. I,] p. 151.)

or speaker's mind with the end which he is aiming at. The reason is, that the various ideas of the train are not solitary in his mind, but there coexists with all of them (in a greater or less degree of constancy according to the quality of the mind) the highly interesting idea of the end in view: and the presence of this idea causes each of the ideas which pass through his mind while so engaged, to suggest such of the ideas associated with them as are also associated with the idea of the end, and not to suggest those which have no association with it. The ideas all follow one another in an associated train, each calling up by association the one which immediately follows it; but the perpetual presence or continual recurrence of the idea of the end, determines, within certain limits, which of the ideas associated with each link of the chain shall be aroused and form the next link. When we come to the author's analysis of the power of the Will over our ideas, we shall find him taking exactly this view of it.

Concerning the simultaneous existence of many ideas in the mind, and the manner in which they modify each other's exercise of the suggesting power, there is an able and instructive passage in Cardaillac's *Etudes Elémentaires de Philosophie*, which has been translated and quoted by Sir William Hamilton in his *Lectures*, and which, being highly illustrative of the preceding remarks, I think it useful to subjoin.

Among psychologists, those who have written on Memory and Reproduction with the greatest detail and precision, have still failed in giving more than a meagre outline of these operations. They have taken account only of the notions which suggest each other with a distinct and palpable notoriety. They have viewed the associations only in the order in which language is competent to express them; and as language, which renders them still more palpable and distinct, can only express them in a consecutive order, can only express them one after another, they have been led to suppose that thoughts only awaken in succession. Thus, a series of ideas mutually associated, resembles, on the doctrine of philosophers, a chain in which every link draws up that which follows; and it is by means of these links that intelligence labours through, in the act of reminiscence, to the end which it proposes to attain.

There are some, indeed, among them, who are ready to acknowledge, that every actual circumstance is associated to several fundamental notions, and consequently to several chains, between which the mind may choose; they admit even that every link is attached to several others, so that the whole forms a kind of trellis,—a kind of network, which the mind may traverse in every direction, but still always in a single direction at once,—always in a succession similar to that of speech. This manner of explaining reminiscence is founded solely on this,—that, content to have observed all that is distinctly manifest in the phenomenon, they have paid no attention to the under-play of the latescent activities,—paid no attention to all that custom conceals, and conceals the more effectually in proportion as it is more completely blended with the natural agencies of mind.

Thus their theory, true in itself, and setting out from a well-established principle, the Association of Ideas, explains in a satisfactory manner a portion of the phenomena of Reminiscence; but it is incomplete, for it is unable to account for the prompt, easy, and varied operation of this faculty, or for all the marvels it performs. On the doctrine of the philosophers, we can explain how a scholar repeats, without hesitation, a lesson he has learned, for all the words are associated in his mind according to the order in which he has studied them; how he demonstrates a geometrical theorem, the parts of which are connected together in the same manner; these and similar reminiscences of simple successions present no difficulties which the common doctrine cannot resolve. But it is impossible, on this doctrine, to explain the rapid and certain movement of thought, which, with a marvellous facility, passes from one order of subjects to another, only to return again to the first; which advances, retrogrades, deviates, and reverts, sometimes marking all the points on its route, again clearing, as if in play, immense intervals; which runs over, now in a manifest order, now in a seeming irregularity, all the notions relative to an object, often relative to several, between which no connection could be suspected; and this without hesitation, without uncertainty, without error, as the hand of a skilful musician expatiates over the keys of the most complex organ. All this is inexplicable on the meagre and contracted theory on which the phenomena of reproduction have been thought explained. . . .

To form a correct notion of the phenomena of Reminiscence, it is requisite that we consider under what conditions it is determined to exertion. In the first place it is to be noted that, at every crisis of our existence, momentary circumstances are the causes which awaken our activity, and set our recollection at work to supply the necessaries of thought. In the second place, it is as constituting a want, (and by *want* I mean the result either of an act of desire or of volition) that the determining circumstance tends principally to awaken the thoughts with which it is associated. This being the case, we should expect, that each circumstance which constitutes a want, should suggest, likewise, the notion of the object, or objects, proper to satisfy it; and this is what actually happens. It is, however, further to be observed, that it is not enough that the want suggests the idea of the object; for if that idea were alone, it would remain without effect, since it could not guide me in the procedure I should follow. It is necessary, at the same time, that to the idea of this object there should be associated the notion of the relation of this object to the want, of the place where I may find it, of the means by which I may procure it, and turn it to account, etc. For instance, I wish to make a quotation: This want awakens in me the idea of the author in whom the passage is to be found which I am desirous of citing; but this idea would be fruitless, unless there were conjoined, at the same time, the representation of the volume, of the place where I may obtain it, of the means I must employ, etc.

Hence I infer, in the first place, that a want does not awaken an idea of its object alone, but that it awakens it accompanied with a number, more or less considerable, of accessory notions, which form, as it were, its train or attendance. This train may vary according to the nature of the want which suggests the notion of an object; but the train can never fall wholly off, and it becomes more indissolubly attached to the object, in proportion as it has been more frequently called up in attendance.

I infer, in the second place, that this accompaniment of accessory notions, simultaneously suggested with the principal idea, is far from being as vividly and distinctly represented in consciousness as that idea itself; and when these accessories have once been completely blended with the habits of the mind, and its reproductive agency, they at length finally disappear, becoming fused, as it were, in the consciousness of the idea to which they are attached. Experience proves this double effect of the habits of reminiscence. If we observe our operations relative to the gratification of a want, we shall perceive that we are far from having a clear consciousness of the accessory notions; the consciousness of them is, as it were, obscured, and yet we cannot doubt that they are present to the mind, for it is they that direct our procedure in all its details.

We must, therefore, I think, admit that the thought of an object immediately suggested by a desire, is always accompanied by an escort more or less numerous of accessory thoughts, equally present to the mind, though, in general, unknown in themselves to consciousness; that these accessories are not without their influence in guiding the operations elicited by the principal notion; and it may even be added that they are so much the more calculated to exert an effect in the conduct of our procedure, in proportion as, having become more part and parcel of our habits of reproduction, the influences they exert are further withdrawn, in ordinary, from the ken of consciousness. . . . The same thing may be illustrated by what happens to us in the case of reading. Originally each word, each letter, was a separate object of consciousness. At length, the knowledge of letters and words and lines being, as it were, fused into our habits, we no longer have any distinct consciousness of them, as severally concurring to the result, of which alone we are conscious. But that each word and letter has its effect,—an effect which can at any moment become an object of consciousness,—is shewn by the following experiment. If we look over a book for the occurrence of a particular name or word, we glance our eye over a page from top to bottom, and ascertain, almost in a moment, that it is or is not to be found therein. Here the mind is hardly conscious of a single word, but that of which it is in quest; but yet it is evident, that each other word and letter must have produced an obscure effect, which effect the mind was ready to discriminate and strengthen, so as to call it into clear consciousness, whenever the effect was found to be that which the letters of the word sought for could determine. But if the mind be not unaffected by the multitude of letters and words which it surveys, if it be able to ascertain whether the combination of letters constituting the word it seeks, be or be not actually among them, and all this without any distinct consciousness of all it tries and finds defective; why may we not suppose,—why are we not bound to suppose, that the mind may, in like manner, overlook its book of memory, and search among its magazines of latescent cognitions for the notions of which it is in want, awakening these into consciousness, and allowing the others to remain in their obscurity?

A more attentive consideration of the subject will show, that we have not yet divined the faculty of Reminiscence in its whole extent. Let us make a single reflection. Continually struck by relations of every kind, continually assailed by a crowd of perceptions and sensations of every variety, and, at the same time, occupied by a complement of thoughts; we experience at once, and we are more or less distinctly conscious of, a considerable number of wants,—wants, sometimes real, sometimes factitious or imaginary,— phenomena, however, all stamped with the same characters, and all stimulating us to act with more or less of energy. And as we choose among the different wants which we would satisfy, as well as among the different means of satisfying that want which we determine to prefer; and as the motives of this preference are taken either from among the principal ideas relative to each of these several wants, or from among the accessory ideas which habit has established into their necessary escorts;—in all these cases it is requisite, that all the circumstances should at once, and from the moment they have taken the character of wants, produce an effect, correspondent to that which, we have seen, is caused by each in particular. Hence we are compelled to conclude, that the complement of the circumstances by which we are thus affected, has the effect of rendering always present to us, and consequently of placing at our disposal, an immense number of thoughts; some of which certainly are distinctly recognised, being accompanied by a vivid consciousness, but the greater number of which, although remaining latent, are not the less effective in continually exercising their peculiar influence on our modes of judging and acting.

We might say, that each of these momentary circumstances is a kind of electric shock which is communicated to a certain portion, to a certain limited sphere, of intelligence; and the sum of all these circumstances is equal to so many shocks which, given at once at so many different points, produce a general agitation. We may form some rude conception of this phenomenon by an analogy. We may compare it, in the former case, to those concentric circles which are presented to our observation on a smooth sheet of water, when its surface is agitated by throwing in a pebble; and, in the latter case, to the same surface when agitated by a number of pebbles thrown simultaneously at different points.

To obtain a clearer notion of this phenomenon, I may add some observations on the relation of our thoughts among themselves, and with the determining circumstances of the moment.

1° Among the thoughts, notions, or ideas which belong to the different groups attached to the principal representations simultaneously awakened, there are some reciprocally connected by relations proper to themselves; so that, in this whole complement of coexistent activities, these tend to excite each other to higher vigour, and consequently to obtain for themselves a kind of pre-eminence in the group or particular circle of activity to which they belong.

2° There are thoughts associated, whether as principals or accessories, to a greater number of determining circumstances, or to circumstances which recur more frequently. Hence they present themselves oftener than the others, they enter more completely into our habits, and take, in a more absolute manner, the character of customary or habitual notions. It hence results, that they are less obtrusive, though more energetic, in their influence, enacting, as they do, a principal part in almost all our deliberations; and exercising a stronger influence on our determinations.

3° Among this great crowd of thoughts, simultaneously excited, those which are connected with circumstances which more vividly affect us, assume not only the ascendant over others of the same description with themselves, but likewise predominate over all those which are dependent on circumstances of a feebler determining influence.

From these three considerations we ought, therefore, to infer, that the thoughts connected with circumstances on which our attention is more specially concentrated, are those which prevail over the others; for the effect of attention is to render dominant and exclusive the object on which it is directed, and during the moment of attention it is the circumstance to which we attend that necessarily obtains the ascendant.

Thus, if we appreciate correctly the phenomena of Reproduction or Reminiscence, we shall recognise, as an incontestable fact, that our thoughts suggest each other not one by one successively, as the order to which language is astricted might lead us to infer; but that the complement of circumstances under which we at every moment exist, awakens simultaneously a great number of thoughts; these it calls into the presence of the mind, either to place them at our disposal, if we find it requisite to employ them, or to make them co-operate in our deliberations by giving them, according to their nature and our habits, an influence, more or less active, on our judgments and consequent acts.

It is also to be observed, that in this great crowd of thoughts always present to the mind, there is only a small number of which we are distinctly conscious: and that in this small number we ought to distinguish those which, being clothed in language, oral or mental, become the objects of a more fixed attention; those which hold a closer relation to circumstances more impressive than others; or which receive a predominant character by the more vigorous attention we bestow on them. As to the others, although not the objects of clear consciousness, they are nevertheless present to the mind, there to perform a very important part as motive principles of determination; and the influence which they exert in this capacity is even the more powerful in proportion as it is less apparent, being more disguised by habit.*

(Vol. II, pp. 69–79.)

\*    \*    \*    \*    \*

*Sir William Hamilton's *Lectures on Metaphysics*, Vol. II, Lecture xxxii [pp. 250–8]. [Hamilton is translating from Jean Jacques Séverin de Cardaillac, *Etudes élémentaires de philosophie*, 2 vols. (Paris: Firmin Didot, 1830), Vol. II, pp. 124–38.

[*In dealing with abstract relative terms, James Mill calls attention to a peculiarity
in "abstract terms formed from the relative concrete terms"; the abstract of one
relative term "always connotes the abstract of the other," for example,* priority
*and* posteriority *"connote" one another. He continues (Vol. II, pp. 82–3):*] *This
constitutes a distinction, worth observing, between the force of the abstracts
formed from the pairs of relatives which consist of different names, as* prior,
posterior; *cause, effect; father, son; husband, wife;*—*and those which consist of
the same name, as* equal, equal; *like, like; brother, brother; friend, friend; and so
on.* Priority *and* Posteriority *make together a compound name of something, of
which, taken separately, each is not a name;* Causingness *and* Causedness, *the
abstracts of* cause *and* effect, *make up between them the name of something, of
which each by itself is not a name, and so of the rest. The case is different with such
abstracts as* likeness, equality, friendship, *formed from pairs which consist of the
same name. When we call A* like, *and B* like; *the Abstract,* likeness, *formed from
the one, connotes merely the abstract,* likeness, *formed from the other. Thus, as*
priority *and* posteriority *make a compound name, so* likeness *and* likeness, *make a
compound name. But as* likeness *and* likeness *are merely a reduplication of the
same word,* likeness *taken once very often signifies the same as* likeness *taken
twice.* Priority *never signifies as much as* priority *and* posteriority *taken together;
but* likeness *taken alone very often signifies as much as* likeness, likeness, *taken
both together.* Likeness *has thus a sort of a double meaning. Sometimes it signifies
only what is marked by the abstract of one of the pair, "like, like;" sometimes it
signifies what is marked by the abstracts of both taken together. The same
observation applies to the abstracts* equality, inequality; *sameness, difference;*
brotherhood, sisterhood; *friendship, hostility; and so on.*

The exposition here given of the meaning of abstract relative names is in substance
unexceptionable; but in language it remains open to the criticism I have, several
times, made. Instead of saying, with the author, that the abstract name drops the
connotation of the corresponding concrete, it would, in the language I prefer, be
said to drop the denotation, and to be a name directly denoting what the concrete
name connotes, namely, the common property or properties that it predicates: the
likeness, the unlikeness, the fact of preceding, the fact of following, etc.

When the author says that abstract relative names differ from other abstract
names in not being wholly void of connotation, inasmuch as they connote their
correlatives, *priority* connoting *posteriority*, and *posteriority priority*, he deserts
the specific meaning which he has sought to attach to the word *connote*, and falls
back upon the loose and general sense in which everything implied by a term is said
to be connoted by it. But in this large sense of the word (as I have more than once
remarked) it is not true that non-relative abstract names have no connotation.
Every abstract name—every name of the character which is given by the
terminations *ness*, *tion*, and the like—carries with it a uniform implication that
what it is predicated of is an attribute of something else; not a sensation or a thought

in and by itself, but a sensation or thought regarded as one of, or as accompanying or following, some permanent cluster of sensations or thoughts. (Vol. II, p. 83.)

*     *     *     *     *

[*James Mill comments that*] Causation *has the same meaning with* Power, *except that it connotes present time;* Power *connotes indefinite time*.

The term *Causation*, as the author observes, signifies causingness and causedness taken together, but I do not see on what ground he asserts that it connotes present time. To my thinking, it is as completely aoristic as *Power*. *Power*, again, seems to me to express, not causingness and causedness taken together, but causingness only. Some of the older philosophers certainly talked of passive power, but neither in the precise language of modern philosophy nor in common speech is an effect said to have the power of being produced, but only the capacity or capability. The power is always conceived as belonging to the cause only. When any co-operating power is supposed to reside in the thing said to be acted upon, it is because some active property in that thing is counted as a con-cause—as a part of the total cause. (Vol. II, p. 85.)

*     *     *     *     *

[*Near the end of "Abstract Relative Terms," Sect. 2 of Chap. xiv, James Mill avers (Vol. II, pp. 86–7) that just as* Noun *is*] *the name of a certain class of words, so* Relation, *is the name of a certain class of words.*

  *It is not, however, meant to be affirmed, that* relative *and* relation, *are not names which are also applied to things. In a certain vague, and indistinct way, they are very frequently so applied. This, however, is, strictly speaking, an abuse of the terms, and an abuse which has been a great cause of confusion of ideas. In this way, it is said, of two brothers, that they are relative; of father and son, that they are relative; of two objects, that they are relative in position, relative in time; we speak of the relation between two men, when they are father and son, master and servant; between two objects, when they are greater, less, like, unlike, near, distant, and so on.*

  *What, however, we really mean, when we call two objects relative (and that is a thing which it is of great importance to mark) is, that these objects have, or may have, relative names.* [*J.S. Mill's note comes at the end of the Section.*]

The application of the word *Relative* to Things is not only an offence against philosophy, but against propriety of language. The correct designation for Things which are called by relative names, is not *Relative*, but *Related*. A Thing may, with perfect propriety both of thought and of language, be said to be related to another thing, or to have a relation with it—indeed to be related to all things, and to have a prodigious variety of relations with all; because every fact that takes place, either in Nature or in human thought, which includes or involves a plurality of Things, is the *fundamentum* of a special relation of those Things with one another: not to mention the relations of likeness or unlikeness, of priority or posteriority, which exist between each Thing and all other Things whatever. It is in this sense that it is said, with truth, that Relations exhaust all phenomena, and that all we know, or can know, of anything, is some of its relations to other things or to us. (Vol. II, p. 88.)

\* \* \* \* \*

[*In "Numbers," Sect. 3 of Chap. xiv, James Mill says that Numbers "are not names of objects," but of "a certain process," that of addition.*] One, *is the name of this once performed, or of the aggregation begun;* two, *the name of it once more performed;* three, *of it once more performed; and so on. The words, however, in these concrete forms, beside their power in noting this process, connote something else, namely, the things, whatever they are, the enumeration of which is required.*

*In the case of these connotative, as of other connotative marks, it was of great use to have the means of dropping the connotation; and in this case, it would have been conducive to clearness of ideas, if the non-connotative terms had received a mark to distinguish them from the connotative. This advantage, however, the framers of numbers were not sufficiently philosophical to provide. The same names are used both as connotative, and non-connotative; that is, both as abstract, and concrete; and it is far from being obvious, on all occasions, in which of the two senses they are used. They are used in the connotative sense, when joined as adjectives with a substantive; as when we say two men, three women; but it is not so obvious that they are used in the abstract sense, when we say three and two make five; or when we say fifty is a great number, five is a small number. Yet it must, upon consideration, appear, that in these cases they are abstract terms merely; in place of which, the words* oneness, twoness, threeness, *might be substituted. Thus we might say,* twoness *and* threeness *are* fiveness. [*The words "to be a name of" do not occur in this part of the* Analysis, *though attributing them to James Mill, as J.S. Mill does in the following note appended to the passage, fairly represents his usage.*]

The vague manner in which the author uses the phrase "to be a name of" (a vagueness common to almost all thinkers who have not precise terms expressing the two modes of signification which I call *denotation* and *connotation*, and employed for nothing else) has led him, in the present case, into a serious misuse of terms. Numbers *are*, in the strictest propriety, names of objects. *Two* is surely a name of the things which *are* two, the two balls, the two fingers, etc. The process of adding one to one which forms two is connoted, not denoted, by the name *two*. Numerals, in short, are concrete, not abstract, names: they denote the actual collections of things, and connote the mental process of counting them. It is not *twoness* and *threeness* that are *fiveness*: the *twoness* of my two hands and the *threeness* of the feet of the table cannot be added together to form another abstraction. It is two balls added to three balls that make, in the concrete, five balls. Numerals are a class of concrete general names predicable of all things whatever, but connoting, in each case, the quantitative relation of the thing to some fixed standard, as previously explained by the author. (Vol. II, pp. 92–3.)

\* \* \* \* \*

[*The first paragraph of "Privative Terms," Sect. 4 of Chap. xiv, to which J.S. Mill's note is attached, reads:*] Privative terms are distinguished from other terms, by this; that other terms are marks for objects, as present or existent; privative terms are marks for objects, as not present or not existent.

The author gives the name of *Privative terms* to all those which are more commonly known by the designation of Negative; to all which signify non-existence or absence. It is usual to reserve the term *Privative* for names which signify not simple absence, but the absence of something usually present, or of which the presence might have been expected. Thus *blind* is classed as a privative term, when applied to human beings. When applied to stocks and stones, which are not expected to see, it is an admitted metaphor.

   This, however, being understood, there is no difficulty in following the author's exposition by means of his own language. (Vol. II, p. 99.)

\* \* \* \* \*

[*James Mill chooses* silence *as an example of a "privative term," saying (Vol. II, p. 103):*] Silence *is the absence of sound, either all sound, which is sometimes its meaning; or of some particular sound, which at other times is its meaning. Sound is the name of a well-known something, as present. Silence is the name of the same well-known something, as absent. The first word, is the name of the thing, and its presence. The second, is the name of the thing, and its absence. In the case of the combination marked by the first, namely, the thing and its presence, the thing is the prominent part, and the presence generally escapes attention. In the case of the second, the thing and its absence, the absence is the important part, and the thing is feebly, if at all, attended to.* [*James Mill also discusses* ignorance, *and* absent *(joined with a "particular name" ), and concludes with the following passage, to which J.S. Mill's note is appended:]* The word Nothing, Nihil, *is another* generical *Privative Term. That this word has a very important marking power, every man is sensible in the use which he makes of it. But if it marks, it names; that is, names something. Yet it seems to remove every thing; that is, not to leave anything to be named.*

*The preceding explanations, however, have already cleared up this mystery. The word* Nothing *is the Privative Term which corresponds to* Every Thing. Every Thing *is a name of all possible objects, including their existence.* Nothing *is a name of all possible objects, including their non-existence.*

The analysis of the facts, in all these cases, is admirable, but I still demur to the language. I object to saying, for instance, that *silence* is "the name of sound and its absence." It is not the name of sound, since we cannot say Sound is silence. It is the name of our state of sensation when there is no sound. The author is quite right in saying that this state of sensation recalls the idea of sound; to be conscious of silence as silence, implies that we are thinking of sound, and have the idea of it without the belief in its presence. In another of its uses, *Silence* is the abstract of *Silent*; which is a name of all things that make no sound, and of everything so long as it makes no sound; and which connotes the attribute of not sounding. So of all the other terms mentioned. *Nothing* is not a name of all possible objects, including their non-existence. If *Nothing* were a name of objects, we should be able to predicate of those objects that they are Nothing. *Nothing* is a name of the state of our consciousness when we are not aware of any object, or of any sensation. (Vol. II, pp. 105–6.)

\* \* \* \* \*

*[James Mill remarks in his discussion of privative terms, that* space *has been] regarded as singularly mysterious. The difficulty which has been found in explaining the term, even, by those philosophers who have approached the nearest to its meaning, seems to have arisen, from their not perceiving the mode of signification of Abstract Terms; and from the obscurity of that class of sensations, a portion of which we employ the word* extended *to mark. The word* space *is an abstract, differing from its concrete, like other abstracts, by dropping the connotation. Much of the mystery, in which the idea has seemed to be involved, is owing to this single circumstance, that the abstract term,* space, *has not had an appropriate concrete. We have observed, that, in all cases, abstract terms can be explained only through their concretes; because they note or name a part of what the concrete names, leaving out the rest. If we were to make a concrete term, corresponding to the abstract term* space, *it must be a word equivalent to the terms "infinitely extended." From the ideas included under the name "infinitely*

*extended," leave out* resisting, *and you have all that is marked by the abstract* SPACE.

There is great originality as well as perspicacity in the explanation here given of *Space*, as a privative term, expressing, when analysed, the absence of the feeling of resistance in the circumstances in which resistance is frequently felt, namely, after the sensations of muscular action and motion. The only part of the exposition to which I demur is the classing of *Space* among abstract terms. I have already objected to calling the word *line*, when used in the geometrical sense, an abstract term. I hold it to be the concrete name of an ideal object possessing length but not breadth. In like manner a Space may be said to be the concrete name of an ideal object, extended but not resisting. The sensations connoted by this concrete name, are those which accompany the motion of our limbs or of our body in all directions: and along with these sensations is connoted the absence of certain others, *viz.* of the muscular sensations which accompany the arrest of that motion by a resisting substance. This being the meaning of *a* Space, *Space* in general must be a name equally concrete. It denotes the aggregate of all Spaces. (Vol. II, p. 111.)

\* \* \* \* \*

[*Connecting the idea of infinity with that of space, James Mill discusses its origins, and concludes:*] *The idea of a portion more, adhering, by indissoluble association, to the idea of every increase, in any or in all directions, is the idea of "infinitely extended," and the idea of "infinitely extended," the connotation dropped, is the idea of Infinite Space. It has been called a simple idea (so little has the real nature of it been understood); while it is thus distinctly seen, to be one of the most complex ideas, which the whole train of our conscious being presents. Extreme complexity, with great closeness of association, has this effect—that every particular part in the composition is overpowered by the multitude of all the other parts, and no one in particular stands marked from the rest; but all, together, assume the appearance of* ONE. *Something perfectly analogous occurs, even in sensation. If two or three ingredients are mixed, as wine and honey, we can distinguish the taste of each, and say it is compound. But if a great many are mixed, we can distinguish no one in particular, and the taste of the whole appears a simple peculiar taste.*

This explanation of the feeling of Infinity which attaches itself to Space, is one of the most important thoughts in the whole treatise; and, obvious as its truth is to a mind prepared by the previous exposition, it has great difficulty in finding entrance into other minds.

Every object is associated with some position: not always with the same position, but we have never perceived any object, and therefore never think of one, but in some position or other, relative to some other objects. As, from every position, Space extends in every direction (*i.e.* the unimpeded arm or body can move in any direction), and since we never were in any place which did not admit of motion in every direction from it, when such motion was not arrested by a resistance; every idea of position is irresistibly associated with extension beyond the position: and we can conceive no end to extension, because the place which we try to conceive as its end, raises irresistibly the idea of other places beyond it. This is one of the many so-called Necessities of Thought which are necessities only in consequence of the inseparableness of an association: but which, from unwillingness to admit this explanation, men mistake for original laws of the human mind, and even regard them as the effect and proof of a corresponding necessary connexion between facts existing in Nature. (Vol. II, pp. 113–14.)

\*     \*     \*     \*     \*

[*In "Time," Sect. 5 of Chap. xiv, James Mill remarks:*] *Of* TIME *itself we conceive, that it is never still. It is a perpetual flow of instants, of which only one can ever be present. The very idea of Time, therefore, is an idea of successions. It consists of this, and of nothing else.*

*But there are no real successions, save successions of objects, that is of feelings in our minds.*

There is an unusual employment of language here, which if attention is not formally drawn to it, may embarrass the reader. By objects are commonly meant, those groups or clusters of sensations and possibilities of sensation, that compose what we call the external world. A single sensation, even external, and still less if internal, is not called an object. In a somewhat larger sense, whatever we think of, as distinguished from the thought itself and from ourselves as thinking it, is called an object; this is the common antithesis of Object and Subject. But in this place, the author designates as objects, all things which have real existence, as distinguished from the instants of mere Time, which, as he is pointing out, have not; and a puzzling effect is produced by his applying the name Object, in even an especial manner, to sensations: to the tickings of a watch, or the beatings of a patient's pulse.[120] (Vol. II, p. 117.)

\*     \*     \*     \*     \*

[120]The examples appear in the text, Vol. II, p. 118.

*[J.S. Mill's note is attached to the end of the section on time.]*

As is shewn in the text, *Time* is a name for the aggregate of the successions of our feelings, apart from the feelings themselves. I object, however, in the case of *Time*, as I did in the case of *Space*, to considering it as an abstract term. *Time* does not seem to me to be a name (as the author says) for the pastness, the presentness, and the futureness of our successive feelings.[121] It is rather, I think, a collective name for our feeling of their succession—for what the author called, in a previous section, the part of the process "which consists in being sensible of their successiveness," for which part, he then said, "we have not a name."[122] This taking notice of the successiveness of our feelings, whether we prefer to call it a part of the feelings themselves, or another feeling superadded to them, is yet something which, in the entire mass of feeling which the successive impressions give us, we are able to discriminate, and to name apart from the rest. A perception of succession between two feelings is a state of consciousness *per se*, which though we cannot think of it separately from the feelings, we can yet think of as a completed thing in itself, and not as an attribute of either or both of the two feelings. Its name, if it had one, would be a concrete name. But the entire series of these perceptions of succession has a name, *Time*; which I therefore hold to be a concrete name.

However inextricably these feelings of succession are mixed up with the feelings perceived as successive, we are so perfectly able to attend to them, and make them a distinct object of thought, that we can compare them with one another, without comparing the successive feelings in any other respect. We can judge two or more successions to be of equal, or of unequal, rapidity. And if we find any series of feelings of which the successive links follow each other with uniform rapidity, such as the tickings of a clock, we can make this a standard of comparison for all other successions, and measure them as equal to one, two, three, or some other number of links of this series: whereby the aggregate Time is said to be divided into equal portions, and every event is located in some one of those portions. The succession of our sensations, therefore, however closely implicated with the sensations themselves, may be abstracted from them in thought, as completely as any quality of a thing can be abstracted from the thing.

The apparent infinity of Time the author, very rightly, explains in the same manner as that of Space. (Vol. II, pp. 133–5.)

\* \* \* \* \*

[121]*Ibid.*
[122]*Ibid.*, p. 81 (in Sect. 2).

[*At the end of "Motion," Sect. 6 (pp. 142–6) of Chap. xiv, a lengthy note by Bain appears (pp. 146–51); J.S. Mill's note follows Bain's.*]

It will be both useful and interesting to the inquiring reader, if I add to the analysis of these very complex ideas by the author of the present treatise, and to that by Mr. Bain, the analysis given of them by the other great living master of the Association psychology, Mr. Herbert Spencer. The following passages are from his *Principles of Psychology*. First, of Resistance:

On raising the arm to a horizontal position and keeping it so, and still more on dealing similarly with the leg, a sensation is felt, which, tolerably strong as it is at the outset, presently becomes unbearable. If the limb be uncovered, and be not brought against anything, this sensation is associated with no other, either of touch or pressure.

This is the sensation of Muscular Tension.

Allied to the sensation accompanying tension of the muscles, is that accompanying the act of contracting them—the sensation of muscular motion. . . . While, from the muscles of a limb at rest, no sensation arises; while, from the muscles of a limb in a state of continuous strain, there arises a continuous sensation which remains uniform for a considerable time; from the muscle of a limb in motion, there arises a sensation which is ever undergoing increase or decrease, or change of composition.

When we express our immediate experiences of a body by saying that it is *hard*, what are the experiences implied? First, a sensation of pressure, of considerable intensity, is implied; and if, as in most cases, this sensation of pressure is given to a finger voluntarily thrust against the object, then there is simultaneously felt a correspondingly strong sensation of muscular tension. But this is not all: for feelings of pressure and muscular tension may be given by bodies which we call soft, provided the compressing finger follows the surface as fast as it gives way. In what then consists the difference between the perceptions? In this; that whereas when a soft body is pressed with increasing force, the synchronous sensations of increasing pressure and increasing muscular tension are accompanied by sensations of muscular movement; when a hard body is pressed with increasing force these sensations of increasing pressure and tension are *not* accompanied by sensations of muscular movement. Considered by itself, then, the perception of softness may be defined as the establishment in consciousness of a relation of simultaneity between three series of sensations—a series of increasing sensations of pressure; a series of increasing sensations of tension; and a series of sensations of motion. And the perception of hardness is the same, with omission of the last series. (Pp. 212–13.)

Of Extension; and first, of Form or Figure:

It is an anciently established doctrine that Form or Figure, which we may call the most complex mode of extension, is resolvable into relative magnitude of parts. An equilateral triangle is one of which the three sides are alike in magnitude. An ellipse is a symmetrical closed curve, of which the transverse and conjugate diameters are one greater than the other. A cube is a solid, having all its surfaces of the same magnitude, and all its angles of the same magnitude. A cone is a solid, successive sections of which, made at right angles to the axis, are circles regularly decreasing in magnitude as we progress from base to apex. Any object described as narrow is one whose breadth is of small magnitude when compared with its length. A symmetrical figure is a figure in which the homologous parts on opposite sides are equal in magnitude. Figures which we class as similar to each other, are such that the relation of magnitude between any two parts of the one, is equal to the relation of magnitude between the corresponding parts of the other. Add to which, that an alteration in the form of anything, is an alteration in the comparative sizes of some of its parts—a change in the relations of magnitude subsisting between them and the other parts, and that by continuously altering the relative magnitudes of its parts, any figure may be changed indefinitely. Hence, figure being wholly resolvable into relations of magnitude, we may go on to analyze that out of which these relations are formed—magnitude itself. (Pp. 224–5.)

### Next, therefore, of Magnitude:

What is a magnitude, considered analytically? The reply is, It consists of one or more relations of position. When we conceive anything as having a certain bulk, we conceive its opposite limiting surfaces as more or less removed from each other; that is, as related in position. When we imagine a line of definite length, we imagine its termini as occupying points in space having some positive distance from each other; that is, as related in position. As a solid is decomposable into planes; a plane into lines; lines into points; and as adjacent points can neither be known nor conceived as distinct from each other, except as occupying different places in space—that is, as occupying not the same position, but relative positions—it follows that every cognition of magnitude, is a cognition of one or more relations of position, which are presented to consciousness as like or unlike one or more other relations of position. (P. 226.)

### And finally, of Position:

This analysis of itself brings us to the remaining space-attribute of body—Position. Like magnitude, Position cannot be known absolutely; but can be known only relatively. The notion of position is, in itself, the notion of relative position. The position of a thing is inconceivable, save by thinking of that thing as at some distance from one or more other things. The essential element of the idea will be best seen, on observing under what conditions only, it can come into existence. Imagine a solitary point A, in infinite space; and suppose it possible for that point to be known by a being having no locality. What now can be predicated respecting its place? Absolutely nothing. Imagine another point B to be added. What can now be predicated respecting the two? Still nothing. The points having no attributes save position, are not comparable in themselves; and nothing can be said of their relative position, from lack of anything with which to compare it. The distance between them may be either infinite or infinitesimal, according to the measure used; and as, by the hypothesis, there exists no measure—as space contains nothing save these two points; the distance between them is unthinkable. But now imagine that a third point C is added. Immediately it becomes possible to frame a proposition respecting their positions. The two distances, A to B, and A to C, serve as measures to each other. The space between A and B may be compared with the space between A and C; and the relation of position in which A stands to B becomes thinkable, as like or unlike the relation in which A stands to C. Thus, then, it is manifest that position is not an attribute of body in itself, but only in its connection with the other contents of the universe.

It remains to add, that relations of position are of two kinds: those which subsist between subject and object; and those which subsist between either different objects, or different parts of the same object. Of these the last are resolvable into the first. It needs but to remember, on the one hand, that in the dark a man can discover the relative positions of two objects only by touching first one and then the other, and so inferring their relative positions from his own position towards each; and on the other hand, that by vision no knowledge of their relative positions can be reached save through a perception of the distance of each from the eye; to see that ultimately all relative positions may be decomposed into relative positions of subject and object.

These conclusions—that Figure is resolvable into relative magnitudes; that Magnitude is resolvable into relative positions; and that all relative positions may finally be reduced to positions of subject and object—will be fully confirmed on considering the process by which the space-attributes of body become known to a blind man. He puts out his hand, and touching something, thereby becomes cognizant of its position with respect to himself. He puts out his other hand, and meeting no resistance above or on one side of the position already found, gains some negative knowledge of the thing's magnitude—a knowledge which three or four touches on different sides of it serve to render positive. And then, by continuing to move his hands over its surface, he acquires a notion of its figure. What, then, are the elements out of which, by synthesis, his perceptions of magnitude and figure are framed? He has received nothing but simultaneous and successive touches. Each touch established a relation of position between his centre of consciousness and the point touched. And all he can know respecting magnitude and figure—that is, respecting the relative position of these points to each other—is necessarily known through the relative positions in which they severally stand to himself.

Our perceptions of all the space-attributes of body being thus decomposable into perceptions of position like that gained by a single act of touch; we have next to inquire what is contained in a perception of this kind. A little thought will make it clear that to perceive the position of anything touched, is really to perceive the position of that part of the body in which the sensation of touch is located. Whence it follows that our knowledge of the positions of objects, is built upon our knowledge of the positions of our members towards each other—knowledge both of their fixed relations, and of those temporary relations they are placed in by every change of muscular adjustment. That this knowledge is gained by a mutual exploration of the parts—by a bringing of each in contact with the others—by a moving over each other in all possible ways; and that the motions involved in these explorations, are known by their reactions upon consciousness; are propositions that scarcely need stating. But it is manifestly impossible to carry the analysis further without analysing our perception of motion. Relative position and motion are two ideas of the same experience. We can neither conceive motion without conceiving relative position, nor discover relative position without motion. In the present, therefore, we must be content with the conclusion that, whether visual or tactual, the perception of every statical attribute of body is resolvable into perceptions of relative position which are gained through motion. (Pp. 226–9.)

In further prosecution of the analysis:

How do we become cognizant of the relative positions of two points on the surface of the body? Such two points, considered as coexistent, involve the germinal idea of Space. Such two points disclosed to consciousness by two successive tactual sensations proceeding from them, involve the germinal idea of Time. And the series of muscular sensations by which, when self-produced, these two tactual sensations are separated, involve the germinal idea of Motion. The questions to be considered then are—In what order do these germinal ideas arise? and—How are they developed?

. . . Taking for our subject a newly-born infant, let us call the two points on its body between which a relation is to be established, A and Z. Let us assume these points to be anywhere within reach of the hands—say upon the cheek. By the hypothesis, nothing is at present known of these points; either as coexisting in Space, as giving successive sensations in Time, or as being brought into relation by Motion. If, now, the infant moves its arm in such a way as to touch nothing, there is a certain vague reaction upon its consciousness—a sensation of muscular tension. This sensation has the peculiarity of being indefinite in its commencement; indefinite in its termination; and indefinite in all its intermediate changes. Its strength is proportionate to the degree of muscular contraction. Whence it follows that as the limb starts from a state of rest, in which there is no contraction; and as it can reach a position requiring extreme contraction only by passing through positions requiring intermediate degrees of contraction; and as the degrees of contraction must therefore form a series ascending by infinitesimal increments from zero; the sensations of tension must also form such a series. And the like must be the case with all subsequent movements and their accompanying sensations; seeing that, be it at rest or in action, a muscle cannot pass from any one state to any other without going through all the intermediate states. Thus, then, the infant, on moving its arm backwards and forwards without touching anything, is brought to what we may distinguish as a nascent consciousness—a consciousness not definitely divisible into states; but a consciousness the variations of which pass insensibly into each other, like undulations of greater or less magnitude. And while the states of consciousness are thus incipient—thus indistinctly separated, there can be no clear comparison of them; no thought, properly so called; and consequently no ideas of Motion, Time, or Space, as we understand them. Suppose, now, that the hand touches something. A sudden change in consciousness is produced—a change that is incisive in its commencement, and, when the hand is removed, equally incisive in its termination. In the midst of the continuous feeling of muscular tension, vaguely rising and falling in intensity, there all at once occurs a distinct feeling of another kind. This feeling, beginning and ending abruptly, constitutes a definite state of consciousness; becomes, as it were a *mark* in consciousness. By similar experiences other such marks are produced; and in proportion as they are multiplied, there arises a possibility of comparing them, both in respect to their degrees and their relative positions; while at the same time, the feelings of muscular tension being, as it were, divided out into lengths by these superposed marks, become similarly comparable; and so there are acquired materials for a simple order of thought. Observe, also, that while these tactual sensations may, when several things are touched in succession, produce successive marks in consciousness, separated by intervening muscular sensations, they may also become continually coexistent with these muscular sensations; as when the finger is drawn along a surface. And observe further, that when the surface over which the finger is drawn is not a foreign body, but some part of the subject's body, these muscular sensations, and the continuous tactual sensation joined with them, are accompanied by a series of tactual sensations proceeding from that part of the skin over which the finger is drawn. Thus, then, when the infant moves its finger along the surface of its body from A to Z, there are simultaneously impressed upon consciousness three sets of sensations—the varying series of sensations proceeding from the muscles in action; the series of tactual sensations proceeding from the points of the skin successively touched between A and Z; and the continuous sensation of touch from the finger-end. . . . As subsequent motions of the finger over the surface from A to Z always result in the like simultaneous sets of sensations, these, in course of time, become indissolubly associated. Though the series of tactual sensations, A to Z, being producible by a foreign body moving over the same surface, can be dissociated from the others; and though, if the cheek be withdrawn by a movement of the head, the same motion of the hand, with its accompanying muscular sensations, may occur without any sensation of touch; yet, when these two series are linked by the tactual sensation proceeding from the finger-end, they necessarily proceed together; and become inseparably connected in thought. Whence it obviously results that the series of tactual sensations A to Z, and the series of muscular sensations which invariably accompanies it when self-produced, serve as mutual equivalents; and being two sides of the same experience, suggest each other in consciousness.

Due attention having been paid to this fact, let us go on to consider what must happen when something touches, at the same moment, the entire surface between A and Z. This surface is supplied by a series of independent nerve-fibres, each of which at its peripheral termination becomes fused into, or continuous with, the surrounding tissue; each of which is affected by impressions falling within a specific area of the skin; and each of which produces a separate state of consciousness. When the finger is drawn along this surface these nerve-fibres A, B, C, D . . . Z, are excited in succession; that is—produce successive states of consciousness. And when something covers, at the same moment, the whole surface between A and Z, they are excited simultaneously; and produce what tends to become a single state of consciousness. Already I have endeavoured to shew in a parallel case, how, when impressions first known as having sequent positions in consciousness are afterwards simultaneously presented to consciousness, the sequent positions are transformed into coexistent positions, which, when consolidated by frequent presentations, are used in thought as equivalent to the sequent positions.* . . . As the series of tactual impressions A to Z, known as having sequent positions in consciousness, are, on the one hand, found to be equivalent to the accompanying series of muscular impressions; and on the other hand, to the simultaneous tactual impressions A to Z, which, as presented together, are necessarily presented in coexistent positions; it follows that these two last are found to be the equivalents of each other. A series of muscular sensations becomes known as equivalent to a series of coexistent positions; and being habitually joined with it, becomes at last unthinkable without it. Thus, the relation of coexistent positions between the points A and Z (and by implication all intermediate points) is necessarily disclosed by a comparison of experiences: the ideas of Space, Time, and Motion, are evolved together. When the successive states of consciousness A to Z, are thought of as having relative positions, the notion of Time becomes nascent. When these states of consciousness, instead of occurring serially, occur simultaneously, their relative positions, which were before sequent, necessarily become coexistent; and there arises a nascent consciousness of space. And when these two relations of coexistent and sequent positions are both presented to consciousness along with a series of sensations of muscular tension, a nascent idea of Motion results.

The development of these nascent ideas, arising as it does from a still further accumulation and comparison of experiences, will be readily understood. What has been above described as taking place with respect to one relation of coexistent positions upon the surface of the skin—or rather, one linear series of such coexisting positions, is, during the

*"Objects laid upon the surface will come to be distinguished from each other by the relative lengths of the series they cover; or, when broad as well as long, by the groups of series which they cover. . . . By habit these simultaneous excitations, from being at first known indirectly by translation into the serial ones, will come to be known directly, and the serial ones will be forgotten: just as in childhood the words of a new language, at first understood by means of their equivalents in the mother tongue, are presently understood by themselves; and if used to the exclusion of the mother tongue, lead to the ultimate loss of it." (Pp. 222–3.) We see that "a set of [nervous] elements may be excited simultaneously as well as serially; that so, a *quasi* single state of consciousness becomes the equivalent of a series of states; that a relation between what we call coexistent positions thus represents a relation of successive positions, and that this symbolic relation being far briefer, is habitually thought of in place of that it symbolizes; and that, by the continued use of such symbols, and the union of them with more complex ones, are generated our ideas of . . . extension—ideas which, like those of the algebraist working out an equation, are wholly unlike the ideas symbolized, and which yet, like his, occupy the mind to the entire exclusion of the ideas symbolized." (P. 224.)

same period, taking place, with respect to endless other such linear series, in all directions over the body. The like equivalence between a series of coexistent impressions of touch, a series of successive impressions of touch, and series of successive muscular impressions, is being established between every pair of points that can readily be brought into relation by movement of the hands. Let us glance at the chief consequences that must ultimately arise from this organization of experiences.

Not only must there gradually be established a connection in thought between each *particular* muscular series, and the *particular* tactual series, both successive and simultaneous, with which it is associated; and not only must there, by implication, arise a knowledge of the special muscular adjustments required to touch each special part, but, by the same experiences, there must be established an indissoluble connection between muscular series in general and series of sequent and coexistent positions in general, seeing that this connection is repeated in every one of the particular experiences. And when we consider the infinite repetition of these experiences, we shall have no difficulty in understanding how their components become so consolidated, that even when the hand is moved through empty space, it is impossible to become conscious of the muscular sensations, without becoming conscious of the sequent and coexistent positions—the Time and Space, in which it has moved.

Observe again, that as, by this continuous exploration of the surface of the body, each point is put in relation not only with points in some directions around it, but with points in all directions—becomes, as it were, a centre from which radiate lines of points known first in their serial positions before consciousness, and afterwards in their coexistent positions—it follows, that when an object of some size, as the hand, is placed upon the skin, the impressions from all parts of the area covered being simultaneously presented to consciousness, are placed in coexistent positions before consciousness: whence results an idea of the superficial extension of that part of the body. The idea of this extension is really nothing more than a simultaneous presentation of all the impressions proceeding from the various points it includes, which have previously had their several relative positions measured by means of the series of impressions separating them. Anyone who hesitates respecting this conclusion, will, I think, adopt it, on critically considering the perception he has when placing his open hand against his cheek—on observing that the perception is by no means single, but is made up of many elements which he cannot think of all together—on observing that there is always one particular part of the whole surface touched, of which he is more distinctly conscious than of any other—and on observing that to become distinctly conscious of any other part, he has to traverse in thought the intervening parts; that is, he has to think of the relative positions of these parts by vaguely recalling the series of states of consciousness which a motion over the skin from one to the other would involve. (Pp. 257–63.)

These three different expositions of the origin of our ideas of Motion and Extension, by three eminent thinkers, agreeing in essentials, and differing chiefly in the comparative degrees of development which they give to different portions of the detail, will enable any competent reader of such a work as the present to fill up any gaps by his own thoughts. Many pages of additional commentary might easily be written; but they would not add any important thought to those of which the reader is now in possession; and belonging rather to the polemics of the subject than to its strictly scientific exposition, they would jar somewhat with the purely expository character of the present treatise.

I will only further recommend to particular attention, the opinion of Mr.

Spencer, also adopted by Mr. Bain, that our ascribing simultaneous existence to things which excite successive sensations, is greatly owing to our being able to vary or reverse the order of the succession. When we pass our hands over an object, we can have the tactual and muscular sensations in many different orders, and after having them in one order, can have them in another exactly the reverse. They do not, therefore, become associated with each other in a fixed order of succession, but are called up in any order with such extreme rapidity, that the impression they leave is that of simultaneousness, and we therefore hold the parts of tangible objects to be simultaneous. (Vol. II, pp. 151–63.)

\*     \*     \*     \*     \*

*[J.S. Mill's note comes at the end of "Identity," Sect. 7 of Chap. xiv.]*

The author has avoided an error in the mode and order of the enquiry, which has greatly contributed to make the explanations given by psychologists of Personal Identity, so eminently unsatisfactory as they are. Psychologists have almost always begun with the most intricate part of the question. They have set out by enquiring, what makes me the same person to myself? when they should first have enquired what makes me the same person to other people? or, what makes another person the same person to me? The author of the *Analysis* has done this, and he easily perceived, that what makes me the same person to others, is precisely what makes a house, or a mountain, the same house or mountain to them to-day which they saw yesterday. It is the belief of an uninterrupted continuity in the series of sensations derivable from the house, or mountain, or man. There is not this continuity in the actual sensations of a single observer: he has not been watching the mountain unintermittedly since yesterday, or from a still more distant time. But he believes, on such evidence as the case affords, that if he had been watching, he should have seen the mountain continuously and unchanged during the whole intervening time (provided the other requisites of vision were present—light to see it by, and no cloud or mist intervening): and he further believes that any being, with organs like his own, who had looked in that direction at any moment of the interval during which he himself was not looking, would have seen it in the same manner as he sees it. All this applies equally to a human object. I call the man I see to-day the same man whom I saw yesterday, for the very reason which makes me call the house or the mountain the same, *viz.*, my conviction that if my organs had been in the same position towards him all the time as they are now, and the other conditions necessary for seeing had been present, my perception of the man would have continued all the time without interruption.

If we now change the point of view, and ask, what makes me always the same person to myself, we introduce, in addition to what there was in the other case, the entire series of my own past states of consciousness. As the author truly says, the evidence on which I accept my own identity is that of memory. But memory reaches only a certain way back, and for all before that period, as well as for all subsequent to it of which I have lost the remembrance, the belief rests on other evidence. As an example of the errors and difficulties in which psychologists have involved themselves by beginning with the more complex question without having considered the simpler one, it is worth remembering that Locke makes personal identity consist in Consciousness, which in this case means Memory;[123] and has been justly criticized by later thinkers for this doctrine, as leading to the corollary, that whatever of my past actions I have forgotten, I never performed—that my forgotten feelings were not *my* feelings, but were (it must therefore be supposed) the feelings of somebody else. Locke, however, had seen one part of the true state of the case; which is, that *to myself* I am only, properly speaking, the same person, in respect of those facts of my past life which I remember; but that I nevertheless consider myself as having been, at the times of which I retain no remembrance, the same person I now am, because I have satisfactory evidence that I was the same to other people; that an uninterrupted continuity in the sensations of sight and touch caused or which could have been caused to other people, existed between my present self and the infant who I am told I was, and between my present self and the person who is proved to me to have done the acts I have myself forgotten.

These considerations remove the outer veil, or husk, as it were, which wraps up the idea of the Ego. But after this is removed, there remains an inner covering, which, as far as I can perceive, is impenetrable. My personal identity consists in my being the same Ego who did, or who felt, some specific fact recalled to me by memory. So be it: but what is Memory? It is not merely having the idea of that fact recalled: that is but thought, or conception, or imagination. It is, having the idea recalled along with the Belief that the fact which it is the idea of, really happened, and moreover happened to myself. Memory, therefore, by the very fact of its being different from Imagination, implies an Ego who formerly experienced the facts remembered, and who was the same Ego then as now. The phenomenon of Self and that of Memory are merely two sides of the same fact, or two different modes of viewing the same fact. We may, as psychologists, set out from either of them, and refer the other to it. We may, in treating of Memory, say (as the author says) that it is the idea of a past sensation associated with the idea of myself as having it. Or we may say, in treating of Identity, (as the author also says), that the meaning of Self is the memory of certain past sensations. But it is hardly allowable to do both. At least it must be said, that by doing so we explain neither. We only show that the two things are essentially the same; that my memory of having ascended Skiddaw on a given day, and my consciousness of being the same person who

---

[123]Locke, *Essay*, Vol. I, pp. 86–7 and 94–6 (Bk. II, Chap. i, Sects. 9 and 19).

ascended Skiddaw on that day, are two modes of stating the same fact: a fact which psychology has as yet failed to resolve into anything more elementary.

In analysing the complex phenomena of consciousness, we must come to something ultimate; and we seem to have reached two elements which have a good *prima facie* claim to that title. There is, first, the common element in all cases of Belief, namely, the difference between a fact, and the thought of that fact: a distinction which we are able to cognize in the past, and which then constitutes Memory, and in the future, when it constitutes Expectation; but in neither case can we give any account of it except that it exists; an inability which is admitted in the most elementary case of the distinction, *viz.* the difference between a present sensation and an idea. Secondly, in addition to this, and setting out from the belief in the reality of a past event, or in other words, the belief that the idea I now have was derived from a previous sensation, or combination of sensations, corresponding to it, there is the further conviction that this sensation or combination of sensations was my own; that it happened to myself. In other words, I am aware of a long and uninterrupted succession of past feelings going as far back as memory reaches, and terminating with the sensations I have at the present moment, all of which are connected by an inexplicable tie, that distinguishes them not only from any succession or combination in mere thought, but also from the parallel successions of feelings which I believe, on satisfactory evidence, to have happened to each of the other beings, shaped like myself, whom I perceive around me. This succession of feelings, which I call my memory of the past, is that by which I distinguish my Self. Myself is the person who had that series of feelings, and I know nothing of myself, by direct knowledge, except that I had them. But there is a bond of some sort among all the parts of the series, which makes me say that they were feelings of a person who was the same person throughout, and a different person from those who had any of the parallel successions of feelings; and this bond, to me, constitutes my Ego. Here, I think, the question must rest, until some psychologist succeeds better than any one has yet done in shewing a mode in which the analysis can be carried further. (Vol. II, pp. 172–5.)

\* \* \* \* \*

*[Chap. xv, "Reflection," is concluded by J.S. Mill's note.]*

To reflect on any of our feelings or mental acts is more properly identified with *attending* to the feeling, than, (as stated in the text) with merely having it.[124] The author scarcely recognises this as a difference. He sometimes indeed seems to

[124]*Analysis*, Vol. II, p. 176.

consider attention as mental repetition; but in his chapter on the Will, we shall find that he there identifies attending to a feeling with merely having the feeling. I conceive, on the contrary, (with the great majority of psychologists) that there is an important distinction between the two things; the ignoring of which has led the author into errors. What the distinction is, I have endeavoured to shew in my note to the chapter on Consciousness; and the subject will return upon us hereafter.[125] (Vol. II, pp. 179–80.)

\* \* \* \* \*

[*Chap. xvii, "Pleasurable and Painful Sensations," consists of only four short paragraphs; J.S. Mill's note is appended at the end.*]

In the case of many pleasurable or painful sensations, it is open to question whether the pleasure or pain, especially the pleasure, is not something added to the sensation, and capable of being detached from it, rather than merely a particular aspect or quality of the sensation. It is often observable that a sensation is much less pleasurable at one time than at another, though to our consciousness it appears exactly the same sensation in all except the pleasure. This is emphatically the fact in cases of satiety, or of loss of taste for a sensation by loss of novelty. It is probable that in such cases the pleasure may depend on different nerves, or on a different action of the same nerves, from the remaining part of the sensation. However this may be, the pleasure or pain attending a sensation is (like the feelings of Likeness, Succession, etc.) capable of being mentally abstracted from the sensation, or, in other words, capable of being attended to by itself. And in any case Mr. Bain's distinction holds good, between the emotional part or property of a sensation (in which he includes the pleasure or pain belonging to it) and its intellectual or knowledge-giving part.[126] It must be remembered, however, that these are not exclusive of one another; the knowledge-giving part is not necessarily emotional, but the emotional part is and must be knowledge-giving. The pleasure or pain of the feeling are subjects of intellectual apprehension; they give the knowledge of themselves and of their varieties. (Vol. II, pp. 185–6.)

\* \* \* \* \*

[125]See pp. 138–41 above and 247–50 below.
[126]Bain's note to Chap. xvi of the *Analysis*, Vol. II, p. 182.

*[Again J.S. Mill's note appears at the end of a chapter, "Ideas of the Pleasurable and Painful Sensations, and of the Causes of Them" (Chap. xix).]*

The principal doctrine of this chapter is, that Desire, and Aversion, are nothing but the Idea of a pleasurable sensation, and the Idea of a painful sensation: which doctrine is then qualified by saying, that a desire is the idea of a pleasure associated with the future, an aversion the idea of a pain associated with the iuture.[127]

But according to the whole spirit of the author's speculations, and to his express affirmation in the beginning of the next chapter,[128] the idea of any sensation associated with the future, constitutes the Expectation of it: and if so, it rested with him to prove that the expectation of a pleasure, or of a pain, is the same thing with the desire, or aversion. This is certainly not conformable to common observation. For, on the one hand, it is commonly understood that there may be desire or aversion without expectation; and on the other, expectation of a pleasure without any actual feeling of desire: one may expect, and even look forward with satisfaction to, the pleasure of a meal, although one is not, but only expects to be, hungry. So perfectly is it assumed that expectation, and desire or aversion, are not necessarily combined, that the case in which they are combined is signified by a special pair of names. Desire combined with expectation, is called by the name of Hope; Aversion combined with expectation is known by the name of Fear.

I believe the fact to be that Desire is not Expectation, but is more than the idea of the pleasure desired, being, in truth, the initiatory stage of Will. In what we call Desire there is, I think, always included a positive stimulation to action; either to the definite course of action which would lead to our obtaining the pleasure, or to a general restlessness and vague seeking after it. The stimulation may fall short of actually producing action: even when it prompts to a definite act, it may be repressed by a stronger motive, or by knowledge that the pleasure is not within present reach, nor can be brought nearer to us by any present action of our own. Still, there is, I think, always, the sense of a tendency to action, in the direction of pursuit of the pleasure, though the tendency may be overpowered by an external or an internal restraint. So also, in aversion, there is always a tendency to action of the kind which repels or avoids the painful sensation. But of these things more fully under the head of Will.[129] (Vol. II, pp. 194–5.)

\*     \*     \*     \*     \*

[127]Vol. II, p. 193.
[128]*Ibid.*, p. 197.
[129]See pp. 244–6 below.

*[In Chap. xx, "The Pleasurable and Painful Sensations, Contemplated as Passed or as Future," James Mill says (Vol. II, p. 197) that in] anticipation, as in memory, there is, first, the complex idea . . .; next, the passage of the mind forwards from the present state of consciousness, the antecedent, to one consequent after another, till it comes to the anticipated sensation. [He illustrates by the anticipation of an inflicted burn, and concludes (p. 198) by mentioning] the association with this idea of the events, one after another, which are to fill up the intermediate time, and terminate with his finger placed in the flame of the candle. The whole of this association, taken together, comprises the idea of the pain as his pain, after a train of antecedents.*

*The process of anticipation is so precisely the same, when the sensation is of the pleasurable kind, that I deem it unnecessary to repeat it.*

This is the first place in which the author gives his analysis of Expectation; and his theory of it is, as all theories of it must be, the exact counterpart of the same person's theory of Memory. He resolves it into the mere Idea of the expected event, accompanied by the "idea of the events, one after another," which are to begin with the present moment, and end with the expected event. But in this case, as in that of Memory, the objection recurs, that all this may exist in the case of mere Imagination. A man may conceive himself being hanged, or elevated to a throne, and may construct in his mind a series of possible or conceivable events, through which he can fancy each of these results to be brought about. If he is a man of lively imagination, this idea of the events "which are to fill up the intermediate time" may be at least as copious, as the idea of the series of coming events for a year from the present time, which according to the author's theory I have in my mind when I look forward to commencing a journey twelve months hence. Yet he neither expects to be hanged, nor to be made a king, still less both, which, to bear out the theory, it would seem that he ought.

The difference between Expectation and mere Imagination, as well as between Memory and Imagination, consists in the presence or absence of Belief; and though this is no explanation of either phenomenon, it brings us back to one and the same real problem, which I have so often referred to, and which neither the author nor any other thinker has yet solved—the difference between knowing something as a Reality, and as a mere Thought; a distinction similar and parallel to that between a Sensation and an Idea. (Vol. II, pp. 198–9.)

*        *        *        *        *

*[The penultimate paragraph of Chap. xx reads:] When a pleasurable sensation is contemplated as future, but not certainly, the state of consciousness is called*

*Hope. When a painful sensation is contemplated as future, but not certainly, the state of consciousness is called Fear.*

The author's definitions of Hope and Fear differ from those offered in my note (p. 194).[130] He considers these words to signify that the pleasure or the pain is contemplated as future, but without certainty. It must be admitted that the words are often applied to very faint degrees of anticipation, far short of those which in popular language would be spoken of as Expectation: but I think the terms are not inconsistent with the fullest assurance. A man is about to undergo a painful surgical operation. He has no doubt whatever about the event; he fully intends it; there are no other means, perhaps, of saving his life. Yet the feeling with which he looks forward to it, and with which he contemplates the preparations for it, are such as would, I think, by the custom of language, be designated as fear. Death, again, is the most certain of all future events, yet we speak of the fear of death. It is perhaps more doubtful whether the fully assured anticipation of a desired enjoyment would receive, in ordinary parlance, the name of Hope; yet some common phrases seem to imply that it would. We read even on tombstones "the sure hope of a joyful immortality."

A still more restricted application of the word Fear, also justified by usage, is to the case in which the feeling amounts to a disturbing passion; and to this meaning Mr. Bain, as will be seen in a future note, thinks it desirable to confine it.[131] (Vol. II, pp. 199–200.)

*    *    *    *    *

[*In Sect. 1 of Chap. xxi, "The Causes of Pleasurable and Painful Sensations, Contemplated as Passed, or as Future," James Mill considers the "immediate causes." He remarks (Vol. II, p. 201):*] *It may be regarded as remarkable, that though the idea or thought of a disagreeable sensation, as passed, is nearly indifferent, the thought of the cause of a painful passed sensation is often a very interesting state of consciousness.* [*He continues (p. 202):*] *The idea of the cause of a painful sensation is so closely associated with that of the sensation, that the one never exists without the other. But this is not all. The anticipation of the future from the passed, is so strong an association, that, in interesting cases, it is indissoluble. The thought of the Cause of a passed painful sensation, is the idea of an antecedent and a consequent. The idea of the passed antecedent and consequent is instantly followed by that of a future antecedent and consequent; and thus the feeling partakes of the nature of the anticipation of a future painful*

---

[130]P. 215 above.
[131]Bain's note is in *Analysis*, Vol. II, pp. 204–5.

*sensation. [J.S. Mill's note appears at the end of the paragraph from which these sentences are taken.]*

The difference here brought to notice between the very slight emotion excited in most cases by the idea of a past pain, and the strong feeling excited by the idea of the cause of a past pain, will be confirmed by every one's experience; and is rightly explained by the author, as arising from the fact that what has caused a past pain has an interest affecting the future, since it may cause future pains. It is noticeable that the author nowhere explains why the thought of a pain as future is so much more painful, than the thought of a past pain when detached from all apprehension for the future; why the expectation of an evil is generally so much worse than the remembrance of one. This fact might have made him doubt the sufficiency of his theory of Memory and Expectation; since, according to his analysis, neither of them is anything but the idea of the pain itself, associated in each case with a series of events which may be intrinsically indifferent; and if there were no elements in the case but those which he has pointed out, no sufficient reason is apparent why there should be any inequality of painfulness between the remembrance and the expectation. (Vol. II, pp. 202–3.)

*   *   *   *   *

*[Pointing out that the opinion was first expressed by Dugald Stewart, James Mill affirms] that there is no conception, that is, idea, without the momentary belief of the existence of its object.*

This is the place where the author most clearly enunciates the doctrine which is the indispensable basis of his theory of Belief, *viz.* that there is no idea "without the momentary belief of the existence of its object." This opinion, as the author observes, is maintained also by Dugald Stewart;[132] but I have never seen any positive evidence in its favour. All which has been established is, that the belief *may* have momentarily existed, although immediately afterwards forgotten, and replaced by disbelief. But no proof of this momentary existence has been given, except that it is supposed that what is not believed to be real cannot cause strong emotion (terror, for instance), nor prompt to outward action. Yet nothing can be more certain than that a mere idea can exercise direct power over our nerves of motion, and through them, over the muscles; as the author shows by examples further on.[133] It is true that, as Mr. Bain has pointed out,[134] this power of an idea over the active energies is the only germ of belief which exists originally, and the

[132]Stewart, *Elements*, Vol. I, pp. 140–2 (Chap. iii).
[133]*Analysis*, Vol. II, pp. 337–43.
[134]In his note, *ibid.*, Vol. I, pp. 394–9.

foundation of the power of Belief in after life; but it is not the less true that the power of Belief as it exists in after life, stands broadly distinguished from the power of the Fixed Idea, and that this last may operate not only without, but in defiance of, a positive Belief. That a contrary belief has momentarily intervened is a mere conjecture, which can neither be refuted nor proved. (Vol. II, p. 211.)

\* \* \* \* \*

[*In Sect. 2 of Chap. xxi, in dealing with remote causes of pleasure and pain, James Mill says:*] *The idea of a man enjoying a train of pleasures, or happiness, is felt by every body to be a pleasurable idea. The idea of a man under a train of sufferings or pains, is equally felt to be a painful idea. This can arise from nothing but the association of our own pleasures with the first idea, and of our own pains with the second. We never feel any pains and pleasures but our own. The fact, indeed, is, that our very idea of the pains or pleasures of another man is only the idea of our own pains, or our own pleasures, associated with the idea of another man. This is one not of the least important, and curious, of all cases of association, and instantly shews how powerfully associated trains of ideas of our pains and pleasures must be with a feeling so compounded.*

That the pleasures or pains of another person can only be pleasurable or painful to us through the association of our own pleasures or pains with them, is true in one sense, which is probably that intended by the author, but not true in another, against which he has not sufficiently guarded his mode of expression. It is evident, that the only pleasures or pains of which we have direct experience being those felt by ourselves, it is from them that our very notions of pleasure and pain are derived. It is also obvious that the pleasure or pain with which we contemplate the pleasure or pain felt by somebody else, is itself a pleasure or pain of our own. But if it be meant that in such cases the pleasure or pain is consciously referred to self, I take this to be a mistake. By the acts or other signs exhibited by another person, the idea of a pleasure (which is a pleasurable idea) or the idea of a pain (which is a painful idea) are recalled, sometimes with considerable intensity, but in association with the other person as feeling them, not with one's self as feeling them. The idea of one's Self is, no doubt, closely associated with all our experiences, pleasurable, painful, or indifferent; but this association does not necessarily act in all cases because it exists in all cases. If the mind, when pleasurably or painfully affected by the evidences of pleasure or pain in another person, goes off on a different thread of association, as for instance, to the idea of the means of giving the pleasure or relieving the pain, or even if it dismisses the subject and relapses into the ordinary course of its thoughts, the association with its own self may be, at the time, defeated, or reduced to something so evanescent that we cannot tell whether it was momentarily present or not. (Vol. II, pp. 217–18.)

*       *       *       *       *

[*The first two sub-sections of Chap. xxi, Sect. 2, are entitled "Wealth, Power, and Dignity, and Their Contraries, Contemplated as Causes of Our Pleasures and Pains" (Vol. II, pp. 207–14), and "Our Fellow-Creatures Contemplated as Causes of Our Pleasures and Pains" (pp. 214–30). A note by Bain is appended at the end of the latter; J.S. Mill's note follows immediately.*]

The two preceding subsections are almost perfect as expositions and exemplifications of the mode in which, by the natural course of life, we acquire attachments to persons, things, and positions, which are the causes or habitual concomitants of pleasurable sensations to us, or of relief from pains: in other words, those persons, things, and positions become in themselves pleasant to us by association; and, through the multitude and variety of the pleasurable ideas associated with them, become pleasures of greater constancy and even intensity, and altogether more valuable to us, than any of the primitive pleasures of our constitution. This portion of the laws of human nature is the more important to psychology, as they show how it is possible that the moral sentiments, the feelings of duty, and of moral approbation and disapprobation, may be no original elements of our nature, and may yet be capable of being not only more intense and powerful than any of the elements out of which they may have been formed, but may also, in their maturity, be perfectly disinterested: nothing more being necessary for this, than that the acquired pleasure and pain should have become as independent of the native elements from which they are formed, as the love of wealth and of power not only often but generally become, of the bodily pleasures, and relief from bodily pains, for the sake of which, and of which alone, power and wealth must have been originally valued. No one thinks it necessary to suppose an original and inherent love of money or of power; yet these are the objects of two of the strongest, most general, and most persistent passions of human nature; passions which often have quite as little reference to pleasure or pain, beyond the mere consciousness of possession, and are in that sense of the word quite as disinterested, as the moral feelings of the most virtuous human being.

The author, then, has furnished a most satisfactory and most valuable explanation of certain of the laws of our affections and passions, and has traced the origin and generation of a great number of them. But it must be remarked of the whole exposition, that it accounts truly, but only partially, for this part of human nature. It affords a sufficient theory of what we may call the mental, or intellectual element of the feelings in question. But it does not furnish, nor does the author anywhere furnish, any theory of what may be called the animal element in them. Yet this is no unimportant ingredient in the emotional and active part of human nature: and it is one greatly demanding analysis. Let us take the case of any of the passions: and as one of the simplest as well as one of the most powerful of them, let us take the emotion of Fear. The author gives no account of Fear but that it is the idea of a painful sensation, associated with the idea of its being (more or less uncertainly) future. Undoubtedly these elements are present in it; but do they account for the peculiar emotional character of the passion, and for its physiological effects, such as pallor, trembling, faltering of the voice, coldness of the skin, loss of control over the secretions, and general depression of the vital powers? The case would be simpler if these great disturbances of the animal functions by the expectation of a pain were the same in kind as the smaller modifications produced by the mere idea. This, however, is by no means the case; Ideas do produce effects on the animal economy, but not those particular effects. The idea of a pain, if it acts on the bodily functions at all, has an action the same in kind (though much less in degree) as the pain itself would have. But the passion of fear has a totally different action. Suppose the fear to be that of a flogging. The flogging itself, if it produced any physical demonstrations, would produce cries, shrinkings, possibly muscular struggles, and might by its remoter effects disturb the action of the brain or of the circulation; and if the fear of a flogging produced these same effects, in a mitigated degree, the power of fear might be merely the power of the idea of the pain. But none of these are at all like the characteristic symptoms of fear: while those characteristic symptoms are much the same whatever be the particular pain apprehended, and whether it be a bodily or a purely mental pain, provided it be sufficiently intense and sufficiently proximate. No one has ever accounted for this remarkable difference, and the author of the *Analysis* does not even mention it. The explanation of it is one of those problems, partly psychological and partly physiological, which our knowledge of the laws of animal sensibility does not yet enable us to resolve. In whatever manner the phenomena are produced, they are a case of the quasi-chemistry of the nervous functions, whereby the junction of certain elements generates a compound whose properties are very different from the sum of the properties of the elements themselves.

This is the point which the author's explanations of the emotional part of human nature do not reach, and, it may even be said, do not attempt to reach. Until, however, it is reached, there is no guarantee for the completeness of his analysis of even the mental element in the passions: for when the effect exhibits so much which has not, in the known properties of the assigned cause, anything to account for it, there is always room for a doubt whether some part of the cause has not been left out of the reckoning. This doubt, however, does not seriously affect the most important of the author's analyses, *viz.* those which, without resolving the emotions themselves into anything more elementary, expound their transfer by association from their natural objects to others; with the great increase of intensity and persistency which so often accompanies the transfer, and which is in general quite sufficiently accounted for by the causes to which the author refers it. (Vol. II, pp. 233–6.)

\*    \*    \*    \*    \*

[*In discussing the views of Archibald Alison (1757–1839), expounded in his* Essays on the Nature and Principles of Taste *(Edinburgh: Bell and Bradfute; London: Robinson, 1790), James Mill says:*] *I shall not follow Mr. Alison in his illustrations of the beauty and sublimity felt in the tones of the human voice, or in the composition of sounds, called Music; because I have no doubt but it will be allowed that they derive the whole of what is called their expression,—in other words, their power of pleasing,—from the associations connected with them.*

What the author thinks himself dispensed from either proving or illustrating because he has no doubt that it will be allowed, is, on the contrary, one of the most disputable parts of his theory. That very much of the pleasure afforded by Music is the effect of its expression, *i.e.* of the associations connected with sound, most people will admit: but it can scarcely be doubted that there is also an element of direct physical and sensual pleasure. In the first place, the quality of some single sounds is physically agreeable, as that of others is disagreeable. Next, the concord or harmony of pleasant sounds adds a further element of purely physical enjoyment. And thirdly, certain successions of sounds, constituting melody or tune, are delightful, as it seems to me, to the mere sense. With these pleasures those of the associated ideas and feelings are intimately blended, but may, to a certain extent, be discriminated by a critical ear. It is possible to say, of different composers, that one (as Beethoven) excels most in that part of the effect of music which depends on expression, and another (as Mozart) in the physical part.[135]

That the full physical pleasure of tune is often not experienced at the first hearing, is a consequence of the fact, that the pleasure depends on succession, and therefore on the coexistence of each note with the remembrance of a sufficient number of the previous notes to constitute melody: a remembrance which, of course, is not possessed in perfection, until after a number of repetitions proportioned to the complexity and to the unfamiliar character of the combination. (Vol. II, pp. 241–2.)

\*    \*    \*    \*    \*

[135]Ludwig van Beethoven (1770–1827) and Wolfgang Amadeus Mozart (1756–91) were (not surprisingly) two of Mill's favourite composers. Mill himself took great pleasure in playing and improvising on the piano.

[*James Mill quotes approvingly Alison's views on the associations contributing to the pleasures of colour.*]

The elements contributed by association are certainly more predominant in the pleasure of colours than in that of musical sounds; yet I am convinced that there is a direct element of physical pleasure in colours, anterior to association. My own memory recals to me the intense and mysterious delight which in early childhood I had in the colours of certain flowers; a delight far exceeding any I am now capable of receiving from colour of any description, with all its acquired associations. And this was the case at far too early an age, and with habits of observation far too little developed, to make any of the subtler combinations of form and proportion a source of much pleasure to me. This last pleasure was acquired very gradually, and did not, until after the commencement of manhood, attain any considerable height. The examples quoted from Alison do not prove that there is no original beauty in colours, but only that the feeling of it is capable, as no one doubts that it is capable, of being overpowered by extraneous associations.

Whether there is any similar organic basis of the pleasure derived from form, so far at least as this depends on proportion, I would not undertake to decide.

The susceptibility to the physical pleasures produced by colours and musical sounds, (and by forms if any part of the pleasure they afford is physical), is probably extremely different in different organisations. In natures in which any one of these susceptibilities is originally faint, more will depend on association. The extreme sensibility of this part of our constitution to small and unobvious influences, makes it certain that the sources of the feelings of beauty and deformity must be, to a material extent, different in different individuals. (Vol. II, pp. 246–7.)

\*     \*     \*     \*     \*

[*J.S. Mill's note appears at the end of "The Objects Called Sublime and Beautiful, and Their Contraries, Contemplated as Causes of Our Pleasures and Pains," Sect. 3 (Vol. II, pp. 230–52) of Chap. xxi.*]

The objection commonly made to the psychological analyses which resolve Beauty into association, is that they confound the Beautiful with the merely agreeable. This objection is urged, for example, by Coleridge, in his *Biographia Literaria*.[136] He admits, with every one else, that things not in themselves agreeable, are often made agreeable by association; that is, the pleasantness which

[136]The passage actually appears in Coleridge's "On the Principles of Sound Criticism Concerning the Fine Arts" (1814), in Joseph Cottle, *Early Recollections; Chiefly Relating to the Late Samuel Taylor Coleridge*, 2 vols. (London: Longman, *et al.*, 1837), Vol. II, pp. 226–7. This essay is reprinted in some editions of *Biographia Literaria*.

belongs to the ideas with which they are associated, adheres to themselves: but this cannot, it is asserted, be the cause of their producing the particular emotion to which we attach the name of Beauty; because, as no feeling of beauty belongs to the ideas that are supposed to generate the emotion, no such feeling can be transferred from them to what they are associated with.

Any one who has studied the *Analysis* up to this point, is aware of the inconclusiveness of this last argument. That a complex feeling generated out of a number of single ones, should be as unlike to any of those from which it is generated, as the sensation of white is unlike the sensations of the seven prismatic colours, is no unexampled or rare fact in our sensitive nature.

But it will also, I think, be found, in the case of our feelings of Beauty, and still more, of Sublimity, that the theory which refers their origin mainly to association, is not only not contradictory to facts, but is not even paradoxical. For if our perceptions of beauty and sublimity are of a more imposing character than the feelings ordinarily excited in us by the contemplation of objects, it will be found that the associations which form those impressions are themselves of a peculiarly imposing nature. This is apparent even from Alison; and if the author of the *Analysis* had written later, he might have referred to a deeper thinker than Alison, and a more valuable because an unconscious witness to the truth of the Association theory. Mr. Ruskin, with profounder and more thoughtful views respecting the beauties both of Nature and of Art than any psychologist I could name, undertakes, in the second volume of *Modern Painters*, to investigate the conditions of Beauty. [137] The result he brings out is, that every thing which gives us the emotion of the Beautiful, is expressive and emblematic of one or other of certain lofty or lovely ideas, which are, in his apprehension, embodied in the universe, and correspond to the various perfections of its Creator. He holds these ideas to be, Infinity, Unity, Repose, Symmetry, Purity, Moderation, and Adaptation to Ends. And he is, in my judgment, to a very considerable degree successful in making out his case. Mr. Ruskin, it is true, never thinks of inferring that our feelings of Beauty are the actual consequence of our having those elevating or cheering ideas recalled to us through manifold channels of association. He deems the emotion to be arbitrarily attached to these ideas by a pre-established harmony. But the evidence which he adduces goes far to prove the other point. If he succeeds, as I think he does, in showing that the things which excite the emotions of beauty or sublimity are always things which have a natural association with certain highly impressive and affecting ideas (whether the catalogue which he has made of those ideas is correct and complete or not), we need no other mode of accounting for the peculiar character of the emotions, than by the actual, though vague and confused, recal of the ideas. It cannot be deemed surprising that a state of consciousness made up of

[137]John Ruskin, *Modern Painters*, 5 vols. (London: Smith, Elder, 1851–60), Vol. II, pp. 39–82.

reminiscences of such ideas as Mr. Ruskin specifies, and of the grand and interesting objects and thoughts connected with ideas like those, must be of a more elevated character, and must stir our nature to a greater depth, than those associations of common-place and every-day pleasures, which often combine with them as parts of the mass of pleasurable feeling set up in us by the objects of Nature and Art. In a windy country, a screen of trees so placed as to be a barrier against the prevailing winds, excites ideas of warmth, comfort, and shelter, which belong to the "agreeable," as distinguished by Coleridge from the Beautiful; and these enter largely into the pleasurable feeling with which we contemplate the trees, without contributing to give them the peculiar character distinctive of aesthetic feelings. But besides these there are other elements, constituting the beauty, properly speaking, of the trees, which appeal to other, and what we are accustomed, not without meaning, to call higher, parts of our nature; which give a stronger stimulus and a deeper delight to the imagination, because the ideas they call up are such as in themselves act on the imagination with greater force.

As is observed by the author of the *Analysis*, the exposition in detail of the associations which enter into our various feelings of the sublime and beautiful, would require the examination of the subject on a scale not suited to the character nor proportioned to the dimensions of this Treatise.[138] Of all our feelings, our acquired pleasures and pains, especially our pleasures, are the most complex; resulting from the whole of our nature and of our past lives, and involving, consequently, a greater multitude and variety of associations than almost any other phenomena of the mind. And among our various pleasures, the aesthetic are without doubt the most complex. It may also be remarked, and is a considerable confirmation of the association theory, that the feelings of beauty or sublimity with which different people are affected by the contemplation of the same object, are evidently as different, as the pleasurable associations of different persons with the same object are likely to be. But there are some ingredients which are universally, or almost universally, present, when the emotions have their characteristic peculiarity; and to which they seem to be mainly indebted for the extraordinary power with which they act on the minds which have the greatest susceptibility to them. These ingredients are probably more numerous and various than is commonly suspected; but some of the most important and powerful of them are undoubtedly pointed to, and illustrated with great force, in the discussion which I have mentioned, by Mr. Ruskin; to whose work I willingly refer the psychological student, as a copious source of at least far-reaching suggestions, and often of much more.

Supposing that all Beauty had been successfully analysed into a lively suggestion of one or more of the ideas to which it is referred by Mr. Ruskin, the question would still remain for psychologists, why the suggestion of those ideas is

[138]Vol. II, pp. 251–2.

so impressive and so delightful. But this question may, in general, be answered with little difficulty. It is no mystery, for example, why anything which suggests vividly the idea of infinity, that is, of magnitude or power without limit, acquires an otherwise strange impressiveness to the feelings and imagination. The remaining ideas in Mr. Ruskin's list (at least if we except those which, like Moderation, are chiefly ancillary to the others, by excluding what would jar with their effect) all represent to us some valuable or delightful attribute, in a completeness and perfection of which our experience presents us with no example, and which therefore stimulates the active power of the imagination to rise above known reality, into a more attractive or a more majestic world. This does not happen with what we call our lower pleasures. To them there is a fixed limit at which they stop: or if, in any particular case, they do acquire, by association, a power of stirring up ideas greater than themselves, and stimulate the imagination to enlarge its conceptions to the dimensions of those ideas, we then feel that the lower pleasure has, exceptionally, risen into the region of the aesthetic, and has superadded to itself an element of pleasure of a character and quality not belonging to its own nature. (Vol. II, pp. 252–5.)

\*     \*     \*     \*     \*

*[J.S. Mill's note appears at the end of Chap. xxii, "Motives," Sect. 1, "Pleasurable or Painful States, Contemplated as Consequents of Our Own Acts" (Vol. II, pp. 256–62).]*

A Motive is that which influences the will; and the Will is a subject we have not yet arrived at the consideration of. Meanwhile, it is here shewn that a motive to an act consists in the association of pleasure with the act; that a motive to abstain from an act, is the association of pain with it; and we are prepared to admit the truth deduced therefrom, that the one or the other motive will prevail, according as the pleasurable or the painful association is the more powerful. What makes the one or the other more powerful, is (conformably to the general laws of association) partly the intensity of the pleasurable or painful ideas in themselves, and partly the frequency of repetition of their past conjunction with the act, either in experience or in thought. In the latter of these two consists the efficacy of education in giving a good or a bad direction to the active powers.

In further elucidation of Motives, I cite the following passages from the First Appendix to the author's *Fragment on Mackintosh*[139] (pp. 389–90):

[139]*A Fragment on Mackintosh: Being Strictures on Some Passages in the Dissertation by Sir James Mackintosh, Prefixed to the Encyclopaedia Britannica* (London: Baldwin and Cradock, 1835). James Mill was attacking James Mackintosh (1765–1832), *Dissertation on the Progress of Ethical Philosophy, Chiefly during the Seventeenth and Eighteenth Centuries* (Edinburgh: n.p., 1830).

A motive is something which moves—moves to what? To action. But all action, as Aristotle says, (and all mankind agree with him) is for an end.[140] Actions are essentially means. The question, then, is, what is the end of action? Actions, taken in detail, have ends in detail. But actions, taken in classes, have ends which may be taken in classes. Thus the ends of the actions which are subservient to the pleasures of sense, are combined in a class, to which, in abstract, we give the name sensuality. The class of actions which tend to the increase of power, have a class of ends to which we give the name ambition, and so on. When we put all these classes together, and make a *genus*; that is, actions in general; can we in like manner make a genus of the ends; and name ends in general?

If we could find what the several classes of ends; sensuality for example; ambition; avarice; glory; sociality, etc.; have in common, we could.

Now, they have certainly this in common, that they are all agreeable to the agents. A man acts for the sake of something agreeable to him, either proximately or remotely. But agreeable to, and pleasant to; agreeableness, and pleasantness, are only different names for the same thing; the pleasantness of a thing is the pleasure it gives. So that pleasure, in a general way, or speaking generically; that is, in a way to include all the species of pleasures, and also the abatement of pains; is the end of action.

A motive is that which moves to action. But that which moves to action is the end of the action, that which is sought by it; that for the sake of which it is performed. Now that, generically speaking, is the pleasure of the agent. Motive, then, taken generically is pleasure. The pleasure may be in company or connection with things infinite in variety. But these are the accessaries; the essence, is the pleasure. Thus, in one case, the pleasure may be connected with the form, and other qualities of a particular woman; in another, with a certain arrangement of colours in a picture; in another, with the circumstances of some fellow-creature. But in all these cases, what is generical, that is the essence, is the pleasure, or relief from pain.

A motive, then, is the idea of a pleasure; a particular motive, is the idea of a particular pleasure; and these are infinite in variety.

Another question is, in what circumstances does the idea of a pleasure become a motive? For it is evident, that it does not so in all. It is only necessary here to illustrate, not to resolve the question. First, the pleasure must be regarded as attainable. No man wills an act, which he knows he cannot perform, or which he knows cannot effect the end. In the next place, the idea of the particular pleasure must be more present to the mind, than any other of equal potency. That which makes the idea of one pleasure more potent than another; or that which makes one idea more present to the mind than another, is the proximate cause of the motive, and a remote cause of the volition. The cause of that superior potency, or of that presence to the mind, is a cause of the volition, still more remote, and so on.

(Vol. II, pp. 262–4.)

\* \* \* \* \*

[*Discussing the idea of Country as a motive, James Mill says:*] *There are cases, though rare, in which this motive has existed in extraordinary force; in which men have been found capable of sacrificing every thing for their country. This happens*

[140]Aristotle, *Physics* (Greek and English), 2 vols., trans. Philip H. Wicksteed and Francis M. Cornford (London: Heinemann; Cambridge, Mass.: Harvard University Press, 1929), Vol. I, pp. 170–2.

*most readily in times of great excitement; that is, when public opinion holds out a great reward; and when the object rather is, to ward off some great calamity, than to obtain an accession of good.*

It is too limited a view of the effect of "times of great excitement" in intensifying the patriotic feelings, to identify it with the influence of a more than usual reward held out by public opinion. That fact often contributes its share, but there are other causes fully as effectual. In times of excitement, the idea of Country, the ideas of all the interests involved in it, and of the manner in which those interests will be affected by our action or by our forbearance to act, exist in the mind in greater intensity, and are recalled with far greater frequency, than in ordinary times. Moreover, the fact that a feeling is shared by all or many of those with whom we are in frequent intercourse, strengthens, by an obvious consequence, all the associations, both of resemblance and of contiguity, which give that feeling its force. This is the well-known influence of sympathy, so strikingly evinced by the vehement feelings of a crowd. To these might be added another influence, belonging rather to physiology than to psychology. When the nervous system has been highly strung up by the influence of any strong feeling, it seems to become more acutely sensible to feeling of any sort, those feelings excepted which jar with, and are counteracted by, the prevailing tone of the system. (Vol. II, pp. 274–5.)

\*    \*    \*    \*    \*

*[J.S. Mill's note is appended to the end of Chap. xxii, Sect. 2.]*

This Section is devoted to an exposition of the manner in which facts which are not pleasures or pains, but causes of pleasures or of pains, become so closely associated in thought with the pains and pleasures of which they are causes, as not only to become themselves pleasurable or painful, but to become also, by their association with acts of our own by which they may be brought about, motives of the greatest strength. The value of a due understanding of this fact, both for the purposes of psychological science and for those of practical education, is evidently very great: and the author, to whose mind the bearings of speculative philosophy on the practical interests of the human race were ever present, has not failed to make some ethical and political applications of the psychological truth which he has here so excellently illustrated. (Vol. II, pp. 278–9.)

\*    \*    \*    \*    \*

[*James Mill, discussing love of fame as a motive, comments:*] *That we have plea-surable associations of great potency, with this manifestation of the favour-able disposition of others towards us, is matter of common and constant experi-ence. It is called, in its more remarkable states, the* LOVE OF FAME, *and is known to operate as one of the most powerful motives in our nature. One of its cases is a remarkable exemplification of that high degree of association, which has been already explained, and to which we have frequently had occasion to advert, in explaining other phenomena; the degree which constitutes belief, and which gives to that belief, even when momentary, and instantly overruled by other associations, a powerful effect on our actions.*

*Not only that Praise of us, which is diffused in our lives, and from which agreeable consequences may arise to us, is delightful, by the associated ideas of the pleasures resulting from it; but that Praise, which we are never to hear, which will be diffused only when we are dead, and from which no actual effects can ever accrue to us, is often an object of intense affection, and acts as one of the most powerful motives in our nature.*

*The habit which we form, in the case of immediate praise, of associating the idea of the praise with the idea of pleasurable consequences to ourselves, is so strong, that the idea of pleasurable consequences to ourselves becomes altogether inseparable from the idea of our Praise. It is one of those cases in which the one Idea never can exist without the other. The belief, thus engendered, is of course encountered immediately by other belief, that we shall be incapable of profiting by any consequences, which posthumous fame can produce: as the fear, that is, the belief of ghosts, in a man passing through a churchyard at midnight, may be immediately encountered by his settled, habitual belief that ghosts have no existence; and yet his terror, not only remains for a time, but is constantly renewed, as often as he is placed in circumstances with which he has been accustomed to associate the existence of ghosts.*

The case here put, that of the desire of posthumous fame, affords no real support to the author's doctrines, that a high degree of association constitutes belief, and that belief is always present when we are determined to action. The case is merely one of many others, in which something not originally pleasurable (the praise and admiration of our fellow-creatures) has become so closely associated with pleasure as to be at last pleasurable in itself. When it has become a pleasure in itself, it is desired for itself, and not for its consequences; and the most confirmed knowledge that it can produce no ulterior pleasurable consequences to ourselves will not interfere with the pleasure given by the mere consciousness of possessing it, nor hinder that pleasure from becoming, by its association with the acts which produce it, a powerful motive. It is a frequent mode of talking, to speak of the desire of posthumous fame in a kind of pitying way, as grounded on a delusion; as a desire which implies a certain infirmity of the understanding. Those who thus speak must be prepared to apply the same disparaging phrases to the interest taken in the welfare of others after our own death; for in that case also, no beneficial consequences to ourselves personally can ever follow from the realization of the object of our desire. But there is nothing at variance with reason in the associations which make us value for themselves, things which we at first cared for only as means to other ends; associations to which we are indebted for nearly the whole both of our virtues, and of our enjoyments. That he who acts with a view to posthumous fame has a belief, however momentary, that this fame will produce to him some extraneous good, or that he shall be conscious of it after he is dead, I shall not admit without better evidence than I have ever seen or heard of. (Vol. II, pp. 295–6.)

*     *     *     *     *

[*Concerning "dispraise," James Mill comments:*] *It not unfrequently happens, that the idea of the unfavourable sentiments of mankind, becomes more intolerable than all the consequences which could result from them; and men make their escape from life, in order to escape from the tormenting idea of certain consequences, which, at most, would only diminish the advantages of living.*

They do not seek death to escape from the idea of any *consequences* of the unfavourable sentiments of mankind. The mere fact of having incurred those unfavourable sentiments has become, by the adhesive force of association, so painful in itself, that death is sometimes preferred to it. There is often no thought of the consequences that may arise from the unfavourable sentiments; and when consequences are thought of, they are usually rather those which are mere demonstrations of feeling, and owe their painfulness to the sentiment of which they are demonstrations, than those which directly grate upon our senses or are injurious to our interests. It is true that a vague conception of the many unpleasant consequences liable to arise from the evil opinion of others, was the crude matter out of which the horror of the thing itself was primitively formed: but, once formed, it loses its connexion with its original source. (Vol. II, p. 297.)

*     *     *     *     *

[*James Mill asserts, on the authority of Adam Smith,*[141] *that*] *in minds happily trained, the love of Praiseworthiness, the dread of Blameworthiness, is a stronger*

---

[141]*The Theory of Moral Sentiments* (1759), 6th ed., 2 vols. (London: Strahan and Cadell; Edinburgh: Creech and Bell, 1790), Vol. II, pp. 284–330 (Pt. III, Chap. ii).

*feeling, than the love of actual Praise, the dread of actual Blame. It is one of those cases, in which, by the power of the association, the secondary feeling becomes more powerful than the primary. In all men, the idea of praise, as consequent, is associated with the idea of certain acts of theirs, as antecedent; the idea of blame, as consequent, with the idea of certain acts of theirs, as antecedent. This association constitutes what we call the feeling, or notion, or sentiment, or idea (for it goes by all those names), of Praiseworthiness, and Blameworthiness.*

This paragraph, unexplained, might give the idea that the author regarded praiseworthiness and blameworthiness as having the meaning not of deserving praise or blame, but merely of being likely to obtain it. But what he meant is, that the idea of *deserving* praise is but a more complex form of the association between our own or another person's acts or character, and the idea of praise. To deserve praise, is, in the great majority of the cases which occur in life, the principal mode of obtaining it; though the praise is seldom accurately proportioned to the desert. And the same may be said of blame. A powerful association is thus, if circumstances are favourable, generated between deserving praise and obtaining it; and hence between deserving praise, and all the pleasurable influences on our lives, of other people's good opinion. And this association may become sufficiently strong to overcome the direct motive of obtaining praise, where it is to be obtained by other means than desert; the rather, as the desire of undeserved praise is greatly counteracted by the thought that people would not bestow the praise if they knew all. That what has now been stated was really the author's meaning, is proved by his going on to say, that praiseworthiness and blameworthiness, as motives to action, have reference "not to what is, or to what shall be, but to what ought to be, the sentiments of mankind." (Vol. II, pp. 298–9.)

*     *     *     *     *

*[At the end of Chap. xxiii, "The Acts of Our Fellow-Creatures, Which Are Causes of Our Pains and Pleasures, Contemplated as Consequents of Our Own Acts" (the running title is "Moral Sense"), a long note by Bain (Vol. II, pp. 302–7) is followed by J.S. Mill's.]*

I

It had been pointed out, in a preceding chapter, that Wealth, Power, Dignity, and many other things which are not in their own nature pleasures, but only causes of pleasures and of exemption from pains, become so closely associated with the pleasures of which they are causes, and their absence or loss becomes so closely associated with the pains to which it exposes us, that the things become objects of love and desire, and their absence an object of hatred and aversion, for their own sake, without reference to their consequences.[142] By virtue of the same law of association, it is pointed out in the present chapter that human actions, both our own and those of other people, standing so high as they do among the causes both of pleasure and of pain to us (sometimes by their direct operation, and sometimes through the sentiments they give birth to in other persons towards ourselves) tend naturally to become inclosed in a web of associated ideas of pleasures or of pains at a very early period of life, in such sort that the ideas of acts beneficial to ourselves and to others become pleasurable in themselves, and the ideas of acts hurtful to ourselves and to others become painful in themselves: and both kinds of acts become objects of a feeling, the former of love, the latter of aversion, which having, in our minds, become independent of any pleasures or pains actually expected to result to ourselves from the acts, may be truly said to be disinterested. It is no less obvious that acts which are not really beneficial, or not really hurtful, but which, through some false opinion prevailing among mankind, or some extraneous agency operating on their sentiments, incur their praise or blame, may and often do come to be objects of a quite similar disinterested love or hatred, exactly as if they deserved it. This disinterested love and hatred of actions, generated by the association of praise or blame with them, constitute, in the author's opinion, the feelings of moral approbation and disapprobation, which the majority of psychologists have thought it necessary to refer to an original and ultimate principle of our nature. Mr. Bain, in the preceding note, makes in this theory a correction, to which the author himself would probably not have objected, namely, that the mere idea of a pain or pleasure, by whomsoever felt, is intrinsically painful or pleasurable, and when raised in the mind with intensity is capable of becoming a stimulus to action, independent, not merely of expected consequences to ourselves, but of any reference whatever to Self; so that care for others is, in an admissible sense, as much an ultimate fact of our nature, as care for ourselves; though one which greatly needs strengthening by the concurrent force of the manifold associations insisted on in the author's text. Though this of Mr. Bain is rather an account of disinterested Sympathy, than of the moral feeling, it is undoubtedly true that the *foundation* of the moral feeling is the adoption of the pleasures and pains of others as our own: whether this takes place by the natural force of sympathy, or by the association which has grown up in our mind between our own good or evil and theirs. The moral feeling rests upon this identification of the feelings of others with our own, but is not the same thing with it. To constitute the moral feeling, not only must the good of others have become in itself a pleasure to us, and their suffering a pain, but this pleasure or pain must be associated with our own acts as producing it, and must in this manner have become a motive,

---

[142]Vol. II, pp. 207–30 (Chap. xxi).

prompting us to the one sort of acts, and restraining us from the other sort. And this is, in brief, the author's theory of the Moral Sentiments.

The exhaustive treatment of this subject would require a length and abundance of discussion disproportioned to the compass and purposes of a treatise like the present, which was intended to expound what the author believed to be the real mode of formation of our complex states of consciousness, but not to say all that may and ought to be said in refutation of other views of the subject. There are, however, some important parts of the author's own theory, which are not stated in this work, but in a subsequent one, of a highly polemical character, the *Fragment on Mackintosh*: and it may be both instructive and interesting to the reader to find the statement here. I therefore subjoin the passages containing it.

Nature makes no classes. Nature makes individuals. Classes are made by men; and rarely with such marks as determine certainly what is to be included in them.

Men make classifications, as they do every thing else, for some end. Now, for what end was it that men, out of their innumerable acts, selected a class, to which they gave the name of moral, and another class, to which they gave the name of immoral? What was the motive of this act? What its final cause?

Assuredly the answer to this question is the first step, though Sir James saw it not, towards the solution of his two questions, comprehending the whole of ethical science; first, what makes an act to be moral? and secondly, what are the sentiments with which we regard it?[143]

We may also be assured, that it was some very obvious interest which recommended this classification; for it was performed, in a certain rough way, in the very rudest states of society.

Farther, we may easily see how, even in very rude states, men were led to it, by little less than necessity. Every day of their lives they had experience of acts, some of which were agreeable, or the cause of what was agreeable, to them; others disagreeable, or the cause of what was disagreeable to them; in all possible degrees.

They had no stronger interest than to obtain the repetition of the one sort, and to prevent the repetition of the other.

The acts in which they were thus interested were of two sorts; first, those to which the actor was led by a natural interest of his own; secondly, those to which the actor was not led by any interest of his own. About the first sort there was not occasion for any particular concern. They were pretty sure to take place, without any stimulus from without. The second sort, on the contrary, were not likely to take place, unless an interest was artificially created, sufficiently strong to induce the actor to perform them.

And here we clearly perceive the origin of that important case of classification . . . the classification of acts as moral and immoral. The acts, which it was important to other men that each individual should perform, but in which the individual had not a sufficient interest to secure the performance of them, were constituted one class. The acts, which it was important to other men that each individual should abstain from, but in regard to which he had not a personal interest sufficiently strong to secure his abstaining from them, were constituted another class. The first class were distinguished by the name moral acts; the second by the name immoral.

The interest which men had in securing the performance of the one set of acts, the

[143]Mackintosh, *Dissertation*, p. 8.

non-performance of the other, led them by a sort of necessity to think of the means. They had to create an interest, which the actor would not otherwise have, in the performance of the one sort, the non-performance of the other. And in proceeding to this end, they could not easily miss their way. They had two powers applicable to the purpose. They had a certain quantity of good at their disposal; and they had a certain quantity of evil. If they could apply the good in such a manner as to afford a motive both for the performance and non-performance which they desired, or the evil, in such a manner as to afford a motive against the performance and non-performance which they wished to prevent, their end was attained.

And this is the scheme which they adopted; and which, in every situation, they have invariably pursued. The whole business of the moral sentiments, moral approbation, and disapprobation, has this for its object, the distribution of the good and evil we have at command, for the production of acts of the useful sort, the prevention of acts of the contrary sort. Can there be a nobler object?

But though men have been thus always right in their general aim, their proceedings have been cruelly defective in the detail; witness the consequence,—the paucity of good acts, the frequency of bad acts, which there is in the world.

A portion of acts having been thus classed into good and bad; and the utility having been perceived of creating motives to incite to the one, and restrain from the other, a sub-classification was introduced. One portion of these acts was such, that the good and evil available for their production and prevention, could be applied by the community in its conjunct capacity. Another portion was such, that the good and evil available could be applied only by individuals in their individual capacity. The first portion was placed under the control of what is called law; the other remained under the control of the moral sentiments; that is, the distribution of good and evil, made by individuals in their individual capacity.

No sooner was the class made, than the rule followed. Moral acts are to be performed; immoral acts are to be abstained from.

Beside this the general rule, there was needed, for more precise direction, particular rules.

We must remember the fundamental condition, that all rules of action must be preceded by a corresponding classification of actions. All moral rules, comprehended in the great moral rule, must relate to a class of actions comprehended within the grand class, constituted and marked by the term moral. This is the case with grand classes in general. They are subdivided into minor classes, each of the minor classes being a portion of the larger. Thus, the grand class of acts called moral has been divided into certain convenient portions, or sub-classes, and marked by particular names, Just, Beneficent, Brave, Prudent, Temperate; to each of which classes belongs its appropriate rule that men should be just, that they should be beneficent, and so on. . . .

In the performance of our duties two sets of cases may be distinguished. There is one set in which a direct estimate of the good of the particular act is inevitable; and the man acts immorally who acts without making it. There are other cases in which it is not necessary.

The first are those, which have in them so much of singularity, as to prevent their coming within the limits of any established class. In such cases a man has but one guide; he must consider the consequences, or act not as a moral, or rational agent at all.

The second are cases of such ordinary and frequent occurrence as to be distinguished into classes. And everybody knows . . . that when a class of acts are performed regularly and frequently, they are at last performed by habit; in other words, the idea of the act and the performance of it follow so easily and speedily that they seem to cohere, and to be but one operation. It is only necessary to recall some of the more familiar instances, to see the mode of this formation. In playing on a musical instrument, every note, at first, is found by an effort. Afterwards, the proper choice is made so rapidly as to appear as if made by a mechanical process in which the mind has no concern. The same is the case with moral acts. When they have been performed with frequency and uniformity, for a sufficient length of time, a habit is generated. . . .

When a man acts from habit, he does not act without reflection. He only acts with a very rapid reflection. In no class of acts does a man begin to act by habit. He begins without habit; and acquires the habit by frequency of acting. The consideration, on which the act is founded, and the act itself, form a sequence. And it is obvious from the familiar cases of music and of speaking, that it is a sequence at first not very easily performed. By every repetition, however, it becomes easier. The consideration occurs with less effort; the action follows with less effort; they take place with greater and greater rapidity, till they seem blended. To say, that this is acting without reflection, is only ignorance, for it is thus seen to be a case of acting by reflection so easily and rapidly, that the reflection and the act cannot be distinguished from one another. . . .

Since moral acts are not performed at first by habit, but each upon the consideration which recommends it; upon what considerations, we may be asked, do moral acts begin to be performed?

The question has two meanings, and it is necessary to reply to both. It may be asked, upon what consideration the men of our own age and country, for example, at first, and before a habit is formed, perform moral acts? Or, it may be asked, upon what consideration did men originally perform moral acts?

To the first of these questions every one can reply from his own memory and observation. We perform moral acts at first, from authority. Our parents tell us that we ought to do this, ought not to do that. They are anxious that we should obey their precepts. They have two sets of influences, with which to work upon us; praise and blame; reward and punishment. All the acts which they say we ought to do, are praised in the highest degree, all those which they say we ought not to do, are blamed in the highest degree. In this manner, the ideas of praise and blame become associated with certain classes of acts, at a very early age, so closely, that they cannot easily be disjoined. No sooner does the idea of the act occur than the idea of praise springs up along with it, and clings to it. And generally these associations exert a predominant influence during the whole of life.

Our parents not only praise certain kinds of acts, blame other kinds; but they praise us when we perform those of the one sort, blame us when we perform those of the other. In this manner other associations are formed. The idea of ourselves performing certain acts is associated with the idea of our being praised, performing certain other acts with the idea of our being blamed, so closely that the ideas become at last indissoluble. In this association consist the very important complex ideas of praise-worthiness, and blame-worthiness. An act which is praiseworthy, is an act with the idea of which the idea of praise is indissolubly joined; an agent who is praiseworthy is an agent with the idea of whom the idea of praise is indissolubly joined. And in the converse case, that of blame-worthiness, the formation of the idea is similar.

Many powerful circumstances come in aid of these important associations, at an early age. We find, that not only our parents act in this manner, but all other parents. We find that grown people act in this manner, not only towards children, but towards one another. The associations, therefore, are unbroken, general, and all-comprehending.

Our parents administer not only praise and blame, to induce us to perform acts of one sort, and abstain from acts of another sort, but also rewards and punishments. They do so directly; and, further, they forward all our inclinations in the one case, baulk them in the other. So does everybody else. We find our comforts excessively abridged by other people, when we act in one way, enlarged when we act in another way. Hence another most important class of associations; that of an increase of well-being from the good-will of our fellow-creatures, if we perform acts of one sort, of an increase of misery from their ill-will, if we perform those of another sort.

In this manner it is that men, born in the social state, acquire the habits of moral acting, and certain affections connected with it, before they are capable of reflecting upon the grounds which recommend the acts either to praise or blame. Nearly at this point the greater part of them remain, continuing to perform moral acts and to abstain from the contrary, chiefly from the habits they have acquired, and the authority upon which they originally acted; though it is not possible that any man should come to the years and blessing of reason, without perceiving, at least in an indistinct and general way, the advantage which mankind derive from their acting towards one another in one way, rather than another.

We come now to the second question, *viz.* what are the considerations upon which men originally performed moral acts? The answer to this question is substantially contained in the explanation already given of the classification of acts as moral and immoral.

When men began to mark the distinction between acts, and were prompted to praise one class, blame another, they did so, either because the one sort benefited, the other hurt them; or for some other reason. If for the first reason, the case is perfectly intelligible. The men had a motive, which they understood, and which was adequate to the end. If it was not on account of utility that men classed some acts as moral, others as immoral, on what other account was it?

To this question, an answer, consisting of anything but words, has never been returned.

It has been said, that there is a beauty, and a deformity, in moral and immoral acts, which recommended them to the distinctions they have met with.

It is obvious to reply to this hypothesis, that the mind of a savage, that is, a mind in the state in which the minds of all men were, when they began to classify their acts, was not likely to be much affected by the ideal something called the beauty of acts. To receive pain or pleasure from an act, to obtain, or be deprived of, the means of enjoyment by an act; to like the acts and the actors, whence the good proceeded, dislike those whence the evil proceeded; all these were things which they understood.

But we must endeavour to get a little nearer to the bottom of this affair.

In truth, the term beauty, as applied to acts, is just as unintelligible to the philosopher, as to the savage. Is the beauty of an act one thing; the morality of it another? Or are they two names for the same thing? If they are two things, what is the beauty, distinct from the morality? If they are the same thing, what is the use of the name morality? It only tends to confusion.

But this is not all. The beautiful is that which excites in us the emotion of beauty, a state of mind with which we are acquainted by experience. This state of mind has been successfully analysed, and shewn to consist of a train of pleasurable ideas, awakened in us by the beautiful object.

But is it in this way only that we are concerned in moral acts? Do we value them for nothing, but as we value a picture, or a piece of music, for the pleasure of looking at them, or hearing them? Everybody knows the contrary. Acts are objects of importance to us, on account of their consequences, and nothing else. This constitutes a radical distinction between them and the things called beautiful. Acts are hurtful or beneficial, moral or immoral, virtuous or vicious. But it is only an abuse of language, to call them beautiful or ugly.

That it is jargon, the slightest reflection is sufficient to evince; for what is the beauty of an act, detached from its consequences? We shall be told, perhaps, that the beauty of an act was never supposed to be detached from its consequences. The beauty consists in the consequences. I am contented with the answer. But observe to what it binds you. The consequences of acts are the good or evil they do. According to you, therefore, the beauty of acts is either the utility of them, or it is nothing at all;—a beautiful ground on which to dispute with us, that acts are classed as moral, not on account of their utility, but on account of their beauty.

It will be easily seen, from what has been said, that they who ascribe the classification of acts, as moral, and immoral, to a certain taste, an agreeable or disagreeable sentiment which they excite (among whom are included the Scottish professors Hutcheson, and Brown, and David Hume himself, though on his part with wonderful inconsistency)[144]—hold the same theory with those who say, that beauty is the source of the classification of moral acts. Things are classed as beautiful, or deformed, on account of a certain taste, or inward sentiment. If acts are classed in the same way, on account of a certain taste or inward sentiment, they deserve to be classed under the names beautiful, and deformed; otherwise not.

I hope it is not necessary for me to go minutely into the exposure of the other varieties of jargon, by which it has been endeavoured to account for the classification of acts, as moral and immoral. "Fitness" is one of them. Acts are approved on account of their fitness. When fitness is hunted down, it is brought to bay exactly at the place where beauty was. Fitness is either the goodness of the consequences, or it is nothing at all.

The same is the case with "Right Reason," or "Moral Reason." An act according to moral reason, is an act, the consequences of which are good. Moral reason, therefore, is another name, and not a bad name, for the principle of utility.*

The following passage from another part of the same work, is also very much to the purpose.

The terms moral and immoral were applied by men, primarily, not to their own acts, but the acts of other men. Those acts, the effects of which they observed to be beneficial, they desired should be performed. To make them be performed, they, among other things they did, affixed to them marks of their applause; they called them, good, moral, well-deserving; and behaved accordingly.

Such is the source of the moral approbation we bestow on the acts of other men. The source of that which we bestow on our own is twofold. First, every man's beneficial acts, like those of every other man, form part of that system of beneficial acting, in which he, in common with all other men, finds his account. Secondly, he strongly associates with his own beneficial acts, both that approbation of other men, which is of so much importance to him, and that approbation which he bestows on other men's beneficial acts.

It is also easy to shew what takes place in the mind of a man, before he performs an act, which he morally approves or condemns.

What is called the approbation of an act not yet performed, is only the idea of future approbation: and it is not excited by the act itself; it is excited by the idea of the act. The idea of approbation or disapprobation is excited by the idea of an act, because the approbation would be excited by the act itself. But what excites moral approbation or disapprobation of

---

[144]Francis Hutcheson (1694–1746), "An Inquiry Concerning the Original of Our Ideas of Virtue or Moral Good," in *An Inquiry into the Original of Our Ideas of Beauty and Virtue* (London: printed Darby, 1725), pp. 101–24; Brown, *Lectures*, pp. 550–7; Hume, *An Inquiry Concerning the Principles of Morals* (1751), in *Essays and Treatises*, Vol. II, pp. 223–9 (Sect. 1), and 339–49 (App. A).

*Fragment on Mackintosh*, pp. 247–65.

an act, is neither the act itself, nor the motive of the act; but the consequences of the act, good or evil, and their being within the intention of the agent.

Let us put a case. A man with a starving wife and family is detected wiring a hare on my premises. What happens? I call up the idea of sending him to prison. I call up the ideas of the consequences of that act, the misery of the helpless creatures whom his labour supported; their agonizing feelings, their corporal wants, their hunger, cold, their destitution of hope, their despair: I call up the ideas of the man himself in jail, the sinking of heart which attends incarceration; the dreadful thought of his family deprived of his support; his association with vicious characters; the natural consequences,—his future profligacy, the consequent profligacy of his ill-fated children, and hence the permanent wretchedness and ruin of them all. I next have the idea of my own intending all these consequences. And only then am I in a condition to perform, as Sir James says, the "operation of conscience." I perform it. But in this case, it is, to use another of his expressions, "defeated."[145] Notwithstanding the moral disapprobation, which the idea of such intended consequences excites in me, I perform the act.

Here, at all events, any one may see, that conscience, and the motive of the act, are not the same, but opposed to one another. The motive of the act, is the pleasure of having hares; not in itself a thing anywise bad. The only thing bad is the producing so much misery to others, for securing that pleasure to myself.

The state of the case, then, is manifest. The act of which I have the idea, has two sets of consequences; one set pleasurable, another hurtful. I feel an aversion to produce the hurtful consequences. I feel a desire to produce the pleasurable. The one prevails over the other. . . .

. . . Nothing in an act is voluntary but the consequences that are intended. The idea of good consequences intended, is the pleasurable feeling of moral approbation; the idea of bad consequences intended is the painful feeling of moral disapprobation. The very term voluntary, therefore, applied to an act which produces good or evil consequences, expresses the antecedence of moral approbation or disapprobation.*

I will quote one short passage more, in correction of the very vulgar error, that to analyse our disinterested affections and resolve them into associations with the ideas of our own elementary pleasures and pains, is to deny their reality.

Sir James must mean, if he means anything, that to trace up the motive affections of human nature to pain and pleasure, is to make personal advantage the only motive. This is to affirm, that he who analyses any of the complicated phenomena of human nature, and points out the circumstances of their formation, puts an end to them.

Sir James was totally ignorant of this part of human nature. Gratitude remains gratitude, resentment remains resentment, generosity generosity in the mind of him who feels them, after analysis, the same as before. The man who can trace them to their elements does not cease to feel them, as much as the man who never thought about the matter. And whatever effects they produce, as motives, in the mind of the man who never thought about the matter, they produce equally, in the minds of those who have analysed them the most minutely.

They are constituent parts of human nature. How we are actuated, when we feel them, is matter of experience, which every one knows within himself. Their action is what it is, whether they are simple or compound. Does a complex motive cease to be a motive whenever it is discovered to be complex? The analysis of the active principles leaves the

[145]Mackintosh, *Dissertation*, p. 181.
*Fragment on Mackintosh*, pp. 375–8.

nature of them untouched. To be able to assert, that a philosopher, who finds some of the active principles of human nature to be compound and traces them to their origin, does on that account exclude them from human nature, and deny their efficiency as constituent parts of that nature, discovers a total incapacity of thinking upon these subjects. When Newton discovered that a white ray of light is not simple but compound,[146] did he for that reason exclude it from the denomination of light, and deny that it produced its effects, with respect to our perception, as if it were of the same nature with the elementary rays of which it is composed?*

## II

The reluctance of many persons to receive as correct this analysis of the sentiments of moral approbation and disapprobation, though a reluctance founded more on feeling than on reasoning, is accustomed to justify itself intellectually, by alleging the total unlikeness of those states of mind to the elementary ones, from which, according to the theory, they are compounded. But this is no more than what is observed in every similar case. When a complex feeling is generated out of elements very numerous and various, and in a corresponding degree indeterminate and vague, but so blended together by a close association, the effect of a long series of experiences, as to have become inseparable, the resulting feeling always seems not only very unlike any one of the elements composing it, but very unlike the sum of those elements. The pleasure of acquiring, or of consciously possessing, a sum of money (supposed not to be desired for application to some specific purpose,) is a feeling, to our consciousness, very different from the pleasure of protection against hunger and cold, the pleasure of ease and rest from labour, the pleasure of receiving consideration from our fellow-creatures, and the other miscellaneous pleasures, the association with which is admitted to be the real and only source of the pleasure of possessing money. In the case, then, of the moral sentiments, we have, on the one hand, a *vera causa* or set of causes, having a positive tendency to generate a sentiment of love for certain actions, and of aversion for certain others; and on the other hand, those sentiments of love and aversion, actually produced. This coincidence between the sentiments and a power adequate to produce them, goes far towards proving causation. That the sentiments are not obviously like the causes, is no reason for postulating the existence of another cause, in the shape of an original principle of our nature.

In a case, however, of so great interest and importance, a rigid adherence to the canons of inductive proof must be insisted on. Those who dispute the theory are entitled to demand that it shall conform strictly to the general law of cause and effect, which is, that the effect shall occur with the cause, shall not occur without the cause, and shall bear some proportion to the cause. Unless it can be shown that

[146]Isaac Newton, *Optics; or, A Treatise of the Reflections, Inflections and Colours of Light*, in *Opera*, Vol. IV, pp. 21–42.
*Fragment on Mackintosh*, pp. 51–2.

when the effect is not produced, the cause is either absent, or counteracted by some more powerful agency; and unless, when there is any marked difference in the effect, a difference can be shown in the cause, sufficient to account for it; the theory must give way, or at least, cannot be considered as proved.

The principal case in which the effect is absent, notwithstanding the apparent presence of the cause assigned for it, is anticipated by the author, and provided for after his manner, in the first of the passages quoted from the *Fragment on Mackintosh*. There are actions (he observes) as beneficial as any others, which yet do not excite the moral sentiment of approbation; but it is because the spontaneous motives to those beneficial acts are in general sufficient: as to eat when we are hungry, or to do a service for which we are to be amply paid. There are, again, actions of a very hurtful character, but such that the spontaneous motives for abstaining from them may be relied on, without any artificial addition: such, in general, are acts destructive of one's own life or property. But even in these cases the hurtful acts may become objects of moral reprobation, when, in any particular case, the natural deterrents prove insufficient for preventing them.

The author seems to think that the difference here pointed out, is explained by the fact that the moral sentiment is in the one case needed, in the other not needed, for producing the useful or averting the hurtful act; that, in short, we are made to have the feeling, by a foresight that our having it will operate usefully on the conduct of our fellow-creatures. I cannot accept this explanation. It seems to me to explain everything about the moral feelings, except the feelings themselves. It explains praise and blame, because these may be administered with the express design of influencing conduct. It explains reward and punishment, and every other distinction which we make in our behaviour between what we desire to encourage, and what we are anxious to check. But these things we might do from a deliberate policy, without having any moral feeling in our minds at all. When there is a moral feeling in our minds, our praise or blame is usually the simple expression of that feeling, rather than an instrument purposely employed for an end. We may give expression to the feeling without really having it, in the belief that our praise or blame will have a salutary effect; but no anticipation of salutary effects from our feeling will ever avail to give us the feeling itself: except indeed, what may be said of every other mental feeling—that we may talk ourselves into it; that the habitual use of the modes of speech that are associated with it, has some tendency to call up the feeling in the speaker himself, and a great tendency to engender it in other people.

I apprehend, however, that there is another, and more adequate reason why the feeling of moral approbation is usually absent in the case of actions (or forbearances) for which there are sufficient motives without it. These actions are done, and are seen to be done, by everybody alike. The pleasant associations derived from their usefulness merge, therefore, in our feelings towards human life and towards our fellow-creatures generally, and do not give rise to any special association of pleasure with given individuals. But when we find that a certain person does beneficial acts which the general experience of life did not warrant us in counting upon—acts which would not have been done by everybody, or even by most people, in his place; we associate the pleasure which the benefit gives us, with the character and disposition of that individual, and with the act, conceived as proceeding from that specially beneficent disposition. And obversely, if a person acts in a manner from which we suffer, but which is such as we should expect from most other people in a parallel case, the associations which his acts create in our minds are associations with human life, or with mankind in general; but if the acts, besides being of a hurtful kind, betoken a disposition in the agent, more hurtful than we are accustomed to look for in average men, we associate the injury with that very man, and with that very disposition, and have the feeling of moral disapprobation and repugnance.

There is, as already intimated, another condition which those who hold the Association theory of the moral sentiments are bound to fulfil. The class of feelings called moral embraces several varieties, materially different in their character. Wherever this difference manifests itself, the theory must be required to show that there is a corresponding difference in the antecedents. If pleasurable or painful associations are the generating cause, those associations must differ in some proportion to the difference which exists in what they generate.

The principal case in point is the case of what is called Duty, or Obligation. It will probably be admitted that beneficial acts, when done because they are beneficial, excite in us favourable sentiments towards the agent, for which the utility or beneficial tendency of the actions is sufficient to account. But it is only some, not all, of these beneficial acts, that we regard as duties; as acts which the agent, or we ourselves if we are the persons concerned, are bound to do. This feeling of duty or obligation, it is contended, is a very different state of mind from mere liking for the action and good will to the agent. The association theory may account for the two last, but not for the former.

I have examined this question in the concluding chapter of a short treatise entitled *Utilitarianism*. The subject of the chapter is "the connexion between Justice and Utility."[147] I have there endeavoured to shew what the association is, which exists in the case of what we regard as a duty, but does not exist in the case of what we merely regard as useful, and which gives to the feeling in the former case the strength, the gravity, and pungency, which in the other case it has not.

I believe that the element in the association, which gives this distinguishing character to the feeling, and which constitutes the difference of the antecedents in the two cases, is the idea of Punishment. I mean the association with punishment, not the expectation of it.

No case can be pointed out in which we consider anything as a duty, and any act

[147]Chap. v of *Utilitarianism* (1861), in *CW*, Vol. X, pp. 240–59.

or omission as immoral or wrong, without regarding the person who commits the wrong and violates the duty as a fit object of punishment. We think that the general good requires that he should be punished, if not by the law, by the displeasure and ill offices of his fellow-creatures: we at any rate feel indignant with him, that is, it would give us pleasure that he should suffer for his misconduct, even if there are preponderant reasons of another kind against inflicting the suffering. This feeling of indignation, or resentment, is, I conceive, a case of the animal impulse (I call it animal because it is common to us with the other animals) to defend our own life and possessions, or the persons whom we care for, against actual or threatened attack. All conduct which we class as wrong or criminal is, or we suppose it to be, an attack upon some vital interest of ourselves or of those we care for, (a category which may include the public, or the whole human race): conduct which, if allowed to be repeated, would destroy or impair the security and comfort of our lives. We are prompted to defend these paramount interests by repelling the attack, and guarding against its renewal; and our earliest experience gives us a feeling, which acts with the rapidity of an instinct, that the most direct and efficacious protection is retaliation. We are therefore prompted to retaliate by inflicting pain on the person who has inflicted or tried to inflict it upon ourselves. We endeavour, as far as possible, that our social institutions shall render us this service. We are gratified when, by that or other means, the pain is inflicted, and dissatisfied if from any cause it is not. This strong association of the idea of punishment, and the desire for its infliction, with the idea of the act which has hurt us, is not in itself a moral sentiment; but it appears to me to be the element which is present when we have the feelings of obligation and of injury, and which mainly distinguishes them from simple distaste or dislike for any thing in the conduct of another that is disagreeable to us; that distinguishes, for instance, our feeling towards the person who steals our goods, from our feeling towards him who offends our senses by smoking tobacco. This impulse to self-defence by the retaliatory infliction of pain, only becomes a moral sentiment, when it is united with a conviction that the infliction of punishment in such a case is conformable to the general good, and when the impulse is not allowed to carry us beyond the point at which that conviction ends. For further illustration I must refer to the little Treatise already mentioned. (Vol. II, pp. 307–26.)

\*　　\*　　\*　　\*　　\*

[*In Chap. xxiv, "The Will," when distinguishing between the effects of external and internal sensations, James Mill remarks:*] *in general, as it is easy to conceive, the internal sensations are a leading cause of such actions as take place in the internal organs of the Body.*

The actions which take place in the interior of the body are not always, nor perhaps even generally, produced by sensations. A large portion of them are not preceded by any sensation of which we are aware, and have been ascertained to depend on nerves not terminating in the brain, which is the seat of sensation, but stopping at the spinal cord. These actions are inferred to be the results of a mere physical stimulus, operating either upon the local nerves, or upon the spinal ganglions with which those nerves communicate, and not attended with any consciousness.

Many of the instances which the author goes on to enumerate, of muscular action excited by sensation, are, in all probability, cases of this description. The muscular action is directly excited by the physical irritation of the nerves, and any sensation which accompanies it is not its cause, but a simultaneous effect. (Vol. II, p. 331.)

\* \* \* \* \*

*[James Mill (Vol. II, pp. 352–4) calls attention to a "double operation" in]* the *formation and execution of motives. The first association starts from the pleasure. The idea of the pleasure is associated with its immediate cause, that cause with its cause, and so on, till it reaches that act of ours which is the opposite end of the train. The process may stop here, and in that case the motive does not excite to action. If it excites to action, the process is exactly reversed. In the first process of association, the pleasure was the first link in the chain, the action the last; in the second process, the action is the first, the pleasure the last. When the first process only is performed, the association is called* MOTIVE. *When the second is performed it is called* WILL.

*A difficulty, however, presents itself. The first process terminates in an Idea of the action. The second process commences with an Idea of the action. The Idea of the action is thus excited twice. But the first time it is not followed by the action; the second time it is. How is this to be reconciled with the supposed constancy of connexion between the muscular action and the Idea which produces it? The difficulty is solved by observing, that the phrase, "Idea of the action," has two meanings. There are two Ideas, very different from one another, to both of which we give the name, "Idea of the action." Of these Ideas, one is the outward appearance of the action, and is always a very obvious Idea. The other is the copy of those internal sensations which originally called the muscles into action, to which, from habit of not attending to them, we have lost the power of attending. This last is by no means an obvious Idea. And the mind passes from it so quickly, intent upon the action which is its result, that it is almost always swallowed up in the mass of association. It constitutes, in fact, one of the most remarkable instances of that class of links in a chain, which, how important soever to the existence of the chain, are passed over so rapidly, that the existence of them is hardly ever recognised.*

*This last Idea alone, is that upon which the contraction of the muscle is consequent. In the process of association which we call the motive, as described above, the first of the two above-mentioned ideas of the action, that of its outward appearance, is the idea excited. If the association stops there, the motive is inoperative; if the association does not stop there, but the idea of the outward appearance of the action, calls up that other, the idea of the internal feelings of the action, the motive is then operative, and we are said* TO WILL.

*If we are asked, how an Idea, as that of the outward appearance of an act, should at one time excite an idea, as that of the internal feelings of the act, at another time not excite it, we can only refer to the laws of association, as far as they have been ascertained. We know there are certain cases of association, so strong, that the one Idea never exists without calling up the other. We know there are other cases in which an Idea sometimes does, and sometimes does not, call up such or such an Idea. Sometimes it is easy to trace the cause of this variety; sometimes difficult.*

This analysis of the power of the Will over muscular action is substantially that of Hartley, though more clearly and forcibly stated, and more amply illustrated. In the field of mental philosophy this is the point at which Hartley approached nearest to the most advanced thoughts of his successors, and left least for them to do beyond the task of commentators and defenders.[148]

The doctrine of Hartley on the Will may be summed up in the following propositions. 1. All our voluntary movements were originally automatic: meaning by automatic, involuntary, and excited directly by sensations. 2. When a sensation has the power of exciting a given muscular action, the idea of that sensation, if sufficiently vivid, will excite it likewise. 3. The idea of the sensation which excites an automatic action of the muscles, persists during the action, and becomes associated with it by contiguity, in such a manner as to be itself, in its turn, excited by any vividly recalled idea of the muscular act. 4. The following is what takes place in voluntary motion. The idea of the end we desire, excites by association the idea of the muscular act which would procure it for us. The idea of this muscular act excites, by association, the idea of the sensation which originally excited the same muscular action automatically. And lastly, the idea of this sensation excites the action, as the sensation itself would have done. 5. These associations being formed gradually, and progressively strengthened by repetition, this gives us the explanation of the gradual and slow process whereby we gain what is called command of our muscles; *i.e.* the process by which the actions, originally produced automatically by sensations, come to be produced,

[148]See Hartley, *Observations*, Vol. I, p. 371.

and at last, to be easily and rapidly produced, by the ideas of the different pleasurable ends to which those muscular actions are the means.   6. In this chain of association, as is so often the case in chains of association, the links which are no otherwise interesting to us than by introducing other links, gradually drop out of consciousness, being, after many repetitions, either forgotten as soon as felt, or altogether thrown out; the latter being the supposition which Hartley apparently favours. The link that consists in the idea of the internal sensations which excited the muscular action when it was still automatic, being the least interesting part of the whole series, is probably the first which we cease to be aware of. When the succession of the ideas has become, by frequent repetition, extremely prompt, rapid, and certain, another link tends to disappear, namely, the ideas of the muscular feelings that accompany the act. A practised player, for example, on a keyed instrument, becomes less and less conscious of the motions of his fingers, until there at last remains nothing in his consciousness to shew that the muscular acts do not arise without any intermediate links, from the purpose, *i.e.* the idea in his mind, which made him begin playing. At this stage the muscular motion, which, from automatic, had become voluntary, has become, from voluntary, what, in Hartley's phraseology, is called secondarily automatic; and it seems to be his opinion that the ideas which have disappeared from consciousness, or at all events from memory, have not been (as maintained by Stewart)[149] called up, and immediately afterwards forgotten, but have ceased to be called up; being, as it were, leapt over by the rapidity with which the succeeding links rush into consciousness.

This theory, as we have seen, is adopted, and more fully worked out, by the author of the *Analysis*. He proves, by many examples, that sensations excite muscular actions; that ideas excite muscular actions; and that, when a sensation has power to excite a particular muscular action, the idea of the sensation tends to do the same. It is true that many, if not most, of what he presents as instances of muscular action excited by sensations, are cases in which both the sensation and the muscular action are probably joint effects of a physical cause, a stimulus acting on the nerves. This misapprehension by the author reaches its extreme point when he declares traumatic tetanus to be produced not by the wound but by the pain of the wound; and cramps to be produced by sensations, instead of merely producing them.[150] But the error is quite immaterial to the theory of the Will; the two suppositions being equivalent, as a foundation for the power which the idea of the muscular sensation acquires over the muscular action. Whether the sensation is the cause of the automatic action, or its effect, or a joint effect of the cause which produces it—on all these hypotheses the sensation and the action are conjoined in such a manner, as to form so close an association by contiguity that the idea of the

[149]Stewart, *Elements*, Chap. ii, in Vol. I, esp. p. 120.
[150]*Analysis*, Vol. II, p. 333 (Chap. xxiv).

sensation becomes capable of exciting the action. This being conceded, it follows, by the ordinary laws of association, that whatever recals the idea of the sensation, tends, through the idea, to produce the action.

Now, there is nothing so closely associated with the idea of the muscular sensation, as the idea of the muscular act itself, such as it appears to outward observation. Whatever, therefore, calls up strongly the idea of the act, is likely to call up the idea of the accompanying muscular sensation, and so produce the act. But the idea of the act is called up strongly by anything which makes us desire to perform it; that is, by an association between it as a means, and any coveted pleasure as an end. The act is thus produced by our desire of the end; that is (according to the author's theory of desire) by our idea of the end, when pleasurable; which, if an end, it must be. The pleasurable association may be carried over from the ultimate end to the idea of the muscular act, through any number of intermediate links, consisting of the successive operations, probably in themselves indifferent, by which the end has to be compassed; but this transfer is strictly conformable to the laws of association. When the pleasurable association has reached the muscular act itself, and has caused it to be desired, the series of effects terminates in the production of the act. What has now been described is, in the opinion of the author, the whole of what takes place in any voluntary action of the muscles. At the close of the chapter we shall consider whether there is any part of the facts, for which this theory does not sufficiently account.[151] (Vol. II, pp. 354–8.)

\*    \*    \*    \*    \*

[*In his chapter on the will, James Mill examines (Vol. II, pp. 362–72) the process of "Attention." He initially explains it thus (p. 362):*] *We seem to have the power of attending, or not attending to any object; by which is meant, that we can Will to attend to it, or not to attend. By attending to an object, we give it the opportunity of exciting all the ideas with which it is associated. By not attending to it we deprive it of more or less of that opportunity. And if the will has this power over every idea in a train, it has thence a power, which may be called unlimited, over the train.* [*He later remarks (p. 363):*] *A painful or a pleasurable sensation is a peculiar state of mind. A man knows it, only by having it; and it is impossible that by words he can convey his feeling to others. The effort, however, to convey the idea of it, has given occasion to various forms of expression, all of which are greatly imperfect. The state of mind under a pleasurable or painful sensation is such, that we say, the sensation engrosses the mind; but this really means no more than that it is a painful or pleasurable sensation; and that such a sensation is a state of mind very different*

[151]See pp. 250–2 below.

*from an indifferent sensation. The phrase, engrossing the mind, is sometimes exchanged for the word* Attention. [*J.S. Mill's note comes at the end of the further analysis of the process.*]

The account here given of Attention, though full of instructive matter, I cannot consider to be at all adequate. When it is said that a sensation, by reason of its highly pleasurable or painful character, engrosses the mind, more is meant than merely that it is a highly pleasurable or painful sensation. The expression means, first, that when a sensation is highly pleasurable or painful, it tends, more or less strongly, to exclude from consciousness all other sensations less pleasurable or painful than itself, and to prevent the rising up of any ideas but those which itself recals by its associations. This portion of the facts of the case is noticed by the author, though not sufficiently prominent in his theory. But there is another portion, altogether untouched by him. Through this power which the sensation has, of excluding other sensations and ideas, it tends to prolong its own existence; to make us continue conscious of it, from the absence of other feelings which if they were present would either prevent us from feeling it, or would make us feel it less intensely; which is called diverting our attention from it. This is what we mean when we say that a pleasurable or painful idea tends to fix the attention. We mean, that it is not easy to have, simultaneously with it, any other sensation or idea; except the ideas called up by itself, and which in turn recal it by association, and so keep it present to the mind. Becoming thus a nearly exclusive object of consciousness, it is both felt with greater intensity, and acquires greater power of calling up, by association, other ideas. There is an increase both in the multitude, the intensity, and the distinctness of the ideas it suggests; as is always the case when the suggesting sensation or idea is increased in intensity. In this manner a sensation which gets possession of our consciousness because it is already intense, becomes, by the fact of having taken possession, still more intense, and obtains still greater control over the subsequent train of our thoughts. And these also are precisely the effects which take place when, the sensation not being so pleasurable or painful as to produce them of itself, or in other words to fix the attention, we fix it voluntarily. All this is as true of Ideas as of Sensations. If a thought is highly painful, or pleasurable, it tends to exclude all thoughts which have no connexion with it, and which if aroused would tend to expel it—to make us (as we say) forget the pain or the pleasure. By thus obtaining exclusive possession of the mind, the pleasurable or painful thought is made more intense, more painful or pleasurable; and, as is the nature of pains and pleasures, acquires, in consequence, a greater power of calling up whatever ideas are associated with it. All this is expressed by saying that it fixes the attention. And ideas which are not of themselves so painful or pleasurable as to fix the attention, may have it fixed on them by a voluntary act. In other words, the will has power over the attention.

But how is this act of will excited, and in what does it consist? On this point the author's analysis is conclusive, and admirable. The act, like other voluntary acts, is excited by a motive; by the desire of some end, that is, of something pleasurable; (including in the word *pleasurable*, as the author does, exemption from pain). What happens is, that, the idea on which we are said to fix our attention not being of itself sufficiently pleasurable to fix it spontaneously, we form an association between it and another pleasurable idea, and the result then is that the attention is fixed. This is the true account of all that we do when we fix our attention voluntarily; there is no other possible means of fixing it. It thus appears, that the fixing of attention by an act of will depends on the same law, as the fixing it by the natural pleasantness or painfulness of the idea. Of itself the idea is not pleasant or painful, or not sufficiently so to fix the attention; but if it were considerably more pleasant or painful than it is, it would do so. It becomes considerably more pleasurable by being associated with the motive—that is, by a fresh association of pleasure with it—and the attention is fixed. This explanation seems complete.

It may be said, however, by an objector, that this accounts only for the case in which the voluntary attention flows easy and unimpeded, almost as if it were spontaneous; when the mere perception that the idea is connected with our purpose—with the pleasurable end which suggested the train of thought, at once and without difficulty produces that exclusive occupation of the mind with it, which is called fixing the attention. But it often happens that the mere perception of its connexion with our purpose is not sufficient: the mind still wanders from the thought: and there is then required a supplementary force of will, in aid of association; an effort, which expends energy, and is often both painful and exhausting.

Let us examine, then, what takes place in this case. The association of the thought with the pleasurable end in view, is sufficient to influence the attention, but not sufficient to command it. The will, therefore, has to be called in, to heighten the effect. But in this case, as in every case, the will is called into action by a motive. The motive, like all other motives, is a desire. The desire must be either the same desire which was already felt, but made more effectual than before, or another desire superadded to the first. The former case presupposes the latter: for the desire which was not sufficient to fix the attention firmly on that which is the means to its fulfilment, cannot be sufficient to call forth the voluntary effort necessary for fixing it: some other desire must come to its assistance. What, then, is this other desire? The question is not difficult. The present is one of the complex cases, in which we desire a different state of our own desires. By supposition, we do not care enough for the immediate end, that is the idea of it is not sufficiently pleasurable, or the idea of its frustration sufficiently painful, to exert the force of association required. But we are dissatisfied with this infirmity of our desires: we wish that we cared more for the end: we think that it would be better for us if either this particular end, or our ends generally, had greater command over our thoughts and actions than they have. There is thus called up, by our sense of the insufficiency of our attention in the particular case, the idea of another desirable end—greater vigour and certainty in our mental operations. That idea superadds itself to the idea of the immediate end, and this reinforcement of the associating power at last suffices to fix the attention. Or (which is the same thing in effect) the painful idea is called up, of being unable to fix our attention, and being in consequence thwarted generally in our designs; and this pain operates, in the same manner as a pleasure, in fixing our attention upon the thought which, if duly attended to, will relieve us from the oppressive consciousness.

It will be asked, whence come the sense of laborious effort, and the subsequent feeling of fatigue, which are experienced when the attention does not fix itself spontaneously, but is fixed with more or less difficulty by a voluntary act? I conceive them to be consequences of the prolongation of the state designated by the author, in the text, as a state of unsatisfied desire. [152] That state, whatever view the psychologist takes of it, is a condition of the brain and nerves, having physiological consequences of great importance, and drawing largely on that stock of what we call nervous energy, any unusual expenditure or deficiency of which produces the feeling of exhaustion. The waste of energy, and the subsequent exhaustion, are greatest when the desire seems continually on the point of obtaining its gratification, but the gratification constantly eludes it. And this is what actually happens in the case supposed. The attention continually fastens on the idea which we desire to attend to, but, from the insufficient strength of the pleasurable or painful association, again deserts it; and the incessant alternation of hope and disappointment produces, as in other cases, the nervous disturbance which we call the sense of effort, and which is physiologically followed by the sensations of nervous exhaustion. It is probable that whatever is not muscular in the feeling which we call a sense of effort, is the physical effect produced by a more than usual expenditure of nervous force: which, reduced to its elements, means a more than usually rapid disintegration and waste of nervous substance.

Let me here remark, that the recognition, by the author of the *Analysis*, of a peculiar state of consciousness called a state of unsatisfied desire, conflicts with his doctrine that desire is nothing but the idea of the desired pleasure as future. In what sense is it possible to speak of an unsatisfied idea? If even we insert the omitted element of Belief, and resolve desire not into the mere idea, but into the expectation of a pleasure; though we might rationally speak of an unsatisfied expectation, it would only mean an expectation not fulfilled, in other words, an expectation of pleasure not followed by the pleasure; an expectation followed by a mere negation. How a pleasant idea, followed, not by a pain, but by nothing at all, is converted into a pain, the pain of unsatisfied desire, remains to be explained: and the author has not pointed out any associations which account for it. If it be said that the expectation is perpetually renewed and perpetually disappointed, this is

---

[152]*Analysis*, Vol. II, p. 362 (Chap. xxiv).

true, but does not account for more than a continual alternation between a pleasant idea and no idea at all. That an element of pain should enter into unsatisfied desire, is a fact not explained by the author's theory; and it stands as evidence that there is in a desire something inherently distinct from either an idea or an expectation. (Vol. II, pp. 372–7.)

\*    \*    \*    \*    \*

[*J.S. Mill's note (which is followed, pp. 382–95, by an extensive one of Bain's) comes at the end of the chapter on the will.*]

The analysis contained in this chapter affords, as it appears to me, a sufficient theory of the manner in which all that we denominate voluntary, whether it be a bodily action or a modification of our mental state, comes to be produced by a motive, *i.e.* by the association of an idea of pleasure or of exemption from pain with the act or the mental modification. But there is still an unexplained residuum which has not yet been brought to account. There are some bodily movements the consequence of which is not pleasure, but pain. Painful states of consciousness, no less than pleasurable ones, tend to form strong associations with their causes or concomitants. The idea, therefore, of a pain, will, no less than that of a pleasure, become associated with the muscular action that would produce it, and with the muscular sensations that accompany the action; and, as a matter of fact, we know that it does so. Why, then, is the result not merely different, but contrary? Why is it that the muscular action excited by association with a pleasure, is action towards the pleasure, while that excited by association with a pain is away from the pain? As far as depends on the law of association, it might seem that the action, in both cases, would be towards the fact with which the action is associated. There are some remarkable phenomena in which this really happens. There are cases in which a vivid imagination of a painful fact, seems really to produce the action which realizes the fact. Persons looking over a precipice are said to be sometimes seized with a strong impulse to throw themselves down. Persons who have extreme horror of a crime, if circumstances make the idea of committing it vividly present to their mind, have been known, from the mere intensity of their horror, to commit the crime without any assignable motive; and have been unable to give any account of why they committed it, except that the thought struck them, that the devil tempted them, and the like. This is the case of what is sometimes called a fixed idea; which has a sort of fascinating influence, and makes people seek what they fear or detest, instead of shunning it. Why is not this extremely exceptional case the common one? Why does the association of pain with an act, usually excite not to that act, but to the acts which tend to prevent the realization of the dreaded evil?

It seems, that as the author has had to admit as an ultimate fact, the distinction between those of our sensations which we call pleasures and those which we call pains, considered as states of our passive sensibility, so also he would be compelled to admit, as a fact unreached by his explanations, a difference between the two in their relation to our active faculty; an attraction in the one case, and a repulsion in the other. That is, he must admit that the association of a pleasurable or painful idea (at all events when accompanied by a feeling of expectation) with a muscular act, has a specific tendency to excite the act when the idea is that of a pleasure, but, when it is the idea of a pain, has a specific tendency to prevent that act, and to excite the acts that are associated with the negation of the pain. This is precisely what we mean when we say that pleasure is desired, that pain is an object of aversion, and the absence of pain an object of desire. These facts are of course admitted by the author: and he admits them even as ultimate: but, with his characteristic dislike to multiply the number of ultimate facts, he merges them in the admitted ultimate fact of the difference between pleasure and pain. It is chiefly in cases of this sort—in leading him to identify two ultimate facts with one another, that his love of simplification, in itself a feeling highly worthy of a philosopher, seems to mislead him. Even if we consent to admit that the desire of a pleasure is one and the same thing with the idea of a pleasure, and aversion to a pain the same thing with the idea of a pain—it remains true that the difference which we passively feel, between the consciousness of a pleasure and that of a pain, is one fact, and our being stirred to seek the one and avoid the other is another fact; and it is just this second fact that distinguishes a mere idea of something as future, from a desire or aversion. It is this conscious or unconscious reference to action, which distinguishes the desire of a pleasure from the idea of it. Desire, in short, is the initiatory stage of volition. The author might indeed say, that this seeking of the sensation is involved in the very fact of conceiving it as pleasant; but this, when looked into, only means that the two things are inseparable; not that they are, or that they can ever be thought of, as identical; as one and the same thing.

It appears, then, that there is a law of voluntary action, the most important one of all, which the author's explanations do not attempt to reach. Yet there is no necessity for accepting that law as ultimate. A theory resolving itself into laws still more fundamental, has been propounded by Mr. Bain in his writings, and a masterly statement of it will be found in the succeeding note. If, as I expect, this theory makes good its footing, Mr. Bain will be the first psychologist who has succeeded in effecting a complete and correct analysis of the Will.

In the same note will be found an analysis of the case of an *idée fixe*—the most striking case of which, is that of a terrific idea, exceptionally drawing the active power into the direction which leads towards the dreaded catastrophe, instead of, as usual, into the opposite direction. This peculiar case obliges us to acknowledge the coexistence of two different modes in which action may be excited. There is the normal agency of the ideas of a pleasure and a pain, the one determining an action towards the pleasure, the other an action away from the pain; and there is the general power of an extremely strong association of any kind, to make the action follow the idea. The reason why the determination of action towards a pain by the idea of the pain is only exceptional, is, that in order to produce it, the general power of a strong association to excite action towards the fact which it recals, has to overcome the specific tendency of a painful association to repel action from that fact. But the intensity of the painful idea may be so great, and the association of the act with it so strong, as to overpower this repulsive force by a greater attractive force: and it is then that we find the painful idea operating on action in a mode contrary to the specific property which is characteristic of it, and which it usually obeys.

It has been suggested, that the intensity with which the mind sometimes fixes upon a frightful idea, may operate by paralysing for the time being the usual voluntary efforts to avoid pain, and so allowing the natural impulse to act on a predominant idea to come into play. (Vol. II, pp. 379–82.)

*   *   *   *   *

[*Chap. xxv, "Intention," concludes the* Analysis. *J.S. Mill's note comes at the end of the examination of the term, and before the final five paragraphs in which, by way of peroration, James Mill places this theoretical work in relation to the practical studies that would complete the "Doctrine of the Human Mind."* ]

This chapter is devoted to clearing up the confusion and disentangling the ambiguity connected with the word *Intention*. And it fully attains the purpose, save where the refusal to admit any difference between expectation and a strong association, throws a certain haze over an operation into which they both enter.

*Intention*, when the word is used in reference to our future conduct, is well characterized by the author as "the strong anticipation of a future will."[153] It is an unfaltering present belief that we shall hereafter will a particular act, or a particular course of action. There may be, over and above this belief, an intention "that nothing shall occur to hinder that intention of its effect;" "the intention not to frustrate an existing intention." The author thinks that "this second intention is included in the first:" but it is not necessarily so. It is the first intention, fortified by some additional motive which creates a special desire that this particular desire and intention should continue. It is another case of what the author never recognizes, the desire of a desire.

*Intention*, when we are said to intend the consequences of our actions, means the foresight, or expectation of those consequences; which is a totally different thing

[153]*Ibid.*, p. 398. The following quotations are from the same passage.

from desiring them. The particular consequences in question, though foreseen, may be disagreeable to us: the act may be done for the sake of other consequences. Intention, and motive, are two very different things. But it is the intention, that is, the foresight of consequences, which constitutes the moral rightness or wrongness of the act. Which among the many consequences of a crime, are those, foresight of which constitutes guilt, and non-foresight entitles to acquittal, depends on the particular nature of the case. We may say generally, that it is the hurtful consequences. When the question arises judicially, we must say it is the consequences which the law intended to prevent. Reverting to the author's illustration;[154] a person who gives a drug to a patient, who dies in consequence, is not guilty (at least of an intentional crime) if he expected good consequences, or no consequences at all, from its administration. He is guilty, if he expected that the consequence would be death; because that was the consequence which the legislator intended to prevent. He is guilty, even if he thought that the death of the patient would be a good to the world: because, though the law did not intend to prevent good to the world, it did intend to prevent persons from killing one another. Judged by a moral instead of a legal standard, the man may be innocent; or guilty of a different offence, that of not using his thinking faculty with sufficient calmness and impartiality, to perceive that in such a case as that of taking life, the general presumption of pernicious consequences ought to outweigh a particular person's opinion that preponderant good consequences would be produced in the particular instance. (Vol. II, pp. 401–2.)

[154]*Ibid.*, p. 400.

# BOTANICAL WRITINGS

## 1840–61

# Botanical Writings

## Calendar of Odours

### APRIL 1840

*Memories of Old Friends, Being Extracts from the Journals and Letters of Caroline Fox, from 1835 to 1871*, ed. H.N. Pym, 2nd ed., 2 vols. (London: Smith, Elder, 1882), Vol. I, pp. 166–7. Headed: "A Calendar of Odours, Being in Imitation of the Various Calendars of Flora by Linnaeus and Others." Concluded: "To Miss Caroline Fox, from her grateful friend, J.S. Mill." As unpublished, not in Mill's bibliography. Mill, accompanied by his mother and his sisters Clara and Harriet, was at Falmouth from 16 March to 10 April 1840, during the last illness of his brother Henry, who died there of tuberculosis on 4 April. He prepared the calendar for Caroline Fox during the last week of his stay.

THE BRILLIANT COLOURING of Nature is prolonged, with incessant changes, from March till October; but the fragrance of her breath is spent before the summer is half ended. From March to July an uninterrupted succession of sweet odours fills the air by day and still more by night, but the gentler perfumes of autumn, like many of the earlier ones here for that reason omitted, must be sought ere they can be found. The Calendar of Odours, therefore, begins with the laurel, and ends with the lime.

*March*—Common laurel.

*April*—Violets, furze, wall-flower, common broad-leaved willow, apple-blossom.

*May*—Lilac, night-flowering stocks and rockets, laburnum, hawthorn, seringa, sweet-briar.

*June*—Mignonette, bean-fields, the whole tribe of summer roses, hay, Portugal laurel, various species of pinks.

*July*—Common acacia, meadow-sweet, honeysuckle, sweetgale or double myrtle, Spanish broom, lime.

In latest autumn, one stray odour, forgotten by its companions, follows at a modest distance—the creeping clematis which adorns cottage walls; but the thread of continuity being broken, this solitary straggler is not included in the Calendar of Odours.

# Rare Plants in West Surrey

## JUNE 1841

*Phytologist*, I (June 1841), 30. No. 3 in Art. IX, "Varieties; Original and Select"; under this heading appeared the editor's selection of extracts from correspondents' letters listing stations at which specimens were found. Signed "J.S. Mill; Kensington, June 1, 1841." Not republished. Identified in Mill's bibliography only in the general note, "Various lists of plants found in different parts of England, in a monthly publication, called the Phytologist during 1841" (MacMinn, p. 53).

RIBES RUBRUM AND NIGRUM, the former in many places, the latter abundantly in one place, by the side of the Mole near Esher: perfectly wild and completely naturalized. Turritis glabra, abundant and fine by the road-side between Hampton and Sunbury. Diplotaxis tenuifolia, a rare plant in Surrey, is very abundant above Walton Bridge. Cerastium arvense, on banks by the side of the Thames below Walton Bridge.

# Isatis Tinctoria

## JUNE 1841

*Phytologist*, I (June 1841), 30. No. 4 in Art. IX, "Varieties; Original and Select." Signed "*Id*. [i.e., J.S. Mill; Kensington,] June 8, 1841." Not republished. For the identification in Mill's bibliography, see "Rare Plants in West Surrey" above. The square brackets are those of the *Phytologist*'s editor.

ISATIS TINCTORIA is now growing in prodigious luxuriance in the chalk-quarries close to the town [of Guildford]. It grows (in many instances) out of clefts in the precipitous chalk cliff, and makes almost a *bush* of flowers from the same root. Geranium lucidum I again found in my old locality, near St. Catherine's Hill.

# Notes on Plants Growing in the Neighbourhood of Guildford, Surrey

## AUGUST 1841

*Phytologist*, I (Aug. 1841), 40–1. Art. XIV. Signed "J.S. Mill, Esq." Not republished. For the identification in Mill's bibliography, see "Rare Plants in West Surrey" above.

IMPATIENS FULVA. At whatever period introduced, this plant is now so thoroughly naturalized, that it would be pedantry any longer to refuse it that place in the

English Flora, which has been accorded on less strong grounds to many plants originally introduced from abroad. For many miles by the side of the Wey, both above and below Guildford, it is as abundant as the commonest river-side plants, the Lythrum Salicaria or Epilobium hirsutum; and my friend Mr. Henry Cole[1] informs me that it is found in various places by the same river all the way to its junction with the Thames. It is equally abundant on the banks of the Tillingbourne, that beautiful tributary of the Wey; especially at Chilworth, where it grows in boundless profusion: and near Albury, where I saw it for the first time in 1822. The plant stated by Sir J.E. Smith to be growing near Guildford,[2] under the name of Impatiens Noli-me-tangere, is doubtless no other than this plant. The Noli-me-tangere, which I have seen growing about Windermere, in the Pyrenees, and in Switzerland, is very distinct from this.

*Geranium lucidum*; in most of the lanes about Guildford.

*Fumaria capreolata*; near Losely, and by the roadside between Guildford and Merrow.

*Fumaria parviflora*; in corn-fields on the summit and southern declivity of the Hog's Back; and in lanes at its foot.

*Valerianella dentata* (or Fedia dentata); corn-fields on the chalk hills on both sides of Guildford, abundantly.

*Isatis tinctoria*; in great perfection in the chalk-pits close to the town, on the Shalford road; as noticed in *The Phytologist*, p. 30.[3]

*Hippuris vulgaris*; in one of the ponds in Clandon Park.

*Bupleurum rotundifolium.* This plant grew, last summer, in a corn-field on the brow of the hill by the path leading from Guildford to Martha's Chapel. The field having been sown this summer with a green crop, which was removed early, the plant cannot now be found.

*Campanula hybrida*; abundant in the lower part of the same field.

*Corydalis claviculata.* This plant formerly grew close to Martha's Chapel, but I have sought for it this year in vain.

*Dipsacus pilosus*; most abundant near Chilworth, especially in the hanging wood.

*Androsaemum officinale*; near Albury, but sparingly.

*Saponaria officinalis*; near Shere.

*Stellaria glauca.* This interesting and elegant plant grows in marshy meadows by the river Wey, near the foot of St. Catherine's Hill.

*Menyanthes trifoliata*; now (whatever may formerly have been the case) a rare

---

[1]Henry Cole (1808–82) was a close friend of Mill's, especially in the late 1820s and early 1830s, when they went on walking tours together, during which Mill initiated Cole into the pleasures of field botany.

[2]This statement by James Edward Smith (1759–1828) has not been located; he gives only northern locations for *Impatiens noli-me-tangere* in his *English Flora*, 4 vols. (London: Longman, *et al.*, 1824–29).

[3]See "Isatis Tinctoria," p. 258 above.

plant in Surrey. It grows on Gomshall Common, in the vale of Albury; where I also once found a double variety of Cardamine pratensis.

*Papaver hybridum*; in corn-fields between Guildford and Martha's Chapel. Papaver dubium is as common in the neighbourhood as P. Rhoeas.

*Lepidium sativum*; naturalized by the side of the Wey.

*Nasturtium sylvestre* and *Barbarea praecox*: not unfrequent by the side of the Wey.

*Rhamnus catharticus* and *Frangula*; the former not unfrequent on the downs, the latter abundant in a wood near Compton.

*Orobanche major*; at Martha's Chapel.

*Listera Nidus-avis*; in a heathy wood between Guildford and Martha's Chapel. With this exception I have not been able to find near Guildford any of the less common Orchideae so numerous near Dorking.

*Salvia verbenaca*. St. Catherine's Hill; Merrow Church-yard; and various other places.

*Cistopteris fragilis* and *Asplenium Ruta-muraria*. These ferns grow in considerable abundance on a wall by the road-side at Albury, where I first found them in 1824, and again this summer.

*Marchantia polymorpha*; on the perpendicular face of the cutting on the road to Godalming, at the foot of St. Catherine's Hill. Geranium lucidum grows on an old wall on the opposite side of the road.


# Cnicus Forsteri

## SEPTEMBER 1841

*Phytologist*, I (Sept. 1841), 61. No. 21 in Art. XXIII, "Varieties; Original and Select," Signed "J.S. Mill; Kensington, July 13, 1841." Not republished. For the identification in Mill's bibliography, see "Rare Plants in West Surrey" above.

CNICUS FORSTERI I saw growing by hundreds last month in a piece of marshy ground formerly part of Ditton Common; at least it was the plant I previously found near Weybridge and sent to Sir W. Hooker.[1] It was growing with various numbers of flowers from one up to four, each on a separate and generally a long stalk. On comparing it with the books both English and foreign, and especially with Decandolle's description of his Cirsium anglicum[2] (our Cnicus pratensis), I have little doubt that it is merely a variety of that, and that C. Forsteri, as you suggested, has no existence as a species.

[1]William Jackson Hooker (1785–1865), one of Britain's leading botanists, and Director of Kew Gardens.

[2]Augustin Pyrame de Candolle (1778–1841), Swiss botanist whose influential "natural" system of botanical classification is given in detail in the work Mill refers to: *Prodromus*

# Additional Guildford Stations

## SEPTEMBER 1841

*Phytologist*, I (Sept. 1841), 64. No. 32 in Art. XXIII, "Varieties; Original and Select." Signed "J.S. Mill; Kensington, August 24, 1841." Not republished. For the identification in Mill's bibliography, see "Rare Plants in West Surrey" above.

SINCE THE PUBLICATION of the list of Guildford plants in the last number of *The Phytologist*,[1] Fumaria claviculata has been refound in its old locality, Martha's Chapel, and likewise on the extensive common near Shalford, called Blackheath. Epipactis latifolia has been found at the Sheepleas, and Cuscuta Europaea in an osier holt by the river Wey, a short distance above Guildford, entwined round nettles, the Spiraea Ulmaria, and the osiers themselves.

# Polygonum Dumetorum

## NOVEMBER 1841

*Phytologist*, I (Nov. 1841), 91. No. 58 in Art. XXXIII, "Varieties." Signed "J.S. Mill; Kensington, October 3, 1841." Not republished. For the identification in Mill's bibliography, see "Rare Plants in West Surrey" above.

POLYGONUM DUMETORUM grows copiously in the hedges on more than one part of the road from the Woking-Common station to Guildford.*

---

*systematis naturalis regni vegetabilis, sive enumeratio contracta ordinum generum specierumque plantarum huc usque cognitarum, juxta methodi naturalis normas digesta*, 19 vols. (Paris: Treuttel and Würtz, *et al.*, 1824–72), Vols. I-VII having appeared by the time Mill was writing. The reference is to Vol. VI, p. 650.

[1]See "Notes on Plants Growing in the Neighbourhood of Guildford, Surrey," pp. 258–60 above.

*This is one of those odd plants which we can never expect to find in the same spot two years in succession. At least such is the case so far as we are taught by our observation of its habits in the neighbourhood of Reigate. Previously to the year 1836, when we had the good fortune to detect it, Polygonum dumetorum was not known as a Reigate plant; in the following year it was found in one or two other stations; from one at least of these it has entirely disappeared, but to make amends has sprung up in the greatest abundance in a locality some miles from either of those previously occupied by it. We are always glad to record the stations of such plants, wherever they may choose temporarily to take up their residence. [Note by the editor of the *Phytologist*.]

# Rarer Plants of the Isle of Wight

## NOVEMBER 1841

*Phytologist*, I (Nov. 1841), 91–2. No. 59 in Art. XXXIII, "Varieties." Signed "J.S. Mill." Not republished. For the identification in Mill's bibliography, see "Rare Plants in West Surrey" above.

I OBSERVED the following less common plants in the Isle of Wight, during a week's tour in July, some years ago.[1]

### MARITIME PLANTS

Matthiola, (no doubt) incana, or Cheiranthus incanus, in inaccessible places on
   Compton Cliffs, Freshwater Bay. The same plant grows most abundantly in
   places overhanging the sea on the promontory of Posilipo, and other similar
   situations near Naples, where it flowers copiously in February, and little
   children collect bouquets of the plant at great apparent risk, to sell to passers
   by.

| | |
|---|---|
| Cakile maritima | Atriplex littoralis |
| Adenarium (Arenaria) peploides | Beta maritima |
| Pyrethrum maritimum (Ryde) | Euphorbia Peplis (Sandown Bay) |
| Convolvulus Soldanella (sands near | Arundo arenaria |
|    Yarmouth) | Triticum Nardus |
| Salsola Kali (Ryde) | |

### SALT MARSHES NEAR YARMOUTH

| | |
|---|---|
| Althaea officinalis | Salicornia herbacea |
| Tamarix gallica | Chenopodium maritimum |

### IN A MARITIME BOG AT EASTON, NEAR FRESHWATER

| | |
|---|---|
| Ranunculus Lingua | Scirpus maritimus |
| Epipactis palustris | Cladium Mariscus |

### MISCELLANEOUS

Poa bulbosa. Alum Bay.
Mentha rotundifolia. This plant, so common on the continent, but comparatively
   so unfrequent in England, grows on the Undercliff, in a maritime situation,
   near Puckaster Cove.

[1]For Mill's journal of the walking tour in 1832 during which he recorded some of these stations, see *CW*, Vol. XXVII, pp. 557–611.

Lathyrus sylvestris and Rubia peregrina. Common in hedges on the Undercliff. The former grows in profusion on the landslip near Bonchurch.

Iris foetidissima. As common on the Undercliff, and (if I recollect right) in other parts of the island as in Devonshire.

Inula Helenium. By the side of a lane between Yarmouth and Freshwater Bay, but sparingly.

PLANTS COLLECTED SHORTLY AFTERWARDS ON THE COAST OF HAMPSHIRE, OPPOSITE TO THE ISLE OF WIGHT

Atriplex portulacoides. Abundant in salt marshes at Lymington.

Bartsia viscosa and Fumaria capreolata. Roadside between Lymington and Exbury.

Euphorbia stricta. Cornfields near Beaulieu river.

Campanula hederacea. New Forest, near Ashurst Lodge.

Parnassia palustris, Drosera longifolia and Myrica Gale. In various parts of the Forest.

# Corrections and Additions in Mr. Mill's List of Plants in the Isle of Wight

JANUARY 1842

*Phytologist*, I (Jan. 1842), 132–3. No. 97 in Art. XLV, "Varieties." Signed "J.S. Mill; Kensington, December 20, 1841." The corrections and additions are to the previous item, pp. 262–3 above. Not republished. Not listed in Mill's bibliography.

LINE 34, for *Triticum Nardus* read *T. junceum*. Tamarix gallica, (line 37) has most probably been introduced into the locality near Yarmouth. Poa bulbosa (line 42) must be erased from the list: the mistake arose from an imperfect specimen of a grass from Alum Bay having been compared by a friend with continental specimens of Poa bulbosa, in its viviparous state. The Alum Bay plant was afterwards found to be an Agrostis. To the plants growing in salt marshes at Yarmouth, add Triglochin maritimum and Potamogeton pectinatum. To those of the New Forest add Triglochin palustre.

# The Phytologist; a Botanical Magazine

DECEMBER 1843

*Westminster Review*, XL (Dec. 1843), 524–5. Running title: "Miscellaneous Notices." Signed "S." Not republished. Identified in an incomplete entry in Mill's bibliography as "A short notice of 'The Phytologist' in the Miscellaneous Notices of the Westminster Review for December 1843 (No.   )" (MacMinn, p. 56).

WE THINK it highly desirable that such lovers of botany as are not yet aware of the fact, should be apprised that there has now existed, for nearly two years, a botanical magazine, at the low price of one shilling. This little periodical is not intended to compete with the large works which are addressed to the scientific public, and are the appointed vehicles for the more recondite discoveries and discussions of vegetable physiology. Without excluding such discussions when they can be brought within the limits of the work, the *Phytologist* addresses itself less to scientific physiologists than to naturalists in the more popular acceptation of the term; and especially to such as wander over the hills and fields of our native country in search of its rarer plants, or who delight in observing their habits and peculiarities. Of the merits of the work in this capacity it is almost a sufficient recommendation that Mr. Newman, the author of the accurate and interesting *History of British Ferns*, has made its pages the vehicle for giving to the botanical public, as a sequel to that work, a similar history of the British Lycopodiaceae Equisetaceae, and adjacent families, which is now nearly complete, and not inferior in excellence to the *British Ferns*.[1] In the genus Equisetum especially, Mr. Newman has corrected serious mistakes, and cleared up important ambiguities.

The *Phytologist* has contained various interesting and valuable discussions on other British plants, as, for example, that by which it was for the first time conclusively shown, by Mr. Luxford and others,[2] that the Monotropahypopitys is not, as it was so long supposed to be, a parasitical plant. The value of this journal to local collectors of plants is very great, as almost every number contains a local flora, or catalogue of the plants growing in some particular district. An account is also regularly given of the contents of the more interesting papers read before the Linnaean Society, and published in its transactions. And under the head of Varieties, admission is given to the briefest notice of any fact interesting to the lover of botany.

We are the more desirous of calling the attention of our botanical readers to this periodical, as we perceive with regret a statement in a recent number that it does not yet pay its expenses, and without an increase of its sale cannot be much longer continued.[3] It will be a real discredit to the growing class of botanical amateurs, if

[1]"A History of the British Lycopodia and Allied Genera," *Phytologist*, I (June-Nov. 1841), 1–7, 17–20, 33–6, 49–51, 65–7, and 81–6, by Edward Newman (1801–79), proprietor of the *Phytologist* 1841–54, and author of *A History of British Ferns* (London: Van Voorst, 1840).
[2]"Botanical Notes," *Phytologist*, I (Aug. 1841), 43–4, by George Luxford (1807–54), printer and botanist, who edited the *Phytologist* from its inception until his death.
[3]The statement appears on the cover of the issue for June 1843.

they suffer so useful a medium for mutual communication among themselves to perish for want of the very trifling support which would continue it in existence.

# Notes on the Species of Oenanthe
## FEBRUARY 1845

*Phytologist*, II (Feb. 1845), 48–9. Signed "J.S. Mill / Kensington, January, 1845." Not republished. Not listed in Mill's bibliography.

THE READERS of *The Phytologist*, and all botanists, are much indebted to Mr. H.C. Watson for his careful, and I believe accurate investigation, in the January number, of the three species of Oenanthe, hitherto confounded under the names of peucedanifolia and pimpinelloides (*Phytol*. ii. 11).[1] I have long been convinced that there was some unknown quantity to be determined among the English species of this very interesting genus, which has until lately received very little critical investigation in this country. It is not generally known that one of these three species grows abundantly in so familiar and much frequented a locality as Battersea fields. I have observed it there for more than twenty years past, in a small patch of grass land, which is passed through in crossing the fields diagonally from Nine Elms, at an acute angle with the direction of the river. Valeriana dioica and Polygonum Bistorta grow copiously near the spot. I have never yet been able to procure the fruit, as the grass is always cut before the plant is out of flower. But the leaves, the tubers, and the bracteae, agree in their characters with Mr. Watson's Oe. Smithii, and quite differ from those of Oe. Lachenalii. The same plant, or one apparently the same, has been seen by me many years ago, as well as lately, in meadows adjoining the river Wey, near Weybridge. Neither of these stations appears to be known to Mr. Watson; to whom I can also contribute an authentic station for his Oe. pimpinelloides, viz. a maritime bog at the little village of Bishopstone, near Seaford, in Sussex, where I gathered unquestionable specimens in July, 1827.[2]

While I am on the subject of this genus, I should be glad if any of your correspondents could inform me whether they have ever found the Oe. crocata with the yellow acrid juice, which until lately has been attributed to it by all botanists. I have examined numberless living specimens of the plant in Surrey, and

[1]Hewett Cottrell Watson (1804–81) known as the father of British topographical botany, "Some Account of the Oenanthe pimpinelloides, and peucedanifolia of English Authors," *Phytologist*, II (Jan. 1845), 11–15.
[2]For Mill's journal of the walking tour in 1827 during which he collected specimens, see *CW*, Vol. XXVII, pp. 455–75.

other counties around London, for the express purpose, and have never, in any one single instance, discovered the smallest vestige of such a juice. The assertion is a curious example of the servile manner in which even scientific observers copy each other's statements, without verifying them.

# Correction of an Error in the "Notes on the Species of Oenanthe"

## APRIL 1845

*Phytologist*, II (Apr. 1845), 116. Signed "J.S. Mill, Kensington, March, 1845." The reference is to the previous item, pp. 265–6 above. Not republished. Not listed in Mill's bibliography.

SINCE my note on the species of Oenanthe was printed (*Phytol.* ii. 48), my specimens from Battersea, Weybridge and Seaford have had the advantage of being examined by Mr. Watson. That gentleman confirms my statement respecting the Battersea and Weybridge plants, which he decides to be his Oenanthe Smithii, the peucedanifolia of Smith. The plant from Seaford, which I had classed as the pimpinelloides, he pronounces to be Oenanthe Lachenalii; and he has fully satisfied me, both by his high authority, and by a comparison of specimens with which he has most courteously supplied me, that I was previously unacquainted with the true Oe. pimpinelloides.

# Observations on Isatis Tinctoria and Other Plants

## MAY 1856

*Phytologist*, n.s. I (May 1856), 331–2. The first entry under the heading "Botanical Notes, Notices, and Queries," which is also the running title. Signed "J.S.M." Not republished. Identified in Mill's bibliography only in the general note, "Botanical Notes signed J.S.M. in the second series of the Phytologist, No. 13, for May 1856, and in many subsequent numbers" (MacMinn, p. 88).

IN THE "Descriptive British Botany," publishing in the *Phytologist*, it is stated, under the initials of Mr. Irvine, that he has never observed *Isatis tinctoria* (except an occasional straggler) on the west side of the river Wey.[1] It will be agreeable to

---

[1]Alexander Irvine (1793–1873), who accompanied Mill on botanical field trips, editor of the *Phytologist* 1855–63, issued eight-page consecutively numbered fascicles as supplements to the journal from 1855 to 1858; these are gathered under the title *British Botany*. The reference actually derives from information supplied in an article by Edward Newman in the *Phytologist*, I (Nov. 1841), 82.

this accurate and trustworthy investigator of localities (by whose indications many others as well as myself must have been often guided to rare plants) to be informed that this fine plant grew in the utmost profusion in 1849 (and doubtless grows still) in the great chalk-quarry near Compton, on the south side of the Hog's Back, a place easily overlooked by a passing botanist from being masked by a Larch-wood in front.

It is also stated that *Iberis amara* grows in fields in Berkshire—Pangbourne and Streatley.[2] The range of this very local plant is considerably wider than these words would import, as it is also found in Oxfordshire and Buckinghamshire; especially, and most plentifully, in the range of country north of the Thames, from Henley to Maidenhead.

My experience agrees with that of your Tring correspondent (p. 105) as to the botanical poverty of the Chiltern Hills,[3] a fact the more remarkable as the southern portion of the same chalk district is one of the richest in the midland counties. *Alchemilla vulgaris* however grows in the woods of Chequers; and I have found *Paris quadrifolia* in a woody ravine adjoining Stokenchurch Common. *Buxus sempervirens* helps to adorn the steep chalky declivities near Ellesborough, and grows also on the hills between Tring and Dunstable. *Pyrola minor* I have gathered on the same range of hills, further south, near Nettlebed; and in great profusion in various parts of the woody region towards Wycombe and Marlow.

As you have thought it worth while to print a new Surrey locality for *Lycopodium Selago*,[4] which has been found in that county by several botanists, you will perhaps allow me to mention one which I believe not to be generally known. The *Lycopodium* grows in considerable abundance on the east side of a sort of pass through and over Chobham Ridges, leading in the direction of Frimley. The path goes directly through the large field which Mr. Watson, some years ago, pointed out as a habitat of *Arnoseris pusilla*;[5] and in the same field I found, in October, 1849, a moderate quantity of *Linaria purpurea*, a plant of which the indigenousness has been doubted, but this situation closely resembles the continental localities of the plant.

The *Phytologist* very judiciously directs much of its attention to the geographical distribution of plants. On this subject much may be learnt by the careful examination of a single county, and there are counties and even smaller districts in England which deserve particular notice as forming the transition between two distinct botanical regions, or combining portions of both. The Isle of Wight is an example of the first kind, Surrey of the second. That county, besides its great

[2]Irvine, "Fields in Berkshire (Pangbourne and Streatley), and Kent (Greenhithe)," *British Botany*, p. 57.
[3]Anon., "Notes of a Day's Botanizing about Tring, Herts, June 29, 1855," *Phytologist*, n.s. I (Sept. 1855), 105–8. Mill is responding partly to Irvine's questioning (*ibid.*, p. 108) of the correspondent's finding.
[4]Not located.
[5]Not located.

variety of geological structure and of vegetation as thereon dependent, contains within its narrow limits an eastern and what may be termed a sub-western flora. The domain of the latter is the tract of heath and sand extending from Esher and Moulsey diagonally to Hindhead and Haslemere. While a great proportion of the plants of the eastern region are wanting in this, it possesses many which are not found further east, and is still more distinctly characterized by the abundance of several, of which only stragglers are found in the region of Croydon, Godstone, Reigate, and Dorking. It is the chosen seat of *Apera Spica-Venti*; *Silene anglica*; *Hypochoeris glabra* (which abounds there, while I have seen it nowhere else in Surrey except a few straggling plants on Reigate Heath); *Erysimum cheiranthoides* and *Marrubium vulgare* (both found near Reigate, but in no similar abundance); *Athyrium Filix-foemina*, more profuse there than elsewhere; *Myrica Gale*; *Senecio sylvaticus*; *Geranium lucidum*; *Rhynchospora alba*; I believe I might add *Hieracium rigidum*, but the Surrey *Hieracia*, though less numerous, require revision as much as those of Yorkshire. *Campanula Rapunculus* is plentiful in one corner of the district. Among its varieties are *Campanula patula*; *Comarum Palustre*; the two *Elatines*, *Hydropiper* and *hexandra*; *Chaetospora nigricans*, which I had the good fortune to rediscover in its old recorded locality, Bagshot Heath; *Hippuris vulgaris*; *Utricularia minor*; *Arnoseris pusilla*; *Linaria purpurea*; *Leonurus Cardiaca*; *Allium vineale*; *Zannichellia palustris*; *Ceterach officinarum*.

Has *Calamintha Nepeta* been ever really found in Surrey? Several botanists have thought they had found it, but by no search in the localities indicated have I discovered anything nearer to it than *Calamintha officinalis*. A *Calamintha* taller than *officinalis*, but with much smaller leaves, resembling those of *Origanum vulgare*, and with a stem not erect, but ascending from a bend near the root, which I believe to be *C. Nepeta*, I have seen in various places on the Continent, among others especially near Rouen; and this plant grows, or did grow in 1843, by the side of the road from Marlow to Hedsor and Clifden. I last year recognized what seemed the same plant (but did not botanically examine it) between Eynsford and Farningham, in Kent. Perhaps some one among your correspondents, who has attended to the subject, would give your readers the benefit of his experience.

# Plants Growing Wild in the District of Luxford's *Reigate Flora*

### JUNE 1856

*Phytologist*, n.s. I (June 1856), 337–43. The heading continues, after the title above: "Omitted Both in That Work and in the Supplementary List by Mr. Holman, Published in the Old Series of the *Phytologist* in September, 1841." Running title: "Reigate Flora." The references are to Luxford's *A Flora of the Neighbourhood of Reigate, Surrey, Containing the Flowering Plants and Ferns* (London: Van Voorst; Reigate: Allingham, 1838), and Henry Martin Holman, "Additions to Luxford's *Reigate Flora*," *Phytologist*, I (Sept. 1841), 1–4. Six errors presumably arising from the printer's misreading of Mill's hand were identified in the October number (see "Reigate Plants" below): "north-eastern" erroneously for "south-eastern" (269.29), "Maiden Park" for "Marden Park" (271.3), "rocks of Box Hill" for "roots of Box Hill" (271.6), "Woodbatch" for "Woodhatch" (271.9), "Wenham Mill" for "Wonham Mill" (271.29 and 273.33), and "Godbroke" for "Gadbroke" (272.42); these corrections are all made in the text below. Signed "J.S. Mill." Not republished. For the identification in Mill's bibliography, see "Observations on Isatis Tinctoria and Other Plants" above.

(THE DISTRICT extends from Leith Hill on the west, to Godstone and its neighbourhood on the east.)

*Thalictrum flavum*. By the Mole below Sidlow Bridge.

*Ranunculus parviflorus*. On the steepest part of Brockham Hill, in Elder thickets about half-way up the hill, abundantly.

*Fumaria capreolata*. Near Buckland, by the footpath leading to the chalk hills.

*Nasturtium sylvestre*. Most plentiful in the dry bed of the Mole, between Mickleham and Leatherhead, and in streams north of Leatherhead.

*Barbarea praecox*. By the road from Dorking to Capel, near the commencement of the Holmwood.

*Arabis hirsuta*. Juniper Hill, Mickleham Downs, Box Hill, and other parts of the chalk hills near Dorking. This plant is so characteristic of the Surrey Hills, that its not having been found in the immediate neighbourhood of Reigate is a curious anomaly.

*Erysimum cheiranthoides*. Copiously in a cultivated field near Doover's Green, to the left of the Brighton road. By the Mole, near the footpath from Betchworth to Brockham. (This plant, common in the north-western half of the county, is rare in the south-eastern.)

*Camelina sativa*. Among wheat in the open upland fields between Ashtead and Leatherhead, in one spot, plentifully, 1849.

*Spergula nodosa*. On the grassy slope of Box Hill, plentifully.

*Geranium pyrenaicum*. About Leatherhead, Dorking, and Reigate, not unfrequent.

*Petroselinum segetum*. By the side of the Brighton road, on the ascent of Cockshot Hill, sparingly, 1845.

(*Archangelica officinalis*, banks of the Mole, near Brockham, I hesitate to insert, not having seen it there since 1824, and being unable to answer for my having correctly determined it at that distant date.)

*Caucalis daucoides*. In a cornfield adjoining Norbury Park, on the summit of the hill (1822).

*Onopordon Acanthium*. Merstham. This fine Thistle occurs in many other parts of the county, but I have not observed it elsewhere in the Reigate district.

*Silybum marianum*. Corner of Earlswood Common, near the church (1845), but possibly an outcast. This Thistle, being rather frequent in the adjoining parts of Kent, will probably be found permanently established somewhere in East Surrey.

*Hypochaeris glabra*. Sparingly on Reigate Heath, near the race-course (1849). One of the characteristic plants of the north-western district of Surrey.

*Campanula Rapunculus*. In a shady lane on Cockshot Hill, sparingly (1845).

*Verbascum Lychnitis*. Sparingly at the foot of the chalk-coomb near Quarry Farm. I have found this handsome Mullein nowhere else below the hills, though not uncommon above them, both in East Surrey and in West Kent.

*Mentha rotundifolia*. Ashtead Park.

*Melissa officinalis*. Sparingly in Coldharbour Lane, Dorking (1849). This naturalized plant has now several authentic stations in Surrey. The only one known to me in which it is sufficiently abundant to hold out much promise of permanency, is a bank by the private road which connects the high-road from Kingston to Leatherhead, with the church and village of Chessington.

*Chenopodium rubrum* (or *urbicum*?). By the road from Reigate to Dorking, near Betchworth; also near Nutfield.

*Sagittaria sagittifolia*. In the Mole at the foot of Box Hill.

*Lemna polyrrhiza*. Dorking mill-pond; and ditches in various places.

*Potamogeton perfoliatus*. In the Mole near Sidlow Bridge.

*Potamogeton pusillus, β. major* (*compressus*, Sm.). Ditch in the valley of Nutfield Marsh.

*Luzula sylvatica*. In the wood below Headley Church, towards Walton-on-the-hill.

*Scirpus caespitosus*. Earlswood Common.

*Carex divulsa*. Cockshot Hill and other places.

*Carex pallescens*. In long grass on the south side of the Merstham ponds (1849). This rich locality, unexplored at the time of the publication of Luxford's *Flora*, contains *Typha angustifolia* (in the western pond), *Epipactis palustris* (in ditches adjoining), *Astragalus Glycyphyllos* (on the border of Warwick Wood), and *Lathyrus sylvestris* (clustering on the copse itself).

*Carex binervis*. Broadmoor (Leith Hill).

*Carex vesicaria*. In the Mole, at Sidlow Bridge.

(*Carex axillaris* has been found near the foot of Colley Hill by Mr. Hanson, of Reigate.)[1]

*Avena fatua*. Found near Littleton in 1845.

---

[1]Not otherwise identified, though a William Hanson had earlier contributed to the *Phytologist*.

*Koeleria cristata*. Brockham Hill (1824). Not found (to my knowledge) since that time in the Reigate district; but grows abundantly above the hills, between Warlingham and the Woldingham and Marden Park district.

*Catabrosa aquatica*. Ditches at Leatherhead, near the great rise of clear water in the bed of the Mole.

*Brachypodium pinnatum*. About the roots of Box Hill; and copiously by the grassy side of the road from Epsom to Headley, between Hundred-acre Field and the great chalk-pit at Ashtead.

*Triticum caninum*. Hedges by the roadside between Woodhatch and Sidlow Bridge.

*Equisetum sylvaticum*. In the swampy wood below Coldharbour on the north side of the range (one of the finest Fern localities in Surrey, especially for *Osmunda*).

*Equisetum palustre*. Frequent in ponds and by wet roadsides. Its omission in Luxford's *Flora* can only be accidental.

*Chara vulgaris*. In a clear pool by the footpath from Wray Common to the Merstham Road. On the top of the chalk-hills between Walton and Headley Heaths.

*Chara flexilis*. In the great rise of water at Leatherhead.

The following are omitted stations of Plants included in the *Flora*, or in Mr. Holman's Supplementary List:—

*Aquilegia vulgaris*. On the summit of Box Hill, in the wood; and in other woods, as well as by the sides of fields, near Dorking.

*Berberis vulgaris*. Near the summit of either Reigate Hill or Colley Hill, in 1826 or 1827: not seen since that time.

*Corydalis claviculata*. About the base of Boar Hill, and in the swampy wood north of Coldharbour.

*Cardamine amara*. In the swamp at Whiggey; near Buckland; by the stream above Wonham Mill; and (sparingly) in various places near Dorking.

*Thlaspi arvense*. On the summit of Redstone Hill (1848).

*Reseda Luteola*. Along the foot of the chalk hills towards Godstone.

*Viola palustris*. In the swamp at Whiggey, copiously. At the lower extremity of Broadmoor, and in the ravine which descends from Leith Hill to Wotton.

*Dianthus Armeria*. In the vale of Mickleham.

*Silene anglica*. Border of a field, in the bottom intervening between Walton and Headley Heaths.

*Hypericum Androsaemum*. Near the cascade of Fillbrook, in the grounds of Tillingbourne, at the foot of Leith Hill.

*Hypericum Elodes*. In a bog at Coldharbour, and in wet parts of Broadmoor.

*Geranium Pratense*. By the Mole near Mickleham, sparingly.

*Radiola Millegrana*. Abundant near the summit of Leith Hill.

*Rhamnus cathartica.* Box Hill, Mickleham Downs, and other places on the chalk hills.

*Rhamnus Frangula.* In the woody and bushy parts of Boar and Leith Hills.

*Genista tinctoria.* Found in 1822 near Dorking, on the side next Boar Hill; the exact place forgotten. This plant is rather abundant near the Godstone railway station, and being common in Kent, both above and below the hills, is likely to be found near Reigate; probably in the Weald.

*Anthyllis Vulneraria.* Chalk hills towards Godstone.

*Lathyrus Nissolia.* In a shaw near Doover's Green, to the left of the high-road.

*Lathyrus sylvestris.* This very ornamental plant is not confined to Warwick Wood, but clothes the thickets and hangs in festoons at intervals along the base of the chalk hills nearly to Godstone.

*Spiraea Filipendula.* Abundant on Mickleham Downs, Box Hill, etc.

*Tormentilla reptans.* Holmwood.

*Rubus Idaeus.* Summit of Box Hill. Boar Hill.

*Rosa rubiginosa.* Box Hill. Mickleham Downs. Chalk hills towards Godstone.

*Epilobium angustifolium.* Boar Hill.

*Sedum acre.* In dry, bare places on the steep sides of Brockham Hill. Box Hill. Juniper Hill, and the intervening ravine.

*Silaus pratensis.* Plentiful in meadows near Dorking; Betchworth and Reigate.

*Asperula cynanchica.* Very common on the chalk hills near Dorking.

*Valeriana dioica.* Bog near the Mole at Brockham.

*Erigeron acris.* Lower slopes of Buckland Hill. Box Hill, copiously. Westhumble.

*Gnaphalium sylvaticum, β (S. rectum).* Betchworth Hill. Kingswood warren. Boar Hill woods.

*Serratula tinctoria.* Woods about Headley and Walton.

*Phyteuma orbiculare.* Mickleham Downs. In the great Ashtead chalk-pit, plentiful. On the ridge of the chalk hills between Merstham and Catherham in abundance.

*Ligustrum vulgare.* Box Hill. Leith Hill woods.

*Vinca minor.* Copiously, and certainly wild, in a hollow road on the south slope of Park Hill. I have this winter found it in an exactly similar situation (the steep side of a deep cutting in a sandy soil), about a mile from St. Mary Cray, on the road to Chelsfield, in Kent. I notice this circumstance as bearing on the question respecting the indigenousness of the plant.

*Chlora perfoliata.* Copiously on Box Hill, Buckland Hill, and the chalk hills near Quarry Farm, between Merstham and Godstone.

*Menyanthes trifoliata.* Bogs about Leith Hill.

*Atropa Belladonna.* Norbury Park; Brockham Hill; steep chalky side of Box Hill. Profusely about the roots of the hills near Quarry Farm.

*Hyoscyamus niger.* Lane between Brockham and Gadbroke.

*Orobanche major*. Summit of the hill named Dorking's Glory (1823).

*Antirrhinum Orontium*. Frequent in the Weald.

*Pedicularis palustris*. Leith Hill.

*Veronica montana*. Woods about Boar and Leith Hills.

*Salvia verbenaca*. Near Leatherhead.

*Scutellaria minor*. Abundant on Leith Hill.

*Nepeta Cataria*. Sidlow Bridge. Road to Buckland.

*Ajuga Chamaepitys*. Brockham Hill, and between Leatherhead and Headley.

*Anagallis tenella*. Leith Hill abundantly.

*Littorella lacustris*. New Pond on Earlswood Common.

*Euphorbia stricta*. By the Mole near Betchworth Park Mill, sparingly (1845). Fields near Woolver Farm, in the Weald. Field adjoining Earlswood Common. Field at the foot of Boar Hill, near Coldharbour Lane. I have some difficulty in believing the identity of this plant with the hairy *Euphorbia platyphylla*.

*Orchis Morio*. Meadows about Headley, Mickleham, and Reigate occasionally.

*Aceras anthropophora*. Profusely on Colley and Buckland Hills, and between Box Hill and Juniper Hill.

*Ophrys apifera*. Copiously in the same localities as the last, and on the lower slopes of the hills near Quarry Farm.

*Ophrys muscifera*. Same localities, and chalk hills near Godstone.

*Epipactis latifolia*. Copse to the right of the Merstham Road, beyond Wray Common. Box Hill.

*Epipactis purpurata*. Grove near Merstham Church, sparingly.

*Allium ursinum*. Woods of Marden Park most profusely.

*Actinocarpus Damasonium*. Ponds on Headley and Walton Heaths in abundance.

*Butomus umbellatus*. In the Mill-pond at Dorking; and in the bed of the Mole between Mickleham and Leatherhead, abundant.

*Triglochin palustre*. In ditches near the rise of water at Leatherhead.

*Lemna trisulca*. Pool in a dense thicket a little beyond the Merstham ponds.

*Lemna gibba*. In Dorking Mill-pond so abundantly as to be piled up in heaps on the edge.

*Scirpus setaceus*. Earlswood Common. Ravines of Leith Hill.

*Carex paniculata*. In boggy shaws at Wonham Mill.

*Carex stellulata*. Leith Hill.

*Carex flava*. Broadmoor.

*Carex pendula*. Boggy wood between Reigate Heath and the Buckland Road. Most abundant at the foot of the chalk hills near Oxted.

*Carex Pseudo-cyperus*. In the pond of Gatton Park (1826 or 1827).

*Triodia decumbens*. Reigate Heath. Broadmoor. Abundant on the summit of Leith Hill.

*Molinia caerulea*. Broadmoor.

*Nardus stricta*. Leith Hill.

*Equisetum fluviatile*. Profusely by the Merstham Road and in Gatton Park.

*Lastrea Oreopteris*. Leith Hill, copiously; and about the roots of Boar Hill towards Coldharbour Lane.

*Polystichum aculeatum* and *angulare*. Lanes in the valley of Nutfield Marsh. In the swampy wood north of Coldharbour, already mentioned.

*Athyrium Filix-foemina*. Leith Hill, abundantly. Reigate Heath. Thicket near Littleton. Hedges by the Buckland Road. Swampy wood north of Coldharbour.

*Asplenium Trichomanes*. On trunks of trees near Betchworth.

*Blechnum boreale*. Leith Hill, Boar Hill, etc., copiously.

*Osmunda regalis*. Foot of Boar Hill (north side). In the swampy wood north of Coldharbour, forming large and tall thickets visible at a great distance.

# Note on West Surrey Plants
## JULY 1856

*Phytologist*, n.s. I (July 1856), 392. Appeared in the section entitled "Botanical Notes, Notices, and Queries." Signed "J.S.M." Not republished. For the identification in Mill's bibliography, see "Observations on Isatis Tinctoria and Other Plants" above.

IF YOU print my *Plantae Rariores* of North-western Surrey,[1] it may be as well to add *Cirsium anglicum* (Carduus pratensis), which has two good habitats in the district; and also (though belonging to its extreme point) that decidedly western plant *Scilla autumnalis*, which I have seen growing on Moulsey Hurst, where it grew in Ray's time.[2]

# Reigate Plants
## OCTOBER 1856

*Phytologist*, n.s. I (Oct. 1856), 460–1. The article begins with a list of the six errata in "Plants Growing Wild in the District of Luxford's *Reigate Flora*," that are corrected in its text above. Running title: "Reigate Plants." Signed "J.S. Mill." Not republished. For the identification in Mill's bibliography, see "Observations on Isatis Tinctoria and Other Plants" above.

THIS LIST of plants is in a great degree superseded by the new *Reigate Flora*, just

---

[1]See the previous item, "Plants Growing Wild in the District of Luxford's *Reigate Flora*," pp. 268–74 above.

[2]John Ray (1627–1705), pioneer field botanist.

published by Mr. Brewer;[1] which, as might be expected, contains most of the plants which I have mentioned, with many others which I had not detected. I had however the good fortune of finding some which have escaped even Mr. Brewer. Of one of these (*Catabrosa aquatica*) I have observed a new station, much nearer to Reigate, even since the publication of Mr. Brewer's work, viz. in the swamp at Whiggey, on the west side of the Brighton road, at a very short distance from the stile: so difficult is it to exhaust this rich botanical district, in which I do not believe there is anywhere a square quarter of a mile not containing one or several rare plants.

Might I take the liberty of asking Mr. Brewer, through your journal, whether *Alchemilla vulgaris* is set down as growing in "damp meadows on the banks of the Mole, and in other places in the neighbourhood of Dorking,"[2] from his own observation, or on the authority of Luxford's *Flora*?[3] I have always suspected a mistake on the part of Mr. Luxford's informant, not as to the plant, but the locality, as I can hardly imagine that a plant so conspicuous, and incapable of being mistaken for any other, can exist in some abundance in that neighbourhood without my having seen it in thirty-five years' botanical knowledge of the locality.

Permit me to ask a similar question respecting *Carex teretiuscula* near Whiggey, which has been suspected to be an error of Mr. Luxford.[4]

Mr. Brewer locates *Carex ovalis* in "damp situations on Reigate Heath and Redhill."[5] To these may be added Earlswood Common, which is at present covered with it.

In my list I omitted one of the habitats of *Sagittaria sagittifolia*—near the Merstham ponds.

---

Has any of your correspondents attended to *Veronica* with the variegated corolla of *V. agrestis* and the large flower of *V. Chamaedrys*? It is not very uncommon in Surrey, and I last year observed it in great abundance in cornfields on the heights overtopping Smitham bottom, between Croydon and Beggar's Bush. Is this a permanent variety of *agrestis*? and is it not often mistaken for *V. Buxbaumii*, reports of which are now starting up everywhere, though wanting not only the uniformly blue colour of *Buxbaumii*, but the broadly divergent lobes of the fruit?

---

[1] *A New Flora of the Neighbourhood of Reigate, Surrey, Containing the Flowering Plants and Ferns of the District, with Their Localities, Times of Flowering, etc. And a List of the Mosses* (London: Pamplin, 1856), by James Alexander Brewer (1818–86). The work was reviewed in the same number of the *Phytologist*, pp. 434–5, with a reference to Mill's article of June, "Plants Growing Wild in the District of Luxford's Reigate Flora," pp. 268–74 above.

[2] Brewer, *A New Flora*, p. 19.

[3] Not located.

[4] Not located.

[5] Brewer, *A New Flora*, p. 123.

# Plants Growing on and near Blackheath

## APRIL 1857

*Phytologist*, n.s. II (Apr. 1857), 93. Appeared in the section entitled "Botanical Notes, Notices, and Queries." Signed "J.S.M." Not republished. For the identification in Mill's bibliography, see "Observations on Isatis Tinctoria and Other Plants" above.

TORILIS NODOSA.—On the grassy slope above Hyde Vale.

*Trifolium striatum.*—Very abundantly along the road crossing the heath diagonally towards Morden College, and the prolongation of that road into Blackheath Park (June, 1856).

*Trifolium* (or *Trigonella*) *ornithopodioides.*—Very scantily by the same road, in front of the Paragon, in 1853. Not seen since; but Blackheath being one of the recorded stations of this small inconspicuous plant, it probably still exists on some other part of the heath.

*Tragopogon porrifolius.*—In some abundance in a corner of a meadow by the prolongation (already mentioned) of the diagonal road into Blackheath Park. The plant has been completely established in the locality for some years past. There is nothing to show its origin; but it is to be feared that the progress of building will shortly root it out.

*Senecio viscosus.*—A weed on the glebe-land at Lee, in profusion (1851). The land is now covered with houses, but the plant has survived this peril, being still found in considerable quantity by the roadside.

# Late (Early?) Flowering Plants: Plants in Flower in the District of Eltham and Chiselhurst, in November, 1857

## JANUARY 1858

*Phytologist*, n.s. II (Jan. 1858), 319–20. Headed as title. Running title: "Late (Early?) Flowering Plants." Signed "J.S. Mill." Not republished. For the identification in Mill's bibliography, see "Observations on Isatis Tinctoria and Other Plants" above.

| | | |
|---|---|---|
| Ranunculus acris. | Tormentilla reptans. | Centaurea nigra. |
| Ranunculus repens. | Tormentilla officinalis. | Lapsana communis. |
| Papaver Rhoeas. | Fragaria vesca. | Hypochoeris radicata. |
| Fumaria officinalis. | Geium urbanum. | Taraxacum Dens-leonis. |
| Capsella Bursa-pastoris. | Spiraea Ulmaria. | Leontodon hispidus. |

Sisymbrium officinale.
Sinapis arvensis.
Raphanus Raphanistrum.
Spergula arvensis.
Arenaria serpyllifolia.
Stellaria media.
Stellaria graminea.
Cerastium triviale.
Lychnis vespertina.
Malva sylvestris.
Malva rotundifolia.
Geranium pusillum.
Geranium robertianum.
Ilex Aquifolium.
Ulex europaeus.
Spartium scoparium.
Trifolium repens.
Trifolium pratense.
Vicia sepium.
Rosa arvensis.
Rubus discolor.
Rubus corylifolius?
Polygonum Persicaria.
Rumex obtusifolius.
Rumex pratensis?
Euphorbia Peplus.

Epilobium montanum.
Pimpinella Saxifraga.
Aethusa Cynapium.
Sison Amomum.
Heracleum Sphondylium.
Pastinaca sativa.
Anthriscus sylvestris.
Lonicera Periclymenum.
Hedera Helix.
Cornus sanguinea.
Bellis perennis.
Anthemis nobilis.
Maruta Cotula.
Chrysanthemum segetum.
Leucanthemum vulgare.
Achillea Millefolium.
Senecio vulgaris.
Senecio viscosus.
Senecio aquaticus.
Senecio Jacobaea.
Carduus acanthoides.
Cirsium arvense.
Euphorbia helioscopia.
Urtica urens.
Glyceria fluitans.

Oporinia autumnalis.
Hieracium Pilosella.
Sonchus asper.
Sonchus oleraceus.
Campanula rotundifolia.
Erica cinerea.
Erica Tetralix.
Calystegia sepium.
Solanum nigrum.
Veronica agrestis.
Veronica Buxbaumii.
Lamium album.
Lamium purpureum.
Galeobdolon luteum.
Ballota foetida.
Stachys Betonica.
Stachys sylvatica.
Thymus Serpyllum.
Clinopedium vulg. *Sm.*
Prunella vulgaris.
Chenopodium album.
Plantago Coronopus.
Poa annua.
Lolium multiflorum.
Alopecurus agrestis.

In flower in December:

Ranunculus repens.
Capsella Bursa-pastoris.
Sinapis arvensis.
Raphanus Raphanistrum.
Stellaria media.
Stellaria graminea.
Geranium robertianum.
Ilex Aquifolium.
Ulex europaeus.
Rubus discolor.
Rubus corylifolius?

Tormentilla reptans.
Fragaria vesca.
Spiraea Ulmaria.
Pimpinella Saxifraga.
Aethusa Cynapium.
Sison Amomum.
Heracleum Sphondylium.
Cornus sanguinea.
Bellis perennis.
Maruta Cotula.
Achillea Millefolium.

Senecio vulgaris.
Taraxacum Dens-leonis.
Oporinia autumnalis.
Helminthia echioides.
Sonchus asper.
Sonchus oleraceus.
Lamium album.
Lamium purpureum.
Ballota foetida.
Euphorbia Peplus.

The following may be added to the list of December flowering plants:

| | | |
|---|---|---|
| Ranunculus acris. | Hypochoeris radicata. | Euphorbia exigua. |
| Alliaria officinalis. | Senecio Jacobaea. | Urtica urens. |
| Stellaria Holostea. | Solanum nigrum. | Poa annua. |
| Cerastium triviale. | Veronica agrestis. | Glyceria fluitans. |
| Lonicera Periclymenum. | Veronica Buxbaumii. | Dactylis glomerata. |

All of these which are not in the list for November (except perhaps *Euphorbia exigua*) are freshly come out.

# Hutchinsia Petraea

## MAY 1858

*Phytologist*, n.s. II (May 1858), 446. Appeared in the section entitled "Botanical Notes, Notices, and Queries," which also serves as running title. Signed "J.S.M." Not republished. For the identification in Mill's bibliography, see "Observations on Isatis Tinctoria and Other Plants" above.

PLANTS in bloom on March 29: *Anemone nemorosa, Veronica hederaefolia, Nepeta Glechoma, Salix Caprea*, and *Taxus baccata. Hutchinsia* is very fine and abundant in the old place.

# Leucojum Aestivum

## JULY 1858

*Phytologist*, n.s. II (July 1858), 510. Appeared in the section entitled "Botanical Notes, Notices, and Queries," which also serves as running title. Signed "J.S.M., May 17, 1858." Not republished. For the identification in Mill's bibliography, see "Observations on Isatis Tinctoria and Other Plants" above.

I HAVE SELDOM ENJOYED a greater botanical pleasure than in finding yesterday, for the first time, the *Leucojum* in the Plumstead Marshes. I had always missed it hitherto by seeking for it *above* Greenwich, according to the fallacious indication (no doubt true once) of Curtis and Smith.[1] I was delighted to see that in two

---

[1]William Curtis (1746–99), *Flora Londinensis; or, Plates and Descriptions of Such Plants as Grow Wild in the Environs of London*, 2 vols. (London: Curtis and White, 1775–98), fasc. 5, text to plate 23. The reference to Smith is less clear: in fact James Edward Smith, in his *English Flora*, Vol. II, p. 130, locates the plant "between Greenwich and Woolwich," that is, below Greenwich. (In the same place Smith quotes Curtis's citation of the Isle of Dogs' station.)

different swamps, both already well known to me, this beautiful plant exists in such profusion that all the botanists in England would scarcely exhaust it; and as both places are within the practising-ground of the Arsenal, they are not likely to be drained and built over.

## Clifton Plants
### JULY 1858

*Phytologist*, n.s. II (July 1858), 512. Appeared in the section entitled "Botanical Notes, Notices, and Queries," which also serves as title. Signed "J.S.M., May 26, 1858." Not republished. For the identification in Mill's bibliography, see "Observations on Isatis Tinctoria and Other Plants" above.

I HAVE JUST returned from Bristol, where I found *Arabis stricta*, *Trinia vulgaris*, *Potentilla verna*, *Geranium sanguineum*, *Convallaria Polygonatum*, the last not yet in flower.

## Plants on Sherborn Sands, Blackheath, and Other Stations
### SEPTEMBER 1858

*Phytologist*, n.s. II (Sept. 1858), 554–5. Appeared in the section entitled "Extracts from Correspondence," which also serves as running title. Signed "J.S.M.," dated "June 22nd." Not republished. For the identification in Mill's bibliography, see "Observations on Isatis Tinctoria and Other Plants" above.

. . . I FOUND *Elymus* abundant about Sherborn Sands, which, it may be new to you to hear, are now shut up; but the key can be had for asking for, without the bore of an attendant. I have investigated the corner of Blackheath, and soon sighted *Geranium pratense*. Being thus satisfied that I was in the right place, I sought and found, among a profusion of *Trifolium striatum* and *minus*, three *Medicagines*, being *lupulina*, *maculata*, and another, prostrate, with spinous fruit and unstained leaves. This last could not be *minima*, as it was far from having entire stipules; but on comparing it with undoubted specimens of *maculata*, though I could find no difference in the fruit, I flattered myself that there was somewhat more of *denticulation* on the stipules, and that it might be *denticulata*. But alas! next day I found others exactly like, except that they had *no* more denticulation, and here and there a *trace* of stain on the leaves. On the whole, I fear this is not the *denticulata* of foreign botanists, or else, as you surmise, theirs does not differ from *maculata*. I do not think there are any other *Medicagines* in the locality this year.

I see in *British Plants* you date the discovery of *L. Martagon* in Headley Copse from 1840.[1] If so, I can claim earlier discovery, as I have known it there from 1826. For a year or two it puzzled me grievously, as I dared not think it could be *Martagon*; but about 1829 I found it in flower, and, I believe, wrote to Sir W. Hooker about it; but he, as you know, repudiated it as a British plant.[2] I should like to know if I was also the first to notice *Impatiens fulva*. I found it below the bridge at Albury, in 1822, but mistook it for *Noli-me-tangere*. *Apropos*, I searched last Monday the skirts of Weston Wood for *Arundo Epigejos*, but fruitlessly. I see you consider *Adiantum* a maritime plant;[3] I suppose therefore it is so in the British Islands; but I have never known it as such, its habitats in the Alps, Italy, etc., being those of *Scolopendrium*,—damp walls, vaults, very shady and moist ruins, the spray of waterfalls, etc., and in no way affecting maritime localities.

# Some Derbyshire Plants

## SEPTEMBER 1858

*Phytologist*, n.s. II (Sept. 1858), 556. Appeared in the section entitled "Extracts from Correspondence," which also serves as running title. Signed "J.S.M.," dated "July 23rd, 1858" and (in the text) "July 30th, 1858." Not republished. For the identification in Mill's bibliography, see "Observations on Isatis Tinctoria and Other Plants" above.

. . . I HAVE BEEN OUT for a few days, with some botanical results. You have probably found, like myself, that when one goes to a neighbourhood known for rare plants one seldom finds those one seeks for: one finds others which one did not expect. It has not so happened with me this time, for during a day at Matlock I found one of the two special rarities of that place, *Thlaspi virens*, Bab. (*alpestre*, Sm.), still not entirely out of flower; and I have plenty for you as well as myself, if you would like to have any. The other plants worth mentioning which I found at Matlock were *Arenaria verna*, still spangling the hillsides with its blossoms; *Cardamine impatiens*, plentiful; *Convallaria majalis, Arabis hirsuta, Campanula*

---

[1]In his *Illustrated Handbook of the British Plants* (London: Nelson, 1858), Irvine gives Headley Copse as a station, but without a date. The reference may be to his *Introduction to the Science of Botany*, 5 pts. (London: Nelson, 1858), p. 297, where he vaguely says to see the *Phytologist* "as above"; much earlier, however, Luxford (then editor) had, in an appended note to a communication from Newman, reported the same station for Lilium Martagon in Surrey in 1826 (*Phytologist*, I [Sept. 1841], 62).

[2]Mill did not write to W.J. Hooker until 26 January, 1831, about his discovery in 1829 (*EL, CW*, Vol. XII, pp. 69–70). Hooker's repudiation of Lilium Martagon as a British plant is in the 6th ed. of his *British Flora; Comprising the Phaenogamous, or Flowering Plants, and the Ferns* (1st ed., 1830) (London: Longman, *et al.*, 1850), p. 444.

[3]Irvine, *Illustrated Handbook*, p. 183.

*latifolia*, and *Geranium pratense*, all in abundance: its usual northern substitute, *G. sylvaticum*, I did not see.

Other plants in Derbyshire:—*Silene nutans*, Dovedale and Wyedale; *Vaccinium Vitis-idaea*, Chatsworth; *Rosa villosa* and *R. tomentosa*, Monsal Dale and its vicinity; *Myrrhus odorata*, Millersdale; also, I believe, between Castleton and Hathersage; *Cochlearia officinalis* and *Thalictrum flexuosum* (or rather, perhaps, *T. calcareum*), abundant on rocks above Castleton; *Viola lutea* (which I prefer calling, with De Candolle, *V. sudetica*,[1] as it has a blue variety), on all mountains and hills near Castleton; the blue variety occasionally; *Polypodium calcareum*, in clefts of rocks between Bakewell and Buxton; *Cystopteris fragilis*, in similar situations there, and near Castleton; *Carduus heterophyllus*, plentiful in wet ground by the river Wye, near Cowdale turnpike, two miles from Buxton, on the Bakewell Road; *Polemonium coeruleum*, on rocks by the same road, one mile from Buxton, but so difficult to be got at that I only secured one specimen. . . .
—July 30th, 1858. I will send *Silene* along with *Thalictrum*. My specimens are not from Dovedale, though I saw the plant there, but from Wyedale, about a mile above Ashford, near Bakewell. The leaf of the *Viola* from New Brighton is very much like that of some specimens I brought from Italy under the name of *V. montana* or *Ruppii*, both of which are considered forms of *canina*. . . .—Among the Derbyshire plants which I saw I omitted *Allium vineale*, near Matlock (at the very top of the High Tor), and *Saxifraga hypnoides*, in various places, but always much past flower, even in places where *Cardamine pratensis* was still flowering.

# Linaria Purpurea

### SEPTEMBER 1858

*Phytologist*, n.s. II (Sept. 1858), 566. Appeared in the section entitled "Botanical Notes, Notices, and Queries," which also serves as running title. Signed "J.S.M." Not republished. For the identification in Mill's bibliography, see "Observations on Isatis Tinctoria and Other Plants" above.

TOUCHING the *murality* of *Linaria purpurea*, the only two places where I have seen it undoubtedly wild were cornfields: one near Frimley, in Surrey, in the large cornfield noted by Mr. Watson as a station of that thumping plant *Arnoseris pusilla*;[1] the other was on the Mont des Alouettes, a richly cultivated eminence in

---

[1]Candolle, *Prodromus*, Vol. I, p. 302.

[1]This reference, identical to that in "Observations on Isatis Tinctoria and Other Plants," p. 267 above, has not been located.

La Vendée, along with *Lathyrus angulatus*, a plant which will probably some day find its way here as an agrarian plant. The exact similarity of the habitat in these two cases satisfied me that *L. purpurea* has as much right to be considered a British as a French plant.

# Faversham Plants

## OCTOBER 1858

*Phytologist*, n.s. II (Oct. 1858), 597–8. Entitled "Extracts from Correspondence," part of "Botanical Notes, Notices, and Queries," which serves as running title. Signed "Very truly yours, J.S.M.," dated "August 11, 1858." Not republished. For the identification in Mill's bibliography, see "Observations on Isatis Tinctoria and Other Plants" above.

. . . I HAVE MADE my projected excursion to Faversham, and have been rewarded by finding *Peucedanum* in the very place mentioned in Smith's *English Flora*,[1] a very little way out of the town, on the east bank of the river or creek which descends from it to the sea. It is so abundant as to be in no danger of extirpation, and, as you have never been there, it is worth while going to see it. The other plants I found in that neighbourhood are *Calamintha Nepeta*, almost as profusely as you have described your having found it in Essex;[2] *Verbascum Lychnitis* on a wall, and *Hippuris vulgaris*. I next went to the Isle of Sheppey, where I enriched myself with *Inula crithmoides*, a plant I never before saw growing. I saw also *Spartina stricta*, and I should like to consult you on an erect Chenopodiaceous plant. I cannot even tell if it is an *Atriplex* or a *Chenopodium*. The enlarged calyx has not yet appeared, but perhaps it is not sufficiently advanced, though it sheds small, flat, dark-coloured seeds in abundance. When passing Strood, I went down to the old place by the river and found *Lepturus*, which I never happened to find in England before. The place is sadly cut up, not only by the railway, but still worse by brickmaking: however, there is still abundance of all the plants that used to be there—even *Glaux maritima*—except *Juncus maritimus*, which I did not see. I shall be happy to send you specimens of *Peucedanum* or *Inula*.

# Lepidium Ruderale

## APRIL 1859

*Phytologist*, n.s. III (Apr. 1859), 127. Appeared in the section entitled "Botanical Notes, Notices, and Queries," which serves as the running title. Signed "J.S.M." Not republished.

[1]Smith, *English Flora*, Vol. II, p. 100.
[2]Irvine, "Calamintha Nepeta, *Clairv.*," *Phytologist*, n.s. II (June 1857), 131–2.

For the identification in Mill's bibliography, see "Observations on Isatis Tinctoria and Other Plants" above.

LEPIDIUM RUDERALE, stated in the Report of the Greenwich Natural History Society[1] to have been growing, last year, in the lane which goes out of the south-west corner of Kidbrook Common, is there in profusion this year also; and so many-seeded a plant having found a locality propitious to it, has every chance of remaining there till the botanist's crack of doom, "a trowell ticking against a brick."[2]

*Mentha Pulegium,* another plant in the Society's general list, is flourishing round a small pond on the eastern edge of Chiselhurst Common.

I have had a day in Tilgate Forest, and have succeeded in finding *Cicendia.* As it was not abundant, I was sparing of it.

## Wallflower Growing on the Living Rock
### MAY 1860

*Phytologist,* n.s. IV (May 1860), 160. Appeared in the section entitled "Botanical Notes, Notices, and Queries," which serves as running title. Signed "J.S.M." Not republished. For the identification in Mill's bibliography, see "Observations on Isatis Tinctoria and Other Plants" above.

IT SEEMS TO BE NOTICED as remarkable (see *Phytologist,* vol. iv, p. 6) that Mr. Sim found *Cheiranthus Cheiri* on the living rock.[1] It grows profusely on the precipitous part of St. Vincent's Rock, at the end next Bristol.

## Spring Flowers of the South of Europe: Remarks on Some of the Spring Flowers of the South of Europe, and on Their Representatives in the British Isles
### OCTOBER 1860

*Phytologist,* n.s. IV (Oct. 1860), 289–96. Running title: "Spring Flowers of the South of Europe." Signed "J.S.M." Not republished. Identified in Mill's bibliography as "An article

[1]Not located.
[2]Not located.

[1]Irvine had noted, in "Address to the Contributors, etc.," *Phytologist,* n.s. IV (Jan. 1860), 6, this report by John Sim (ca. 1812–93), a soldier-naturalist.

headed 'Spring Flowers of the South of Europe' in the Phytologist for October 1860"
(MacMinn, p. 93).

THE ENGLISH BOTANIST who has resided or travelled in the countries of southern
Europe, and has filled his herbarium with the treasures of their copious Flora, must
often have thought, with almost envious regret, of the comparative poverty of our
own. But as we have no power to change the lot which in this matter the general
arrangements of Nature have assigned to us, we shall do well to look at its brighter
side, and find matter for congratulation in some points of superiority which our
indigenous Flora, meagre though it be in comparison with those of France and
Italy, nevertheless possesses over the richest regions of the basin of the
Mediterranean. Two of these points have particularly impressed me in the course
of a tolerably extensive wandering over the south of Europe, and I will
communicate them here for the benefit of those who may not already have adverted
to them.

The first is our pre-eminence in Ferns. Though the species of Phaenogamous
plants in (for instance) the French Flora, outnumber ours almost in the ratio of four
to one, the species of Ferns in the two countries are about equally numerous, and
indeed nearly identical. In the excellent Flora of MM. Grenier and Godron the only
Ferns which are not (under the same or some other name) included in the fourth
edition of Mr. Babington's *Manual*, are two *Nothoclaenae*, *N. Marantae* and
*vellea* (the last found only in Corsica), *Pteris cretica* (also confined to Corsica),
*Cheilanthes odora*, and *Scolopendrium Hemionitis*.[1] Two more, *Ophioglossum
lusitanicum* and *Grammitis leptophylla*, are, as British plants, limited to the
Channel Islands. On the other hand, *Lastrea Foenisecii*, *Hymenophyllum Wilsoni*,
and *Trichomanes radicans*, among the most precious of our ferny treasures, have
not hitherto been discovered in France. We are thus scarcely outnumbered in
species of Ferns by the whole of France, Corsica included. But when we compare
this country, not with all France, but with the part of it which in most branches of
botany we have greatest reason to envy,—the Mediterranean provinces,—we find
that they, in this particular department, have cause to envy *us*, their powerful sun
and dry atmosphere, to which they owe their vegetable riches, being unfavourable
to the growth of nearly all the more beautiful Ferns. It is only the damper, Atlantic
provinces of France, the west and north-west, which offer any parallel in this
particular to our green commons and moist hedgesides. Our numerous Lastreas,
our Lady-Fern, our Polystichums, our Blechnum, our Osmunda, in the true South
are scarcely to be met with out of the mountains. Our Sussex *Hymenophyllum*,

[1]Jean Charles Marie Grenier (1808–75) and Dominique Alexandre Godron (1807–80),
*Flore de France, ou Description des plantes qui croissent naturellement en France et en
Corse*, 3 vols. (Paris: Baillière, 1848–56), Vol. III, pp. 623–42; and Charles Cardale
Babington (1808–95), *Manual of British Botany, Containing the Flowering Plants and
Ferns Arranged According to the Natural Orders* (London: Van Voorst, 1843).

except an indication in Corsica, is known as a French plant solely in Brittany. Even our common Brake, the *Pteris aquilina*, is rarely met with in the plains of the Mediterranean region. The only Ferns which are at all widely diffused in that portion of France, are the Ceterach, which, as in our western counties, abounds on walls and rocks; the commoner Aspleniums (*Trichomanes, Ruta-muraria*, and *Adiantum-nigrum*), the universal *Polypodium vulgare*, and, most beautiful of all, the Maidenhair, *Adiantum Capillus-Veneris*, which haunts the spray of falling water, and lines all cavities which combine dampness with depth of shade. Here, then, is one of the loveliest families of the Vegetable Kingdom, one of those which by their verdure, grace, and conspicuousness, and by their abundance in climates suited to them, do most to beautify the face of nature, and in which the opulent South cannot be for a moment compared in wealth with our modest northern latitudes.

Another advantage which we possess, and which has not perhaps been so much remarked upon, is our striking superiority over the South, considered generally, in the flowery beauty of our spring. We are indeed greatly surpassed in the mere number of species which flower at that, as at every other season. But the multitude and splendour of gregarious flowering plants which constitute the floral brilliancy of the South, and to which our mild summer can show nothing comparable, does not really begin until the *Cisti* are in bloom. Nearly the whole glory of an English April and May is derived from plants which, universal with us, are scarcely, or not at all, known in the South, except as mountain plants. We may count on our fingers the few ornaments of our spring which are common to us with the Mediterranean provinces of France. They possess the Celandine and the Sweet Violet in abundance. They have our Daisy, and our three common Buttercups, *R. repens*, *R. acris*, and *R. bulbosus*. *Cardamine pratensis* is found, but not, as with us, in almost every wood or hedge; only in irrigated meadows and by the sides of streams. Our common *Symphytum* abounds, and so does the common *Polygala*; and, best of all, the Blackthorn and the Whitethorn are as much at home in their hedges and thickets as in ours. Now, however, I am at the end of the list. I do not believe I have omitted anything of importance. On the other hand, mark the catalogue of our spring plants which (except in the mountains, or in some very peculiar localities) do not grow in the southern countries of Europe.

Of wood plants they have neither our Wood Anemone (*A. nemorosa*), nor our Wood Sorrel (*Oxalis Acetosella*), nor our Woodruff (*Asperula odorata*), nor our Primrose (*Primula vulgaris*), nor our Hyacinth (*Endymion nutans*), nor our Lily-of-the-valley (*Convallaria majalis*), nor the graceful *Adoxa Moschatellina*, nor the beautiful *Allium ursinum*. Of meadow plants they want the Cowslip (*Primula veris*), the Daffodil (*Narcissus Pseudo-narcissus*), the Marsh Marigold (*Caltha palustris*), and both our early Orchides, *O. mascula* and *O. Morio*. Of the plants which adorn our hedges and banks, they have neither the Wood Violet (*V. canina*, or *V. sylvatica*), the wild Strawberry (*Fragaria vesca*), the delicate

*Ranunculus auricomus*, the elegant white *Potentilla Fragariastrum*, the starry *Stellaria Holostea*, the fragrant Ground-ivy (*Nepeta Glechoma*), the cheerful *Mercurialis perennis*, nor the bright-eyed Germander Speedwell (*Veronica Chamaedrys*). There are but few of our water plants which flower in spring, but they want the loveliest of these, *Hottonia palustris*. Of early heath plants they have neither our Bilberry (*Vaccinium Myrtillus*), nor our brightly coloured *Pedicularis sylvatica*. Among flowering trees they have not at all, or but rarely, either the Crab-apple (*Pyrus Malus*) or the splendid White Beam-tree of our chalk-hills, the *Pyrus Aria*. A still greater deficiency is the absence of the two plants which by their masses of deep yellow, convert many of our spring landscapes into the likeness of Turner's pictures—the Furze (*Ulex europaeus*) and Broom (*Sarothamnus scoparius*). The former they do not possess at all, the latter nowhere in the plains, except occasionally about the roots of the mountain ranges.

It will be said, if they have not these plants, they have equivalents: and this is true, but the equivalents are seldom equally beautiful, and scarcely ever so abundant and so universal. The case of the Anemones is one of the most favourable which can be cited. The equivalent of *Anemone nemorosa* in central Italy is *A. apennina*, one of the doubtful plants of our Flora; and this is certainly as beautiful and nearly as abundant, where it prevails, as *A. nemorosa*, but it prevails only in a limited range. In southern Italy the place is occupied by the starlike *A. hortensis*. But neither of these is found, except as a rarity, in the south of France. The blue and red Anemone of our gardens, *A. coronaria*, is the most widely diffused of all the Anemones of the South, and in the places where it is most abundant, it is one of the most gorgeous flowers of the year. But this, though commoner than the two others, is but partially distributed in Mediterranean France. The substitutes for our Broom and Furze are much more inadequate. There is a small Furze, *Ulex provincialis*, (*parviflorus* of Grenier and Godron,)[2] extremely local in its distribution, neither so large nor so beautiful as our dwarf Furze, and which can at most be allowed to pair off with *Genista anglica*. In almost every part of Europe, however, there is some prickly Leguminous plant, which in early spring colours the landscape with its yellow blossoms. In Sicily it is *Calycotome spinosa*, formerly a Cytisus. In the south of France and the neighbouring provinces of Spain, it is *Genista Scorpius*, a low bush, whose thorny branches, spreading on every side, are very rough to handle. Later in the year those regions are dotted over with the stately and powerfully fragrant *Spartium junceum*, the Spanish Broom of our gardens; but this is a summer ornament, a plant of the Cistine period. Still later the *Genista tinctoria* displays itself with a beauty and luxuriance far greater than in our colder climate. Advancing from the plains to the mountain regions of the Cevennes and the eastern Pyrenees, and leaving the *Spartium junceum* at their foot, we come first upon the English Broom in the lower zone of the mountains, among the Chestnut and Beech woods; then, above these, another Broom, more

---

[2]Grenier and Godron, *Flore*, Vol. I, p. 344.

bushy, tougher, coarser, but still beautiful, *Sarothamnus purgans*. All these plants are highly gregarious, and colour great spaces of country in a similar manner to our Furze and Broom; but, if we except *S. junceum*, they are far inferior. Not one of them has either the height, the size of flowers, the delicate enamel-like polish of corolla, nor combines so rich a verdure with its golden inflorescence, as those matchless ornaments of our spring.

The *Narcissi* are perhaps the greatest riches of the vernal meadows in the South. The Daffodil is indeed absent, but *N. poeticus* is frequent, though nowhere but in the mountains have I seen it in any profusion: the meadows of the Pyrenees are positively white with its blossoms. Some of the many-flowered species of this genus are met with in the plains; in some localities *N. Tazetta* is frequent; the gorgeous *N. stellatus*, or *orientalis*, is found in others; and there is a *Narcissus* near Naples—probably *N. serotinus*—in flower all the winter, and with which I have seen the plain of Paestum quite covered in February. All these, however, are very local. *Veronica Teucrium* comes near in beauty to *V. Chamaedrys*, but is scarcely equal to it, and not nearly so universal. *Oxalis corniculata* (itself a British plant) is a poor substitute for *Oxalis Acetosella*; while, for the Primrose, Cowslip, Hyacinth, Woodruff, and Lily-of-the-valley, there is no equivalent at all. When we consider the exquisite beauty of all these, and the immense abundance of the three first in almost all neighbourhoods, and of the two last in some, the assertion will not appear paradoxical that the South, with all its number and variety of species, is on the whole poorer in those flowering plants which make spring beautiful, than our otherwise less favoured botanical region of the earth.

In what precedes, I have been speaking of the south of Europe generally. But there are particular places in it which, from local circumstances, combine much of the character of northern vegetation with that of the more sunny regions which surround them, and these places are the paradise of the botanist, as they are of the lover of Nature. I will endeavour to give an account of one of these, and will begin by describing its situation, since this determines the main peculiarities of its botanical character, and the richest Flora is almost always found among the most splendid scenery.

Whoever has been at Rome is familiar with at least the appearance of the group of noble though not very lofty mountains (for, indeed, it is visible from many streets of the city,) which stands isolated at some distance from the sea on one side, and from the mountain barrier of the Campagna on the other, and is the delight of painters by the aerial purple tint with which it fills up one-half of the southern side of the landscape. Almost all the part of these mountains which is visible from Rome is clothed with thick forests, but nearly their whole base on the northern and western sides is studded, at a small elevation above the plain, with a succession of small towns which, and their neighbourhood, are the resort of the richer Romans and resident foreigners during the unhealthy season. Omitting Frascati and other places which face to the north, the western base is occupied by Albano, La Riccia, and Gensano: Albano, which forms the angular point, being alone visible from

Rome. Both in scenery and in vegetation this place, more, perhaps, than any other in Italy, combines the peculiar character and features of southern Europe with a large share of those of England. Its elevation is sufficient to command the whole breadth of the Campagna, and a considerable space of sea beyond. The view from the western side of the town has the solemn, though not sombre, but cheerful, stateliness characteristic of Italian landscape, while on the land side the forests range from the summits of the mountains to the very border of the town, and on the boundary which separates the two regions, an avenue of full-grown forest trees, so rare in most parts of the Continent, stretches along the whole length of the winding road leading from Albano to the beautiful village of Castel Gandolfo, situated on the rim of the crater which holds the blue volcanic lake of Albano. Beyond Castel Gandolfo are grassy downs, which combine with the forest to produce the likeness of verdant England in the centre of Italy, and the resemblance extends to botany as well as to scenery. The spring Flora of this region is of an almost English character, though the particular species are mostly such as are either rare, or do not grow at all in England. On the downs of Castel Gandolfo are found *Hesperis* (now *Arabis*) *verna*, with its flower resembling Virginia Stock, and one of the most graceful of the *Irides*, *I. tuberosa*. Along the circuit of the lake, *Lunaria biennis*, the "Honesty" of our cottage-gardens, exhibits its lilac, cross-like flowers, and its large, flat, almost nummular, pods. Nearer to the town, *Lithospermum purpureo-coeruleum* puts forth its bright, metallic-looking blossoms. The woods abound with the yellow *Anemone ranunculoides*; the light-blue *Scilla bifolia*, with its hyacinth-like leaves; *Pulmonaria officinalis*, another plant of cottage-gardens, and indigenous in England, with its flowers of various hues on the same stalk, and its broadly-spotted leaves; the snowy *Allium pendulinum*; the rarer of our two species of Solomon's-seal (*Convallaria multiflora*); one of the smaller *Aristo-lochiae* (*A. longa*); the four-whorled and delicate-leaved *Asperula taurina*, a plant of the Alps; and the smaller of the two English *Symphyta*, *S. tuberosum*. Further on in the woods, towards La Riccia, we meet with *Narcissus poeticus*. Further still, near Gensano, we come upon the Bladder-nut of our shrubberies, *Staphylea pinnata*; *Dentaria bulbifera*, one of the finest of our rarer indigenous plants; and the blue Iris of our gardens, *I. germanica*. If we would ascend the highest member of the mountain-group, the Monte Cavo, we must make the circuit of the north flank of the mountains by Marino, on the edge of the Alban Lake, and Rocca di Papa, a picturesque village in the hollow mountain-side, from which we climb through woods abounding in *Galanthus nivalis* and *Corydalis cava*, to that summit which was the *arx* of Jupiter Latialis, and to which the thirty Latian cities ascended in solemn procession to offer their annual sacrifice. The place is now occupied by a convent, under the wall of which I gathered *Ornithogalum nutans*, and from its neighbourhood I enjoyed a panoramic view, surely the most glorious, in its combination of natural beauty and grandeur of historical recollections, to be found anywhere on earth.

The eye ranged from Terracina on one side to Veii on the other, and beyond Veii to the hills of Sutrium and Nepete, once covered by the Ciminian forests, then deemed an impenetrable barrier between the interior of Etruria and Rome. Below my feet, the Alban mountain, with all its forest-covered folds, and in one of them the dark-blue lake of Nemi: that of Albano, I think, was invisible. To the north, in the dim distance, the Eternal City; to the west, the eternal sea; for eastern boundary, the long line of Sabine mountains, from Soracte, past Tibur, and away towards Praeneste. The range then passed behind the Alban group, and became invisible, but reappeared to the south-east as the mountain-crescent of Cora and Pometia, enclosing between its horns the Pontine marshes, which lay spread out below as far as the sea-line, extending east and west, from Terracina in the bay of Fondi, the Volscian Anxur, to the angle of the coast where rises suddenly, between the marshes and the sea, the mountain promontory of Circeii, celebrated alike in history and in fable. Within the space visible from this one point the destinies of the human race were decided. It took the Romans nearly five hundred years to vanquish and incorporate the warlike tribes who inhabited that narrow tract, but this being accomplished, two hundred more sufficed them to complete the conquest of the world.

# Botany of Spain.
# A Few Days' Botanizing in the
# North-Eastern Provinces of Spain,
# in April and May, 1860

## AUGUST 1861–FEBRUARY 1862

*Phytologist*, n.s. V (Aug., Oct., Nov., Dec., 1861), 225–36, 296–303, 327–30, 356–62, and VI (Feb., 1862), 35–45. Running title: "Botany of Spain." The sub-headings in the text indicate the serial divisions; the printer's error in the last, numbering it "IV" rather than "V," has been corrected, and the many emendations indicated by Mill in the Somerville College copies of the articles have been accepted (see App. G for a list). Not signed, but identified in the table of contents as by Mill. Mill was accompanied on the trip by his step-daughter, Helen Taylor (1831–1907). Not republished. Identified in Mill's bibliography as "A series of papers entitled 'A few days Botanizing in the North Eastern Provinces of Spain in April and May 1860' published in the Phytologist for August, October, November, December 1861 and January [sic] 1862" (MacMinn, p. 94).

## No. I. Catalonia

THERE IS HARDLY ANY COUNTRY IN EUROPE whose floral treasures are less known to botanists than those of Spain. That country has produced few indigenous botanists. She possesses, practically speaking, no local Flora; the only one known to Europe being the old, rare, and costly work of Cavanilles, in which, along with such of the native plants as were known in his time, descriptions and figures are given of the American and other exotics cultivated in the Madrid Botanical Garden.[1] There is another book, which the present writer had never heard of, but which he saw on a bookstall at Barcelona; a *Flora of Spain*, bearing a date soon after the middle of the last century, in which the names given to species are Linnaean, but the genera are arranged on the simple and primitive plan of alphabetical order.[2] M. Boissier, to whom the botany of the Mediterranean basin is so much indebted, has made excursions in several parts of Spain, the botanical results of which have been published.[3] And this is nearly all which has been done for Spanish botany. Yet the country is one of the most largely endowed in our quarter of the globe, with the conditions on which variety of indigenous vegetation depends. It reaches further south than any country in Europe; the rock of Gibraltar being some fifty miles nearer to the Equator than the most southern promontories of Sicily or Greece. The low latitude of the northern provinces, compared with England, Germany, and the greater part of France, is more than compensated by their mountainous character, which renders their vegetation a copious sample of all northern climates, to the Arctic inclusive. Modern investigation has shown that there is as marked a difference between the western and eastern Floras, as between the northern and southern; and of this distribution also, both branches are fully represented in the Peninsula. Its northern and western coasts, especially if we include Portugal, are the typical example of the western or Atlantic Flora; while the dry eastern districts, from the Pyrenees to Carthagena (and no doubt the south coast also), belong in all respects to the Mediterranean portion of the eastern botanical region. Of soils there are all varieties, from the richest alluvion to the barest granitic or calcareous rock; and the proportion of waste is probably unequalled in any European country, Greece and Turkey excepted.

That a country with these attractions to botanists, should have been so little explored by them, is an effect, doubtless, of the same causes which have made, until lately, the resort of travellers thither, for any but commercial purposes, comparatively infrequent; the disturbed state of the country through civil war, the danger from banditti, and the absence of the facilities for travelling afforded by roads, inns, and means of conveyance. The first two of these hindrances have completely, and, it is to be hoped, permanently disappeared. Civil wars are ended, and brigands are now never heard of. The remaining difficulties are in a course of

---

[1] Antonio José Cavanilles (1745–1804), *Icones et descriptiones plantarum, quae aut sponte in Hispania crescunt*, 6 vols. (Madrid: Royal Printer, 1791–1801).

[2] Almost certainly José Quer y Martinez (1695–1764), *Flora Española ó historia de las plantas que se crian en España*, 4 vols. (Madrid: Ibarra, 1762–64).

[3] Pierre Edmond Boissier (1810–85), *Voyage botanique dans le midi de l'Espagne pendant l'année 1837*, 2 vols. (Paris: Gide, 1839–45).

rapid removal. Security and freedom—for in spite of the imperfections of her institutions and of her administration, Spain is a free country—are producing their natural fruits. The impulse given to the national mind by political emancipation; the freedom of speaking and printing which has been enjoyed for nearly a generation; the downfall of the Inquisition, and the decline of the great enemy of modern ideas, the Catholic hierarchy (for Spain, though still a Catholic, is no longer a priest-ridden country) have brought that fine people once more into the full current of European civilization. In the material department of national improvement, Spain is rapidly recovering her lost ground. Instead of the desolate and neglected appearance which we are taught to expect, every province which I visited, except the naturally arid and unfertile plain of Aragon, wore the appearance of diligent and careful agriculture, and not unfrequently of active and successful manufacturing industry. The soil of Spain will soon be completely intersected by railroads. The lines from Madrid to Valencia and Alicante, from Cadiz through Xeres and Seville to Cordova, are open throughout. Of those from Madrid to the French frontier, at both extremities of the Pyrenean chain, large portions have been opened, as well as many shorter and branch railways. The common roads are now numerous, and some of them good. The diligences surprise one by their number. Their rapidity was already noted at a time when the state of the road seemed hardly compatible with that quality. But what most surpassed my expectation was the inns. My experience is indeed limited to a few provinces. There, however, they are not only, in the great towns, very tolerable, but even in small roadside places we found them equal to the small country inns of France. The hotels of Madrid, indeed, cannot be compared to those of the great towns of France, and are inferior to those of some places in Spain itself; but Madrid, except in being the seat of the government and Court, is the capital of Castile rather than of Spain. At Barcelona, Valencia, and Zaragoza, there are hotels about on a par with those of provincial towns of secondary rank in France; while not only at places like Tarragona or Guadalaxara, but even at an insignificant village like Alcolea, on the plateau of Castile, a hamlet distinguished by nothing but by being one of the stopping-places of the diligences from Madrid to Zaragoza, we found a roadside inn at which it was possible to sleep and even to make some stay in comfort. I should not indeed advise any one to travel in these provinces in the months of August and September, both on account of the heat, and of the plague of insects which might at that season be expected. But these months are later or earlier than a botanist in the south of Europe has any inducement to travel. Botanists, walking tourists, and all who are accustomed to penetrate into the nooks and corners of a country, will find Spain, in the present day, no more closed to them than any other part of Europe.

I should not presume to offer as worthy of attention, such fragmentary notices as I could pick up in a mere run through any country whose botany was known, and which possessed local Floras. Even as regards Spain, my passing observations have little of the value which would belong to those of a profound botanist. My only qualifications are delight in the subject, and some acquaintance with a considerable portion of the general Flora of Southern Europe. I have therefore to apologize beforehand for many deficiencies, and doubtless for some errors. It requires a really good botanist to investigate the plants of a country, with a universal "Species Plantarum" for his sole guide: neither can a traveller carry about with him De Candolle's *Prodromus* and Kunth's *Enumeratio*,[4] which, moreover, even joined together, are not complete; and to determine plants by them afterwards from dried specimens, is a task of which every one knows the difficulty. The books I had with me were the *Flore de France*, by Grenier and Godron; Woods' *Tourist's Flora* (in which Spain is not included);[5] and by way of a general Flora, the Compendium of Persoon,[6] which, notwithstanding the extreme brevity and frequent want of precision of its descriptions, enabled me to determine some plants which I could not otherwise have identified. I must premise further, that the only mode of travelling in Spain (except on horseback) being by public conveyances, want of time, and of information as to halting-places, confined us for the most part to journeys from one large town to another; and the rapid pace of the diligences precluded even that common resource of Continental travelling, taking advantage of hills for pedestrian exploration of roadsides. My experience therefore of Spanish botany was mostly confined to the immediate vicinity of considerable towns. Of the intermediate spaces I saw, in general, only what could be seen from a diligence drawn by from ten to sixteen mules at full gallop, or through the windows of a railway carriage; and thus, although I passed a whole month in Spain, I had but a few days of real botanizing during that period, which extended from the middle of April to the middle of May, in an extremely backward season. It is a proof of the botanical riches of the country, that with only these opportunities and such imperfect qualifications, I can still furnish a respectable list of plants.

The province which I first visited, and of which I saw most, was Catalonia; which, both botanically and geologically, may serve as a representative of the whole north-east region of Spain. It differs from Aragon and Valencia chiefly in being more mountainous. Its northern portion is a confused heap of mountains; and all the way to Barcelona these come down to, or very near, the sea. Towards Barcelona they open out into a crescent of no great depth, leaving a semicircular plain, in the centre of which, on the sea, stands this fine city, rich in the signs of

[4]Carl Sigismund Kunth (1788–1850), *Enumeratio plantarum omnium hucusque cognitarum*, 5 vols. in 6 (Stuttgart and Tübingen: Cotta, 1833–50).

[5]Joseph Woods (1776–1864), *The Tourist's Flora: A Descriptive Catalogue of the Flowering Plants and Ferns of the British Islands, France, Germany, Switzerland, Italy, and the Italian Islands* (London: Reeve, *et al.*, 1850).

[6]Christiaan Henrik Persoon (1761–1836), *Synopsis plantarum, seu enchiridium botanicum*, 2 vols. (Paris: Cramer, *et al.*, 1805–07).

prosperous industry, and hemmed in by a girdle of populous villages as prosperous as itself. Close beside it, on a hill cultivated to the top, is the celebrated but not formidable-looking fortress of Monjuich, the scene of so many exploits in the old wars. The plain is rich and fertile, without artificial irrigation, at least in the usual Spanish manner, by canals. Such irrigational apparatus as I saw (all of which was quite close to Barcelona) consisted of those curious irrigation-towers, the work of the Saracens, which form a conspicuous, and, at first sight, a puzzling feature in the country about Palermo. The plain is crossed here and there by gullies, cut deep into the soil by the torrents of rain which must descend at certain seasons from the adjacent mountains.

The conditions of soil and climate in Catalonia, are much the same as in the Mediterranean provinces of France, and the botany accordingly is very similar. It is the country of the Olive, the Fig, the Vine, and, further south, of the spreading and shady but stiff-leaved Caruba (*Ceratonia Siliqua*) but not of the Orange and the Myrtle. The aloe (*Agave americana*), and the Prickly Pear (*Cactus Opuntia*) are found; but not, as in Sicily, in wild abundance, forming a great feature in the landscape. The first chiefly appears in the form of hedges (as in Roussillon); and the Cactus I did not observe further north than Tarragona. There too I first came upon the Palmetto (*Chamaerops humilis*), the dwarfish representative of the mighty family of *Palmae*; that stiff low prickly bush which half covers with its *chevaux-de-frise* of fan-like leaves the vast wastes of Sicily. It abounds also on the line of road from Tarragona to Valencia, and its fibres are made into a kind of matting, the production of which is part of the domestic industry of the country. The plants of the Catalonian landscape were chiefly those of the rocky calcareous wilds of Languedoc and Provence, called locally *Garrigues*, from the provincial name (according to M. Léonce de Lavergne) of the dwarf evergreen Oak which covers them;[7] the *Quercus coccifera*, in which the *Kermes* insect, the European variety of the cochineal, elaborates its brilliant dye. This, and *Quercus Ilex*, are the principal representatives of the old Order *Amentaceae*. *Pistacia Lentiscus*, the Mastic-tree of Scripture[8] (to my surprise I saw little of the still finer *P. Terebinthus*, though equally or more common in the south of France); the fragrant Tree-Heath (*Erica arborea*); the still more powerfully odorous woody Thyme (*Thymus vulgaris*), inferior in beauty, but superior in odour to our *T. Serpyllum* (which grows there also); that common southern plant, the Rosemary (*Rosmarinus officinalis*); the Spanish Broom of our gardens (*Spartium junceum*) with its intoxicating perfume; the prickly Broom of the south of France (*Genista Scorpius*), which though humbler in stature than our tall Furze, colours the

---

[7]Louis Gabriel Léonce Guilhard de Lavergne (1809–80), economist and politician, *Economie rurale de la France depuis 1789* (1860), 2nd ed. (Paris: Guillaumin, 1861), p. 281.

[8]In the Apocryphya, Susanna, 54.

landscape in spring with similar masses of brilliant yellow, while it projects its sword-like flowering branches vertically and laterally, like the dwarf autumnal Furze of our commons; these form the most conspicuous clothing of the uncultivated ground in the coast region of Catalonia. The honeyed *Koniga maritima*, in flower at all seasons, and especially after other flowers have disappeared, covers the ground, both waste and cultivated, to great distances from the sea; and another winter plant, *Diplotaxis erucoides* (which is brought into Rome by cartloads in full flower throughout January), adorns the cultivated lands with its light-grey cruciform blossoms. If to these we add several species of *Cistus* and *Helianthemum* (of which hereafter), a tolerably complete idea is given of the vegetation, as it exhibits itself at this season to an eye merely wandering over the face of the country.

To proceed to local details; the plants of Barcelona may be divided into those of the plain, and those of the crescent of low calcareous mountains which overlook it. The brightest flower of the plain, in these spring months, is *Hypecoum procumbens*, a Papaveraceous plant, with a flower like that of *Chelidonium majus*, and about as large, though the plant itself is small in comparison. It has a long, crooked pod, and its leaves are cut like those of an *Erodium*. Notwithstanding the name *procumbens*, the plant, though spreading, is erect, and grows copiously among the corn, in appearance like an agrarian *Ranunculus*, of greater size and finer quality than *R. arvensis*. I found this plant in other parts of Spain, and I had already found it near Perpignan. I will not affirm that some of it may not be *H. grandiflorum*, if there be any real difference between the two. I met with another undoubtedly different *Hypecoum* further south, which will be commemorated in its place. Of *Ranunculi* I noticed near Barcelona only *R. bulbosus*, and the aquatic but not batrachian species *muricatus*, allied to *sceleratus*, but with a fruit of a somewhat similar character to *arvensis*. A fine *Fumaria*, with large white and purple flowers (which I also saw near Perpignan), seemed to be *muralis* of Grenier and Godron;[9] but those authors, I observe, have on reconsideration decided their plant to be not one species but three, none of them the true *muralis* of Sonder.[10] The *Cruciferae* I noticed were those common plants of southern France, *Sisymbrium irio* and *obtusangulum*, and *Lepidium Draba*. *Reseda Phyteuma*, a plant nearly resembling *odorata*, but without its smell, was here, as in most parts of the south of Europe, abundant. This plant reaches so far north in France, that it might well have been looked for in England. The family *Geraniaceae* is represented by *Erodium malachoides*. *Oxalis corniculata*, and the brittle bush *Coriaria myrtifolia*, with its currant-like racemes clothing its dry-looking branches long before the leaves come out, are here common. Of Leguminous

[9]*Flore de France*, Vol. I, p. 67.
[10]Otto Wilhelm Sonder (1812–81), *Flora Hamburgensis* (Hamburg: Kittler, 1851), p. 385.

plants, the most worthy of notice is *Lathyrus Ochrus*, a procumbent species, with large oval leaflets, (like a greater and paler *L. Aphaca*,) which haunts, as in Sicily, low moist places in the alluvial ground. The place of our *Lotus corniculatus* is taken by another Sicilian plant, the equally yellow and not less elegant *L. ornithopodioides*. Another Leguminous plant, with oval leaflets and round leaf-life stipules, is *Arthrolobium* (formerly *Ornithopus*) *scorpioides*. Of *Rosaceae*, the principal is that happily ubiquitous shrub, the Hawthorn; I did not examine whether in both its forms or only in one. It is curious that the form *monogyna* is sometimes the only one found in a large tract of country. According to Gussone, there is no other in Sicily.[11] The only *Potentilla* I saw was *P. verna*, which is rather frequent. The Composites were those common in the south: *Sonchus tenerrimus*, like our common Sowthistle, but much more fragile and delicate; *Picridium vulgare*, with its urceolate flowers and hard scarious phyllaries; that ornament of banks, *Urospermum Dalechampii*, and the coarser *U. picroides*; the small Marigold, *Calendula arvensis*; this last is found as far north as Normandy, and I believe no botanist knows, any more than myself, why it does not grow in Kent. Who can tell why *Specularia Speculum*, the Venus's Looking-glass of our gardens, comes up to the very Straits of Dover as a cornfield plant, while, though so generally cultivated in England, we never see it wild, even as an escape from culture?—or why *Orlaya grandiflora*, which I have gathered in cornfields between Boulogne and St. Omer, should not be found in England at all?—or why that commonest of Continental weeds, even on the sands opposite the English coast, *Eryngium campestre*, should be the rarest of rare plants in England, and should not spread even when introduced as a ballast plant. These secrets of vegetation will, perhaps, be some day unveiled. The only Thistles in flower near Barcelona, at this early season, were the same as in Sicily; *Carduus pycnocephalus* (allied to *C. tenuiflorus*) and the elegant *Galactites tomentosa*. Of *Boragineae*, I observed the common Borage, and a fine *Echium*, perhaps the *violaceum* of the Channel Islands, but it was not sufficiently advanced to enable me to distinguish it with perfect certainty from *E. plantagineum*, one of the handsomest of the tribe, which, as well as others, has been confounded under the name *violaceum*. The *Scrophularineae* were *Antirrhinum Orontium*; the brilliantly yellow *Linaria supina*; *Scrophularia peregrina* of Italy and Sicily; *S. canina* of southern and middle Europe. The genus *Euphorbia* was largely represented: *E. Peplus* and *helioscopia* of course; those fine plants *serrata* and *Characias*, the first common in the south of France, the second everywhere in the South (*E. Cyparissias* and *gerardiana*, so frequent in southern Europe, I did not see); but the principal *Euphorbia* of the plain of Barcelona is *E. terracina*, less striking in appearance

[11]Giovanni Gussone (1787–1866), author of *Florae siculae synopsis exhibens plantas vasculares in Sicilia insulisque adjacentibus huc usque detectas*, 2 vols. (Naples: Tramater, 1842–43), which is cited below, though this reference has not been located.

than some of these, but more curious when examined. The calycinal glands characteristic of the genus, which in this, as in many other species, are of a crescent form, are terminated in *E. terracina* by a pair of setae, exactly resembling the antennae of an insect. The *Monocotyledoneae* which I noted were that common weed *Muscari comosum*, the wild original of one of the ornaments of our gardens, and *Asphodelus fistulosus*, the smallest European species of its genus, not general in the south of France, though not unknown there, but most plentiful here as well as in Sicily. Of Ferns, no abundance could be expected in these dry climates, but the Ceterach grew plentifully here and elsewhere, as did also the Maidenhair (*Adiantum Capillus-Veneris*), wherever there was local dampness and depth of shade.

The mountain Flora of Barcelona is much more copious, and as I explored it twice, at some interval of time, I can give a rather fuller account of it. Apart from their form and composition, these heights would scarcely be entitled to a more ambitious name than that of hills. The range, at least this part of it, is of small breadth, and the line of summit looks down upon a wide extent of country, rugged and rocky enough, but of little elevation, though varied with occasional eminences, among which the lofty and many-pinnacled ridge of Monserrat is supreme. The rocks of the maritime range are calcareous, like those of Bas-Languedoc and Provence, and the mountain sides are cut through by deep ravines, of which the gullies that intersect the plain are a continuation. The rocks, though in most parts thickly clothed with bushy shrubs, show few trees, except a pine-grove here and there. The species of the Pine I did not verify, but it had the aspect of *P. halepensis*, the common Pine of the Mediterranean provinces of France. The remaining wood was chiefly *Ilex*, kept low and bushy by the woodcutters. The floral treasures of this range are considerable. *Leguminosae* are the most abundant. Besides the thorny *Genista Scorpius* and the Spanish Broom, I noticed two other plants of kindred character: the Furze which fills so large a place in the winter Flora of Provence (*Ulex parviflorus*, or *provincialis*), and the thorny Cytisus, which covers Sicily in March with its yellow blossoms, *Calycotome spinosa*, unless I am mistaken in this last, which was not yet in flower. Of non-thorny Cytisi there were as many as three: *C. candicans* (*Genista* of some authors), one of the most elegant, and here the most flowery of this elegant genus; *C. triflorus*, a shrub of the height of a man, which blackens in drying, and with which all who have botanized near Naples must be familiar; and the dwarfish *C. argenteus* (by some called *Argyrolobium linnaeanum*), one of the *Garrigue* plants of the south of France. *Anthyllis* was represented by *A. tetraphylla*, a Palermo plant; *Trifolium*, by the well-named *T. stellatum*; *Medicago* by several, which, for want of sufficiently developed fruits, I did not determine, but which were apparently some of the common ones of the south of France,—*M. minima, denticulata, praecox, Gerardi, orbicularis*, or *marginata*. The commonest of the *Coronillae* of southern France, *C. Emerus*, made a large display of its loosely hung blossoms. Here, as everywhere in Spain, the *Hippocrepis comosa*, the charm of English chalk hills, brought pleasant remembrances of the floral beauties of Surrey and Kent, though often, doubtless, confounded with *H. glauca*, a plant equally common, and if specifically different, perfectly resembling *comosa* in habit and general appearance. The *Lathyri* were represented by the delicate and slender *L. setifolius*, and the large-flowered *L. Clymenum* (*tenuifolius* of Gussone),[12] which I have also found at Perpignan and at Palermo. *Vicia* presented me with *V. tenuifolia* of Roth,[13] an improved likeness of *V. Cracca*; and the much less beautiful *triflora* of Tenore,[14] the first plant I met with which is not a native of France. *Astragalus* offered a species rather insignificant in appearance, *A. sesameus*, a plant not unlike, at the first glance, to *Bisserrula Pelecinus*; and another, the commonest, but one of the most gorgeous of this splendid genus, which grows in Normandy, and ought to grow in Kent, *A. monspessulanus*. My Catalonian specimens were not of the usual colour, but paler, and with a mixture of yellow; a character attributed to the neighbouring *A. incanus*, but not, so far as I know, to any form of *monspessulanus*; this plant, however, seemed to possess the essential characters of the more common species. Among *Leguminosae* not yet in flower, I may mention two common plants of southern Europe, the bushy *Dorycnium suffruticosum*, with its small round heads of pale flowers, which I have known to whiten at a distance large spaces of ground; and the trefoiled *Psoralea bituminosa*, with its elegant flowering clusters, and long axillary peduncles.

The greatest ornaments however of these bushy hills were the *Cisti*, which form in some places a great part of the whole vegetation. Without reckoning Helianthemums, there were four species of *Cistus* proper; bushes covered all over with large and brilliant blossoms; the decumbent *salviaefolius*, with its milk-white cups; the erect *albidus*, with its grey foliage and delicate mallow-coloured flowers, larger than the largest wild Rose; the stiffish, narrow-leaved *monspeliensis*, with flowers rather smaller than *salviaefolius*, flat and wheel-like, instead of cup-shaped; and a rarer species than any of these, *C. Ledon*, which, with *monspeliensis*, by their viscous touch, and rich resinous smell, form a transition to the real European Gum Cisti, *C. ladaniferus* and *laurifolius*. The *Cisti*, happily for Spanish landscape, are, like the *Ericae*, gregarious plants, and, of all *Cisti* I know, none are so gregarious as *C. Ledon*. Near Perpignan, and on the plateau of Morières, near Avignon, it covers acres of ground. Of *Corolliflorae* not previously mentioned, I noticed a *Verbascum*, probably *V. Boerhavii*; the deep blue *Lithospermum purpurocaeruleum*, not unknown in England, and one of the most frequent as well as beautiful of the wood and thicket plants of the South in April

---

[12]*Florae siculae*, Vol. II, p. 278.
[13]Albrecht Wilhelm Roth (1757–1834), *Tentamen florae germanicae*, 3 vols. in 4 (Leipzig: Müller, 1788), Vol. I, p. 309.
[14]Michele Tenore (1780–1861), *Catalogus plantarum horti regii Neapolitani ad annum 1813*, 2 pts. (Naples: Trani, 1813, 1819), p. 112.

and May; *Veronica Teucrium*, which vies with, if it does not surpass our beautiful *Chamaedrys*; that curious plant, *Lavandula Stoechas*, named, like several other plants, from the isles of Hyères, but tolerably general in the south of Europe; and *Stachys hirta*, a plant in France confined to the extreme south-eastern corner. Other plants in flower were, a rare but rather dull-looking *Polygala*, *P. rupestris*, growing in clefts of the rocks; *Paronychia argentea*, one of the ornaments of Sicily, carpeting the ground with its silvery inflorescence and herbage; *Osyris alba*, a scraggy bush of the family *Eleagneae*, abundant in the South, which, covered at this season with yellow blossoms, fills the air all around with a powerful fragrance like that of the *Galia*. At the back of the ridge, looking towards the north and north-west, I came upon plants of a decidedly English character. *Euphorbia Characias* and *serrata* were replaced by *E. amygdaloides*; and I found here the first Orchid I saw in Spain, *Cephalanthera ensifolia*, a rare, but still a British species. Our common wild Strawberry was occasionally visible. These were nearly all the plants of interest which I saw in flower. Most of the *Compositae* were not yet in a state to be recognizable. The only ones in flower were *Senecio vulgaris* and *viscosus*. *Inula viscosa*, and *Phagnalon* (or *Conyza*) *saxatile* were distinguishable. The plants not in flower included several of the most characteristic shrubs of southern Europe: the gorgeous Pomegranate, the evergreen *Phillyraea media*, the common *Arbutus* (*A. Unedo*), and one of the most powerfully and sweetly odoriferous of European climbers, which retains its fragrance for many years in the herbarium, *Smilax aspera*. To these let me add the perfoliate *Lonicera implexa*, and another Honeysuckle, which was probably *etrusca*, the other common one of the South; for our Woodbine is in southern Europe a mountain plant, and our garden *L. caprifolium* I have seen wild only in Italy. The curious *Asparagus acutifolius*; *Bupleurum rigidum*, one of the oddest species of a genus already anomalous among Umbellifers; and *Daphne Gnidium*, an ornament of late summer and autumn, complete the list of my observations in the Barcelona mountains, with the exception of Monserrat, the copious botany of which I keep for a separate notice.

Many of the plants above enumerated, I afterwards met with in the same line of country further north, where another evergreen oak, the Cork tree (*Quercus Suber*), abounds, and its produce is an important article of commerce. Here, too, the English Broom, *Sarothamnus scoparius*, makes its appearance, even in the plain, at least near the foot of the mountains. Other common English plants, *Stellaria Holostea*, *Chrysanthemum segetum*, *Centaurea Cyanus*, are abundantly visible to the passing eye, together with *Lavandula Stoechas*, *Cistus albidus* and *salviaefolius*, *Ulex parviflorus*, *Euphorbia terracina* and *amygdaloides*, *Muscari comosum*, and an *Ononis*, probably *Natrix*. In the woody hills near Gerona, in the middle of May, I had a botanical walk of considerable interest. A deep shady wood of deciduous trees afforded the beautiful *Geum sylvaticum* (otherwise *atlanticum*). This, with *Onobrychis supina*, and the dwarfish and quaint *Lithospermum apulum*, I observed nowhere else in Spain. I found also (besides many of the Barcelona plants) the beautiful *Allium roseum*, the rush-like *Aphyllanthes monspeliensis*, with its large and curiously lined azure flowers, the narrow-leaved *Phillyraea* (*P. angustifolia*) of our shrubberies; a *Sideritis*, (I believe *S. hirsuta*); and a characteristically southern tree of the family *Urticeae*, *Celtis australis*, the *Micocoulier* of the south of France: not to mention *Helleborus foetidus*, *Aquilegia vulgaris*, *Alyssum calycimum*, *Potentilla reptans*, and sundry common *Ranunculi* and *Helianthema*.

## No. II. Tarragona, Valencia, Zaragoza [1]

THE PLACE IN SPAIN which added most to my Barcelona stock of plants, was Tarragona; a fortified town, picturesquely situated on a hill overlooking a broad space of sea from north to south, and commanding westward a wide stretch of uneven rocky ground, in which cultivation and waste are blended in varying proportions. I will not lengthen the record by speaking again of any plant mentioned in my former paper, except *Dorycnium suffruticosum*, *Lonicera implexa*, and *Phagnalon saxatile*, all of which I here found in flower; and except the Prickly Pear and Palmetto, which I have already mentioned that I first saw at this place. Here too was another *Cistus*, with large white flowers, *Cistus umbellatus*, a *Helianthemum* of some writers; and growing copiously on a wild rocky hill, the original *Gladiolus* of our flower-gardens, *G. byzantinus*, far more beautiful, to my thinking, than the spotted ones of modern introduction. This plant I had only before seen wild at Floridia, near Syracuse. It is not a plant of the French Flora, though France can boast of several species of this fine genus. The one I best know, *G. communis* of Bertoloni, *segetum* of Grenier and Godron,[15] which grows profusely in the corn at Avignon and elsewhere, is of a paler colour than *G. byzantinus*, with petals of more unequal length, and hung more loosely together. The *G. communis* of the French botanists I do not know.[16]

But Tarragona supplied too great a harvest of botanical treasures to be catalogued wtihout some sort of arrangement. To begin, then, at the beginning, I will first mention *Clematis Flammula*, the decumbent though climbing species of the south of Europe; where however the more luxuriant Clematis of our own hedges and thickets is also not unfrequent. This last I do not remember seeing in Spain, except at Monserrat. Of Fumitories there were two, the *parviflora*, and a less common plant, with a dense oval head of dark flowers, *F. spicata*. The remaining *Thalamiflorae* which I noticed were those common *garrigue* Helian-

[15] Antonio Bertoloni (1775–1869), *Flora italica*, 10 vols. (Bologna: Masi, 1833–54), Vol. I, pp. 227–9; and Grenier and Godron, *Flore de France*, Vol. III, p. 248. (Grenier and Godron refer to Bertoloni's identification at Vol. III, p. 227.)
[16] Grenier and Godron, Vol. III, p. 248.

themums, the white *H. pilosum* (allied to *polifolium*) and that very variable plant, the bright-yellow *H. italicum*; three species of *Silene*, *S. quinquevulnera*, *S. hispida* (I believe) of Desfontaines, recognized by the *Flore de France* only as a Corsican plant,[17] and a third (*S. turbinata*), not in the French Flora at all, which will be more particularly mentioned hereafter; *Althaea hirsuta*, a plant rather general in the South; *Erodium romanum*, still more common, resembling a large-flowered *E. cicutarium*, without a stem; and one of the common Rues of the south of France (with the characteristic odour), *Ruta angustifolia*. Of *Leguminosae* there was still greater variety. To many of the Barcelona species were added *Lotus edulis*, with its thick curved pods, a plant which I had found in Sicily; and a *Melilotus*, I believe *sulcata*; the densely downy *Medicago marina*, the only beach plant in flower here at this period of the season; a *Scorpiurus*, probably the common species, *S. subvillosa*, though its backward condition disables me from speaking positively; and a *Hippocrepis*, much more curious than the *comosa*, *H. ciliata*, whose slender, jointed, crescent-shaped pods are scooped out on the inner side in bay-like, nearly circular indentations, penetrating beyond the middle of the breadth, and justifying the title of Horse-shoe Vetch. This plant was long confounded with *H. multisiliquosa*, L., which it seems is a different species; but those who have seen our plant side by side with *H. unisiliquosa*, will feel tempted to persist in giving it the contrasted name. The next in order of the plants which I noticed, is the blue *Asperula arvensis*. The *Compositae* included the common Immortelle of the *garrigues*, *Helichrysum Stoechas*; a *Santolina* (I believe) which I also found further south, but which I will not venture to name; the brilliant *Chrysanthemum coronarium*, only coming into flower; a most delicate little plant, the annual Daisy (*Bellis annua*), more daintily coloured but more humble-looking than even its better-known sister; and lastly, one of the most curious of the *Cynareae*, *Leuzea conifera*, not six inches high, with a flower occupying half its length, like a yellowish-white cone, with a small opening at the top. The *Corolliflorae* were many and interesting: the exquisitely coloured *Anagallis caerulea*; the splendid *Convolvulus althaeoides*, in size resembling *C. sepium*, L., in colour, *C. arvensis*; the creeping *Echium calycinum*, one of the least beautiful of its handsome tribe; our common Snapdragon, *Antirrhinum majus*, which here and in Languedoc is as splendid as in English flower-gardens; *Linaria triphyllos*, a plant of cultivated ground, and its taller but less conspicuous sister, *L. simplex*; one of the handsomest of the genus *Orobanche*, *O. speciosa*, in the same field as the *Linaria* first mentioned; *Plantago Lagopus*, and the rarer and more curious *P. albicans*; and six of the family *Labiatae*, being *Mentha rotundifolia*; the common Lavender, *Lavandula Spica*; that common plant of the south of Europe, *Sideritis romana*; *Salvia clandestina* (otherwise *horminoides*), an ally of *S. verbenaca*;

[17]René Louiche Desfontaines (1750–1833), *Catalogus plantarum horti regii Parisiensis*, 3rd ed. (Paris: Chaudé, 1829), p. 263; and Grenier and Godron, Vol. I, p. 205.

*Micromeria graeca*, one of a small-leaved, wiry genus, detached from *Satureia*, and characteristic of the extreme south of Europe; and, last of all, the magnificent *Phlomis Lychnitis*, covered with a grey down all over, except the large bright-yellow flowers. This genus counts, I believe, only three European species, which are at the head of European *Labiatae* in the size and brilliancy combined with the multitude of their flowers. One of the species, *P. Herba-venti*, is widely and rather copiously branched, forming, though herbaceous, a kind of small bush; it is found at Montpellier and other places in the south of France. Our species, *P. Lychnitis*, has a simple stem, with great whorls of flowers, like those of the taller and still more magnificent ornament of Sicily and Greece, *P. fruticosa*. The *Apetalae* I noticed were *Euphorbia flavicoma*, *segetalis*, and *Paralias* (the last not yet in flower); an *Urtica* of the *pilulifera* section, possibly *pilulifera* itself, which I did not stop to determine; and the picturesque *Passerina hirsuta*, not a beach plant, but seldom or never found far from the sea, and which in February hangs in profusion from the cliffs of Bagnoli, on the approach to Pozzuoli from Naples. Of Monocotyledonous plants the handsomest I saw, except the *Gladiolus*, was a plant looking like a *Scilla* or *Hyacinthus*, and with small pendent flowers, of a bluish colour (if I remember right) while growing, but turning red in drying. The petals, which are united at the base, consist of three shorter and broader, alternating with and included within the same number of longer. This I decided to be *Uropetalum serotinum* (*Lachenalia serotina* of some authors). I found but one specimen. A more singular plant was an Asparagus, of which more hereafter. These, with *Juncus acutus*, on wet ground near the sea, and two grasses, *Gastridium lendigerum* and the beautiful *Lamarckia aurea* (which, in spite of its name, is, at least until withered, rather silvery than golden), complete the record of the best and richest herborization (that of Monserrat excepted) which I have made on Spanish soil. Properly however it was not one, but two herborizations on the same ground, at an interval of about a fortnight.

From each of the other centres at which I halted in my journey, I made but one botanizing expedition. The results however were not without interest.

The plain, well named Huerta (garden) of Valencia, has been often described. It is a rich mass of cultivation, fertilized by the elaborate system of irrigation for which it is indebted to the Moors, consisting of canals traversing the country above its level, from which large or small ramifications are carried into or along the edge of every field. The rivers, which from the shortness of their course are nowhere considerable, are so drained by the canals that in summer they may be crossed dry-shod as they approach the sea. A region of this character is seldom favourable to the botanist; and the mountains, if that name may be given to the heights which support the great plateau of Castille, are too far off to be within reach of an ordinary excursion. The wild plants therefore were chiefly those of cultivated ground, or of the damp borders of streams; of the former class, two were especially abundant and conspicuous: *Allium roseum*, which had delighted me on the hills of Patras and elsewhere, with its umbels of brilliant flowers; and a tall large-flowered *Silene*, with something of the port and colour of the elegant *Lychnis Viscaria*. This plant, which is not in the French Flora, I make out to be *S. turbinata* of Gussone.[18] Of more common plants I observed *Anagallis arvensis*, and a frequent corn plant in eastern and southern Europe, *Saponaria Vaccaria*. The waterside species which I remarked were *Euphorbia pilosa*, a large species, in a dense greyish coat, which frequents similar situations in the valley of the Rhone, and other parts of the South; the universal *Iris Pseudacorus*; and a gigantic *Thalictrum*, which I had not the means of determining. This is a poor tale of plants for so southern a region; but after about an hour's walk, I came to a patch of rocky ground, which, being above the region of the irrigation, had remained in the state of *garrigue*, or had only vines and olives growing on it, and this furnished me with plants of a different order and greater variety. Here I first saw the lurid and night-odorous Stock of English greenhouses, *Matthiola tristis*, a plant which also grows in Provence. The *garrigue* abounded with the narrow-leaved and silvery *Convolvulus Cneorum*, bringing reminiscences of Megara and Corinth. A *Hedysarum*, I believe *H. humile*, made its appearance in small quantity, as did the uniformly grey and downy *Mercurialis tomentosa*, unlike the dark-green hue of the two English species, and with its fructification not spiked but clustered or solitary. Here I again saw *Hippocrepis ciliata* and *Smilax aspera*. The decumbent *Alkanna tinctoria* (formerly a *Lithospermum*) spread out as usual its stems close to the ground, with their terminal clusters of blue flowers, and their thick covering of leaves, incrusted underneath with the dense calcareous soil in which the plant delights. In the herbarium it sometimes stains the paper with a violet dye. I found here, though in small quantity, a species not French (*angustifolia*, I believe), of the very southern genus *Sideritis*, which, by its wiry look and the spinous induration of its sepals, speaks plainly of the arid climates in which it flourishes. But the strangest plant I saw was a bushy mass of Thorns, exactly resembling a small furze-bush in winter, when without traces of leaves; until, on looking for the yellow papilionaceous blossoms, I perceived instead a profusion of small greenish hexandrous flowers, pendent on short thin footstalks from near the axillae of the wiry and thorny sprays projecting from the stem. By the aid of Persoon I identified this as a plant of Spain, and especially of this part of it, *Asparagus horridus*.[19] It is the same which I afterwards found, in my way back, at Tarragona.

The only other noticeable plant which I saw at Valencia was the stately *Asphodelus ramosus*, of which I had seen at Tarragona a few roots (as I believed) still far from flowering. It does not seem to be a common plant in these parts of Spain, though widely spread in the Mediterranean region. It abounds in many parts of Languedoc and Provence, near Rome and in some other parts of Italy; and in

[18]Gussone, *Florae siculae*, Vol. I, p. 491.
[19]Persoon, *Synopsis plantarum*, Vol. I, p. 371.

Sicily it, together with the Palmetto, covers nearly all the uncultivated ground. I am afraid, indeed, that the meadows, celebrated by poets, from which Proserpine was carried off while gathering flowers with her attendant maidens, were in truth no other than these Asphodel wastes, which, notwithstanding the beauty of the plant, are by no means so pleasing to the eye or the mind as a real English or mountain meadow. This Asphodel is now called by French botanists *A. microcarpus*. It is confined to the hotter districts of Europe. There is another species or race, called by them *A. subalpinus*, which covers in large masses the middle regions of some of the higher Pyrenees, and it is said also of the Alps. On a superficial view this is not distinguishable from the former. *A. albus* is also a French species, and there is another allied to it, which has only of late become known in France itself, for it is not mentioned by De Candolle. It was seen by the present writer in its native place before the publication of the third volume of Grenier and Godron, in which it is for the first time distinguished and described.[20] It has been named by them *A. sphaerocarpus*, and I will venture to make it the subject of a short digression.

Perhaps English botanists may some day turn their steps towards a region not yet much frequented by them, but which has many claims to their notice,—the peninsula of Brittany. The tour of this province is one of the most attractive short Continental excursions which an Englishman can make. In the first place, it is about the cheapest; a consideration no less important to botanists than to others, their pursuit not being one of those which bring in a golden harvest. The inn charges, when once fairly within the peninsula, are (or were half-a-dozen years ago) less than two-thirds of the ordinary scale of travelling in France. Besides being the cheapest, this excursion is one of the most beautiful of those which are easily and quickly accessible, and its style of beauty is that which English people usually prefer. The interior resembles, more nearly than anything else on the Continent, the wilder and rockier parts of England, while the coast scenery rivals that of Cornwall. The journey also naturally combines with a visit to that corner of the British dominions so interesting to an English botanist and to a political economist, the Channel Islands. The north coast of Brittany has not, as far as I could observe, much of botanical attraction, if we except the neighbourhood of Dinan, which produces *Galeopsis villosa*, *Gratiola officinalis*, *Sinapis Cheiranthus*, *Sedum album*, *reflexum*, and *rubens*, *Tragopogon porrifolius*, and others. But the southern coast, from the peninsula of Penmarch to the Loire, unites the attraction of rare plants with that of its unrivalled Druidical remains. Among these last, the traveller will scarcely fail to visit those of the peninsula of Locmariaker; and if he does so, it should not be from Auray, but from Vannes, in a boat down the river, and across the gulf or inland sea known as the Mer de Morbihan. Among the numerous islands (the popular imagination reckons three hundred and sixty-five)

---

[20]Grenier and Godron, Vol. III, pp. 223–4.

with which the sea is studded, he will doubtless land on a small one bearing the name of Gâvr Innis, and containing one of the rarest of Druidical monuments, a chamber entirely covered in, smaller certainly than the remarkable one near Saumur, but excelling it in being subterraneous, and (what is still more important) solitary. This island is full of the Asphodel in question. I was told that it grows on several of the other islands, and that its white flowers (replaced when I saw it in June by red fruits) are the glory in spring of this marine region. The authors of the *Flore de France* enumerate four other localities, all in the west or west centre of France, but three of these four have a mark of interrogation attached to them by the authors.[21]

## No. III. Tarragona, Valencia, Zaragoza [2]

FROM VALENCIA TO MADRID we travelled all the way by railroad, and had no opportunity of botanizing, except an hour's walk at the point where the Valencia branch meets the Alicante line. This point is Almansa, in the kingdom of Murcia, and the railway-station is in the very field of battle, where the English arms sustained one of the few defeats they underwent in the war of Marlborough and Queen Anne.[22] To write the name Almanza is in every way a mistake; it is spelt with an *s*, and that letter in Spanish is never sounded like *z*. The shabby-looking little country town, which I only saw from outside, is still, probably, much what it was then. The adjacent country was mostly, at this season, in a freshly-ploughed state, and my botanizing was limited to a strip of ground between two lines of cultivation. There, however, I found *Adonis autumnalis*, *Sisymbrium Irio* and *Sophia*, *Erysimum perfoliatum*, a *Camelina* (I believe *sylvestris*), *Hypecoum procumbens*, a single plant of another *Hypecoum*, *H. pendulum*, the curiously podded *Enarthrocarpus arcuatus*, and the fine dark-coloured Poppy, *Roemeria hybrida*. It is remarkable (and could scarcely have happened at any season but early spring) that all the plants I saw were of the three neighbouring families, *Ranunculaceae*, *Papaveraceae*, and *Cruciferae*.

While at Madrid I did not botanize; the time we passed there was occupied with the town itself, and especially its almost unrivalled picture-gallery, which they who have not seen are unacquainted with one of the two great schools of painting of the world. The neighbouring country is a treeless and bushless expanse of corn—a uniform green in spring, a melancholy stubble in autumn—comprising the lofty plateau of Castille, of which the monotonous swell has neither the variety of hills nor the imposingness of a real plain. It is as unpromising to the botanist as it

[21]*Ibid.*, p. 224.
[22]During the reign of Queen Anne (1665–1714), in the War of the Spanish Succession, the British troops, under John Churchill (1650–1722), Duke of Marlborough, were defeated on 25 April, 1707, at Almansa.

is unattractive to the lover of nature, to whose eye everything about the capital of *todas las Españas* is wearisome, save at the few points from which he can look over the north edge of the plateau, across a broad valley, to the snowclad mountains of Guadarrama, by the blasts from which sentries are said to have been frozen to death at the gates of Queen Isabella's palace.[23]

My next botanizing was in a walk in the dusk near Guadalaxara, the place where the railway from Madrid towards Zaragoza at that time terminated; it has since been extended further. This little town is made imposing by the vast château of the Mendozas, a building which tells of Spain in what are called her great ages, being in reality the ages by which she was ruined. The only new plant which met my eye was *Reseda undata*, now identified with *R. alba*, a plant of our gardens, sometimes found in England as an escape from culture, to me indissolubly associated with the place where I first saw it, the ruins of Nero's Golden House.[24]

I was more successful at Alcolea, the small village mentioned in my former paper,[25] halfway between Guadalaxara and Calatayud, the first considerable town in Aragon. The plants which were here in flower, were those of a much earlier time of year, owing to the great elevation of the plateau on which, though now drawing near to its eastern boundary, we still were. Though it was the 1st of May, *Genista scorpius* (which near Avignon begins to flower in February) had not yet expanded its buds. *Erysimum perfoliatum* also, was not yet in flower. *Hutchinsia petraea*, the plant of St. Vincent Rocks and Eltham churchyard, was there; *Potentilla verna*, another Clifton plant; two Crucifers which grow near Rome and flower in March, *Arabis verna* and the less beautiful *Calapina Corvini*; another *Arabis*, probably *ciliata*; two *Veronicae* of the earliest spring, *hederaefolia* and *triphyllos*; an *Alyssum*, new to me, which I believe to be *A. perusianum*, a plant noted in the *Flore de France*, with only one habitat (in the Eastern Pyrenees);[26] *Ceratocephalus falcatus*, formerly classed as a Ranunculus, whose small flower gives birth to an oval head of scythe-shaped carpels, sometimes equalling in dimensions all the rest of the plant; and last of all, abounding among the young corn, a plant of the Order *Primulaceae*, with a small bright flower sunk in the hollow of a very large calyx, which I did not at first see to be a lowland species of the highland genus *Androsace*; it is *A. maxima*, which I found again at Zaragoza, and the seeds of which are said in the country to be edible. Of plants not in flower I noted only a *Euphorbia* and the formidable Thistle *Picnomon Acarna*.

From Zaragoza, the prosperous capital of a backward province, noted for its glorious siege and for its two splendid cathedrals, I made a successful herborization. The immediate vicinity contains abundance both of waste and

---

[23]Isabella of Castile (1451–1504), co-regent with King Ferdinand.

[24]Clodius Caesar Nero (37–68 A.D.), Roman Emperor 54–68 A.D., built this enormous palace, adorned with gems and Greek masterpieces, after the great fire of Rome in 64 A.D.

[25]See p. 291 above.

[26]Grenier and Godron, Vol. I, pp. 118–19.

cultivated land, dry rocky garrigue, and low arable, fertilized by water tumbling in cascades from sluices in a broad canal carried along a very high embankment. Of plants already mentioned I noted *Roemeria hybrida, Fumaria spicata, Mathiola tristis, Lepidium Draba, Sisymbrium obtusangulum* and *Irio,* two *Helianthema, Genista Scorpius,* and I believe *Calycotome spinosa, Hippocrepis ciliata* and *comosa, Vicia triflora, Paronychia argentea, Helichrysum Stoechas, Thymus vulgaris* (a variety with a lemon scent), *Plantago Lagopus* and *albicans, Mercurialis tomentosa, Asphodelus fistulosus,* and a small variety of *A. ramosus.* I have hardly anywhere seen *Ranunculus repens* so magnificent. The following were new to me, in Spain at least:—an Adonis, I believe *A. microcarpa; Papaver hybridum* in profusion; the richly-coloured *Glaucium corniculatum* (otherwise *phoeniceum*), a plant also of Avignon; a cruciferous siliculose plant of dried-up appearance, not unlike in aspect to an advanced state of *Alyssum campestre* or *calycinum,* but which proved on examination to be *Berteroa incana;* a tall *Reseda* allied to *lutea,* I believe *R. fruticulosa;* to *Hippocrepis ciliata* was added a larger species, with pods similarly jointed and scooped out, *H. unisiliquosa;* the spreading *Hedypnois polymorpha,* with its clumsy club-like peduncles; the red-flowered and downy-coated *Cynoglossum cheirifolium,* one of the handsomest of its tribe; a fine dark-flowered *Teucrium,* not in the French Flora,—I made it out to be *T. thymifolium;* lastly, a tiny grass, with a round, rather prickly head, *Echinaria capitata.*

At Lerida my botanizing was limited to a single field, but in that small space (besides *Alyssum calycinum* and the beautiful *Anchusa italica* of our gardens, a common cornfield plant in Spain and all over southern Europe as high up as Burgundy on the east and La Vendée on the west) I found four plants which I did not see elsewhere in Spain; two species of Silene, *S. conica,* and the rarer, more stately, and larger-flowered *S. conoidea;* a less handsome, not to say ugly, Boragineous plant, *Nonnea ventricosa,* one of the roughest of its rough tribe, without the usual lustrous beauty of their flowers; and the rather vulgar-looking sister of an otherwise most elegant race, *Malcolmia africana.*

Between Lerida and Tarragona I saw from the diligence the following plants, scattered in abundance over the country:—*Roemeria hybrida, Lepidium Draba, Cistus* (if I mistake not) *umbellatus, Ulex parviflorus, Convolvulus althaeoides, Cynoglossum cheirifolium, Mercurialis tomentosa,* a Gladiolus, and the blue *Aphyllanthes monspeliensis.* To these I will subjoin the following, which seemed universal in the parts of Spain which I have botanically visited:—*Adonis autumnalis, Lychnis vespertina, Agrostemma Githago, Vicia sativa, Scandix Pecten-Veneris, Maruta Cotula, Podospermum laciniatum, Hieracium sylvaticum,* or some of the many species (or supposed species) allied to it, *Anchusa italica, Lycopsis arvensis, Lithospermum arvense* and *officinale, Plantago Coronopus* and *lanceolata.* And here ends Spanish botanizing, with the exception of a visit to Monserrat, and two days at the end of May in the Spanish Pyrenees, of which I will endeavour to give some account in a future number of the *Phytologist*.[27]

## No. IV. Monserrat

THE CELEBRATED MOUNTAIN Monserrat (which there is no good reason for writing with the French orthography, Montserrat), consists of a long range of many summits, which from their peak-like and serrated appearance, when seen from far off, might be supposed to be of slate. The greater is the surprise of the traveller when he finds on approach, that the whole mountain is composed of pudding-stone, and that the turrets and pinnacles are not pointed, but rounded. The highest summit is stated to be 3800 feet above the sea, from which its distance is not great, and the mountain is a conspicuous object from the coast road, south of Barcelona. From the northern, or rather north-eastern coast, it could also be seen for a considerable space, were not the view intercepted by intervening high ground. From the range behind Barcelona, a fine view of it may be had; but at an angle which does not give it the advantage of its entire length. It is only from the Tarragona road, at a considerable distance from Barcelona, that it can be seen spread out lengthwise in its full dimensions. On a ledge in a receding hollow (or coomb) of the mountain, nearly in the middle of its length, and seemingly about the middle of its height (though really much lower), stands the famous monastery. Like the other monasteries of Spain, once so wealthy and powerful, it is now shorn of its glories; but it is still inhabited by a few monks, though in a number disproportioned to the size and aspect of the edifice, and their hospitality is extended to travellers to the extent of lodging, but not of food; which last is supplied at a tolerable *restaurant* within the precincts of the convent, the utility of which establishment atones for its violation of the *religio loci*. The lodging in the convent itself is gratuitous; but travellers who can afford it, make a donation (also gratuitous) to the funds of the convent. The sleeping chambers, or cells, are neat, sufficiently commodious, beautifully clean, and the views from their windows magnificent. The one which I occupied looked across the hollow of the mountain, upon the splendidly wooded other horn of the crescent, then vocal with numerous nightingales. A copious spring, which issues from the mountain just outside the gateway, had, no doubt, a share in originally deciding the locality of the convent.

The easiest way to Monserrat from Barcelona is by the Manresa railway, one of the four which diverge from that city. From the railway station to the mountain there is a broad and good carriage-road, by means of which tourists and pilgrims are landed in the very yard of the convent, from that universal symbol and

---

[27]Actually the separate accounts (the next two sections) appeared in two numbers, those for December 1861 and February 1862.

instrument of modern civilization, an omnibus. If this commodious mode of access makes the expedition less romantic, it does not make the place less beautiful. The prosaic vehicle winds its way up the mountain-side through, for the South, a rather dense wood, which, more or less open, according as the woodcutters have been more or less recently in operation, covers a great part of the mountain, both in its higher and lower regions. There is another mode of approach at the southern end of the mountain from the Martorell station of the Valencia railway; but on this side there is neither carriage nor road, but a mule-path only, and travellers must make their way up the mountain and along its side to the convent, either on foot or mounted. Beyond the monastery there is no road higher up; but mountain paths are not deficient. The path to the top, after a stiff climb, leads for a considerable distance along a wooded ravine hemmed in by summits of a pillar-like or sugar-loaf character. The view from the highest of these includes the greater part of Catalonia, northward to the Pyrenees, westward and southward towards the Segre and the Ebro.

I can hardly speak in sufficiently strong terms of the profusion and variety of the flowers, southern and northern, Mediterranean, subalpine, and almost alpine, which covered the mountain-side when I saw it; not always in separate regions, but often mixed together on the same spot. It is fitting to begin with the trees and shrubs, which, still more than flowers, give the general character to a landscape. The *Quercus Ilex* and *coccifera* of the South (the latter not so plentiful as in many other places) are combined with the Holly (*Ilex Aquifolium*) of the North. A denizen of both equally, the Box-tree (*Buxus sempervirens*), here attains a lofty growth. The Juniper of our chalk downs (*Juniperus communis*) is joined with *J. phoenicea*, a Southern and a *garrigue* plant. With *Celtis australis*, the *Micocoulier*, a Mediterranean tree, is found the Mountain Ash (*Pyrus Aucuparia*) of the North. Another flowering rosaceous shrub, *Amelanchier vulgaris*, abounds, as it usually does where there are clefts in calcareous rocks, from the stony hills of Provence to the chalk cliffs above the Seine in Normandy. The Laurustinus (*Viburnum Tinus*), a plant of Italy and the south of France, is side by side with another of the same genus, *V. Lantana*, the Wayfaring-tree of our chalk hills. *Phillyrea media* and *Rhamnus Alaternus*, natives of the *garrigue*, which reach English shrubberies, are accompanied by the Mastic, *Pistacia Lentiscus*, the Terebinth, *P. Terebinthus*, and the universal *Hedera Helix*.

But the flowers of Monserrat are more various and remarkable than the wood products. I have seen few places in the South where the vernal wood-flowers are so abundant. The blue colour is that which predominates. The lovely *Hepatica*, of which the pink is rare compared with the far more beautiful blue variety, glistens from under every thicket. A flower of still deeper blue, our early *Polygala calcarea*, helps perhaps even more to colour the mountain-side. *Viola canina* is in like profusion; as is also, in the barer places, the peculiarly Southern *Aphyllanthes monspeliensis*, a leafless plant (as the name indicates), of the Order *Junceae*, but which, wherever it grows, studs the ground with ornamental blue flowers, each division of the corolla marked by a midrib of a deeper blue. In the lower regions of the mountain, *Linum narbonense* expands its still finer and larger blue flowers, the most magnificent of their tribe. In the shady woods, our Columbine, *Aquilegia vulgaris*, is not unfrequent. Another of the most abundant flowers is *Globularia vulgaris*, a plant unknown to England (though not requiring a very Southern climate), whose round heads are also blue, though of a less beautiful tint. Another plant of the same genus, *G. Alypum*, is also here met with, a more decidedly Southern species, though rarer even in the South than *G. vulgaris*. Of flowers other than blue, one of the most plentiful—it is so indeed wherever it grows in the Pyrenees, the Cevennes, or the burning rocky wastes of the Mediterranean—is the rosy *Saponaria Ocymoides*, with its masses of blossom carpeting the ground. *Anthyllis Vulneraria* is frequent; that is, its red-flowered variety, much the commonest in the South. Of *Cisti* I only saw the purple *C. albidus*, the most beautiful of the common species, and only matched by the very similar *C. villosus*, which supplies its place in Sicily and Greece. But there were numerous *Helianthema*, among which one white (probably *H. apenninum*) and several yellow, which, not feeling quite certain that I have determined them rightly, I forbear to name. The red Valerian, *Centranthus ruber* (which we possess, though probably naturalized, in Greenhithe chalk-pits and other places in Kent), here showed its dark-red masses; a fact rather exceptional, for I have found *C. angustifolius* much more common, both in the French Alps, the Pyrenees and the mountains of the south of France. On a turfy part of the mountain-side, at a considerable elevation, I found *Ranunculus gramineus*, a handsome and rather rare plant allied to *R. Flammula and Lingua*; and at a height above that, *Arbutus Uva-ursi* (now *Arctostaphylos*) spread out its luxuriant stems and pitcher-like flowers. The small yellow Narcissus, *N. juncifolius*, formerly confounded with *N. Jonquilla*, grew copiously in the same region; and near the summit of the mountain (on the grassy ledge on which are the ruins of the highest hermitage, that named after St. Jerome),[28] *N. biflorus*, more beautiful than even *N. poeticus*, filled the air with rich fragrance.

But the plant most associated with Monserrat is *Ramondia pyrenaica*, known to those who have botanized at Gavarnie, Esquierry, and other places in the Higher Pyrenees, as one of the most exquisite vegetable productions of that mountain chain. This plant, the only European representative of the Order *Cyrtandraceae*, was earliest known and described (under the name *Verbascum Myconi*) as a Monserrat plant; these excepted, it has, I believe, no other known habitat. I was fortunate enough to find on a rock, a plant or two already in flower; not on the higher part of the mountain, but on its lower slope, very near the carriage-road.

---

[28]St. Jerome (ca. 340–420 A.D.), after whom the hermitage was named, had been a hermit in the wastes of Chalcis, near Antioch, 373–79 A.D.

Though I possessed far more beautiful specimens collected on the rocky side of the torrent at Gavarnie, it gave me great pleasure to find it in what, if not its first abode, is at least the first place in which it was scientifically recognized.

The remaining plants which I observed on Monserrat I shall enumerate in the usual order. They are doubtless but a small part of the botanical riches of the mountain, so many plants being, at this early time of the year (the second week of May, in a very backward season), not only not in flower, but not yet recognizable. Of *Ranunculaceae*, there were *Clematis Vitalba* and two *Thalictra*; one of these had not even begun to flower; another, in the lower region of the mountain, and in very small quantity, had barely begun, and I could not with certainty determine it. Its appearance is not the usual one of a *Thalictrum*, and if a French species, it must be *T. tuberosum*. *Ranunculus gramineus* I have mentioned, to which add *R. bulbosus* and *Helleborus foetidus*. Of Crucifers, I saw *Arabis sagittata, Gerardi*, and *Turrita*; *Cardamine hirsuta*; *Biscutella laevigata* abundantly, the smooth, though hard form, which justifies the name (not *B. ambigua*, the common one of the South, now generally accounted a variety of the former); an *Erysimum*; *Sisymbrium Irio, Columnae*, and *obtusangulum*; *Diplotaxis erucoides*; and, of course, *Alyssum calycinum*, and *Lepidium Draba*. The *Resedae* were represented by *R. Phyteuma* and *R. fruticulosa*. The *Caryophylleae*, by *Silene italica*, with other large and small species of that genus, not in flower; and an *Arenaria* unknown to me. Of *Oxalideae*, I noticed *O. corniculata*; of *Geraniaceae*, only two Erodiums, *E. ciconium* and *malachoides*. *Leguminosae* were, as usual, abundant. Besides *Calycotome spinosa* and *Genista Scorpius*, there was a light-green dwarf *Genista*, one of several species which have leaves on the upper part and only thorns on the lower part; the real Spanish broom, *G. hispanica*. The *Cytisi* were *C. argenteus*, and that bush of golden flowers, *C. sessilifolius*. The *Astragali* were *A. monspessulanus*, and a species with pods like large hooks, *A. hamosus*. Besides these, and the *Anthyllis* already mentioned, there were *Dorycnium suffruticosum*, *Lotus corniculatus, Psoralea bituminosa, Coronilla Emerus, Hippocrepis comosa* (unless I mistook *H. glauca* for it), *Arthrolobium scorpioides*, and *Lathyrus setifolius*. Of *Rosaceae*, besides several Roses not yet in flower, there were *Pyrus communis, Potentilla verna*, the wild Strawberry (*Fragaria vesca*), and *Poterium Sanguisorba*. Umbellifers, at this season, I could scarcely expect to find; I only noticed, of course not in flower, the common Fennel (*Foeniculum vulgare*) and the tall *Bupleurum fruticosum*, with its large, entire, coriaceous leaves. I observed *Momordica Elaterium*, the European representative of the Cucumber tribe; several Honeysuckles, *Lonicera implexa, Xylosteum*, and perhaps others; various Sedums, one apparently *altissimum*, and a *Rubia*, probably *peregrina*; none of these however were in flower. Several Galiums were, but I did not stop to determine them. The *Compositae* which I was able to recognize at this season were, *Pallenis* (formerly *Buphthalmum*) *spinosa, Calendula arvensis, Urospermum Dalechampii* and *picroides*, (all common plants); *Crepis albida*, a fine mountain plant, which seemed as much at home here as in the Pyrenees; a *Santolina*, and, I believe, a *Phagnalon*; the last two not yet in flower. The Heaths were *Erica arborea*, and another (probably *multiflora*) out of flower. Of *Primulaceae*, I only noticed *Anagallis arvensis*. Of *Boragineae*, an early-flowering Order, there were several: *Asperugo procumbens* exhibited its ugly form in luxuriant tangled masses, under the walls of the convent. On the mountain-side the handsome *Lithospermum fruticosum* put forth its blue funnel-shaped flowers. *Echium vulgare* and *Borrago officinalis* make up the list. Of the Order *Solaneae* I only remarked *Hyoscyamus niger*, a plant very widely diffused, though seldom abundant in any of its localities (an English station, the chalk-hill near Boxley, is an exception). There was a *Verbascum*, resembling *V. Thapsus, Antirrhinum majus*, and an *Orobanche* of a blood-red colour. *Labiatae*, a numerous Order on the calcareous wastes of the South, were rather frequent, and later in the year there are, no doubt, many more. *Lavandula Spica* and *Phlomis Lychnitis* were there, but not yet in flower; *Thymus vulgaris* and *Rosmarinus officinalis* of course; *Salvia clandestina*; a *Teucrium* not in flower, I believe the dark-coloured one which I had found near Zaragoza; *Sideritis hirsuta*, one of the goodliest of its stiff genus. Of Plantains, I saw only the common *Plantago Cynops*. Of *Apetalae*, only *Daphne Laureola*, and four *Euphorbiae*, *E. Characias, serrata, amygdaloides*, and another. The *Monocotyledoneae*, besides those previously mentioned, were *Orchis mascula*; *Gladiolus byzantinus* (in the hot lower regions); the furze-like *Asparagus* (*A. horridus*), which I first found at Valencia; *Tamus communis*; *Smilax aspera*; *Ruscus aculeatus*, a plant which looks more congenial to the South than to the damp thickets which shelter it in our own country; *Convallaria Polygonatum*; *Asphodelus ramosus* and *fistulosus*, and lastly, though not yet in flower, *Lilium Martagon*, that ornament of mountain woods on the continent of Europe, which though existing in profuse abundance in several similar localities in our south-eastern counties, an idle scrupulosity so long kept out of our British Floras.

Here I am obliged to end what is no doubt a very scanty sample of the treasures by which, a botanist able to visit Monserrat repeatedly and at various seasons, might hope to have his labour rewarded. There only remains to be recorded a two days' excursion in the Spanish Pyrenees, and my memoranda of Spanish botany will have been exhausted.

## No. V. Spanish Pyrenees; Andorra

A SHORT EXCURSION from the French to the Spanish side of the Pyrenees, about a fortnight after the termination of our tour in Spain, yielded some botanical acquisitions which deserve to be added to the brief records already given of Spanish botany. The interval had been passed in the richest botanical districts of

the Eastern Pyrenees, but with results unexpectedly scanty, the backwardness of
the season having deprived me of the majority of the plants which I might
otherwise have reasonably expected. I hoped that on the southern side of the chain
I might have better fortune; nor was I altogether disappointed.

We crossed the watershed of the Eastern Pyrenees at the head of the long oblique
valley of the river Tet, which during the greatest part of its length forms, not a
right, but an acute angle with the general direction of the mountain-chain. The
range is crossed, not by a pass, but by a considerable breadth of gently sloping and
waving corn country, which, though flanked by lofty summits and dark fir woods,
is as easily traversable by an army as Salisbury Plain, and an invasion of either
country from the other at this point would meet with no physical obstacles near the
summit, whatever they might possibly find in the defiles lower down. Accordingly, the deficiency of natural is made up, on the French side at least, by artificial
defences. A green knoll on the border of the waving country is crested by one of the
most strongly fortified military posts in the country, the town of Mont Louis,—for
a town in all respects it is, though with only a few hundred inhabitants,—
overtopped by a citadel, the work of Vauban,[29] larger than the town itself. At this
point the French territory projects for some miles on the Spanish side of the
Pyrenees, as the Spanish territory does on the French side about the head-waters of
the Garonne. French Cerdagne, as it is still popularly called, forms a richly
cultivated valley, or rather, inclined plane, of such width as to make the high
mountains which bound it appear what I might almost call distant. This fertile
slope is terminated by a little stream, which separates Bourg-Madame, the frontier
village in the French territory, from Puycerda, the capital of Spanish Cerdagne, a
genuine Spanish town of some importance, on a height which projects far into the
valley, and commands, from a small planted promenade on its southern side, a
view over the Spanish part of the valley and the adjoining mountains, which it was
worth the whole journey to see. From Puycerda to Urgel, the chief place in this part
of the Spanish Pyrenees, is a long day's journey on foot or on muleback. The
valley differs from mountain valleys in general in being more picturesque in the
descent than in the ascent, the upper extremity, as may be gathered from what has
already been said, being the tamest instead of the boldest part of its Alpine
panorama. The beauty seemed always to increase as we descended the valley,
Urgel itself being the most beautiful place in the whole descent.

The Flora of this district, as usual on the southern declivities of mountain
ranges, is a mixture of mountain plants with those of the plains below. In the upper
part of the valley the meadows have the floral magnificence characteristic of the
Pyrenees, where the open mountain pastures in June, before the grass has been cut
or the cattle driven in among them, are often one mass of bloom, giving its colour

[29]After the peace of Nimegen (1678) the border fortifications of France were put in the
hands of Sébastien le Prestre de Vauban (1633–1707); Mount Louis was built in 1679.

to the mountain sides from a great distance. The meadows for many miles below Puycerda were of this character. They were as white with *Narcissus poeticus* as English meadows at the same season are yellow with Buttercups. In other places the dark variety of Columbine (*Aquilegia vulgaris*) divided the honours with the Narcissus, or engrossed the larger part; while several Umbellifers in full flower contributed a different kind of white colour to the mixture, particularly *Chaerophyllum hirsutum*, with a plant resembling *Pimpinella magna*, and, I believe, *Ligusticum pyrenaeum*; the fruits of neither being yet in a state to admit of their being determined. The other plants of which I made a note are the following:

Of *Ranunculaceae*, the finest, besides the Columbine, was *Adonis flammea*, with flowers of the same bright colour but greater size than those of *A. autumnalis*. *A. pyrenaica*, though common among the corn near Bourg-Madame, I did not see on the Spanish side of the frontier. The remaining *Ranunculaceae* were *Clematis Vitalba* and *Flammula*, *Helleborus foetidus* (a plant universal in the Pyrenees), and *Caltha palustris*. The *Papaveraceae* I saw were *Papaver Rhoeas*, *Chelidonium majus*, and *Hypecoum procumbens*. There were, as usual, many Crucifers. Of Alyssums, there were (besides *A. calycinum*) the plant which I had found at Alcolea, and called *A. perusianum*, and a yellow species akin to *montanum*, *A. cuneifolium*. *Erysimum lanceolatum*, a frequent plant of the Pyrenees, was there, with its large bright yellow flowers; and three *Sisymbria*, *S. Sophia*, *obtusangulum*, and a common Pyrenean species, with a mass of flowers succeeded by long spikes of slender highly curved pods, *S. austriacum*, the most common variety of which is otherwise known as *Sinapis pyrenaica*. The only *Arabis* I noticed was, I believe, *Gerardi*. The *Biscutella* was not the Monserrat species (or variety), but the common Mediterranean plant, *B. ambigua*. I had previously found in the valley of the Tet, near Fonpedrouze, a much rarer species, *B. cichoriifolia*, resembling the former in little except the twin shields, from which the genus derives its name. Of other *Siliculosae*, I noted *Iberis amara*, *Thlaspi arvense*, *Lepidium heterophyllum*, the plant of which our *L. Smithii* is classed by French botanists as a variety,[30] and the stately spreading *Neslia paniculata*, with its nearly globular pods. The genus Cistus seemed wanting in this district, though one of its noblest species, a Gum-Cistus, *C. laurifolius*, abounds where it was less to be looked for, on the sloping side of the corresponding French valley, a short distance below Mont Louis. The only Helianthemum I saw was either *H. vulgare* or one of the plants which are sometimes reckoned varieties of it. As might be expected, there were *Reseda Phyteuma* and *fruticulosa* and *Polygala vulgaris*. The *Caryophylleae* visible were *Saponaria ocymoides* and *vaccaria*, the common *Lychnis vespertina* and *Agrostemma Githago*, *Silene inflata*, and the elegant *S. saxifraga*, with its funnel-shaped flowers, so common in the mountain valleys of the south of Europe. There were two splendid Linums, *L. narbonense* and a

---

[30]Grenier and Godron, Vol. I, pp. 149–50.

smaller plant with paler flowers, which I suppose to be *decumbens*, intermediate between *tenuifolium* and *suffruticosum*. The *Malvaceae* were the common *Malva rotundifolia* and *sylvestris*. The *Geraniaceae* were *Erodium cicutarium*, *Geranium Robertianum*, *sanguineum*, and *pyrenaicum*. The name of the last, mysterious to those to whom it is only known as a plant of Surrey and Kent, is intelligible to those who have seen its abundance in the Pyrenees. The Wild Vine (*Vitis vinifera*) spread its climbing stems and grasping tendrils over the bushes.

Of *Calyciflorae*, I begin with the Terebinth-tree, *Pistacia Terebinthus*. *Leguminosae* were, as usual, one of the most abundant of all the Orders. Along with the *Genista Scorpius* of the plains there was *G. sagittalis* of the mountains, and *G. pilosa* of both; all plants which by their beauty do credit to this fine genus. Of *Cytisi*, there was the beautiful *C. sessilifolius*. The only Trefoils I observed were *T. pratense* and *repens*; but the prevailing Medicago was a special plant of the Eastern Pyrenees, *M. suffruticosa*. The *Viciae* were in number five: *V. sativa*, *sepium*, *cracca*, a glorious dark-purple species (*V. onobrychioides*), and the duller-coloured *V. pannonica*. *Lotus corniculatus* and *Hippocrepis comosa* abound here as everywhere. I saw but one Astragalus, I believe *A. purpureus*, a purple-flowered, erect, rather dwarfish plant, approaching to *A. hypoglottis*. I conclude the Order with the small decumbent Sainfoin of southern Europe, *Onobrychis supina*. Of the Order *Rosaceae*, there were *Crataegus Oxyacantha*, *Amelanchier vulgaris*, and *Poterium Sanguisorba*; but the genus *Rosa*, above all, was in profusion. The town of Urgel is in the midst of a sort of garden of wild Roses: every hedge and enclosure is loaded with them in a quantity and of a size to which I never saw even an approach elsewhere. The species must be numerous, but I regret my inability to record them. The fatigue of the journey, the multitude of other plants to determine and put into paper, and the difficulty of dealing with this genus without the fruit and without proper books, deterred me from the attempt. *Rosa tomentosa*, or some species near to it, appeared to be one, and another resembled, in the appearance of its stem, *R. spinosissima*, but with much larger flowers; in fact, as I have already mentioned, the size of the Roses was quite as remarkable as their profuse abundance.

*Saxifraga Aizoon*, now in full flower, one of the common mountain species of the Alps and Pyrenees, dotted the rocks of the valley with its white rosettes of spatulate coriaceous leaves. Sedums were numerous: among others, *S. acre*, *Telephium*, and (though not in flower) *altissimum*, like a large white-flowered *S. reflexum*. Another plant of the same Order, *Umbilicus pendulinus*, as common on moist rocks and walls in the south of Europe as in our western counties, was also present. *Bryonia dioica* was visible, and *Paronychia serpyllifolia*, a mountain species, takes the place of *P. argentea*. Of Umbellifers, besides those already mentioned, I saw *Heracleum Sphondylium* (unless it was the very similar *H. pyrenaicum*), *Bupleurum rotundifolium*, and, I believe, *Orlaya platycarpa*. The Cornel-tree (*Cornus sanguinea*) was as common here as elsewhere. Of the Order

*Caprifoliaceae*, there were the common Elders (*Sambucus nigra* and *Ebulus*), and two Honeysuckles, *Lonicera implexa* of the plains, and *Xylosteum* of the mountains. There were the blue *Asperula arvensis* and several *Galia*; two *Valerianeae*, *V. officinalis* and *Centranthus angustifolius*; *Dipsacus sylvestris*, and a *Knautia*, apparently a variety of *K. arvensis*.

*Compositae* were of course less numerous than in the plains or at a later period of the year. There were, however, several. *Achillea odorata*, a plant of southern Europe, like a dwarf *A. Millefolium*, with a sweet smell of camomile, was one. With this was a Santolina, probably *S. Chamaecyparissias*, an *Artemisia*, probably *campestris*, and the universal *Leucanthemum vulgare*. Of Thistles on this occasion I have no note. The Centauries were *C. Cyanus*, *C. Scabiosa*, and another species, not uncommon on the less elevated mountains of the South, *C. pectinata*, deriving its name from the comb-like structure of its involucral appendages. Of Cichoraceous *Compositae*, I noticed *Scorzonera humilis*, *Tragopogon pratensis*, a Hieracium (*H. murorum*?), the fine blue Lactuca of Continental cornfields, which almost reaches our own latitudes, *L. perennis*, and two much rarer plants, both of which I only found within a short distance of Urgel, one in the bed of the torrent, a stiff, widely branched plant, coated all over with a fine white wool, which I guessed rather than ascertained to be *Andryala macrocephala* of Boissier;[31] and, growing within the spray of a waterfall, a Sonchus, with undivided leaves, allied to *S. maritimus*, which was certainly *S. crassifolius*.

Passing now to the *Corolliflorae*, I did not find in this day's journey either *Gentianeae* or *Primulaceae*, plants which, for the most part, require higher elevations, or at least cooler and moister valleys. *Vincetoxicum officinale*, so abundant on calcareous soils, even far north, and which ought to grow in England, was there; so also Privet (*Ligustrum vulgare*), a plant equally at home in north and south; and the only European Jasminum, *J. fruticans*, a yellow species, and rather frequent in the south of France, but not beyond the Mediterranean region. Our northern Ash, *Fraxinus excelsior*, grows here, which, in the south, is principally a mountain tree. I saw no *Convolvulus*, except *C. arvensis*, though I should have expected *C. cantabrica*, which comes up as high, or higher, in other southern mountains. The *Boragineae* were not remarkable: *Echium vulgare*, *Lithospermum arvense* and *officinale*, *Anchusa italica*, *Lycopsis arvensis*, and our common Cynoglossum, *C. officinale*. The *Solaneae* were *Solanum Dulcamara*, as common in the south as in the north, and *Hyoscyamus niger*. There were several Verbascums, *V. floccosum* apparently being one. *Scrophularineae* and *Labiatae* were, as might be expected, the most numerous Orders; of the former there were *Scrophularia canina* and *nodosa*, *Rhinanthus glaber*, *Veronica Teucrium* and *serpyllifolia*, the stately *Digitalis lutea*, *Linaria supina*, and two Antirrhinums proper—the pale-flowered *A. Asarina*, which, as in many other parts of the

[31]Boissier, *Voyage botanique*, Vol. II, p. 393.

Pyrenees, hangs like tapestry on the perpendicular rocks, and *A. latifolium*, looking like a yellow variety of *majus*. The *Labiatae* were *Lavandula Spica* and *Mentha sylvestris* (the British plant so common in Switzerland), *Salvia clandestina*, and another (I believe *phlomoides*), our ugly *Ballota foetida*, *Lamium maculatum*, *Stachys recta*, which, like *Digitalis lutea*, reaches northward as far as Normandy; both the Thymes, *T. vulgaris* and *Serpyllum*; and in great abundance a common Sideritis, *S. scordioides*. *Globularia nana*, as elsewhere in the Pyrenees, coated the rocks with its small leaves, its numerous heads of flowers, and its clumsy woody stems, so creeping that they seem adherent to the soil. An Armeria, seemingly *A. plantaginea*, represented the Order *Plumbagineae*; and *Plantago* was represented by *P. media*, and the mountain species, *P. carinata*.

Of *Apetalae*, the most worthy of notice was *Aristolochia Pistolochia*, with its almost black flowers, one of the smallest species of this curious genus. The *Polygoneae* were *Polygonum Bistorta*, as abundant as it usually is in moist mountain meadows, *Rumex acetosa*, and *R. scutatus*, with its singular leaves, a plant as common in the vineyards near Coblentz as in the south of Europe. The *Euphorbiae* were *E. serrata*, *Cyparissias*, *Characias*, the polished *E. nicaeensis*, and another, to me unknown. To these may be added the shrubs or trees, *Quercus coccifera*, *Buxus sempervirens*, and *Celtis australis*.

The *Monocotyledoneae* were finer than I expected, and finer than I found in my next day of botanizing. There were *Orchis mascula*, *O. galeata* (by some reduced to *militaris*, but the form of the flower, admirably figured by Woods,[32] is decidedly different), *Aceras anthropophora*, which recalled pleasing memories of the Surrey hills; *Narcissus poeticus*, as already mentioned; one of the plants common to alpine and maritime situations, *Allium Schoenoprasum* (but I am not sure this plant does not belong to the next day's district); the Grasses, *Bromus tectorum*, *Briza media*, *Aegilops ovata*, *Melica Magnolii*; and the Ferns, *Asplenium Trichomanes* and *Adiantum Capillus-Veneris*.

Urgel, properly La Seu (or Seo) de Urgel, better known locally as La Seu simply (*the See*, its bishop having for many centuries been one of the chief princes of the country), is the most characteristic, old-looking, and picturesque of small Spanish towns. We entered it after nightfall. I shall never forget the moonlight look of its dark streets, its *jalousies* and overhanging balconies. The situation is one of the most glorious in the whole Pyrenees. It lies far down in the long valley which we had been a day and a half in descending; but the valley does not open to the plain; it is crossed, and, in appearance, closed a little below the town, by a low range, with a striking peaked outline, which regaled our eyes as we saw it before us during the latter half of our day's journey, and appeared more beautiful still when seen from the promenade outside the walls of Urgel, or from the terrace or *loggia* of our very Spanish, but quite habitable inn. All experienced travellers know how much the

[32]Woods, *The Tourist's Flora*, p. 351 and Fig. 5.

beauty of a range of mountains, under a glaring sun, is improved by seeing it on its shady side. Of the little narrow plain into which the valley expands immediately round Urgel, I can say nothing botanically, except to repeat that it is a perfect paradise of Roses.

We had decided to find our way back to France by the valley of Andorra. Of this curious middle-age republic, independent equally of Spain and France, though under their joint protectorate, a description may be read in the *Edinburgh Review* for April last.[33] The writer has given a very interesting account of its history and of its institutions; but he seems somehow to imagine that he is the discoverer of Andorra, at least to Englishmen. It was however explored as long ago as about 1824, by two eminent English botanists—Mr. Bentham and Mr. Walker Arnott; the former of whom, in the narrative of his tour in the Pyrenees, prefixed to his valuable catalogue of their plants, gave a clear and succinct description of the country.[34] Since then it has been occasionally visited by English tourists, one of whom, Mr. Erskine Murray, devoted to it no small portion of his well-known book.[35] Respecting the institutions of the country, much was left for the reviewer to do; and he has done it, to all appearance, well. He makes one statement, however, which I hope is not correct, that "in this republic education is a thing almost unknown."[36] I cannot affirm that this is not the fact; but the standard French *Guide to the Pyrenees*, the elaborate volume of Joanne, affirms that "l'instruction publique est plus répandue en Andorre que dans les territoires voisins de l'Ariége et d'Urgel; les écoles sont gratuites, et la plupart des jeunes gens aisés vont faire leurs études à Toulouse ou à Barcelone."* The reviewer's description of the local features of the country is that of one who has only visited it from the French side. He says it is "isolated by mountains on every frontier."[37] This is neither more nor less true of the Val d'Andorre than it is of every other Pyrenean valley. None of them have more than one outlet into the plain. Andorra is simply the upper end of a

---

[33]John William Wilkins (b. 1829), "The Republic of Andorre," *Edinburgh Review*, CXIII (Apr. 1861), 345–59.

[34]George Arnott Walker Arnott (1799–1868), a Scottish botanist and colleague of Hooker's, published extensively on foreign plants; on the trip mentioned he accompanied George Bentham (1800–84), nephew of Jeremy Bentham, who first stimulated Mill's interest in botany during a trip to the Pyrenees in 1821 (see *CW*, Vol. XXVI, No. 1). Bentham's *Catalogue des plantes indigènes des Pyrénées et du Bas Languedoc* (Paris: Huzard, 1826), contains a descriptive preface, pp. 15–55.

[35]James Erskine Murray (1810–44), Scottish lawyer, *A Summer in the Pyrenees*, 2nd ed., 2 vols. (London: Macrone, 1837), Vol. I, pp. 94–170, esp. 161–70.

[36]Wilkins, p. 355.

*Public education in Andorre is superior to that of Ariego and Urgel. Instruction is gratuitous; pupils can easily complete their studies at Toulouse or Barcelona. [Adolphe Laurent Joanne (1823–81), *Itinéraire descriptif et historique des Pyrénées de l'Océan à la Méditerranée* (Paris: Hachette, [1858]), p. 561.]

[37]Wilkins, pp. 346–7.

Spanish valley (one of several which meet at Urgel), with the addition of two other valleys branching out of it. From France of course they can only be reached across the main chain, but the access from Spain is not more difficult nor mountainous than that to any other place in the Pyrenees.

In the lower or Spanish part of the valley the plants were chiefly those which I had seen in the descent from Puycerda, with one or two additional, particularly *Phalangium Liliago*, an elegant white-flowered plant of the Order *Asphodeleae*, and a fine Thistle, which I had seen in a former year on the Spanish side of another of the Pyrenean passes, *Cirsium rivulare*. When however we entered Andorra, the Flora soon assumed a far more mountain character, though here also occasionally varied by southern plants, the most remarkable of which was a Maple, *Acer monspessulanum*, with three-lobed coriaceous leaves. To begin at the beginning, *Trollius europaeus* now raised its globular heads in the rich meadows; and I saw, for the first time in Spain, two mountain *Ranunculi*, *R. Villarsii*, L., towards the head of the valley, and the tall white *R. aconitifolius*, the stateliest of its tribe. Of Crucifers there were now a *Barbarea* (probably *B. arcuata*), *Arabis thaliana* and *turrita*, *Sinapis Cheiranthus*, *Nasturtium pyrenaicum*, which, in spite of its name, is not a peculiarly Pyrenean plant; and one which is more so, *Cardamine latifolia*, like a greatly magnified *C. pratensis*, with leaves shaped like those of the Watercress. Two of our common Violets now appeared, *Viola canina* and *V. tricolor*; while to *Silene Saxifraga* was added *S. nutans*, and a very beautiful common plant of the Alps and Pyrenees, *S. rupestris*, as well as *Stellaria Holostea* and *Cerastium arvense*. Along with *Geranium Robertianum* and *pyrenaicum* there was in abundance *G. sylvaticum* of the English mountains. I saw also *Oxalis corniculata*. A tall bush, belonging to the Flora of the high mountains, *Rhamnus alpinus*, was here in full flower. The *Leguminosae* were fewer than usual; they included the Broom of the middle region of the southern mountains, *Sarothamnus purgans*, *Coronilla Emerus*, the stiff, but not inelegant *Trifolium montanum*, *Astragalus monspessulanus*, and the red variety of *Anthyllis Vulneraria*. Of *Rosaceae*, there were added to those already recorded, *Rosa rubiginosa*, *Potentilla verna*, and *Alchemilla vulgaris*. Of *Saxifragae*, besides *S. Aizoon*, there was our beautiful *S. granulata* (a mountain plant in the south of Europe), and a far rarer species than either, *S. media*. The Umbellifers appeared to be the same as in the previous day. To the common Elders was added *Sambucus racemosa*, now in full flower; it bears red instead of black fruit, and in that state I had found it in some of the forests near the Rhine, especially that of Stolzenfels, near Coblenz. Of *Rubiaceae*, I only noted *Galium cruciatum*. The only additional plant of the Order *Compositae* (except the *Cirsium* previously mentioned) was *Achillea chamae-melifolia*, a plant of the Eastern Pyrenees. The *Corolliflorae* also were mostly those which I had seen in the other valley. I must however add *Pinguicula grandiflora*, a plant common in the Pyrenees, often mistaken for a Violet by the non-botanical traveller; the exquisite *Primula farinosa*, of the Alps and the north of England; the large Alpine Forget-me-not (*Myosotis alpestris*); a tall *Pedicularis*, *P. verticillata*, growing profusely in the meadows near the principal village of the Republic; and, lastly, *Marrubium vulgare*. Of *Polygona*, besides *P. Bistorta*, there was a peculiar and curious mountain species with panicled inflorescence, *P. alpinum*. *Rumex scutatus* re-appeared, with *R. Acetosella*. Among monocotyledonous plants, *Paradisia Liliastrum* reigned supreme; a stately plant, with flowers of the purest white, of the shape and almost the size of a Hemerocallis, which Pyrenean tourists will see abundant, at its season, in the Vallée de Lys, near Bagnère de Luchon. *Narcissus poeticus* was as plentiful as ever; *Platanthera bifolia* was another ornament; *Muscari comosum* made its appearance, and in the lower and warmer part of the valley our blue garden Iris (*I. germanica*) grew. A *Veratrum*, probably *V. album*, so common in the Alps and Jura, not yet in flower, raised its strong, thick, green stems. The following plants, all of which were common to this with the preceding valley, I will simply enumerate:

| | | |
|---|---|---|
| Clematis Vitalba. | Reseda fruticulosa. | S. Telephium (and others). |
| Caltha palustris. | Saponaria ocymoides. | Umbilicus pendulinus. |
| Aquilegia vulgaris. | Erodium cicutarium. | Lonicera Xylosteum. |
| Helleborus foetidus. | Medicago suffruticosa. | Achillea odorata. |
| Chelidonium majus. | Lotus corniculatus. | Tragopogon pratensis. |
| Sisymbrium Sophia. | Crataegus Oxyacantha. | Fraxinus excelsior. |
| Sisymbrium obtusangul. | Amelanchier vulgaris. | Convolvulus arvensis. |
| Sisymbrium austriacum. | Bryonia dioica. | Lithospermum arvense. |
| Lepidium heterophyllum. | Sedum dasyphyllum. | Cynoglossum officinale. |
| Hyoscyamus niger. | Stachys hirta. | Euphorbia serrata. |
| Veronica Teucrium. | Lamium maculatum. | Euphorbia Cyparissias. |
| Veronica serpyllifolia. | Sideritis scordioides. | Orchis mascula. |
| Rhinanthus glaber. | Globularia nana. | Bromus tectorum. |
| Scrophularia canina. | Armeria plantaginea. | |
| Mentha sylvestris. | Buxus sempervirens. | |

At the foot of the ascent to the lofty pass (the Col de Puymaurin) we encountered in profusion four of the most interesting plants we had yet seen; the tall *Anemone alpina*, with its great flowers, of the sulphur-coloured variety (which I have found the commonest both in the Alps and Pyrenees); the mountain Umbellifer (*Meum athamanticum*), a plant rare in the English mountains, common in the Pyrenees and Cevennes; *Orchis sambucina*, with its great spikes of flowers, both purple and yellow; and the delicately beautiful *Tulipa Celsiana*, also a plant of the Cevennes. As we wound our way up the face of the mountain towards the Col, we came among decidedly Alpine plants; the three Gentians which light up the lofty pastures with their dark blue flowers, *G. acaulis* and *verna*, known to all Alpine explorers; *G. pyrenaica*, peculiar to the Eastern Pyrenees; the small white-flowered *Ranunculus pyrenaicus*, the lovely *Hepatica*, *Crocus vernus*, and a pink *Androsace*, common on the Pyrenean summits, long confounded with *A. carnea* of the Alps, but to be described, as I am told, in the Supplement to the *Flore de France*, under the name of *A. Lagerii*.[38] One plant, though I did not see it till just on the French side of the pass, I cannot help mentioning, and with this I close my list: that exquisitely fringed and strangely coloured plant, one of the most delicate of Alpine vegetable products, the plant so much admired by Mr. Ruskin, *Soldanella alpina*.[39] From this place a long and gradual descent brought us into the beautiful valley of the Ariége; and being now in a country well explored, and possessed of excellent Floras, I at last end this long memorandum, and finally take my leave.

# Verbascum Thapsiforme

## OCTOBER 1862

*Phytologist*, n.s. VI (Oct. 1862), 314. Appeared in the section entitled "Botanical Notes, Notices, and Queries." In the "Communications Received" section a letter from Mill is mentioned (*ibid.*, p. 320); the quoted words are presumably from that (non-extant) letter. Not republished. Not listed in Mill's bibliography.

OUR ESTEEMED CORRESPONDENT "J.S.M." in his homeward journey saw much of *Verbascum thapsiforme* between Vienna and Switzerland, in "the Austrian Highlands, where, like many other plants, it grows much more luxuriantly than in the North." Some good examples of this species have been seen in the Chelsea Botanic Garden.

---

[38]Not located.
[39]John Ruskin, *Modern Painters*, Vol. II, pp. 86, 104–5.

# MEDICAL REVIEWS

## 1834, 1842

# Medical Reviews

## Dr. King's Lecture on the Study of Anatomy
### NOVEMBER 1834

*Monthly Repository*, VIII (Nov. 1834), 817–18. Subtitled: "Delivered at the reopening of the School founded by the late Joshua Brooks, Esq. October 1, 1833." In the "Critical Notices" section. A review of *The Substance of a Lecture Designed as an Introduction to the Study of Anatomy Considered as the Science of Organization: and Delivered at the Reopening of the School, Founded by the late Joshua Brookes, Esq. October 1st, 1833* (London: Longman, *et al.*, 1834), by Thomas King (1802–39). Unsigned. Not republished. Identified in Mill's bibliography as "A brief notice of Dr. King's lecture on the study of anatomy; in the Monthly Repository for November 1834" (MacMinn, p. 42).

DR. KING'S LECTURE is an excellent specimen of the lucid and methodical exposition and philosophic views of the nature of classification which characterise the French anatomists and physiologists. It also contains a surprising quantity, considering its shortness, of the most important elementary facts of the human organization, explained in a manner peculiarly well suited, not only to learners, but even to non-medical readers. Dr. King has evidently some of the highest qualities of an able teacher.

## Carpenter's Physiology
### JANUARY 1842

*Westminster Review*, XXXVII (Jan. 1842), 254. Headed with the title of the book reviewed: "*Principles of General and Comparative Physiology, intended as an Introduction to the study of Human Physiology, and as a guide to the Philosophical pursuit of Natural History*, by William B. Carpenter, M.D., Lecturer on Physiology in the Bristol Medical School, etc. Second Edition, 1841. [London:] Churchill." In the "Miscellaneous Notices" section. Signed "S." Not republished. Identified in Mill's bibliography as "A short notice of Dr. Carpenter's Principles of General and Comparative Physiology, in the Westminster Review for January 1842" (MacMinn, p. 54).

THIS IS A BOOK to which justice cannot be done without a much fuller notice than can be given in this part of our journal, and we shall probably return to it in a future number. The author (who is the son of the late respected Dr. Lant Carpenter, of Bristol, and who, though still a young man, has long been known as a physiologist of eminence)[1] has not only accumulated in this work a richer store of the mere facts of the science than we believe is to be obtained in the same compass elsewhere, but has displayed in an eminent degree one of the principal attributes of a philosopher, as distinguished from a mere man of science, the power of generalizing. To the experienced reader, it is already some indication of this quality, that Dr. Carpenter includes in his design the physiology of plants as well as of animals, the best physiologists being now convinced that so far as respects mere organic life, the formation, nutrition, and reproduction of the living body (independently of the superadded casualties of sensation and voluntary motion), there is no fundamental distinction between the animal and vegetable creation, but both are governed by essentially the same organic laws, variously modified by circumstances.

In Dr. Carpenter's book this and a large body of similar truths are established and illustrated with a very uncommon degree of philosophic power, and the work may be considered as a clear exposition of the highest generalities yet arrived at in the science of life. As such breadth of speculation and reach of philosophy, applied to this subject, have not hitherto been often exemplified in this country, English writers having remained greatly inferior in this highest scientific attribute to the physiologists of France and Germany, it is highly creditable to our scientific and medical public that Dr. Carpenter's work has been warmly welcomed and highly applauded by almost all the professional periodicals,[2] and by most of those scientific authorities whose praise confers real honour.

[1]William Benjamin Carpenter (1813–85) was the son of Lant Carpenter (1780–1840), a Unitarian preacher, polemicist, and schoolmaster.

[2]See, e.g., the anonymous reviews in the *British and Foreign Medical Review*, VII (Jan. 1830), 168–85, and the *Medical Gazette*, 2 Feb., 1839, 675–8.

# APPENDICES

# Appendix A

## Wills and Deed of Gift
### 1853–72

Principal Registry of the Family Division, Somerset House, London, and Archives Départementales de Vaucluse. Mill's first will, indited on 23 May, 1853, after his marriage two years earlier to Harriet Hardy Taylor, was subject to a codicil entered on 14 February, 1872, some thirteen and a half years after her death in 1858 and nearly a year before his. Meanwhile, on his acquiring French property after her death, he drew up the first of his French wills on 14 February, 1859; he confirmed this and added codicils on 11 January, 1864, and 21 January, 1867; finally on 27 February, 1869, he drew up a "Donation" giving the French property to Helen Taylor, his stepdaughter, who in effect was his sole beneficiary in both England and France.

### 23 May, 1853

This is the last Will and Testament of me John Stuart Mill of the East India House in the City of London and of Blackheath Park in the County of Kent First I nominate and appoint my dearest Wife Harriet Mill[1] her daughter Miss Helen Taylor William Ellis[2] of the Marine Indemnity Assurance Office Great Winchester Street in the aforesaid City of London and of Champion Hill in the Parish of Camberwell in the County of Surrey Esquire and William Thomas Thornton[3] of the East India House aforesaid and of Marlborough Hill Saint Johns Wood in the County of Middlesex Esquire joint Executrixes and Executors of this my will And I bequeath the sum of fifty pounds to each of them the said Harriet Mill Helen Taylor William Ellis and William Thomas Thornton And as to all the real estate to which at the time of my decease I shall be entitled in possession remainder reversion or expectancy or in or over which I have a disposing power and all the rest and residue of my personal estate and after payment thereout of my debts and funeral and testamentary expenses and the legacies herein before bequeathed I give devise

[1]Harriet Taylor Mill (née Hardy) (1808–58), who following the death in 1849 of her first husband, John Taylor, married Mill in 1851, after an intimate friendship that began in 1830.
[2]William Ellis (1800–81), an insurance executive, economist and educational reformer, had been a friend of Mill's since the early 1820s.
[3]William Thomas Thornton (1813–80), economist, was from 1836 employed with Mill in the Examiner's Office of the East India Company.

bequeath and appoint the same and every part thereof unto my said wife her heirs executors administrators and assigns for her and their own absolute use and benefit And in the event of my said wife Harriet Mill departing this life in my lifetime I give and bequeath the same and every part thereof unto her daughter the said Helen Taylor her heirs executors administrators and assigns for her and their own absolute use and benefit In witness whereof I have hereunto set my hand this twenty third day of May one thousand eight hundred and fifty three

J.S. Mill

Signed and acknowledged by the above named John Stuart Mill as and to be his last Will and Testament in the presence of us present at the same time who at his request in his presence and in the presence of each other have hereunto subscribed our names as witnesses
Robt. S. Gregson Solr. 8 Angel Court Throgmorton St. London

Geo. Wm. Walker his Clerk.

**14 February 1872**

This is a Codicil to the last Will of me John Stuart Mill of No. 10 Albert Mansions Victoria Street in the City of Westminster Esquire dated the twenty third day of May one thousand eight hundred and fifty three Whereas by my said Will I gave and devised all my real estate and all the residue of my personal estate to my late dearest wife Harriet Mill and in the event of her dying in my lifetime I gave and bequeathed the same unto her daughter Miss Helen Taylor for her absolute use and benefit and I appointed my said late wife the said Helen Taylor William Ellis and William Thomas Thornton to each of whom I bequeathed the sum of fifty pounds Executors thereof And whereas I have made several Codicils to my said Will And whereas since the date of my said will my said dear wife has departed this life and her remains have been interred in a Tomb or Vault in the public Cemetery of the Town of Avignon in France Now I do hereby revoke all the codicils I have ever made to my said will and I also revoke the said appointment of executors in the said will made and also the said legacies to each of such executors thereby given and in case my stepdaughter Miss Helen Taylor shall survive me then and in such case I nominate and appoint her to be the sole Executor or Executrix of my said Will and of any Codicil thereto and devise bequeath and confirm to her her heirs executors administrators and assigns All and singular the real and personal estate of whatsoever nature kind and description I may die seised or possessed of or entitled to for her and their own proper use and benefit absolutely I also nominate and appoint the said Helen Taylor to be my literary Executor or Executrix of my said Will and of any Codicil thereto with full and absolute power and license to her to edit all or any of my literary works and to publish all or any of my manuscripts as she in her sole discretion may think fit And whereas in these days no one is secure against attempts to make money out of his memory by means of pretended biographies I therefore think it necessary to state that I have written a short account of my life which I leave to the absolute charge and controul of my said stepdaughter Miss Helen Taylor to be published or not at her will and discretion[4] and in the event of her death in my lifetime to the charge and controul of William Thomas Thornton of No. 23 Queens Gardens Hyde Park Square on condition that he publishes the same within two years of my decease And I hereby declare that all papers and materials available for an account of my life are in the possession of my said stepdaughter and of her only and that no other person has such knowledge of either my literary or private life as would qualify him or her to write my biography In the event of the said Helen Taylor predeceasing me then and in such case I nominate and appoint the said William Thomas Thornton and William Ellis of No. 6 Lancaster Terrace Regents Park in the said County of Middlesex Esquire to be the Executors and Trustees of my said Will and of any Codicil thereto and subject to the said Helen Taylor predeceasing me as aforesaid I make the following bequests and dispositions I bequeath to my stepson Algernon Taylor of Tetsworth in the County of Oxford Esquire the sum of one thousand pounds I bequeath to Elizabeth Taylor Mary Taylor and John Cyprian Taylor[5] the two daughters and son of the said Algernon Taylor the respective sums of one thousand pounds each Provided always that in case at my death the said Elizabeth Taylor Mary Taylor and John Cyprian Taylor or any of them shall be under the age of twenty one years then I direct that their respective legacies of one thousand pounds each or the legacies or legacy of such of them as shall be then minors or a minor shall be retained by the said William Thomas Thornton and William Ellis or other the trustees or trustee for the time being of my said will and any codicil thereto Upon trust to pay the same respectively to them her or him when and if they she or he shall attain the age of twenty one years And upon further trust in the meantime to invest the same in any of the modes of investment hereinafter specified and pay the interest dividends and income thereof to their her or his father or guardians or guardian for their her or his benefit and advantage And I declare that the receipt of their said father guardians or guardian as the case may be shall be an effectual discharge for such interest dividends and income and every part thereof Provided always and I hereby further declare that if the said Elizabeth Taylor and Mary Taylor or either of them shall be married at my death or shall marry previously to their or her attaining the said age of twenty one years then and in such case and

[4]Helen Taylor fulfilled this obligation by publishing Mill's *Autobiography* in October 1873 after his death on 7 May of that year.

[5]Algernon Taylor (1830–1903), second son of Harriet and John Taylor, whose wife Ellen had died in 1864, and their three children, Elizabeth (1861–1924), Mary (1863/4–1918), who became the literary executor of Helen Taylor and so custodian of Mill's surviving papers in 1907, and John Cyprian (1862–1939).

thereupon I declare that the said William Thomas Thornton and William Ellis and the survivor of them and the executors and administrators of such survivor or other the trustees or trustee for the time being of my said will and any codicil thereto shall hold the said two legacies of one thousand pounds each or the said legacy of such one of them the said Elizabeth Taylor and Mary Taylor as shall be then so married or shall so marry as aforesaid Upon trust to invest the same in the names or name or under the legal control of them or him the said trustees or trustee for the time being in any of the public stocks or funds or Government securities of the United Kingdom or India or upon freehold copyhold leasehold or chattel real securities in England or Wales or in or upon the stocks funds shares debentures mortgages or securities of any Corporation Company or Public Body in the United Kingdom or India in which my estate or any part thereof may be invested at the time of my decease but not in any other mode of investment and may from time to time vary or transpose such stocks funds shares and securities into or for others of any nature hereby authorised at their or his discretion And shall pay the interest dividends and income thereof during the lives or a life of such married legatees or legatee respectively as the case may be to such person or persons as they or she respectively may from time to time notwithstanding coverture appoint by any writing under their or her hands or hand respectively but not by any mode of anticipation and in default of such appointment into their or her hands respectively for their or her sole and separate use respectively independently and exclusive of their or her husbands or husband respectively and their or his debts control and engagements respectively but so that they or she respectively shall not dispose thereof in any mode of anticipation And the receipts in writing of them or her respectively or of such person or persons as they or she respectively shall appoint to receive the said interest dividends and income in manner aforesaid but not in any mode of anticipation shall notwithstanding coverture be effectual discharges for the same And from and after their or her deaths or death respectively shall stand possessed of and interested in the said legacies or legacy respectively or the stocks funds shares and securities representing the said legacies or legacy respectively and the interest dividends and income thereof respectively Upon and for such trusts intents and purposes and in such manner as they or she respectively by their or her last wills or will codicils or codicil or other testamentary writings or writing respectively to be duly executed notwithstanding coverture shall direct or appoint and in default of such direction or appointment and so far as any such direction or appointment if incomplete shall not extend In trust for the person or persons who under the statutes made for the distribution of the estates of intestates would under the decease of them or her the said Elizabeth Taylor and Mary Taylor respectively be entitled to their or her personal estate respectively in case they or she had died possessed of the same respectively intestate and without having been married and to be divided between or amongst the same persons if more than one respectively in the shares in which the same would under the same statutes be divided between or amongst them respectively And I declare that in case the said Elizabeth Taylor Mary Taylor and John Cyprian Taylor or any of them shall not attain the age of twenty one years or in the case of the said Elizabeth Taylor and Mary Taylor or either of them failing to attain such age and without having contracted marriage then and in each such case I direct that the same legacies or legacy as the case may be shall be held upon such and the like trusts for the benefit of the survivors in equal shares or for the survivor if but one as are hereinbefore declared in respect to the legacy of one thousand pounds given to each of them I bequeath to the said William Thomas Thornton and William Ellis their executors administrators and assigns the sum of two thousand five hundred pounds Upon trust to invest the same in any of the securities hereinbefore mentioned with reference to the investments of the said legacies of one thousand pounds each in favour of the said children of the said Algernon Taylor together with the like powers of varying and transposing from time to time such investments or any of them And to pay the interest dividends and income thereof during the life of my sister Mary Elizabeth Colman[6] the wife of Charles Colman Esquire to such person or persons as she the said Mary Elizabeth Colman may from time to time notwithstanding coverture appoint by any writing under her hand but not by any mode of anticipation and in default of such appointment into her own hands for her sole and separate use independently and exclusively of the said Charles Colman and of any future husband but so that she shall not dispose thereof in any mode of anticipation and the receipts in writing of the said Mary Elizabeth Colman or of such person or persons as she shall appoint to receive the said dividends interest and income thereof in manner aforesaid but not in any mode of anticipation shall notwithstanding coverture be effectual discharges for the same And from and after the death of the said Mary Elizabeth Colman upon and for such trusts intents and purposes and in such manner as the said Mary Elizabeth Colman shall by her last will or any codicil or testamentary writing to be by her duly executed notwithstanding coverture direct or appoint and in default of such direction or appointment and so far as any such direction or appointment if incomplete shall not extend In trust for the person or persons who under the statutes made for the distribution of the estates of intestates would at the decease of the said Mary Elizabeth Colman be entitled to her personal estate in case she had died possessed of the same intestate and widow and to be divided between or amongst the same persons if more than one in the shares in which the same would under the same statutes be divided between or amongst them I bequeath to Minnie daughter of the said Charles and Mary Elizabeth Colman the sum of one thousand pounds and to Stuart Colman Henry Colman and Archibald Colman sons

[6]Mary Elizabeth Colman (née Mill) (1822–1913), Mill's youngest sister, married Charles Frederick Colman in 1847, and had by him the four children mentioned below, Marion (known as Minnie), Stuart, Henry, and Archibald. It will be noted that none of his other surviving sisters is mentioned in the will (his three brothers had all died unmarried before the date of the codicil).

of the said Charles and Mary Elizabeth Colman the sum of five hundred pounds each Provided always that in case at my death the said Minnie Colman Stuart Colman Henry Colman and Archibald Colman or any of them shall be under the age of twenty one years the said legacies hereinbefore bequeathed to them or the legacies or legacy of such of them as shall then be minors or a minor shall be retained by the said William Thomas Thornton and William Ellis or the executors and trustees for the time being of my said will and any codicil thereto Upon trust to pay the same to them him or her when and if they he or she shall attain the age of twenty one years And upon further trust in the meantime to invest the same respectively in any of the investments hereinbefore specified and pay the interest dividends and income thereof respectively to the said Mary Elizabeth Colman or to such person or persons as she shall notwithstanding coverture direct or appoint for their his or her benefit and advantage and her or her appointees receipts alone shall be sufficient discharges for the same but in case of her death during my lifetime or subsequently without having made any such direction or appointment as last aforesaid then Upon trust to pay such interest dividends and income during the respective minorities of the said Minnie Colman Stuart Colman Henry Colman and Archibald Colman to their respective Guardians and to be applied by them for their respective benefits and the receipts of such guardians shall be sufficient discharges for the same Provided always and I hereby further declare that if the said Minnie Colman shall be married at my death or shall marry previously to her attaining the said age of twenty one years then and in such case and thereupon I declare that the said William Thomas Thornton and William Ellis and the survivor of them and the executors and administrators of such survivor or other the trustees or trustee for the time being of my said will and any codicil thereto shall invest the said legacy of the said Minnie Colman in any of the investments hereinbefore specified with the like powers of varying and transposing the same and any of them and shall stand possessed of and interested in the stocks funds shares and securities and the interest dividends and income thereof Upon and for the same and the like trusts intents and purposes and in the same and the like manner as are hereinbefore declared respecting the said legacies and the funds stocks shares and securities representing such legacies and the interest dividends and income thereof hereinbefore bequeathed in favor of the said Elizabeth Taylor and Mary Taylor in the event of their being married at my death or marrying previously to their attaining the age of twenty one years in the same manner in every respect as if the same trusts were here repeated in totidem verbis mutatis mutandis And I declare that if the said Minnie Colman Stuart Colman Henry Colman and Archibald Colman or any of them shall not attain the age of twenty one years or in the case of the said Minnie Colman failing to attain such age and without having contracted marriage then and in such case the same legacies or legacy as the case may be shall be held upon such or the like trusts for the survivors in equal shares or for the survivor if but one as are hereinbefore declared in respect of the respective legacies given to each of them I bequeath the sum of five hundred pounds to the Governors Treasurers or other proper Officers of the "Royal Society for the prevention of Cruelty to Animals" whose Offices are at No. 105 Jermyn Street Saint James Westminster in the said County of Middlesex for the benefit of that Institution and I declare that the receipt of the Treasurer for the time being of the said Royal Society for the prevention of Cruelty to Animals shall be an effectual discharge for the same legacy which I direct to be paid out of my pure personal estate I bequeath the like sum of five hundred pounds to the Treasurer or other the proper Officers of the "Land Tenure Reform Association" whose Offices are at No. 9 Buckingham Street Strand in the said County of Middlesex for the benefit of that Institution and I declare that the receipt of the Treasurer for the time being of the said "Land Tenure Reform Association" shall be an effectual discharge for the same legacy which I direct to be paid out of my pure personal estate I bequeath to the said William Thomas Thornton and William Ellis their executors administrators and assigns the sum of three thousand pounds in trust for such one of the now existing Universities of Great Britain and Ireland as shall be or at the time of my death shall have been the first in point of time to throw open all its degrees to female students such sum of three thousand pounds to be paid out of my pure personal estate to the Chancellor Governors Trustees or other proper Officers of such University within six calendar months after my decease or as the case may be immediately upon such degrees being thrown open as aforesaid in trust to endow a fellowship to which only females shall be eligible And in like manner I bequeath in favour of such University the further sum of three thousand pounds to be paid out of my pure personal estate in trust to endow therewith two scholarships to be held by female students exclusively And I direct that in the meantime and until the fulfilment of such conditions as aforesaid the said William Thomas Thornton and William Ellis and the survivor of them and the executors and administrators of such survivor or other the trustees or trustee for the time being of my said will and any codicil thereto shall stand possessed of the said two sums of three thousand pounds and three thousand pounds Upon trust to invest the same in any of the stocks funds shares and securities hereinbefore mentioned with the like powers as hereinbefore mentioned of varying and transposing all or any of such investments And shall from time to time accumulate the interest dividends and income thereof in the way of compound interest by investing the same and the resulting income thereof in or upon any such investments as are hereinbefore mentioned all which accumulations shall go in addition to and accretion of and be held upon the same trusts as are hereby declared of and concerning the said sums of three thousand pounds and three thousand pounds Provided always and I hereby declare that in case the aforesaid conditions shall not be fulfilled within the space of twenty years after my death then and in such case I direct that the same legacies of three thousand pounds and three thousand pounds and the accumulations aforesaid shall be applied by the trustees for the time being of my said will and any codicil thereto in whatever way they in their absolute and uncontrolled discretion judge most beneficial to the education of women I bequeath all copyrights I may die possessed of to John Morley[7] of Pitfield Down Puttenham near Guildford in the County of Surrey Esquire his executors administrators and assigns Upon trust to apply the proceeds thereof in aid and support of some periodical publication which shall be open to the expression of all opinions and shall have all its articles signed with the name of the writer and subject to the fulfilment of such conditions on the part of any such periodical publication I leave the selection of such publication to the said John Morley and subject to the trust aforesaid I declare that the said John Morley his executors or administrators shall stand possessed of and interested in all such said copyrights and the proceeds thereof In trust for such person or persons as the said John Morley shall by his last will or any codicil or testamentary writing to be by him duly executed give or bequeath the same subject nevertheless to the same trusts as those under which the said John Morley himself held the said copyrights and the proceeds thereof during his lifetime I bequeath to the said William Thomas Thornton and William Ellis the sum of one hundred pounds each I direct that all the legacies hereinbefore bequeathed shall be paid free of all legacy and succession duties and that the duty on the legacies given to the said Society for the prevention of Cruelty to Animals to the said Land Tenure Reform Association and to the said University shall be paid out of my pure personal estate And I hereby direct and declare that all manuscripts letters and copies of letters to and from me which may be in my possession at my death shall belong exclusively to and be at the disposal of my literary executor and should I not before my death have made a selection of such of them as it may be useful or interesting to publish I hereby authorize and request my said literary executor to make such a selection the letters so selected either by myself or by my said literary executor to be published with the aforesaid memoir of my life whenever the said memoir shall be published and all my other letters to be destroyed unless my said literary executor shall desire to retain them or any of them And in case the said Helen Taylor shall die before me or if she shall survive me but die without having nominated by will a successor to her self as my literary executor then I appoint the said William Thomas Thornton to be my literary executor and I direct that the above mentioned memoir of my life and all other manuscripts and writings left by me on which I shall have written the words "For Publication" and signed such words with my name shall be published with all convenient expedition And I declare that the profits if any that may arise from such publication by the said William Thomas Thornton shall go and belong to the said William Thomas Thornton his executors administrators and assigns absolutely for his and their own use and benefit I devise and bequeath all my real estate whatsoever and wheresoever charged in aid of my personal estate with my funeral

---

[7]John Morley (1838–1923), editor, author, and later statesman, had been an admirer and adherent of Mill's since 1865.

and testamentary expenses debts and legacies other than charitable legacies and all my residuary personal estate including as well real as personal estate over which I have or shall have at the time of my death a general power of appointment unto and to the use of the said William Thomas Thornton his heirs executors administrators and assigns absolutely And I declare that the trustees or trustee for the time being of my said will and any codicil thereto shall have the fullest powers of apportioning blended trust funds and of determining whether any moneys are to be treated as capital or income and generally of determining all matters as to which any doubt difficulty or question may arise under or in relation to the execution of the trusts of my said will or any codicil thereto And I declare that every determination of the said trustees or trustee in relation to any of the matters aforesaid whether made upon a question formally or actually raised or implied in any of the acts or proceedings of the said trustees or trustee in relation to the premises shall bind all parties interested under my said will and any codicil thereto and shall not be objected to or questioned upon any ground whatsoever And I hereby declare that the receipt of the said trustees or trustee for the time being acting in the execution of the trusts of my said will and any codicil thereto for any moneys payable to them or him by virtue thereof or in the execution of the trusts or powers thereof shall effectually discharge the person or persons paying the same therefrom and from being bound to see to the application or being answerable for the loss or misapplication thereof Provided always and I hereby declare that if the said trustees hereby constituted or either of them shall die in my lifetime or if they or either of them or any trustee or trustees to be appointed as hereinafter provided shall after my death die or go to reside permanently abroad or desire to be discharged or refuse or become incapable to act then and in every such case it shall be lawful for the surviving or continuing trustees or trustee for the time being and for this purpose every refusing or retiring trustee shall if willing to act in the execution of this power be considered a continuing trustee or for the acting executors or executor administrators or administrator of the last surviving or continuing trustee to appoint a new trustee or new trustees in the place of the trustee or trustees so dying or going to reside permanently abroad or desiring to be discharged or refusing or becoming incapable to act as aforesaid and upon every or any such appointment as aforesaid the number of trustees may be augmented or reduced but so that the number thereof be not less than two And upon every such appointment all the moneys stocks funds shares and securities if any then vested in the trustees or trustee for the time being or in the executors or administrators of the last surviving or continuing trustee shall be so assigned and transferred that the same may be vested in the surviving or continuing trustee or trustees jointly with such new trustee or trustees or in such new trustee or trustees solely as the case may require And every trustee appointed as aforesaid may as well before as after the said trust premises if any shall have been so vested act or assist in the execution of the trusts and powers of my said will and any codicil thereto as fully and effectually to all intents and purposes as if I had hereby constituted him a trustee Provided always and I hereby declare that the trustees for the time being of my said will and any codicil thereto shall be respectively chargeable only for such moneys stocks funds shares and securities as they shall respectively actually receive notwithstanding their respectively signing any receipt for the sake of conformity and shall be answerable and accountable only for their own acts receipts neglects and defaults respectively and not for those of each other nor for any banker broker or other person with whom or into whose hands any trust monies or securities may be deposited or come nor for dispensing wholly or partially with the investigation or production of the lessor's title on lending money on leasehold securities nor for otherwise lending on any security with less than a marketable title nor for the insufficiency or deficiency of any stocks funds shares or securities nor for any other loss unless the same shall happen through their own wilful default respectively And also that the said trustees or trustee for the time being may reimburse themselves and himself or pay and discharge out of the trust premises all expenses incurred in or about the execution of the trusts or powers of my said will and any codicil thereto I devise and bequeath all the estates which at my death shall be vested in me upon any trusts or by way of mortgage and of which I shall at my death have power to dispose by will unto the said William Thomas Thornton and William Ellis their heirs executors and administrators respectively according to the nature thereof respectively upon the trusts and subject to the equity of redemption which at my death shall be subsisting or capable of taking effect therein respectively but the money secured on such mortgages shall be taken as part of my personal estate And whereas I have already made and executed in France a Will disposing of my estate and property situate in that Country now I do hereby confirm such will and do declare that nothing in my said will dated the twenty third of May one thousand eight hundred and fifty three or in this Codicil contained save and except as to the said hereinbefore mentioned manuscripts letters and copies of letters shall affect or be deemed to affect any of the dispositions and contents generally of my said will so made in France as aforesaid it being my express desire and intention that my said will dated the twenty third of May one thousand eight hundred and fifty three and this Codicil shall not extend to embrace or dispose of save as to such manuscripts letters and copies of letters as aforesaid the estate and property disposed of or dealt with in such said will so made by me in France as aforesaid or any property or estate situate and being in France whereof I may die possessed or entitled to Lastly I desire and direct that my mortal remains may be buried in the said tomb of my dear wife in the said Cemetery at Avignon and that the same shall on no account or pretext whatsoever be buried in any other place wheresoever In witness whereof I have set my hand to this Codicil contained in eight sheets of paper this fourteenth day of February one thousand eight hundred and seventy two

J.S. Mill

Signed and acknowledged by the said John Stuart Mill as and to be a Codicil to his last Will and Testament in the presence of us present at the same time who in his presence at his request and in the presence of each other have hereunto subscribed our names as witnesses the alterations opposite which our initials are placed having been first made

Robt. S. Gregson Solr. 8 Angel Court Throgmorton Street London
Theophilus Wm. Starkey 8 Angel Court Solicitor Clerk to Mr. R.S. Gregson

Proved at London with a Codicil 5th September 1873 by the Oath of Helen Taylor Spinster the sole Executrix named in the said Codicil to whom Administration was granted.

## 14 February, 1859

Testament
L'an mil huit cent cinquante neuf et le quatorze février.

Par-devant nous Paul Giéra,[8] notaire à Avignon, soussigné, et en présence des témoins ci-après nommés également soussignés;

A Comparu

M. John Stuart Mill, rentier, demeurant à Blackheath Park près de Londres.

Lequel étant sain d'esprit, ainsi qu'il en est apparu à nous notaire et témoins, a dicté à nous notaire, qui l'avons écrit desuite de notre main, en présence des dits témoins et tel qu'il nous l'a dicté, le testament dont la teneur suit:

[a] Sans entendre révoquer le testament que j'ai fait en Angleterre à la date du vingt trois mai mil huit cent cinquante trois, testament que j'entends au contraire maintenir et confirmer; Je lègue et laisse à ma fille adoptive, Hélène Taylor, fille de ma défunte épouse

1° Un pavillon et la terre sur laquelle il est construit, en nature de jardin, labour et vigne de la contenance d'environ vingt neuf ares quatre vingt huit centiares, situé sur le territoire d'Avignon, clos de St-Véran ou de la Folie que j'ai acquis de M. Mouzin suivant acte du dix huit novembre dernier reçu par le dit Me Giéra. Pour le posséder et en jouir dès le jour de mon décès sans être astreinte à en demander délivrance.

2° le terrain que j'ai acquis dans le cimetière St Véran d'Avignon, ainsi que le tombeau que j'y [b]fais édifier[b].

[8]The notary Paul Giéra (1816–61) was one of the group of seven Provençal poets who, in 1854, had formed the group called *les félibres*. His son, Jules, and their successor, Michel Baulieu, continued to serve as notaries to Mill and Helen Taylor.

[a][*cancelled*] Je lègue et laisse
[b–b][*cancelled*] ai fait édifier

Je désire être inhumé dans ce tombeau.

Je désire que ma fille adoptive et son frère <sup>c</sup>Algernon Taylor<sup>c</sup> y soient également inhumés.

J'entends que dans le cas où ma fille adoptive ne disposerait pas de ces propriétés ou de l'une d'elles, celles ou celle dont elle n'aura pas disposé appartiennent après elle au Conseil Presbytéral de l'Eglise réformée à Avignon, à charge par le dit Conseil de maintenir le tombeau, et de l'entretenir en bon état; ainsi que les plantations que ma fille ou moi y aurons faites.

A cet effet je lègue éventuellement les dits objets au dit Conseil presbytéral.

C'est ma volonté dont je requiers acte.

Ainsi fait et passé à Avignon dans un salon au premier étage de notre maison d'habitation rue Banasterie en présence de Mrs Jean Xavier Louis Duprat, négociant, Jean Etienne Ernest Duprat, négociant, Jean Emmanuel Duprat, employé de la Banque de France, et Jean Xavier Emile Duprat, commis négociant, tous domiciliés et demeurant à Avignon, témoins requis et signés avec le testateur et nous notaire.

Le présent testament et tout le contenu ci-dessus a été lu par nous notaire au testateur en présence des dits témoins qui ont assisté sans désemparer.[9]

J.S. Mill

### 11 January, 1864

Testament

L'an mil huit cent soixante quatre et le onze Janvier.

Devant nous Me Jules Giéra, notaire à Avignon soussigné, et en présence des témoins ci-après nommés également soussignés;

a comparu

Mr John Stuart Mill, propriétaire rentier demeurant et domicilié à Blackheat Parc, près de Londres.

Lequel étant sain d'esprit, ainsi qu'il en est apparu à nous notaire et témoins, a dicté à nous notaire, qui l'avons écrit de suite de notre main, en présence des dits témoins et tel qu'il nous l'a dicté, son testament dont la teneur suit:

Je déclare confirmer dans tout leur contenu les dispositions écrites dans mon testament reçu par Me Paul Giéra notaire à Avignon le quatorze février mil huit cent cinquante neuf et à ces dispositions j'ajoute les suivantes en forme de codicile.

Je lègue et laisse à ma fille adoptive Hélène Taylor, fille de ma défunte épouse

1° un corps de terre en nature de prés situé sur le territoire d'Avignon quartier des Fontaines de la contenance d'environ vingt neuf ares et tel que je l'ai acquis de

---

[9][In margin:] Rayé sept mots nuls aux présentes.

<sup>c–c</sup>[*an addition noted in the margin*]

dame Anne Rozan épouse Martin suivant acte reçu par Me Jules Giéra le douze Septembre mil huit cent soixante deux,

2° un autre corps de terre, partie en nature de pré partie en vigne et jardin situé sur les mêmes territoires et quartier, attenant au précédent, et tel que je l'ai acquis de Mrs Challe frères, Marandon, Perrier et Raymond suivant acte reçu par Me Jules Giéra le quatre Janvier courant,

3° enfin je lui lègue également tous les immeubles que je pourrais acquérir par la suite sur le territoire d'Avignon

pour jouir du tout à dater du jour de mon décès et en disposer à sa volonté.

Tel est ma volonté dont je requiers acte.

Ainsi fait et passé à Avignon en l'étude de nous notaire, en présence de MM. Albert Roche aspirant au notariat, M. Paulain Malosse, élève de notaire, M. Charles Morénas tourneur, Charles Bontour sacristain de la paroisse St Pierre, tous les quatre domiciliés et demeurant à Avignon, témoins requis et signés avec le testateur et nous notaire.

Sur notre interpelation les témoins ont déclaré qu'ils sont majeurs citoyens français qu'ils jouissent de leurs droits civils et qu'ils ne sont ni parents ni alliés au degrés prohibés par la loi soit du testateur soit de la légatrice.

le présent testament et tout le contenu a été lu par nous notaire au testateur en présence des témoins dénommés qui ont assisté sans désemparer.

J.S. Mill

## 21 January, 1867

Testament

L'an mil huit cent soixante sept et le *<sup>d</sup>*vingt-un*<sup>d</sup>* Janvier.

Devant nous Me Jules Giéra, notaire à Avignon, soussigné, et en présence des témoins ci-après nommés, également soussignés

a Comparu

Mr John Stuart Mill, propriétaire rentier, demeurant et domicilié à Blackheat Parc, près Londres.

lequel, étant sain d'esprit, ainsi qu'il en est apparu à nous notaire et témoins, a dicté à nous notaire, qui l'avons écrit desuite de notre main, en présence des dits témoins et tel qu'il nous l'a dicté, son testament codicile, dont la teneur suit:

Je déclare confirmer dans tout leur contenu les dispositions écrites dans mon testament, reçu par Me Paul Giéra le quatorze février mil huit cent cinquante neuf et dans le codicile de ce testament reçu par Me Jules Giéra le onze janvier mil huit cent soixante quatre

et à ces dispositions j'ajoute les suivantes toujours en forme de codicile.

---

*<sup>d–d</sup>*[*cancelled*] dix huit

Je lègue et laisse à ma fille adoptive Mlle Hélène Taylor, fille de ma défunte épouse

tous les biens meubles et immeubles que je posséderai en France à mon décès et notamment les immeubles que je possède ou posséderai à Avignon ou sur son territoire, avec tous les objets mobiliers, valeurs industrielles ou deniers comptant qui se trouveront dans mes maisons d'habitation à Avignon au moment de mon décès, sans exception ni réserve, donnant au mot objet mobilier et biens meubles, le sens le plus large que comporte la loi.

pour jouir du tout à dater du jour de mon décès et en disposer à sa volonté.

Ces nouvelles dispositions ne pourront nuire aux dispositions supplémentaires exprimées dans mon testament reçu par Me Paul Giéra.

Telle est ma volonté dont je requiers acte.

Ainsi fait et passé à Avignon en l'étude de nous notaire, en présence de M. Jean Agricol Brouchier Commissaire aux inhumations, M. Jean Antoine Chaspoul, propriétaire rentier, M. Albert Roche, aspirant au notariat, et M. Joseph Céylan sous-sacristain de la paroisse St Pierre, tous les quatre domiciliés et demeurant à Avignon.

Témoins requis et signés avec le testateur et nous notaire.

les dits témoins sur notre interpelation ont chacun dit être majeurs, français, jouissant de leurs droits civils, et non parents ou alliés du testateur et de la légataire.

le présent testament et tout le contenu a été lu par nous notaire au testateur en présence des témoins qui ont assisté sans désemparer.[10]

J.S. Mill

## 27 February, 1869

### Donation

Stuart Mill à Taylor

L'an mil huit cent soixante *neuf* et le vingt sept février.

Devant Me *Michel dit Baulieu*, licencié en droit, notaire à Avignon, en présence des deux témoins ci-après nommés, tous soussignés,

### A Comparu

Monsieur John Stuart Mill, rentier, demeurant à Blackheath Park, près de Londres.

Lequel a par les présentes, fait donation entrevifs

A Melle Hélène Taylor, propriétaire rentière, domiciliée à Londres, demeurant actuellement à Avignon, *sa belle fille*,

[10][In margin:] Rayé trois mots nuls dans le cours de l'acte.

*e–e*[*cancelled*] huit et le
*f–f*[*in the margin, replacing the cancelled name* Jules Giéra]
*g–g*[*an addition noted in the margin*]

Ici présente et acceptant expressément

Des biens dont la désignation suit:

1° Un pavillon et la terre sur laquelle il est construit en nature de jardin, labour et vignes, de la contenance d'environ vingt neuf ares quatre vingt huit centiares, situé sur le territoire d'Avignon, clos de St Véran ou de la folie, confrontant au levant Cade, au midi le chemin de la folie, au couchant les hoirs Boyer, au nord Martin née Rozan ou le donateur.

Le comparant a acquis ledit immeuble de M. Pierre Alexis Mouzin, propriétaire ancien boulanger et Marie Thérèse Drôme, son épouse, demeurant à Avignon, suivant acte du dix huit novembre mil huit cent cinquante huit, Paul Giéra notaire à Avignon, transcrit au bureau des hypothèques d'Avignon le vingt trois du même mois, et a payé le prix de cette vente, suivant quittance reçu par M. Paul Giéra, le quinze février mil huit cent cinquante neuf.

2° Une pièce de terre en nature de pré, situé sur le territoire d'Avignon, quartier des fontaines, de la contenance de vingt neuf ares, limitée au nord par Maradon, le donateur et autres, au midi la terre ci-dessus, au levant Cade, au couchant Martin-Rozan.

Cette terre fut acquise par le donateur de Madme Anne Rozan, épouse de Louis Charles Martin, propriétaire cultivateur, demeurant à Avignon, suivant acte reçu par Me Giéra <sup>h</sup>notaire à Avignon<sup>h</sup>, le douze septembre mil huit cent soixante deux, transcrit au bureau des hypothèques d'Avignon, le vingt quatre septembre même année, vol. 423, no. 67. Le prix fut payé comptant.

3° Une terre partie en nature de pré et partie labourable située sur le territoire d'Avignon, quartier du pont des deux eaux et des fontaines, d'une contenance d'environ soixante dix sept ares trente cinq centiares, y comris une petite parcelle séparée et en dépendant d'environ cinq ares dix centiares. Le plus grand de ces deux corps confronte au levant et au midi Joseph Rozan, au couchant Lubière, au nord une traverse; la petite parcelle confronte au levant et au midi Toussaint Ferrière, au couchant Richard, au nord Lubière. Les bâtiments construits sur ladite terre font aussi partie de la donation.

4° Une parcelle de terre en nature de pré de la contenance de quarante ares dix sept centiares, située sur le territoire d'Avignon, clos des fontaines, faisant du no. 291 de la section H.H. du plan cadastral, et confrontant au levant M. Cléments, au midi le donateur, au couchant Marandon, au nord un chemin d'exploitation.

5° Une pièce de terre en prairie située sur le même territoire, même clos des fontaines, et une langue de terre complantée en saules située au couchant de ladite prairie dont elle est séparée par une distance de quatorze mètres; de la contenance ensemble de trente quatre ares quatre vingt centiares. La prairie confronte au levant Marandon, au midi Martin dit la vierge, au couchant Ferrier ou le donateur, au nord les hoirs Ytier; la langue de terre confronte au couchant un canal d'arrosage, au levant Ferrier.

---

<sup>h–h</sup>[*in the margin, replacing the cancelled word* soussigné]

6° Une terre en nature de pré, située sur le même territoire et quartier, d'une contenance de quarante un ares quatre vingt dix huit centiares, confrontant au levant Raymond, au midi le donateur, au couchant Martin dit la vierge et autres, au nord les hoirs Ytier.

Ces quatre derniers immeubles ont été acquis par le donateur; savoir:

la première, de Etienne Trophine Isidore Marandon, boulanger, demeurant à Avignon;

la deuxième, de MM. Antoine Challe, André Challe, et Valentin Challe, frères, marchands d'huiles et de fromages, demeurant à Avignon;

la troisième, de M. Paul Joseph Marie dit Raymond, propriétaire rentier, demeurant à Avignon;

la quatrième, de M. Jean Pierre Ferrier, propriétaire cultivateur, demeurant sur le territoire d'Avignon, quartier de Courtine;

le tout suivant acte reçu par Me Giéra, *i* le quatre Janvier mil huit cent soixante quatre, transcrit au bureau des hypothèques d'Avignon, le vingt un janvier, même année, vol. 437, no. 82.

Le prix de la vente relatif aux propriétés aliénées par Challe, Raymond et Ferrier fut quittancé dans l'acte; le prix de la parcelle vendu par Marandon a été payé suivant actes des dix novembre et quatorze décembre mil huit cent soixante quatre et quatorze mars mil huit cent soixante cinq, notaire Me Giéra.

7° enfin les meubles et objets mobiliers décrits et estimés à la somme de deux mille cent quarante cinq francs en un état dressé par les parties à la date de ce jour, lequel devant être enregistré en même temps que ces présentes est demeuré ci-joint, après avoir été certifié véritable par les parties, et que dessus il a été apposé une mention la constatant signée des parties et du notaire, et des témoins.

Les immeubles sont donnés en l'état où ils se trouvent et avec toutes leurs dépendances, sans exception ni réserve, et *j*sans*j* garantie tant de la mesure exprimée que du bon état des bâtiments; mais avec garantie de tous troubles, évictions et autres empêchements quelconques, le donateur s'y obligeant expressément.

### Jouissance

La donataire aura la propriété des objets donnés, et elle en prendra la jouissance par la perception à son profit des loyers, fermages et revenus, le tout à compter d'aujourd'hui.

Elle se reconnaît en possession des meubles et objets mobiliers donnés.

### Les Soussignés

Monsieur John Stuart Mill, rentier, demeurant à Blackheath Park, près de Londres, d'une part

*i*[*cancelled*] soussigné,
*j-j*[*cancelled*] moins

Et Mademoiselle Hélène Taylor, propriétaire rentière, domiciliée à Londres, demeurant à Avignon, sa belle fille, d'autre part.

Dressent ainsi qu'il suit l'Etat descriptif et estimatif des meubles et objets mobiliers dont M. Mill doit faire donation à Melle Taylor; lequel sera annexé à l'acte de donation.

| | |
|---|---:|
| Quatre bibliothèques, six cent cinquante francs | 650 |
| Six tapis, deux cent septante cinq francs | 275 |
| Cinq tables, cent cinquante francs | 150 |
| Un canapé, quatre vingt dix francs | 90 |
| Deux fauteuils, soixante francs | 60 |
| Dix chaises, quarante francs | 40 |
| Une commode, trente francs | 30 |
| Trois lits, trois cent vingt cinq francs | 325 |
| Un chiffonnier, cent dix francs | 110 |
| Un paravent, quinze francs | 15 |
| Neuf cent quatre vingt deux volumes | |
| Quatre cents francs | 400 |
| Total des objets inventoriés ci dessus | —— |
| Deux mille cent quarante cinq francs | 2145 |

Fait à Avignon, le vingt sept février mil huit cent soixante neuf.

John Stuart Mill                                      Helen Taylor

## Conditions

La donataire acquittera les impôts de toute nature des immeubles donnés, à partir d'aujourd'hui.

Elle supportera les servitudes passives pouvant grêver ces immeubles, sauf à s'en défendre et à profiter de celles actives, s'il en existe, à ses risques et périls, sans que cette stipulation puisse conférer à des tiers plus de droits que ceux qu'ils pourraient avoir en vertu de la loi ou de titres réguliers non prescrits.

Elle entretiendra pour le temps qui reste à courir les baux verbaux ou écrits qui peuvent avoir été consentis par le donateur, de manière à ce que celui ci ne soit point inquiété à cet égard.

M. Mill déclare qu'une partie des terres données est affermie à M. Antoine Bathelemy, aubergiste, demeurant à Avignon, suivant acte reçu par Me Giéra, le vingt un décembre mil huit cent soixante quatre, dont la donataire déclare avoir parfaite connaissance.

## Déclarations

M. Mill déclare

Qu'il n'est personnellement dans aucun des cas spécifiés dans les articles 2121 et 2124 du Code Napoléon.

Que les formalités de purge légale ont été remplies sur la vente consentie par Mouzin, ainsi qu'il résulte du dépôt fait au greffe du tribunal d'Avignon, le vingt cinq novembre mil huit cent cinquante neuf, de la notification fait aux personnes désignées par la loi, par exploit de Berlandier huissier, du sept décembre suivant, et de l'insertion au Mémorial de Vaucluse du neuf du même mois, enregistré le quinze, fol. 88, case 1 par Ravoux qui a perçu deux francs vingt centimes.

Que ces mêmes formalités ont été remplies sur les ventes consenties par Marandon, les frères Challe, et Ferrier, ainsi qu'il résulte de pièces déposées aux minutes de Me Giéra, le vingt *ᵏ*sept*ᵏ* septembre mil huit cent soixante cinq.

Qu'il n'y avait pas lieu à purger d'hypothèques légales les terres vendues par dame Martin et par Raymond.

Enfin que tous les immeubles ci-dessus sont entièrement libres d'hypothèques.

## Titres

Le donateur a remis à la donataire qui le reconnaît:

1° Tous les actes de vente ci-dessus mentionnés, dans lesquels se trouve établie l'origine de la propriété de chacun des immeubles donnés.

2° Tous les titres de propriété plus anciens, ainsi que les pièces de purge légale et les certificats après *ˡ*transcription et purge*ˡ*.

3' et le bail consenti à Barthelemy, et plus haut mentionné.

## Evaluation

Pour la perception du droit d'enregistrement, les parties évaluent les immeubles donnés à un revenu annuel de mille cinquante francs.

## Election de domicile

Pour l'exécution des présentes, les parties font élection de domicile, à Avignon, en l'étude de Me *ᵐ*Baulieu*ᵐ*.

## Dont acte en minute

Fait et passé à Avignon, en l'étude, en présence de MMrs Jean François Puy, élève de notaire et Charles Morénas, tourneur, tous deux demeurant et domiciliés à Avignon.

Témoins instrumentaires requis.

Et après lecture, les parties ont signé avec les témoins et le notaire.

La lecture du présent acte par le notaire et la signature par les parties ont eu lieu en la présence réelle des deux témoins instrumentaires.[11]

John Stuart Mill
Helen Taylor

---

[11][In margin:] Approuvé dix sept mots rayés nuls.

*ᵏ⁻ᵏ*[*cancelled*] cinq
*ˡ⁻ˡ*[*cancelled*] la formalité hypotheq
*ᵐ⁻ᵐ*[*cancelled*] Giéra ou de son successeur

# Appendix B

## The Vixen, and Circassia

### APRIL 1837

*London and Westminster Review*, V & XXVII (Apr. 1837), 196–209. Headed: "Art. VIII. / The Vixen and Circassia. / 1. *Voyages aux Indes-Orientales par le Nord de l'Europe, les Provinces du Caucase, la Géorgie, l'Arménie, la Perse, etc., etc.*, par M. Charles Bélanger [1805–81]. [4 vols.] Paris [: Bertrand], 1836–37 [1834–38]. London, Dulau and Co. [not located]. / 2. *A Geographical, Statistical, and Commercial Account of the Russian Ports in the Black Sea, the Sea of Asoph, and the Mouth of the Danube. From the German. With an Appendix, containing the Official Report, lately published, of the European Commerce of that Empire in 1835*. [London:] Schloss [and Richardson], Great Russell Street. 1837." Signed "B.T." Not listed in Mill's bibliography. Mill sent a set of the *London and Westminster Review* to the Foxes of Falmouth, with annotations indicating authorship; the set has not been located, but some attributions are given in *Memories of Old Friends, Being Extracts from the Journals and Letters of Caroline Fox, from 1835 to 1871*, ed. H.N. Pym, new and rev. ed. (London: Smith, Elder, 1883), pp. 102–4. (The mention of the gift is in Vol. I, p. 158 in the 2nd ed.) In that list, this article is said to be marked "J.S. Mill and C. Buller" (p. 103). It seems likely that Mill wrote the opening paragraphs (perhaps the first four pages), and the conclusion, and collaborated in the rest with Buller, the main author.

THE SUBJECT of the above works has acquired a very great momentary interest, from the late seizure of a British vessel by the Russians on the coast of Circassia. The capture of the *Vixen* has been known in this country for two months: but since that period the public has been vainly looking to its ministers for any vindication of the national interests, or any explanation of the apparent wrong done to them. The matter has been frequently urged on the notice of the House of Commons, in the shape of questions and passing remarks.[1] It has very lately been brought forward in a more precise shape by Mr. Roebuck, in moving for papers relative to the transaction.[2] These papers were refused by Lord Palmerston, on the ground which is now taken by every Secretary for the Foreign Department—that of pending negotiations:[3] the silence of the noble Lord was approved by many of those

---

[1]See *PD*, 3rd ser., Vol. 37, cols. 133, 134 (6 Feb., 1837), and 165 (9 Mar., 1837).

[2]John Arthur Roebuck (1801–79), Motion on the Vixen—Treaty of Adrianople (17 Mar., 1837), *ibid.*, col. 628.

[3]Henry John Temple (1784–1865), Speech on the Vixen—Treaty of Adrianople, *ibid.*, cols. 630–6.

gentlemen, who think it their duty to utter their cuckoo note of agreement in a common absurdity: the required information was refused; and no explanation whatever was given. The admission of such a reason as sufficient to justify the withholding such information is equivalent to depriving the House of Commons of all control over the foreign policy of the country. In former times—in that of the transaction, for instance, respecting Nootka Sound, the naval force of the country was kept on so low a footing as to compel Ministers to have recourse to Parliament on the first prospect of any disturbance of our foreign relations.[4] But with a fleet so large as to admit of our carrying on even a war on a moderate scale, a minister may indulge for a long time the natural official aversion to responsibility to Parliament. He may, if he chooses it, involve the nation half-way in a war, or he may let slip irrecoverably the proper opportunity for vindicating the national interests. Parliament has no control over him. While the public feeling is strong on any subject concerning the foreign relations of the country, the Foreign Minister may refuse all information, and consequently disable the public from exercising any control over his measures. When the public interest in the matter has exhausted itself, the Minister has only to inform an indifferent audience of his necessarily final decision of a matter over which the House of Commons has not previously had, and cannot thereafter exercise, any control.

We have not yet learned from Lord Palmerston the ground on which this seizure of British property, this interruption of British commerce, are justified. The *Vixen* has been seized, and condemned: this we know; but for what offence, and by what authority, and with what right, we know not. We know not whether the Russian Government defends this act on the fact of its being done in the course of a blockade of a hostile country, and the consequent application of those principles of maritime blockade, which this country laboured to establish during the last war, and of which, however we may agree with Mr. Roebuck as to their utter injustice and impolicy,[5] the original and most zealous assertors have no right to demand the renunciation from others till they have set the example themselves. If this be the ground assumed, we know not how far it is supported by the facts of the case; whether the blockade had been sufficiently notified; whether it was enforced by sufficient naval means. But we cannot yet make out whether the seizure of the *Vixen* is not justified on grounds perfectly contrary, and perfectly inconsistent with these: whether Russia does not look on Circassia not as a hostile but a subject country: whether she does not claim to exercise a sovereign right over its trade and internal regulations; and whether the offence of the *Vixen* is not stated to be the violation of the Russian regulations of police, trade, or quarantine. In this case, we know not how this claim of sovereignty is supported; or how these sanatory, fiscal,

[4]See the debate on the King's Message respecting Captures at Nootka Sound (5–6 May, 1790), in *The Parliamentary History of England*, ed. William Cobbett and John Wright, 36 vols. (London: Bagshaw, Longmans, 1806–20), Vol. XXVIII, cols. 769–82.

[5]See Roebuck, speech of 17 Mar., 1837, col. 622.

or police regulations were notified so publicly as to justify the punishment of foreigners for a violation of them. And on all these matters the public may expect to be enlightened when it shall not care about the matter: when our commercial interests in the Black Sea, and our moral influence on its shores, shall have been annihilated, and it shall please the Russian Government to do us similar wrong with similar impunity in some other part of the world.

We are aware that we have been using language of a kind from which we have always hitherto been averse; and our readers will believe that we have caught the prevailing epidemic of an exaggerated fear of Russia. But this is not the case. Of the Russian power we have as little fear as ever, because we form as low an estimate of it as ever. We believe, as we always have believed, that the political influence of Russia is in many respects detrimental, and most seriously detrimental, to the interests of European freedom and civilization; and that its designs of aggrandisement are of a most extensive and pernicious nature. But we are compelled to assert the impolicy of involving one country in hostilities for the interests of other nations: and, with whatever reluctance we may abandon the interests of any independent people to the power of this barbarous despotism, we must confess that the blood and treasure, and commercial prosperity of Englishmen must not be perilled in the chances of what would be an obstinate and uncertain struggle for continental interests. The Russian designs of aggrandisement still inspire us with little terror, because these extensive designs appear to rest on very inadequate means of execution. We see no reason to believe that Russia could at present inflict the slightest permanent injury on us; or that any acquisition, which she has any chance of making, would materially increase her power of coping with us. We would not rush into the certain evils of war with a country which contributes so large a proportion to our foreign commerce, in order to avert distant and fancied chances of collision.

But the mere regard for our own interests, which induces us to deprecate hostilities resulting from idle fears, or an overstrained alarm for our dignity, prompts us to repel with the utmost vigour and celerity any actual attack on the interests of our countrymen, or any attempt to diminish our national power. We would not enter on a war with Russia to avert some fancied chance of a future attack on our Indian possessions. But an interference with our present commerce is a present evil. The maintenance of the rights of our merchants, and of the security of our commerce, is a matter which we must contend for. An Englishman[6] has lost the cargo and hulk of the *Vixen*: English sailors have been maltreated: our merchants will consequently expect similar treatment, and will therefore be deterred from the trade with Circassia. Our merchants will lose this trade, our manufacturers this market. Here is an injury which we ought to resent, in order to procure reparation to our countrymen who have in this particular instance

[6]George Bell and Co. owned the *Vixen*.

sustained loss,—in order to give a sense of security to those of our countrymen who are, under present circumstances, likely to be deterred from engaging in a profitable trade.

But we view this matter as an insult; and in that light likely to do us more hurt than we should experience from submitting to the actual injury. It is true that the whole trade of the Black Sea (as far as it is affected by this transaction) would not in twenty years be equivalent to the loss of a two-years' war with so valuable a commercial connexion as Russia; and if the Court of St. Petersburgh were doggedly bent on merely excluding us from commerce with the Caucasus, it would be a question worthy of our serious consideration, whether it would be worth our while to enforce justice by war. But this act of the Russian Government is but one proof among many of a spirit of insolence and encroachment, which threatens us, if unchecked, with more serious injuries. We know that we are using terms full of danger: and when we think of the follies that nations have committed on the score of national honour, we feel almost inclined to repent of having expressed resentment at a national insult, which a country of the undoubted strength and courage of Great Britain can well afford to let pass. But this is of the class of insults which imply injury; which, in fact, aggravate the mischief of a slight injury by showing the existence of a disposition to inflict more. The Russian Government inflicts this injury because it hates us and because it fancies we cannot help submitting to that, and even worse, at her hands. If we submit to this, the spirit of hostility which is known to actuate the Government—not the people—will soon find an opportunity for some other encroachment or some other vexation of greater magnitude; and it is best in these cases to check the first outbreak of an aggressive spirit even in trifling matters, because the aggressor, after all, is as loth actually to embark in war for a slight object as the nation which is aggrieved. The sum of these, and other similar encroachments, which will follow this if it succeeds, will become serious: the only thing which can prevent a further progress in the series, is the showing Russia, by our conduct in the present instance, that she can only continue at the cost of war. The earlier we do this, the less we lose before we do it. This barbarous and unprincipled despotism cannot comprehend forbearance springing from any motive but fear; and we must show Russia that it has not the hold on us of which it would make so unmerciful a use. But we need not anticipate the evils of war. Russia cannot maintain a six-weeks' war against England. Mr. Roebuck did not exaggerate when he said that the English would in a very brief period of time sweep the military and commercial marine of Russia off the seas, and compel the Emperor, at the hazard of his crown and his life, to accept our terms.[7] He might have added, that two British squadrons, at the Dardanelles and the Sound, might starve the Russian empire.

[7]Roebuck, speech of 17 Mar., 1837, col. 623; the Emperor was Czar Nicholas I (1796–1855).

How long Lord Palmerston will allow, or, rather, will be permitted to allow, this matter to remain suspended on the tardy deliberations of lawyers, and the purposed procrastinations of diplomacy, it is not for us to say. In the mean time, it will be of some service to show what ought to be done; and the work which we have placed at the head of this article throws some light on one of the important questions involved in the affair of the *Vixen*; namely, the right of Russia to the acknowledgment by other nations of her sovereignty of the Caucasus.

It was about the beginning of the present century that the Czars began to form any steady system of policy for the aggrandisement of their dominions in the mountainous districts between the Black Sea and the Caspian; several of the Circassian tribes, indeed, had become the allies or vassals of Russia about the close of the sixteenth century, but they were neglected or betrayed; and, about the beginning of the last century, most of them embraced the Mahommedan faith. In 1723, Peter the Great,[8] anxious to secure for his subjects the navigation of the Caspian Sea, and, as he hoped, a large portion of the trade with India, concluded a treaty with Ismael Bey, the ambassador of Shah Támásp, by which it was stipulated that the Russian Emperor should expel the Afghans, and establish Támásp upon the throne of Persia, in return for which service the Persian prince agreed to cede to his ally the towns of Derbend and Bakú, with the provinces of Daghestan, Shirwán, Ghilán, and Asterabad.[9] Two years after, the Court of St. Petersburgh, unscrupulously violating the promises made to Támásp, concluded a partition treaty with the Court of Constantinople, by which the Russians were to obtain all the Caspian Provinces from the country of the Turkomans to the conflux of the Kuŕ and the Araxes.[10] The districts thus perfidiously acquired were found to be unprofitable and expensive: they were abandoned at the first summons of Nadir Shah.[11] But the projects of establishing empire over the Caucasian and Caspian provinces were renewed when the sovereign of Georgia, in 1783, declared himself a vassal of the Russian empire; and they have been still more steadily prosecuted since Georgia was definitely united to Russia in 1806.[12]

To estimate justly the peculiar character of this mountain region, it is of more importance to examine its materials physically than geographically: the races that

[8]Czar of Russia (1672–1725).

[9]Ismael Beg (d. ca. 1740), ambassador of Shah Tahmasp II (1704–40), was instrumental in securing the Treaty of Alliance between Russia and Persia, signed at St. Petersburg, 12 September, 1723 (in *Consolidated Treaty Series*, Vol. XXXI, pp. 423–8).

[10]Treaty between Russia and Turkey, signed at Constantinople, 23 June, 1724 (*ibid.*, pp. 487–94).

[11]Nadir Quli Beg (1687–1747), known as Nadir Shah.

[12]Heraclius II (d. 1798) put himself under Russian protection by the Treaty between Georgia and Russia, signed at Fortress George, 24 July, 1783 (in *Consolidated Treaty Series*, Vol. XLVIII, pp. 413–28). Eastern Georgia was annexed in December 1800 and much of western Georgia in October 1804. Perhaps the reference is to the beginning of the Russo-Turkish war of 1806–12.

inhabit these districts are of more importance to the inquirer than the structure of their country; and again, the nature of the mountains and rivers is a matter requiring more minute investigation than the circumstances of their position.

Beginning at the western side of the Caucasian provinces, between the Black Sea and the mountain-chain, we find a singularly warlike and unconquered race, the Abassians. Their country is full of defiles, where a few brave men may bid defiance to an host: they have been from remote ages robbers by land and pirates by sea: they have been attacked by every power that ever aimed at establishing supremacy in the Black Sea, but they have never wholly lost their rude independence. Identity of usages and great similarity of language seem to connect them with the Circassians on the northern declivity of the Caucasus; but from the remotest ages of history a singular tradition has prevailed which traces their origin to an Egyptian colony established by Sesostris[13] at the mouth of the Phasis. Herodotus declares that the Colchians or Abassians related the circumstance themselves,* and he mentions several coincidences in colour, physical constitution, language and usages; dwelling chiefly on the practice of circumcision, which was common to the two nations.[†] Whatever may have been their origin, they have been always averse to civilization, and they have gradually retired into their mountain fastnesses before the Georgian race, branches of which have expelled the Abassians from Imeretia and Mingrelia.

On the northern declivity of the Caucasus are found the tribes of the

[13]One of the legendary Pharoahs of Egypt, dating from the beginning of the second millenium B.C.

*He adds: "the Phoenicians and Syrians of Palestine confess that they learned this practice (of circumcision) from the Egyptians; but the Syrians who dwell on the rivers Thermodon and Parthenius assert that they recently derived the practice from the Colchians." [Herodotus (ca. 484–420 B.C.), the Greek historian; see *Herodotus* (Greek and English), trans. A.D. Godley, 4 vols. (London: Heinemann; New York: Putnam's Sons, 1926–30), Vol. I, p. 393 (II, 104).] This theory has been revived in our own day by Mr. Klaproth, who asserts that he recognised several Coptic words in the idioms of the north-western Caucasus. [Heinrich Julius von Klaproth (1783–1835), *Tableau historique, géographique, ethnographique et politique du Caucase* (Paris: Ponthieu, 1827), pp. 8–9.] We are far, however, from receiving this evidence as conclusive; we are of those who believe that the immediate derivation of the Coptic from the ancient language of Egypt is anything but proved; and we should much rather attribute these similarities to the Cherkessian Mamlukes who so long were the masters of Egypt. "During the five hundred and fifty years," says Volney ([Constantine François de Chasseboeuf, comte de Volney (1757–1820),] *Voyage en Syrie* [*et en Egypte*, 2 vols. (Paris: Volland, and Desenne, 1787), Vol. I,] pp. 99, 101), "that the Mamlukes were in Egypt, no one of them became founder of an existing line; there was not a single family existing in the second generation; all their children died young. The means by which they were perpetuated are the same as those by which they were established; that is to say, by fresh importations of slaves from their native country (Circassia)." This would lead us to reverse the order of causation, and conclude that the Copts derived the words common to both nations from the Cherkessians.

[†]Herodotus, *Euterpe*, Lib. II. See 103, 104, and 105. [*Herodotus*, Vol. I, pp. 391–3.] It

Cherkessians or Circassians, equally remarkable for their ferocity and beauty. Klaproth has informed us that they are divided into five classes, princes, nobles, freedmen of nobles, freedmen of freedmen, and slaves.[14] Their form of government is aristocratic, but the wars between the *beharichs*, or petty princes, render the country almost perpetually a prey to anarchy. Some of the tribes profess Christianity, others Mahommedanism, others jumble the two creeds together, and few pay any regard to the moral principles of either. But Klaproth has not done full justice to their daring and desperate valour, nor does he notice the great value that they set on martial achievements. In fact a prince cannot be confirmed in the privileges of his birth until he has given some signal proof of his heroism. Colonel Rottier, who served several campaigns as a Russian officer in the Caucasian wars, mentions many instances of Cherkessian bravery or temerity. On one occasion a young *beharich* with three friends resolved to cut through a Russian column:* the daring prince effected a passage, but his three followers were slain.

Rottier adds: "even the women of this warlike nation follow their husbands to the field, not merely to dress wounds, or rouse the courage of the men, but to combat by their side."[15] This certainly tends to prove that the history of the Amazons is not quite fabulous. Most readers are aware that Zonoras relates, that on the field of battle where Pompey conquered the Albanians, cuirasses were found, which could only have belonged to women; and Procopius relates a similar circumstance of a battle between the Romans and the Huns.[16] But in more modern times some Cherkessian tribes having been repulsed in an attack on the people of

---

is also mentioned by Valerius Flaccus.

Cunabula gentis
Colchidos hic ortusque tuens; ut prima Sesostris
Intulerit rex bella Getis; ut clade suorum
Territus, hos Thebas patriumque reducat ad amnem,
Phasidis hos imponat agris, Colchosque vocari
Imperet.

(*Argonaut* [Gaius Valerius Flaccus (d. ca. 90 A.D.); see *Valerius Flaccus* (Latin and English), trans. J.H. Mozley (London: Heinemann; Cambridge, Mass.: Harvard University Press, 1934), pp. 274], V, 417–22.)

[14]Klaproth, *Travels in the Caucasus and Georgia*, trans. F. Shoberl (London: Colburn, 1814), p. 314.

*The Colonel uses a phrase common to the Irish peasants, when attacking a rival faction: "he swore he'd let daylight through the column." [Translated from Bernard Eugène Antoine Rottiers (1771–1858), *Itinéraire de Tiflis à Constantinople* (Brussels: Tarlier, 1829), p. 18.]

[15]*Ibid.*

[16]For the tale concerning Gnaeus Pompeius (106–48 B.C.), see Plutarch, *Life of Pompey*, in *Lives*, Vol. V, p. 209, a Greek passage that Joannes Zonaras used in his Ἐπιτομὴ Ἱστοριων; for Procopius (ca. 326–66 A.D.), see *Procopius* (Greek and English), trans. H.B. Dewing, 7 vols. (London: Heinemann; New York: Macmillan, 1914–40), Vol. V, pp. 77–9 (VIII, iii, 10).

Karatchai, several suits of armour were brought to the prince of that country, taken from the corpses of women who had fallen in the battle. "Each consisted of a helmet, braces, and a cuirass composed of small steel plates. A vest of woollen stuff, of a bright red colour, was attached to the cuirass, and reached about half way down the leg."* The Circassians regret the abolition of their slave-trade; to them, indeed, a state of slavery is any thing but terrible; the greater part of the population being serfs, have nothing to fear from a change in their condition: the young men are encouraged to offer themselves for sale by the anecdotes they hear of the exalted posts to which their countrymen have attained in Egypt and Turkey; and the girls, prisoners at home, and forced to work, hope that their charms may win them a more prosperous fate in another land. The prohibition of this traffic is consequently felt as a grievance, and it is a principal cause of their intense hatred of the Russian power. Lieutenant Conolly, one of the latest British travellers through these regions, gives a very lively picture of the state of the garrisons sent to control those fierce mountaineers:

The Russians do not yet command free passage through the Caucasus; for they are obliged to be very vigilant against surprise by these Circassian sons of the mist, who still cherish the bitterest hatred against them. In some instances, the Russian posts on the right of the defile were opposed to little stone eyries perched upon the opposite heights; and when any number of the Caucasians were observed descending the great paths on the mountain side, the Russian guards would turn out and be on the alert. Not very long before our arrival we learned that a party of Circassians had, in the sheer spirit of hatred, lain in ambush for a return guard of some sixteen Cossacks, and killed every man.

Such facts seem to argue great weakness on the part of the Russians; but great have been the difficulties they have contended with, in keeping the upper hand over enemies whose haunts are almost inaccessible to any but themselves. Several colonies of these ferocious mountaineers have been captured and transplanted to villages of their own in the plains, where they are guarded, and live as sulkily as wildbeasts; and a general crusade, if I may be allowed the expression, has been talked of for some years past, to sweep such untameable enemies from the mountains, and settle them on the plains in the interior of Russia.†

North and east of the Caucasus, between the river Terek and the Caspian sea, are tribes still more barbarous and more hostile. The principal are the Chetchentzes and the Lesghies, but there are several others. Though they differ in language and in origin, their usages are alike, and the description of one will serve for the rest.

The Lesghies, whose name is formidable even at the gates of Astrachan, inhabit the north of Daghestan, and are all Mohammedans. In the year 684 the Saracens, headed by Mushlimeh, the brother of the Khaliph Walid,[17] obtained possession of Georgia, and continued to hold it, in spite of their incessant wars with the mountain tribes, until the year 732. During this interval several nomade tribes came from the

---

*[Translated from] *Recueil de Voyages dans le Nord*, [ed. Jean Frédéric Bernard (d. 1752), 10 vols. (Amsterdam: Bernard, 1715–38),] Vol. VII, pp. 180–1.

†Conolly's Travels [Arthur Conolly (1807–42), *Journey to the North of India*, 2 vols. (London: Bentley, 1834)], Vol. I, pp. 9–10.

[17]Caliph Walid I (675–715 A.D.) and his brother Maslama (d. 739 A.D.)

sterile plains of central Asia to colonise these fertile valleys. Wandering hordes are still found in Daghestan, who have preserved, in whole or in part, the language of their Saracenic ancestors. Most of the Lesghies also in their appearance, manners, and idiom, exhibit marks of a mixed descent. There have been few descriptions published of this remarkable people: war alone discloses their character, and almost their existence, for it is rarely that the Russians have dared to penetrate their forests and mountains.

In Pompey's age the Lesghies, called Albanians, from their river Albanus, still known by the name of Al-sú, or The White Water, though repulsed and decimated by the Roman armies, remained unsubdued, and continued to defy the victorious legions. Since that time the mixture of their race with the Saracenic colonists has served to augment their natural vigour, and strengthen their love of independence.

In the year 1741 Nadir Shah invaded Daghestan, to revenge the blood of his brother Ibrahaim Khan,[18] who had been slain in an attack of the Lesghies. Colonel Rottier assures us that the memory of this conqueror's exploits is still preserved in the popular songs of the Caucasus,*—but he never engaged in a more hazardous enterprise. The mountaineers defended themselves with the most desperate bravery, and the rugged nature of the whole country of Daghestan made it almost impossible to subdue them. The bravest troops of the Persian army sunk under the fatigues of this harassing war, and the Lesghies having threatened to put themselves under the protection of Russia, Nadir returned from this expedition with very partial success and very great loss.

Jonas Hanway has preserved a copy of the letter which the Lesghies addressed on this occasion to the Russian general;† it enclosed a summary of their forces, which is sufficiently curious.

|  |  |
|---|---|
| Ahmed Khan, the Ousmai, has | 12,000 men. |
| The Horda of Aparz | 13,000 |
| Ahmed Khan Beg of Shunketén | 2,700 |
| In the districts of Kanshukúl | 8,000 |
| In Aby | 5,000 |
| In Abugal and Kalashky | 7,000 |
| In Karack or Karacarta | 7,500 |
| In the districts of Kusti | 500 |
| In Kly | 2,500 |
| In Gedat | 4,000 |
| In Kongide | 1,000 |
| And in Kubada | 1,000 |
| Total | 66,200 |

[18]Muhammad Ibrahim Khan (d. 1738).
*Rottiers, pp. 47–8. [The preceding two paragraphs closely follow Rottiers, pp. 46–7.]
†Hanway's Travels [Jonas Hanway (1712–86), *An Historical Account of the British Trade over the Caspian Sea* (1753), 2nd ed., 2 vols. (London: Osborne, *et al.*, 1754)], Vol. II, pp. 410–11. [Ahmed Khan, the Ousmai, and Ahmed Khan, of Shunketén, both fl. 1741.]

Sir John Malcolm* thinks this estimate greatly exaggerated; but it must be received, not as the amount that could actually be brought into the field, but as the census of all the fighting men in the different divisions of Daghestan. A Russian journal estimates the population of the Lesghian provinces at half a million;[19] and if this be at all near the truth, we cannot think the number of men stated as fit for service at all out of proportion.

From time immemorial the Lesghies have subsisted on plunder: when they cannot obtain employment from the Sultan, the Shah, or the Tartar Khans at war with Russia, they pour down on the plains of Georgia, as the highlanders of yore into the Lennox.

Issuing in spring from their impregnable fastnesses and mountains covered with snow, they principally infest Karthlinia and the lovely district of Kisiché Búdhi. They select their position near the fords of rivers, or in the woods bordering on defiles, or in the ruins of old monasteries; there they wait for the shepherd and his flock, the merchant's caravan, or even the single traveller. They often venture to seek their prey in villages, and even in towns: they carry off the inhabitants as prisoners, ransom them, or keep them as slaves. The difficulty of preventing the flight of the latter has induced them to adopt an operation invented by the most ingenious ferocity. They guard them during the first days of their captivity with apparent negligence, and impose on them such severe tasks that a great many attempt to escape. Unacquainted with the localities, the fugitives are easily retaken, and to prevent a renewal of the effort, the Lesghian makes an incision under his captive's heel, and thrusts chopped horse-hair into the wound. The cut soon cicatrises over this foreign body, and seems completely healed; but the wretch thus punished feels a painful tingling every time that he rests on his heel, and during the rest of his life is forced to walk on tiptoe.[†]

Though the Lesghies profess to be guided by the Koran, they unscrupulously violate some of its precepts. They are very fond of wine and brandy. During the war of 1812 a division of them, infuriated with liquor, broke through a Russian brigade, and when a fresh regiment came up, the conquered and conquerors were found stretched side by side, the former dead and the latter drunk. Colonel Rottier mentions several examples of their bravery, their ferocity, and their religious enthusiasm; but we have before us more recent information in the shape of an official report on the military operations against the Mussulman mountaineers of the Caucasus, translated from the Russian by the lamented Klaproth for the Asiatic society of Paris.[‡] This war, which was scarcely heard of in Europe, began in 1828, and ended in 1832. A brief account of it will better illustrate the condition of the Cherkessians and the Lesghies than any laboured dissertation.

*[John Malcolm (1769–1833),] *History of Persia*, [2 vols. (London: Murray, 1815),] Vol. II, p. 95n.
[19]Not located.
[†]Rottiers, pp. 48–9.
[‡]["Rapport officiel sur les opérations de guerre contre les montagnards, Musulmans du Caucase," trans. Klaproth,] *Nouveau Journal Asiatique*, No. 61 [2nd ser., XI (Jan. 1833), 18–30.]

In the year 1828 several tribes of Daghestan demanded that the Russian tribunals should be abolished and justice administered by Mohammedan courts. Their discontent was stimulated by Shah Kazi Mollah,[20] a native of Húmry, a village in the western territories of the Lesghians: he had the art to persuade his countrymen that he was a prophet destined to restore the purity of Islam, and he soon found himself at the head of 6000 followers, whom he named Múrids or disciples. Being defeated by the Russian general Rosen,[21] he sought refuge with the Chetchentzes, the Galgaï, and the Karaboulak; fierce tribes that inhabit the mountainous districts near the sources of the Sunja, the Martan, and the Aksai. His pretensions were accredited by these barbarous hordes, and he taught his disciples that their first duty was the extermination of the Russians. Several villages were destroyed, detachments cut off, and stragglers massacred or enslaved. In 1831 he fought no less than six pitched battles with the imperial troops; and though the Russians assert that he was invariably defeated, we find that his influence and power were greatly strengthened, so that at the beginning of 1832 his authority was not only recognised by the insurgents of Daghestan, but by several tribes in Kabarda, and even in Kuban.

Baron Rosen, with a numerous and well-appointed army, was sent to suppress this dangerous revolt. He entered the country of the Chetchentzes, and stormed their principal village Ghermentchouk. One incident will serve to show the obstinate resistance made by these enthusiastic mountaineers.

After the village had been occupied, a body of about fifty men, conducted by the Mollah Abd-er-rahman, one of the most determined partisans of Kazi Mollah, was cut off from the rest, and surrounded in a large house. These fellows had no hope of safety: but when they were summoned to surrender, they thundered out verses of the Koran, as is their custom when they devote themselves to death. Then working loop-holes through the walls, they opened a well-supported and well-directed fire upon their assailants. Several grenades thrown down the chimney exploded in the interior of the house, but failed to shake their resolution. Orders were at length given to set fire to the place. Eleven of them, half suffocated by the smoke, came out and surrendered; a few others sword in hand threw themselves on our bayonets; but far the greater part perished with Abd-er-rahman chaunting to the last their song of death.*

From the country of the Chetchentzes the Russians next marched into the Lesghian districts. Here they encountered physical obstacles not less formidable than the desperate valour of the warriors previously described. If, indeed, the road to Húmry be a specimen of Caucasian communications, the military occupation of these countries is all but impossible.

The road to Húmry from the territory of the Chetchentzes presents incredible difficulties. It ascends from Karanai to the snowy summit of a lofty mountain, and then descends in a winding direction about four wersts (three miles) over the scarped side of a mountain, along

[20]Shah Gazi Muhammed (ca. 1793–1832).
[21]Grigory Vladmirovich Rozen (1781–1841).
*[Translated from] "Rapport officiel," pp. 23–4.

precipices and across rocks: it is only the breadth of an ordinary footpath. It afterwards passes about the same distance over the narrow projections of rocks, where there are no means of going from one to the other but by ladders, with which it is necessary to come provided. Afterwards it joins another road coming from Erpeli, between two walls of perpendicular rock, when it becomes still narrower and more rugged. And finally, in front of the village of Húmry, it is crossed by three walls, the first of which is flanked by towers. The whole side of the mountain is cut into terraces, so judiciously arranged as to afford the means of making the most effective resistance.*

The Lesghians deemed this pass impregnable, and they might easily have made it so; but relying too much on its difficulties, they neglected to guard it, contenting themselves with exclaiming, "the Russians can only come here, as the rain does, by falling from heaven."[22] Favoured by a thick fog, the Russians occupied the mountains in front of Húmry, and after a furious cannonade, carried the village by storm. The final scene is too characteristic of Lesghian valour to be omitted:

After the soldiers had carried the first wall, it was not possible for the garrisons of the towers to escape. Still they refused to surrender; but on the contrary, became more obstinate in their resistance. General Veliaminov opened a heavy cannonade on the ramparts in front of the towers; but as the bandits still kept up their fire, a body of volunteers, from the corps of sappers and miners, stormed the forts, and put the mountaineers who defended them to the sword. Amongst those who fell were Kazi Mollah and his most distinguished partisans: their bodies, pierced with bayonets, were recognised next morning by their countrymen. Night put an end to the conflict, and our advanced guard halted between the third wall and the village. On the morning of the 30th of October, 1832, the Russian troops entered into Húmry.†

To complete this "strange eventful history,"[23] we must quote the proclamation issued by the Russian Major-General, to inform the Lesghians of his success:

The justice of God has overtaken Kazi Mollah, the preacher of false doctrines, the enemy of peace. This scoundrel, his principal adherents, and a number of wretches that he had deceived, have been exterminated by the victorious Russian army in the celebrated defiles of Húmry, long believed impregnable.

May this example serve as a warning to all disturbers of the public tranquillity! May they, listening to the voice of penitence, have recourse to the powerful Russian government, and our mighty Emperor, in his gracious condescension, will mercifully grant them pardon. But whoever shall hereafter dare to form rebellious plots shall feel the utmost rigour of the laws. Neither mountains, nor forests, nor ravines, will shelter the traitor. The triumphant Russian troops will penetrate everywhere, and everywhere punish the disobedient. The Galgaï, the Ilczkerians, the Chetchentzes, and others, have experienced this truth! He that hath ears to hear, let him hear and understand!‡

---

*[Translated from] *ibid.*, pp. 24–5.

[22]Translated from *ibid.*, p. 26.

†[Translated from] *ibid.*, p. 28. [The Russian general was Alexei Veliaminov (1783–1838).]

[23]William Shakespeare (1564–1616), *As You Like It*, II, vii, 164; in *The Riverside Shakespeare*, ed. G. Blakemore Evans (Boston: Houghton Mifflin, 1974), p. 382.

‡"Rapport officiel," p. 30. [The proclamation was issued by V.D. Volkhovsky (1778–1841).]

We have lately seen a gentleman just returned from Astrachan, who assures us that Kazi Mollah's sect is not yet extinct, and that the Lesghies continue to exhibit their former fanaticism and hatred of the Russian rule. They are also as inveterately hostile to the Georgians as ever; and their hatred is returned with interest. The Georgians form ambushes for the Lesghians who traverse their country on the road to Turkey, saying, "These Mussulman dogs constantly assault and pillage us:" on the other hand, the Lesghians make forays into Georgia, declaring, "These Christian dogs formerly hunted us in our mountains, under the pretence of converting us." Thus all over the world a difference of religion is held to justify turpitude and atrocity.*

South of the Caucasus, Russia possesses Georgia, Imeretia, Mingrelia, and the greater part of Armenia. The Georgians voluntarily submitted to the Russian yoke to escape from the capricious tyranny of the Persians; and though they felt very bitterly the perfidious cruelty displayed to their princes, they continued unswerving in their allegiance until 1812, when a Georgian army, sent against the Aghabziké, was sacrificed by the incapacity or treachery of the Russian general:[24] this national wrong, followed by an onerous system of fiscal regulations, provoked a revolt, which was quelled in blood; but its spirit still survives. Georgia is a fertile country, and Tiflis, its capital, is a thriving city; but the inhabitants are governed by foreigners, who look upon the vice-royalty as a punishment rather than an honour. Indeed, it is notorious that a southern government is regarded by the Court of St. Petersburgh as a species of honourable exile.[†]

*Before quitting the Lesghians, we must notice the singular tradition of a Genoese colony having been established in their country. The town of Akusha, on the river Koisa, contains about 1000 families. Colonel Gaerber, who travelled through these countries in 1728, asserts that they called themselves Frankî. At the present day they are distinguished from the rest of their countrymen by their manufacturing skill. They make excellent fire-arms, sabres, and daggers; they also fabricate coats of mail, inlaid with gold and silver; and they coin imitations of Persian, Turkish, and even Russian money. Akusha is regarded as a kind of neutral republic by the surrounding hordes; its citizens enjoy the privileges of self-government, annually electing a council of ten to rule their little state. They have a tradition of being descended from Genoese mariners, shipwrecked on the coast about the time of the capture of Constantinople by the Turks; but their language retains no traces of such an origin. [The reference is to Johann Gustar Gaeber, "Nachrichten von denen an der westlichen Seite der Caspischen See," in *Sammlung russischen Geschichte*, ed. Gerhard Friedrich Müller, 9 vols. (St. Petersburg: Kayserl. Academie der Wissenschaften, 1732–64), Vol. IV, pp. 57–79; the source is probably Rottiers, who gives the reference on p. 59.]

[24]Alexander Tormasoff (1752–1819).

[†]The natural fertility of Georgia and Russian Armenia is very great; corn, wine, and oil are produced abundantly; fruit trees cover the hills and encircle the forests; apples, pears, and cherries, are produced in the north, while the more genial climate of the south ripens the pomegranate, the fig, the nectarine, and the peach. But Russia derives little benefit from this bounty of nature; the empire does not import raw produce, it has an abundant supply within for the limited wants of its population.

The commercial importance of the Caucasian isthmus must be estimated from its system

From the above details, the reader will be able to form a just conception of the true character of the dominion which it is pretended that Russia possesses over the mountain tribes of the Caucasus. Russia has long endeavoured to render those tribes subject to her, but she is now as far as ever from having succeeded. Still more absurd is it to pretend that Turkey was sovereign to these regions, and ceded them to Russia by the treaty of Adrianople.[25] What Turkey never had, she could not part with. The Caucasian tribes were not subject to Turkey, they were subject to no one; they have never been conquered, and dominion over them, how often soever it may have been claimed, has never yet been enforced. It is on the laws of war, therefore, and not on the internal regulations of the Russian empire, that the seizure of the *Vixen* must, if at all, be defended. Whether British traders can be excluded from Circassia on the plea of a blockade, is a question which remains to be discussed; on the plea of quarantine, revenue, or police, they certainly cannot. Russia cannot legislate for Circassia on any of these points, for Circassia is not Russian.

---

of rivers; these have been strangely misrepresented both in ancient and in modern times; the Romans were taught to believe them a highway to India, and some speculators in our own day have thought it possible to restore this supposed commercial route. But a glance at the map must convince every body who can reason, that the altitude of their sources and the nature of their course, must render them wholly unfit for internal navigation. The Rion or Phasis is blocked up by a sand-bank which prevents the entrance of large vessels, and its rapidity prevents even boats from going higher than a few miles from the mouth. Amara, Poti, and Redout Koulé, are poor harbours, and can never obtain any great commercial importance. The Kúr, which it is proposed to unite with the Phasis, never has been and never can be a trading route. In spring when the snow melts, and after the autumnal rains, it flows with the rapidity of a torrent: in some places it is sunk between precipices, in others the banks are so low that inundations are of frequent occurrence, as for instance, in the neighbourhood of Tiflis. Add to this its great and numerous windings; the rocks, the quicksands, and the stumps of trees that impede its channel, and the drift-wood which the floods bring down from the mountains. All these circumstances render it at present impossible to ascend the Kúr for more than a few miles from its point of junction with the Araxes. An enormous expenditure of money and labour might open the river for about eighty or ninety miles, but no human power could clear the channel a hundred miles farther; that is to say, to Ganja or Elizabethpol. Indeed the Russians themselves are now aware of this fact: Erivan, not Tiflis, is their chief mart for overland commerce, and the *St. Petersburgh Gazette* has more than once hinted that the true route of trade between the Black Sea and Central Asia must be conducted by the Batumi and the Araxes. [For a reference to such reports, see *The Times*, 18 Mar., 1837, p. 3.]

[25]Treaty of Peace between Russia and Turkey, signed at Adrianople, 14 September, 1829 (in *Consolidated Treaty Series*, Vol. LXXX, pp. 83–96).

# Appendix C

## The Spanish Question

### JULY 1837

*London and Westminster Review*, V & XXVII (July 1837), 165–94. Headed: Art. VIII. / *Spain.* By Henry David Inglis, Esq. [1795–1835], 2 vols. Second Edition. [London:] Whittaker & Co. [1837.] / *Sketches in Spain.* By Captain Samuel Edward Cook [1787–1856]. [London:] T. & W. Boone [1834]. / [Anon.,] *Policy of England towards Spain.* [London:] Ridgway [1837]. / [William Walton (1784–1857),] *Reply to the Anglo-Christian Pamphlet, Entitled Policy of England towards Spain.* [London:] Hatchard [1837]. / [John Richardson (1796–1852),] *Movements of the British Legion* [(1836), 2nd ed. London: Simpkin, Marshall;] Macrone [; Wilson, 1837]. / *The Basque Provinces.* By Edward Bell Stephens, 2 vols., unpublished [London: Whittaker, 1837]. / *The Andalusian Sketch-Book.* [Probably *The Andalusian Annual*, ed. Michael Burke Honan, 2nd ed.] London. Macrone, 1837. / *Sketches of the War for Constitutional Liberty in Spain and Portugal*; interspersed with Scenes and Occurrences Abroad and at Home. By Charles Shaw, Esq. [1795–1871], K.C.T.S., and Colonel Portuguese Service, late Brig.-Gen. in the Service of the Queen of Spain, 2 vols., with Portraits of Admiral Napier and General Evans. Colburn: London, 1837. / *Shaw's Memoirs*, unpublished. [Issued with the previous work as *Personal Memoirs and Correspondence of Colonel Charles Shaw, K.C.T.S., etc., of the Portuguese Service, and Late Brigadier-General, in the British Auxiliary Legion of Spain; comprising A Narrative of the War for Constitutional Liberty in Portugal and Spain, from its Commencement in 1831 to the Dissolution of the British Legion in 1837*, 2 vols. (London: Colburn, 1837).] Signed: "T.E." Listed in Mill's bibliography as "Part of the article on Spanish affairs in the same number of the same review" as his review of Carlyle's *French Revolution* (MacMinn, p. 49).

BUCCANEERS AND SLAVE-DEALERS were the first to discover that there was a geographical distribution of moralities as well as of animals; they found that common honesty, like its emblem, the common house-dog, degenerated sadly as it approached the line; that piracy and kidnapping flourished in the same temperature as beasts of prey and venomous reptiles. Their charts regulated their morals; every observation to determine their latitude was a lesson in ethics, and the sun's altitude gave an accurate measure of the height to which it was lawful to extend their violence. Of late years moral geography has been permitted to fall a little into oblivion; the world even seemed disposed to believe that the essence of principle is its universality; that virtue and vice depend neither upon parallels nor meridians;

and that Humboldt's isothermal lines mark temperature only,[1] and do not convey the slightest information respecting a nation's capacity for justice and freedom. Thanks to those eminent philosophers, Mr. Maclean and Mr. Grove Price,[2] this spreading delusion is on the point of being dispelled; the philosophical discoveries of the slavers and buccaneers will be worthily supported by our modern Conservatives, ever steady advocates of

> The good old rule, the simple plan,
>      That they should take who have the power,
>      And they should keep who can.[3]

These sages and their followers have established, that in all countries north of the fiftieth degree of northern latitude, Popery is an abomination, whose endurance calls loudly to heaven for vengeance, and municipal institutions nuisances that ought to be abated; but when we pass to the south of that mystic line, the horror of Popery changes into a profound respect for his Catholic Majesty, a sincere veneration for that ancient conservative institution, the Inquisition, and a burning zeal that would consign liberal gainsayers to an *auto-da-fé*.[4] Some ascribe this apparent discrepancy to the delight of these gentlemen in abstractions; their zeal is for the church, *any* church, *quocumque modo* church; the church, which in their minds is a more abstract idea than even that of a lord mayor without a gold chain and fur robe (which was so puzzling to Martinus Scriblerus),[5] seeing that it includes not the notions of religion, creed, or discipline. And this theory derives

---

[1]Friedrich Wilhelm Heinrich Alexander, Freiherr von Humboldt (1769–1859), devised the first chart indicating equal temperatures.

[2]See Donald Maclean (1800–74), Speech on the Affairs of Spain (18 Apr., 1837), *PD*, 3rd ser., Vol. 37, cols. 1394–1411; and Samuel Grove Price (1793–1839), Speech on Spain (10 Mar., 1837), *ibid.*, cols. 249–56.

[3]William Wordsworth (1770–1850), "Rob Roy's Grave" (1807), in *Poetical Works*, 5 vols. (London: Longman, *et al.*, 1827), Vol. III, p. 26 (ll. 37–40).

[4]The "Spanish Question" involved both Spain and Portugal. In the former, Ferdinand VII (1784–1833) had in 1830 revoked the Salic law (introduced in 1713 by Philip V [1683–1746]) of exclusive male succession to make his young daughter Isabella (1830–1904) queen, with his wife, Maria Christina de Bourbon (1806–78) as regent. This settlement was disputed by Ferdinand's brother, Don Carlos Maria Isidro de Bourbon (1788–1855). His challenge failed, partly through the intervention of a British force, and a more democratic constitution was forced on Maria Christina in 1837.
In Portugal, John VI, who died in 1826, left his daughter Isabel Maria as regent for his son Pedro IV of Portugal and Pedro I of Brazil (1798–1834), Duke of Braganza, who tried in that year to surrender the Portuguese crown to his seven-year-old daughter, Maria del Gloria (1819–53), provided she marry his brother, Don Maria Evarist Miguel (1802–66). After their betrothal, Miguel became king in 1828, but she returned to Brazil and Pedro came back to Portugal in 1831 when he unseated Miguel and restored Maria's claims.

[5]Alexander Pope (1688–1744), *et al.*, *Memoirs of the Extraordinary Life, Works, and Discoveries of Martinus Scriblerus* (1741), in *Works*, ed. Joseph Warton, *et al.*, 10 vols. (London: Priestley, 1822–25), Vol. VI, p. 111.

some confirmation from a recent version of some of these philosophers' speeches into tolerable rhyme, and plainer reason than these gentlemen ordinarily use:

> The church is in danger, alas!
> The church is in danger, alas!
>     Which church? Pho! you fool!
>     The creed is no rule,
> Be it Koran, or Bible, or mass, or mass,
> Be it Koran, or Bible, or mass!
>
> The church is in danger, alas!
> The church is in danger, alas!
>     The church which we cry for,
>     The church we will die for,
> Is the church in which priests can amass, amass,
> The church in which priests can amass!
>
> The TRUE church is Popish in Spain;
> In Portugal Popish again;
>     In fine, to be brief,
>     That church is the chief
> Which boasts of the largest domain, domain,
> Which boasts of the largest domain!
>
> Then here's to the church, in despite
> Of the knaves who for liberty write!
>     Great Mammon's the Lord
>     By all churches ador'd,
> And the church that's establish'd is right, is right,
> The church that's establish'd is right!
>
> Then toast inquisitions in Spain!
> Drink Tories and churchmen again,
>     Put a foot on the people,
>     Add a yard to the steeple,
> And cry from the pulpit, amen, amen!
> And cry from the pulpit, amen![6]

But this explanation, though it may show why Popery may be a blessing in Spain, and a curse in Ireland, throws no light on the second point, municipal institutions; it leaves us still to guess why west of us all local privileges and local self-government should be swept away, while south of us the *fueros* of the Biscayans, however useless to themselves or pernicious to the rest of Spain, must be supported even at the hazard of placing the Peninsula beyond the pale of civilization. Our first theory therefore claims the preference,—that Messrs. Maclean and Price (with their followers, the Inglises, Goulburns, Peels,

---

[6]Not identified; probably written by White for the occasion. The catch-phrase, "The church is in danger," originated in a debate in the House of Commons in 1704; see Cobbett, *Parliamentary History*, Vol. VI, cols. 479–511.

Hardinges, and unchanged* Burdetts), have revived the neglected science of moral geography, to the great edification and advantage of the present and all future generations; that they have given to its principles a strength, a permanence, and an extension not contemplated by the original authors, and that they may therefore claim rather to be its founders than its revivers. *Sumite superbiam quaesitam meritis.*[7]

Whatever other reflections may be justly excited by the late debates on Spanish affairs,[8] we cannot help congratulating our country on the extraordinary growth of the philanthropic virtues which was exhibited on the Tory benches, and the near prospect of the conversion in particular of some of our military senators to quakerism. The morality of warfare has been discussed with an ethical rigour, and at the same time a sentimental eloquence, which would not have disgraced the classic shades of the Academy. Hear how wisely and philosophically our military Plato, Sir Henry Hardinge, discusses this delicate point of morals:

There was another mode of viewing this subject—namely, as affecting the moral character of this country, which, in his opinion, was a matter of high consideration. It remained a matter of deep consideration for the inhabitants of this Christian country whether his Majesty's Ministers and that House should allow men, the natives of this country, to become accustomed to shed the blood of their brother men in a quarrel in which they were not interested. It was a matter of deep consideration whether, by such proceedings as those he alluded to, they should train up our countrymen to scenes of bloodshed and murder, which had never been approached in any modern warfare.[9]

So many of our half-pay officers have exchanged general orders for holy orders that the church militant is no longer a questionable phrase among us, and this piece of sermonizing may probably be designed to announce the gallant officer as a candidate for the mitre. The late Archbishop of Cashel[10] began life as a

---

*An old joke slightly varied supplies a better epithet than that which has been applied to himself by the once popular baronet:

> From all his former friends estranged,
> How can he say he stands "unchanged?"
> 'Tis a mistake, as all may see,
> In the "unchanged" omit the *c*.

[The doggerel has not been located; for the claim, see Francis Burdett (1770–1844), Speech to a Deputation of the Electors of Westminster, *The Times*, 6 May, 1837, p. 6. The other M.P.s referred to are Henry David Inglis, Henry Goulburn (1784–1856), Robert Peel (1788–1850), and Henry Hardinge (1785–1856).]

[7]Horace (65–8 B.C.), *Odes*, in *Odes and Epodes* (Latin and English), trans. C.E. Bennett (London: Heinemann; Cambridge, Mass.: Harvard University Press, 1964), p. 278 (III, xxx, 14–15).

[8]See *PD*, 3rd ser., Vol. 37, cols. 223–86 (10 Mar., 1837), cols. 1329–1460 (17 and 18 Apr., 1837); Vol. 38, cols. 1–170 (19 and 21 Apr., 1837).

[9]Hardinge's speech (*ibid.*, Vol. 37, cols. 1329–53; 17 Apr.) is reported in the *Morning Chronicle*, 18 Apr., p. 2, from which the quotation appears to be taken.

[10]Charles Brodrick (1761–1822).

midshipman in the navy, at a time when Lord Gambier had not commenced his efforts to substitute psalms for oaths, and tracts for cards,[11] and when the name of temperance societies was unknown to our sailors; yet in his instance the quarterdeck was found to supply as good a system of preparatory education as the universities, and the cockpit sent forth a prelate that would not have disgraced the cloister. Here assuredly is a precedent which will more than justify Sir Henry's elevation; the camp is as good a school for clerical instruction as a man-of-war, and a dean has informed us, that

> To give a young gentleman right education,
> The army's the only good school in the nation.[12]

To our extract from this probationary sermon we must add the commentary of another eminent moralist, Lord Mahon, especially as he gives us history to aid philosophy, and illustrates "wise saws" by "modern instances":[13]

In the debate last evening one principal point under discussion was how far historical precedent could be adduced to justify the present policy of Great Britain. Upon that point he believed scarcely any precedent had been adduced except from the dark ages of our history, when it was not unusual for men to engage in war in the service of foreign powers, without any regard to the interests of their sovereign or country in its issue. At that time soldiers of this character were termed mercenaries, a term which he would not apply to the British Legion in Spain, because he was aware that the spirit of that term had been misunderstood by many persons, and he did not at all mean to insinuate that the persons who formed part of that legion were actuated—as the expression was supposed to imply—by none but mercenary motives. So far from intending any imputation of this kind, he believed that the intentions of those individuals were honourable; and so believing, he would be the last person to cast a stigma upon them in their absence. But he did say this—that looking at the position in which Great Britain was placed, this legion stood in a situation in which British soldiers ought not to stand—a position for which he could only find a parallel in the mercenaries he had alluded to in the darker ages of our history. When we thus revived one of the features in our ancient and less civilized history, we could hardly be surprised to see the laws against witchcraft, and the old penal code, which were scarcely less barbarous, called also into existence. He hoped that in future the progress of our advancing civilization would be marked by humanity, and a respect for human life.[14]

The abstract moral question, how far the trade of a soldier is consistent with the duties of a man and a Christian, is here very unnecessarily mooted. We have no objection to anything which can possibly be said in denunciation of medicines, if

[11]James Gambier (1756–1833), an admiral of the fleet with limited sea-faring experience, had tried to apply his strict Methodist views in the navy.

[12]Jonathan Swift, "The Grand Question Debated" (1732), in *Works*, ed. Walter Scott, 19 vols. (Edinburgh: Constable; London: White, *et al.*, Dublin: Cumming, 1814), Vol. XV, p. 154.

[13]William Shakespeare, *As You Like It*, II, vii, 156; in *The Riverside Shakespeare*, p. 382.

[14]Philip Henry Stanhope (1805–75), Viscount Mahon, Speech on the Affairs of Spain (18 Apr., 1837), reported in the *Morning Chronicle*, 19 Apr., p. 3.

we can first get rid of diseases. We are quite ready to join in the cry of "No prisons," when the thieves shall all be converted to the faith of "No thieving;" but when the cry comes from the friends and partisans of the thieves, we like it not. War may be stigmatized universally, and we are quite ready to give our vote for its abolition in a universal congress of mankind: but while the enemies of freedom are allowed to levy their vassals, embattle their slaves, and organize their dupes, assuredly the friends of freedom have a right to employ their own thews and sinews to check the onward flow of barbarism and tyranny.[15]

But Lord Mahon asks for modern precedents; this worthy aspirant to the honours of the Historical Muse can find no parallel to the service of the British Legion, save in the darker periods of our history:—The reign of Queen Elizabeth is not wont to be accounted such, nor are Sir Philip Sidney and Sir Horatio Vere generally reckoned among "mercenaries" and "buccaneers."[16] There are, indeed, some more modern transactions which Lord Mahon may have had in his eye:—It is not very long since Indian savages were taken into British pay to butcher our brethren in America; and history of no very ancient date records, that the emissaries of an English king[17] were seen in the soldier-market of every petty German despot, bargaining as coolly as carcase-butchers in a shambles, for Hessians, Hanoverians, Brunswickers, and Saxons, to crush men fighting for privileges dearer and more valuable than the Biscayan *fueros*, because they were the rights of mankind, and not those of a petty province. If General Evans[18] be a mercenary for accepting pay from Queen Isabella, what name must be given to George III, paying blood-money and head-money to margraves and landgraves for the hire of their subjects? We do not like moral maxims which go just so far, and no farther, than suits the interest of the moralizer.

Mr. Walton puts the objection in a much more tangible shape, and with him we readily join issue:

Among men, acts must be estimated not merely by their moral turpitude, but by their effect on society, and what can be more generally mischievous, what better calculated to put everything under the yoke of violence, than to propagate opinions by the sword, and apply to politics, what formerly prevailed in religious matters, the fanatical bloody spirit of forcible proselytism? My gallant countryman knows by experience the miseries of war, and can he really think himself justified in inflicting them on the numerous Spaniards who happen to differ from him on points of internal Spanish policy? What would become of society, if every political enthusiast, not satisfied with oppressing our patience by tedious harangues, should force his foolish fancies on our acceptance by military violence?[19]

[15]The phrase "thews and sinews" appears to have originated with Walter Scott (1771–1832); see *Rob Roy*, 3 vols. (Edinburgh: Constable, 1818), Vol. I, p. 60 (Chap. iii).

[16]Elizabeth I (1533–1603), reigned 1558–1603; Philip Sidney (1554–86) and Horace Vere (1565–1635) were famed for their military valour.

[17]George III (1738–1820).

[18]George de Lacy Evans (1787–1890), leader of the British Legion in Spain, who was also M.P. for Westminster.

[19]Walton, *A Reply*, p. 148.

Against such doctrine as this we have not a word to say: whoever excites civil war, whoever rebels against an established government, unless he has so plainly the majority with him that he succeeds almost without a struggle, acts under a terrible responsibility. But we beg to inform Mr. Walton that the Legion went to assist not rebels, but an established government; not to excite but to suppress a civil war. Mr. Walton should preach to his friend Don Carlos. A sermon against thieving should not be addressed to the thief-catcher, but to the thief.*

*Nothing was more surprising in the late debate than the anxiety exhibited by some of the Conservative orators for the morals of the Legion! It was feared that they would be contaminated by the pernicious examples of Spanish cruelty daily before their eyes; their tender sympathies would be blunted, their generous hearts hardened, and all the noble feelings with which they were suddenly invested in one of Lord Francis Egerton's fits of poetic enthusiasm, would have disappeared like Goethe's spirit in his lordship's translation of the *Faust*! [*Faust: A Drama, by Goethe, and Schiller's Song of the Bell*, trans. Francis Leveson Gower (later Egerton; 1800–57) (London: Murray, 1823). *Faust*, by Johann Wolfgang von Goethe (1749–1832), appeared in German in 1808 (Pt. I) and 1833 (Pt. 2).] We should like to know, from these soft-hearted moralists, when they first discovered that war was a trade not likely to foster the growth of humanity, and at what period the soldiers of the Legion, long described as the vilest outcasts, became objects of such virtuous care. We do not attempt to hide our detestation of the barbarities that have been perpetrated in the Spanish contest, but, as Lord Palmerston justly said, "Unfortunately, history told them that in all times, whether in peace or in war, the character of the Spanish nation was more cruel and bloodthirsty than that of any other nation in Europe. Let them look to their conquest of America—to all the wars that had taken place in Spain—from the war of Succession down even to 1815, and they would see that their conduct was stained by atrocities which inflicted a deeper disgrace on humanity than the conduct of any other nation on earth. One of the effects of the regeneration of Spain, through the force of constitutional government, was, that, by generating a public opinion they would improve the Spanish character, and put an end to atrocities like these." [Temple, Speech on the Affairs of Spain (19 Apr., 1837), reported in the *Morning Chronicle*, 20 Apr., p. 2.] But the Conservatives may take comfort; the legionaries have not been brutalized: at Irun and Fontarabia they exhibited a degree of forbearance and moderation, which could scarcely have been expected after the publication of the Durango degree. [See Don Carlos, "Royal Decree" (20 June, 1824), *The Times*, 2 July, 1835, p. 6.]

The only attempt made to defend this Durango decree, which is without a precedent in the annals of modern warfare, came from that eminent professor of ethics, Mr. Maclean; it was however reprobated by many on the opposition side of the house, and by none more forcibly than Sir Henry Hardinge. [See Maclean, speech of 18 Apr., 1837, and Hardinge, speech of 17 Apr., 1837.] But though the defence of this brutal ordinance has been abandoned in parliament, we still find attempts made to justify it in Carlist pamphlets and journals. It is fortunately unnecessary for us to do more than quote an authority which the persons with whom we have to deal will readily confess to be of great weight. The *Standard*, a journal conducted with more than ordinary ability, and remarkable for its adherence to the darkest shade of Orange politics, thus speaks of what it honestly calls the butchering decree of Durango: "Every one knows that Don Carlos is not a *de facto* King; but, if not *de facto* King of Spain, he has no more right to enforce the laws of the Basque provinces—the pretext for the Durango decree, and for the murders committed in pursuance of it—than has the correspondent of the *Morning Post* or *Morning Herald*. He is, as Charles Edward [the Young Pretender (1720–88)] said of himself, as yet a self-commissioned adventurer,

The doctrine, that the soldiers and officers of the Legion fought in a quarrel in which they were not interested, and in the issue of which "the interests of their sovereign or country" were not involved, is false at both points. Without entering into the niceties of the case, there was not one among them who did not know that he was fighting for free institutions against despotism; for Reformers against Tories, at home and abroad. Such a quarrel is not one in which Englishmen or Irishmen are not "interested." And as to the indifference of the Spanish contest to "the interests of their sovereign and country," it was a contest in which both sovereign and country had found sufficient inducements either of interest, or of duty, for binding themselves by treaty to a direct and positive co-operation. It may be meant to assert, though the intention is disclaimed, that the officers and soldiers of the Legion sold their services for pay, without caring for the justice of the cause. Among so large a body this must no doubt be true of no inconsiderable proportion; but so it is of all military bodies; for instance, of those who have entered the British army as officers or soldiers at any period during the last hundred years. The Legion at least knew what they were hired to fight for; but those who enter the British army are hired (we say it not invidiously, but to express what no one will deny, that they

---

supporting his own title, just as General Evans is an adventurer, commissioned by the Queen, supporting the title of her Majesty. Now, there are evils enough necessarily attendant upon this war of adventurers without allowing it to familiarize the soldiers of modern Europe with the bloody sacrifices of barbarous times; and it is the business of all Europe to see that he who first attempts to introduce usages repugnant to the authorised laws of war be visited with an European chastisement. The justification attempted to be set up by one of our contemporaries—namely, the assertion that Don Carlos is menaced with a felon's death—is no justification at all. Every claimant of a throne already occupied *de facto*, if he press his claims by force, is, by the universal practice of mankind, regarded as a traitor, and exposed to the penalty of death, if defeated and captured. But are we to be told, therefore, that the supporters of a *de facto* prince, whether natives or foreigners, justly forfeit their lives? The law of England, which merely echoes the rule of common sense with the law of nations, has for three hundred and fifty years distinctly declared that the defence or service of a *de facto* Government can never constitute a crime. But away with all this quibbling apology for a brutal decree, which none but an inbred savage could fulminate— which none but a worse than butcher, an amateur hangman, could enforce in a single instance. Thanks to Heaven, the whole tendency of modern war has for centuries run to the mitigation of the horrors inseparable from any form of the military contest. Our Generals—and we include Frenchmen, Germans, and even Russians, in speaking of the Generals of our time—our Generals have frequently had to apologise for advantages sacrificed, and triumphs foregone, through considerations of humanity. This Carlos, this pretender to a throne, but without commission or acknowledgment from any authorised Sovereign, would re-plunge us in the carnage puddle of unpitying and unsparing slaughter. But—
> Gore-moistened trees shall perish in the bud,
> And, by a bloody death, shall die the man of blood.

[*Standard*, 28 Mar., 1837, p. 2; the concluding quotation is from Walter Scott, *The Vision of Don Frederick: A Poem* (Edinburgh: Ballantyne, 1811), p. 41 (Canto XLII, ll. 8–9).]

enter it from the ordinary motives from which men engage in any other profession,) they are hired, we say, to fight, they know not for what; certainly, in any of our wars since Queen Anne's time,[20] for no good: perhaps to fight against, not for, the cause of free institutions. The good Major Cartwright[21] laid down his commission rather than fight against the Americans; how few, in the British army, have shown similar virtue; yet how many, both in the American and in the French war, must have felt that the cause they were in arms against was that which ought to prevail! The Tory moralist, who deems these honourable men, and General Evans and his followers adventurers, must be a very pretty illustration of the doctrine of Helvetius, that our notions of virtue are corollaries from our notions of our own interests.[22]

But a more complicated question than the morality of the Legion's conduct is the value of its services. There is no use in disguising our belief that the friends of liberty in Spain and England have been disappointed by the general results of the expedition, and that the successes of our countrymen have neither been so early nor so decisive as had been expected. It was clearly the knowledge of this feeling that animated the supporters of Sir Henry Hardinge's motion.[23] The time chosen for the debate was the moment when temporary failure was likely to produce temporary unpopularity. This point was eloquently urged by Mr. Ward:

He asked them, why was not the policy of the Government with regard to Spain made the subject of complaint during the present session till now? He asked in what material point the line of policy pursued in consequence of the quadruple alliance[24] was changed, so as to cause the present motion? (Cheers.) There were precisely the same grounds for the motion. (Cheers.) They had been threatened with it during the whole of the recess—(cheers); they had heard nothing but denunciations of the policy of the Noble Lord (Palmerston) from every organ of the Conservatives. They had been told up to the first day of the session of the expensive mode of intervention, of the neglect of British interests, and of the incapacity of the Noble Lord the Secretary for Foreign Affairs. What was the result of all this? It happened that three days before the meeting of Parliament intelligence was received of a victory gained by the combined forces of the Queen of Spain and the British Legion. And so great was the reaction which attended the receipt of this intelligence, and so great was the interest excited in the public mind by the gallantry of our fellow-countrymen in Spain, that the Right Hon. Baronet the Member for Tamworth, feeling that the moment was very unpropitious for such a discussion, quelled some little symptoms of insubordination, and availed himself of the very first opportunity that the forms of the House allowed to express his admiration of the conduct and gallantry of the brave men who had successfully defended

[20]Anne (1665–1714), reigned 1702–14.

[21]John Cartwright (1740–1824), the ultra-Radical.

[22]Claude Adrien Helvétius (1715–71), *De l'esprit* (Paris: Durand, 1758), e.g., pp. 53–5.

[23]Hardinge, Motion on the Affairs of Spain (17 Apr., 1837), *PD*, 3rd ser., Vol. 37, cols. 1352–3.

[24]See "Treaty between His Majesty, the Queen Regent of Spain, the King of the French, and the Duke of Braganza, Regent of Portugal," *PP*, 1834, LI, 299–309.

Bilbao.[25] (Cheers.) The Hon. Member for Sandwich (Mr. Grove Price)[26] and the Hon. and Learned Member for Oxford (Mr. Maclean), of whose devotion to the cause of absolutism there could not be the least doubt, submitted in silence to the course pursued by the Right Hon. Baronet the Member for Tamworth. He would ask, what prevented the Hon. and Gallant Officer (Sir H. Hardinge) from bringing forward this motion on that occasion, and what encouraged him to do so now? (Loud cheers.) The simple fact was, that success no longer beamed so decisively on the cause of liberty in the Peninsula. (Great and continued cheering.) This was the first time that he had heard in the British House of Parliament that a fair ground for abandoning an ally was that he was unfortunate. (Loud cheers.) He had heard often the opposite argument used. He had heard the misfortunes of those with whom we were in alliance stated, and never unsuccessfully, as a plea for additional struggles and exertion on our part. (Cheers.) It was reserved for the Hon. and Gallant Officer (Sir H. Hardinge) to reverse this, and to make the want of success a plea for shamefully abandoning the engagements to which we were solemnly bound by treaty.[27]

But though success has nothing to do with the policy of the quadruple treaty, it is a very important element in the Spanish controversy; for if the British Legion be useless, if its presence in the Peninsula does not very materially promote the Queen's cause, it is doing incalculable mischief to the cause it was embodied to serve. The Duke of Wellington's reasoning on this head is conclusive, and his speech, when the question was deliberated in the Lords, points out errors of system, the more to be lamented as they cannot be denied.[28]

Military criticism by a person at a distance from the scene of operations is equally difficult and ungracious. Before questioning the prudence of the conduct of General Evans, or the wisdom of his operations, we must be acquainted with the circumstances of his position. According to his adversaries, the materials of the British Legion were the worst possible. Mr. Walton, and he is more temperate in his description than the majority of the Carlist writers, says, "that the privates were the lowest and vilest of our urban rabble, refined or still further debased (for I know not which term to choose) by a mixture of Irish peasants. Among them might be here and there scattered a disbanded soldier."[29] The soldiers were certainly undisciplined, and were therefore likely to evince little patience in suffering, and to lose subordination under the smart of disappointment. Did these raw recruits, on their landing, find comfortable quarters, proper rations, and regular pay? On the contrary, all parties confess that they had to endure more privations and misery than those which disorganised the veterans of Wellington in his retreat from Burgos. It is highly creditable to the perseverance and fortitude of General Evans, that under such circumstances he has been able to keep his men together as a

[25]Peel, Speech on the Address in Answer to the King's Speech (31 Jan., 1837), *PD*, 3rd ser., Vol. 36, cols. 50–6.
[26]Samuel Grove Price (1793–1839).
[27]Henry George Ward (1797–1860), Speech on the Affairs of Spain (18 Apr., 1837), reported in the *Morning Chronicle*, 19 Apr., p. 3.
[28]Arthur Wellesley (1769–1852), Duke of Wellington, Speech on Spain (21 Apr., 1837), reported in the *Morning Chronicle*, 22 Apr., pp. 1–2.
[29]Walton, *A Reply*, p. 138.

# The Spanish Question

military body at all; and in every examination of his conduct, this great difficulty must be allowed to have its full weight. It is also uncertain how far his actions have been controlled by Spanish orders, influenced by Spanish counsels, or misled by Spanish promises of co-operation. But, after having made every fair allowance for the difficulties of the position in which General Evans was placed, the disappointments he experienced, and the frequent failure of the promises on which he relied, we must reluctantly confess that his strategetic skill seems far inferior to his perseverance, fortitude, and spirit. The Duke of Wellington's criticisms on the movements of the legion appear to be too well founded:

After a certain period,—he believed, as soon as the original money was expended,—the corps was sent down to join the other troops in the neighbourhood of Vittoria. They remained there during the winters of 1835 and 1836, struggling with every possible distress! but a crisis was approaching—it became necessary that Great Britain should take a more active part in the war—that something should be done to produce some effect in a certain place called the Stock Exchange. Accordingly this corps, towards the spring of the year, was brought to Santander and St. Sebastian, and employed in the relief of the blockade which had been maintained for some time by Guibelalde.[30] It was then found absolutely necessary to raise this blockade, and the British squadron, under the command of a most active and able officer,[31] for whom he (the Duke of Wellington) entertained the highest respect, employed their 68-pounders, and forced in the works of the Carlist line on 6th of May. What was the effect? The blockade was still maintained a little further off, out of the reach of the fire of the British fleet, and there it had remained up to the present time. Excepting this, he defied the noble lord[32] to show any single advantage which had been gained of any description from that day to this. The whole distance that the blockade had been removed was one mile. General Evans might have left the Carlists in their original position without any inconvenience whatever being felt by the town, because he (the Duke of Wellington) happened to know that the communication by sea could not have been prevented, even if the whole British fleet had been blockading the places, instead of being stationed there to give facility to the communication. The whole inconvenience felt by the town from the position the Carlists had taken up was, neither more nor less than, that some ladies and gentlemen were prevented taking the waters. He would say further, that his firm belief was, that the connexion between the legion and the fleet had been injurious to the military affairs of the Queen of Spain. That was his decided opinion, from what he knew of the nature of the country, and more particularly from the position which was the strength of Don Carlos. There was one point which military men perfectly understood, and that was, that if great corps were to act together, there must be a communication between them. If there were no communication, then the attempt at co-operation would in all probability lead to such disasters as had occurred at Hernani; and it was to him most surprising that General Evans, who appeared an able man, and deserving of the confidence of his Majesty's Government, and the Queen of Spain, with the experience he had had, of the difficulty of carrying on communications in that country, should not have felt the danger of his position, and placed himself in communication with the corps with which he was co-operating, instead of being at a distance from his Majesty's fleet.[33]

[30]Bartolomé Guibelalde, "commandante general" of the Carlists 1836–38.
[31]Lord John Hay (1793–1851).
[32]William Lamb (1779–1848), Lord Melbourne.
[33]Wellesley, speech of 21 Apr., pp. 1–2.

Indeed the best tacticians disapprove of his entire plan of operations, both in conception and execution; they say, "that he had no business to go to Vittoria; being there, he had no business to come back; he had no business in Bilbao, which is a dangerous position for an army; he failed at Fontarabia in his first attack for want of *coup d'oeil* and promptness," and his recent success scarcely atones for his error. He appears indeed to have made every attack, and fought every action, till within the last three months, without any object in view except the immediate battle. Hence all his proceedings are desultory, all his actions isolated, his victories unproductive of permanent result, and not unfrequently followed by rout or retreat. This defect appears especially conspicuous in his only positive disaster, at Hernani, which was principally occasioned by the General's not rightly considering his position; he fought his way with great energy and determination to the heights overlooking Hernani, but when these were attained he seems to have regarded the future as a matter of little import. Major Richardson not unjustly remarks,

Surely the experience of the past, at that very same Hernani, ought to have satisfied the Lieutenant-General that an attempt would be made to turn his flanks and gain his rear the moment a forward movement was made upon the town. This is the Carlist system of warfare; and favoured as they are by the hilly and wooded character of the country, nothing is more easy of accomplishment. It was precisely in this manner they attempted and had very nearly succeeded in turning us during the reconnoissance upon Hernani in 1835.[34]

The circumstances of the battle have been stated with tolerable accuracy by Lord Alvanley:

On the 1st of March the general had under him a combined force of 13,000 men, besides the aid of 400 British marines and 20 guns. On the 15th they had taken the heights above Hernani: his position was on those heights. On his right his position was very strong, and on his left was the village of Astigarraga, which was not occupied. As he (Lord Alvanley) understood the attack upon Hernani, it was this. It was commenced about nine in the morning; the troops were very much fatigued by the operations of the two or three preceding days. About half past eleven a column of about 4,000 Carlists, who had advanced by forced marches to the action, attacked the rear of General Evans, by the bridge of Astigarraga, of which they took possession. The Carlist force marched steadily forward, and the consequence was that the army under General Evans retired before their pursuers in the greatest disorder. So little, however, were the Carlists aware of the retreat, that it was at first taken to be a *ruse de guerre*, and had they pursued the flying force with vigour they would have gained a greater victory. When the Carlists were upon the heights, the soldiers under the English general they distinctly saw, like an undisciplined mob, rushing onwards towards the outer works of St. Sebastian. It was but justice, however, to add, that from the general to the lowest officer, every effort was made by them to quell the panic which had seized the troops, but without effect—and every means they could devise was resorted to, in order to retrieve what had been thus just lost. Undoubtedly it might be asked where was the reserve which ought to have been kept? It appeared that no reserve had been made.[35]

[34]Richardson, *Movements of the British Legion*, pp. 312–13.
[35]William Arden (1789–1849), Lord Alvanley, Speech on Spain (21 Apr., 1837), reported in the *Morning Chronicle*, 22 Apr., p. 1.

The panic was the simple result of surprise; the Carlists appear to have pushed their battalions across the bridges of the Uramea almost without interruption, and nearly the first intimation of their presence was the impetuous and unexpected attempt to turn the extreme left, where General Chichester's[36] brigade was stationed. But the Carlist reinforcement did not arrive until nine o'clock, there was therefore sufficient time to secure the heights, which are strong and well wooded, by *abattis* and field-works. General Evans should have remembered that his was the accessary, not the principal army, and he should, therefore, have taken measures to secure and defend the advantages he had gained until he could communicate with the principal army (Espartero's),[37] and ascertained its true position. This communication might have been made in two or three days by sea, and in a less time by land, if General Evans had been sufficiently prudent to establish any secret channels of intelligence. The subsequent conduct of the legion has sufficiently retrieved its character from the imputation of cowardice, to which it was exposed by the panic at Hernani; but even yet we are unable to perceive in the General's movements any proof of his having formed a fixed and comprehensive plan for his campaign.

Able strategists, acquainted with the country which is the seat of war, are of opinion that the true line of operations by General Evans would have been along the French frontier of St. Sebastian; establishing strong fortified points as he moved, until the communication with Pampeluna was secure. He would thus have cut off the Carlists from their French succours and resources; he would have been able to obtain from France supplies of provisions and the munitions of war for his own men; the enemy would have been forced to attack him in his chosen position, instead of his being compelled to attack them on the ground which they had previously selected as most favourable to their operations. To the employment of the greater part of the Queen's forces in this quarter there is one apparent objection of some moment,—the road to Madrid would have been left open, and the Carlists would have had an opportunity of making a dash on the capital. But this might have been obviated by having one compact, well-equipped field corps, constantly concentrated near the Ebro, ready to move under a good commander, and meet the Carlists whenever they attempted to make a push in that direction.

But here another and rather a difficult question presents itself; have the Spaniards a good commander? Espartero certainly is not such, or he would never have attacked at Bilbao on the side he did; nor, having gained his battle there, would he have suffered the enemy to rally after their defeat, when a vigorous pursuit would have destroyed them as a military body. Narvaez shewed both talent and energy, but he is in disgrace;[38] the rest are men incapable of acting without

---

[36]Lieutenant-General Charles Chichester (1795–1847).

[37]Baldomero Espartero (1792–1879), commander of the Spanish troops.

[38]Ramon Maria Narvaez (1800–68), in charge of the "Army of the Centre," had been successful against the Carlists near Acros in November 1836, but when a brigade of his

instruction, which they will not submit to receive. It is not necessary to attribute the failures of Cordova, Sarsfield, and others, to treachery; the experience of the Peninsular war has taught us that Spanish armies make a great figure on paper, and rarely anywhere else. When closely examined, their numbers begin to illustrate the theory of vanishing fractions; their equipments bring to mind the Irish metaphor of being "clothed with nakedness," and their capacity of motion, described as that of the hare, scarcely equals the tortoise. Things have not altered for the better since the days of Sir John Moore,[39] and Spanish emblazonment must be always taken with, what the heralds call, an abatement.

General Evans has now quitted the legion, and in a farewell address has given a summary of its history,[40] to which we know of no parallel but that of the celebrated King of France, who,

> With fifty thousand men,
> Marched up the hill, and then marched down again.[41]

The strictures of Richardson, Shaw, and Hall, on the conduct of the legion,[42] are not half so severe as the implied censures of the commander himself; his enumeration of its services merely recites battles without an object, and victories without a result; the logical blunder of argument in a vicious circle, receives the stratagetic exemplification of movement in a vicious circle; nothing is proved by the one, nothing accomplished by the other. Carlos, we are told, has abandoned Biscay; the Queen's troops are close upon his track; his ruin, nay, his capture, is certain. Two days elapse, and, lo, Carlos is in Catalonia, the cradle of fanaticism; the British Legion, without officers or organization; Espartero gone to look for the Carlists "round about Estella:" Oraa[43] opening a passage for the factious from Barbastro, in obedience to his country's proverb, "build a silver bridge for thine enemy;" and Baron de Meer taking care, if possible, not to hurt the cause to which he is openly opposed, and secretly attached.[44] In fact, the Spanish army, like the British Horse-guards,[45] is independent of the reforming government, and hence,

---

army defected to the revolutionary forces he was unable to capitalize on the victory; consequently he lost control of the army.

[39]The British General (1761–1809) famed for his campaign in the Peninsula during the Napoleonic wars.

[40]Reported in the *Morning Chronicle*, 17 June, 1837, p. 3.

[41]Cf. the version of the satire on Henri IV (1553–1610) in *The Oxford Dictionary of Nursery Rhymes*, ed. Iona and Peter Opie (Oxford: Clarendon Press, 1951), p. 176.

[42]Richardson, *Movements of the British Legion*; Shaw, *Personal Memoirs*; Herbert Byng Hall (1805–83), *Spain; and the Seat of War in Spain* (London: Colburn, 1837).

[43]Marcelino Oráa y Lecumberri (1788–1851) was a general in Narvaez' army. The invading army of Don Carlos crossed the river Arga and defeated Oraá's forces at Barbastro on 1 June, 1837.

[44]Baron Ramon De Meer (b. 1787), Viceroy of Navarre and commander of the army of Catalonia.

[45]I.e., the British Army command.

every liberal movement is paralysed, and faction allowed to gather its chief strength from the culpable weakness and contemptible cowardice of its adversaries.

Into the disputes between General Evans and his officers we have no wish to enter: whether he has succumbed to the Spanish ministry, and sacrificed the claims of his followers to please the Court of Madrid; whether they have expected too much, and betrayed their disappointment by acts of insubordination, are questions it would not be fair to discuss on *ex parte* evidence, though there is sufficient variance in the charges made against the discipline of the General, for us to see that some of them, at least, have been coloured by passion and prejudice, and that the character of others might be materially altered by explanation. But this scarcely concerns the public, and has no connection whatever with the object of our article. That object requires that we should here take our leave of General Evans and the Legion, and pass to a subject of greater moment,—the conduct of our own Government with reference to the Spanish contest; the principles of foreign policy properly applicable to the case, and how far the Quadruple Treaty, and the measures which have been taken in execution of it, are in conformity to those sound principles.

An opinion has been advanced, and ably supported, by one of the most distinguished advocates of the popular cause in Parliament, Mr. Roebuck, which condemns altogether any interference of one country in the internal commotions of another; and holds, that England should meddle with other nations only when other nations meddle with her, by impeding her commerce, or plundering the property of her people.[46]

We cannot subscribe to this doctrine; nor can we help regretting that a man of so much eminence among that section of the popular party in England, with whom alone the friends of freedom throughout Europe can be expected to sympathize, should have published to all Europe an opinion so calculated to alienate that sympathy; or confirm the opinion already so deeply rooted of our selfishness as a nation, by seeming to shew that the only party among us who might have been deemed an exception to that selfishness, is not so; an opinion, moreover, so contrary to the spirit of the present times, which is not less than in the time of the Reformation, a spirit of mutual helpfulness, a sense of common interest, among persons of congenial opinions in all nations.

Nevertheless, all rational friends of popular institutions should be ready, whenever necessary, to express, in their most emphatic terms, their adherence to as much as is true of Mr. Roebuck's proposition; namely, the condemnation of wars of propagandism. Self-defence justifies much: Revolutionary France, standing at bay against all the despots in Europe, had the amplest justification for invoking, in the name of universal liberty, the aid of every disturbed spirit in

[46]Roebuck, Speech on the Affairs of Spain (19 Apr., 1837), *PD*, 3rd ser., Vol. 38, cols. 18–23.

Europe, who might respond to the call. But if the despots would have let France alone, France would not have been justified in raising, merely for the promotion of free institutions, a war of opinion against the despots. The attempt to establish freedom by foreign bayonets is a solecism in terms. A government which requires the support of foreign armies cannot be a free goverment. If a government has not a majority of the people, or at least a majority of those among the people who care for politics, on its side; if those who will fight for it, are not a stronger party than those who will fight against it, then it can only have the name of a popular government; not being able to support itself by the majority, it must support itself by keeping down the majority, it must be a despotism in the name of freedom; like the Directorial Government of France, which decimated its representative bodies, and sent all opposition journalists to Cayenne, in defence of Liberty and the Revolution.[47] There is a party of really sincere patriots on the continent of Europe, who look back to the Convention as their model,[48] and avowedly seek to govern for the *interest* of the majority by the *agency* of a patriotic and energetic minority: but we have no faith in the government of a few, even when they speak in the name of the many, nor do we believe in the stability of representative institutions when the people, who are to be represented by them, do not care sufficiently about them to fight for them. Nobody will long enjoy freedom when it is necessary for another to assert it for him.

We hold it, therefore, as an inviolable principle that an enslaved people should be left to work out their own deliverance. But of this principle it is a necessary part, that if unaided, they shall also be unhindered. If free nations look on inactive, despots must do so too. Non-interference is not a principle at all unless it be adopted as a universal principle. If freedom cannot be established by foreign force, it does not, therefore, follow, that by foreign force it should be allowed to be crushed.

If it were possible, as it will be in time, that the powers of Europe should, by agreement among themselves, adopt a common rule for the regulation of wars of political opinion, as they have already adopted so many for the regulation of their private quarrels, it is easy to see what the purport of the agreement should be. When a struggle breaks out anywhere between the despotic and the democratic principles, the powers should never interfere singly; when they interfere at all, it should be jointly, as a general European police. When the two parties are so unequal in strength that one can easily prevail, and keep the other down, things should be allowed to take their course. If parties are nearly balanced, and general

[47]Loi concernant les mesures de salut public prises relativement à la conspiration royale (19 fructidor, an V [5 Sept., 1797]), Bull, 142, No. 1400, *Bulletin des lois de la république française*, 2nd ser., Vol. IV, pp. 7–10; and Loi qui ordonne la déportation des journalistes royaux (22 fructidor, an V [8 Sept., 1797]), Bull. 143, No. 1405, *ibid.*, pp. 12–14.

[48]I.e., the French National Convention, elected by a wide suffrage, which sat from 20 Sept., 1792, until 26 Oct., 1795, governing through its committees.

anarchy or protracted civil war, is likely to ensue, the powers should interfere collectively, and force the combatants to lay down their arms and come to a compromise, and should send their own troops against the party that refused to do it. This is no idle speculation: it has been twice done within ten years: once in Greece; and again, in Holland and Belgium. Much contemptuous sarcasm was expended some years ago upon the conference and its several hundred protocols.[49] Doubtless these were much more ridiculous than as many pitched battles, but a trifle more humane. We regard those ridiculed protocols as constituting the most important step in European civilization, which has been taken for generations past. They were a sign that with the growth of humanity, and also the interests of commerce and the arts of peace, war, long the sport of despots, had become such an object of fear and detestation to the governments of Europe, both free and despotic, that they would not suffer it to exist in the smallest corner of Europe, if it could be prevented; rather should the jarring interests of constitutional and despotic monarchies, which, in other days, would have admitted of no compromise, be discussed quietly over a table, and adjust themselves by talk, as they best could, that so all might combine and send a kind of European Constabulary to Antwerp to part the combatants, and handcuff the more obstinate fellow of the two, who would not submit and have the cause tried by a sort of European Sessions of the Peace. Is this a small thing, does the reader think, in the history of European civilization? It is simply the first step towards getting rid of war; a beginning towards doing for public wars what was done for private wars when tribunals were established to adjudicate the quarrels from which those wars arose, and a police to execute the decision.

The case of Don Carlos and the Queen of Spain is parallel to that of Greece, and to that of Holland and Belgium; exactly the kind of dispute which might be, and ought to be, put down by European interference. Other prospect of its termination there seems none; neither party, according to all appearances, can hope to subdue the other; neither will hear of any proposition for a peaceful settlement; the exasperation must grow, must become more and more furious, until human beings are changed into savage beasts, all kinds of raging passions being kindled, not only between the actual combatants, but among all persons throughout Spain who find their means of subsistence rendered precarious, and their hopes of a settled government blighted by Carlists or traitors, or Moderates or Exaltados, or whatever persons they happen to consider responsible for the protraction of the struggle. If

---

[49]See *Protocols of the Conferences* [of 4 Nov., 1830, and 1 Oct., 1832] *Held at London, between the Plenipotentiaries of Austria, France, Great Britain, Prussia, and Russia*, *PP*, 1833, XLII, 1–551. The earlier agreements were, as regards Greece, the Anglo-Russian protocol of 4 Apr., 1826, and the subsequent Treaty of London, 6 July, 1827, which France also signed; and, as regards Belgium, the agreement amongst England, France, Russia, Austria, and Prussia, at the London Conference of December 1830, with the subsequent protocol of 20 Jan., 1831, and the treaty of 5 Nov., 1831.

ever there was a call demanding a similar intervention to that which took place at Antwerp, this does. But intervention of the same sort, and by the same parties, there cannot now be.

For we have been speaking only of what would be desirable if all the powers of Europe could agree that no one of them should interfere singly; that the principle of not interfering, except by common consent, and the joint act of all Europe, should be adopted and enforced by all other nations, against any power which might choose to infringe it. But this principle (we need hardly say) has not been adopted. Russia has interfered in Poland, Austria (a still more unequivocal case) in Modena and the Papal dominions. In these circumstances, England and France had two courses open to them. One was to enforce non-interference, and go to war with Russia, unless she withdrew from Poland; with Austria, unless she withdrew from all parts of Italy, not included in her own possessions. This would have been in itself the most eligible course, most conformable to the principles of sound international moralists; but as it would have implied a European war and its attendant evils, evils far greater than any good which could have been done to Poland or Italy, we think this course was very rightly avoided. Another course remained for adoption: As Austria and Russia had been suffered to interfere, unopposed, in the internal affairs of independent states in the East of Europe, so might England and France assume the power of interfering, to the exclusion of the despotic powers in the West of Europe; and the right to do, singly, whatever might with propriety be done, in Spain and Portugal, by a Congress of all Europe. This course was adopted, and its result was the Quadruple Treaty. The Quadruple Alliance was formed when Don Carlos and Don Miguel were both in Portugal; it was an agreement between the guardians of the young Queens to save them from the machinations of their uncles, and was ratified by the Kings of France and England,[50] on the very reasonable ground that the restoration of tranquillity to the Peninsula was necessary to preserve the peace of Europe. The design of the treaty is very clearly expressed in the preamble:

Her Majesty the Queen-Regent of Spain, during the minority of her daughter, Isabella II, Queen of Spain, and his Imperial Majesty the Duke of Braganza, Regent of the kingdoms of Portugal and the Algarves, in the name of Queen Donna Maria II, intimately convinced that the interest of the two Crowns imperiously demand the immediate and vigorous exertion of their mutual efforts for terminating hostilities, which heretofore had for their object the overthrow of her Portuguese Majesty's throne, and now afford countenance and support to discontented subjects of the kingdom of Spain: their said Majesties, desirous at once to secure the means of restoring peace and internal prosperity to their dominions, and to establish on a reciprocal and solid basis the bonds of future amity between the two states, have agreed to unite their forces, for the purpose of obliging the Infante Don Carlos of Spain, and the Infante Don Miguel of Portugal, to evacuate the territories of the latter kingdom.[51]

[50]Louis Philippe (1773–1850) and William IV (1765–1837).
[51]Cf. the wording in "Treaty between His Majesty, the Queen Regent of Spain, the King of the French, and the Duke of Braganza, Regent of Portugal," *PP*, 1834, LI, 300.

The official answer of the British King, when appealed to, declares the design of the ratifying powers,

> The two latter Sovereigns, taking into consideration the interest with which the safety of the Spanish Monarchy must always inspire them, and animated with the most ardent desire for the restoration of peace both to the Peninsula and Europe, and his Britannic Majesty taking into further consideration the special obligations which result from his ancient alliance with Portugal, have consented to act as parties to the said treaty.[52]

Before the ratification was completed, this treaty produced a decisive effect; Don Miguel abandoned Portugal, and Carlos, surrounded by Don Pedro's troops, had no means of escape but by seeking refuge on board a British ship of war. He was received without any stipulations on either side, and he at least has had no reason to complain that his confidence was violated. There are circumstances to be explained respecting the residence of Don Carlos in London, which we fear would not bear a very rigid scrutiny. It is not in our power to remove the veil by which they are covered, but there are some grounds for suspicion that the refusal of Carlos to resign his pretensions on assurance of protection and a pension, was encouraged, if not dictated, by some members of an anti-national party in Great Britain. In the meantime the rebellion burst forth in the Northern provinces; it was instigated by the monks, it was supported by the organized bands of smugglers, it was recruited from the neighbouring districts, which abound with idle and discontented peasants, habituated to a wandering life from the continued disorganization of Spain. The folly of Castanon, who published a proclamation,[53] abolishing the *fueros* without any instructions direct or implied from the government, gave the insurgents a pretext for their rebellion, and furnished them with a popular war-cry, a matter of vast importance in a civil war. Carlos secretly escaped from England, passed through France undetected, we are not quite sure that we can say, unsuspected, and appeared in the midst of the insurgents, where his presence gave unity to their desultory operations. This was an unforeseen case; it did not, therefore, come within the letter of the Quadruple Treaty, but it manifestly is included in its spirit. Spain and Portugal are both included in the words of the preamble; Carlos was assuredly more likely to disturb the tranquillity of the Peninsula in Biscay than Portugal, and it must be remembered that, but for the timely protection afforded him by a British vessel, his opportunities of doing mischief would have been brought to an abrupt termination. The additional articles were, in fact, nothing more than an adaptation of the original treaty to altered circumstances; and the new stipulations were strictly limited by the circumstances; no one article has been pointed out which does not of necessity arise from the new position taken by the Pretender. But though many of the conservative orators adhered to the policy of the Quadruple Treaty, which the Duke of Wellington

[52]*Ibid.*, pp. 300–2.
[53]General Federico Castanon y Lorenzana (1770–1836); his proclamation is in Carmelo de Echegaray, *Compendio de las instituciones forales de Guipúzcoa* (San Sebastian: Disputación de Guipúzcoa, 1925), pp. 292–3.

himself had sanctioned during his late brief tenure of office, they insisted that the present ministers had gone beyond their engagements, by permitting the marines to serve on land, and by directing Lord John Hay to take every opportunity of co-operating with the Queen's forces. If the British naval force did not co-operate with the royalists, what would be the meaning of his "Britannic Majesty *acting as a party* to the Quadruple Treaty?" The additional article binds us to aid the Queen with military stores and a naval force;[54] but how is the naval force to be employed? A blockade without a declaration of war every publicist knows would be clearly illegal. Blockade is a belligerent right that can only be exercised by principals, the attempt to enforce it by auxiliaries is contrary to the law of nations and the law of England. As Carlos has no fleet, assistance by a naval force could not possibly mean that we should attack a non-existent navy; the limits of our obligations must consequently be measured by the mode in which a naval force is usually employed along a line of coast in co-operation with a land force. Now, in every such conjuncture recorded in English history, the employment of marine forces on shore went to a greater extent than the aid given to the Queen's armies by Lord John Hay.\*

The Quadruple Treaty was a well-aimed attempt to put down, in its early stages, a civil war, which threatened, if not so put down, to become that scourge to the Peninsula, and deformity in the sight of Europe, which, in spite of the interference, it has since become. The occasion is now more urgent, and the interference, which has hitherto taken place, not sufficient. What follows? That the Quadruple Treaty was wrong? No: but that something much more decisive, something going the full length of what was done between Holland and Belgium, would now be justifiable; and advisable, if it can be done consistently with the general peace of Europe.

We are ignorant whether such a joint interference, by France and England, as would enable them to put down the civil war, and constitute them judges of the concessions to be made to the insurgent provinces, would be consented to by

[54]See Art. III of "Treaty between His Majesty," pp. 304–6.

\*The example of the French Government has indeed been quoted [by Hardinge, speech of 17 Apr., 1837, col. 1349; and by Maclean, speech of 18 Apr., 1837, cols. 1399–1400, and 1408] in condemnation of the conduct pursued by the British ministry; undoubtedly Louis Philippe has taken a very different view from our ministers, of the obligations of the Quadruple Treaty; but M. Thiers has concentrated into a brief space all that need be said to characterize the spirit in which their obligations have been interpreted, and fulfilled by a man who can endure anything rather than institutions arising from popular movements, although to them he owes his throne. "Look at the Treaty," said M. Thiers; "Portugal gave an army, England a naval force, and France gave nothing but promises. These promises evidently meant succour. If they were given and meant succour, then to refuse it was to break the Treaty. If the promises were given and meant nothing, then the French Government has meanly sought to dupe England and Europe." [Louis Adolphe Thiers (1797–1866), Speech in the Chamber of Deputies (14 Jan., 1837), reported in the *Morning Chronicle*, 17 Jan., p. 2.]

France; or if consented to, would be possible without provoking a war with the other powers of Europe. That evil would far outweigh the good which, in this instance, would be obtained by hazarding it. We pretend not to decide the question, for we are in ignorance of some of the material circumstances; but we would impress, with all the energy in our power, upon those with whom the decision depends, that an interference, of the kind we have suggested, is the only satisfactory *denoûement* which seems possible to the present anarchy in the Peninsula, that it should be attempted at the very earliest moment at which it would be practicable, without a civil war: and that anything short of this, however required by the faith of treaties already concluded, is now of proved inefficacy, and is a mere paltering with the difficulties of the case.

Before we close this article, it is perhaps advisable to add a few remarks on the substantial merits of the quarrel to which the civil war owes its origin. For every part of the Spanish question has been made a subject of angry controversy; and most (though, to their credit be it said, not all) of the Tory writers[55] and orators, have not been ashamed to contend, that the Spanish liberals are fighting, not *for*, but *against*, both liberty and legitimacy; trampling upon the one, as embodied in the *fueros* of the Basque provinces, and the other, as incarnated in the worthy author of the Durango decree.

The latter point at least is speedily disposed of. Carlos's pretended right rests upon the Salic law, which had never the force of law in Spain. The Salic law was not the ancient rule of succession, it was first introduced by the Bourbon, Philip V, the great grandfather of Don Carlos. Females could always succeed in Castille, Leon, and Portugal; it was by a marriage with the heiress of Navarre that a King of France obtained a claim to that kingdom,[56] and though females were excluded in Arragon, yet it was through a Princess[57] that its inheritance passed to the Counts of Catalonia. It was by the right of female succession that the house of Austria reigned in Spain; it was by the same right that the Bourbons themselves occupied the throne. It formed a part of the Partidas,[58] or system of constitutional law, which Philip swore to observe on his succession to the throne.

The Salic law could only be established in two ways, by the old forms of the constitution, or by the despotic will of the sovereign. If the advocates of Don Carlos take their stand on the former ground, the answer is, that the forms as well as the substance of the constitution were violated when Philip V established his law

[55]See, e.g., Archibald Alison (1792–1867), "The Spanish Contest," *Blackwood's Magazine*, XLI (May 1837), 573–99, esp. 577.

[56]Jeanne of France and Navarre (1273–1305) and Philip IV (1268–1314).

[57]Petronilla (1137–64) married Raymond Berenger IV, Count of Barcelona, who ruled Catalonia.

[58]*Las siete partidas del rey Alfonso*, 3 vols. (Madrid: La imprenta real, 1807), Vol. II, pp. 132–3 (Part II, Title xv, Law 2).

of agnation,[59] and that, conscious of its invalidity, he did not register it in the form usual with similar acts; while again, if we pass over the Cortes of 1789[60] as secret and irregular, we have the Cortes of Cadiz in 1812,[61] representing the nation and acting in the name of the King, which abolished the decree of Philip, restored the ancient law *de Partidas*, and re-established the right of female succession to the crown. Finally, the decree of Ferdinand, constituting his daughter his successor,[62] was just as regularly sanctioned by a Cortes as Philip's law of agnation. If, on the other hand, the Sovereign's will be regarded as despotic in Spain, the question is at an end, for Carlos must confess that Ferdinand had a right to rule the succession as he liked; and this view seems to have been taken by the King's confessor and his minister Calomarde,[63] when, during his dangerous illness at La Granja in 1832, they seduced him to sign a new will, settling the crown on Don Carlos. Ferdinand's recovery disconcerted their plan, but their effort plainly shows that the partisans of Don Carlos at that time felt that the Salic law was a very weak support to their favourite's claims. If Carlos appeals to the constitution, the question is decided against him; the will of the Sovereign is against him; and what is of far more importance than either, a majority of the nation is against him.

Greatly as circumstances have changed since 1830, Inglis's account of Spain in that year contains the most accurate information respecting the state of public opinion in the Peninsula that is yet available to English readers.* The only correction to be made in his estimate of parties is the addition of the Moderates to the Liberals, and the alienation from the Carlists of a portion of the Castilian

---

[59] Auto-acordado of May 1713.

[60] See *Pragmatica-Sancion en Fuerza de Ley Decretada por el Señor Rey Don Carlos a peticion de las cortes del año de 1789, y Mandada publicar por S.M. Peinante para la Observancia Perpetua de la Ley Segunda, Título quince, partida segunda, que establece la sucesion regular en la corona de España* (Madrid: Imprenta real, 1830). In it Charles IV overturned the Salic law of Philip V.

[61] See *Constitución política de la monarquía Española. Promulgada en Cadiz á 19 de marzo de 1812* (Cadiz: Imprenta real, 1812), Title IV, c. II, Art. 177.

[62] See *Pragmatica*, n 60 above.

[63] Francisco Tadeo Calomarde (1773–1842).

*A new edition of this interesting work has just been published, with an additional chapter on the recent changes in Spain, which is both an accurate and impartial *resumé* of recent events in Spanish history. ["Introduction," Vol. I, pp. xiii-xliv.] We have learned with pleasure that the travels in the footsteps of Don Quixote, prepared for the press by the author a little before his lamented decease, will be published in the course of the year. From the specimens that appeared in one of the Magazines, we doubt not that this will be joyous news to the admirers of the hero of Cervantes. [For Inglis' travels in the path of the hero of Miguel de Cervantes Saavedra's *The History and Adventures of the Renowned Don Quixote*, see "Recent Rambles in the Footsteps of Don Quixote," *Englishman's Magazine*, I (Apr., May, June, and Aug., 1831), 84–90, 208–16, 328–35, and 592–601; republished as *Rambles in the Footsteps of Don Quixote* (London: Whittaker, 1837).]

peasantry. He is a less picturesque writer than Lord Carnarvon,[64] but his weakness of colouring is more than compensated by his accuracy of outline; above all, he is impartial, for though a liberal in sentiment, he carried the fear of being warped by prejudice to such an excess, that he not unfrequently seems to have given the weight of his authority to the opposite side. Experience, however, has proved the truth of his statements respecting Spain and Ireland, the two unfortunate countries whose destinies have been the plague of parties and the bane of politicians. An author publicly praised by Lord Aberdeen[65] must assuredly be received as a fair witness by the Conservatives, and his evidence is highly valuable on that part of the Spanish question connected with the province, which is the principal seat of war, the peculiar situation of Biscay, and the nature of the *fueros*, or privileges enjoyed by its inhabitants. Are the *fueros* valuable in themselves, or are they mere empty flatteries to national pride? Is their preservation consistent with the establishment of constitutional freedom throughout the Peninsula? Are they cherished by the Biscayans themselves? The latter point again resolves itself into the double enquiry, are the *fueros* popular with all the Biscayans, or only with a part? and what part?

We need not go very deep into history to discover the value of a name as the watchword of party in civil warfare; the possessive pronoun has cost the English nation too large a sum for any doubt to exist respecting its price; the phrase *our* colonies in America, and *our* kingdom of Ireland, repeated by every English peasant, as if the mystic pronoun conferred on him some unknown advantage of ownership, has cost us millions of debt, the total loss of one country, and not a little difficulty in the preservation of the other. Now, in some particulars, "our *fueros*" are just as worthless to the Biscayans, as "our colonies" were to the English peasants; the King of Spain, for instance, is only *lord* of Biscay, just as the Queen of England is only a Duchess in Lancashire and a Countess in Cheshire. Our palatine counties have suffered the nominal distinction to fall into oblivion, but the Biscayans attach some importance to a difference of title which flatters and fosters the feelings of independence. It was one of the errors of the constitutionalists to disregard these prejudices in favour of forms, childish perhaps, but not injurious, and in their love of conformity, to abolish those playthings which delight children of a larger growth, and serve to keep them from mischief. With the vulgar and the ignorant, exclusive possession of anything greatly enhances its imaginary worth; had the *fueros* been common to all the provinces of the Peninsula, they would lose

[64]Henry John George Herbert (1800–49), Earl of Carnarvon, *Portugal and Gallicia, with a Review of the Social and Political State of the Basque Provinces: and a Few Remarks on Recent Events in Spain*, 2 vols. (London: Murray, 1836).
[65]The praise of Inglis by George Hamilton Gordon (1784–1860), Lord Aberdeen, minister under Wellington and Peel, has not been located.

the greater part of their fictitious value, and even now the gallant defence made by the citizens of Bilbao proves that, though they have not lost their hold over the minds of the peasants in the interior, they are more justly appreciated by the mercantile classes. But in the present state of the contest, the abolition of the Basque privileges can scarcely be considered as staked on the issue; it is rather desired to extend such of them as are advantageous to all the inhabitants of the Spanish Peninsula. This no doubt will be offensive to the pride of some Biscayans, for the same reason that Catholic Emancipation was odious to the Irish Orangemen; they will no longer be able to triumph in the degradation of their neighbours. From the earliest ages despots have found supporters by using the argument of the affectionate parent—"Take your physic, Tommy, and you shall have the dog to kick;" but liberals presume to think that Tommy might be cured in a better way.

No objection exists to the retention of any *fueros* which merely gratify hereditary pride; those that are really useful elements of government have been adopted in the Spanish Constitution, but there are some useless to the Biscayans themselves, but prejudicial to the rest of the community, which artful men have succeeded in blending with those that are innocent and advantageous. The provinces have the privilege of importing foreign goods, free of duty, but they are not permitted to transmit them to the rest of Spain; custom-houses are placed upon the frontiers of Castille; and the same system of prevention and of smuggling necessarily result, which are found on the Swiss and Belgian frontiers of France. Mr. Inglis records a circumstance which proves that the Basques are not the only persons interested in the maintenance of this anomaly:

I had been told that on entering Old Castille we should be subjected to a rigorous Custom-house search; but in Spain, such matters always depend upon circumstances. A Colonel in the Spanish service chanced to occupy a seat in the diligence; and no Custom-house officer in Spain dare to put a person holding a military commission to a moment's inconvenience. The consequence was, that in place of being detained three hours upon the bridge, until every packet should be lowered and opened, the Colonel merely thrust his arm out of the window; and the Custom-house officers, seeing around his wrist the proofs of his military rank, doffed their caps, and stood back; and the diligence passed on.[66]

The demi-official pamphlet entitled *The Policy of England towards Spain*, declares that the question of the *fueros* "resolves itself into the highly unromantic one of a tariff."[67] But though *unromantic*, it is essentially connected with the commercial prosperity of the country; the anomalies of a double financial system have proved ruinous to the trade of the Basque as well as the Castilian provinces; they have rendered smuggling a regular hereditary profession; they have been the chief cause of the dilapidation of the public finances, and the low estimation of

[66]Inglis, *Spain*, Vol. I, p. 45.
[67]Anon., *The Policy of England towards Spain*, p. 24.

private commerce; but they have been profitable to corrupt officials, to a set of desperadoes long at enmity with law; in fine, to the greater part of those who form the strength of the army of Don Carlos. Their effect on the general prosperity of Biscay is very well described in the pamphlet to which we have alluded:

The Basque Provinces, in short, as a necessary consequence of their privileges, have long been treated, with respect to commerce, as a foreign nation by the rest of Spain. They were forbidden to trade with the Americans—Spanish colonial goods were not allowed to be imported direct to their ports—their vessels were looked upon as foreign, and the Basques, moreover, were placed upon the same footing as foreigners with respect to those productions of Spain which are absolutely necessary to them for their own consumption; while their own productions, being treated as foreign, were subject to enormous duties upon entering Castille.

The consequences of such a state of things may be easily conceived; they are the same as exist in some other countries at this moment. The sea-port towns and the manufacturers are hostile to a system which destroys foreign trade and excludes their productions from a profitable market, while the inland people and those who dwell upon the frontier are violent in support of the system, which necessarily creates the enormous smuggling trade by which they have enriched themselves.

There accordingly exists throughout the exempted provinces every variety of opinion respecting their privileges, some desiring to be altogether assimilated to the rest of Spain, others claiming to be put upon a commercial equality with the neighbouring provinces; while a third, and the most numerous party, not venturing to put forward their real motives against any change of a commercial system which is manifestly injurious to their country, clamour for the absolute maintenance of the privileges, and under the mask of patriotism advocate their right to fill their own pockets by smuggling.[68]

We should have the same controversy in kind, though not in degree, were our own government to equalize the spirit-duties in England and Ireland; and we saw some examples of it when free trade in silk was under discussion.[69] The gains of contraband traffic are always sweeter than those of honest trade; the peasants along the frontiers of Castille have found smuggling lucrative, and they fight for a sovereign who promises to perpetuate it along with the other abuses of the old system; the citizens of Bilbao find the *fueros* ruinous to their commerce, and therefore they contend for a government that holds out some promise of reformation. This point is ably stated in the pamphlet from which we have quoted:

But if the Basques are fighting *for* their privileges, what is it that the town of Bilbao has been fighting *against*? Can we have a greater proof that it is fanaticism, and not *fueros* that maintains the cause of Don Carlos than the heroic conduct of Bilbao in its different sieges, though this once flourishing and most loyal town may be supposed to have as much interest as any other part of the country in the maintenance of Biscayan privileges? And yet Bilbao has resisted all the forces of Don Carlos, commanded by his best officers and aided by foreign engineers, being an open town without fortifications, and, as a military position, pronounced indefensible. It has held out contrary to all the rules of art, solely by the native

[68]*Ibid.*, pp. 22–3.
[69]See *PD*, new ser., Vol. 14, cols. 733–859 (23–24 Feb., 1826).

valour and resolution of its inhabitants, who, wonderful to relate, have resolved rather to perish amidst the ruins of their houses than yield to the generous champion of their country's privileges; and is not this single fact enough to sweep away all the nonsense which is talked about privileges and *fueros*?[70]

Before the present contest began, Bilbao contained citizens anxious for the regeneration of their country. Mr. Inglis declares,

I heard several of the most respectable inhabitants of Bilbao express openly much dissatisfaction at the political debasement of Spain, and breathe ardent wishes for the diffusion of intellectual and religious light; but they added, what my own knowledge has since fully confirmed, that I should not find in any other part of Spain the same enlightened views as I had found in Biscay.[71]

From the character of the Biscayan provinces, we naturally turn to the character of the new Spanish government. Is it such as to afford the lovers of freedom good and reasonable grounds for hope, that the success of the Christinos will lead to the permanent establishment of good institutions in the Peninsula? We cannot maintain the affirmative without some great and even disheartening qualifications. Isabella has shewn some of that jealousy towards free institutions which characterizes the policy of Louis Philippe; her Estatuto Real was little better than a mockery; her acceptance of the Constitution was more than reluctant.[72] But the great consolation is, that the Queen and the Apostolicals have gone too far in hostility to admit of their differences being reconciled; her safety is so completely identified with the triumph of the constitutionalists, that we see no reason to fear her imitating the treachery of her late husband. Adolphe de Bourgoing, a steady partisan of Don Carlos, describes her as clever and ambitious,* and he mentions some anecdotes of her management of her husband which seem to justify his opinion:

Naturally diffident, Ferdinand VII feared that his Queen would not intermeddle in the affairs of the State. That young Princess did not care to show any desire of taking an active part in politics. A Neapolitan, and remarkable for her tact, she accustomed her husband, by the tenderness of her care, and the constancy of her caresses, to feel uneasy when absent from her side. She at first used to withdraw at the precise moment he received his Ministers, affecting great reserve and a perfect indifference to political affairs; but she took care that her apartment should be in the immediate vicinity of the Council Chamber. She, for a time, permitted the King to remain alone, but soon, complaining that her solitude was wearisome, and that she could not endure his absence, she declared that she could not be so long separated from him. Thenceforth she used to come into the council-chamber, pretending to

---

[70]Anon., *The Policy of England towards Spain*, pp. 26–7.

[71]Inglis, *Spain*, Vol. I, p. 20.

[72]*Estatuto real para la convocación de las Cortes Generales del Reino* (10 Apr., 1834) (Madrid: De Burgos, 1834); *Constitución de la monarquía española* (8 Jan., 1837) (Madrid: n.p., 1837).

*[Adolphe de Bourgoing,] *L'Espagne: souvenirs de 1823 et 1833* [(Paris: Dufart, 1834), pp. 299–300].

say some tender things to him, as if she feared that he had been wearied by grave and tedious discussion; when she retired she left the door of his room open, and thus apparently apart, without being really absent, she took an active share in all the ministerial deliberations. Finally, she came and openly took her seat in the council, declaring that she could not endure separation from her well-beloved husband and king. From participating in the deliberations, she finally proceeded to directing them altogether, at least her voice was always potential and decisive.

Mr. Inglis testifies to the influence she thus acquired over the mind of Ferdinand; his affection even burst forth in "a right merry and conceited jest," and as it is the first and last we have seen recorded of this monarch, we shall extract the anecdote:

I happened to be walking one day in the Balle de Alcala, when the royal carriage drove up to the door of the Cabinet of Natural History, and being close by, I stopped to see the King and Queen. The King stepped from the carriage first; he then lifted from the carriage a large poodle dog, and then the Queen followed, whom, contrary no doubt to royal etiquette, his Majesty did not hand, but lifted and placed on the pavement; and then turning to the crowd who surrounded the carriage, he said to them, "*Pesa menos el matrimoni*;" which means, matrimony is a lighter burden than the dog,—a very tolerable *jeu d'esprit* to have come from Ferdinand VII.[73]

From all that we have been able to learn, the personal character of the Queen does not seem to justify a very high degree of confidence in her sincerity or her firmness. Let us now look to those by whom she is surrounded. The most casual reader of the debates in the Cortes must feel convinced, that there is very little statesmanlike talent in the leading public men of Spain; too many of them remind us of Churchill's censure of Mossop, they

> To particles affix emphatic state,
> While principles ungrac'd like lackeys wait.[74]

Arguelles, Galliano, Mendizabel, and Valdez, have, however, shewn a fair share of skill in the business of politics;[75] the last especially is an able financier; but still we cannot hide from ourselves, that the Liberals show a want of practical acquirements, which must long expose them to great inconvenience, and perhaps not unfrequently endanger their cause. But before giving full scope to censure, it is only fair to take into account the paucity of individuals, in the subordinate and working departments of the government, untainted by corrupt practices. A country to which we have referred more than once in the course of this article affords sad proof of the difficulties that beset the progress of reformation, when ancient and

---

[73]Inglis, *Spain*, Vol. I, p. 97.

[74]Cf. Charles Churchill (1731–64), *The Rosciad* (London: Flexney, 1761), pp. 20–1 (ll. 521–2), attacking the actor, Henry Mossop (1729–73).

[75]Liberal politicians, exiled after their share in the government of 1820–23, who returned after the death of Ferdinand VII in 1833: Agustin Argüelles (1776–1844), António Alcala Galiano (1789–1865), Juan Alvarez Mendizabel (1790–1853), and José Lúcio Travassos Valdez (1787–1862).

profitable abuses have made the whole body of inferior functionaries interested in the maintenance of corruption. It is now notorious that intrigues against Lord Grey's government were formed every day in the Castle of Dublin, that underlings were combined to baffle the designs of their superiors, and that by their machinations Tory rule was perpetuated under a Reform ministry.[76] Liberality in political opinion is apt to be connected with exalted views of human nature, and the zealous philanthropist rarely makes the abatements in his estimate of humanity, necessarily required by the effects of misrule and the habits produced by the practice of corruption. The Spanish patriots are not the only Liberals who have suffered from neglecting St. Paul's advice, "Despise not the day of small things."[77]

Our chief ground for hope, however, is in the Spanish people: Captain Cook, who had better opportunities of estimating the real nature of public opinion than most travellers have enjoyed, declares,

The Queen's party comprises, almost without exception, every man of talent or information in Spain. Nearly all the nobility, all the military men of rank and station, and nearly all the others; every man and woman in the country who is *at par*, and all above it. In fact, almost every one who can read or write; no inconsiderable number even of the clergy and amongst the constituted bodies. In short, all the *mind* of Spain is arrayed in favour of the present government, not because it was the *will* or *interest* of the late King to change the succession, but because it is the real law of the country, and that it is a question of good or bad government. . . . So widely spread was the feeling in favour of the change of system (in 1833), that of a most extended acquaintance I had through the country in every station of life, from the highest downwards, of every profession and calling, I should be puzzled now to point out a single male or female who was a Carlist.[78]

We have a striking verification of this testimony from Don Carlos himself; he has found that Absolutism is no longer, even in Biscay, a good gathering cry, and he has attempted to revive his waning popularity by the promise of a Constitution!

We have no fear, therefore, of the success of the Carlists; our fear is of a prolonged civil war, growing disorganization in the country, and such a dispersion of all the elements of peaceful society as shall render a stable government for many years to come an impossility in the Peninsula. It is to prevent these evils, that we invoke the early interference of England and France, for a peaceful termination of the struggle.

General Shaw's Memoirs have reached us as this article was going through the press. Restricted as we are in space and in time, it is impossible to bestow on them more than a few cursory observations. His letters, published as they were written,

[76]The ministry of Charles Grey (1764–1845), formed 16 Nov., 1830, broke up in 9 July, 1834, because of difficulties over Ireland: Dublin Castle was the government centre in Ireland.

[77]Not St. Paul, but Zechariah, 4:10.

[78]Cook, *Sketches in Spain*, Vol. I, pp. 330–1.

may be taken as the testimony of a witness favourable to General Evans; and their evidence fully confirms our opinion that though a gallant soldier, the commander of the British Legion is deficient in foresight, in energy, and in prudence; that, in short, he wants the qualities necessary to ensure a successful campaign—a far different thing from a successful battle. He left England without having appreciated the difficulties of the position he was to occupy. Like our Ministers in the late war, he seems to have placed implicit confidence in Spanish boasts; and if he escaped such a calamity as the retreat to Corunna, it must be attributed rather to the stupidity of the Carlists than to the merits of the Christinos or their auxiliaries. Accustomed to have "great means at their command,"[79] engineering in a small way was not much to the taste of the British officers, and they neglected what Don Pedro[80] used to call "substitutions," which, however despicable in the eyes of a martinet, must ever be of importance in desultory warfare. Notwithstanding the "voluminous staff"[81] appointed by the Commander-in-Chief, there was from the beginning a confusion and want of system which would have been ruinous, if the Legionaries had not proved themselves superior in character and conduct to the regular British troops in the retreat from Burgos. One instance of the dangerous unsteadiness at head-quarters must be noticed:

While at Velorado a circumstance occurred which gave me a great deal of uneasiness, and which was the cause, perhaps, more than any other circumstance, of interfering with discipline, because it hurt that respect for the "dignity of office," without which no subordination can exist. On the 25th of November I got an official letter from the Adjutant-General, finishing, "Sergeant-Major Dwyer, 4th Regiment, having been promoted to the rank of acting Adjutant and Ensign in the 7th Regiment, you will please to order him into head-quarters, and to report himself at this office with as little delay as possible." On getting this letter I instantly sent for Dwyer to my quarters, ordered him, to his astonishment, to cut off his stripes as sergeant-major, then took him by the hand and wished him joy, and regretted that I could not ask him to dine with me, as he must start for Briviesca immediately.—He was of course proud and gratified, and away he went. His situation in the 4th Regiment was immediately filled up; and, two days afterwards, he came into my quarters weeping, to say he was sent back to his regiment as a sergeant, and that he was ashamed to show his face among his old comrades after such a disgrace. He seemed, as far as I had been able to judge, a good soldier; and, to prove that I had nothing to do with this, I read to him his official appointment, and advised him to take his disappointment, as I had done about the generalship, and all would be right. But, no; I saw his spirit was broken.*

The best criticism on the proceedings of the Legion and its commander is a prophecy; it is contained in a letter from Colonel W. Napier, the fearless author of

---

[79]Shaw, *Personal Memoirs*, Vol. II, p. 451.

[80]I.e., Pedro IV of Portugal.

[81]Shaw, *Personal Memoirs*, Vol. II, p. 452.

*[*Ibid.*, pp. 456n–7n.] Dwyer afterwards deserted near to Vittoria, taking with him eleven of the Grenadiers of the 4th regiment fully equipped and armed, and became an officer of Don Carlos, and was very active and successful in getting more of the Legion to follow him.

the *History of the Peninsular War*,[82] addressed to General Shaw's brother, and dated Bath, 28th September, 1835:

What you say of Evans's situation does not surprise me. I have always looked to Spanish hospitals as the ultimate bivouac of his auxiliaries. While Evans remains in towns near the sea coast, and the enemy will face him in the field, I have little doubt that he will get the best of this squabble as soon as his men are disciplined. He is bold and prompt; though I do not much approve of his ensconcing himself in Bilbao, which I told him before he went, he would find a bad position. He should rather keep to St. Sebastian, and move to the French frontier, from whence he can, *if he has money*, get his supplies cheaply and securely, and yet operate upon the rear of the Carlists; for instance, I would rather have made a forced march from St. Sebastian by Mondragon upon Durango, and so have fallen from the high ground upon the rear of the Carlists, than have moved out of Bilbao to meet them from the low ground. I suppose, however, his men are still too much of a mob to try such a march. What he will do when he has to take the field permanently I cannot conceive.

Ten thousand men are an army; an army to move must have mules and convoys; will the Spaniards, who cannot pay their own men, pay his? Then will come the disputes and jealousies of his Spanish generals. Nous verrons!

I remain, dear Sir, etc.

W. Napier.[83]

We have no wish, even if we had time, to enter into all the details of mismanagement described by General Shaw; the besetting sin of the expedition was an obstinate adherence to British regulation, which the peculiar nature of the Spanish service rendered wholly inapplicable. Money, munitions of war, means of transport, were not to be had when the moment arrived that rendered them all necessary; while general orders, issued as if in mockery, prescribed the most minute regulations respecting food and sleep, when each man had nothing but his length of damp earth or handsomely cut stone for his bed, and the heartiest curses of the commissariat for his supper. In short, too many officers went out as if they were only going "to play at soldiery," and when they discovered the difference between mimic display and stern realities, they were found wanting in the qualities of manly endurance which their position so peremptorily required.

[82]William Francis Patrick Napier (1785–1860), *History of the War in the Peninsula and in the South of France, from the Year 1807 to the Year 1814*, 6 vols. (London: Murray, 1828–40).

[83]Letter to T. George Shaw (28 Sept., 1835), in Shaw, *Personal Memoirs*, Vol. II, p. 460.

# Appendix D

## Questions before the Select Committee on Metropolitan Local Government

### 1867

"Third Report from the Select Committee on Metropolitan Local Government, etc.; together with the Proceedings of the Committee, Minutes of Evidence, and Appendix (20 May, 1867), *PP*, 1867, XII, 443–660. The Report covers the Committee's meetings on 5, 6, 26, and 28 March; 1, 4, 8, 11, and 30 April; and 2 and 6 May. Mill attended all the sessions, with the exception of the initial deliberations on 28 February, which were not reported.

### 28 March, 1867
*William Corrie*[1]

[*John Locke*[2] *put forward in his questions the position that, as he had been arguing for a decade, the jurisdiction of the Corporation of the City of London should be extended throughout the whole metropolis.*]

775. Supposing that what the honourable Member for Southwark has proposed, namely, to have but one municipality for the whole metropolis, were thought to impose too much upon one body, and that instead of that every one of the Parliamentary districts of London were made a municipality by itself, there being also a general body which represented the City fairly, as well as each of those municipal bodies, and which might take the place of the Metropolitan Board of Works, would not that remove all difficulties?—*That would be my own opinion; I think that such an enormous Corporation as that suggested by the honourable Member for Southwark, would be unworkable, and difficulties would arise from the localities not being attended to, whereas if the municipalities were scattered about, each would attend to its own local wants, and then there might be some such plan as is suggested by the honourable Member of forming a board, in which all would have confidence.*

---

[1]William Corrie (1806–81), Remembrancer of the City of London from 1864, had been an original member of the Metropolitan Board of Works. He had appeared earlier before the Committee; see *CW*, XXIX, 443.

[2]John Locke (1805–80), M.P. for Southwark, a member of the Committee.

[*In response to Locke, the witness said that there might be ten mayors with one Lord Mayor.*]

777. Supposing that each of those municipalities, the City included, had the control of the numbering and the naming of the streets, and all matters of that extremely local character, and that matters which were regarded as concerning the metropolis generally were put in the hands of a representative body, so constituted that every one of the municipalities, the City including, should be duly and fairly represented in it, do you think that all the powers of the Board of Works should be transferred to this body; and that, in fact, the Board of Works might in some measure be considered as merging in it; would such an arrangement meet your views, and do you think that it would be acceptable to the City?—*I have no means of ascertaining what would be acceptable to them; but I think if you had municipalities in the way suggested by the honourable Member, the work of any great board would be very little; indeed, I think it would resolve itself, principally, perhaps, into the entertainments and matters of that sort, and you might very well leave that where it is; but such a board as is suggested, with representation by municipalities in a sort of federal council, might work.*

778. You do not think that there are any circumstances sufficiently common to the whole metropolis to be properly transferred to that central body, except the duty of giving entertainments?—*In my own opinion I think not. I think most of those things which the Metropolitan Board of Works execute would be better done generally by the Corporation of London and those other municipalities. Supposing there were a municipality for Westminster, for instance, they could attend to all the matters there, and I almost think myself, although of course it is merely my private opinion, that for any great undertakings you might come to Parliament on each occasion.*

[*The Chairman, Acton Smee Ayrton, M.P. for the Tower Hamlets, asked a number of questions about the inconvenience of different jurisdictions over thoroughfares, specifically instancing the problems connected with a great fall of snow (such as had occurred the previous Christmas).*]

796. Do you not think that, on the supposition which I have referred to, it would still be necessary to have some central body which was bound to look after the interest of the whole metropolis, and which should have the power of compelling those municipalities to do their duty in any such cases as clearing the streets, supposing they neglected or omitted to do it?—*I certainly think it would be an advantage to have some authority to compel those who neglected their duties to perform them.*

### Benjamin Scott[3]

[*Appearing on behalf of the Corporation of the City of London, Scott responded to the Chair with a number of statistics concerning the policing of the City of*

[3]Benjamin Scott (1814–92), Chamberlain of the City of London from 1858, had also appeared earlier before the Committee; see *CW*, XXIX, 443–4.

*London. In particular Scott challenged the way in which the number of inhabitants of the City was calculated.*]

835. In making a comparative estimate per head of the City police and the general police of the metropolis you contended with great reason that the population of the City ought not to be counted merely as a population which sleep there and are reckoned in the census, but that the day population should be taken into account; but is it not carrying that argument rather too far when you contend that those frequenting the City besides being added to the population of the City should be subtracted from the population of the remainder of the metropolis, because although they may frequent the City, still they live and pass the greater part of their time in some other district; and consequently do you not think that they ought to be counted both as the population of the City and also as the population of the metropolis generally?—*I have considered, after a great deal of thought upon the subject, that first a portion of them ought to be added to the City (not the whole of them), that the City population should then be added to that of the Metropolis; and that then you should deduct from the whole those who will be absent in another place. They cannot be in both places at once.*

836. They could not be in two places at once; but they could be in the City during a part of their time and elsewhere during another part, and therefore they count, I take it, as part of the population of the other districts as well as of the City for police purposes?—*They are included in the census tables in the metropolis, because the census is there taken at the maximum, whereas, the census is always taken in the City at the extreme minimum. It is very difficult, indeed, to ascertain what would be the right proportion so as to contrast them. All I contend now, is, that Sir Richard Mayne has gone to the extreme of testing it unfairly as regards the City of London, because he has not made any allowance for the day population, and has made no allowance for any frequenters whatever.*[4]

837. I do not object to that argument, but only to what seems to be carrying it, perhaps, rather beyond its fair limits?—[*The inhabitants of the City, wishing better protection, choose to pay a higher price for a more efficient police. Mayne's figures are absurd: according to them,*] *every adult person in the City, male and female, must have been in prison over three times during their natural lives;* [*and each inhabitant must have been guilty of a grave crime, such as wounding with intent, shooting, stabbing, and garotting, once a year. Proper counting of actual and transient inhabitants destroys these conclusions.*]

## 1 April
*James Medwin*[5]

[*The Chair established the witness's identity, and Mill began the substantive questions.*]

[4]Richard Mayne (1796–1868), Chief Commissioner of Police from 1850, later appeared before the Committee to refute Scott; see p. 406 below.

[5]James Medwin, a bootmaker, was a vestryman in St. James's parish.

915. You are a vestryman of St. James'?—*I am; I became so very soon after the passing of the Metropolis Local Management Act.*[6]

916. You have therefore considerable knowledge of the administration of other parts of the metropolis as well as of the City?—*I am a member of the Court of Common Council, and I have been so for seven or eight years. I have had the opportunity, certainly, of becoming well acquainted with the working of the municipal system in the City and the working of the vestry system outside the City.*

917. Have you formed any opinion as to the merits of those systems, and the amendments of which they might be susceptible?—*I have formed an opinion; and the opinion taken as a whole is, that the vestry system, especially taken in connection with the Metropolitan Board, is a failure. I have come to the conclusion that no trust property in the country is managed more economically or better than the trust property which is managed by the Corporation, as trustees; and not only is it managed faithfully and well and economically, but I think that it is managed with great intelligence and efficiency. I am quite clear that that is the case in contrast with many trusts with which I am acquainted, and I believe it to be so taken as a whole.*

[*After an intervention concerning the responsibilities of corporations as trustees, Mill resumed his line of questioning.*]

919. As you have begun a statement regarding the City, will you continue that subject, and state your opinions fully upon the City administration, before proceeding to that of the vestries?—[*Medwin argued from his own experience that the Corporation in this respect was much better than the vestries because the quality of its members was much higher: they gave more time to the business, had more confidence in one another, and had higher intelligence and social position. Further, its composition had improved over the past thirty or forty years. In response to other questions, he indicated the benefits that might result from the sale of trust properties. The questioning then turned to the way in which a central body might be chosen. Medwin was in favour of annual elections, a principle to which Lord John Manners objected, on the grounds that major works requiring many years to complete should be overseen by experienced members.*]

964. Do you not think that a large majority of the members of the central board, unless they had given great dissatisfaction to their constituents, would be almost certain to be re-elected, so that in all probability no actual interruption of the works in progress would take place by its transfer from the hands of those who have acquired some knowledge of it, to those who are entirely inexperienced?—*I would answer that question by saying that in the large works which we have in hand in the City, such as the construction of the Holborn Valley Viaduct, and the Smithfield*

[6]18 & 19 Victoria, c. 120 (1855). Sect. 31 set up the Metropolitan Board of Works; the vestries' powers were established by Sects. 67–134.

*Meat Market, the members are returned frequently year after year to the same committee, and we find the advantage of doing it.*

[*After further questions by others on the Committee about the period of service and the likely quality of Members, Mill returned to the comparison of the Corporation with the vestries.*]

973. I think I understand you to state that, in your opinion, the members of the Corporation of the City of London have, in their character for intelligence, improved very much of late years.?—*Very much.*

974. Do you think the same has been the case with regard to the members of vestries?—*I think there has been a deterioration, and practically we have found a difficulty every year in getting a candidate in St. James's, Westminster. He is hunted for, and he gives his consent through being entreated, in fact solicited, as a personal favour, to become a candidate, and then he seldom comes in many cases.*

975. Then do you think it is more and more difficult to induce the most desirable class of men to become vestrymen?—*I do.*

976. How do you account for the increasing difficulty in that respect?—*I think that if the difficulty has been gradually increasing during the last 10 years, it is fair to assume that it will go on for the next 10 years.*

977. Can you give the Committee any idea of what are the causes of this increasing reluctance to become members of vestries?—*No, excepting that the major part of the works of an important character, and which give dignity and character to the bodies who execute them, do not fall into the hands of the vestries for execution, but the works which give a little honour are taken from them and done by the Metropolitan Board of Works.*

978. Do you think the office of vestryman is considered an office of much less importance than it used to be?—*I think so.*

979. And you think that that objection would not exist in the case of municipalities?—*I think so.*

980. Particularly if the functions of the central body were of the very restricted character which you seem to anticipate?—*Yes.*

981. Do you not think that there are other things besides the main drainage which would properly come under the jurisdiction of the central body, for instance, a matter which has excited a good deal of discussion, and is now before Parliament, namely, the regulation of the traffic of the metropolis;[7] do you not think that regulations for that purpose might advantageously be made by such a central body as you are proposing?—*It might, but the position and necessities of one borough so differ from the position and necessities of another borough, that if you legislate for the borough of Westminster, you would enact regulations which*

---

[7]"A Bill, Intituled, an Act for Regulating the Traffic in the Metropolis, and for Making Provision for the Greater Security of Persons Passing through the Streets; and for Other Purposes," 30 Victoria (27 Mar., 1867), *PP*, 1867, VI, 423–35.

*would be extremely inconvenient for the borough of the Tower Hamlets, or for the borough of Greenwich; and therefore though a central board might be entrusted with those things, I do not think that in such matters a necessity arises for one board or against separate jurisdictions.*

982. On the other hand, do you not think there is a great advantage in having those regulations, as far as convenience admits, uniform, in order that people may know what regulations they have to observe, and may not have to commit to memory a great many different systems of regulations?—*That would be a great advantage, no doubt.*

983. You have made some general remarks upon the administration by vestries, but I do not think you have made any full statement on the subject; will you state in a few words what you consider to be the defects of the present system, which you would wish to remedy by substituting municipalities for vestries?—*I think that in vestries there is wanting the bond of pecuniary results and interests which bind many committees and bodies of men together, and under which they work effectually; there are other societies which are brought together by a desire to do good, and in those a feeling of philanthropy is the bond, but I know of no bond of that kind, or of any other sufficient kind operating upon the minds of vestrymen, so as to secure the intelligence of a parish or district, and that love for the work which I see evinced elsewhere.*

984. Then in the Corporation of London, I suppose you think that the desire to keep up the credit of the Corporation is the bond of union which you desiderate in the other cases?—*I do.*

985. And you do not think that that desire exists in the case of vestries?—*I do not.*

986. But you think that it would exist in the case of municipalities?—*I do.*

987. You think that there would be a general feeling for the honour and credit of the municipality which does not exist with regard to a parish or vestry?—*That is my opinion. I think they would have greater power. A municipality would not exist long without either obtaining by Act of Parliament, or from other sources, some opportunity for their members to come together occasionally for social purposes, for conversaziones, or for lectures. Something of that sort would grow out of every municipality, and would constitute a bond of union and an inducement of an interested character to bring people into the new corporations, which do not exist now or in the case of the vestries.*

988. You think the vestries are not sufficiently large or important bodies to excite that feeling?—*They are not, and important works are denied to them.*

[*A varied series of questions led to comparison with municipal arrangements on the Continent.*]

1127. Do you know that in Paris the municipality is entirely nominated by the Crown?—*I have understood that it is a representative of the Crown, and not of the people.*

**4 April**

*Sir John Thwaites*[8]

[*The questioning of Thwaites having covered many issues, Mill set out on a path of his own.*]

1387. You stated, did you not, that there was considerable difficulty in inducing owners of property to take such an interest in the proceedings of the Board as to be willing to serve as members of it?—*With regard to the Metropolitan Board of Works, that was not my statement.*

1388. Perhaps you will be so good as to say what your statement was?—*My statement had reference to the district boards and vestries.*

1389. You stated, I believe, that they were not willing to become members of district boards and vestries; but do you think they would be unwilling to give votes for district boards or vestries, or for the Metropolitan Board of Works, if votes were assigned to them in their character of owners; do you think that if there were a provision that owners of property, as well as occupiers, should have votes in virtue of their property, they would be unwilling to give votes, whether by voting papers, or otherwise?—*Then they would vote as residents and as owners of property also.*

1390. They might be owners of property in one district, and residents in another, and in that case perhaps there would be no absurdity of their having votes for both; is there not at present a Bill before Parliament, promoted by the Board of Works, under which a metropolitan improvement rate would be raised, half of which would fall upon the owners?[9]—*That is so.*

1391. Do you not think that, if a rate can be levied by the Board, a portion of which has to be paid by owners, it would be just that the owners, as such, should have a voice in a choice of the body which imposes those rates?—*I have gone to the full length already of admitting that it would be a great advantage to the district, and to us, if owners would take their proper share in the government of the metropolis.*

1392. Do you not think that, if rates were imposed upon them as owners, that would give them a motive to interest themselves more in local business?—*Then it is a very strong argument in favour of the Bill which we have introduced, that it will create activity in a direction where it has been very sluggish.*

1393. Is there any way which you could suggest by which owners of property, as such, might be represented upon the Metropolitan Board of Works?—*I confess having given the subject very earnest attention, that I can point out to the Committee no machinery by which such persons can be specially represented as owners of property.*

[8]John Thwaites (1815–70) was Chairman of the Metropolitan Board of Works from 1855 to his death. He had testified earlier before the Committee; see *CW*, XXIX, 437–42.

[9]In Clause 3 of "A Bill to Make Better Provision for the Raising of Money to Be Applied in the Execution of Works of Permanent Improvement in the Metropolis," 30 Victoria (26 Feb., 1867), *PP*, 1867, IV, 203–6. The Bill was brought in by Ayrton and Tite.

1394. Is not that a considerable objection to the present mode of choosing the Board of Works, namely, by delegation from the vestries; because if the Board of Works were chosen directly by the ratepayers, there would be no difficulty, I apprehend, in enabling the owners of property, as well as the occupiers, to give votes in the election of the Board of Works; whereas there is a difficulty, undoubtedly, in introducing a representation of the owners of property, when the members of the Board of Works are elected by the vestries, who are themselves elected by the occupiers only?—*No doubt; unless the owners of property would exercise their influence, which they can exercise if they have the disposition, by electing a different class of persons from those who are at present on the vestries and district boards, which would accomplish their object indirectly, I admit.*

1395. In that case, the influence which any individual's vote would have might be extremely small in proportion to the degree in which his interest as an owner might be at stake; because he might be a very large owner, and still he would only have a vote as a single occupier?—*That would be so.*

1396. Is any inconvenience experienced in the proceedings of the Board of Works from the insufficient number of the Board?—*I think not.*

1397. Do you think that there is no special reason for any increase of the number, except that which might arise from the new districts?—*An increased representation of 8 or 10 members would not affect the principle which I hold to be important in an executive and deliberative body, viz., that you should not get beyond a certain number, otherwise you would not get through your business. The members of our Board, when they meet, meet for the purpose of the dispatch of business, and we have so much to attend to that we have not much time for talking.*

1398. Do you think that the present number of the Board of Works, or something like it, hits the correct medium between a number which is insufficient for the business and a number which is so great as to cause a loss of time in mere discussion?—*Yes; I mean that as regards the question of whether you should have five or six representatives of property, if I rightly understand the term, or owners of property, or representatives of owners of property, added to our Board, I should not have the slightest objection whatever. All we want is respectable, and intelligent, and honourable men in the discharge of their duty.*

[*The history of conflict over improvements between the Crown and the Board of Works was discussed, and Thwaites agreed that the Crown might, because of its large property in the metropolis, be represented on the Board.*]

1406. Do you not think that the interest of the owners of property in a locality is more closely and more permanently connected with the interests of the locality than the interest of the mere occupiers?—*No doubt they have a permanent stake, and an interest beyond that of a mere occupier who may be a yearly tenant.*

1407. Is it not the case that many improvements are often desirable in a locality, the advantage of which will not be likely to be reaped within the average terms for which occupiers may hold their occupation, but which will be advantageous ultimately to the owner?—*Yes.*

1408. In that case is it not important that owners should be represented upon any body which has the power of making those improvements; and are not improvements very often delayed because they depend upon the occupiers, and the occupiers have not a sufficiently long interest in their occupation to render it worth their while to incur any expense for those improvements?—*No doubt if you could induce that class of persons to take an active part in the local government of the metropolis, great good would result from it.*

[*It was asserted that there was some disinclination of owners to serve on district boards, but Thwaites indicated that the problem did not exist in the case of the Board of Works.*]

1412. The owners of compounded property, I apprehend, on the contrary very often do serve upon the vestries and district boards, do they not?—*I believe that in some vestries they are very numerous.*

1413. And it is understood that they are not that portion of the vestries and district boards, whose influence is exercised to the greatest public advantage?—*No doubt.*

[*Considerable discussion arose over the representation of owners on the Board, especially concerning the difficulty of identifying various classes of owners.*]

1432. Would not the Parliamentary Register show who are the freeholders, and who are the leaseholders, or the owners of property in a certain district, above a certain value, to which value it might perhaps be expedient to restrict the right of voting?—*There would be no difficulty in ascertaining the number of freeholders, which would be very large; but the difficulty is in ascertaining the beneficial leaseholders who have great interest in metropolitan property, and adapting the machinery to give them a representative.*

## 8 April

*Henry Letherby*[10]

[*The questioning dwelt on the overcrowded housing conditions of the poor, and the powers of the Commissioners of Sewers, guided by the advice of the Medical Officer who made inspections. Letherby's observation was that following the Sanitary Act of 1866,[11] conditions had much improved, and he believed that in the City of London there were no houses in which sleeping lodgers covered the floors.*]

1607. Are you speaking of common lodging-houses, or of others?—*The common lodging-houses of the City of London are different from those outside*

[10]Henry Letherby (1806–76) was Medical Officer of Health under the City Commissioners of Sewers from 1855.

[11]29 & 30 Victoria, c. 90 (1866).

the City. *The common lodging-house outside the City of London is occupied by tramps for the night, and is under the supervision of the police, but a common lodging-house within the City, is also a place in which the rooms are let at 3*s. 6d. *per week or less; and so advantageous has been this supervision and control by reason of the provisions of the City Sewers Act, that it was made the subject of a clause in the Sanitary Act of 1866.*[12]

1608. So that a very large number of houses occupied by the poorer classes have been placed under your control, and have been inspected by you?—*Yes.*

### William Haywood[13]

[*Discussion of the most equitable way of taxing services such as road cleaning and sewers turned to a comparison of costs in poor areas and in affluent ones such as St. George's, Hanover Square.*]

1822. There would be also a much smaller length of street in the highly-rated districts, would there not?—*I think not. You will find that in the highly-rated districts the houses are very close together indeed; and the streets in those districts bear a very large proportion to the whole area. In the case of the City of London, in a square mile there are nearly 50 miles of thoroughfares, and probably something like 25 per cent. of the whole area is street. I think in St. George's, Hanover-square, you would find a very great length of street in relation to the whole area; and those streets are of a very important nature, as regards the whole public, and not only as regards that locality.*

### John Francis Bontems[14]

[*The witness asserted that many of the difficulties of vestry government, as illustrated in Islington, would be avoided in larger municipalities.*]

1892. Do you find that inconveniences arise from the small extent of the districts under the present vestry administration?—*Yes; in speaking of the advantages which I anticipate from the proposed municipalities, I shall refer to that point.*

### 11 April
*William Corrie* (recalled)

[*Corrie cited the Acts and parliamentary amendments that tended to show that, since the establishment of the Metropolitan Board of Works, the jurisdiction of the City of London was separate and distinct from that of the Board, sewers being an exception.*]

[12]11 & 12 Victoria, c. 112 (1848), frequently renewed and amended, led to Clause 35 in 29 & 30 Victoria, c. 90.

[13]William Haywood (1821–94), an architect and civil engineer, was Chief Engineer to the Commissioners of Sewers from 1846.

[14]John Francis Bontems, a vestryman of Islington, was a member of the Common Council of the Corporation of London and of the City Sewer Commission.

1974. Has it ever been maintained of the Metropolis Board of Works that they have the power in question under Acts of Parliament previous to this one?[15]— *They know that they have not the power, as the honourable Member for Bath says; they would say, "Our sewers ceased at Holborn Bars, and therefore we thought it very desirable to have this power."* [16]

1975. It is an undisputed point, is it not, that the Metropolitan Board of Works had no power within Holborn Bars previously to this Act which did not give them any such powers?—*Precisely; that is how it is. I have not troubled the Committee with the names of private Acts of Parliament, in which the same sort of things have been done, because they are very often inserted by promoters at the request of different parties, and perhaps there is no great authority in them; but this is a case in which the question was distinctly raised and discussed before Committees of the two Houses of Parliament, and no attempt was made by the Board of Works to go to either House to try to reverse the decision of the Committee.*

[*The witness continued to assert that the separation of jurisdictions was proper.*]

1990. I presume that you mean that those local improvements which are for the interest of the inhabitants of the City, and which concern them only, should be exclusively made by the City authorities; you do not mean that improvements of a larger character, which extend to other districts of the metropolis, as well as to the City, should be made exclusively by the City, or by the local authorities of those other districts; and that there should be no general body whatever empowered to make such improvements?—*My opinion is this: I think first of all that these local improvements ought to be in the hands of the local authorities; I cannot imagine any great case in which the parties must not come to the Legislature upon that subject; and I think that the proper time to determine who is to do the work would be, when they come before the Legislature. It would not do to entrust any local authority with the power of raising sums of money as was proposed, and is proposed this year by the Metropolitan Board of Works and all the metropolis, I believe, are protesting against that power being given to them.*

1991. But assuming that it would not be proper to have any of those great improvements made without obtaining the authority of the Legislature for making them, that authority, if given, must be given to some executive body or other; and do you not think that when the improvement is one which regards the whole metropolis, the body that is entrusted with executing it, ought to be one that has

---

[15]I.e., the legislation proposed by James Beal, and earlier given to the Committee, "A Bill Intituled 'An Act for the Establishment of Municipal Corporations within the Metropolis,'" App. 9 of the "Second Report," *PP*, 1866, XIII, 619–28.

[16]William Tite (d. 1873), M.P. for Bath 1855–73, a member of the Committee, actually said (question 1972) not that the sewers, but the Board's "authority," ceased at Holborn Bars.

authority over the metropolis throughout?—[*On the supposition that a proposal was made to Parliament to make a great street running east and west through the City,*] *if I might humbly suggest what the proper course would be, I should say that it would be to appoint some persons from both districts, to appoint some from the City, and some from outside, and to let them execute the work; I do not think for such works as that any central body is necessary.*

1992. Would you have a special body constituted for the whole metropolis, for the express purpose of that particular improvement?—*Suppose it ran from Westminster through the City, and supposing Westminster were then a municipality, I would let the Corporation of Westminster and the Corporation of London execute that work jointly, and that would then be, I think, a very good body for doing it; but I do not see that the inhabitants of Woolwich or of Hampstead would be wanted at all to assist in such a matter.*

1993. Do you not think that a great line of communication of this sort, to use your example, would be materially for the advantage, not only of the particular districts through which it might pass, but of all the districts which would be enabled to communicate with one another through it? Do you not think that, for instance, a great street passing through the City, and through Westminster, would be of great use to the Kensington and Chelsea districts, and also to the Finsbury and Tower Hamlets districts?—*Then, I say again, let the Legislature determine what parties are interested, and let those parties be represented.*

[*The case of the Thames Embankment being instanced, Corrie argued that it was an exception, and maintained again his position about the propriety of the current arrangements.*]

2000. Would you not think it very desirable that there should be some authority charged with the express duty of planning and originating the improvements which may be necessary in a great town like the metropolis?—*My idea upon that is this; you will always find projectors; it would not be the Board of Works, or the City of London, or the central authority, it would be some clever projector who would come and lay this plan before them, and then it would be carried out afterwards.*

2001. No doubt all proposals for improvements originate with some individual or other, but would you think it desirable to leave the whole business of suggesting the improvement, and of getting together the people who are to bring such improvements before the Legislature entirely to individuals?—*I do not see the necessity, but, however, I do not wish to combat that suggestion; but I wish to say, that I feel very confident that the Metropolitan Board of Works ought not to be that authority; I think they ought to be elected for the express purpose, and also elected directly by the ratepayers.*

[*In particular, Corrie asserted, the localities most concerned in improvements could be outvoted on the Board by representatives of distant districts.*]

2008. Do you think that, in the case of such an improvement as that which you mentioned of a street passing through the City and through Westminster, but which would benefit other parts of the metropolis and not only those two districts, it would be just to expect that the City and Westminster should, or do you think they would voluntarily, consent to defray the expense of this work by rates borne wholly by themselves and not paid by other parts of the metropolis?—*I think if it were shown, as is suggested by the question, that other parts of the metropolis were interested, they would in some way or other have to contribute towards it: and the Legislature would then determine how far those other districts were to be represented according to the contributions which they might make.*

2009. The Legislature might fix a maximum of rates which it should be allowable to levy on the metropolis generally, or on any of its parts; but as they could not fix the exact sum, I apprehend they must confide to some authority or other the power of levying the rate; and, as they would probably not be willing to vest in the representatives of the City and of Westminster the power of levying rates on other parts of the metropolis, would it not be necessary that they should appoint some special authority representing the whole metropolis for that purpose?—*I intended to say, I think, that it would be a good plan if this were done; but I do not think it is necessary that you should keep up this central authority, for perhaps once or twice in the course of a century an improvement of this sort being made, because it is kept up at great expense. However, I do not express my opinion at all upon that subject.*

[*Further questioning dwelt on the specific powers of the Board.*]

2020. Upon your construction of the Act[17] the local authorities of the different districts can make those improvements with the consent of the Metropolitan Board of Works, but the Metropolitan Board of Works cannot itself make them?—*The Metropolitan Board of Works cannot itself make them. They have no power to do so.*

## Thomas John Bedford[18]

[*Mill initiated the questioning of Bedford.*]

2077. Are you an Officer of the Corporation?—*I am a Commissioner of Sewers. It has been stated that the right of pre-emption operated in the City of London as a bar in carrying out our local improvements under the Act of Parliament;[19] I say, in reply, as a member of the Commission, that we never found anything of the kind, and never had the point raised. It never operated to the slightest extent against our carrying out our full powers. Our powers are almost unlimited, and we had a decision in the Court of Chancery last year which confirmed that view. We have very large powers, and we exercise them very fully. Nothing stops us but want of*

[17]25 & 26 Victoria, c. 102 (1862), esp. Sect. 72.

[18]John Thomas Bedford (1812–1900) was a Member of the City Court of Common Council from the Ward of Farrington Without.

[19]Particularly by Committee members during the questioning of William Corrie on 11 April; see "Third Report," 568 ff.

*funds. I may say that, at the present moment, we have laid down and commenced lines in the City of London, which will cost to carry out between £800,000 and £900,000. No right of pre-emption ever stops us for one single day.*

2078. I understand the right of pre-emption to consist merely in the obligation which the City of London is under, to give the owner of the land the first offer of buying back any portion of that land which is not wanted by them for their improvements?—*Quite so.*

2079. But if they refuse to buy it back, then it is open to the public in the same manner as if no right of pre-emption had ever existed?—*Quite so.*

[*Tite intervened with questions about specific cases, concerning which the witness denied there had been any hindrance.*]

2085. The City is not bound to sell land to the original owner of it at his own price, but only at the same price which they can obtain for it from others?—*A fair market price.*

[*Discussion turned to taxation, which the witness said had reached beyond its proper maximum in much of the City, and argued that the burden should be equalized.*]

2095. Is there any other subject connected with the general question of the government of the metropolis to which you wish to direct the attention of the Committee?—*I may say that the Metropolitan Board of Works is exceedingly unpopular in my neighbourhood. I do not know that they deserve it; but it is because all the increased taxation springs from them.*

2096. So that you consider that a great portion of the City of London is generally over-taxed, and therefore they dislike any authority over them which imposes more taxes?—*Quite so. With regard to the local government of the metropolis, having given some little attention to the matter, I may say that I should generally approve of municipalities for the Parliamentary boroughs, and that some body emanating from them for special objects might be appointed where the matters in hand affected the whole metropolis. That seems to be the popular opinion out of doors wherever I go.*

[*Bedford argued for direct representation on municipal bodies, asserting that larger ones would attract better candidates than at present in the vestries.*]

2121. Do you think that the extent of the suggested municipalities, as compared with the extent of the districts under the district boards, would have much to do with the result which you anticipate?—*I should think so.*

*Benjamin Scott* (recalled)
[*Once more Mill began the questioning.*]

2154. You gave the Committee on a former occasion a great deal of information upon the subject of the local administration of the City;[20] but you have turned your

---

[20]In his earlier evidence; see "Third Report," 493 ff.

attention, I believe, to the more general question of improving the local administration of the metropolis; will you kindly put the Committee in possession of your opinions upon that subject?—*I shall be very happy to do so; but previously to doing it, I was requested to put in two documents, which I had not with me, on a former occasion; the first is a list of the improvements and public works conducted by the Corporation, of which Mr. Corrie in his evidence gave a very insufficient account. The account includes all public works and improvements from the date of the building of Blackfriars Bridge.*

[*Scott outlined the history and general state of improvements planned by the City Corporation, and mentioned other documents that he could supply.*]

2160. Have you another paper to put in?—[*The witness handed in a paper concerning the new street from Blackfriars to the Mansion House.*]

[*It was established that business failure was a disqualification for membership in the City Corporation and courts of the livery companies.*]

2170. Will you kindly enter into the general subject of the municipal government of the metropolis?—[*Having given much thought to the matter for some thirty-seven years, Scott asserted that the only satisfactory government of the metropolis would result from enfranchising all the districts' municipal institutions. Originally the City expanded by the addition of "Out Wards," but parliament became jealous of the City and tried, vainly, to prevent its further expansion. The result was that the areas that grew up around the City did not have the municipal institutions that they needed and that were found in much less significant municipalities through the kingdom.*]

[*The history of Southwark was discussed as a specific instance.*]

2203. In what particular form would you give municipal government to the metropolis?—*I am disposed to think that it is too large to create one corporation out of. Parliament seems already to have settled that principle in dividing Manchester and Salford into two municipalities.*

[*Scott affirmed that the size of the proposed metropolitan municipality would not be a genuine threat to parliament.*]

2205. You do not think there would be any difficulty in keeping such a body within its proposed functions, namely, those of local government only?—[*There would be no true difficulty; the instinct of the people was for good government, and the "trading class" generally represented on municipal bodies wanted only "peace, quiet, and order" for themselves and for the protection of trade. The main practical problem lay in the proper division of the whole into districts: ten would be best, with the parliamentary and municipal boundaries coinciding. It would also be convenient to extend the rural boundaries of the metropolis to*] take in the collection of the coal duty, and then the coal duty would be expended in the district taxed, and the parties who pay the duty would be represented.

2206. Does not the coal duty extend to such a very great distance from the metropolis proper, that the effect would be to introduce so large a population as would interfere with the purposes of the municipality?—*It extends for a radius of several miles further in most places. The coal duty boundary, according to a Return placed before the House of Commons, extends from 13 or 14 miles to 16 miles from Charing-cross, whereas the proposed limits of Mr. Beal's Bill extend from about 9 to 12 miles, I think, from Charing-cross. There would be an addition of a good deal of geographical territory, but very little would have to be added as regards population and rateable value.*

2207. Do you think that, to make the district from which the funds were derived co-extensive with the authority that would dispose of those funds, would be an advantage which would overcome any disadvantage there might be in including a rural population?—[*Yes: one advantage is that the police boundary is cotermi-nous with the coal duty boundary. It would be very inconvenient to introduce another anomaly when trying to reduce them.*]

2209. Do you think it important that the divisions of the metropolis should be the same for all kinds of public business?—*As far as possible. I think that if any alteration is made, an attempt should be made to introduce something like uniformity of administration, and uniformity of boundary.*

2210. What are your opinions as to the manner in which those municipal bodies should be constituted and elected?—*I think, generally, that the principle which exists in the provinces, and in the City of London, and which has been tested for very many centuries, should be applied to London. If the vestry system is better than the municipal system, then Manchester and Birmingham should have a central board appointed by the vestries, and the municipal system should be superseded. But I apprehend, no doubt, that at present Parliament is satisfied with municipal administration, as it exists in the large towns; and I conceive that there can be no valid reason offered why it should not be introduced into the metropolis.*

[*Questioning turned to the placing and extent of control in officers, particularly over the police.*]

2235. You say that you would have a court of quarter sessions in each municipality; would you have the administration of justice conducted by stipendiary magistrates, or by the ordinary magistrates of the municipality?—*I prefer, personally, the elective system, and, I think, that it works well; but the stipendiary system is working well in the provinces, and I think that is a matter of detail and not a matter of principle.*

*John Jones*[21]

[*Jones not being a very responsive witness, establishment of his credentials as a vestryman took several questions.*]

2267. Your district is included in the Strand Union, I presume?—*Yes.*

2268. So that it does not exercise the ordinary power of a vestry?—*We elect officers to the district board.*

---

[21]John Jones, a watchmaker, was a vestryman from the Strand.

[*Jones's grievance centred on the government's refusal to pay its proper share of rates for Somerset House, which occupied about half of his parish in the Strand. In his view, a larger municipality would be better able to establish equitable taxation.*]

2270. What do you propose with a view to give you this greater authority?—*I think that if we had had an organised authority for the district, such as the City of London have, we should have had a power at once to be attended to, but the several parishes just going up very feebly, each of them by itself, are very little noticed.*

2271. Do you think that a municipality would be more listened to by the Government and by Parliament?—*I do think that a municipality, as being a larger power, would be more listened to by the Government and by Parliament than a parish, and naturally enough.*

2272. Have you any other suggestions to make to the Committee?—*Then I think that it is also very unreasonable that a resident in London, and a man holding a moderate position in the world, and who is able to understand things, should be dictated to, and be told to pay so much towards a county rate in which he has no voice whatever; I, as one of the parish, have to do with the making of the poor rate, but in the case of the county rate, without any communication, we are bidden by some central authority over which we have no control, to add so many pounds to our rate book, to provide for a county rate. Now I think that that is a position in which citizens of this metropolis ought not to be; we ought to be under no such subservience as that any power should be able to tell us how much to give without our having any voice in the matter.*

2273. Do you think that the whole metropolis should be itself a county, and should vote its own county rate?—*I claim the power of appointing those men who have the power of dictating county rates to me. I claim the power also of having a voice in the management of those men who claim a police rate from me; and, I think it a reasonable claim, that every citizen ought to have the power of asking by what right they put those burdens upon us, and that they should also account to us as to whether those things are wisely expended which we have contributed as part of the rates. That is what I should like to know in the first instance. I sent up some months ago to know at the police office how many men were supplied to my parish. We pay in my parish, which is a very small one, some 280l. a year; and I wanted to know how many men it furnished for our district; but the police had no orders to give any answer; I consider that that was rather an inferior kind of answer to what I ought to receive, and therefore, I consider that all tradespeople who are resident in Westminster ought to be able to ask with authority how the money taken from us is disposed of, and so hearing that this matter was before you, I came.*

[*In response to the Chair, Jones said larger municipalities would provide evidence as to which candidates were fit for parliament.*]

2275. I understand you to say that you think properly constituted local bodies are a useful training school for Members of Parliament?—*That is right: and that men would be understood for what they are worth if they passed before us in different gradations of duty.*

2276. This is, in your opinion, one of the particular advantages of properly constituted local government, which you consider that the vestry government is not?—*Just so. I think it is very feeble.*

2277. Is it your opinion that the vestry does not bring forward persons and make them known to the public, who would be useful to the public in capacities of a more elevated kind; but that municipal government does do so?—*Entirely. I think it is all part of a general system.*

## 30 April
*Richard Mayne*

[*Mayne objected strenuously to the imputation by Scott that Mayne had, by omitting murder, distorted the evidence of crime in the metropolitan district as compared to the City of London;[22] he explained that he had omitted it because murder was not generally a crime the police could prevent, and handed in a paper dealing with murder.*]

2310. There is no personal imputation against you conveyed in those words of Mr. Scott; he only objects to the principle upon which you proceed?—*I am the person who has done what he says is unfair.*

2311. There is no imputation upon your intention, or upon your honesty at all. An objection is taken to the principle, which is stated to be unfair in its operation?—*I am sure that no such imputation could properly have been made; but the words of that passage seem to bear the meaning, that I omitted the class which was against me, in order to make my comparison unfair as against the City.*

[22]See p. 391 above.

# Appendix E

## Mill at the Political Economy Club
### 1840–65

*Political Economy Club*, VI (London: Macmillan, 1921), gives information about the history of the Club, with the topics proposed and the members present for the discussions. The following list gives the topics Mill proposed, with the dates of the meetings. He of course frequently attended discussions initiated by others.

### 1840
6 February

What would be the effect produced upon Wages, if the rich should adopt the practice of expending a large portion of their income on menial servants and retainers, and a smaller portion in the purchase of Commodities?

### 1841
4 March

What is the most convenient definition of the word *Demand*?

6 May

According to what principle is the benefit of the Trade between two nations shared between those two nations?

### 1842
2 June

To what extent has any country the power of making another independent country pay a portion of its Taxes?

### 1843
2 February

Is not the exportation of British Capital a cause, and almost a necessary condition, of its continued increase at home?

1 June

Is Political Economy a Science *à priori*, or what is commonly called a science of facts?

**1844**

5 December

Was Ricardo correct in stating that "the same rule which regulates the relative value of Commodities in one country, does not regulate the relative value of the Commodities exchanged between two or more countries"?[1]

**1845**

3 April

Under what conditions, and to what extent, ought Governments to exercise a directing or regulating power over the operations of Private industry; and in connection with it?

**1846**

2 April

Is the Rent of Mines governed by similar principles with the Rent of Land?

7 May

What are the circumstances which regulate the Prices of the different kinds of Agricultural produce relatively to one another?

**1847**

1 April

What measures can be adopted to avert, as far as possible, the dangerous consequences of the Irish Poor Law proposed by the present Government?

2 December

Under what circumstances is it desirable to maintain a Surplus revenue for the purpose of paying off a National Debt?

**1848**

2 March

What are the essential differences between Bank Notes and other forms of credit?

4 May

Would it not be highly conducive to the economical and moral improvement of the Labouring Classes that the workmen should be, as far as possible, associated in the Profits of Industrial undertakings, and what means can be devised of giving a greater degree of extension to this principle?

[1]David Ricardo, *On the Principles of Political Economy and Taxation* (London: Murray, 1817), p. 156.

**1849**

1 February

What is the most equitable mode of assessing an Income Tax?

6 December

What are the most desirable changes to be made in our system of Taxation?

**1850**

4 April

Does the progress of Wealth and Industry, under the present social institutions of Europe, tend to an increasing agglomeration of capital in large masses, or to the dispersion of such masses?

**1851**

6 February

Would not the most eligible mode of relieving the Handloom Weavers from their habitually depressed condition, be their formation into Home colonies, combining agriculture with their present employment?

3 July

Does a business in which the Returns are slow, employ with equal capital as much labour, and add as much to the produce of the country, as a business in which the Returns are quick?

**1852**

4 March

Is the purchase of commodities produced by Labour equivalent in its effect on Wages, and on the Labour market, to the Direct purchase of Labour?

2 December

What are the necessary conditions of a just Income Tax?

**1853**

3 February

Is Direct preferable to Indirect taxation?

5 May

Is the claim made on behalf of the Irish Tenantry to hold their farms in perpetuity at a rent fixed by valuation, admissible in any shape, or under any conditions?

**1855**

6 December

What are the nature and extent of the relief which the present generation obtains at the expense of posterity, by raising the supplies necessary for War expenditure, by means of Loans instead of by means of Taxation?

## 1856
3 April

Does the purchase of Commodities for Unproductive consumption contribute to the employment of Labour, in the same degree as the expenditure of an equal sum in direct payment of Wages to unproductive Labourers?

4 December

Is it incumbent on the Bank of England to restrict its discounts, on the Setting in of a Drain of Gold, without reference to the causes in which that Drain originates?

## 1857
7 May

By what laws are Retail Prices and Profits determined?

## 1858
3 June

Under what circumstances would a fall in the exchangeable value of Gold, as a consequence of the recent discoveries, justify any alteration in the Standard so as to affect existing Contracts?

## 1861
11 April

What is the value of Moral Education to Economical Improvement; and conversely, what are the bearings of Economical Prosperity on Moral Excellence?

## 1863
27 March

What is the best definition of Productive and Unproductive Labour, and of Productive and Unproductive Consumption?

3 July

Is the word *Capital* most properly used to designate certain kinds of Wealth, namely, Food, Implements, and Materials; or should it rather be applied to all Wealth, of whatever kind, which is, or is intended by its owner to be, applied to the purpose of Reproduction?

## 1865
7 July

Does the high rate of Interest in America and in new Colonies indicate a corresponding high rate of profits? and if so, What are the causes of that high rate?

# Appendix F

## Textual Emendations

IN THIS LIST, following the page and line numbers, the reading of the copy-text is given first, and then the amended reading in square brackets, with an explanation if required. If there is no explanation, it may be assumed that there is an obvious typographical error, or else that the change is made for sense or for consistency within the item. Typographical errors in versions other than the copy-text are ignored. "SC" signifies Somerville College, Oxford.

7.8–9   editor . . . author [Editor . . . Author]
7.10    MSS. [manuscripts]
7.12    inmately [intimately]
8.25    ugred [urged]
14.22   themeslves [themselves]
22.6    cross-examination. [cross-examination."]
23.30   things [thing]
25.35   *temperance* [*temperate*] [*as in* Source]
49.4    lord [Lord]
60.19   it. [it?]
67.4    occasien [occasion]
84.20   mistated [mis-stated]
134.9   *etc.* [etc.] [*as in* Source]
134.10  être [*être*]
134.14  contenu, etc. [contenu. . . .] [etc. *signals the omission of the remainder of the passage*]
148.23  section 6 [section 5] [*as in fact*]
172.2   facts [parts] [*as in* Source]
202.1   resisting [*resisting*] [*emphasis reversed in this ed.*]
204.4   time [Time] [*for consistency*]
205.15  rises [arises] [*as in* Source]
206.27  locality, what [locality. What] [*as in* Source]
207.3   magnitude [Magnitude] [*as in* Source]
207.16  position [positions] [*as in* Source]
207.32  In [For] [*as in* Source]
223.5   association [association.] [*as in* Source]
231.1   Dread [dread]
240.3   shewn [shown] [*as elsewhere in paragraph*]
243.23  with an idea [with an Idea]

253.1     foreseen [foreseen,]
264.23    parasetical [parasitical]
265.10    peucidanifolia [peucedanifolia]
266.2     siugle [single]
268.16    rarieties [varieties]
269.29    north-eastern [south-eastern] [*corrected by JSM in later article*]
271.3     Maiden [Marden] [*corrected by JSM in later article*]
271.6     rocks [roots] [*corrected by JSM in later article*]
271.9     Woodbatch [Woodhatch] [*corrected by JSM in later article*]
271.29    Wenham [Wonham] [*corrected by JSM in later article*]
272.42    Godbroke [Gadbroke] [*corrected by JSM in later article*]
273.33    Wenham [Wonham] [*corrected by JSM in later article*]
285.21–2  not all [not at all]
294.30    Sender [Sonder] [*printer's error?*]
299.34    γ. *spicata*] [*F. spicata*] [*corrected by JSM in SC copy*]
300.14    *comesa* [*comosa*] [*corrected by JSM in SC copy*]
300.23    north [south] [*corrected by JSM in SC copy*]
301.3     *Lychnites* [*Lychnitis*] [*corrected by JSM in SC copy*]
301.7     concisely [copiously] [*corrected by JSM in SC copy*]
301.9     *Lychnites* [*Lychnitis*] [*corrected by JSM in SC copy*]
301.11    *digitalis* [*segetalis*] [*corrected by JSM in SC copy*]
302.7     Rhine [Rhone] [*corrected by JSM in SC copy*]
304.6     where [when] [*corrected by JSM in SC copy*]
304.8     enumerated [enumerate] [*corrected by JSM in SC copy*]
304.34    mountainous [monotonous] [*corrected by JSM in SC copy*]
305.23    March; [March,]
307.33    Mauresa [Manresa] [*corrected by JSM in SC copy*]
309.8     decidely [decidedly]
309.38    find in [find on] [*corrected by JSM in SC copy*]
310.25    *S. hispanica* [*G. hispanica*] [*corrected by JSM in SC copy*]
310.33–4  find, . . . course, [find; . . . course]
311.14    *Lychnites* [*Lychnitis*] [*corrected by JSM in SC copy*]
311.17    *Siderites* [*Sederitis*] [*corrected by JSM in SC copy*]
311.35    No. IV [No. V] [*as in fact*]
314.15    *crassa* [*cracca*] [*corrected by JSM in SC copy*]
317.3     that is [that it is]
318.19    liked [like]
318.24    *S. sylvaticum* [*G. sylvaticum*] [*corrected by JSM in SC copy*]
323.17    non-medica [non-medical]
*330.30*    respresenting [representing]
*334.18*    Society to [Society for]
*334.21*    manscripts [manuscripts]
*345.2*     *Indes Orientales* [*Indes-Orientales*]
*345.3*     *Georgie, l'Armenie, la* [*Géorgie, l'Arménie, et la*]
*345.3*     Belanger [Bélanger]
*353.38*    66,200 [66,200'] [*restyled in this ed.*]
*359.2*     H.D. Inglis [Henry David Inglis]
*359.3*     J. Cook [Samuel Edward Cook] [*as in fact*]
*359.9*     E.B. Stephens [Edward Bell Stephens]
*360.18*    *quocunque* [*quocumque*]

*366n.7*   contemparories [contemporaries

*369.17*   Giubelalde [Guibelalde]

*375.10*   that the [that with the]

*375.11*   peace, long [peace, war, long]

*375.34*   Moderate [Moderates]

*376.27*   Spain [England] [*as in fact*]

*382.9*   Orangemen, [Orangemen:]

*382.19*   imparting [importing]

*384.10*   confimed [confirmed]

*387.35*   broken.* [broken."*] [*restyled in this ed.*]

*391.19–20*   count; I take it [count, I take it]

*393.21*   *gives* [*give*]

*399.7–8*   the many [them any]

*404.20*   provinces; [provinces,]

# Appendix G

## Index of Persons, and Works Cited, with Variants and Notes

LIKE MOST NINETEENTH-CENTURY AUTHORS, Mill is cavalier in his approach to sources, sometimes identifying them with insufficient care, and occasionally quoting them inaccurately. This Appendix is intended to help correct these deficiencies, and to serve as an index of names and titles (which are consequently omitted in the Index proper). Included here also are (at the end of the appendix and listed alphabetically by country) references to parliamentary documents and to statute laws. The material otherwise is arranged in alphabetical order, with an entry for each person or work reviewed, quoted, or referred to in the text proper and in Appendices A–E (the page numbers in the appendices are given in italic type). Anonymous articles in newspapers are entered in order of date under the title of the particular newspaper. References to mythical and fictional characters are excluded. The following abbreviations are used: *ADB* (*Allgemeine deutsche Biographie*), *DBF*, (*Dictionnaire de biographie française*), *DBI* (*Deutscher Biographischer Index*), *DNB* (*Dictionary of National Biography*), *EB* (*Encyclopaedia Britannica*, 11th ed.), *EUI* (*Enciclopedia Universal Ilustrada*); *GDU* (Larousse, *Grand dictionnaire universel du XIXe siècle*), *GE* (*Grande encyclopédie*), *JMP* (Judd, *Members of Parliament*), *MEB* (Boase, *Modern English Biography*), *PD* (*Parliamentary Debates*), *PP* (*Parliamentary Papers*), SC (JSM's library, Somerville College, Oxford), *WWBMP* (*Who's Who of British Members of Parliament*), *WWG* (*Who Was Who in the Greek World*), *WWR* (*Who Was Who in the Roman World*).

The entries take the following form:

1. Identification of persons: birth and death dates are followed by a standard biographical source; if no source isated, available details are given in a note.

2. Identification of works: author, title, etc. in the usual bibliographic form.

3. Notes (if required) giving information about JSM's use of the source, indication if the work is in his library, Somerville College, Oxford, and any other relevant information.

4. Lists of the pages where works are reviewed, quoted, and referred to.

5. In the case of quotations, a list of substantive variants between Mill's text and his source, in this form: Page and line reference to the present text. Reading in the present text] Reading in the source (page reference in the source).

The list of substantive variants also attempts to place quoted passages in their contexts by giving the beginnings and endings of sentences. The original wording is supplied where Mill has omitted two sentences or less; only the length of other omissions is given. There being uncertainty about the actual Classical texts used by Mill, the Loeb editions are usually cited.

NOTE:  see Cockayne's *Complete Peerage*. The exact source of JSM's quotation has not been located, but the report in the *Morning Chronicle* has similarities; also reported in *PD*, 3rd ser., Vol. 38, cols. 125–31.
QUOTED: *370*

ARGÜELLES, AGUSTIN (1776–1844). Referred to: *385*

ARISTOTLE (384–322 B.C.; *WWG*). Referred to: 97, 103

———— *The Metaphysics* (Greek and English). Trans. Hugh Tredennick. 2 vols. London: Heinemann; New York: Putnam's Sons, 1933.
REFERRED TO: 103

———— *Physics* (Greek and English). Trans. Philip H. Wicksteed and Francis M. Cornford. 2 vols. London: Heinemann; Cambridge, Mass.: Harvard University Press, 1929.
NOTE: the reference is in a quotation from James Mill's *Fragment, q.v.*
REFERRED TO: 227

———— *Posterior Analytics*. In *Posterior Analytics, Topica* (Greek and English). Trans. Hugh Tredennick and E.S. Forster. London: Heinemann; Cambridge, Mass.: Harvard University Press, 1960, 24–261.
REFERRED TO: 103

ARNOTT, GEORGE ARNOTT WALKER (1799–1868: *DNB*). Referred to: 317

AYRTON, ACTON SMEE (1816–86; *DNB*). Referred to: *390*


BABINGTON, CHARLES CARDALE (1808–95; *DNB*). *Manual of British Botany, Containing the Flowering Plants and Ferns Arranged According to the Natural Orders*. London: Van Voorst, 1843.
NOTE: 5th ed. (London, 1862) formerly in SC.
REFERRED TO: 284

BACON, FRANCIS (1561–1626; *DNB*). *Maxims of the Law* (1630). In *Works*. Ed. James Spedding, *et al*. 14 vols. London: Longman, *et al*., 1857–74, VII, 308–87.
NOTE: the quotation is in a quotation from Phillipps, *q.v.* for the collation.
QUOTED: 80

BAILEY, SAMUEL (1791–1870; *DNB*). Referred to: 156

———— *A Letter to a Philosopher, in Reply to Some Recent Attempts to Vindicate Berkeley's Theory of Vision, and in Further Elucidation of Its Unsoundness*. London: Ridgway, 1843.
REFERRED TO: 156

———— *A Review of Berkeley's Theory of Vision, Designed to Show the Unsoundness of That Celebrated Speculation*. London: Ridgway, 1842.
REFERRED TO: 156

BAIN, ALEXANDER (1818–1903; *DNB*). Referred to: 102, 103

———— *The Emotions and the Will* (1859). 2nd ed. London: Longmans, Green, 1865.
REFERRED TO: 102, 138, 140–1, 155, 160, 178, 192, 251

———— *Mental and Moral Science. A Compendium of Psychology and Ethics*. 2 vols. London: Longmans, Green, 1868.
QUOTED: 192

———— Notes to James Mill's *Analysis*.
REFERRED TO: 102, 103, 109, 111, 115, 116, 122, 138, 153, 155, 157, 158, 159, 160, 205, 214, 217, 218, 250, 251

———— *The Senses and the Intellect* (1855). 2nd ed. London: Longmans, Green, 1864.
NOTE: in SC is the 3rd ed. (London: Longmans, *et al*., 1868).

—— *A Treatise on Judicial Evidence, Extracted from the Manuscripts of Jeremy Bentham Esq. by M. Dumont. Translated into English.* London: Baldwin, Cradock and Joy, 1825.
QUOTED: 13–14, 17, 60
REFERRED TO: 3, 14–15, 57

BERKELEY, GEORGE (1685–1753; *DNB*). Referred to: 156

—— *An Essay towards a New Theory of Vision* (1709). In *Works*. 3 vols. London: Priestley, 1820, I, 225–316.
REFERRED TO: 156, 163

BERNARD, JEAN FRÉDÉRIC (d. 1752). *Recueil de voyages au nord, contenant divers mémoires très utiles au commerce et à la navigation.* 10 vols. Amsterdam: Bernard, 1715–38.
NOTE: the passage is in "Relation de la Colchide, ou Mingrellie, par le P. Archange Lamberti," VII, 136–302.
QUOTED: *352*
*352.2–5* "Each . . . leg."] [*translated from:*] C'étoient des casques, des cuirasses, et des brassars faits de plusieurs petites lastres de fer, couchées les unes sur les autres: celles de la cuirasse et des brassars r'entroient les unes sur les autres et obeïssoient ainsi aisément aux mouvemens du corps. A la cuirasse étoit attachée une espece de cotte qui leur alloit jusqu'à mi-jambe, d'une étoffe de laine semblable à notre serge, mais d'un rouge si vif, qu'on l'eut prise pour de très-belle escarlotte. (VII, 180–1)

BERTOLONI, ANTONIO. *Flora italica, sistens plantas in Italia et in insulis circumstantibus sponte nascentes.* 10 vols. Bologna: Masi, 1833–54.
REFERRED TO: 299

BEST, WILLIAM DRAPER (Baron Wynford) (1767–1845; *DNB*). Referred to: 81
BIBLE.
NOTE: the reference at *361* is in a quotation.
REFERRED TO: 77, *361*

—— Apocrypha: Susanna. Referred to: 293

—— John.
NOTE: the quotation is indirect.
QUOTED: 63
63.12–13 Whence comes it that any one loves darkness better than light, except it be that his deeds are evil?] And this is the condemnation, that light is come into the world, and men loved darkness rather than light, because their deeds were evil. (3:19)

—— Matthew.
NOTE: the quotation is indirect.
QUOTED: 9
9.25–6 signs of the times,] O *ye* hypocrites, ye can discern the face of the sky; but can ye not *discern* the signs of the times? (16:3)

—— Zechariah.
NOTE: the quotation is indirect; attributed in the text to St. Paul.
QUOTED: *386*
*386.10–11* Despise not the day of small things.] For who hath despised the day of small things? for they shall rejoice, and shall see the plummet in the hand of Zerubbabel with those seven; they are the eyes of the Lord, which run to and fro through the whole earth. (4:10)

BLACKBURNE, FRANCIS (1705–87; *DNB*). Referred to: 20

—— *The Confessional; or, A Full and Free Inquiry into the Right, Utility, Edification and Success of Establishing Systematical Confessions of Faith and Doctrine in Protestant Churches.* London: Bladon, 1766.
REFERRED TO: 20

8 vols. London: Dodsley (Vols. I–III), Rivington (Vols. IV–VIII), 1792–1827, III, 19–321.
QUOTED: 106
106.9   a delightful vision.] [*paragraph*] It is now sixteen or seventeen years since I saw the queen of France, then the dauphiness, at Versailles; and surely never lighted on this orb, which she hardly seemed to touch, a more delightful vision. (110)

CALOMARDE, FRANCISCO TADEO (1773–1842; *EUI*). Referred to: *380*

CANDOLLE, AUGUSTIN PYRAME DE. *Prodromus systematis naturalis regni vegetabilis, sive enumeratio contracta ordinum generum specierumque plantarum huc usque cognitarum, juxta methodi naturalis normas digesta.* 19 vols. Paris: Treuttel and Würtz, 1824–38 (Vols. I–VII); Fortin, Masson, 1844–45 (Vol. VIII); Masson, 1846–72 (Vols. IX–XIX).
REFERRED TO: 260, 281, 292, 303

CARDAILLAC, JEAN JACQUES SÉVERIN DE (1766–1845; *DBF*). *Etudes élémentaires de philosophie.* 2 vols. Paris: Firmin Didot, 1830.
NOTE: the quotation, in translation, is taken from Hamilton's *Lectures, q.v.* for the collation.
QUOTED: 193–6

CARLILE, RICHARD (1790–1843; *DNB*). Referred to: 54

CARLOS MARIA ISIDRO DE BOURBON, DON (1788–1855; *EB*).
NOTE: the reference at *365n–6n* is in a quotation from the *Standard*; that at *369* is in a quotation from Wellesley; that at *376* is in a quotation from the "Quadruple Treaty."
REFERRED TO: *359–88 passim*

—————— "Royal Decree" (20 June, 1835), *The Times*, 2 July, 1835, 6.
NOTE: quoted in English; also quoted in Walton, 153, *q.v.*
REFERRED TO: *365n*

CARNARVON, LORD. See Henry Herbert.

CAROLINE (of England) (1768–1821; *DNB*). Referred to: 81

CARPENTER, LANT (1780–1840; *DNB*). Referred to: 324

CARPENTER, WILLIAM BENJAMIN (1813–85; *DNB*). *Principles of General and Comparative Physiology, Intended as an Introduction to the Study of Human Physiology, and as a Guide to the Philosophical Pursuit of Natural History* (1839). 2nd ed. London: Churchill, 1841.
REVIEWED: 323–4

—————— *Principles of Human Physiology* (1842). 6th ed. Ed. Henry Power. London: Churchill, 1864.
REFERRED TO: 106

CARTWRIGHT, JOHN (1740–1824; *DNB*). Referred to: *367*

CASHEL, ARCHBISHOP OF. See Charles Brodrick.

CASTANON Y LORENZANA, FEDERICO (1770–1836; *EB*). Referred to: *377*

CAVANILLES, ANTONIO JOSÉ. *Icones et descriptiones plantarum, quae aut sponte in Hispania crescunt.* 6 vols. Madrid: Royal Printer, 1791–1801.
REFERRED TO: 290

CAVENDISH, HENRY (1731–1810; *DNB*). Referred to: 96

—————— "Experiments on Air, Read Jan. 15, 1784," *Philosophical Transactions of the Royal Society of London*, LXXIV (1784), Pt. I, 119–53.
REFERRED TO: 96

COLMAN, ARCHIBALD.
NOTE: JSM's nephew.
REFERRED TO: *331, 332*

COLMAN, CHARLES FREDERICK.
NOTE: JSM's brother-in-law.
REFERRED TO: *331, 332*

COLMAN, HENRY.
NOTE: JSM's nephew.
REFERRED TO: *331, 332*

COLMAN, MARY ELIZABETH (née Mill) (1822–1913).
NOTE: JSM's sister.
REFERRED TO: *331, 332*

COLMAN, MARION ("Minnie").
NOTE: JSM's niece.
REFERRED TO: *331, 332*

COLMAN, STUART.
NOTE: JSM's nephew.
REFERRED TO: *331, 332*

COMYNS, JOHN (d. 1740; *DNB*). *A Digest of the Laws of England* (1762–67). Ed. Anthony Hammond. 5th ed. 8 vols. London: Butterworth, *et al.*, 1822.
NOTE: this ed. used in Bowring's ed. of Bentham's *Works*.
REFERRED TO: 24

CONOLLY, ARTHUR (1807–42). *Journey to the North of India, Overland from England, through Russia, Persia, and Affghaunistaun.* 2 vols. London: Bentley, 1834.
QUOTED: *352*

*Consolidated Treaty Series.* See Clive Parry.

COOK, SAMUEL EDWARD (later Widdrington) (1787–1856; *MEB*). *Sketches in Spain during the Years 1829, 30, 31, & 32; Containing Notices of Some Districts Very Little Known; of the Manners of the People, Government, Recent Changes, Commerce, Fine Arts, and Natural History.* 2 vols. London: Boone, 1834.
NOTE: incorrectly identified in heading as J. Cook; title-page incorrectly reads S.S. Cook.
REVIEWED: *359–88*
QUOTED: *386*
*386.15* "The Queen's party comprises, almost without exception, every] The party who support the Queen are not a mere faction, but it comprises every (I, 330)

COPERNICUS, NICOLAUS (1473–1543; *EB*). *De revolutionibus orbium coelestium libri VI.* Nuremberg: Petreium, 1543.
REFERRED TO: 164–5

CORRIE, WILLIAM (1806–81; *MEB*). Questioned: *389–90, 398–401*

CURTIS, WILLIAM (1746–99; *DNB*). *Flora Londinensis; or, Plates and Descriptions of Such Plants as Grow Wild in the Environs of London.* 2 vols. London: Curtis and White, 1775–98.
REFERRED TO: 278

DALLAS, ROBERT (1756–1824; *DNB*). Referred to: 81

DARWIN, ERASMUS (1731–1802; *DNB*). Referred to: 98

——— *Zoonomia; or, The Laws of Organic Life* (1794–96). 3rd ed. 4 vols. London: Johnson, 1801.
NOTE: in SC.
REFERRED TO: 98

from Wellesley; the first at *370* is in a quotation from Richardson; the second at *370* is in a quotation from Arden; that at *388* is in a quotation from Napier.
REFERRED TO: *364–88 passim*

———— Farewell Speech to the Army, *Morning Chronicle*, 17 June, 1837, 3.
REFERRED TO: *372*

FERDINAND VII (of Spain) (1784–1833; *EB*).
NOTE: husband of Maria Christina; father of Isabella II; brother of Don Carlos. The references at *384–5* are in a quotation from de Bourgoing, the second at *385* is in a quotation from Inglis, that at *386* is in a quotation from Cook.
REFERRED TO: *380, 384, 384–5, 385, 386*

FINCH, HENEAGE (Earl of Aylesford) (1647?–1719; *DNB*). Referred to: 58

FINDLATER, ANDREW (1810–85; *DNB*). Referred to: 103

———— Notes to James Mill's *Analysis*.
REFERRED TO: 103, 133

FOSTER, JOHN (Baron Oriel) (1740–1828; *DNB*). Referred to: 49

FOX, CAROLINE (1819–71; *DNB*). Referred to: 257, *345*

———— *Memories of Old Friends, Being Extracts from the Journals and Letters of Caroline Fox, from 1835 to 1871.* Ed. H.N. Pym. 2nd ed. 2 vols. London: Smith, Elder, 1882.
QUOTED: 257, *345*

FRENCH (Mr.).
NOTE: not allowed to appear as a witness in the Earl of Warwick's trial.
REFERRED TO: 56

GAERBER, JOHANN GUSTAV. "Nachrichten von denen an der westlichen Seite der Caspischen See zwischen Astrachan und dem Flusse Kur befindlichen Völkern und Landschaften, und von derselben Zustande in dem Jahre 1728." In *Sammlung russischer Geschichte.* Ed. Gerhard Friedrich Müller. 9 vols. St. Petersburg: Kayserl. Academie der Wissenschaften, 1732–64, IV, 1–147.
NOTE: see Rottiers.
REFERRED TO: *357n*

GALIANO, ANTÓNIO ALCALÁ (1789–1865).
NOTE: appears in the text as Galliano. See *EUI* under Alcalá.
REFERRED TO: *385*

GALILEI, GALILEO (1565–1642; *EB*). *Dialogo . . . sopra i due massimi sistemi del mondo tolemaico, e copernicano.* Florence: Landini, 1632.
REFERRED TO: 164–5

———— *Sidereus nuncius.* Venice: Baglionum, 1610.
REFERRED TO: 164–5

GALLIANO. See Galiano.

GALVANI, LUIGI (1737–98; *EB*). "De viribis electricitatis in motu musculari commentarius," *De Bononiensi Scientiarum et Artium Instituto atque Academia Commentarii* (1791), VII, 363–418.
REFERRED TO: 28

GAMBIER, JAMES (Baron) (1756–1833; *DNB*). Referred to: *363*

GAY, JOHN (1699–1745; *DNB*). Referred to: *98*

———— *Dissertation Concerning the Fundamental Principle and Immediate Criterion of*

*Virtue, as Also the Obligation to, and Approbation of It. With Some Account of the Origin of the Passions and Affections.* Prefixed to William King (1650–1729), *Essay on the Origin of Evil.* Cambridge: Thurlbourn, 1731.
REFERRED TO: 355, 356, 357

GEORGE III (of England) (1738–1820; *DNB*). Referred to: *364*

GIÉRA, PAUL (1816–61; *EB*). Referred to: 337, 338, 339, 340

GILBERT, GEOFFREY. *The Law of Evidence* (1717). 2nd ed. London: Owen, 1760.
QUOTED: 41, 83
REFERRED TO: 7n

41.28    nobody . . . verdict, who had . . . contrary:] [*paragraph*] But this Rule of giving Verdicts in Evidence on the same Point, is to be taken with great Restriction; for no Body . . . Verdict that had . . . contrary; and therefore if a Termor for Years had recover'd against *B.* the Reversioner might give such Verdict in Evidence, for *B.* has no Prejudice, because he hath the Liberty to Cross-examine the Witnesses, and to attaint the Jury, and 'tis fit the Reversioner should make use of the Verdict, and have Benefit by it, since he had been dispossess'd by the Verdict, if it had gone against the Termor, and therefore he may offer it in Evidence; so if there were Tenant for Life, the Reversion in Fee, and *B.* brings his Action in Ejectment against the Tenant for Life, and a Verdict is given against the Plaintiff, it seems that the Reversioner might have given this in Evidence against *B.* because he would have been prejudiced in Case *B.* had recovered, for his Reversion would have been turned to a naked Right in him. (34–5)

83.3–4   "a diagram" . . . "for the demonstration of right"] [*paragraph*] And first of Records: These are the Memorials of the Legislature, and of the King's Courts of Justice, and are authentick beyond all Manner of Contradiction: They are (if a Man may be permitted a Simile from another Science) the proper Diagrams for the Demonstration of Right, and they do constantly preserve the Memory of the Matter that it is ever permanent and obvious to the View, and to be seen at any Time in all the Certainty of Demonstration, in as much as the Record, as is observed elsewhere, can never be proved* [*footnote: *More notorious.*] *per notiora,* for Demonstration is only appealing to a Man's own Conceptions, which can never be done with more Conviction than where you draw the Consequence, from what is already† [*footnote: †Granted.*] *concessum,* and consequently, there can be no greater Demonstration in a Court of Justice, than to appeal to its own Transactions. (7)

GLADSTONE, WILLIAM EWART (1809–98; *DNB*). Referred to: 168

GODWIN, WILLIAM (1756–1836; *DNB*). *Things As They Are; or, The Adventures of Caleb Williams* (1794). 4th ed. 3 vols. London: Simpkin and Marshall, 1816.
NOTE: in SC.
QUOTED: 59

GOETHE, JOHANN WOLFGANG VON (1749–1832; *EB*). *Faust* (1808, 1833).
NOTE: as the reference is to the translation by Egerton (*q.v.*), no edition is cited.
REFERRED TO: *365n*

GORDON, GEORGE HAMILTON (Earl of Aberdeen) (1784–1860; *DNB*). Referred to: *381*

GOULBURN, HENRY (1784–1856). Referred to: *361*

GREGSON, ROBERT S.
NOTE: JSM's solicitor; not otherwise identified.
REFERRED TO: *328, 337*

GRENIER, CHARLES (1808–75; *DBF*), and DOMINIQUE ALEXANDRE GODRON (1807–80; *DBF*). *Flore de France, ou Description des plantes qui croissent naturellement en France et en Corse.* 3 vols. Paris: Baillière, 1848–56.
REFERRED TO: 284, 286, 294, 299, 300, 303, 304, 305, 313

GREY, CHARLES (Earl) (1764–1845; *DNB*).
NOTE: the reference is to his administration.
REFERRED TO: *386*

426 *Appendix G*

GREY, WILLIAM DE (1st Baron Walsingham) (1719–81; *DNB*).
NOTE: the quotation is in a quotation from Phillipps, taken from Howell, *State Trials*.
QUOTED: 40

GROTE, GEORGE (1794–1871; *DNB*). Referred to: 100, 103

———— "John Stuart Mill on the Philosophy of Sir Wm. Hamilton," *Westminster and Foreign Quarterly Review*, LXXXV (Jan. 1866), 1–39.
REFERRED TO: 100

———— Notes to James Mill's *Analysis*.
REFERRED TO: 103

GUIBELALDE, BARTOLOMÉ (fl. 1837).
NOTE: the reference is in a quotation from Wellesley.
REFERRED TO: *369*

GUSSONE, GIOVANNI. *Florae siculae synopsis exhibens plantas vasculares in Sicilia insulisque adjacentibus huc usque detectas. Secundum systema Linneanum dispositas.* 2 vols. Naples: Tramater, 1842–43.
REFERRED TO: 295, 297, 302

HALL, HERBERT BYNG (1805–83; *MEB*). *Spain; and the Seat of War in Spain.* London: Colburn, 1837.
REFERRED TO: *372*

HAMILTON, WILLIAM (1788–1856; *DNB*). Referred to: 117, 150

———— "Dissertations on Reid." In *The Works of Thomas Reid*. Ed. William Hamilton. Edinburgh: Maclachlan and Stewart; London: Longman, *et al.*, 1846, 910–17.
REFERRED TO: 121, 155

———— *Lectures on Metaphysics and Logic.* Ed. Henry Longueville Mansel and John Veitch. 4 vols. Edinburgh and London: Blackwood, 1859–60.
NOTE: the quotation is of Hamilton's rendering of Cardaillac's *Etudes, q.v.*
QUOTED: 193–6
REFERRED TO: 117, 118
193.30   attain.] attain. [*footnote omitted*] (II, 250)
193.41   setting out] departing (II, 251)
194.11   explained. . . .] explained."ᵃ [*footnote indicator missing in 1st ed., but footnote—here omitted—to Cardaillac. There is no ellipsis in Hamilton's text, but he was omitting a passage from Cardaillac, as Mill indicates by his marks of ellipsis*] (II, 252)
194.15   thought.] thought. [*footnote omitted*] (II, 252)
195.3   consciousness. . . .] consciousness." [*footnote to Cardaillac omitted; no gap in Hamilton, whose own words follow, but Mill is indicating an omission from Cardaillac, quotation from whom recommences in the next paragraph*] (II, 254)
195.8   effect, which] effect, and which (II, 254)
195.26   occupied by] occupied with (II, 255)
195.42   acting.] acting. [*footnote omitted*] (II, 256)
196.43   habit."] habit." [*footnote omitted*] (II, 258)

HANSON, WILLIAM .
NOTE: of Reigate; not otherwise identified.
REFERRED TO: 270

HANWAY, JONAS (1712–86; *DNB*). *An Historical Account of the British Trade over the Caspian Sea: with the Author's Journal of Travels from England through Russia into Persia; and back through Russia, Germany and Holland. To Which Are Added, The Revolutions of Persia during the Present Century, with the Particular History of the Great Usurper Nadir Kouli* (1753). 2nd ed. 2 vols. London: Osborne, *et al.*, 1754.
NOTE: this would appear to be the ed. cited. Vol. II, from which the quotation comes, is entitled: *The*

*Revolutions of Persia: Containing the Reign of Shah Sultan Hussein; the Invasion of the Afghans and the Reigns of Sultan Mir Maghmud and His Successor Sultan Ashreff; with the History of the Celebrated Usurper Nadir Kouli, from His Birth in 1687, 'till His Death in 1747; and Some Particulars of the Unfortunate Reign of His Successor Adil Shah.*

QUOTED: *353*

*353.27*   Horda] tribe^e [*footnote:*] ^cHorda. (II, 411)

*353.28*   Beg] lord^f [*footnote:*] ^fBeg. (II, 411)

*353.23*   Karack or Karacarta] Carack^g [*footnote:*] ^gThese I presume are the Caracaita, who distressed Nadir's army so much. (II, 411).

*353.33–4*   In the . . . 2,500] [*entered on one line, with total 3,000*] (II, 411)

*353.35*   In Gedat . . . 1,000] [*entered on one line, with total 6,000*] (II, 411)

*353.37*   66,200] 66,200^h] [*footnote:*] ^hThis number seems greatly to exceed what these people have been generally thought able to bring into the field, tho' the several divisions of them may have easily created mistakes as to their strength. (II, 411)

HARDINGE, HENRY (Viscount) (1785–1856; *DNB*).

NOTE: the reference at *368* is in a quotation from Ward.

REFERRED TO: *362, 368*

———— Speech on the Affairs of Spain (17 Apr., 1837; Commons), *PD*, 3rd ser., Vol. 37, cols. 1329–33.

NOTE: also reported in *Morning Chronicle*, 18 Apr., 1837, 2, from which the quotation appears to have been taken. The reference at *368* is in a quotation from Ward.

QUOTED: *362*

REFERRED TO: *367, 368*

HARDWICKE, LORD. See Philip Yorke.

HARRISON, SAMUEL BEALEY (1802–67; *MEB*). *Evidence: Forming a Title of the Code of Legal Proceedings, According to the Plan Proposed by Crofton Uniacke, Esq.* London: Butterworth, 1825.

QUOTED: 75, 76, 86

REFERRED TO: 7n

76.17–30   "By accounting . . . tolls . . . [*paragraph*] By paying tithes . . . tithes. [*paragraph*] Where . . . rector . . .[*paragraph*] In . . . title . . . end. [*paragraph*] In an action of ejectment . . . expired."] 16. By accounting . . . *tolls* . . . [*paragraph*] 17. By paying *tithes* . . . tithes. [*paragraph*] 18. By receiving tithes, a *clergyman* precludes himself from disputing the fact of his being the parson, in an action against him for non-residence. [*paragraph*] 19. Where . . . *rector* . . . [*paragraph*] 20. In . . . *title* . . . end. [*paragraph*] 21. By submitting to a *distress* for rent, stated in the notice of distress to be due from the defendant as tenant to the distrainer, a defendant in an action of use and occupation, admits the tenancy, and is precluded from disputing the title of the plaintiff. [*paragraph*] 22. In actions of *ejectment* . . . *expired*. (9–10)

HARTLEY, DAVID (1705–57; *DNB*). Referred to: 98, 99, 102

———— *Observations on Man, His Frame, His Duty, and His Expectations.* 2 pts. Bath: Leake and Frederick; London: Hitch and Austen, 1749.

NOTE: in SC.

REFERRED TO: 98, 99, 101–2, 118, 121–2, 139, 244–5

HAY, JOHN (Lord) (1793–1851; *DNB*).

NOTE: the reference at *369* is in a quotation from Wellesley.

REFERRED TO: *369, 378*

HAYWOOD, WILLIAM (1821–94; *DNB*). Questioned: *398*

HEINECCIUS, JOHANN GOTTLIEB (1681–1741; *ADB*). *Elementa juris civilis, secundum ordinem institutionum et pandectarum* (1727). In *Operum ad universam juris prudentiam.* 8 vols. Geneva: Cramer Heirs and Philibert Bros., 1744–49, V, 1–812.

NOTE: in SC.

REFERRED TO: 92

HELVÉTIUS, CLAUDE ADRIEN (1715–71; *GDU*). *De l'esprit*. Paris: Durand, 1758.
REFERRED TO: *367*

HENRI IV (of France) (1553–1610; *GDU*). Referred to: *372*

HERACLIUS II (of Georgia) (d. 1798; *EB*). Referred to: *349*

HERBERT, HENRY JOHN GEORGE (Earl of Carnarvon) (1800–49; *DNB*). *Portugal and Gallicia, with a Review of the Social and Political State of the Basque Provinces: and a Few Remarks on Recent Events in Spain*. 2 vols. London: Murray, 1836.
REFERRED TO: *381*

HERODOTUS (ca. 484–420 B.C.; *WWG*). *Herodotus* (Greek and English). Trans. A.D. Godley. 4 vols. London: Heinemann; New York: Putnam's Sons, 1926–30.
NOTE: this ed. used for ease of reference. Two Greek and Latin eds. (Glasgow: Foulis, 1761; and Edinburgh: Laing, 1806) formerly in SC.
QUOTED: *350n*
REFERRED TO: *350n*

HOBBES, THOMAS (1588–1679; *DNB*). Referred to: 97, 129, 134, 150

———— "Computation or Logic" (in Latin, 1655). Part I of *Elements of Philosophy: The First Section, Concerning Body*. In *The English Works of Thomas Hobbes*. Ed. William Molesworth. 11 vols. London: Bohn, 1839–45, I, 1–90.
REFERRED TO: 137, 181

———— *Leviathan; or, The Matter, Form, and Power of a Commonwealth Ecclesiastical and Civil* (1651). In *Works*, III.
REFERRED TO: 129, 129–30, 133

HOLMAN, HENRY MARTIN. "Additions to Luxford's *Reigate Flora*," *Phytologist*, I (Sept. 1841), 51–4.
REFERRED TO: 268n, 271

HOLME-SUMNER, GEORGE (1760–1838; *JMP*). Speech on Commitments by Magistrates (2 Mar., 1824; Commons), *PD*, n.s. Vol. X, cols. 646–7.
REFERRED TO: 48

———— Speech on Commitments and Convictions (27 May, 1824; Commons), *PD*, n.s. Vol. XI, col. 908.
REFERRED TO: 48

HOLROYD, GEORGE SOWLEY (1758–1831; *DNB*). Referred to: 81

HOLT, JOHN (1642–1710; *DNB*). Referred to: 58

HOMER (ca. 700 B.C.; *WWG*). *The Iliad* (Greek and English). Trans. Augustus Taber Murray. 2 vols. London: Heinemann; Cambridge, Mass.: Harvard University Press, 1924.
NOTE: formerly in SC was *Iliad and Odyssey* (Greek), 2 vols. (Oxford, 1800).
REFERRED TO: 132

———— *The Odyssey* (Greek and English). Trans. Augustus Taber Murray. 2 vols. London: Heinemann; New York: Putnam's Sons, 1919.
NOTE: formerly in SC was *Iliad and Odyssey* (Greek), 2 vols. (Oxford, 1800).
REFERRED TO: 132

HOOKER, WILLIAM JACKSON (1785–1865; *DNB*). Referred to: 280

———— *British Flora; Comprising the Phaenogamous, or Flowering Plants, and the Ferns* (1830). 6th ed. London: Longman, *et al.*, 1850.
REFERRED TO: 280

HORACE (Quintus Horatius Flaccus) (65–8 B.C.; *WWR*). *Odes*. In *Odes and Epodes* (Latin

and English). Trans. C.E. Bennett. London: Heinemann; Cambridge, Mass.: Harvard University Press, 1964, 1–347.
QUOTED: *362*
*362.5–6 Sumite . . . meritis.*] Sume . . . meritis et mihi Delphica / lauro cinge volens, Melpomene, comam. (278; III, xxx, 14–16)

HOWELL, THOMAS BAYLEY (1768–1815; *DNB*), and THOMAS JONES HOWELL (d. 1858; *DNB*), eds. *A Complete Collection of State Trials and Proceedings for High Treason and Other Crimes and Misdemeanours from the Earliest Period to the Year 1783, with Notes and Illustrations: Compiled by T.B. Howell, Esq., F.R.S., F.S.A., and Continued from the Year 1783 to the Present Time by Thomas Jones Howell, Esq.* 34 vols. London: Longman, *et al.*, 1809–28.
REFERRED TO: 40n, 49, 58

HUMBOLDT, FRIEDRICH WILHELM HEINRICH ALEXANDER, FREIHERR VON (1769–1859; *ADB*). Referred to: *360*

HUME, DAVID (1711–76; *DNB*). Referred to: 98

———— *An Inquiry Concerning Human Understanding.* In *Essays and Treatises on Several Subjects* (with this title, 1758). New ed. 2 vols. London: Cadell; Edinburgh: Bell and Bradfute, and Duncan, 1793, II, 17–183.
NOTE: in SC. The reference is to Section X, "Of Miracles," II, 124–47.
REFERRED TO: 31

———— *An Inquiry Concerning the Principles of Morals* (1751). In *Essays and Treatises*, II, 222–376.
NOTE: the reference is in a quotation from James Mill's *Fragment, q.v.*
REFERRED TO: 237

HUMPHREYS, JAMES (d. 1830; *DNB*). Referred to: 9, 9n

———— *Observations on the Actual State of the English Laws of Real Property, with the Outlines of a Code.* London: Murray, 1826.
REFERRED TO: 9, 9n

HUTCHESON, FRANCIS (1694–1746; *DNB*). "An Inquiry Concerning the Original of Our Ideas of Virtue or Moral Good." In *An Inquiry into the Original of Our Ideas of Beauty and Virtue; in Two Treatises.* London: printed Darby, 1725, 99–276.
NOTE: the reference is in a quotation from James Mill's *Fragment, q.v.*
REFERRED TO: 237

IBRAHIM KHAN. See Muhammad Ibrahim Khan.

INGLIS, HENRY DAVID (1795–1835; *DNB*). Referred to: *361, 381*
———— *Rambles in the Footsteps of Don Quixote.* London: Whittaker, 1837.
NOTE: selections first published in *Englishman's Magazine* as "Recent Rambles in the Footsteps of Don Quixote," Nos. 1–4 (Apr., May, June, and Aug., 1831). The *DNB* mistakenly attributes the articles to the *New Monthly Magazine*.
REFERRED TO: *380n*

———— *Spain.* 2nd ed. 2 vols. London: Whittaker, 1837.
NOTE: 1st ed. entitled *Spain in 1830* (1831), *q.v.* The "new chapter" referred to is the "Introduction" to the 2nd ed., dated March 1837, but not signed; it is not by Inglis, who died in 1835, though he had projected a chapter "On the Present State and Prospects of the Peninsula" (xiii).
REVIEWED: *359–88*
QUOTED: *382, 384, 385*
*382.26* matters] matter [*sic*] (I, 45)
*384.7* I] [*no paragraph*] I (I, 20)

—— *Spain in 1830.* 2 vols. London: Whittaker, 1831.
NOTE: see the preceding entry.
REFERRED TO: *380, 381*

IRVINE, ALEXANDER (1793–1873; *DNB*). Referred to: 266

—— "Address to the Contributors, etc.," *Phytologist*, n.s. IV (Jan. 1860), 1–10.
NOTE: the reference is to Irvine's citation of John Sim, *q.v.*
REFERRED TO: 283

—— *British Botany.* London: Phytologist, 1856–58.
NOTE: issued in consecutively numbered fascicles with issues of the *Phytologist*.
REFERRED TO: 266, 267

—— "Calamintha Nepeta, *Clairv.*," *Phytologist*, n.s. II (June 1857), 131–2.
REFERRED TO: 282

—— *The Illustrated Handbook of the British Plants.* London: Nelson, 1858.
REFERRED TO: 280

—— *Introduction to the Science of Botany.* 5 pts. London: Nelson, 1858.
NOTE: continuously paginated.
REFERRED TO: 280

ISABELLA (of Castile) (1451–1504; *EB*). Referred to: *305*

ISABELLA II (of Spain) (1830–1904; *EB*).
NOTE: the reference at *366n* is in a quotation from the *Standard*; that at *367* is in a quotation from
    Ward; that at *369* is in a quotation from Wellesley; that at *376* is in a quotation from the "Quadruple
    Treaty"; that at *386* is in a quotation from Cook.
REFERRED TO: *360–88 passim*

ISMAEL BEG (d. ca. 1740).
NOTE: appears as Ismael Bey in text.
REFERRED TO: *349*


JEANNE (of France and Navarre) (1273–1305; *GDU*).
NOTE: Queen of Navarre, married Philip IV of France in 1284.
REFERRED TO: *379*

JEFFREYS, GEORGE (Baron Jeffreys of Wem) (1648–89; *DNB*). Referred to: 58

JEROME, ST. (ca. 340–420 A.D.; *EB*).
NOTE: the reference is to the ruined hermitage on Monserrat named after St. Jerome.
REFERRED TO: 309

JOANNE, ADOLPHE LAURENT (1823–81; *GE*). *Itinéraire descriptif et historique des
    Pyrénées de l'Océan à la Méditerranée.* Paris: Hachette, [1858].
QUOTED: 317

JONES, JOHN.
NOTE: a watchmaker, and a vestryman of the Strand district.
QUESTIONED: *404–6*


KAZI MOLLAH. See Gazi Muhammad.

KING, THOMAS (1802–39). *The Substance of a Lecture Designed as an Introduction to the
    Study of Anatomy Considered as the Science of Organization; and Delivered at the
    Reopening of the School, Founded by the Late Joseph Brookes. October 1st, 1833.*
    London: Longman, *et al.*, 1834.
REVIEWED: 323

KINGSTON, DUCHESS OF. See Elizabeth Chudleigh.

KLAPROTH, HEINRICH JULIUS VON (1783–1835). *Tableau historique, géographique,*

*ethnographique et politique du Caucase et des provinces limitrophes entre la Russie et la Perse.* Paris: Ponthieu, 1827.
REFERRED TO: *350n*

———— *Travels in the Caucasus and Georgia, Performed in the Years 1807 and 1808, by Command of the Russian Government.* Trans. F. Shoberl. London: Colburn, 1814.
REFERRED TO: *351*

———— See also "Rapport officiel sur les opérations de guerre contre les montagnards Musulmans du Caucase."

KORAN.
NOTE: the reference at *355* is in a quotation from Klaproth; that at *361* is in quoted verse.
REFERRED TO: *354, 355, 361*

KUNTH, CARL SIGISMUND (1788–1850; *ADB*). *Enumeratio plantarum omnium hucusque cognitarum, secundum familias naturales disposita, adjectis characteribus, differentiis et synonymis.* 5 vols. in 6. Stuttgart and Tübingen: Cotta, 1833–50.
REFERRED TO: 292

LAFAYETTE, MARIE JEAN PAUL ROCH YVES GILBERT DU MOTIER, MARQUIS DE (1757–1834; *GDU*). Referred to: 174

LAMB, WILLIAM (Lord Melbourne) (1779–1848; *DNB*).
NOTE: the reference is in a quotation from Wellesley.
REFERRED TO: *369*

LAROMIGUIÈRE, PIERRE (1756–1837; *GDU*). Referred to: 134

———— *Leçons de philosophie sur les principes de l'intelligence ou sur les causes et sur les origines des idées* (1815–18). 7th ed. 2 vols. Paris: Hachette, 1858.
QUOTED: 134
134.9 *etc.*] etc. (I, 307)
134.9 *est*] est (I, 307)
134.11 voudrais] voudrai (I, 307)
134.12 existe. Le] existe: je veux dire, d'un côté, que l'idée de Dieu et celle d'existence sont inséparables; de l'autre, que l'idée de Virgile et celle de poëte se réunissent en une seule et même idée. Le (I, 307)
134.12 *est*] est (I, 307)
134.14 contenu,"] contenu, du tout à une ou à plusieurs de ses qualités, à un ou à plusieurs de ses points de vue [*footnote omitted*]; en disant l'être est, etc., on n'explique donc pas un mot par ce même mot, une idée par cette même idée. (I, 307)

LAVERGNE, LOUIS GABRIEL LÉONCE GUILHAUD DE (1809–80; *GDU*). *Economie rurale de la France depuis 1789* (1860). 2nd ed. Paris: Guillaumin, 1861.
REFERRED TO: 293

LAW, EDWARD (1st Baron Ellenborough) (1750–1818; *DNB*).
NOTE: the reference at 82 is in a quotation from Phillipps.
REFERRED TO: 49, 82

LAWRENCE, SOULDEN (1751–1814; *DNB*).
NOTE: the quotation is in a quotation from Phillipps, *q.v.* for the collation.
QUOTED: 74

LECLERC, JEAN (1657–1736; *EB*). *Ars critica in qua ad studia linguarum latinae, graecae et hebraicae munitur.* London: Clavel, Childe, and Bell, 1698.
REFERRED TO: 24

LEIBNIZ, GOTTFRIED WILHELM VON (1646–1716; *ADB*).
NOTE: JSM uses the spelling Leibnitz.
REFERRED TO: 129

——— *Dissertatio de stilo philosophico Nizolii* (1670). In *Opera philosophica*. Ed. Johann Eduard Erdmann. 2 pts. Berlin: Eichler, 1840, Pt. I, 55–71.
QUOTED: 129
129.7 "plus quam nominalis."] Ex hac jam regula Nominales deduxerunt, omnia in rerum natura explicari posse, etsi universalibus et formalitatibus realibus prorsus careatur; qua sententia nihil verius, nihil nostri temporis philosopho dignius, usque adeo, ut credam ipsum Occamum non fuisse Nominaliorem, quam nunc est Thomas Hobbes, qui, ut verum fatear, mihi plusquam nominalis videtur. (I, 69)

LETHERBY, HENRY (1806–76; *DNB*). Questioned: *397–8*

LOCKE, JOHN (1632–1704: *DNB*). Referred to: 97

——— *An Essay Concerning Human Understanding* (1690). In *Works*. New ed. 10 vols. London: Tegg, *et al.*, 1823, I–III, 176.
QUOTED: 25–6
REFERRED TO: 32, 124, 144–5, 159, 161, 212
25.30 "All] First, all (III, 52)
25.35 *temperance*] *temperate* (III, 52) [*treated as a typographical error in this ed.*]

——— Letter to Thomas Molyneux, 26 Apr., 1695. In *Works*, IX, 354–7.
REFERRED TO: 159

LOCKE, JOHN (1805–80; *WWBMP*). Referred to: *389*

LOUIS PHILIPPE (of France) (1773–1850; *GDU*). Referred to: *376, 378n, 384*

LUXFORD, GEORGE (1807–54; *DNB*). "Botanical Notes," *Phytologist*, I (Aug. 1841), 43–4.
REFERRED TO: 264

——— Editor's Note, *Phytologist*, I (Sept. 1841), 62.
NOTE: the note is appended to a communication from Edward Newman, reporting the same station for Lilium Martagon in Surrey in 1826. JSM is apparently referring to Irvine, but actually to the *Phytologist*, edited by Luxford before Irvine.
REFERRED TO: 280

——— *A Flora of the Neighbourhood of Reigate, Surrey, Containing the Flowering Plants and Ferns*. London: Van Voorst; Reigate: Allingham, 1838.
REFERRED TO: 268–9, 270, 271

MACAULAY, THOMAS BABINGTON (1800–59; *DNB*). Referred to: 101

——— "Bentham's Defence of Mill: Utilitarian System of Philosophy," *Edinburgh Review*, XLIX (June 1829), 273–99.
REFERRED TO: 101

——— *Critical and Historical Essays, Contributed to the Edinburgh Review*. 3 vols. London: Longman, *et al.*, 1843.
REFERRED TO: 101

——— "Mill's Essay on Government: Utilitarian Logic and Politics," *Edinburgh Review*, XLIX (Mar. 1829), 159–89.
REFERRED TO: 101

——— "Utilitarian Theory of Government, and the 'Greatest Happiness Principle,'" *Edinburgh Review*, L (Oct. 1829), 99–125.
REFERRED TO: 101

McCOSH, JAMES (1811–94; *DNB*). *An Examination of Mr. J.S. Mill's Philosophy, Being a Defence of Fundamental Truth*. London: Macmillan, 1866.
REFERRED TO: 155

MIGUEL, MARIA EVARIST (1802–66; *EB*).
NOTE: the first reference at *376* is in a quotation from the Quadruple Treaty.
REFERRED TO: *376, 377*

MILL, HARRIET TAYLOR (née Hardy) (1808–58). Referred to: *327, 328, 336*

MILL, JAMES (1773–1836; *DNB*). Referred to: *93–253 passim*

———— *Analysis of the Phenomena of the Human Mind* (1829). New ed. with notes illustrative and critical by Alexander Bain, Andrew Findlater, and George Grote. Edited with additional notes by John Stuart Mill. 2 vols. London: Longmans, *et al.*, 1869.
NOTE: in SC. The quotations at 130–1 and 170 are indirect; the second at 201 is summary.
QUOTED: 111, 124, 130, 130–1, 133, 136, 138, 140, 142, 146, 148, 149, 154, 156, 163, 164, 170, 171–2, 172, 176, 186, 191, 201, 204, 216, 228, 231, 252
111.17  "obscure"] The idea of figure which rises, is, of course, more obscure than that of extension; because, figures being innumerable, the general idea is exceedingly complex, and hence, of necessity, obscure. (I, 94)
124.10  "put . . . discretion;"] There is another species of complex ideas which, though derived also from the senses, are put . . . discretion, as the ideas of a centaur, a mountain of gold, of comfort, of meanness; all that class of ideas in short which Mr. Locke has called mixed modes. (I, 137–8)
124.11  "those . . . arbitrarily,"] Ideas, of the third class, those . . . arbitrarily are innumerable; because the combinations capable of being formed of the numerous elements which compose them, exceed computation. (I, 140)
124.11–13  "the . . . combination."] [*paragraph*] As the combinations are formed arbitrarily, or in other words, as the . . . combination, it very often happens, that one man includes something more or something less than another man in the combination to which they both give the same name. (I, 141)
130.16  ."the] It is, that the (I, 165)
133.15–16  "are . . . thing,"] Thus, "rational animal" is precisely the same class as "man;" and they are . . . thing; the one a simple, or single-worded name; the other a complex, or double-worded, name. (I, 171)
133.16–17  "to . . . term,"] When they are used for any other purpose than to . . . term, they are useless, and are denominated identical propositions. (I, 171)
133.17  "such propositions are] Such propositions therefore are (I, 171)
136.16  "the . . . us:"] But the two sides of an algebraic equation are of necessity two marks or two names for the same thing; of which the one on the right-hand side is more distinct, at least to the present purpose of the inquirer, than the one on the left-hand side; and the whole purpose of an algebraic investigation, which is a mere series of changes of names, is to obtain, at last, a distinct name, a name the . . . us, on the right-hand side of the equation. (I, 190)
136.22  "twice . . . angle."] I arrive at this conclusion, as it is called, by a process of reasoning: that is to say, I find out a name "twice . . . angle," which much more distinctly points out to me a certain quantity, than my first name, "amount of the three angles of a triangle;" and the process by which I arrive at this name is a successive change of names, and nothing more; as any one may prove to himself by merely observing the steps of the demonstration. (I, 191)
138.1  "Anciently,"] "A number of men anciently in England had wives in common." (I, 199)
142.22–3  "men . . . names,"] It is thus obvious, and certain, that men . . . names. (I, 260)
142.30–2  "it . . . *and of individual qualities* . . . discourse."] But as the limits of the human memory did not enable men to retain beyond a very limited number of names; and even if it had, as it . . . and of individual qualities, . . . discourse, it was necessary to have contrivances of abridgment; that is, to employ names which marked equally a number of individuals, with all their separate properties; and enabled us to speak of multitudes at once. (I, 260)
146.9  idea . . . when] idea. [*two-paragraph omission*] [*paragraph*] Thus, when (I, 264–5)
148.24–8  There . . . one primarily . . . secondary. . . . white horse . . . primarily . . . secondarily.] There . . . one, *primarily . . . secondary. . . . white horse . . . primarily . . . secondarily.* (I, 33n–4n)
149.17–19  "that in which there is no reference to anything preceding, that in which there is a reference to something preceding, and that in which reference is made to the will of one of the

Persons."] The Indicative is used when no reference is made to any thing which precedes: the Subjunctive, when a reference is made to something which precedes; and the Optative, and Imperative, when the reference is to the state of the will of the speaker or the person spoken of. (I, 155)

154.3  "will not be doubted"] Now these two, 1, the idea of the thing, 2, the idea of my having seen it, combined, make up, it will not be doubted, the whole of that state of consciousness which we call Memory. (I, 329)

154.13–15  "the idea of my present self, . . . and the idea of my past self, . . . self:"] Now in this last-mentioned part of the compound, it is easy to perceive two important elements; *the idea of my present self, . . .* and *the idea of my past self, . . .* self. (I, 330)

156.8  "All men admit."] All men admit, that this, one of the most remarkable of all cases of belief, is wholly resolvable into association. (I, 345)

156.20–1  antecedent," . . . "no . . . dispute"] antecedent, is no . . . dispute. (I, 352)

163.14–15  "we . . . believing"] The sound is heard; the association takes place; we . . . believing that the sound proceeds from a certain place, though we know, that is, immediately recognize, that it proceeds from another. (I, 370)

163.18–19  "in . . . *believe* . . . none:"] In . . . believe . . . none: though we may be sailing rapidly before the wind, she making hardly any progress against it. (I, 371)

163.19  "we *believe*] We BELIEVE (I, 371)

164.2–3  "dread . . . belief," "we] That dread . . . belief, we (I, 372)

171.31–2  "A . . . different."] A . . . different; and being felt to be different, and known to be different, are not two things, but one and the same thing. (I, 334)

171.34–5  "The . . . idea. . . . The] Besides, the . . . idea; of course, the associations are generically different. The (I, 335)

172.29–31  "the . . . association."] I have a sensation; I have an idea; if these two are distinguishable in the having, it is likely that the . . . association; just as when I have two distinguishable sensations, one, for example, of red, and another of black, the copies of them, when brought up by association, are distinguishable. (I, 334–5)

172.34–6  "the . . . seeing and hearing:" . . . "not. . . . But" . . . "myself] The self which is at the antecedent end of the associated train, in the case of sensation, is the . . . seeing or hearing; the self at the antecedent end of the associated train, in the case of ideas, is not. . . . But myself (I, 336)

186.4  when] When (II, 21)

186.5  this other thing] the other (II, 21)

191.19–20  "the . . . thoughts" . . . "that . . . Effect."] Supposing the . . . thoughts to have . . . effect, trains would still have that variety which we experience. (II, 67)

201.12  "the name of sound and] The second [silence], is the name of the thing, and (II, 103)

201.20  "Nothing"] Nothing is a name of all possible objects, including their non-existence. (II, 105)

204.7–8  "which . . . successiveness," . . . "we] In the process which is marked by the relatives prior and posterior, part is noted, part connoted; and the part which is noted, is the part which it is difficult to make a separate object of attention,—the part which . . . successiveness, for which we (II, 81)

216.16  "idea . . . another,"] The remainder is the association with this idea . . . another, which are to fill up the intermediate time, and terminate with his finger placed in the flame of the candle. (II, 198)

216.22  "which . . . time"] [*see preceding entry*]

218.22–3  "without] Secondly, that there is no conception, that is, idea, without (II, 210)

228.4  "times . . . excitement"] This happens most readily in times . . . excitement; that is, when public opinion holds out a great reward; and when the object rather is, to ward off some great calamity, than to obtain an accession of good. (II, 274)

231.24  "not] The case is perfectly analogous to that of the love of posthumous praise, the dread of posthumous blame, and is a still more important principle of action, as it has reference, not (II, 299)

252.25  "the strong] Intention is the strong (II, 399)

252.27–9  "that . . . effect;" "the . . . intention."] If it be asserted that [a Promise] is not only the declaration of an Intention, but the declaration that . . . effect; what is this but the declaration of another intention; the . . . intention? (II, 398)

252.29–30 "this . . . first:"] But this . . . first. (II, 398)

———— *Elements of Political Economy.* London: Baldwin, *et al.*, 1821.
NOTE: 2nd ed. rev., 1824; 3rd ed. rev., 1826.
REFERRED TO: 100

———— *A Fragment on Mackintosh: Being Strictures on Some Passages in the Dissertation by Sir James Mackintosh, Prefixed to the Encyclopaedia Britannica.* London: Baldwin and Cradock, 1835.
NOTE: the 2nd ed. (London: Longmans, *et al.*, 1870) is in SC.
QUOTED: 227, 233–7, 237–8, 238–9
REFERRED TO: 240
227.12 agents] agent (389)
233.37 classification . . . the] classification which, before talking of moral rules, Sir James ought to have well understood; the (249)
234.15 having been thus] having thus been (250)
234.39–40 and so on. . . . In] on. [*ellipsis indicates 4 1/2-page omission*] In (252–6)
234.47 knows . . . that ] knows, even Sir James knew, that (257)
235.5–6 generated. . . . [*paragraph*] When] generated. The meaning of this, however, needs to be a little opened, since in heads like that of Sir James, strange work is apt to be made of it. [*paragraph*] When (257)
235.15–16 another. . . . [*paragraph*] Since] another. Habits of moral acting are habits of obedience to the principle of utility, and are so far from being liable to be prevented or hurt, as poor Sir James would have it, by bringing utility, as he phrases it, "into contact with action," that they can be formed by no other means. [*paragraph*] On the formation of moral habits, reference being had to the confusion in the ideas of Sir James, another word may be necessary. Since (258)
238.22–3 other. . . . [*paragraph*] . . . Nothing] other. And this is what Sir James calls the contact of the conscience and the will. This too, is that precedence of conscience, which he says is a discovery of his own. [*paragraph*] Bless the memory of Sir James! Was he ignorant that this is included in the very definition of a voluntary act? Nothing (377)

———— *The History of British India.* 3 vols. London: Baldwin, *et al.*, 1817 [1818].
NOTE: the 3rd ed., 6 vols. (London: Baldwin, *et al.*, 1826) is in SC.
REFERRED TO: 50, 99

———— Miscellaneous writings. Referred to: 99–100

MILL, JOHN STUART. *Autobiography.* London: Longmans, *et al.*, 1873. In *CW*, I, 1–290.
NOTE: the 2nd ed. (London: Longmans, *et al.*, 1873) is in SC.
REFERRED TO: 329, 334

———— "Bailey on Berkeley's Theory of Vision," *Westminster Review*, XXXVIII (Oct. 1842), 318–36, and XXXIX (May 1843), 491–4. In *CW*, XI, 245–69.
REFERRED TO: 156

———— "Botany of Spain. A Few Days' Botanizing in the North-Eastern Provinces of Spain, in April and May, 1860. No. I. Catalonia," *Phytologist*, n.s. V (Aug. 1861), 225–36.
NOTE: printed at 289–99 above.
REFERRED TO: 305

———— "Botany of Spain. A Few Days' Botanizing in the North-Eastern Provinces of Spain, in April and May, 1860. No. IV. Monserrat," *Phytologist*, n.s. V (Dec. 1861), 356–62.
NOTE: printed at 307–11 above.
REFERRED TO: 307

———— "Botany of Spain. A Few Days' Botanizing in the North-Eastern Provinces of Spain, in April and May, 1860. No. V. Spanish Pyrenees; Andorra," *Phytologist*, n.s. VI (Feb. 1862), 35–45.

MURRAY, JAMES ERSKINE. *A Summer in the Pyrenees* (1837). 2nd ed. 2 vols. London: Macrone, 1837.
NOTE: the 1st ed. was unavailable for reference.
REFERRED TO: 317

MUSHLIMEH. See Maslama.

NADIR QULI BEG (1687–1747; *EB*).
NOTE: known as Nadir Shah.
REFERRED TO: *349, 353*

NAPIER, WILLIAM FRANCIS PATRICK (1785–1860; *DNB*). *History of the War in the Peninsula and in the South of France, from the Year 1807 to the Year 1814.* 6 vols. London: Murray, 1828–40.
REFERRED TO: *387–8*

———— Letter to [T. George] Shaw, 28 Sept., 1835. In Shaw, *Personal Memoirs, q.v.*
QUOTED: *388*
*388.5* and the] and that the (II, 460)

NARVAEZ, RAMON MARIA (1800–68; *EB*). Referred to: *371*

NERO, CLAUDIUS CAESAR (37–68 A.D.; *WWR*). Referred to: 305

NEVIL, EDWARD (Baron) (d. 1705). Referred to: 56

NEWMAN, EDWARD (1801–79; *DNB*). *A History of British Ferns.* London: Van Voorst, 1840.
NOTE: an 1844 ed. is in SC.
REFERRED TO: 264

———— "A History of the British Lycopodia and Allied Genera," *Phytologist*, I (June—Nov. 1841), 1–7, 17–20, 33–6, 49–51, 65–7, 81–6.
REFERRED TO: 264, 266

NEWTON, ISAAC (1642–1727; *DNB*). *Optics; or, A Treatise of the Reflections, Inflections and Colours of Light.* In *Opera quae exstant omnia.* Ed. Samuel Horsley. 5 vols. London: Nichols, 1779–85, IV.
NOTE: the reference is in a quotation from James Mill's *Fragment, q.v.* This ed. used for ease of reference. The so-called "Jesuits' Edition" (Geneva: Barillot, 1739–42) is in SC.
REFERRED TO: 239

———— *Philosophiae naturalis principia mathematica* (1687). In *Opera*, II–III.
REFERRED TO: 95, 96

NICHOLAS I (of Russia) (1796–1855; *EB*).
NOTE: the reference at *356* is in a quotation from Klaproth quoting a proclamation by Major-General Volkhovski.
REFERRED TO: *348, 356*

OPIE, IONA and PETER, eds. *The Oxford Dictionary of Nursery Rhymes.* Oxford: Clarendon Press, 1951.
QUOTED: *372*
*372.13–14* With . . . again.] The King of France went up the hill / With forty thousand men; / The King of France came down the hill, / And ne'er went up again. (176)

ORÁA Y LECUMBERRI, MARCELINO (1788–1851). Referred to: *372*

PALEY, WILLIAM (1743–1805; *DNB*). Referred to: 19

———— *The Principles of Moral and Political Philosophy* (1785). 15th ed. 2 vols. London: Faulder, 1804.

NOTE: in SC. The reference at 59 is in a quotation from Denman.
QUOTED: 19
REFERRED TO: 19, 59
19.23   as, where] as, [*paragraph*] I. Where no one is deceived; which is the case in parables, fables, novels, jests, tales to create mirth, ludicrous embellishments of a story, where the declared design of the speaker is not to inform, but to divert; compliments in the subscription of a letter, a servant's *denying* his master, a prisoner's pleading not guilty, an advocate asserting the justice, or his belief of justice, of his client's cause. In such instances no confidence is destroyed, because none was reposed; no promise to speak the truth is violated, because none was given, or understood to be given. [*paragraph*] 2. Where (207–8)

PALMERSTON, LORD. See Henry John Temple.

PARKER, THOMAS (Earl of Macclesfield) (1666?–1732; *DNB*). Referred to: 69

PARRY, CLIVE, ed. *The Consolidated Treaty Series*. 231 vols. Dobbs Ferry, N.Y.: Oceana Publications, 1969.
NOTE: this ed. used for ease of reference to miscellaneous treaties.
REFERRED TO: *349, 358*

PASCAL, BLAISE (1623–62; *GDU*). Referred to: 134

——— *De l'esprit géométrique* (1658). In Appendix to Vol. II of Laromiguière, *Leçons de philosophie, q.v.*, 467–91.
NOTE: *Oeuvres*, 5 vols. (Paris: Lefèvre, 1819) in SC.
REFERRED TO: 134

PEDRO IV (of Portugal, and Pedro I of Brazil) (Duke of Braganza) (1798–1834; *EUI*).
NOTE: the reference at *376* is in a quotation from the Quadruple Treaty.
REFERRED TO: *376, 377, 387*

PEEL, ROBERT (1788–1850; *DNB*). Referred to: 8, 9, 45, 57, *361, 367*

——— Speech on the Address in Answer to the King's Speech (31 Jan., 1837; Commons), *PD*, 3rd ser., Vol. 36, cols. 50–6.
NOTE: the reference is in a quotation from Ward.
REFERRED TO: *367–8*

PERICLES (d. 429 B.C.; *WWG*). Referred to: 110

PERSOON, CHRISTIAAN HENRIK. *Synopsis plantarum, seu enchiridium botanicum, complectens enumerationem systematicam specierum hucusque cognitarum.* 2 vols. Paris: Cramer (Vol. I), and Treuttel and Würtz (Vol. II); Tubingen: Cotta, 1805–07.
REFERRED TO: 292, 302

PETER I (of Russia) (1672–1725; *EB*).
NOTE: known as Peter the Great.
REFERRED TO: *349*

PETRONILLA (of Aragon) (1137–64; *EB*). Referred to: *379*

PHILIP IV (of France) (1268–1314; *GDU*). Referred to: *379*

PHILIP V (of Spain) (1683–1746; *EB*). Referred to: *379, 380*

PHILLIPPS (or PHILIPPS), SAMUEL MARCH (1780–1862; *DNB*). *A Treatise on the Law of Evidence* (1814). 6th ed. 2 vols. London: Butterworth; Dublin; Cooke, 1824.
NOTE: the quotation at 88 is indirect.
QUOTED: 22, 40, 41, 42, 44–5, 53, 56, 68, 68–9, 70, 74, 78, 79, 79n, 80, 81–2, 82, 83, 86, 87, 88
REFERRED TO: 7n, 39, 40, 42, 45, 49, 51, 54, 55, 73, 89
22.3   "If] [*paragraph*] If (I, 256)
40.1   "that . . . suit in] The objections, then, against the admissibility of such evidence seems to be, first, that the parties are not the same in the civil suit, as in the criminal case; and, secondly, that . . . suit on (I, 319)

40.24 "'of . . . question, nor] But neither the judgment of a concurrent or exclusive jurisdiction is evidence of . . . question, though within their jurisdiction, nor (I, 304)

41.9 "had] [*paragraph*] The general rule is, that a verdict cannot be evidence for either party, in an action against one who was a stranger to the former proceeding, who had (I, 309)

41.28 "'nobody . . . contrary:'"] And Ch. B. Gilbert lays it down, "that nobody . . . contrary." (I, 309)

42.21–2 "that . . . litigation:"] Here it may be observed, the party, against whom the judgment was pronounced, had an opportunity of discharging themselves by proving the liability on a third parish; and this not having been done, and the court of quarter sessions having confirmed the order of removal, the last settlement is adjudged to be in the appellant parish; and this point being once determined, the judgment must be final, that . . . litigation.[4] [*footnote:*] [4]By Holt, C.J. in R. v. Rislip, Salk. 524. 2 Bott, 705. (I, 312)

44.34–45.3 "a decree of . . . law."] [*paragraph*] A decree in . . . law.[1] [*footnote:*] [1]See ante, ch. 2. s. 1. (I, 340–1).

53.14–16 "a person . . . as a subscribing . . . instrument;"] A person . . . as subscribing . . . instrument, [*footnote omitted*] although his evidence is to be received with all the jealousy necessarily attaching to a witness, who upon his oath asserts to be false, what he has by his solemn act attested as true. [*footnote omitted*] (I, 39)

56.17–22 "In . . . case," . . . "one . . . discharge."] In . . . case, above cited, one . . . discharge[4] [*footnote:*] [4]See infra p. 33. on substitution of punishment for burning in the hand. (I, 32)

68.17 "where it seems," . . . "to] [*paragraph*] One other exception appears to have been made in the case of an action for a malicious prosecution, where it seems to (I, 66)

68.33 "'For] Lord Holt C.J. admitted in evidence the oath of the defendant's wife (who was the only person present at the time of the supposed felony, and who, as the report says, could not herself be a witness) to prove the felony committed; "for (I,66)

70.13–14 "The . . . chancery," . . . invariably] But the . . . Chancery invariably (I, 421)

74.2–3 "acknowledgment upon record;" . . . "the] And as it is an acknowledgment on record, the (I, 175)

74.36 "The present] Mr. Justice Lawrence on that occasion said, "Van Dyck and Co., the persons on whose risk the goods were shipped, are in this difficulty; the present (I, 84)

75.8–12 "a letter . . . was held . . . *good evidence* [meaning . . . evidence] of . . . *was . . . prove . . . made:*"] A letter . . . was in this case, held . . . good evidence of . . . was . . . prove, . . . made. (I, 97n)

75.9–11 "where . . . of, the Master of the Rolls *refused to admit*] "Except in one or the other of these ways," said the Master of the Rolls in Fairlie v. Hastings[3], [*footnote:*] [3]10 Ves. 128. [*text:*] "I do not see how they can be evidence against the principal:" and therefore in that case, (where . . . of,) he refused to admit (I, 95)

75.24 "made] [*paragraph*] It must be remembered, that the cases, in which the declarations of an agent have been admitted against the principal, are exceptions to that general rule, which requires evidence to be given upon oath: and the exception is confined to such statements as are made (I, 95)

75.28–30 "it . . . agent:"] But it . . . agent. (I, 96)

78.14–15 "to . . . a written agreement."] [*paragraph*] Parol evidence is not admissible to . . . a deed. (I, 530)

79n.2 "The] And the (I, 515)

79.27–8 "the . . . uncertainty."] [*paragraph*] If a clause in a deed, or will, or any other instrument, is so ambiguously or defectively expressed, that a court of law, which has to put a construction on the instrument, is unable to collect the intention of the party, evidence of the declaration of the party cannot be admitted to explain his intention; but the . . . uncertainty. (I, 519)

80.8–10 "the . . . *matter of specialty . . . of the higher account . . . matter of averment . . . of inferior account* in law."] "Ambiguitas patens," says Lord Bacon[1], [*footnote:*] [1]Bac. Elem. rule 23.] [*text:*] (that is, an ambiguity apparent on the deed or instrument,) "cannot be helped by averment; and the reason is, because the . . . [*none of phrases in italic*] . . . in law; for that were to make all deeds hollow, and subject to averment, and so in effect to make that pass without deed, which, the law appoints, shall not pass but by deed. (I, 519–20).

80.13–14 "would . . . testators:"] So in a case, where the testator made dispositions in his will to several persons, among others to his wife and niece, who were the only women mentioned in the will, and then devised "to her" a particular estate for life, the question was, whether parol evidence could be admitted, to shew which of the two was intended: the Lord Chancellor refused to receive it, on the ground, that it would . . . testators; the Court held, that though the term "her" was relative, it was to be referred in this case to the wife, because in other parts of the will it seemed to relate to the wife; but expressly excluded the parol evidence offered to explain the will.[2] [*footnote:*] [2]Castleton v. Turner; cited 2 Ves. 217. (I, 520)

81.6–7   "the contents] The Judges were of opinion, that the question must be answered in the negative; and the reason of their opinion was, "That the contents (I, 281)

81.25–82.4   a written . . . all; . . . *best evidence* . . . occupation.] A written . . . all; [*footnote omitted*] . . . best evidence . . . occupation. [*footnote omitted*] (I, 486)

82.13–21   The acts of state of . . . Anderson] [*no paragraph*] The acts of state, also, of . . . Anderson[5] [*footnote:*] [5]1 Campb. 65 (a). (I, 382–3)

83.32–7   Records . . . are . . . them. . . . mistake.] Records are . . . them. [*footnote omitted*] . . . mistake. [*footnote omitted*] (I, 299)

83.7–8   "that . . . stated," . . . "as . . . traversable."] [*paragraph*] A record, then, is conclusive proof, that . . . stated; and evidence to contradict it will not be admitted. But it will not be conclusive as . . . traversable.[1] [*footnote:*] [1]Co. Lit. 352.b. (I, 300)

86.12   "different] And, in addition to this argument of inconvenience, the objection taken to the evidence in that case, namely, that it was inapplicable to the point in dispute, appears to be very strong: customs being different (I, 162)

86.18   "'for,' . . . 'if] In the Duke of Somerset's case, Lord Ch. J. Raymond said, he had always looked upon it as a settled principle in the law, that the customs of one manor should not be given in evidence to explain the customs of another; "for, if (I, 161–2)

87.8   "argument of inconvenience,"] [*see entry for* 86.12 *above*]

89.22   the plaintiff in this action must prove that he . . . further, that he . . . possession;] [*paragraph*] The plaintiff, in support of this action, will have to prove, that, at the time of the conversion, he . . . further he . . . possession, and that the goods have been wrongfully converted by the defendant. [*footnote omitted*] (II, 168)

89.26–7   he must prove . . . defendant,] [*paragraph*] The plaintiff is also to prove . . . defendant, this being the main bearing of the action. (I, 168)

89.27–8   the denial . . . then, is a wrongful conversion;] "The very denial . . . then, (said Lord Holt in the case of Baldwin v. Cole) [*footnote omitted*] is an actual conversion, and not only evidence of it, as has been holden: for what is a conversion, but an assuming upon one's self the property and right of disposing of another's goods? (II, 169)

89.28–9   the defendant may shew that the property belonged to him or to . . . claims,] [*paragraph*] Under the general issue of not guilty, the defendant will be at liberty to prove his title to the property in question; for if the property belonged to him, he cannot be charged with a wrongful conversion. Or he may disprove the plaintiff's title, by showing that the goods belonged to . . . claims; thus, if he took the goods out of the plaintiff's possession, it will be a good defence in this action, that he took them by the order of one to whom they belonged. (II, 171)

89.29–30   the plaintiff . . . damages against a third person for a conversion of the same goods,] Or the defendant may prove that the plaintiff . . . damages for a conversion of the same goods, in an action of trover against J.S.; for this recovery vests the property in J.S., and the plaintiff has damages in lieu of the goods; in a second action, therefore, he cannot say, they are his property. [*footnote omitted*] (II, 171–2)

89.31–2   he was . . . parcener,] [*paragraph*] The defendant may also show that he was . . . parcener; one of these co-tenants cannot maintain trover against another, on the account of the unity of possession, which subsists between them; but if one joint tenant, or tenant in common, or parcener, destroy the common property, [*footnote omitted*] or sell the whole without authority, [*footnote omitted*] he will then be liable to this action. (II, 172)

89.32   had a *lien* on the goods,] [*paragraph*] In answer to the proof of a demand and refusal, the defendant may show, that he had a right to detain them under a lien. (II, 173)

*Phytologist*, I (June 1843), cover. Referred to: 264

PINDAR (518?-after 446 B.C.; *WWG*). *The Odes of Pindar Including the Principal Fragments* (Greek and English). Trans. John Sandys. London: Heinemann; Cambridge, Mass.: Harvard University Press, 1946.
NOTE: in SC is Παντα τα πινδαρου σωξομενα. *Omnia Pindari quae extant. Cum interpretatione latina* (Greek and Latin), 2 vols. in 1 (Glasgow: Foulis, 1744).
QUOTED: 132

PLATO (427–347 B.C.; *WWG*). Referred to: 103, *362*

———— *Gorgias.* In *Lysis, Symposium, Gorgias* (Greek and English). Trans. W.R.M. Lamb. London: Heinemann; Cambridge, Mass.: Harvard University Press, 1925, 258–532.
NOTE: in SC is *Opera omnia*, ed. Immanuel Bekker, 11 vols. (London: Priestley, 1826).
REFERRED TO: 180

———— *Parmenides.* In *Cratylus, Parmenides, Greater Hippias, Lesser Hippias* (Greek and English). Trans. H.N. Fowler. London: Heinemann; New York: Macmillan, 1914, 198–330.
REFERRED TO: 103, 141

———— *Phaedo.* In *Euthyphro, Apology, Crito, Phaedo, Phaedrus* (Greek and English). Trans. H.N. Fowler. London: Heinemann; Cambridge, Mass.: Harvard University Press, 1947, 200–402.
REFERRED TO: 103

———— *Protagoras.* In *Laches, Protagoras, Meno, Euthydemus* (Greek and English). Trans. W.R.M. Lamb. London: Heinemann; Cambridge, Mass.: Harvard University Press, 1952, 92–256.
REFERRED TO: 180

———— *Republic* (Greek and English). Trans. Paul Shorey. 2 vols. London: Heinemann; Cambridge, Mass.: Harvard University Press, 1946.
REFERRED TO: 103, 141

———— *Symposium.* In *Lysis, Symposium, Gorgias* (Greek and English). Trans. W.R.M. Lamb. London: Heinemann; New York: Putnam's Sons, 1925, 80–244.
REFERRED TO: 103

———— *Theaetetus.* In *Theaetetus, Sophist* (Greek and English). Trans. H.N. Fowler. London: Heinemann; New York: Putnam's Sons, 1921, 6–256.
REFERRED TO: 180

PLUNKET, WILLIAM CONYNGHAM (Baron) (1764–1854; *DNB*). Referred to: 49

PLUTARCH (fl. A.D. 50–120; *WWG*). "Alexander." In *Lives* (Greek and English). Trans. Bernadotte Perrin. 11 vols. London: Heinemann; Cambridge, Mass.: Harvard University Press, 1914–26, VII, 223–439.
REFERRED TO: 44

———— "Pompey." In *Lives*, V, 116–324.
NOTE: see also Zonaras.
REFERRED TO: *351*

POLLEXFEN, HENRY (1632–91; *DNB*). Referred to: 58

POMPEY (Gnaeus Pompeius) (106–48 B.C.; *WWG*).
NOTE: the reference derives from Zonoras, *q.v.*
REFERRED TO: *351, 353*

POPE, ALEXANDER (1688–1744; *DNB*), *et al. Memoirs of the Extraordinary Life, Works, and Discoveries of Martinus Scriblerus* (1741). In *Works.* Ed. Joseph Warton, *et al.*, 10 vols. London: Priestley, 1822–25, VI, 61–181.
NOTE: in SC.
REFERRED TO: *360*

PRICE, RICHARD (1723–91; *DNB*). Referred to: 17

——— "On the Importance of Christianity, the Nature of Historical Evidence, and Miracles." in *Four Dissertations*. London: Millar and Cadell, 1767, 359–439.
REFERRED TO: 16–18

PRICE, SAMUEL GROVE (1793–1839; *WWBMP*).
NOTE: the reference at *368* is in a quotation from Ward.
REFERRED TO: *361, 368*

——— Speech on Spain (10 Mar., 1837; Commons), *PD*, 3rd ser., Vol. 37, cols. 249–56.
REFERRED TO: *360*

PRIESTLEY, JOSEPH (1733–1804; *DNB*). Referred to: 98

——— *Hartley's Theory of the Human Mind on the Principle of the Association of Ideas, with Essays Relating to the Subject of It*. London: Johnson, 1775.
REFERRED TO: 98

PROCOPIUS (ca. 326–66 A.D.; *WWR*). *Procopius* (Greek and English). Trans. H.B. Dewing. 7 vols. London: Heinemann; New York: Macmillan, 1914–40.
NOTE: this ed. used for ease of reference.
REFERRED TO: *351*

QUADRUPLE ALLIANCE (Treaty). See, under *Parliametary Papers*, "Treaty between His Majesty . . ." (1834).

QUER Y MARTINEZ, JOSÉ (1695–1764; *GDU*). *Flora Española ó historia de las plantas que se crian en España*. 4 vols. Madrid: Ibana, 1762–64.
NOTE: continued by Gomez Ortega, Vols. V—VI (1784).
REFERRED TO: 290

"Rapport officiel sur les opérations de guerre contre les montagnards Musulmans du Caucase," trans. Heinrich Julius Klaproth, *Nouveau Journal Asiatique*, 2nd ser., XI (Jan. 1833), 18–30.
QUOTED: *355, 355–6, 356*
REFERRED TO: *354*
*355.22–32* After . . . death.] [*translated from:*] [*no paragraph*] Après que le village eut été occupé une bande d'à peu-près cinquante hommes, conduite par le moullah *Abdour-rahman*, l'un des partisans les plus déterminés de Kazi moullah, fut coupée du reste de la troupe et cernée dans une grande maison. Ces gens n'avaient aucun espoir de salut; mais lorsqu'on leur proposa de se rendre de bonne volonté, ils entonnèrent des versets du Coran, comme c'est leur usage quand ils se dévouent à la mort, puis, creusant des meurtrières dans les murailles, ils dirigèrent un feu bien nourri et bien ajusté sur les assaillants. Quelques grenades lancées dans la cheminée éclatèrent dans l'intérieur de la maison, mais cela n'ébranla pas leur résolution. Comme il fallait en finir avec leur bravade, l'ordre fut donné de mettre le feu à la maison. Onze d'entr'eux, à moitié suffoqués par la fumée, sortirent et se rendirent; quelques autres, le poignard et le sabre à la main, se précipitèrent sur les baïonnettes de nos guerriers; mais le plus grand nombre périt avec moullah Abdourrahman, en répétant sans interruption le chant de mort. (23–4)
*355.38–356.8* The . . . resistance.] [*translated from:*] Le chemin de Ghumry, qui depuis le pays des Tchetchentses présente des difficultés incroyables, monte depuis *Karanaï* [*footnote omitted*] jusqu'au sommet neigeux d'une haute montagne; ensuite il descend pendant quatre versts en décrivant des sinuosités, sur le penchant escarpé des monts et le long des précipices, à travers des rochers et n'a que la largeur d'un sentier; ensuite, il passe, pendant une distance égale, sur les saillies étroites de rochers, et l'on ne peut aller de l'un à l'autre qu'à l'aide d'échelles dont il faut se munir. Ensuite, lorsque ce chemin s'est joint à un autre venant du village d'*Erpeli* [*footnote omitted*], il se rétrécit toujours davantage entre deux hauts parois de rochers perpendiculaires, et enfin, en avant du village de Ghumry, il est barré par trois murailles dont la première est fortifiée, de chaque côté, d'une petite tour. Le long de la pente de la montagne, plusieurs terrasses ont été très-habilement disposées de manière à opposer la plus vive résistance. (24–5)

*356.11–12*   "the . . . heaven."] [*translated from:*] Ce défilé fameux est réputé inaccessible, et les montagnards disaient proverbialement: "Les Russes n'y pourront arriver que comme la pluie (en tombant du ciel)." (26)

*356.15–24*   After . . . Húmry.] [*translated from:*] Après que nos soldats eurent emporté la première muraille, il ne fut plus possible aux révoltés renfermés dans les petites tours, de se sauver par la fuite. Cependent ils ne voulurent pas se rendre et, au contraire, firent une résistance opiniâtre. Alors le général Veliaminov canonna vivement le rempart qui était en avant de ces tours; mais comme les bandits qui y étaient logés continuaient à tirer comme auparavant, des hommes de bonne volonté tirés du bataillon des sapeurs donnèrent l'assaut à ces fortifications et tuèrent les montagnards qui les défendaient. Parmi eux se trouvaient Kazi moullah et ses partisans les plus dévoués; leurs cadavres, percés de coups de baïonnettes, furent reconnus le lendemain par leurs compatriotes. La nuit mit fin au combat, et notre avant-garde fit halte entre le troisième mur et le village. [*paragraph*] Le 30 octobre, au point du jour, nos troupes entrèrent dans Ghumry. (28)

*356.27–38*   The . . . understand!] [*translated from:*] "La justice de Dieu a atteint Kazi moullah, le propagateur de fausses doctrines, l'ennemi de la paix. Ce fourbe, ses principaux adhérents et une quantité de malheureux qu'il avait trompés ont été exterminés par la victorieuse armée russe dans le fameux ravin de Ghumry regardé comme inaccessible. [*paragraph*] Puisse cet exemple servir d'avertissement à tous les ennemis du repos public! puissent-ils, écoutant la voix du repentir, avoir recours au puissant gouvernement russe, et le grand empereur, dans sa bonté, leur accordera leur pardon! Mais quiconque osera dorénavant tramer des projets coupables, encourra sans miséricorde toute la rigueur des lois. Ni les montagnes, ni les forêts, ni les ravins ne le sauveront. Les troupes russes triomphantes pénétreront partout, partout les désobéissants et les traîtres seront châtiés. Les Galgaï, les Itchkeri, les Tchetchentses, ceux de Ghumry et autres l'ont éprouvé. Quiconque a des oreilles pour entendre, qu'il entende et comprenne!" (30)

RAY, JOHN (1627–1705; *DNB*). Referred to: 274

RAYMOND, ROBERT (Lord) (1673–1733; *DNB*).
NOTE: the quotation is in a quotation from Phillipps, *q.v.* for the collation.
QUOTED: 86

RICARDO, DAVID (1772–1823; *DNB*). Referred to: 100

——— *On the Principles of Political Economy and Taxation*. London: Murray, 1817.
QUOTED: *408*
REFERRED TO: 100
*408.3*   "the] The (156)

RICH, EDWARD (Earl of Warwick, Earl Holland) (1673–1701).
NOTE: see Cockayne's *Complete Peerage*.
REFERRED TO: 56

RICHARDSON, JOHN (1796–1852; *MEB*). *Movements of the British Legion* (1836). 2nd ed. London: Simpkin, *et al.*, 1837.
NOTE: first ed. entitled *Journal of the Movements of the British Legion*.
REVIEWED: *359–88*
QUOTED: *370*
*370.16*   Surely] [*no paragraph*] Surely (312)

RICHERAND, BALTHASAR ANTHELME (1779–1840; *GDU*). *Elements of Physiology* (in French, 1801). Trans. G.J.M. de Lys. Ed. with notes by James Copland. 4th ed. London: Longman, *et al.*, 1824.
REFERRED TO: 106

ROEBUCK, JOHN ARTHUR (1801–79; *DNB*). Speech on the Vixen—Treaty of Adrianople (17 Mar., 1837; Commons), *PD*, 3rd ser., Vol. 37, cols. 621–8.
NOTE: see also his concluding motion on the same date.
REFERRED TO: *346, 348*

——— Motion on the Vixen—Treaty of Adrianople (17 Mar., 1837; Commons), *PD*, 3rd ser., Vol. 37, col. 628.

*364.7* thews and sinews] With all these cares on his mind, my fellow traveller, to judge by his thewes and sinews, was a man who might have set danger at defiance with as much impunity as most men. (I, 60; 3)

—— *The Vision of Don Roderick: A Poem*. Edinburgh: Ballantyne, 1811.
NOTE: the quotation is in a quotation from the *Standard*.
REFERRED TO: *366n*

SENEFELDER, ALOIS (1771–1834; *EB*). Referred to: 38

SHAKESPEARE, WILLIAM (1564–1616; *DNB*). Referred to: 110

—— *As You Like It*. In *The Riverside Shakespeare*. Ed. G. Blakemore Evans. Boston: Houghton Mifflin, 1974, 365–402.
NOTE: this ed. used for ease of reference.
QUOTED: *356, 363*
*356.25* "strange eventful history"] Last scene of all, / That ends this strange eventful history, / Is second childishness, and mere oblivion, / Sans teeth, sans eyes, sans taste, sans every thing. (382; II, vii, 163–6)
*363.13* "wise saws" . . . "modern instances"] And then the justice, / In fair round belly with good capon lin'd, / With eyes severe and beard of formal cut, / Full of wise saws and modern instances; / And so he plays his part. (382; II, vii, 153–7)

—— *Hamlet*. In *The Riverside Shakespeare*, 1135–97.
NOTE: the reference is to the character, Hamlet.
REFERRED TO: 110

—— *Henry IV, Part I*. In *The Riverside Shakespeare*, 842–85.
NOTE: the references at 110 are to Falstaff.
REFERRED TO: 110, 173, 174

—— *Julius Caesar*. In *The Riverside Shakespeare*, 1100–34.
NOTE: the quotation is in a quotation from Denman.
QUOTED: 59
*59.28–9* "let us . . . a feast . . . carcass for the hounds."] And, gentle friends, / Let's kill him boldly, but not wrathfully; / Let's . . . a dish . . . / . . . carcass fit for hounds; / And let our hearts, as subtle masters do, / Stir up their servants to an act of rage, / And after seem to chide 'em. (1113; II, i, 171–7)

SHAW, CHARLES (1795–1871; *MEB*). *Personal Memoirs and Correspondence of Colonel Charles Shaw, K.C.T.S., &c. of the Portuguese Service, and Late Brigadier-General, in the British Auxiliary Legion of Spain; Comprising A Narrative of the War for Constitutional Liberty in Portugal and Spain, from Its Commencement in 1831 to the Dissolution of the British Legion in 1837*. 2 vols. London: Colburn, 1837.
NOTE: the heading of the article gives the title as *Sketches of the War for Constitutional Liberty in Spain and Portugal; Interspersed with Scenes and Occurrences Abroad and at Home*, but gives the same description of the author, the same publisher, date, and no. of vols.; it also lists "*Shaw's Memoirs*, unpublished." There can be little doubt that the title here given encompasses both those listed; see *386–7* for a partial explanation.
REVIEWED: *359–88*
QUOTED: *387, 388*
*387.10* "great means at their command"] [*paragraph*] Once or twice General Reid came down to superintend the construction of the defences of Portugalette; but I could not help remarking that he must have been always accustomed to have great means at his command, and that engineering in this small way very naturally was not at all to his taste, and that he took much more interest in the drill of the Light Brigade. (II, 451)
*387.14* "voluminous staff"] [*paragraph*] I was ordered to Bilbao, where I never saw a better dressed set of officers; but the General's Staff was now so voluminous, that he was obliged to scatter them among the different brigadiers, displeasing thus a great many. (II, 452)

SHAW, T. GEORGE.
NOTE: see also William Napier. Charles Shaw does not identify in his memoirs to which of his brothers Napier's letter was addressed; however, George is a more likely recipient than Patrick, since most of Charles Shaw's letters at this time were addressed to him.
REFERRED TO: *388*

SIDNEY, PHILIP (1554–86; *DNB*). Referred to: *364*

SIM, JOHN (ca. 1812–93).
NOTE: see Alexander Irvine, "Address to the Contributors," 1860.
REFERRED TO: 283

SMITH, ADAM (1723–90; *DNB*). *The Theory of Moral Sentiments, to Which Is Added a Dissertation on the Origin of Language* (1759). 6th ed. 2 vols. London: Strahan and Cadell; Edinburgh: Creech and Bell, 1780.
NOTE: in SC.
REFERRED TO: 230–1

SMITH, JAMES EDWARD (1759–1828; *DNB*). Referred to: 259

——— *The English Flora.* 4 vols. London: Longman, *et al.*, 1824–29.
REFERRED TO: 259, 278, 282

SONDER, OTTO WILHELM (1812–81). *Flora Hamburgensis. Beschreibung der phanerogamischen Gewächse, welche in der Umgegend von Hamburg wild wachsen und häufig cultiviert werden.* Hamburg: Kittler, 1851.
REFERRED TO: 294

SPENCER, HERBERT (1820–1903; *DNB*). Referred to: 102, 159

——— *The Principles of Psychology.* London: Longman, *et al.*, 1855.
QUOTED: 205, 205–6, 206, 206–7, 207–10
REFERRED TO: 102, 139, 140, 159, 160, 184, 211
205.8    "On] [*no paragraph*] On (212)
205.113  pressure." . . . [*paragraph*] "Allied] pressure. [*paragraph*] Allied (212)
205.14   muscular motion. . . . While] *muscular motion.* Concerning the state of consciousness induced by muscular motion, and concerning the ideas of Space and Time which are connected with it in adult minds, something will be said hereafter. For present purposes it will suffice to notice, that while (212)
205.15   rises] arises (212) [*treated as printer's error in this ed.*]
205.18   composition. [*paragraph*] When] composition. [*1-paragraph omission*] 55. When (213)
206.9    "What] [*no paragraph*] Still, however, there remains the question—What (226)
206.12   position. When we imagine] position. When we think of a particular area, we think of a surface whose boundary lines stand to each other in specific degress of remoteness; that is—are related in position. When we imagine (226)
206.29   locality, what] locality. What (226) [*treated as printer's error in this ed.*]
207.23   position] positions (228) [*treated as printer's error in this ed.*]
207.32   In the] For the (229) [*treated as printer's error in this ed.*]
207.37   "How] [*paragraph*] Omitting for the present all consideration of the visual phenomena, let us turn our attention to the question in which centres the whole controversy respecting the genesis of our ideas of Motion, Space, and Time: the question namely—How (257)
207.43   developed? [*paragraph*] . . . Taking] developed. [*paragraph*] Already, in treating of visual extension (58), and the visual perception of space (62), and in showing how serial states of consciousness are consolidated into simultaneous states which become their equivalents in thought, the way has been prepared for answering these questions. The process of analysis partially applied to retinal impressions, has now to be applied, after a more complete manner, to impressions on the body at large. To this end, taking (258)
208.6    as the degrees] as the degree (258) [*printer's error in Source?*]
208.15   them; no] them; no classing of them; no (259)

208.39  finger-end. . . . As] finger-end. Now it might be argued that some progress is made towards the idea of space, in the simultaneous reception of these sensations—in the contemplation of them as coexistent: seeing that the notion of coexistence and the notion of space have a common root; or in other words—seeing that to be conscious of a duality or multiplicity of sensations, is the first step towards being conscious of that duality or multiplicity of points in space which they imply. It might also be argued that as, when the finger is moved back from Z to A, these serial sensations are experienced in a reverse order, there is thus achieved a further step in the genesis of the idea: seeing that coexistent things are alone capable of impressing consciousness in any order with equal vividness. But passing over these points, let us go on to notice, that as (260)

208.50–209.1  consciousness. [*paragraph*] Due] consciousness. [*no paragraph*] Due (261)

209.11  case,] case (58), (261)

209.13  presentations] presentation (261) [*treated as printer's error in this ed.*]

209.14  positions.ᵃ . . . As] positions. [*no footnote*] positions: and it is needless here to repeat the explanation. What it now concerns us to notice is this:—*that as* (261)

209.14–19  As . . . other.] [*in italic*] (261)

209n.1  "Objects] And when, by numberless repetitions, the relation between any one finger and each of the others is established, and can be represented to the mind as a series of a certain length; then we may understand how a stick laid upon the surface so as at the same moment to touch all the fingers from A to Z inclusive, will be taken as equivalent to the series A to Z—how the *simultaneous* excitation of the entire range of fingers, will come to stand for its *serial* excitation—how thus, objects (222)

209n.3  cover. . . . By] cover—and how by (222)

209n.8  We see that "a set of [nervous] elements] We have seen that a set of retinal elements (224)

209n.9  *quasi*] quasi (224)

209n.10  coexistent positions] [*in italic*] (224)

209n.11  successive positions] [*in italic*] (224)

209n.13–14  of . . . extension] of visible extension (224)

*Standard.* Leading article on the Durango Decree, 28 Mar., 1837, 2.
QUOTED: *365n–6n*

STANHOPE, PHILIP HENRY (Viscount Mahon, later Earl Stanhope) (1805–75; *DNB*). Speech on the Affairs of Spain (18 Apr., 1837; Commons), *PD*, 3rd ser., Vol. 37, cols. 1428–38; reported in *Morning Chronicle*, 19 Apr., 1837, 3.
QUOTED: *363, 366*
REFERRED TO: *364*

STARKEY, THEOPHILUS WILLIAM.
NOTE: clerk to JSM's solicitor, R.S. Gregson.
REFERRED TO: *337*

STARKIE, THOMAS (1782–1849; *DNB*). *A Practical Treatise of the Law of Evidence, and Digest of Proofs in Civil and Criminal Proceedings*. 3 vols. London: Clarke, 1824.
REFERRED TO: 7n, 47n, 52, 85n, 89

STEPHENS, EDWARD BELL. *The Basque Provinces: Their Political State, Scenery, and Inhabitants; with Adventures among the Carlists and Christinos*. 2 vols. London: Whittaker, 1837.
REVIEWED: *359–88*

STEWART, DUGALD (1753–1828; *DNB*). Referred to: 163

——— *Elements of the Philosophy of the Human Mind*. 3 vols. London: Strahan and Cadell; Edinburgh: Creech, 1792 (Vol. I). Edinburgh: Constable; London: Cadell and Davies, 1814 (Vol. II). London: Murray, 1827 (Vol. III).
REFERRED TO: 163, 218, 245

SWIFT, JONATHAN (1667–1745; *DNB*). "The Grand Question Debated: Whether Hamilton's Bawn Should be Turned into a Barrack or Malt-House." In *The Works of Jonathan*

*Swift, D.D., Dean of St. Patrick's, Dublin; Containing Additional Letters, Tracts, and Poems, Not Hitherto Published; with Notes and a Life of the Author.* Ed. Walter Scott. 19 vols. Edinburgh: Constable; London: White, *et al.*; Dublin: Cumming, 1814, XV, 148–55.
NOTE: this ed. in SC.
QUOTED: *363*
*363.10*  nation.] nation: / My schoolmaster call'd me a dunce and a fool, / But at cuffs I was always the cock of the school; / I never could take to my book for the blood o' me. (XV, 154)

TAHMASP II (Shah of Persia) (1704–40; *EB*).
NOTE: appears as Támásp in the text.
REFERRED TO:  *349*

TAYLOR, ALGERNON (1830–1903).
NOTE: second son of Harriet and John Taylor.
REFERRED TO: *329, 331, 338*

TAYLOR, ELIZABETH MARY (1861–1924).
NOTE: elder daughter of Algernon Taylor.
REFERRED TO: *329, 330, 331, 332*

TAYLOR, HELEN (1831–1907).
NOTE: JSM's companion on his tour through Spain, and hence included in the narrative "we" at *289–320 passim.*
REFERRED TO: *289–320 passim, 327–44 passim*

TAYLOR, JOHN CYPRIAN (1862–1939).
NOTE: son of Algernon Taylor.
REFERRED TO: *329, 330, 331*

TAYLOR, MARY (1863/4–1918).
NOTE: younger daughter of Algernon Taylor and eventually legatee of JSM's papers.
REFERRED TO: *329, 330, 331, 332*

TEMPLE, HENRY JOHN (Lord Palmerston) (1784–1865; *DNB*).
NOTE: the reference at *D.7* is in a quotation from Ward.
REFERRED TO: *345, 346, 349*

———— Speech on the Vixen—Treaty of Adrianople (17 Mar., 1837; Commons), *PD*, 3rd ser., Vol. 37, cols. 630–6.
REFERRED TO: *345*

———— Speech on the Affairs of Spain (19 Apr., 1837; Commons), *Morning Chronicle*, 20 Apr., 1837, 2. Also in *PD*, 3rd ser., Vol. 38, cols. 59–96.
QUOTED: *365n*
*365.14*  "Unfortunately, history] But, unfortunately, sir, history (2)
*365n.16*  Europe. Let them look to their] Europe. (hear! hear!) Look at their (2)
*365n.17*  America—to all] America—Look at all (2)
*365n.18*  and they would see that their] and you will see that in all cases their (2)
*365n.19*  earth. One] earth. [*paragraph omitted*] One (2)
*365n.19–22*  One of the effects of the regeneration of Spain, through the force of constitutional government, was, that, by generating a public opinion they would improve the Spanish character, and put an end to atrocities like these."] But I trust and hope that one of the results, at least, from the regeneration of Spain, through the medium of a free constitution will be, by the creation of public opinion which such a constitution must produce, that these defects and vices of the national character will, for the future, be corrected. (2)

TENORE, MICHELE (1780–1861; *GDU*). *Catalogus plantarum horti regii Neapolitani ad annum 1813.* 2 pts. Naples: Trani, 1813, 1819.
REFERRED TO: *297*

THIERS, LOUIS ADOLPHE (1797–1866; *GDU*). Speech in the Chamber of Deputies (14 Jan., 1837), *Morning Chronicle*, 17 Jan., 1837, 2.
QUOTED: *378n*
*378n.9* "Look] For, look (2)
*378n.13* has] had (2)

THORNTON, WILLIAM THOMAS (1813–80; *DNB*). Referred to: *327–41 passim*

THWAITES, JOHN (1815–70; *MEB*). Questioned: *395–7*

TITE, WILLIAM (1798–1873; *DNB*). Referred to: *399*

——— Question in "Third Report from the Select Committee on Metropolitan Local Government," *PP*, 1867, XII, 569
QUOTED: *399*
399.4–5 "*Our sewers ceased at Holborn Bars, and therefore we thought it very desirable to have this power.*"] The point was this: that when we got to Holborn Bars our authority ceased, and that was very inconvenient and very undesirable? (569)

TOOKE, JOHN HORNE (1736–1812; *DNB*). Referred to: 103

——— Επεα πτεροεντα; *or, The Diversions of Purley* (1786). 2nd ed. 2 vols. London: Johnson, 1798, 1805.
REFERRED TO: 103

TORMASOFF, ALEXANDER (1752–1819). Referred to: *357*

TRAVASSOS VALDEZ, JOSÉ LÚCIO (1787–1862). Referred to: *385*

TREBY, GEORGE (1644?–1700; *DNB*). Referred to: 56

UNIACKE, CROFTON (1783–1852).
NOTE: Uniacke's "plan" is embodied in his *The New Jury Law: Forming a Title of the Code of Legal Proceedings, According to the Plan Proposed for the Statute Law of the Realm* (London: Clarke, 1825).
REFERRED TO: 7n

VALDEZ. See Travassos Valdez.

VALERIUS FLACCUS, GAIUS (d. ca. 90 A.D.; *WWR*). *Valerius Flaccus* (Latin and English). Trans. J.H. Mozley. London: Heinemann; Cambridge, Mass.: Harvard University Press, 1934.
QUOTED: *351n*
351n.2–7 "Cunabula . . . imperet."] nec minus hinc varia dux lactus imagine templi / ad geminas fert ora fores cunabula . . . imperet; Arsinoen illi tepidaeque requirunt / otia laeta Phari pinguemque sine imbribus annum, / hi iam Sarmaticis permutant carbasa bracis. (274–6; V, 416–24)

VAUBAN, SÉBASTIEN LE PRESTRE DE (1633–1707; *GDU*). Referred to: 312

VELIAMINOV, ALEXEI (1783–1838).
NOTE: the reference is in a quotation from Klaproth.
REFERRED TO: *356*

VERE, HORACE (Baron Vere of Tilbury) (1565–1635; *DNB*).
NOTE: referred to in the text as Horatio Vere.
REFERRED TO: *364*

VIRGIL (Publius Virgilius Maro) (70–19 B.C.; *WWR*).
NOTE: the reference is in a quotation from Laromiguière.
REFERRED TO: 134

VOLKHOVSKY, V.D. (1778–1841).
NOTE: the reference is in a quotation from Klaproth, who refers to him as the major-general.
REFERRED TO: *356*

WELLESLEY, ARTHUR (Duke of Wellington) (1769–1852; *DNB*). Referred to: *368, 377–8*

———— Speech on Spain—Lord John Hay's Despatches (21 Apr., 1837; Lords), *Morning Chronicle*, 22 Apr., 1837, 1–2. Also in *PD*, 3rd ser., Vol. 38, cols. 137–50.
NOTE: Mill's exact source has not been located.
QUOTED: *369*
REFERRED TO: *368*

WELLINGTON, DUKE OF. See Arthur Wellesley.

WILKINS, JOHN WILLIAM (b. 1829). "The Republic of Andorre," *Edinburgh Review*, CXIII (Apr. 1861), 345–59.
QUOTED: 317
REFERRED TO: 317
317.25 "isolated . . . frontier."] Andorre, then, is a republic isolated . . . frontier, included neither in France nor in Spain, but intervening between the two countries, and (so far as their frontiers and government are concerned) by much more ancient than either. (346–7)

WILLIAM IV (of England) (1765–1837; *DNB*). Referred to: *376, 377, 378*

WOODS, JOSEPH (1776–1864; *DNB*). *The Tourist's Flora: A Descriptive Catalogue of the Flowering Plants and Ferns of the British Islands, France, Germany, Switzerland, Italy, and the Italian Islands*. London: Reeve, *et al.*, 1850.
REFERRED TO: 292, 316

WORDSWORTH, WILLIAM (1770–1850; *DNB*). "Rob Roy's Grave" (1807). In *Poetical Works*. 5 vols. London: Longman, *et al.*, 1827, III, 24–30.
NOTE: in SC.
QUOTED: *360*
360.7 The good] For why?—because the good (III, 26; 37)
360.7 rule, the] Rule / Sufficeth them, the (III, 26; 37–8)

YORKE, PHILIP (Earl of Hardwicke and Viscount Royston) (1690–1764; *DNB*). Referred to: 80

ZONARAS, JOANNES (fl. 12th cent.). Επιτομη ιστοριων.
NOTE: the spelling Zonoras appears in the text. Zonaras based his *Epitome* on *Plutarch's Lives* (*q.v.*), among other works.
REFERRED TO: *351*

# PARLIAMENTARY PAPERS

"Report Made to His Majesty by the Commissioners Appointed to Enquire into the Practice of Chancery," *PP*, 1826, XV, 1–120.
REFERRED TO: 8

*Protocols of the Conferences Held at London, between the Plenipotentiaries of Austria, France, Great Britain, Prussia, and Russia*, PP, 1833, XLII, 1–551.
REFERRED TO: *375*

"Treaty between His Majesty, the Queen Regent of Spain, the King of the French, and the Duke of Braganza, Regent of Portugal," *PP*, 1834, LI, 299–309.
NOTE: the Quadruple Treaty, also known as the Quadruple Alliance, signed 22 Apr., 1835. The wording in *PP* differs markedly from that quoted in the text. The reference at *367* is in a quotation from Ward.
QUOTED: *376, 377*

## STATUTES

### ENGLISH

4 Henry VII, c. 13. Clergy Shall Be Allowed but Once. A Convict Person Shall Be Marked with the Letters M or T. A Provision for Them Which Be within Orders (1487).
REFERRED TO: 56

8 Elizabeth, c. 4. An Act to Take Away the Benefit of Clergy from Certain Offenders for Felony (1565).
REFERRED TO: 70

18 Elizabeth, c. 7. An Act to Take Away Clergy from the Offenders in Rape or Burglary, and an Order for the Delivery of Clerks Convict without Purgation (1576).
REFERRED TO: 56

29 Charles II, c. 3. An Act for Prevention of Frauds and Perjuries (1676).
REFERRED TO: 72

7 & 8 William III, c. 3. An Act for Regulating of Trials in Cases of Treason and Misprision of Treason (1695).
REFERRED TO: 70

9 & 10 William III, c. 32. An Act for the More Effectual Suppressing of Blasphemy and Prophaneness (1698).
REFERRED TO: 54

4 George I, c. 11. An Act for the Further Preventing Robbery, Burglary, and Other Felonies, and for the More Effectual Transportations of Felons, and Unlawful Exporters of Wool; and for Declaring the Law upon Some Points Relating to Pirates (1717).
REFERRED TO: 56

19 George III, c. 74. An Act to Explain and Amend the Laws Relating to the Transportation, Imprisonment, and Other Punishment, of Certain Offenders (1779).
REFERRED TO: 56

39 & 40 George III, c. 93. An Act for Regulating Trials for High Treason and Misprision of High Treason, in Certain Cases (28 July, 1800).
REFERRED TO: 70

43 George III, c. 141. An Act to Render Justices of the Peace More Safe in the Execution of Their Duty (11 Aug., 1803).
REFERRED TO: 47

48 George III, c. 129. An Act to Repeal So Much of an Act Passed in the Eighth Year of the Reign of Queen Elizabeth, Intituled, An Act to Take Away the Benefit of Clergy from Certain Offenders for Felony, as Takes away the Benefit of Cergy from Persons Stealing Privily from the Person of Another; and for More Effectually Preventing the Crime of Larceny from the Person (30 June, 1808).
REFERRED TO: 70

53 George III, c. 127. An Act for the Better Regulation of Ecclesiastical Courts in England, and for the More Easy Recovery of Church Rates and Tithes (12 July, 1813).
REFERRED TO: 55

53 George III, c. 160. An Act to Relieve Persons Who Impugn the Doctrine of the Holy Trinity from Certain Penalties (21 July, 1813).
REFERRED TO: 55

5 George IV, c. 41. An Act to Repeal Certain Duties on Law Proceedings in the Courts in Great Britain and Ireland Respectively (28 May, 1824).

NOTE: one of Peel's law reforms.
REFERRED TO: 8, 50, 57

6 George IV, c. 25. An Act for Defining the Rights of Capital Convicts who Receive
Pardon, and of Convicts after Having Been Punished for Clergyable Felonies; for
Placing Clerks in Orders on the Same Footing with Other Persons, as to Felonies; and for
Limiting the Effect of the Benefit of Clergy (20 May, 1825).
NOTE: one of Peel's law reforms.
REFERRED TO: 8, 57

6 George IV, c. 84. An Act to Provide for the Augmenting the Salaries of the Master of the
Rolls and the Vice Chancellor of England, the Chief Baron of the Court of Exchequer,
and the Puisne Judges and Barons of the Courts in Westminster Hall; and to Enable His
Majesty to Grant an Annuity to Such Vice Chancellor, and Additional Annuities to Such
Master of the Rolls, Chief Baron and Puisne Judges and Barons, on Their Resignation of
Their Respective Offices (5 July, 1825).
NOTE: one of Peel's law reforms.
REFERRED TO: 8, 48

6 George IV, c. 96. An Act for Preventing Frivolous Writs of Error (5 July, 1825).
NOTE: one of Peel's law reforms.
REFERRED TO: 8, 45

11 & 12 Victoria, c. 112. An Act to Consolidate and Continue in Force for Two Years and to
the End of the Then Next Session of Parliament, the Metropolitan Commissions of
Sewers (4 Sept., 1848).
REFERRED TO: *398*

18 & 19 Victoria, c. 120. An Act for the Better Local Management of the Metropolis
(14 Aug., 1855).
REFERRED TO: *392*

25 & 26 Victoria, c. 102. An Act to Amend the Metropolis Local Management Acts
(7 Aug., 1862).
REFERRED TO: *401*

29 & 30 Victoria, c. 90. An Act to Amend the Law Relating to the Public Health (7 Aug.,
1866).
REFERRED TO: *397, 398*

## FRENCH

Loi concernant les mesures de salut public prises relativement à la conspiration royale (19
fructidor, an V [5 Sept., 1797]), Bull. 142, No. 1400, *Bulletin des lois de la république
française*, 2nd ser., IV, 7–10.
REFERRED TO: *374*

Loi qui ordonne la déportation des journalistes royaux (22 fructidor, an V [8 Sept., 1797]),
Bull. 143, No. 1405, *Bulletin des lois de la république française*, 2nd ser., IV, 12–14.
REFERRED TO: *374*

## BELGIAN

Code Civil. In *Journal officiel du royaume des Pays-Bas*, Vols. 17–21 (1822–26).
REFERRED TO: 91–2

SPANISH

*Las siete partidas del rey Alfonso el Sabio, cotejadas con varios codices antiguos por la*
   *Real Academia de la Historia* (1263). 3 vols. Madrid: Imprenta Real, 1807.
   NOTE: JSM's reference is to the provision for the succession of daughters to the throne in default of
   sons, Partida II, Title xv, Law 2 (II, 132–3). The *partidas* were the work of Alphonso X, King of
   Castile, in 1263. This law was restored in the Constitution of Cadiz (*q.v.*) in 1812.
   REFERRED TO: *379*

*Constitución política de la Monarquía Española. Promulgada en Cadiz á 19 de marzo de*
   *1812.* Cadiz: Imprenta Real, 1812.
   REFERRED TO: *380*

*Pragmatica—Sancion en fuerza de ley decretada por el Señor Rey Don Carlos Cuarto a*
   *peticion de la cortes del año de 1789, y mandada publicar por S.M. Reinante para la*
   *observancia perpetua de la ley segunda, título quince, partida segunda, que establece la*
   *sucesion regular en la corona de España.* Madrid: Imprenta Real, 1830.
   NOTE: the first reference is to the secret Cortes of 1789, where Charles IV overturned the Salic Law
   instituted by Philip V in 1713; the second is to the promulgation of this decision by Ferdinand VII in
   1830 in his proclamation of his daughter as his successor.
   REFERRED TO: *380*

*Estatuto real para la convocacion de la Córtes Generales del Reino* (10 Apr., 1834).
   Madrid: De Burgos, 1834.
   REFERRED TO: *384*

*Constitución de la monarquía española, decretada y sancionada por las Córtes Generales*
   *en 1837, y adoptada por la Reina gobernadora Doña María Cristina de Borbón* (8 Jan.,
   1837). Madrid: n.p., 1837.
   REFERRED TO: *384*

# Index

The abbreviations JM, JSM, and HT have been used for James Mill, John Stuart Mill, and Helen Taylor respectively. References to the Appendices are in italic. Excluded from the index are geographical names mentioned incidentally, and editorial matter, including answers to JSM's questions and summaries of the passages of Bentham and James Mill annotated by JSM.

Profits: sharing of, *408*; in colonies, *410*; mentioned, *410*

Progress, results of, *409*, *410*

Propositions, verbal, 25–6. *See also* Predication

Psychology: need to find simple laws in, 96–7; JM's contribution to, 97, 99, 101–2

Publicity, value of, 47

Punishment: role of reward and, in forming moral sense, 235–6; justice and, 241–2

Pyrenees: botany of Spanish, 311–17; and botany of Andorra, 317–20

QUAKERS, legal treatment of, 55

Quality, JM on, 189–90

Quantity, JM on, 189, 190–1

READING, physical process of, 139–40, 195

Realists, 144

Reasoning, does not consist of syllogisms, 175

Reflection, JM on, 213–14

Reformation, Protestant, *373*

Reigate, plants in vicinity of, 261n, 269–75

Relation, JM's discussion of terms of, 181–6, 187–91, 197–9

Religion: a weak sanction for truthfulness, 19–21; exclusion on grounds of, 54–5

Reminiscence, Cardaillac on, 193–6

Rent, *408*, *409*

Resemblance: association by, 120–1; and classification, 143–4; JM on, 183–5

Resistance: JM on, 108–9; H. Spencer on, 205

Revolution, justification of, *365*

Rights: Bentham on collation and non-collation of, 12; legal, 88

Roman Catholic Church: in Spain, 291; Tory attitude to, *360–1*

Roman Catholicism: morality of, 19; and exclusion of evidence from the confessional, 65; and Catholic Emancipation, *382*

Rome (ancient), conquest by, 289

Rome (modern), 287

Royal Society for the Prevention of Cruelty to Animals, JSM's bequest to, *333*, *334*

Rules, judicial, 73, 77, 78, 82

Russia: seizes British ship on coast of Circassia, *345–9*, *358*; its expansionist designs, *347*; its relations with Caucasus, *349–58*; and Poland, *376*

ST.-VERAN, JSM's property at, *see* Avignon

Saracens, *352–3*

Science: its advance, by resolution of complex phenomena into simpler, 95–6; and the inconceivable, 165; mentioned, 11

Self. *See* Ego

Sensation: JM on names for, 104–9, 123, 190; distinguished from idea, 109–10, 171–4; JM on, 111, 138, 155, 168, 243; whether can be unconscious, 117–18; and association, 120–1; and attention, 139–40, 214, 247; permanent possibilities of, 168–70, 190, 211; likeness and unlikeness in, 183–4; H. Spencer on new-born baby's, 207–10; pleasure and pain in, 214

Settlement, laws of, 42, 52–3

Sherborn Sands, 279

Sight, JM on, 105–6. *See also* Vision

Slavery: morality under systems of, 18; considered advantageous among Circassians, *352*

Smell: JM on, 104–5, 106; of flowers, 257

Space: JM on, as abstract term, 202; JM's theory of infinite, 202–3; H. Spencer on origin of idea of, 207–10. *See also* Extension

Spain: flora of, 289–90; improved state of (1860), 290; JSM botanizes in, 291–317; intervention of British Legion in Carlist wars of, *362–73*, *387–8*; cruelty in national character of, *365n*; and Quadruple Alliance, *375–9*; issues in Carlist wars in, *379–86*. *See also* Europe

Strood, 282

Sublimity, association theory of, 224–6

Succession, JM on experience of, 185–6, 188

Surrey, plants of, 258–61, 267–75, 280

Syllogism: JM's theory of, 135–6, 175; not type of reasoning, but test of it, 175

Sympathy, 232

TARRAGONA, plants of, 299–301

Taste, JM on sensation of, 106–7

Taxation: of contracts, 23; of justice, 50, 57; mentioned, *407*, *409*, *410*

Terms. See Names

Theft, legal definition of, 89

Thought, trains of, how produced, 191–6

Time: JM on, as abstract term, 204; JM's theory of infinite, 204; H. Spencer on origin of idea of, 207–10; mentioned, 203

Titles, legal, when not to be disputed, 76

Tories: beliefs of, *360–2*; on question of intervention in Spain, *362–3*, *365n*, *367*, *379*; machinations of, *386*

Touch, JM on, 107

Transcendentalists, 162

Treason, English law of, 70

*Trover*, actions for, 89

Turkey: and the Caucasus, *358*; mentioned, 18

# DATE DUE